The
Garland Library
of
War and Peace

The
Garland Library
of
War and Peace

Under the General Editorship of
Blanche Wiesen Cook, *John Jay College, C.U.N.Y.*
Sandi E. Cooper, *Richmond College, C.U.N.Y.*
Charles Chatfield, *Wittenberg University*

The Quakers in Peace and War

An Account of Their Peace Principles and Practice

by
Margaret E. Hirst

with an introduction by
Rufus M. Jones

with a new introduction
for the Garland Edition by
Edwin B. Bronner

Garland Publishing, Inc., New York & London
1972

Library of Congress Cataloging in Publication Data

Hirst, Margaret Esther.
  The Quakers in peace and war.

  (The Garland library of war and peace)
  Reprint of the 1923 ed.
  1. Friends, Society of—History. 2. Pacifism—
History. I. Title. II. Series.
BX7748.W2H5 1972   289.6   70-147671
ISBN 0-8240-0429-9

Printed in the United States of America

Introduction

For more than three centuries the members of the Religious Society of Friends (Quakers) have advocated a pacifist position, not only in peacetime when many people agreed with their principles, but also in wartime when they were left to stand nearly alone, exposed to public censure. This tiny group of less than 200,000 persons scattered around the world has served as an inspiration to others, and their story deserves to be told.

Margaret E. Hirst was the first person to attempt any comprehensive study of Quaker pacifism, and we are indebted to her for what was not only a pioneering effort but an important scholarly volume as well. While her study appeared nearly a half century ago and only tells the story through World War I, it is a landmark volume in the literature of the peace movement. This is the first full reprint of the book although it was condensed by Ruth Freeman and others in the World War II era when an abbreviated edition appeared under the title, Quakers and Peace (Pacifist Research Bureau, Ithaca, New York, 1947).

The book grew out of research while Margaret Hirst started in preparation for a paper she read at the first All-Friends Conference held in London in 1920,

5

INTRODUCTION

a gathering which focused upon peace issues in the aftermath of World War I. She went to the sources for her material regarding the Quaker pacifist testimony in England. She dug through three-centuries-old manuscripts and ill-printed tracts in the library at Devonshire House and also turned to other repositories for information to fill in gaps.[1] Already recognized as a scholar in the fields of economics and classics, she applied her intelligence and training to this new field of peace history and produced a remarkable book. Unfortunately, she was forced to rely on secondary works for the section she wrote on the peace testimony in America, and that part of the volume does not measure up to the rest.

The book was published on both sides of the Atlantic late in 1923, by the Swarthmore Press in London, and the George H. Doran Company in New York. The volume was given a warm reception by reviewers and has been highly regarded ever since. It became the standard reference work on the peace testimony of Quakers and has been quoted and referred to in footnotes for half a century. Only now, with the revived interest in peace history, has a scholar compiled a study to rank alongside of it and to replace the American section of it.

The review in the New York Times *called it the "... first complete and authoritative study to be made of this interesting subject ... a genuine contribution to the religious and social history of the world during the last two and a half centuries" (Jan. 27, 1924, p. 26).*

Without expressing any opinion about the quality of the book, a reviewer in The Nation & The Athenaeum *voiced admiration for the peace testimony of Quakers and dismay regarding the actions of the British government toward pacifists in the Great War (Dec. 1, 1923).* The New Statesman *referred to the volume as ". . . a record of astonishingly brave adherence to an impractical code" (Feb. 9, 1924, p. 522).*

Writing for The Spectator, *E. M. Wrong suggested that the book was rather longer than any a non-Quaker would wish to read and added that Miss Hirst was not an exciting author. Having put the writer in her place, he admitted that ". . . she shows the romance that may attend non-resistance." Wrong doubted the logic of the pacifist position and disagreed with Miss Hirst's belief that Pennsylvania might have remained at peace with the Indians if William Penn's policies had prevailed into the middle of the eighteenth century (Feb. 23, 1924, p. 294). While the book was noticed in other magazines and newspapers, it was not reviewed in the historical journals such as the* English Historical Review *and the* American Historical Review.

The reviewer for the Bulletin of the Friends Historical Association *(now called* Quaker History*) was Rufus M. Jones (1863-1948), the professor at Haverford College who had written the introduction*

INTRODUCTION

to the volume. While praising the book and its author, he added, "My main interest in this book is its possible contribution to the great task of our time, the building of a warless world." In his introduction he had said that the story was not ". . . another Utopia, or a new rainbow dream of the year 2023. It is the actual history of doings and events and practised faiths that are on record." In the Bulletin *he made the same point once again, calling it ". . . the testimony of the actual experience and practice of a new way of life" (Spring, 1924, p. 35). Thus he expressed the hope and optimism which flowered in the 1920s.*

Early in the twentieth century John Wilhelm Rowntree (1868-1905) and Rufus Jones had initiated an ambitious project to publish a comprehensive history of Quakers. Named the Rowntree Series, in honor of the Yorkshire industrialist who died prematurely, seven volumes appeared between 1909 and 1921. Rufus Jones, who carried the major responsibility in this monumental effort, was ably assisted by William Charles Braithwaite (1862-1922), who wrote two definitive volumes on the first half century of Quakerism. These scholarly studies are still regarded as the backbone of any study of the history of Friends and are kept in print, either by the original publishers or by reprint firms.

Thus, when Edward Grubb wrote in his review, "Margaret Hirst has worthily followed up the Rowntree history of Quakerism . . . by an equally thorough and accurate study of what may prove to be our best contribution to Christian life — our belief that the principles of Jesus Christ can be applied in the international relations of men," he offered high praise indeed (The Friend *|London|, Dec. 7, 1923, p. 956). Jones had also said that "it is worthy to rank with the Rowntree series . . . ."*

The book, which is divided into six parts, begins with a thoughtful study of the early experiences of Friends and describes the persecutions suffered in the seventeenth century. Miss Hirst carefully examined the records of the first decade of Quakerism, when the leaders were developing a consistent peace testimony, and it is clear from what she has written that it was not until 1661 that Friends were united on pacifism. Friends have remained firmly attached to a pacifist position ever since that date, both in official statements and in practice, although individual Quakers have not always accepted the peace testimony.

The second part of the volume is devoted to the study of the religious and philosophical grounds of the Quaker peace testimony with special emphasis upon the writings of Isaac Penington (1616-1679), William Penn (1644-1718), Robert Barclay (1648-1690), and John Bellers (1654-1725).

Parts Three and Four of the volume trace the history of the peace testimony in the eighteenth and nineteenth centuries. In the former century the decision to disown those who could not accept the peace testimony was adopted, and this practice was followed until the twentieth century. Nearly half of Part Four is devoted to a study of the career of the great Quaker political figure, John Bright (1811-1889).

Part Five, "Friends Abroad," includes material about Quakers in Europe but is largely about American Friends. More than one-third of the volume is devoted to this section which begins with a full discussion of the colonial period. After examining the peace principles of Quakers in the West Indies and the other mainland colonies, Miss Hirst turns to the familiar story of Pennsylvania. Additional chapters deal with Quakers in the American Revolution and in the nineteenth century, especially in the Civil War years. The section reflects the way in which Quakers perceived their successes and failures as they looked back after more than two centuries.

The final part is a summary of the way in which Friends around the world responded to the challenges of World War I. Several useful lists and documents are published as appendices at the end. While there is an index, Miss Hirst did not compile a bibliography.

Professor Peter Brock, at the University of Toronto, published a monumental volume in 1968, Pacifism in the United States, from the Colonial Era to the First World War *(Princeton Univ. Press) based upon research in original sources and reflecting all of*

INTRODUCTION

the scholarly work in the last half century. In a thirty-four page bibliography he lists primary and secondary sources on American pacifism up to World War I. The chapters dealing with the Quakers were published as a separate paperback in 1970, including bibliographical data about Friends. Professor Brock's work supersedes Part Five of Miss Hirst's volume. He has written a comparable study on pacifism in Europe to appear in 1972 which will contain several chapters on the peace testimony of Friends. Like Miss Hirst, Brock spent considerable time with the original sources, and his bibliography will include publications of more recent times. In a volume covering the entire peace movement he was not able to include the rich detail found in Miss Hirst's volume with its focus on the Quaker movement.

Margaret E. Hirst (1882-1954) was born at Dalton Lodge near Huddersfield and earned her degree at Newnham College, Oxford. Later she studied in Germany, out of which came her first book, a volume of the life and writings of the German free trade advocate, Friedrich List (1789-1846). Four years later, in 1913, her second book appeared, The Story of Trusts. Her brother, Francis W. Hirst (1873-1953), editor of the Economist (London), wrote introductions to both volumes.

Classics, her second field of interest and knowledge, led her into the academic world, where she served as Lecturer in Greek and Latin at the

11

INTRODUCTION

University of Birmingham from 1920 until her retirement in 1947.

In the meantime, she joined Friends in her twenties, attracted by the peace testimony of Quakers, and later publications reflected these interests, especially her major work, The Quakers in Peace and War. In 1945 she published a new study of John Bright, and she also contributed to journals and books of collected essays.

At the time of her death in 1954, one biographical article ended with these words: ". . . though severity was a note in her character the warmth of loyalty and affection was another note, and the two notes blended" (The Friend, Sept. 10, 1954, p. 908). This same blend of severe honesty and warm affection is visible in The Quakers in Peace and War as she examined and described the way in which members of her adopted faith, the Society of Friends, practiced their ancient peace testimony.

Edwin B. Bronner
Department of History
Haverford College

NOTE

[1] *The material designated in the references as "In D.," and formerly located in the Friends' Reference Library, Devonshire House, London, was moved in 1926 to The Library, Friends House, Euston Road, London, N.W. 1 2BJ.*

THE QUAKERS IN
PEACE AND WAR

Swarthmore

THE QUAKERS IN PEACE AND WAR

AN ACCOUNT OF THEIR PEACE PRINCIPLES AND PRACTICE

BY

MARGARET E. HIRST, M.A.

former Scholar of Newnham College, Cambridge
Lecturer in the University of Birmingham

WITH AN INTRODUCTION BY

RUFUS M. JONES, M.A., D. LITT.

Author of " The Inner Life,"
" Later Periods of Quakerism," etc.

Are you faithful in maintaining our Christian testimony against all war as inconsistent with the precepts and spirit of the Gospel ?

(Official Query of the Society of Friends periodically read in its Meetings.)

I told them I lived in the virtue of that life and power, that took away the occasion of all wars (GEORGE FOX, 1650).

LONDON : THE SWARTHMORE PRESS LTD.
RUSKIN HOUSE, 40 MUSEUM STREET, W.C. 1
NEW YORK : GEORGE H. DORAN COMPANY

First published in 1923

Printed in Great Britain by
UNWIN BROTHERS, LIMITED, THE GRESHAM PRESS, LONDON AND WOKING

PREFATORY NOTE

THIS historical study of the Society of Friends in its relation to the peace question was written in part before the War, and neither its plan nor its argument have been influenced by that catastrophe, though its completion and appearance have been delayed. In the chapters dealing with America I have had to rely mainly upon printed sources, in spite of kind help and advice from Friends across the Atlantic. But I trust that the account is accurate as far as it goes. Elsewhere, as will be seen, I have drawn largely from central and local Quaker records, many of which are preserved at the headquarters of the Society of Friends, Devonshire House, Bishopsgate, E.C., while others are still in the possession of the local Meetings. The difficulty has been in selecting from materials so abundant. In most of my citations the spelling and punctuation are modernized.

My aim throughout has been to show the practice of Friends in maintaining their peace testimony, rather than to analyse or defend its basis. I have tried to give a fair picture of all inconsistencies and divergences, and to show the varying emphasis laid on different aspects of the question at different times and under different conditions. Inaccuracies, I fear, there must be in a book ranging over three centuries and two continents, but I trust there are no wilful errors or suppressions. As a member of the Society I fully share its views upon war and the spirit of war, but I have tried to avoid overmuch comment, and to let Friends speak for themselves in their words and works of past and present days. I wished to state the facts, leaving readers to form their own opinion upon them. I am greatly indebted to Dr. Rufus M. Jones for his Introduction and to many Friends and others who have generously helped me by information and critical reading of my manuscript. Without the stores of the Friends' Reference Library, and the unfailing and cheerful help of the late Librarian, Norman Penney, his successor, M. Ethel Crawshaw, and the Staff, this book could never have been written. It is not an official publication of the Society, and for its contents I alone am responsible.

M. E. H.

NOTE ON REFERENCES.

"*In D.*" denotes that the manuscript or book is in the Friends' Reference Library, Devonshire House, Bishopsgate, London.

Camb. Journal = the edition of George Fox's *Journal*, transcribed from the original manuscript, edited by Norman Penney, and published by the Cambridge University Press, 1911.

J.F.H.S. = Journal of the Friends' Historical Society.

INTRODUCTION

HERE is an important piece of historical work worth doing and worthily done. The reader who has known little about the subject before will find the book packed with interesting details and narratives, and the reader who has been long *en rapport* with the main facts will find this account fresh and significant.

We are not asked here to read another Utopia, or a new rainbow dream of the year 2023. It is the actual history of doings and events and practised faiths that are on record. It is, in fact, a book about an experiment, good enough in intention to be called *holy*, and effective enough, at least within the domain of those who tried it, to be called *practical*. Some who would not grant this last claim would, perhaps, now after the unveilings of the years close behind us, at least thank God that a little band of men and women, whether successful or not in the venture, were ready to go out, like St. Francis and his Little Brothers, to try the way of love and peace in a world where hate and war have already had more than a fair chance.

One excellent feature of this book is the absence from it of all special pleading for an abstract theory. There is no attempt to prove that swords can with perfect safety be beaten into productive ploughshares and spears into reaping sickles. It is not a treatise on the elimination of physical force from human society. It is rather the story of a definite adventure, on the part of a group of Christian believers, to take their faith very seriously and to put their religion—their loyalty to Christ—into actual practice as a way of life. Instead of debating in words what the whole world ought to do with its complicated problems, the persons here dealt with have burned their bridges and cut the bands of social entanglement, and have set themselves to exhibit in deeds, even if in small compass, a programme of life which they believed would build a new world, if all men followed it, as they have tried to do.

Many persons—it has now grown to be a multitude—accept this same way of life, this same pacific attitude in the periods between wars. They abhor the methods of war and the effects of it, but

9

too often in the past such persons have found themselves swept into the war-mind, the war-passion, when their nation entered upon a concrete war. The particular war on hand has seemed to them an exception to the general principle. They are caught by the moral slogans, the idealisms of the hour, and they are carried on either into sympathy with it or participation in it. One of the contributions of the Friends, as these pages will show, has been their persistent maintenance of their convictions, their consistent practice of their vision and insight, even in the hard conflict of loyalties. They have formed a Peace Society which has never adjourned and never postponed to a more convenient season its labours for peace.

The most important thing about the experiment is not its magnitude, not its reverberations across the world, but its *spirit*, its exhibition of a new kind of force, the demonstration and power of the way of love and fellowship. We have grown used, almost callous, to compromise in the sphere of religion. We have seen the Evangel of a kingdom of God fitted into the political schemes of great empires and clipped down to meet the demands of a life and civilization still deeply paganized. We have heard it said again and again that Christianity has not so much failed as that it has not yet been tried. It is, therefore, a relief to discover a *remnant* of those that call Christ their divine Leader who actually set about doing, in uncompromising fashion, what He said His followers should do ; who will not hate, who will not kill, who will not join in the work of starving little children to death, but who insist, at whatever risk or sacrifice, upon going on with their programme of love and co-operation, their practice of the kingdom of God, even in the midst of hate and havoc.

This story, which covers two hundred and seventy-five years, has its failures and its trivialities, its blunders and its humorous aspects. Those who have shared in the experiment have no illusions about the difficulties or the blemishes. They are extremely humble over the rôle they have played and the thing they have accomplished. Their one concern has been and is to *keep the faith* and to *follow the gleam.*

> " 'Tis not the grapes of Canaan that repay,
> But the high faith that fails not by the way."

RUFUS M. JONES.

CONTENTS

PAGE

PREFATORY NOTE 7

INTRODUCTION 9

INTRODUCTORY

CHAPTER

I. THE CHRISTIAN CHURCHES AND PEACE 15

PART I

THE SEVENTEENTH CENTURY

II. THE EARLY TESTIMONY, 1643–60 39

III. YEARS OF PERSECUTION, 1660–1702 69

PART II

THE GROUND OF THE PEACE TESTIMONY

IV. EARLY APOLOGISTS FOR PEACE, 1653–64 113

V. ROBERT BARCLAY THE APOLOGIST 134

VI. WILLIAM PENN AND JOHN BELLERS 153

PART III

THE EIGHTEENTH CENTURY

VII. DAYS OF TRADITION, 1702–55 177

VIII. IN TIME OF WAR—ENGLAND AND IRELAND—1755–1815 194

IX. SOME DISOWNMENTS, 1774–1815 225

PART IV

THE NINETEENTH CENTURY

CHAPTER   PAGE
X. Peace and War, 1815–99. 243

XI. John Bright 273

PART V

FRIENDS ABROAD

XII. The West Indies 307

XIII. The American Colonies 327

XIV. Pennsylvania 353

XV. The War of Independence 383

XVI. The United States 416

XVII. Friends in Europe 452

PART VI

CONCLUSION

XVIII. The Twentieth Century 481

APPENDICES

A. List of Soldiers and Sailors who became Friends
before the Year 1660 527

B. The Testimony of the Soldiers, 1657 . . . 530

C. George Fox to Oliver Cromwell, 1654 . . . 532

D. Address to the Emperor of Russia, 1854 . . . 534

E. The Protest of the German Friends against Slavery,
Philadelphia, 1688 536

F. Statistics of Enlistment, 1917 538

Index 539

INTRODUCTORY

Full long our feet the flowery ways
Of peace have trod,
Content with creed and garb and phrase :
A harder path in earlier days
Led up to God.

Too cheaply truths, once purchased dear,
Are made our own ;
Too long the world has smiled to hear
Our boast of full corn in the ear,
By others sown ;

To see us stir the martyr fires
Of long ago,
And wrap our satisfied desires
In the singed mantle that our sires
Have dropped below.

But now the cross our worthies bore
On us is laid.
Profession's quiet sleep is o'er,
And in the scale of truth once more
Our faith is weighed.

The levelled gun, the battle-brand
We may not take :
But calmly loyal we can stand
And suffer with our suffering land
For conscience' sake.

Stanzas from *Anniversary Poem*, 1863, by J. G. Whittier.

CHAPTER I

THE CHRISTIAN CHURCHES AND PEACE

EVEN those whose acquaintance with the Society of Friends, or Quakers, is of the slightest have a general idea that among its doctrines is a belief in the un-Christian nature of war, of which the refusal to take part in war or military training is the corollary. An odd illustration of this opinion is the application by soldiers of the term " Quaker " to a dummy gun, used to draw the enemy's fire, which of course it cannot return. The grounds of this principle among Friends, and their practice of it during nearly three centuries will be set forth in the later chapters of this book. But it is less generally known that the same belief was widely held among early Christians, that it was a tenet of some mediæval and Reformation sects, and is even now maintained by some other Churches, of which the Mennonite body in Russia, Germany, and America is the chief in point of numbers. The following pages give a brief account of the peace views of these non-Quaker bodies—views which were often one cause of the persecutions they endured.

In the Christian Church of the first three centuries there existed a strong body of opinion which, basing itself upon the words of Christ and the spirit of His teaching, held that warfare and bloodshed were impossible for His followers. Professor Harnack, in his short study *Militia Christi*, after making a careful examination of the evidence, came to the conclusion that, at any rate until the time of Marcus Aurelius, the soldier's life was held to be in such obvious conflict with that of the Christian that no Christian entered, and all converted soldiers left, the Army.[1] Justin Martyr, the

---

[1] Harnack says : " Es entstand auch keine ' Soldatenfrage ' : der getaufte Christ wurde eben nicht Soldat " (*Militia Christi*, p. 49). Neander (*Church History*, i. 125) argued that " only a minor party among the Christians " objected to the occupation of a soldier. Rigaltius (Nicholas Rigault) and Beatus Rhenanus,

Apologist, writing in the reign of Antoninus Pius, testifies to the peaceful character of the Christian religion (*First Apology*, 39 ; *Trypho*, 110). He died about A.D. 165, but some later editor appended to his *Apology* an alleged letter from the Emperor Marcus Aurelius to the Senate, in A.D. 174, ordering a general toleration of Christianity, on the ground that when hard pressed by thirst and the enemy his army in Germany was saved by the prayers of a large body of Christians in the Twelfth Legion. Their supplications were followed by a storm which quenched the thirst of the Romans and terrified the enemy into flight. Hence the Legion became known as the " Thundering." Tertullian twice alludes to the story, but though the deliverance is recorded by historians, the Christian element in it is probably false and the letter an invention. The Twelfth Legion had been named the *Fulminata* (Thunderstruck) for generations, and Marcus Aurelius permitted a severe persecution in the South of France in A.D. 177. The letter contains one curious sentence about the Christian soldiers. " They began the battle [i.e. prayer] not by preparing weapons nor arms nor bugles, *for such preparation is hateful to them, on account of the God they bear about in their conscience.*" [1]

But during the next century and a half, as Christianity spread and the early hope of the immediate second coming of Christ faded, the Christians began to make that compromise with the world which was fully carried out by Constantine. The writings of the Fathers and the legends of the Church give abundant testimony that the Christian soldier was no longer an anomaly, and by the year 323 the new faith must have been widespread in the ranks, for how else could Constantine, owing his power to the army, have ventured on the adoption of Christianity as the official religion of the Empire ?

Even in this later period, however, there were great leaders of the Church, for example, Tertullian (born *circa* 160) and

a Humanist friend of Erasmus, both accept Tertullian as a complete opponent of war. " Christianis omnibus ubique militiam interdicit Auctor," says the former in his edition of Tertullian (1634), and the latter : " Haud dubie nunquam credidit futurum Tertullianus ut Christiani mutuis armis concurrerent." A recent study of the question is *The Early Christian Attitude to War*, by Dr. C. J. Cadoux, 1919 (The Swarthmore Press, Ltd.).

[1] Dr. Cadoux (*op. cit.*, pp. 230 foll.), however, considers that " there can be no doubt of the main fact, that in or about A.D. 174 the Legio Fulminata contained a considerable number of Christian soldiers." The miraculous rainfall is represented among the scenes on the Column of Marcus Aurelius at Rome.

Lactantius (born *circa* 270), who maintained the old testimony against the soldier's profession. There were also many occasions on which the devout Christian soldier found himself in opposition to the State and his commanders. Under the *Pax Romana* it was not so much the question of war and battle, as that of his ordinary military duties in time of peace, which roused the Christian's conscience. The military garrison in the provinces was the engine of criminal law ; it was the duty of officers to pronounce and soldiers to execute death sentences, and the early Church, as a whole, included capital punishment among the forms of blood-shedding forbidden by the Gospel. How, again, could a Christian reconcile the *sacramentum*, or military oath of unconditional submission to his Emperor, with the other vow of obedience to his God ? Lastly, the official sacrifices which all soldiers were bound to attend, the worship of past Emperors and of the genius of the living ruler, the reverence paid to the standards, and the constant practice of pagan rites and superstitions, must all have placed a conscientious believer in a delicate and difficult position. Some attempted to compromise, and, while attending pagan ceremonies, protected themselves from their evil influence by making the sign of the Cross. Others took some convenient opportunity of leaving the army. Others simply absented themselves from sacrifice. The result of this last step evidently depended largely on the attitude of the ruling Emperor, and perhaps still more on the temper of the commanding officers. In times of persecution such " nonconformists " were the first to suffer ; in times of peace, even, there are occasional records of martyrdom ; but in many cases the practice must have been tolerated.[1] It must be remembered that conscription, though nominally in force, was little employed, since the army, comparatively small in proportion to the great masses of population within the Empire, found ready recruits among the warlike peoples of the recently conquered northern provinces. In the more settled regions exemption could be purchased with little difficulty. The clearest instance recorded in the martyrology of an objection on Christian grounds to actual warfare occurs in the legend of St. Martin of Tours (born *circa* A.D. 316). Himself a Christian, he was forced into the army by heathen parents, and later his legion was among those stationed on the Rhine to resist the inroads of the barbarians.

---

[1] See various instances in Eusebius, *Church History*, vi. 5, 41 ; vii. 15 ; viii. 4. Lactantius (?), *De mortibus persec.*, 10. Tertullian, *De Corona*, 1.

One day, when a donative, or money gift, was being distributed among the soldiers to hearten them for the coming battle, Martin asked for his discharge. " I am the soldier of Christ, it is not lawful for me to fight." The general taunted him with cowardice, whereupon he offered to stand unarmed next day in the thickest of the battle, to prove his faith in the divine protection. He would have been taken at his word had not the enemy sued for peace, and shortly afterwards he was allowed to leave the army. The story of a young African conscript, martyred under Diocletian in A.D. 295, presents some features of peculiar interest. Brought before the proconsul at Teveste (Tebers, in Algeria), Maximilian, a youth of twenty-one, withstood persuasion, arguments, and threats with his one simple answer, " I am a Christian, I cannot serve," and at last suffered death " with a cheerful countenance." [1]

It is remarkable that even in the third century and the early part of the fourth century the Christian apologists, while admitting that their brethren were serving in the army, still laid down in emphatic terms the incompatibility of war and military service with Christianity. Tertullian, before and after joining the sect of the Montanists (which stood for strict adherence to New Testament teaching), discusses the question at length.

" For what wars should we not be fit, we who so willingly yield ourselves to the sword, if in our religion it were not counted better to be slain than to slay ? " [2]   In the preceding sentence he stated that Christians had filled " the very camp." Again : " How shall a Christian be a fighter, nay, how shall he even serve as a soldier in time of peace, without a sword ? " [3]   In *De Corona*, a work of his Montanist period devoted entirely to the dilemma of the Christian soldier, he recounts every moral and religious objection to adopting the profession, but adds that if one who is already a soldier is converted, his case is different and he may be compared to the soldiers of the New Testament. " Yet, at the same time, when a man has become a believer and faith has been sealed, there

---

[1] Dion the proconsul said : " In the august retinue of our lords Diocletian and Maximian, Constantius and (Galerius) Maximus, there are Christians who are soldiers, and serve as soldiers." Maximilian answered : " They know what is best for themselves ; but I am a Christian, and I cannot do evil things." Dion said : " Those who serve as soldiers, what evil things do they ? " Maximilian answered : " You surely know what they do " (translated from Acta Maximiliani. Ruinart, *Acta Martyrum*, pp. 340 foll.).

[2] *Apologeticus*, 37   [3] *De Idolatria*, 19.

must be either an immediate abandonment of it, which has been the case with many ; or all sorts of quibbling will have to be resorted to in order to avoid offending God, and that is not allowed even outside of military service ; or, last of all, for God, the fate must be endured which a citizen-faith has been no less ready to accept." 1

About A.D. 178 Celsus, in his controversy with the Christians, urged them " to help the Emperor . . . to fight for him ; and if he requires it, to fight under him or lead an army along with him." This appeal, if words mean anything, must mean that Christians were currently believed to have a scruple against military service. Seventy years later Origen's reply admits the fact,2 but argues that since priests are exempted from warfare in order to offer sacrifice with pure hands, Christians have an equal right to exemption, since they all as priests of the One true God offer prayers on behalf of those " fighting in a righteous cause." " And as we by our prayers vanquish all demons who stir up war, and lead to the violation of oaths, and disturb the peace, we in this way are much more helpful to the Emperor than those who go into the field to fight for him. . . . And none fight better for the Emperor than we do. We do not indeed fight under him, even at his command (οὐ συστρατευόμεθα μὲν αὐτῷ, κἂν ἐπείγῃ . . .). But we fight for him in our own army, an army of piety, by our supplications to God." 3 Some of these later Fathers are as emphatic in their condemnation of war as their predecessors. Origen's concession of " a righteous cause " was not admitted by his contempory Cyprian, who described war as " wholesale murder." 4 Lactantius, half a century later, has an eloquent passage condemning the Roman deification of great conquerors and slayers of men.5 More than once he asserts the superiority of spiritual over physical force. " If you meet injustice with patience . . . it will immediately be extinguished, as though you would pour water upon a fire. But if injustice has met with impatience equal to itself, as though overspread with oil, it will excite so great a conflagration,

1 Tertullian, *De Corona*, 11. The Rev. J. Bethune-Baker, in his short study, *The Influence of Christianity on War* (1888), considers that Tertullian's objection to soldiering rested entirely on the pagan associations and practices of the army. But the objection to actual warfare is plainly expressed in *De Corona*.

2 In his *Hom. in Jesu Nave*, 15, he says (on Ephes. vi. 11-17) the apostle knew " nulla nobis jam ultra bella esse carnaliter peragenda."

3 Origen, *Contra Celsum*, viii. 73.

4 Cyprian, *Epistle to Donatus*.

5 Lact., *Divine Institutes*, i. 18.

that no stream can extinguish it but only the shedding of blood." [1]
War, he says elsewhere, though esteemed lawful by the State, is
forbidden to the Christian. [2]

But with the accession of Constantine and the official recognition of Christianity ("that fatal encircling of the cross with the
laurel," as it has been called by a Quaker historian [3]) the leaders of
the Church modified their opinion. Augustine, a hundred years
later, goes far enough to satisfy the most aggressive War Lord. "The
Emperor Julian was an unbeliever, an apostate, an idolater ; yet
Christian soldiers served under him. When indeed a question
arose as to their obedience to Christ, they acknowledged only Him
who is in heaven. Whensoever the Emperor ordered them to
worship idols, or to offer incense, they preferred God to him. But
when he said, ' Draw out the line of battle, march against this or
that nation,'—forthwith they obeyed their King." [4] " Be, even
while warring, a peace-maker," he wrote in another passage. [5] In
his great treatise, The City of God, Augustine included only wars waged
" by the command of God " among the forms of manslaughter not
forbidden by the Sixth Commandment, on which Vives, the Spanish
humanist, commented in his edition of the treatise, that certainly
God never commanded the Christians of sixteenth-century Europe
to engage in their war of mutual destruction. [6]

From this date the official Church raised no protest against
Christian participation in war. Athanasius indeed might assert
that barbarian tribes when converted turned from war to agriculture
and "instead of arming their hands with the sword lift them in
prayer," but his hopes were soon belied by the fanatical wars against
infidels and heretics waged by these converts. [7] Soon ecclesiastical
and civil legislation was needed to restrain priests and bishops from
themselves taking part in the slaughter. Neander gives a naïve

[1] Lact., Divine Institutes, vi. 18, also v. 17, 18.
[2] Ibid., vi. 20.
[3] Backhouse and Tyler, Early Church History, p. 317. The allusion is both
to the legendary vision of Constantine and to his actual adoption of the labarum
or Christian emblem as the standard of Rome. Cp. Gibbon, Decline and Fall,
c. 20. Harnack says of the Vision, " Der Christengott hatte sich als Krieg- und
Siegesgott offenbart " (Militia Christi, p. 87).
[4] Augustine on Psalm cxxiv.
[5] Augustine, Epistle 189.
[6] De Civitate Dei, i. 20.
[7] Athanasius, De Incarn. Verbi, § 51, 2. The Council of Arles, A.D. 314,
in its Third Canon specifically censured deserters from the Army.

account of the conditions which led to the famous capitulary of Charles the Great.[1]

" It being found," he says, " that a very bad impression was made on the minds of the multitude, when clergymen fell wounded or dead in battle, the Emperor Charles was entreated to make a provision against the occurrence of such things in future."   The result was the Capitulary of A.D. 801, to the following effect :—

" That no priest should thereafter engage in battle ; but that two or three chosen bishops should attend the army, with a certain number of priests, who should preach, give the blessing, perform mass, receive confession, attend the sick, administer extreme unction, and take especial care that no man left the world without the communion.   What victory could be hoped for, when the priests, at one hour, were giving the body of the Lord to Christians, and at another were, with their own wicked hands, slaying those very Christians to whom they gave it, or the heathen to whom they ought to have been preaching Christ ? " [2]

This ordinance did not restrain Popes and bishops of the Middle Ages from waging wars like any temporal ruler, but it did emphasize afresh the distinction between clergy and laity which had already been established by the doctrine of a celibate priesthood.   The clear statement that it is sinful for Christian priests, but lawful for Christian laymen to slay their fellow-Christians marks the distance travelled since the second century after Christ.   From the time of Constantine the general protest against Christian participation in war is only voiced by heretical sects, about whom we have unfortunately little definite information, and that little, since it comes mainly from their persecutors, cannot be accepted without question.   Even in the second century heresies appeared, to protest against the growing conformity of the Church to the world.   The reversion to a more simple, and even ascetic, creed began in Phrygia, the home of many Eastern cults.   Its leader, Montanus, gave his name to the sect of which Tertullian was the most famous member, and it is mainly from the latter's strenuous opposition to war and military service that the deduction is drawn that such opposition was a special feature of the Montanist creed.   The body, though persecuted, survived in Asia and North Africa into the fifth century, and may have linked itself on to later heretical movements. Marcion, the founder of the other great heresy of the second

---

[1] Neander, *Church History,* v. 125.   [2] Mansi Concl., t. xiii. f. 1054.

century, was also a native of Asia Minor, from Sinope in Pontus. In his teachings there was much that was wild and strained, largely borrowed from the confused metaphysics of the Gnostics. But a distinguishing feature of his heresy was the rejection of the Old Testament on the ground of its incompatibility with the Gospels and the teachings of St. Paul. The Old Testament God (he argued), harsh and revengeful, urging men to war and cruelty, could not be the Father of the merciful, peace-giving Christ. Rather he was a false power, the Gnostic Demiurge, inferior and opposed to the true God. In fact, Marcion approached the position of the liberal theologian who told his opponent that " your God is my Devil." Origen, who detested war as much as Marcion did, tried to meet the attack on the Old Testament by an attempt at allegory, explaining its frequent wars as types of the Christian struggle against sin and evil.[1] Many Marcionites in time were absorbed into Manichæanism, but the influence of the sect is marked in some later heresies.

Did we know more about a Jewish sect, the Essenes, which arose in the second century before Christ, we might be able to trace its influence also in the early Christian Church. But the accounts given by Philo and Josephus of these ascetic celibate communistic groups, dwelling in villages on the shores of the Dead Sea, do not afford much clue to their origin or development. Among the oaths by which they were bound, one is said to have been " to hurt no man voluntarily or at the command of another," and Philo says expressly that among the trades forbidden to them was the manufacture of weapons or of war equipment.

In the thousand years between Augustine and Luther the Church was disturbed by many groups of " heretics " or dissenters from established orthodoxy. Those which are of interest in relation to the question of peace and war seem, broadly, to belong to two classes. Some, under the influence of the Gnostics and possibly of older Eastern cults, adopted a rigid asceticism, cut themselves off from the ordinary practices of the world, and were accused of secret unhallowed rites and mysteries. They are often described as Manichæans, but some of their extravagances seem to point to a

---

[1] Harnack remarks (*Militia Christi*, p. 26) that neither side in the controversy had any idea of religious evolution—of the possibility of development in man's conception of the Deity. But (he adds) it will always be the glory of the Marcionite Church that it chose rather to sacrifice the Old Testament than to dim the picture of the Father by inserting the lineaments of a God of War.

more remote origin and to be a survival of the taboos and fetishes of primitive races. The other early " dissenters " were groups of earnest believers, drawn together to practise their interpretation of true Christianity. This, they thought, was revealed to them through prayer and meditation, either singly or in united worship, and through study of the New Testament. But the actual points of dissent are curiously the same in all these sects. They tended to exalt the New Testament and belittle the Old, to reject or modify the distinction between priest and layman, and in some cases the ecclesiastical sacraments and ritual. They opposed war, military service and judicial oaths, and denied the right of the State to inflict capital punishment. It is noteworthy that it is against the earlier and less-known sects that the Church controversialists and historians level the most damaging charges—charges which bear a marked resemblance to the distorted opinions about the early Christians held by their pagan neighbours. These early sects are conveniently labelled Gnostic or Manichæan, and Dualistic views are ascribed to them, but in sober fact very little is known about either their origin, their numbers, or their influence.[1]

The Paulicians, who existed in Armenia in the seventh century, may have been descendants of Marcionite communities, if it is true that their name was acquired by the emphasis they laid upon the Pauline writings. Their views spread westward ; in the ninth century they appeared in what is now Bulgaria and Macedonia under the Slav name of " Bogomili," or " Lovers of God." Many of the Christians in Bosnia at the time of the Turkish conquest belonged to this sect, and its views soon met with a welcome in parts of Western Europe, particularly in North Italy and the South of France. Various titles were given to them—Paterini, Publicani, and others of obscure origin—but the most generally accepted was

[1] Ordinary works of reference give some information about the sects briefly mentioned in this chapter. For more detail the reader may be referred to the following : Hastings, *Dictionary of Religion and Ethics* ; Schaff-Herzog, *Encyclopedie* ; Harnack, *History of Dogma* (English translation) ; Rufus Jones, *Studies in Mystical Religion*, 1909 ; *Spiritual Reformers in the Sixteenth and Seventeenth Centuries*, 1914. For the Waldenses. Müller, *Die Waldenses . . . bis zum Anfang des 14 Jahrhunderts* 1886, is a learned work with an exhaustive bibliography of mediæval authorities. ; S. R. Maitland, *Facts and Documents ; . . . illustrative of the Ancient Albigenses and Waldenses*, 1832 ; and H. C. Lea, *History of the Inquisition*, i. 1888, are also valuable ; R. Barclay, *Inner Life of the Religious Societies of the Commonwealth*, 1877, has a mass of information about early Continental and English Baptists, including the Mennonites.

Greek, Cathari, " the pure ones." [1] In Italy Atto, Bishop of Vercelli, denounced them in A.D. 942 for their errors (the tenets mentioned above), and particularly for their assertion that the law of Moses was not a guide to Christians. Since the Crusade of 1208 against the heretics of Southern France was first undertaken against those round Albi in Languedoc, the French Cathari were then and later termed Albigenses, but this was a wider term, and included other sects, especially the Waldenses. The more extreme among the Cathari are said to have practised celibacy, self-mutilation, and fasting, and to have abstained entirely from animal food.

The Waldenses, though undoubtedly influenced by Catharist teaching, looked upon the sect as unorthodox, and did not acknowledge any connection.[2] They had themselves a clear starting-point. In the latter half of the twelfth century Peter de Waldo, a rich merchant of Lyons, translated the New Testament and some writings of the early Fathers into the Romance tongue, and, adopting the doctrine of apostolical poverty, sold his possessions and began to preach a simple gospel. A group of adherents soon gathered round him, from which other preachers went out in apostolic. fashion, two and two. The Waldensians, or " Poor Men of Lyons," as they were sometimes called, spread over Southern France, Italy, and parts of Germany, and their numbers gave grave alarm to the ecclesiastical authorities. Contemporary chroniclers give a curious list of their chief errors, which were : the wearing of sandals " like apostles," the refusal to take oaths or to take human life on any ground, and the assertion that the sacraments could be administered by any believer. This last tenet, however, was certainly

---

[1] According to some the Bosnian heretics were refugees from France and Italy, survivors of the Albigensian persecutions of the thirteenth century. The early Crusaders considered that the " Bulgari " were all heretics. Hence from " Bulgare " came the term of vulgar abuse, *bougre*, which originally meant " heretic." So the German *Ketzer* (also = heretic) comes from the Italian " Gazzari," a corruption of Cathari. M. Emile Gebhart, *Mystics and Heretics in Italy*, p. 54, distinguishes the Paterini, as a local Milanese movement, from the Cathari.

[2] " Nor was the old traditional Church doctrine assailed by the Waldensians. They diverged only in respect of certain doctrines which bore upon practice. . . . The rejection of oaths, of service in war, of civil jurisdiction, of all shedding of blood, seemed to them, as to so many mediæval sects, simply to follow from the Sermon on the Mount" (Harnack, *History of Dogma*, vi. 90 note). The Inquisition of Toulouse in the fourteenth century distinguished between " heretics " (i.e. Cathari) and " Waldenses." Gebhart, *op. cit.*, p. 58, identifies the Italian Waldenses with the " humiliati."

not part of the original doctrine, and does not appear to have been universally held at any time.   Dr. S. R. Maitland, in his acute and critical book on the Waldenses,[1] quotes a treatise, *On the Sects of Modern Heretics*, by Reinerius Saccho (*circa* 1254).   In it is included among the errors of the " Poor Men of Lyons " the belief that " the Pope and all bishops are homicides on account of wars." There is an interesting description of the manner in which heretics " introduce themselves to the notice of the great."   " The heretic draws a comparison between the circumstances of the Church and those of his sect ; saying thus . . . they [the ecclesiastics] fight and make wars, and command the poor to be killed and burned, to whom it is said, ' He that taketh the sword shall perish by the sword.' "   The Crusade of 1208, and later persecutions, scattered the remnants of the Cathari and Waldensians far and wide.   Some turned eastward, to Hungary and Bohemia.   Waldensians joined the " Bohemian Brothers " (to be mentioned later) about the year 1467.   Others, possibly, reached England.   But even in Provence the community lingered on in secret.   A didactic Romance poem of Waldensian teaching, the *Noble Lesson*, is assigned by scholars to the early fifteenth century.   Some of its verses teach pure non-resistance.

The Old Law commands to fight against enemies and render evil for evil ;
But the New says, Avenge not thyself,
But leave vengeance to the heavenly King,
And let those live in peace who do thee harm ;
And thou shalt find pardon with the heavenly King.
The Old Law says, Thou shalt love thy friend, and hate thy enemy ;
But the New says, Thou shalt no more do this ;
But love your enemies, and do good to those who hate you
And pray for them who persecute you, and seek occasion against you ;
That ye may be the children of your Father who is in heaven.
The Old Law commands to punish malefactors ;
But the New says, Pardon all people,
And thou shalt find pardon with the Father Almighty ;
For if thou dost not pardon thou shalt not be saved.

From the end of the fifteenth century onwards the Waldensian communities which had taken refuge in the mountain valleys of Savoy were exposed to persecution and outrage at the hands of Catholic mercenaries at the order of the Pope and the Piedmontese rulers.   Milton's sonnet, " On the late Massacre in Piedmont,"

[1] Maitland, *Facts and Documents Illustrative of . . . the Waldenses*, 1832, pp. 400 foll.

was evoked by one of these atrocities in 1655. The exact date at which the persecuted began to resist by force is doubtful, but from time to time the inhabitants of one of the valleys, maddened by their sufferings, rose to arms, when struggles ensued, conducted by both sides with every circumstance of atrocity. The best-known episode is the war in the French Alpine valleys at the end of the seventeenth century led on the Waldensian side by one of their pastors, Arnaud.[1]

At first efforts were made to win back the Waldensians to the Church by other methods than persecution. Innocent III, a wise and far-seeing statesman, about the time of the Crusade of 1208 formed some " Catholic Poor Men " (or Waldensians reconverted to the Roman Church) into a brotherhood of preaching friars, allowing them freedom from oaths and military service, " so far as this may be done without prejudice or offence to any and with the sanction of the secular arm." Prejudice and malice seem to have prevented the development of the body, but the scheme has a curious resemblance to the Third Order founded a few years later by Francis of Assisi. These Tertiaries were to be laymen and women living according to a simple rule, which included a prohibition against wearing weapons or serving as soldiers. This was at a time when Italy was desolated by public and private war, when robbers swarmed on the high-roads, and duelling was already an obligation for a man of honour. " For nearly seventy years the Tertiaries kept their rule. Sometimes, in the war of town with town, the Italian podestas would call them to serve along with their fellows as soldiers to defend their native cities. But when they would not, the witness of their whole lives agreed with their refusal to be unfaithful to the command of Christ, and their fellow-townsmen had not the heart to punish as criminals the men whom they felt to be their best and most useful citizens." [2] At last the

---

[1] The sympathy evoked in Protestant countries led the sufferers to put forward in the seventeenth century entirely unhistorical claims to a direct continuity of descent from the primitive Church. Waldo was forgotten, and the name Waldenses or Vaudois, derived from the *Valles* in which (it was supposed) the true faith had been kept pure and without addition from the early days of Christianity. In 1658, George Fox urged his fellow Quakers to contribute to a general subscription raised in England for the relief of the Vaudois, but pointed the moral against all persecution in a letter to the Protector and his Government (Fox, *Journal*, 8th edition, i. 435).

[2] T. Edmund Harvey, " St. Francis in History " (*Friends' Quarterly Examiner*, January 1904).

rule was altered : by a Bull of 1289 Pope Nicholas IV allowed them to carry weapons for defence, and to fight " in defence of the Church."

During the fourteenth century the first English voices are heard against war, evoked perhaps by the sufferings of the long struggle with France. Wycliffe's study of the New Testament drew him away from the prevalent standards in civil and religious life. In more than one treatise he attacked war in vigorous terms. " Lord, what honour falleth to a knight that he kills many men ? The hangman killeth many more, and with a better title. Better were it for men to be butchers of beasts than butchers of their fellow-men." [1] These views were adopted by the Lollards, the spread of whose opinions through the work of " poor preachers " is curiously parallel to that of the earlier Waldensians. A Lollard petition to the Parliament of 1395, in stating their views, declared that " all wars were against the principles of the New Testament, and were but murdering and plundering the poor to win glory for kings." One of the accusations against Oldcastle, their chief leader in the time of Henry IV, was his opposition to the French war. About 1445, Reginald Pecock, in his quaintly named *Repressor of Over-Much Blaming of the Clergy*, mentions as a Lollard doctrine that war and capital punishment were unlawful. A late Lollard tract, *The Sum of the Scriptures* (which probably belongs to Tudor times), says : " Men of war are not allowed by the Gospel, the Gospel knoweth peace and not war." [2] The Lollards were popularly supposed to be revolutionaries and conspirators (the same charge was brought against the early Quakers). Wycliffe had an undoubted influence upon Huss, possibly through members of the retinue which Anne of Bohemia, wife of Richard II, brought with her to England. But the Hussite wars, after the martyrdom of the reformer, were not peaceable fruits of his teaching. Yet one body, the Bohemian Brethren, or *Unitas Fratrum*, stood apart from the two main divisions of Hussites. They refused any kind of military service, and it was to them that the refugee Waldensians joined themselves. The Brethren spread into Poland and Moravia, but everywhere they endured bitter persecution, and in the Thirty Years' War were almost extirpated. A remnant from Moravia settled in 1722 upon the estates of a pious nobleman, Count Zinzendorf, at Herrnhut

---

[1] Quoted in *Arbiter in Council*, p. 16.
[2] Rufus Jones, *Studies in Mystical Religion*, p. 365.

in Saxony. The Count soon joined the body, and by him they were again organized into a sect, or, as they preferred to consider, a branch of the Lutheran Church, known in Germany as " Herrn-hüter," or " Brüder," and in England and America as " Moravians." Their virtues and the important influence they have exerted in the cause of the slave, of foreign missions, and through Wesley and Whitefield, upon English religious life, are well known. They are still supposed to be principled against military service and war, but this was denied by English members in the Great War. According to Franklin (in his *Autobiography*) the Pennsylvian Moravians at Bethlehem took vigorous measure of defence after the massacre of their Indian co-religionists at Gnadenhütten.

While these pre-Reformation sects undoubtedly held peace principles, they came into collision with the Church on so many other points of doctrine and practice that this one does not seem to have been the cause of much persecution.

At the dawn of the Reformation some of the most distinguished men of the New Learning were found on the side of peace. Luis Vives, the Spaniard, has been already mentioned. His greater friend Erasmus was one of the most eloquent and earnest exponents of the contradiction between war and Christianity. He opposed a projected war against the Turks with the remark that " the most effective methods of vanquishing the Turks would be to let them see in our lives the light which Christ taught and expressed, to let them feel that we were not lusting for their dominions, nor thirsting for their gold, but seeking their salvation and Christ's glory." [1] Again : " War breeds war ; vengeance is repaid by vengeance. Let us now try the new policy of friendliness and goodwill." [2] And again : " Christians who defend war must defend the dispositions which lead to war ; and these dispositions are absolutely forbidden by the Gospel." [3] But the more powerful sects produced by the Reformation did not include among their tenets any scruple against war. The history of Huguenots in France and of Lutherans in Germany, Scandinavia, and Holland contain many bloody pages. The peace doctrine was left to the despised Baptists, or Anabaptists as they were popularly called. There were many shades of belief

---

[1] Epistle to Volsius, prefaced to *Militis Christiani Enchiridion*, 1518.
[2] *Querela pacis.*
[3] His English friend Colet, Dean of St. Paul's, declared that " an unjust peace is better than the justest war."

and practice among the early Baptists, but two facts stand out clearly. First, the wild spirits who ran riot in Munster in the year 1536 were in no respect typical, though they succeeded in bringing the name of Anabaptist into a disrepute which it retained for more than a century. Secondly, the movement known as " Anabaptism," which included such sects as the Schwenkfeldians and Huterites,[1] was not directly inspired by the sixteenth-century Reformers, but rather was in continuity with pre-Reformation bodies. It would, for example, be a hard matter to disentangle the mutual relations of Lollardry and Anabaptism. As in trade, so in religion, there was much intercourse betweeen England and the Netherlands. Anabaptists from Holland and Germany appear in England as early as the reign of Henry VIII, and they endured martyrdom at the hands of the Tudors. Persecution at home drove many to settle in England under Elizabeth, and, in turn, when William the Silent established religious liberty, the persecuted English Separatists took refuge in Holland.

In 1530 an Ecclesiastical Commission found a sect holding " divers heretical opinions " such as the unlawfulness of war. " Cristen men among themselves have nought to do with the sworde." These may have been Lollards or Anabaptists, but it was an early English Anabaptist who was charged, among other heresies, with asserting : " I am bound to love the Turk from the bottom of my heart." [2]

John Smith (or Smyth), one of the most influential and learned of the first generation of English Baptists, who died in 1612, declared in his *Confession* that Christ called His flock " to the

---

[1] The Schwenkfeldians were followers of Caspar Schwenkfeld, a Silesian nobleman. He joined the Reformation movement in 1525, but his " Quaker " views on the Sacraments and war drew down on him the hatred both of Catholics and Lutherans. His followers were greatly persecuted. In the early eighteenth century one remnant joined the Moravians, and another emigrated to Pennsylvania where a small Church still survives. The Huterites (led by Jacob Hunter) took refuge in Moravia about 1535. English Quakers found them at Pressburg in Hungary in 1661. Their general views were almost identical with the Mennonite Baptists, but they practised communism, and carried their peace principles to the point of refusing payment of war taxes. A few Churches founded by emigrants exist in South Dakota.

[2] Barclay, *Inner Life*, p. 14. Jones, *Studies in Mystical Religion*, pp. 387 foll. Elizabeth burnt two Dutch Anabaptists at Smithfield in 1575. Edmund Wightman, a " Baptist," was burnt for Unitarian opinions at Lichfield in 1612. There were migrations of Separatists from England to Holland from 1593 to 1597, 1604 to 1606 (led by John Smyth), and in 1608. The last group were eventually the " Pilgrim Fathers " of the New World.

following of His unarmed and unweaponed life and of His cross-
bearing footsteps." Smyth was closely connected with the Dutch
Mennonites, and during the early seventeenth century some of the
English Baptist congregations were in rather loose union with the
Dutch Mennonite Church. But a division soon arose between
them concerning war and the use of arms, which was naturally
intensified by the outbreak of the Civil War. Even after the
Restoration, however, there were Baptist congregations who maintained an objection to war, though the Friends considered them
but lukewarm in their testimony.[1]

The Mennonites just mentioned were the most important and
interesting of the sects into which the Continental Anabaptists
developed. Menno Symons was a priest in West Friesland, where
in 1535 there was a fierce persecution and massacre of Anabaptists.
Menno was so struck by the courage and constancy of the martyrs
that he began to inquire into their creed. In 1536 he appeared
as a leader of the moderate party in their protest against the fanatics
of Munster. Soon he had so stamped his personality upon the
Church that it received his name. The Mennonites became established in Holland, France, Switzerland, and Germany. They
practised adult baptism and silent prayer, opposed war, oaths, capital
punishment, and a separate and paid class of ministers, and laid great
stress upon integrity of life and the practice of benevolence.[2] These
characteristics tempted some of their early historians to claim them
as direct descendants of the Waldenses, and the same claim has been
made for the Anabaptists in general. On this it has been said in
a recent treatment of the subject[3] : —

---

[1] A little-known sect, the "Family of Love," founded by a Westphalian,
Henry Nicholas, in Germany and England during Elizabeth's reign, also opposed
war and capital punishment. This body was neither Catholic nor Reformed, and
members were permitted to attend the services of either Church (Barclay, *Inner
Life*, pp. 25 foll., and references there given. Jones, *Studies in Mystical Religion*,
pp. 436 foll.). It died out in England during the Civil War. Barclay in his
Apology (1676) rebukes those who oppose war (probably the Baptists) and yet take
part in the public prayers and thanksgivings for victory.

[2] The Mennonites are sometimes called "Unitarian Baptists," but Menno
appears to have held the orthodox view of the Trinity, though he thought the
term itself unscriptural (Barclay, *Inner Life*, p. 81).

[3] *Encycl. Religion and Ethics*, article "Anabaptists." The Collegiants of
Holland (Spinoza's friends) in the seventeenth century were largely drawn from the
Mennonites and held their views on war. Another Baptist sect, the Tunkers
(i.e. "Dippers"), Dunkers, or Dunkards arose in Westphalia about the year
1708. Persecution drove them to Pennsylvania ten years later. They now

" The similarity in doctrines, spirit, and organization is so marked as almost to compel belief in some sort of historical succession ; and yet the effort to trace this connection has not so far been successful. Moreover, several considerations militate against such a conclusion. (1) The Anabaptists themselves were not conscious of such connection, regarding themselves as the spiritual children of a renewed study of the Bible. (2) All their leaders, so far as their lives were known, came out of the Catholic Church. (3) They had little or no connection with older sects after their rise. These considerations render it probable that they, like the sects of the Middle Ages, are the offspring of a renewed Bible study, and that the similarity is the result of independent Bible study under similar circumstances and controlling ideas."

The testimony against war and oaths caused the Mennonites as much trouble as it did the Quakers later. In all other respects they made excellent and law-abiding citizens, but they were gradually driven out from each country that adopted compulsory military service. In Holland they early obtained complete exemption, but in the excitement of the Dutch Revolution, 1787–97, by which a short-lived Republic was founded, many abandoned their principles and resorted to arms. When the country was overrun by Napoleon the majority submitted to conscription, and the Churches who maintained their old principles gradually emigrated to Canada and the States.[1]

In France the sect mainly settled among the Vosges Mountains. They were exempted by Louis XIV, and protected from the consequences of the Edict of Nantes. In 1793 they petitioned the Assembly concerning military service, and received exemption from combatant duties, but were required to serve in hospitals and transport or to pay a commutation. The Committee of Public Safety, in granting the concession, declared : " We have observed in this people a simple heart and sweetness of character, and we think that a good Government ought to enlist all such virtues for the public good,"—sentiments which were signed, amongst others, by Robe-

number about 100,000 in the United States (where their peace principles were recognized by the law), and there are small bodies in Sweden and Denmark.

[1] The Quaker, Thomas Story, was told at Rotterdam in 1715 that the " Menists . . . still keep up their old testimony against fighting and swearing, yet they are not so lively in worship or so near the truth as they once were " (*Journal*, p. 520). In 1821, another Quaker, Thomas Shillitoe, found the testimony against war " had quite fallen to the ground " (Shillitoe's *Journal*, i. 237).

spierre. Napoleon and later Governments continued the exemption. The sect still existed in the year 1860.[1]

Very early in their history some Dutch Mennonites were allowed by Sigismund, King of Poland, to settle in what is now East Prussia, where they enjoyed religious freedom in return for their skilful cultivation of the land. The sect spread and flourished, but in 1723 Frederick William of Prussia threatened them with military service. So numerous an emigration to Pennsylvania and other parts of America was the result that the project was abandoned. In 1780 Frederick the Great confirmed their privileges. But soon the Prussian Government became alarmed at the increase in their numbers and in the amount of land held by them. In 1787, and again in 1801, regulations were imposed which were designed to check their growth. The consequence was a new emigration, this time to Russia, until the Government was again forced to make concessions.[2] They were exempted from military service during the war of 1813, and retained this privilege until the general conscription law for the North German Confederation in 1867. By a Cabinet order of 1868 the Mennonites were given the choice of accepting non-combatant duties in the Army under the military oath or of emigrating. Opinion in the body was divided. Many emigrated, some accepted the compromise, while others, even in Prussia, maintained their testimony. The emigration to Russia already mentioned was due to that astute monarch Catherine II, who wished for emigrants to cultivate her new conquests, and found her opportunity in the Prussian religious difficulty. She granted the Mennonites free land and a charter of full religious liberty and exemption from military service. This charter was confirmed by her successor, Paul. For eighty years and more these Mennonite colonies flourished exceedingly, and their members were held in high estimation as good farmers and good citizens. The Quakers, William Allen and Stephen Grellet, visited the settlements round the Dnieper in 1819. William Allen, in his *Journal*, gives an attractive account of them, adding that a new migration was expected. " The King of Prussia does not wish to part with them, as they are indeed among the very best of his subjects, but as they cannot bear arms the

---

[1] *Vide* article by W. Tallack in *British Friend*, 1900, p. 242, also Barclay, *Inner Life*, p. 610.

[2] The Mennonites seem always to have fared better than the small body of German Friends which arose in Prussia at the end of the eighteenth century. *Vide post*, Chapter XIV.

popular odium is so strong against them that they are glad to get away." [1]

In the early 'seventies, however, the Russian Government passed a law of universal military service. At once the Mennonites prepared to emigrate, and some of the leading members had reached the United States before the Government intervened. General Todleben, the hero of Sebastopol, told the Czar that he was driving away his best agriculturists, and suggested a compromise. Military service would not be required of Mennonites called up if they would undertake to serve three years in the Forestry Department, and to learn ambulance work in case of need. As in Prussia, some accepted the offer (in this case, of course, the forestry work was civilian in character), but there was a large emigration to America during the years immediately succeeding the law. English Friends helped the poorer Mennonites to leave Russia. In the United States and Canada they were specifically exempted from military service. The Stundist bodies in Russia show marked traces of Mennonite influence.[2] Two other Russian sects deserve notice. Allen and Grellet in 1819 visited bodies of " Molokans " and " Doukhobors " near the Mennonite settlements, and while finding much in common with the former, considered that the latter held unbalanced and dubious opinions. Fifty years later two Yorkshire Friends, Isaac Robson and Thomas Harvey, paid a visit of religious service to South Russia.[3] They too came into contact with the Molokans. One member who claimed to be more than a hundred years old gave the traditional version of their origin. A century before, General Tverchikoff had been sent to London on a mission by the Empress Catherine. There he and one of his under-officers became Quakers. The General dared not reveal his change of mind, but the officer began to preach and to make converts. Catherine heard of the new sect,

---

[1] William Allen, *Life*, ii. 61 foll. An interesting modern account of the Russian body is in Hume, *Thirty-five Years in Russia*, 1915, pp. 55 foll.

[2] The Mennonites are now estimated at 250,000. These include :
  (1) The Dutch body, which has given up the war tenet.
  (2) Those in Prussia, South Germany, and in the States (descendants of South Germans) who leave it an open question, which in practice means, in conscriptionist countries, military service.
  (3) The largest body in Prussia, Russia, Canada, the United States, and a few hundred in Galicia—which maintains the old testimony (*vide* Chapter XVIII, pp. 518–20 for the American Mennonites' attitude during the Great War).

[3] Report of visit (privately printed) 1867. In D.

and after inquiry declared that their principles were those of the Bible and they must be protected. Persecution was their lot, however, in later reigns. Their own name was " Spiritual Christians," " Molokans " or " Milk-eaters " was a nickname derived from their non-observance of the fasts of the Russian Church. At that time (1867) they were exempted from military service, but had to pay heavily for the privilege. Their Quaker visitors thought their objection was not to actual war, but to the ikon worship and other observances inevitable in the Army.

Almost the same story of their own origin is told by the Doukhobors. According to them a retired Prussian non-commissioned officer (probably in Russian service) settled in a village in the Kharkoff district about the year 1740 and founded the sect. But Mr. Aylmer Maude [1] in his study of the Doukhobors doubts the tradition. Possibly it was borrowed from the Molokans, with whom the Doukhobors have at times had some connection. In any case the term " Quaker " has often been applied on the Continent to mystical sects having no connection with Friends. The advocacy of Tolstoy, and their wholesale emigration to Canada, have made the Doukhobors comparatively well known to the English public. Their peace tenets were a late development. When conscription was imposed on the Caucasus in 1887 they submitted, and did not resist service until 1895. Many Russians have adopted Tolstoyan views on war and force, but these do not form a separate sect. A number of these Tolstoyans were imprisoned or banished to Siberia for refusal to serve in the Great War.[2]

There is another Continental sect of more recent growth. The " Nazarenes " appeared in Hungary, Austria and Bohemia after the year 1845, and in thirty years' time numbered several thousands. It is tempting to connect them with the Mennonites, whom they greatly resemble in their tenets, but they appear to have an independent and modern origin. One account naïvely remarks that " it is not to the bearing of arms in itself which they object, but

[1] *A Peculiar People—The Doukhobors.* Mr. Maude also doubts the story of the success of their attitude of non-resistance in winning over the wild tribes of the Caucasus, after their banishment thither in 1841. But for this there seems to be more evidence. The help given to the Doukhobors by Friends is described in Chapter X.

[2] Further details about these sects, some of which even call themselves " Friends " or " Quakers," were given in the *Friend*, January 6, 1923, in an article partly based on a letter from Countess Olga Tolstoy. See also for the treatment of Pacifists in Russia, J. W. Graham, *Conscription and Conscience*, pp. 365–8.

the purpose of killing the enemy, which they regard as anti-Christian." This opposition has brought on them much suffering and imprisonment in Austria and Hungary, though occasionally they have been allowed to give hospital work in lieu of military service. One Nazarene, Peter Zimbricht, of Vienna, was forced into the army in the war of 1866, and dragged from battle to battle with weapons tied upon him. At Königgrätz he was actually sentenced to death, but escaped the penalty. A branch of the sect arose in Serbia about the year 1875, and in that country they have endured frequent and severe imprisonment. Report has it that Nazarenes were shot for refusal to serve in the Great War, both in Hungary and Serbia, but complete information is not as yet available.[1]

After the adoption of conscription in the war by the United Kingdom, appeals to tribunals for exemption reminded the public that, in addition to the Friends, various smaller sects, such as the Christadelphians and the Seventh Day Adventists, which have arisen in the nineteenth century hold principles opposed to war. The Plymouth Brethren are content with an exemption from combatant service. This summary of the history of peace sects in the Christian Church may serve to show that the peace principle is generally held in common with some other very definite views on the obligations of Christianity. It may also remind us that (in the words of a recent study of religious thought) " Quakerism is no isolated or sporadic religious phenomenon. It is deeply rooted and embedded in a far wider movement that had been accumulating volume and power for more than a century before George Fox became a ' prophet ' of it to the English people. And both in its new English, and in its earlier Continental form, it was a serious attempt to achieve a more complete Reformation, to restore primitive Christianity, and to change the basis of authority from external things, of any sort whatever, to the interior life and spirit of man."[2]

---

[1] Details have lately been collected by J. W. Graham, *Conscription and Conscience*, pp. 354–7. *Vide* article on the " Nazarenes " in an extinct periodical, *The Messiah's Kingdom*, 1889, and also an appendix to the *Report* of I. Robson and T. Harvey. The Society of Friends in 1889 sent an address of sympathy to some Nazarenes imprisoned at Belgrade, which reached them just as they were released (*Proceedings of London Yearly Meeting*, 1889, p. 77).

[2] Rufus Jones, *Spiritual Reformers of the Sixteenth and Seventeenth Centuries*, p. 348.

PART I

THE SEVENTEENTH CENTURY

OUR forefathers and predecessors were raised to be a people in a time of great commotions, contests, and wars, begun and carried on for the vindication of religious and civil liberty, in which many of them were zealously engaged, when they received the knowledge of the truth ; but through the influence of the love of Christ in their minds they ceased from conferring with flesh and blood, and became obedient to the heavenly vision, in which they clearly saw that all wars and fightings proceeded from the spirit of this world, which is enmity with God, and that they must manifest themselves to be the followers of the Prince of Peace, by meekness, humility, and patient sufferings.—Address of the Philadelphia Yearly Meeting to Friends in Pennsylvania, 1774.

CHAPTER II

THE EARLY TESTIMONY OF THE SOCIETY
OF FRIENDS

1643–60

THROUGHOUT the sixteen centuries which separated the rise of
the Society of Friends from the days of the Early Church the sects
and teachers just described had maintained a witness for Christian
simplicity in life and doctrine. At times the witness had been
faintly uttered and almost unheeded, but it was never wholly silenced.
It is impossible, however, to trace a direct connection between
these earlier movements and the "great openings" which came
to George Fox, the young Leicestershire shepherd, in the days of
the Civil War.[1] Filled as he was with the conviction that his
spiritual enlightenment was the immediate gift of God, he acknowledged no guidance from men or books. Yet, least of any sect,
can Quakerism be understood apart from the religious and social
conditions amidst which it came into being. It is not only to the
personal experiences of George Fox, but to the general mind of
England in his day, that we must look for an explanation of the
rapid establishment and extension of the Society of Friends under
the Commonwealth and the later Stuarts.

In the years of struggle between Parliament and King, and in those
which followed Charles' execution, a hard Old Testament Calvinism
was dominant. The Army was religious, the Government was
religious, and religion was military and political, bringing the arm
of flesh to reinforce the sword of the Spirit. Episcopalianism was
in hiding, a current running underground, to reappear with gathered
strength at the Restoration ; Puritanism, stern and forbidding,

---

[1] Fox certainly had a good deal of intercourse with Baptists during his six
years (1643–9) of spiritual conflict, and many of his first followers came from
that sect.

though from many aspects full of grandeur, ruled in Church and State. Yet amid its rocks and precipices, where weak heads and hearts at times quailed, falling headlong into awful gulfs of pre-destined sin and reprobation, there rose in places clear springs of spiritual refreshment or the fiery breathings of spiritual ardour. While Presbyterian and Independent wrangled for political supremacy, little companies of " Seekers " met together to wait in silence for the divine teaching, and the Ranter and the Anabaptist, with stammering tongues and strange tremblings, strove to deliver their half-inspired, half-hysterical messages. "To be a Seeker," wrote Cromwell himself, " is to be of the best sect next to a finder ; and such an one shall every faithful, humble seeker be at the end. Happy seeker, happy finder ! " [1] Fox, in the days of his early struggles, met at times with these little bands,[2] and many Seekers at last found rest for their souls within the Society of Friends, or, as William Penn expressed it, " what people had been vainly seeking *without,* with much pains and cost, they by this ministry found *within* . . . the right way to peace with God." [3]

The seed of Fox's teaching fell upon prepared ground. But it would give a false impression, and be gravely unjust to the brave " Publishers of Truth," his friends and fellow-workers, to identify the teaching of the Society exclusively with one man's utterances or to imply that he ever imposed a rigid body of doctrine upon the new sect. A detailed history of the beginnings of Quakerism does not fall within the scope of this study. It has been told by many writers, most recently and fully by W. C. Braithwaite, with first-hand knowledge and quaint simplicity by the Dutch Quaker, William Sewel ; [4] but to understand the basis of " Friends' ancient testimony against wars and fightings " it is necessary to consider the principle which inspired the life and thought of Fox himself and of the community which gathered round him. The early pages of his *Journal* tell of his vain efforts to gain help and comfort from the creeds and teachers of the day. At last (in the year 1647), "when all my hopes in them and in all men were gone, so that I had nothing outwardly to help me, nor could I tell what to do : then, O ! then I heard a voice which said, ' There is one,

[1] Cromwell to Bridget Ireton, October 25, 1646.
[2] Fox, *Journal,* 8th edition, vol. i., ch. i, ii.
[3] *Ibid.,* Preface, p. xxvi.
[4] W. C. Braithwaite, *The Beginnings of Quakerism,* 1912. William Sewel, *History of the Quakers,* 1722.

even Christ Jesus, that can speak to thy condition'; and when I heard it, my heart did leap for joy. . . . For though I read the Scriptures that spoke of Christ and of God; yet I knew Him not but [except] by revelation, as he who hath the key did open, and as the Father of Life drew me to his Son by his Spirit." [1] Soon it became clear to him that the revelation was not for him alone : "With and by this divine power and Spirit of God, and the light of Jesus, I was to bring people off from all their own ways, to Christ, the new and living way, and from their Churches, which men had made and gathered, to the Church in God, the general assembly written in heaven which Christ is the head of : and from the world's teachers, made by men, to learn of Christ." [2]

This revelation, the light of Christ within, is the central truth of Quaker teaching. But to Fox and the early Friends it was no

> Sudden blaze . . . spread o'er the expanse of heaven,

which in one flash unveiled every detail of the road before them. It was rather a clear ray shed on the immediate path, a principle to guide in each new perplexity. It is a strange misreading of Friends' principles which accuses them of too literal reliance upon certain passages of Scripture. The words of Fox are echoed with slight variations by many others in the first generation of the Society, "These things I did not see by the help of man nor by the letter, though they are written in the letter, but I saw them in the light of the Lord Jesus Christ, and by his immediate Spirit and power." [3] Hence it was not primarily by the literal interpretation of certain verses in the Sermon on the Mount that their testimony against wars and fightings arose, but by an inward convincement that such practices were contrary to the Spirit of Christ.

In the years from 1643 to 1647, when Fox was passing through fierce temptations and inward struggles, his friends were ready with suggestions for his cure. Tobacco, psalm-singing, and matrimony were all proposed, but Fox never learned to smoke, his heart was too heavy to allow him to join in songs, and as to marriage— "I told them I was but a lad, and must get wisdom." "Others" (thinking, perhaps, that a drastic change of thought and occupation was necessary) "would have had me into the auxiliary band among

[1] Fox, *Journal*, 8th edition, i. 11, 12.
[2] *Ibid.*, pp. 36, 37.
[3] *Ibid.*, p. 36

the soldiery, but I refused ; and I was grieved that they proffered such things to me being a tender youth." [1]

"Tender," in Fox's vocabulary, means "responsive to spiritual influence," and it may seem natural that his soul should shrink from the confusion and bitterness which prevailed at the outbreak of the Civil War. Yet, perhaps, of all wars that between King and Parliament was the one into which many of the combatants on either side flung themselves with the most selfless devotion to political and religious ideals, and to which they were most fervently urged by their ecclesiastical guides. "I have eaten the King's bread," said Sir Harry Verney to Hyde, "near thirty years and I will not do so base a thing as to forsake him. I choose rather to lose my life." But (he added), "I have no reverence for the bishops for whom this quarrel subsists." *Bellum episcopale*, the war was called in bitterness, but presbyter as well as priest drove men to the battle. "Curse ye Meroz" (the Puritan ministers cried from their pulpits) "because they went not forth to help the Lord against the mighty" ; and as young William Dewsbury heard them, he too was willing to fling away his life on behalf of another King than Charles Stuart.[2] "We are both on the stage,", wrote a Parliamentary leader to his Royalist friend, "and we must act the parts assigned us in this tragedy. Let us do it in a way of honour, and without personal animosities." [3] In England at least the contest was singularly free from the cruelty and rapine which are usually inseparable from war, and which marked with indelible stains the struggles of the time between rival religious systems on the Continent.[4] None the less, Fox saw too clearly the essential nature of war to condone it even under such conditions. But it was not until the strife had dragged on for nine years and had led to the fateful scene at Whitehall and to the horrors of Drogheda and Wexford that he made his first recorded pronouncement on the relations of Christianity and war.

[1] Fox, *Journal*, 8th edition, i. 5, 6. As to tobacco, there is a curious story printed first in *Camb. Journal*, i. 44, how Fox, in 1652, put a proffered pipe for a moment to his mouth, to prove that he was no false ascetic, but had unity with the creation.

[2] Dewsbury, *Works*, pp. 45 foll.

[3] Sir William Waller to Sir Ralph Hopton.

[4] The chief exceptions are to be found in the doings of Rupert's troops at Bristol and Birmingham, and, on the Parliamentary side, in Fairfax's treatment of the Colchester garrison. In Ireland, unhappily, the war was fought on a different level.

In the autumn of 1650, three years after he began to preach his new revelation, the Derby justices had imprisoned him for six months as a blasphemer. During his term of imprisonment his patience and integrity won him many friends. In this same autumn and winter Charles Stuart the younger was rallying his forces for a last venture, and Cromwell's Commissioners were filling up the gaps in the Parliamentary Army by raising local militia under the provisions of the Militia Act passed in July 1650. It is evident from Fox's experience that the Commissioners took a large view of their powers. Thus he tells the story : " So Worcester fight came on, and my time being out of being committed six months to the house of correction : and then they filled the house of correction with persons they had taken up to be soldiers ; and then they would have had me to be captain of them to go forth to Worcester fight and the soldiers cried they would have none but me. So the keeper of the house of correction was commanded to bring me up before the Commissioners and soldiers in the market-place : and there they proffered me that preferment because of my virtue (as they said) with many other compliments : and asked me if I would not take up arms for the Commonwealth against the King ? But I told them I lived in the virtue of that life and power that took away the occasion of all wars : and I knew from whence all wars did rise, from the lust, according to James his doctrine. And still they courted me to accept of their offer, and thought I did but compliment with them, but I told them I was come into the covenant of peace, which was before wars and strifes was ; and they said they offered it in love and kindness to me, because of my virtue, and suchlike : and I told them if that were their love and kindness I trampled it under my feet.

" Then said they, Take him away, gaoler, and cast him into the dungeon among the rogues and felons : which they then did put me into the dungeon among thirty felons in a lousy stinking place without any bed : where they kept me almost a half year, unless it were at times : and sometimes they would let me walk in the garden, for they had a belief of me that I would not go away." [1]

[1] *Camb. Journal,* i. 11, 12. A remarkable fact in this episode is the offer of a command to an untrained man. Fox says more than once on other occasions : " The postures of war I never learned." Apparently, the first offer was some time before the battle, and the Commissioners may have had plans for training their pressed men.

A few weeks later the attempt was renewed, but neither dungeon nor felons had shaken Fox. " Now the time of Worcester fight coming on, Justice Bennet sent the constables to press me for a soldier, seeing I would not voluntarily accept of a command. I told them that I was brought off from outward wars. They came down again to give me press-money, but I would take none. Then I was brought up to Sergeant Holes, kept there a while and then taken down again. After a while the constables fetched me up again, and brought me before the Commissioners, who said I should go for a soldier ; but I told them that I was dead to it. They said, I was alive. I told them, where envy and hatred are, there is confusion. They offered me money twice, but I would not take it. Then they were angry, and committed me close prisoner, without bail or mainprize." [1]

Throughout his life Fox's physical strength and moral influence were recognized, and early in this imprisonment he had shown his power to control his unruly gaol-fellows. Moreover, the magistrates, he tells us, were " uneasy " about him and wished to get rid of him. It was not surprising, therefore, that the new militia levies seemed to offer a way of escape, and that neither magistrates nor Commissioners could understand the ground of the strange Quaker's refusal to serve. As little could they understand the spirit of the letter that he addressed to the magistrates, from his close confinement. " You profess to be Christians, and one of you [2] a minister of Jesus Christ ; yet you have imprisoned me, who am a servant of Jesus Christ. The Apostles never imprisoned any, but were imprisoned themselves. Take heed of speaking of Christ in words, and denying him in life and power. O friends, the imprisoning of my body is to satisfy your wills, but take heed of giving way to your wills, for that will hurt you." [3]

This first Quaker testimony against war struck the keynote for the future. Fox did not linger over the circumstances of the particular war, nor the interpretation of a particular text, but he relied on the contradiction between the spirit of war and the spirit of Christ. Fighting, like persecution, was the negation of Christianity—" denying Christ in life and power." Like the Apostle John, Fox could not reconcile hatred of the brother on earth with

---

[1] Fox, *Journal*, 8th edition, i, 72, 73. This second attempt is not given in the MS. from which the *Camb. Journal* is printed.

[2] Colonel Barton.   [3] *Journal*, i. 73.

love of the Father in heaven. There was also another marked resemblance between the attitude of Fox and that of his later followers. He obviously carried on no peace propaganda among the other conscripts and made no attempt to impose his own convictions upon them. The essence of early Quakerism lay in freedom to follow the inward guide, who would in due season lead the pilgrim into all truth : there was no desire on the part of the human teacher to force his hearers to travel at his own pace or to tread precisely in his footprints. Thus the Quaker " position " on war, as will be seen, came to be adopted at different times as an individual conviction by the first members of the Society.

Fox was released from Derby gaol in the early winter of 1651. The next eight years were for him and other Friends times of apostolic journeyings throughout Great Britain, punctuated by long and painful imprisonments—for blasphemy and heresy, for disturbance of the peace, and for sedition.[1] During these years the teaching spread far and wide, and the number of Friends increased with such rapidity that after the Restoration thousands were cast into gaol on an unjust suspicion of complicity in the Fifth Monarchy rising. Amongst the converts were many soldiers of all ranks, chiefly drawn from the Baptist and Independent members of the Parliamentary Army, although a few Royalist conversions are also recorded. From the scattered allusions in contemporary Quaker writings a list can be made of more than ninety soldiers or ex-soldiers who became Friends, and no doubt there were many others of whom no records remain.[2] These ninety include some of the leaders of the Society, James Naylor, Richard Hubberthorn, William Dewsbury and others, fellow-preachers and fellow-labourers with Fox. Quakerism at this early stage laid down no laws or regula-

---

[1] Among the *Swarthmore MSS.* (i. 40) (in D) there is a copy of a Justice's warrant against Thomas Rawlinson, a Friend, in 1656, which opens thus : " To all mayors, bailiffs, sheriffs, constables, tithing-men and all other officers whom these may concern ; Whereas there was an order issued from this bench for the apprehending of all Rogues and Vagabonds and in particular for the apprehending of all those who pass up and down the country under the name of Quakers as disturbers of the peace of the present Government and as underminers of the fundamentals of religion. . . ." The copyist comments : " This Thomas Rawlinson was going to visit the prisoners at Launceston in Cornwall, and they took him up by the watch and the constable took twenty shillings from him in the night, that he was carrying to the prisoners, and this was the wickedness of the Presbyterians in Oliver's days."

[2] Appendix A, List of soldiers and ex-soldiers who became Friends.

tions for its members, but it is abundantly clear that it soon proved impossible for a Quaker to remain a soldier.[1]

William Dewsbury's experience presents some features of peculiar interest, since his spiritual development ran parallel to that of Fox, yet on entirely independent lines.   He, too, in his perplexed search for truth, turned for help to ministers and preachers, " who only added to my sorrow, telling me to believe in Christ, I knew not where he was." Their exhortations drove him into the Parliamentary army, where he joined with a remnant that claimed to fight for the Gospel, but found among them as much ignorance of the Gospel as in those he had left.   Gradually his mind was turned from painful seekings after outward observances to the Light Within.   " And the word of the Lord came unto me and said, Put up thy sword into thy scabbard, if my kingdom were of this world when would my children fight.   Knowest thou not that, if I need, I could have twelve legions of angels from my Father ? Which word enlightened my heart, and discovered the mystery of iniquity, and that the kingdom of Christ was within ; and the enemies was within, and was spiritual, and my weapons against them must be spiritual, the power of God.   Then I could no longer fight with a carnal weapon, against a carnal man, for the letter, which man in his carnal wisdom had called the Gospel, and had deceived me ; but then the Lord . ; . caused me to yield in obedience, to put up my carnal sword into the scabbard and to leave the Army." [2]

This experience came to Dewsbury in 1645, some years before his first meeting with Fox, but he gladly accepted the Quaker message in 1651, at the same time as James Naylor, formerly quarter-master under General Lambert.   Some soldier-converts were soon brought to a position in which they could no longer fight ; and others found that for other reasons life in the army became impossible for them.   The story of the unnamed soldier who visited Fox in Derby gaol in 1650–1, throws some light on the difficulties both of Quaker soldiers and non-Quaker officers. He was " convinced " by Fox, and began to preach in his regiment. Unluckily his Colonel (Barton) was also a preacher (probably an Independent) and one of the justices who had committed Fox to his prison.   Thus, when the new convert declared that his officers,

[1] W. C. Braithwaite, *Beginnings of Quakerism*, p. 519.
[2] Dewsbury, *Works*, pp. 45–55.

through their treatment of Fox, were " as blind as Nebuchadnezzar," they were not unnaturally annoyed.   Hence, when before the battle of Worcester two Royalists came out from the King's camp with a challenge to any two Parliamentarians, the Quaker was one chosen to meet them.   His companion was killed, but he drove the Royalists back without firing a shot, as he told Fox.   But when the battle was over, " he laid down his arms and saw to the end of fighting "—another instance of individual conviction.[1]   Freedom of preaching in all ranks was a question upon which Cromwell and his officers differed,[2] but even making allowance for the laxer discipline of the day, it was natural that officers should have disliked privates with a turn for drawing unflattering Scripture parallels.

In 1654, when Cromwell assumed the Protectorate, the oath of allegiance was tendered to all soldiers and others employed under Government. This, or rather their own principle against all swearing, cut short the military career of several Quakers, including John Stubbs, who had been convinced when Fox was a prisoner at Carlisle in 1653.[3] Fox relates how some soldiers, who had inclined towards Quakerism, nevertheless took the oath, and how shortly afterwards on a march into Scotland they were fired at by a garrison in mistake for the enemy, and several lost their lives, " which was a sad judgment." [4] This period was one of great testing for soldier-Friends ; probably it was only the cessation of campaigning after the battle of Worcester that permitted them to remain even as long as some did in the Army. From his gaol at Northampton in October 1655 William Dewsbury wrote to Margaret Fell of Swarthmore, the protectress of all Friends in distress, telling her how their friend Captain Bradford had quartered his regiment in the town on its march to London, but when he visited Dewsbury and the other

---

[1] *Camb. Journal*, i. 13.   [2] Carlyle, *Cromwell*, Letter clxii.

[3] A characteristic story of another Carlisle soldier of this period is told by John Whiting in *Persecution Exposed*, 1715, p. 120. William Gibson with some other soldiers from the garrison intended to amuse themselves by breaking up a Quaker meeting. The preaching of Thomas Holmes, however, had such an effect on Gibson " that he stept into them meeting near Thomas, to defend him, and bid any that durst offer to abuse him." He soon joined Friends, left the garrison and became a shoemaker. After three years of " waiting upon God in silence " in this peaceful occupation, he proved an effective and powerful preacher, defending Quakerism by his life and words, and no longer by the strength of his arm.

[4] *Camb. Journal*, i. 142

prisoners the gaoler churlishly refused to admit him, asking him whether he had a command in the Army. " He answered him : Whether I have it matters not in this thing, for this I declare to thee, what command soever I have in the Army my sword shall not open the gaol doors, and if thou do not open them I shall not come in. And in meekness and patience he stood until the Lord commanded the gaoler's spirit, that he let him come in." For the remainder of the regiment's stay the prison was frequented by officers and soldiers who joined in the Friends' meetings.[1]

The Society was already feeling anxiety for the welfare of its members. In 1656 Fox wrote to Friends exhorting them to help and support any soldiers that might be turned out of the Army " for truth's sake." [2] The advice was repeated three years later by a meeting at Horsham of Friends—Kent, Sussex, Surrey and Hampshire. In 1656 also one of the earliest " General " or " Yearly " Meetings to settle the affairs of the Society was held at Balby in Yorkshire. Its Epistle, signed by William Dewsbury and others, and sent out to be read in Friends' meetings, bears witness to the growing care for a consistent behaviour among Friends. Three of its recommendations seem to glance at the Army difficulties. They run as follows :

" 13th. That care be taken as any one is called before outward powers of the nation, that in the light obedience to the Lord be given.
" 14th. That if any be called to serve the Commonwealth in any public service, which is for the public wealth and good, that with cheerfulness it be undertaken, and in faithfulness discharged with God, that therein patterns and examples in the thing that is righteous ye may be to those that are without.
" 15th. That all Friends who have calling and trade do labour in the thing that is good in faithfulness and uprightness, and keep to the yea and nay in all their communications ; and that all who are indebted to the world do endeavour to discharge the same, that nothing they may owe to any man but love one another." [3]

The outward powers of the nation were in no mood to deal tenderly with scruples of conscience. Fox noted in his *Journal*

[1] *Swarthmore MSS.*, iv. 141.
[2] Fox, *Epistles*, 1698, p. 94. *Letters of Early Friends*, p. 284.
[3] *Beginnings of Quakerism*, pp. 411–14.

for 1656 that " O. P [Oliver, Protector] began to harden," [1] and that several Quakers lost their commissions in the Army. The next year there was a drastic purge, particularly among the forces in Scotland and Ireland, where Quakerism had begun to make its way. It found little welcome from the authorities. The Quaker neglect of rank and title was held to be subversive of military discipline, and the refusal to take the oath of allegiance was suspected as the cloak of designs to restore Charles Stuart or to set up the kingdom of the Saints. Monk in Scotland and Henry Cromwell in Ireland, both in person and through their subordinates, cleared the regiments of Friends. Monk assured the Protector (perhaps not yet completely " hardened " and mistrustful of such stern measures) that the Quakers " will prove a very dangerous people should they increase in your Army, and be neither fit to command nor to obey, but ready to make a distraction in the Army and a mutiny upon every slight occasion." [2] Colonel Daniel at Perth reported in a similar strain the sad case of his Captain-Lieutenant Davenport.

" My Captain-Lieutenant is much confirmed in his principle of quaking, making all the soldiers his equal (according to the Levellers' strain) that I daresay in a short time his principles in the Army shall be the root of disobedience. My Lord, the whole world is governed by superiority and distance in relations, and when that is taken away, unavoidably anarchy is ushered in. The man is grown so besotted with his notions, that one may as well speak to stone walls as to him ; and I speak it from my heart, his present condition is the occasion of great trouble to me. He hath been under my command almost fourteen years, and hitherto hath demeaned himself in good order, and many of these whimsies I have kept him from, but now there is no speaking to him. . . There was one example last day when he came to St. Johnston [Perth] ; he came in a more than ordinary manner to the soldiers of my company, and asking them how they did, and the men doing their duty by holding off their hats, he bade them put them on, he expected no such thing from them. My Lord, this may seem to be a small thing, but there lies more in the bosom of it than every one thinks, and though it's good to be humble, yet humility would be known by the demonstration thereof, and where all are equals I expect little obedience in government." [3]

---

[1] *Camb. Journal*, i. 263.   [2] Thurloe, *State Papers*, vi. 136.
[3] *Ibid.*, vi. 167.

Davenport was cashiered by Monk, towards whom he displayed the same principle of equality, refusing "hat-honour" and using the familiar "thou." With him in 1657 several other officers and many soldiers left the Army.[1] Among the Swarthmore Manuscripts at Devonshire House is the copy of a document signed by some of these ejected soldiers, disclaiming the derisive name of Quaker, while admitting "quaking and trembling" which testified to the power of God.[2] There are not many traces of distinctly anti-war testimony, although at Aberdeen one Cornet Ward, who was inclining towards Quakerism, declared that, if he were convinced, "he purposed not to make use of any carnal sword, but was resolved for that thing to lay down his tabernacle of clay." "I fear," wrote Major Richardson, "that these people's principles will not allow them to fight if we stand in need, though it does to receive pay."[3]

Besse, writing with special reference to Ireland, gives a fair summary of the general position. There were many in the Army, he says, "who came to be convinced of the truth gradually, and began publicly to declare against the vices and immoralities of others, and were sensible of the corruptions of the teachers in those times, and bore their testimony against them. This their zeal for virtue and true religion often exposed them to the resentment of their officers and others, who hated reproof, so that some of these faithful monitors were imprisoned, others cashiered and turned out of the Army. And divers of them, as they became further enlightened refused to bear arms any longer, and became able ministers of the truth, and publishers of the gospel."[4] Given a strict disciplinarian in command and a zealous Quaker in the ranks, an explosion was bound to result sooner or later from their contact, and it is strange that many of the converts did not realize earlier the difficulties of their position. Some always cherished a certain pride in their past service and a friendly feeling for their old com-

---

[1] *Camb. Journal*, i. 308.

[2] *Swarthmore MSS.*, iv. 237, see Appendix B. Testimony of the Soldiers.

[3] Thurloe, *State Papers*, vi. 145, 146. William Caton wrote to Fox in 1659 after a visit to Scotland, "that few soldiers at that time came to meetings, excepting some few officers who did decline from Monk, and for the most part . . . were loving to Friends ; for many there was that threw in their commissions while I was there and several were displaced, and great overturnings there was among them" (*Swarthmore MSS.*, iv. 268).

[4] Besse, *Sufferings of the Quakers*, edition 1753, vol. ii. Ireland, 1656.

rades.[1]   In the troubled days between the death of Cromwell and the Restoration, many Quakers, some of them ex-soldiers, addressed pamphlets of earnest exhortation to the Army, and one or two drew a connection between their own expulsion and the present difficulties of Presbyterians and Independents.

In the Navy, at a time when Blake was gaining fresh renown for England on the seas, difficulties of conscience were more urgent. The press-gang was busy, sweeping men on board the ships-of-war. On February 25, 1655/6, Captain Willoughby wrote to the Admiralty Commissioners from Portsmouth, complaining of the poor quality of recruits, men of all trades but seamen, which tends to nothing but to multiply expense.   The pressed men are "the gatherings of the south part of Sussex, sent by four justices of the peace."   The collection is reminiscent of Falstaff's ragged regiment, "a tinker, quaker, two glass-carriers, hatter, chairmaker, and a tanner with his boy, seven years old, and so the Mayor of Southampton supplies at all times."[2]   Whether this pressed Quaker spread his principles in the Navy or not, they had certainly made headway there some months later.   Captain Foster of the *Mermaid*, in October 1656, forwarded to the Commissioners the resignation of his master-gunner.   "He have not acted these two months but have altogether confined himself to his cabin, and have given out to our master-carpenter that no power shall command him to fire a gun as that from thence blood might be spilt, his tenets obliging him thereunto : the which myself with others do find to come nearest to those which are called Quakers, for his carriage towards me and others is without any outward respect, and from a spirit of delusion, as to the denying of ordinances and visible authority." The worthy captain, like Colonel Daniel in Scotland, evidently wished to be rid of a perplexing subordinate, for he added : "I earnestly desire that he may have his will as that I may discharge him with all speed."[3]   The infection spread, however, for in April 1657 Captain Marryot reported to the Commissioners that Thomas Shewell, late boatswain of the *Discovery* and an Admiralty agent at Bristol, had turned Quaker and refused to swear in a case where his witness was required.[4]

[1] Joseph Fuce in *A Visitation by Way of Declaration*, 1659 (D. Tracts 95, 37), says : " I was for many years a private soldier, corporal, and serjeant in the times of the late wars."

[2] *Cal. State Papers, Dom.*, 1655–6, p. 489.

[3] *Extracts from State Papers relating to Friends*, p. 14.

[4] *Ibid.*, p. 27.

In the same month another gunner, from scruples of conscience, wished to be released from his employ. It is not certain that Richard Knowlman, of the *Assistance* frigate lying in the Downs, was a Quaker, but his letter makes it probable. He addressed one of the Commissioners (whose name is lost) because he was reputed to be more favourable to tender consciences than his colleagues and would not be offended by the omission of flattering titles. Knowlman's plea has a rough eloquence of its own. " Friend, I have served this Commonwealth by land and sea very faithfully, to the loss of my limbs, ever since the year 'forty-one, and am willing to continue in this Commonwealth's service so far forth as I may be profitable unto it upon some other account than I am at present, not that I desire to be in a higher place. . . . I shall desire thee as soon as it may be that thou wilt think of some other employment for me : for I am not very free to continue much longer in this : for I desire but a livelihood for I and my wife and children, though it be but a mean one. So the Lord Almighty be thy director and preserver and that thou mayest once come to feed of the true bread of life which will be a continual satisfaction unto thee when all the pomp and glory of the world will pass away." [1] It is tempting to believe that Knowlman had read the Epistle from the General Meeting at Balby, already quoted, but there is no direct evidence that he was a Quaker, nor does any record survive to show whether the busy Commissioner found time to provide him with a new and more innocent post. The next year, in a record of Friends' sufferings presented to Cromwell, two Friends in prison at Winchester, Daniel Baker and Anthony Milledge, are each described as lately a captain of a ship-of-war for the State.[2] Daniel Baker became the owner of a merchant vessel and a leading Friend.

But the instance of Friends' peace principles in the Commonwealth Navy of which the fullest and most interesting record survives is that of Thomas Lurting. This Friend, in his old age, published his experiences under the title *The Fighting Sailor turned Peaceable Christian,*[3] with the express object of commending to others the silent waiting upon God which had been his own guide through life. " For as silence is the first word of command in

[1] *Extracts*, p. 27.
[2] *Ibid.*, pp. 45 foll.
[3] *The Fighting Sailor turned Peaceable Christian : Manifested in the Convincement and Conversion of Thomas Lurting, with a Short Relation of many Great Dangers and Wonderful Deliverances he met withal.* 1710.

martial discipline, so it is in the spiritual ; for until that is come unto, the will and mind of God concerning us cannot be known, much less done."

Born in 1632, at fourteen years of age he was pressed into the wars in Ireland, then fought by sea against Dutch and Spaniards, and by 1657 was boatswain's mate upon the *Bristol* frigate. There he had the oversight of the crew of two hundred men ; one of his duties was to see that they were present at the ship's worship and to compel the unwilling to attend. A few who met in Quaker fashion for silent worship he beat and maltreated for their obstinacy. At Blake's attack on Santa Cruz, Lurting played a gallant part, and his vivid narrative is used by historians as a " source " for that battle. His mind, naturally religious, was affected further by several hairbreadth escapes from death, and, as he grew dissatisfied with the official worship of the ship, he prayed earnestly for guidance. But the first thought that truth might be found among the despised Quakers startled him. " For the reasoning part got up. What, to such a people, that both priests and professors are against ? What, to such a people that I have been so long beating and abusing, and that without just cause ? Death would be more welcome." The very form of the protest showed that the battle was half won, and he soon reached the position that " whether Quaker or no Quaker, peace with God I am for." He confided in one of the Friends, who received him lovingly, but his first attendance at their little meeting caused a great stir on board, calling forth remonstrances from both chaplain and captain. The former said : " Thomas, I took you for a very honest man and a good Christian, but am sorry you should be so deluded," while the captain stood by, " turning the Bible from one end to another, to prove the Quakers no Christians."

Their conduct, however, during a severe epidemic on the ship, changed the captain's opinion, and he soon placed great confidence in them.[1] " When there was any fighting in hand he would say, ' Thomas, take thy friends, and do such and such a thing.' They proved indeed the hardiest men on the ship, but refused to take any plunder. Being come to Leghorn, they were ordered to Barcelona to take a Spanish man-of-war. Lurting's ship opened fire on the castle, and Lurting occupied himself with one corner

[1] This quotation is borrowed from the summary of Lurting's story in W. C. Braithwaite's *Beginnings of Quakerism*, pp. 521-2.

of the place, the guns of which had found the range of the ship. He was on the forecastle, watching the effect of his shot, when it suddenly flashed through him : ' What if thou killest a man ? ' Putting on his clothes, for he had been half-stripped, he walked on the deck as if he had not seen a gun fired, and when asked if he was wounded, said : ' No, but under some scruple of conscience on the account of fighting,' though at that time he did not know that Quakers refused to fight. That night he opened out his new convictions to his friends, who said little, except that, if the Lord sent them well home, they would never go to it again. Soon after one of them went to the captain and asked to be discharged, as he could fight no longer. The captain, a Baptist preacher, said he should put his sword through any man who declined fighting in an engagement, and after further words beat the man with his fist and cane. The time of trial came a little later, when the ship was cruising off Leghorn, and had cleared for action with a vessel bearing down on them, supposed to be a Spanish man-of-war. Lurting and his friends drew together on deck and refused to go to their quarters. The lieutenant went to the captain and reported : ' Yonder the Quakers are all together, and I do not know but they will mutiny, and one says he cannot fight.' The captain, in a fury, dragged Lurting down to his quarters and drew his sword on him. Then the word of the Lord ran through Lurting : ' The sword of the Lord is over him, and if he will have a sacrifice, proffer it him.' Thereupon he stepped towards the captain, fixing his eye with great seriousness on him, at which the captain changed countenance, turned himself about, called to his man to take away his sword, and went off. The ship they expected to fight proved to be a friendly Genoese, and before night the captain sent a message excusing his anger." When Lurting returned to England, he entered the merchant service, but, as will appear, his peaceable principles were several times put to a severe proof.

Nor was it only in the Army and Navy that the peace testimony of Friends led them into conflict with authority. The Militia Acts of Cromwell and his Parliaments proved a heavy burden. In 1649 and 1650 Parliament had re-established the county militia, and it was under the latter Act that George Fox suffered at Derby. In 1655 Cromwell appointed new Militia Commissioners for the English and Welsh counties, upon whom rested the duty of raising a force. The horses, arms, and money required were to be obtained from Royalist estates, and used to equip the well-affected, who were formed into regiments and trained. Those who refused to train were to be fined £20, and the obstinate imprisoned.[1] The policy of mulcting Royalist estates was soon abandoned, but the militia was maintained throughout the Protectorate, and heavy fines " for not sending a man to serve in the train-bands " soon became a common form of Quaker suffering. The earliest known instances are found in records for fines and distraints in kind at Colchester in 1659,[2] but it is almost certain that these were not isolated examples. After the Restoration, when Friends noted their sufferings with great accuracy, these fines are very frequent in all parts of the country. No doubt there were some backsliders like Thomas Ayrey, who " could suffer nothing for truth, for when like to suffer for keeping Christ's command in not swearing, he truckled under and took an oath ; when like to suffer for truth's testimony against fighting and bearing outward arms, he consented to take arms " ;[3] but the great majority stood as firm as Richard Robinson of Countersett, Wensleydale, who had a faithful testimony " against bearing arms or finding a man for the militia, for he was all along charged with finding a man, but always kept very clear, and never after his convincement would pay anything directly or indirectly, but suffered for the same by fines and distresses, frequently encouraging other Friends to stand faithful." [4]

In the troubled days of 1659, when the Commissioners were busy raising new troops, Justice Anthony Pearson, still nominally a Friend, was a Commissioner in the North,[5] and in Bristol seven Friends who were chosen for the office were in a strait how to act, desiring Fox's counsel.[6] " He told them : ' You cannot well leave them, seeing ye have gone among them ; so keep in that which presses and grinds all down to the witness, the power of God ;

[1] Gardiner, *Commonwealth and Protectorate*, iii. 148–9, 171–2. *Cal. State Papers, Dom.*, 1655, Preface, p. viii.

[2] Besse, *Sufferings*, i. 194.

[3] *First Publishers of Truth*, p. 266.

[4] *Ibid.*, p. 314, also p. 308.

[5] Pearson, who lived in Durham, was also a magistrate for Westmorland, and was convinced in 1652–3 on the bench at Appleby, at the trial of Naylor and Howgill. After the Restoration he returned to the Established Church, and died in 1665.

[6] Alexander Parker to Fox, *Swarthmore MSS.*, iii. 143. Parker says : " I have had a great weight on my spirit about it. I see very little, yet something there may be in it. I can neither persuade them to it, nor dissuade them from it."

and therein you will have freedom and wisdom and liberty to declare yourselves over the contrary part that would rule.' But he warned Friends against running into places." [1]

From Cardiff Francis Gawler wrote to Fox, January 26, 1659/60 : [2] " I wass disired by my brother, who is a Jestes, John Gawler, who hath Receued a Commission Come Dowen from ffleetwoode, to be Lefteniente Cornell to one Boushey Mancell of this Conty, who is to raise a Regement of Malisa foote, and if thow sesete aney thing in the theinge that hee should not medell with it ; and if thow arte free, it will be very much unto him to vnderstand a word from thee. His Coronell is a louinge man to frinds, and is very disierus to haue frinds in his Regemente, and my brother is verey Redy and willing to prefer frinds to offeces verey much, bute frinds are not free to medell with it, only Mathew Gibon hath partly Ingaged to bee a Captan (and Another a privat Souldger) of whom we are tender, knowing hee hath noe bade ende in it, but thinkes he may be sarvesabell for truth in it." But this tentative proposal was sternly met by Fox, in whose handwriting the letter is endorsed, " which g f forbad and said it was Contraye to over prensables, for ovr wepenes are spiritall and not Carnall."

In 1664 a paper was drawn up on behalf of Fox and other Friends imprisoned in Lancaster Gaol, which states that the Committee of Safety in 1659 offered him the post of Colonel, " but he denied them all and bade them live peaceable." This paper also describes three of the imprisoned Friends, Thomas Waters, William Wilson, and James Brown, as faithful Royalists, who had suffered for the King in battles, wounds, prisons, and sequestrations, and " never had a penny of pay to this day." [3] Another Royalist Quaker appears in Sewel's pages, where it is told how, in later years, Christopher Bacon of Somerset was taken from a meeting at Glastonbury and brought before the Bishop of Wells, who called him a rebel for meeting contrary to the King's law. Christopher retorted : " Dost thou call me rebel ? I would have thee know that I have ventured my life for the King in the field when such as thou

---

[1] W. C. Braithwaite, *Second Period of Quakerism*, p. 18, quoting from *Swarthmore MSS.*, vii. 157. This letter confirms the fact that some London Friends were serving, " for they were, when I was out of town, put in commission." Fox adds : " There is little but filth and much dirt and dross to be expected among them."

[2] *Swarthmore MSS.*, iv. 219. The document is given in its original spelling as a very perfect example of the phonetics of the time.

[3] *Camb. Journal*, ii. 48–52.

lay behind hedges." By this (says Sewel) he stopped the Bishop's mouth, who did not expect such an answer, and soon dismissed him.[1]

Not all the precautions and warnings of Fox and others, however, could save Friends from falling under the suspicions of the shifting Governments of that strange year 1659, and it was the general misunderstanding of the Quaker position which led Friends to publish more clear and comprehensive statements of their peace principles. Before considering these, a short account must be given of the general attitude of Fox and his adherents to the Commonwealth Government.

The overthrow of parliamentary government by Cromwell in 1653 gave a fresh impetus to conspiracies, both Cavalier and Republican, against his power. He lived for nearly six years longer, and died at last in his bed ; but throughout those years plots were unceasing, and his life was in constant danger. As is usual in times of unrest and treachery, all assemblies, whether religious or secular, whether for business or pleasure, were regarded by the Government with suspicion, and often prohibited beforehand or dispersed by bands of soldiers. Quaker meetings (which, indeed, were at times frequented by wild spirits, Levellers, Ranters or Fifth Monarchy men) were not exempt ; Fox was arrested at Whetstone in Leicestershire and carried to London, where he was told that Cromwell would be satisfied by a signed promise " that he would not take up a sword against the Lord Protector, or the Government as it is now."[2] In response Fox drew up a document,[3] the theological implications of which were sharply canvassed and criticized in later times. From Cromwell's point of view the essential passage was that in which Fox proclaimed his mission " to stand a witness against all violence and against all the works of darkness, and to turn people from the darkness to the light and from the occasion of the magistrate's sword. . . . With the carnal weapon I do not fight, but am from those things dead." He subscribed his name as one " who to all your souls is a friend . . . and a witness against all wicked inventions of men and murderous plots." Another document filled with fervent spiritual exhortation was also conveyed to the Protector, whose interest was sufficiently aroused to make him wish for an interview with the new teacher.[4] Fox was summoned to

---

[1] Sewel, *History*, p. 682.   [2] *Camb. Journal*, i. 161.   [3] Appendix C.
[4] For the letter and interview, *vide Camb. Journal*, i. 161–5, 167–8.

Whitehall before the time of the morning levee, and set forth at length his belief in a free ministry inspired by the Spirit of Christ. Cromwell listened patiently, at times interjecting that "it was very good" or "truth," but at last the room became crowded and Fox took his leave.   As he was turning away, Cromwell caught him by the hand and said, with tears in his eyes : " Come again to my house, for if thou and I were but an hour a day together, we should be nearer one to the other.   I wish thee no more ill than I do to my own soul."   Fox characteristically replied by a warning to listen to the voice of God and to beware of hardness of heart.   After he had withdrawn he received the Protector's message that he was free and might go where he would.   There were Friends and sympathisers with Friends in Cromwell's own household, and the Protector on several occasions intervened to check the zeal of local authorities.[1]   Even in 1658, when many Friends were in prison on various counts, Oliver and his Council sent down advice to local magistrates, " in dealing with persons whose miscarriages arises rather from defects in their understanding than from malice in their wills, to exercise too much lenity than too much severity." [2]

In this first peace document, as definitely as in his speeches at Derby, Fox stated his abhorrence of all war and of the employment of force and violence for political and religious ends, but he now made the further claim that part of his mission was to bring others to the same peaceable state.   He recognized, though within strict limits, the power of the " magistrate's sword " (that is, the civil authority) in preserving order within the State ; but that sword, too, was to pass away with the occasion for it, as all men were turned from evil to follow the inward light.   It must be remembered that the line of demarcation between the civil and the military power was blurred almost out of recognition in the days of the Protectorate.   Soldiers were often put upon police duty, and it was in that capacity that they were ordered to disperse Friends' meetings and to arrest Fox and others.   In this paper Fox repeats to " soldiers that are put in that place " (of maintaining civil order) the advice of John the Baptist [3] given to the Roman soldiers, who themselves were first and foremost policemen, upholding the law and government of Rome in Palestine.   The text has been described as " the

---

[1] He protested in vain against the barbarous punishment inflicted by Parliament on James Naylor in 1657.

[2] *Extracts*, p. 34.   [3] Luke iv. 14.

epitome of the good policeman's character." [1] In the following
year, 1655, when Friends were beginning to suffer on account
of the oath of allegiance, Fox wrote again to the Protector, re-
emphasizing the argument that a magistrate's duty was not to coerce
men's consciences, but to put down open and notorious evil. [2]

A declaration against the use of weapons was apparently made
a test against other suspects. John Lilburne, doughty champion
of political equality and sufferer for his beliefs, had been lying in
gaol first in the Channel Islands and later in Dover Castle. Here
he came into contact with Friends, and his restless, quarrelsome
spirit found help in their peaceable teaching. [3] Cromwell, who
always treated him with some respect, heard of his new leanings,
and offered to release him if he would sign a promise never to draw
a sword against the existing Government. At first Lilburne,
although he knew of Fox's declaration, refused, " because he did
not perfectly approve that point of self-denial." In time his insight
grew clearer, and he published, in May 1655, a paper declaring
his adherence to " the savouriest of people called Quakers," and
that " I am already dead, or crucified, to the very occasions and
real grounds of outward wars and carnal sword-fightings and fleshly
bustlings and contests ; and that therefore confidently I now believe,
I shall never hereafter be a user of a temporal sword more, nor a
joiner with them that do so." But the old Lilburne was not, in
truth, quite dead, for he was careful to explain that this declaration
was not intended to satisfy " the fleshly wills of my great adversaries " nor his " poor, weak, afflicted wife," but to deprive the said
adversaries of any excuse for continuing his imprisonment. Probably
he was somewhat surprised and disappointed when Cromwell
accepted the declaration and set him free. He remained faithful
to Friends' principles, and on his death in 1657 he was buried in
Quaker simplicity. [4]

The difficulties of Friends in the last years of the Protectorate
have already been described, but when Cromwell's death removed
the controlling hand from the affairs of the nation their perplexities
increased amidst the general unsettlement and confusion. Yet
Fox and other Friends continued to journey up and down the

[1] *Arbiter in Council*, p. 518.
[2] *Camb. Journal*, i. 192–4.
[3] In the paper quoted he says that in Dover Castle, " I have really and
substantially found that which my soul hath many years sought diligently after."
[4] Sewel, *History*, Book III.

country, encouraging meetings already established and settling up
new ones, and although their gatherings were often broken up by
troops of soldiers armed with justices' warrants, Fox's *Journal* tells
of "glorious, powerful, heavenly meetings."[1] Early in 1659
Sir George Booth stirred up a Royalist insurrection in Cheshire
which caused general alarm. Some Quakers, or old soldiers with
Quaker leanings, prepared to join the forces led against him by
Lambert. The leaders of the Society were greatly troubled by
this backsliding, and Fox, for weeks at a time, was overcome by
deep depression seeing "how the powers was plucking each other
in pieces."[2] He published several earnest exhortations to "all
Friends everywhere" to keep out of plots and fighting or any interference in matters political The Devil, he wrote emphatically,
is the author and cause of wars and strife : "all that pretend to
fight for Christ are deceived ; for his kingdom is not of this world,
therefore his servants do not fight. Fighters are not of Christ's
kingdom, but are without Christ's kingdom. . . . All such as
pretend Christ Jesus, and confess him, and yet run into the use of
carnal weapons, wrestling with flesh and blood, throw away the
spiritual weapons. . . . Live in love and peace with all men,
keep out of all the bustlings of the world ; meddle not with
the powers of the earth ; but mind the kingdom, the way of
peace."[3]

It was probably the enlistment of these pseudo-Quakers that
gave rise to the rumours which reached the Royalist Secretary
Nicholas, in the autumn of 1659. He had heard (he wrote to
the French Court) that the impious rebels in England were arming
madmen, for three regiments of Quakers, Brownists and Anabaptists
were being raised in London, under the command of Vane, Skippon,
and "White, a famous Quaker from New England."[4] Events,
however, moved steadily towards the restoration of the monarchy :

---

[1] *Camb. Journal*, i. 340, 354.   [2] *Ibid.*, 341.
[3] For these letters, *vide Camb. Journal*, i. 334. *Journal*, 8th edition,
i. 448–51. Fox, *Epistles* (1698), pp. 137, 145.
[4] *Extracts*, p. 116 (*State Papers, Dom.*, J, Foreign Correspondence, Flanders,
vol. 32). White is a name unknown in early Quaker history. The name
"Quaker," however, as a term of reproach was applied to other sects, and the
fighting Quakers may have been Fifth Monarchy men. This may also be the
explanation of a letter from Desborough (April 8, 1660) directing the last attempt
in Wales and the West at organized resistance to the Restoration. "Let the
Quakers," he writes, "have the knottiest piece, for they are resolute in performance
though but rash in advising" (*Extracts*, p. 116, *State Papers, Dom.*, ccxx. 70).

as Fox travelled through the country he found that "great fears and troubles was in many peoples and a looking for the King's coming in and that all things should be altered, but I told them the Lord's power and light was over all and shined over all." [1] The Army was in a state of grave disorder, the soldiers openly taking sides for King or Commonwealth,[2] and both parties found some relief for their feelings in disturbing Friends' meetings. Monk had entered London in February 1659/60, and his old friend and fellow-soldier, Richard Hubberthorn, appealing to him, obtained a brief and emphatic order, which was of some service.

St. James, *9th of March.*
I do require all officers and soldiers to forbear to disturb the peace-able meetings of the Quakers, they doing nothing prejudicial to the Parliament or Commonwealth of England.

George Monk.[3]

But Monk's authority could not prevail everywhere and in many places the trouble continued.[4] The Commonwealth of England was soon to pass away ; in April the Convention Parliament met, the first act of which was to recall the King. In that troubled and excited spring Fox travelled in the West from Bristol to Gloucester, and thence by Tewkesbury to Worcester. "I never saw the like drunkenness," he noted, "as then in the towns, for they had been choosing Parliament-men." [5] These travelling Quaker missionaries roused the suspicions of the authorities at a moment when no man could trust his neighbour, and the new Government was scarcely established before Friends felt its heavy hand. At the end of April 1660, as William Caton and Thomas Salthouse journeyed from Yorkshire, they found "all was on heaps after the apprehending of John Lambert." The Quaker meetings they held brought about their arrest, with that of other Friends. They were treated fairly and, as they could give a satisfactory account of themselves, allowed to proceed on their way. Others were not

---

[1] *Camb. Journal,* i. 347.

[2] W. Caton, who travelled in Scotland in the winter of 1659, wrote to Fox that many officers there had thrown up their commissions, and others had been displaced, and " great overturnings there was among them " (*Swarthmore MSS.,* iv. 268). At Gloucester, Fox found " part of the soldiers were for the King, and another part for the Parliament " (*Camb. Journal,* i. 352).

[3] *Swarthmore MSS.,* iii. 141. *Letters of Early Friends,* 79.

[4] At Balby the regular troops protected the Yearly Meeting against the militia soldiers who wished to break it up (*Camb. Journal,* i. 353-4.)

[5] *Camb. Journal,* i. 352.

so fortunate. A few days later Salthouse reported several arrests in various parts of the country. " The Cavalier Commissioners, of the new militia serve to apprehend Friends and deliver them to the cruel magistrates (so called), as men who gather tumultuous assemblies." [1]

Fox was the chief sufferer. In May 1660 (the exact date is uncertain) constables entered the friendly asylum of Swarthmore Hall, arrested him, and carried him off to await trial at Lancaster.[2] During the journey next day the encounter with a body of Friends on the high road threw his guard into a panic, and they gathered about him, crying out : " Would they rescue him ? Would they rescue him ? " Fox, to reassure them, called out, " Here is my hair, here is my back, here is my cheek, strike on ! " which assuaged their anger. At Lancaster he was brought before Justice (formerly Major) Porter, who inquired : " Why I came down into the country in that troublesome time ? I told him, to visit my brethren. And he said, we had great meetings up and down, and I told him we had so, but I said, our meetings were known throughout the nation to be peaceable." After some more fencing, Fox was committed to Lancaster Castle on the grounds (as he discovered with much difficulty, for a copy of the warrant was withheld from him) that " he was a person suspected to be a disturber of the peace of the nation, a common enemy to his majesty our Lord the King, a chief upholder of the Quakers' sect, and that he with others of his fanatic opinion have of late endeavoured to raise insurrections in this part of the country to the imbruing of the nation in blood." Apparently no witnesses were called in support of these charges, and as soon as Fox learned their terms he drew up a dignified refutation, relating how he had been arrested in 1654 upon a similar charge and how Cromwell had accepted the statement of his peaceable principles. He says twice with emphasis : " The postures of war I never learned," and retorts that the term " fanatic " is more applicable to the " mad, furious, foolish " spirit that relies on force and per-

[1] *Swarthmore MSS.*, i. 320, iii. 179. In iii. 136, 146, 170, are some interesting letters and testimonies of Alexander Parker, who was imprisoned at this time. In the first, an address to the King, he says : " The peace of the King and all the people of England that is in Christ Jesus I am firmly bound to keep and not to disturb. And likewise, all the good and wholesome laws of England, which are grounded upon truth and equity, which are according to the laws of Christ. I own them and am bound to be subject to them and [not] break nor infringe them."

[2] For the whole account of this episode, see *Camb. Journal*, i. 358–84.

secution than to the Quakers. In another letter, addressed personally to Major Porter, he reminded that gentleman of certain episodes in his previous career as a Parliamentarian which, in his new flush of loyalty to the house of Stuart, he would have preferred to have forgotten.[1] That magistrate was in no very happy frame of mind, for, hearing that Margaret Fell and other Friends had appealed directly to the King on Fox's behalf, he had gone to London himself, where he had the ill luck to find that several of those in close attendance on the King were men whose houses and estates he had plundered during the Civil War. They were not backward in reminding him of this, and he hastily returned home, " blank and down."

The Friends working for Fox, amongst them Ann Curtis (whose father, Robert Yeamans, Sheriff of Bristol, had been hung as a Royalist in 1643), succeeded in influencing the King, and obtained a writ for the removal of the case to London. The Lancaster authorities, however, raised so many technical objections that Fox remained some time longer in prison. As usual, he was not idle, but issued many letters and papers, one to encourage Friends who were troubled by the change of Government, and another to the King, surely the strangest petition ever sent by a prisoner awaiting trial : [2]

" Charles, thou came not into this nation by sword, and not by victory of war, but by the power of the Lord. Now if thou do not live in it, thou wilt not prosper, and if the Lord hath shewed thee mercy and forgiven thee and thou dost not shew mercy and forgive, the Lord God will not hear thy prayers nor them that pray for thee. And if thou do not stop persecution and persecutors, and take away all laws that do hold up persecution in religion, but if thou persist in them and uphold persecution, they will make thee as blind as all that have gone before thee, for persecution was ever blind."

The reaction from Puritan rule had already set in, and Fox urges the King to deal sternly with " drunkenness, oaths, pleasure, May-games with fiddlers, drums, trumpets, and set-up Maypoles with the image of a crown on top," or else " the nation will quickly turn to Sodom and Gomorrah."

[1] For example : " Where had that wainscot that he ceiled his house with? Had he it not from Hornby Castle ? "
[2] *Camb. Journal,* i. 361.

If Charles ever read the paper, he probably felt some idle admiration for one who could so plainly speak his mind. Margaret Fell, who studied his character to some purpose during her frequent audiences, wrote to Fox that the Presbyterian leaders, who still hoped to guide Charles' policy, were so bitter against Friends that she believed they over-reached themselves and unwittingly influenced the King towards toleration. "The man is moderate, and I do believe hath an intent in his mind and a desire to do for Friends, if he knew how and not to endanger his own safety. He is dark and ignorant of God, and so anything fears him, but we have gotten a place in his heart that he doth believe we will be true to him." [1]

In October 1660 Fox was allowed by the Sheriff of Lancashire to travel to London with a few Friends, unguarded and carrying a copy of the charges against him. The trial took place before the Lord Chief Justice, Foster, and two other judges, and was fairer and more orderly than most Quaker trials of the time. When the charge of "imbruing the nation in blood, and raising a new war" was read, the judges lifted up their hands in horror or surprise. "Then," says Fox, "I stretched out my arms and said, I was the man that that charge was against, but I was as innocent as a child concerning the charge, and had never learnt any war-postures. And did they think that if I and my faculty had been such men as the charge declares that I would have brought it up with one or two of my faculty against myself? For had I been such a man as this charge declares, I had need of being guarded with a troop or two of horse." No witnesses appeared against Fox, as Major Porter wisely remained in the North, and on October 25, 1660, he was set free.

Indeed, at first the Restoration seemed to offer hopes to the suffering Quakers. In the Declaration of Breda, Charles had promised liberty to tender consciences, and during the first months of his reign several hundred Friends were included in the numbers released from prison in accordance with the Declaration.[2] Several members of the Society had deserved well of the King by loyal service to his father or himself.[3] Richard Hubberthorn, through

---

[1] *Camb. Journal,* i. 373.

[2] Others, however, were imprisoned on other counts.

[3] A Dorset Quaker, Richard Carver, in 1651 carried Charles through the water to the little fishing-smack in which he escaped to France. Besse quotes, under the year 1684, a petition from a Staffordshire Quaker, William Corbett, which he presented to the King in Windsor Park. He claimed a hearing on the

his acquaintance with Monk, obtained an audience with Charles, who, with his usual interest in novelties, questioned him closely on the doctrines and practice of the sect. As he dismissed him, he declared, " None should molest the Quakers, on the word of a King, so long as they lived peaceably." The interview was published by Friends as a pamphlet,[1] several times reprinted in crises when " the word of a King " had snapped asunder like rotten wood. Charles was not naturally cruel, and the Quakers amused him, while they were hated by his own enemies, the Presbyterians. All this predisposed him in their favour, and on several occasions he showed a careless interest in the fortunes of individual Friends. But, as Margaret Fell had seen, he would never put himself to personal inconvenience or endanger his popularity in the cause of justice, and a few months after his accession his hand was forced by an outburst of fanaticism.

The Fifth Monarchy men were political and religious extremists who throughout the Protectorate had reviled Cromwell and his friends with wild bitterness. The study of prophecy had turned heads never, seemingly, very steady, and they believed that the fourth great world monarchy was drawing to its end, to be succeeded by the Fifth Monarchy, the rule of Christ and the Saints. The Fifth Monarchists identified themselves with these elect, while they were more than suspected of attempts to hasten, by the murder of the Protector, the coming of the expected millennium, and they had even attempted a rising in the spring of 1657. The Government they detested did in truth crumble away, but a few months' experience made it clear to them that the reign of the Saints was not to be found in the restored Court at Whitehall. On January 6, 1660/1, their rebellion broke out in London. It was never formidable, being the work of a handful of men, but it threw the Court and Parliament into a panic out of all proportion to the danger.

ground of his services in the Royalist Army, " in the General Lord Capel's own troop, wherein I sustained these wounds, namely, I was shot in my leg at the siege of Wem in Shropshire, and wounded in my left arm at the garrison of the Lord Cholmeley's house in Cheshire, and also cut and dangerously wounded in my head, to the caul of my brain, with a pole-axe at a skirmish at Stourbridge in Worcestershire, and at the same time the thumb of my right hand was cut off." Since those stormy days he had been led to join the " peaceable people " called Quakers, and now applied to the King for relief from the heavy distraints he had suffered under the laws against conventicles. Charles characteristically " read part of it, and then delivered it to another person to read the rest for him," but Besse adds that apparently Corbett obtained no relief.

[1] *Something that lately passed in discourse between the King and R.H.* In D.

Fox, who had remained in the south, was in London at the time. His *Journal* tells the story as it affected Friends :

" It was said there was something drawn up that we should have our liberty [of worship] only it wanted signing. And on the first day there was glorious meetings, and the Lord's truth shined over all, and his power was set over all. And at midnight, soon after, the drums beat and they cried " Arms ! Arms ! ", for the monarchy people were up. And I got up out of bed and in the morning took boat, and came down to Whitehall stairs and went through Whitehall, and they looked strangely upon me. And I went to the Pall Mall and all the city and suburbs were up in arms, and exceeding rude all people were against us." [1]   Neither mob nor magistrates stayed to make much distinction between Quaker and Fifth Monarchist. Not only were many Friends roughly handled in the streets, but when they met for worship the next Sunday wholesale arrests were made. Fox was taken on the Saturday night (January 12th) and searched for arms. The searcher was an old acquaintance, so Fox replied that he knew well enough that he never carried even pocket-pistols, which were the ordinary travelling equipment of the day. He was detained a few hours at Whitehall, but released at the instance of Esquire Marsh, one of the King's attendants, who was often of great service to Friends.

There was a general belief that Friends were in the plot (although Fox says that the ringleaders at their execution denied that any Friends were concerned). Soon the prisons were full, and all Quaker meetings forbidden. None the less, they continued to be held as long as any Friends were left unarrested.[2]

The *State Papers* bear abundant testimony to the blind panic which prevailed. A West Riding magistrate, William Lowther, writes to State Secretary Nicholas on January 12th that Quakers

---

[1] *Camb. Journal*, i. 386–7.

[2] A Committee of both Houses reported in December 1661, after an inquiry into the plot, " that at Huntingdon many met under the name of Quakers, that were not so, and rode there in multitudes at night, to the great terror of his Majesty's good subjects " (Cobbett, *State Trials*, vi. 114). The *State Trials* also quotes from *An Historical Account of all the Trials and Attainders for High Treason*, the assertion that the plotters intended to allow " such Quakers as agreed with them in their millenary notions, as nearest to their sort of enthusiasm, the honour of partaking with them." Few troubled to distinguish Quakers from other new sects. Baxter wrote : " The Quakers were but the Ranters turned from horrid profaneness and blasphemy to a life of extreme austerity " (*Reliquiæ Baxterianæ*, i. 77). See the account of these imprisonments, W. C. Braithwaite, *Second Period of Quakerism*, pp. 9–14.

have held great assemblies in his neighbourhood attended by divers officers of horse and foot, where strange doctrines were broached tending to the overthrow of the Government. In his anxiety he brought the matter before Wakefield Quarter Sessions, and encloses their order of the previous day forbidding such gatherings.[1] Three days later a Wilts magistrate reports that he has arrested nearly thirty Quakers and other desperate fellows, former soldiers of the Parliament. Most of them (surely not the Quakers?) have taken the oath of allegiance, but he still mistrusts them, and proposes to exact in addition security for their good behaviour.[2] Next week, in the East Riding, Sir Robert Hildyard carried on the work. " In searching for arms there was found at Risum [Rysome] in Holderness, in a Quaker's house, divers papers wherein it doth appear that they have constant meetings and intelligence all over the kingdom, and contributions for to carry on their horrid designs, though masked under the specious pretence of religion and piety. I have sent you copies of two of them that you may see it is a real truth. They also keep registers of all the affronts and injuries that is done to any of them, when, where, and by whom. Therefore it doth appear they are an active, subtle people, and it is a great mercy that their designs did produce no more mischief to this kingdom. We shall be careful to prevent their unlawful meetings and to break the knot of them in this town and county." [3]

A few weeks later a careless messenger dropped a letter from one Quaker to another on the high road near Cockermouth. By ill-luck it came into the hands of two zealous local magistrates. In the letter John Dixon told Hugh Tickell, a Cumberland Friend, what collections were decided upon at the last monthly meeting, and begged him to send the contribution from his local meeting with all speed. Both men were arrested, and underwent separate examinations, but the most searching questions could not unearth a conspiracy. The magistrates, however, wrote to Under-Secretary Williamson at Whitehall, enclosing the ill-fated letter, with the suggestion that it should be shown first to the Earl of Carlisle and the local members of Parliament, and then to the Privy Council, and advice sent down how they were to act. " Admit their explanation thereof be truth, and they be as harmless and innocent people as they pretend to be, yet their continued meetings against the King's

---

[1] *Extracts from State Papers*, 117.

[2] *Ibid.*, 123.

[3] *Ibid.*, 127.

Proclamation, their collections among them, and sending many of their faction to several parts beyond the seas and maintaining them (if permitted) may give too great an opportunity to malicious dissatisfied spirits through suchlike pretences to effect their dangerous designs to the prejudice of the present Government." [1]

These are only samples of the action taken by hasty and frightened magistrates all over the country. The net swept wide, and by the end of January thousands of Friends were in prison, and one or two had died of the rough handling they had received. The King and Council were not left in ignorance of the events. Margaret Fell, courageous as ever, obtained audiences of Charles in which she gave him detailed accounts of her people's sufferings (from the records which had so alarmed Sir Robert Hildyard), set forth again their peace principles, and told him plainly that " it concerned him to see that peace should be kept, that so no blood might be shed." [2] Thomas Moor, who also had some influence with the King, helped her in these interviews, from which they returned with the report that Charles was " tender to them." But, as later, at the time of the Popish Plot, Charles was perfectly able to combine a belief in the innocence of political sufferers with an entire disinclination to help them when the tide was running too strongly against them. It was not until the panic had subsided that the prison doors were opened.

Fox and Hubberthorn at the first outbreak of trouble drew up a statement vindicating Friends from any share in the plot. It was confiscated in the printer's hands, but they immediately redrafted it and presented it to the King and Council on January 21, 1660/1. Fox says " it cleared the air," although arrests and imprisonments still continued. [3] In 1684 it was reprinted, to " stand as our certain testimony against all plotting and fighting with carnal weapons," and thus may be taken as the official expression of the early mind of the Society upon the question of peace and of loyalty to the established Government. In a later chapter its tenor is considered, with that of other contemporary Quaker tracts on peace.

---

[1] *Extracts*, pp. 143 foll.   [2] *Camb. Journal*, i. 386.

[3] *Swarthmore MSS.*, i. 44, is a letter from Ellis Hookes, a leading London Friend, to Margaret Fell, describing the wholesale arrests of Quakers and Baptists at their first day meetings. " The King and Council would have Friends promise that they will not take up arms . . . but our answer we have not yet returned, but thou knowest our principle is to live in peace and quietness."

CHAPTER III

YEARS OF PERSECUTION

1660–1702

THE little ark of Quakerism had been launched, and had survived the political tempests of the Protectorate and Restoration, but it still tossed on stormy waters in the reigns of the later Stuarts. Under Charles II Fox and his friends, not without opposition within the body,[1] completed the simple but efficient organization of the Society into co-ordinated groups of local meetings, Monthly and Quarterly, under the oversight of London Yearly Meeting, to which each group sent its representatives. The existence of this organized authority exercising regular discipline over its members was one cause of the gradual recognition of the Society of Friends and the grudging toleration of its worship which was won under James II. But so much of the Quaker testimony brought its holders into direct conflict with the social framework of the day, that liberty of worship in itself did not bring them ease. Their refusal to pay tithes in support of a State Church, to take the oaths of allegiance, and to have any share in military preparations were not condoned even when at length they could assemble on First Day without the expectation that their meeting would be broken up by a rude band of soldiers and the worshippers haled to prison. There was hardly a year of this period in which a Quaker could lead a peaceable life and follow Fox's advice " to keep clear of the powers." Conspiracies at home and war abroad and on the seas sharpened the disfavour with which officials regarded men who

[1] The Wilkinson-Story separation, about the year 1676, was the first of the unhappy disputes which, especially in America, have weakened the testimony of the Society to the power of Christian love. These first seceders, however, formed no separate body, but were either absorbed in other sects or re-admitted to membership after confession of error (vide Braithwaite, *Second Period of Quakerism*, ch. xi. pp. 290 foll.).

would neither swear fealty to the King nor arm to defend the country. And when it came to open hostilities, as in the Monmouth Rebellion of 1685 and the Revolution of 1688, the Quakers were found in neither camp and fell under the suspicion of both parties. But it was under the King who gained his crown by the pledge of liberty to tender consciences that their sufferings were most severe.

The cry of sedition raised against them in 1661 was re-echoed throughout Charles' reign at the rumour of any real or imaginary plot. Fox was again arrested at Swarthmore[1] in 1663, and brought to the justices at Holker Hall on suspicion of complicity in a conspiracy reported to be brewing at that time in the North of England.[2] A Catholic Justice, Middleton, called him a rebel and traitor. Fox's anger flamed up, and " I struck my hand on the table, and told him, ' I had suffered more than twenty such as he or any that was there ; for I had been cast into Derby dungeon for six months together because I would not take up arms against this King at Worcester fight, and was carried up out of my own county by Colonel Hacker before O. C. as a plotter to bring in King Charles in 1654.' " Middleton tried to turn the attack by a sneer, " Did you ever hear the like ? " " Nay," said Fox, " ye may hear it again if ye will. For ye talk of the King, a company of ye, but I have more love to the King for his eternal good and welfare than any of you have." He was then questioned about the plot, and replied that he had heard rumours, but knew nothing of it or of those concerned. Why then, asked the justices, had he warned his followers against it ?

" My reason was," he replied, " because you are so forward to mash the innocent and guilty together, therefore I wrote against it to clear the truth from such things, and to stop all forward foolish spirits from running into such things. . . . I sent a copy of it to the King and Council." He was committed to the sessions at Lancaster, on his refusal to take the oaths of allegiance and supremacy, and imprisoned in Lancaster Gaol, from which he issued another paper against war, plots, and oaths.[3] There he remained for several months, and in 1665 was removed to Scarborough Castle and kept

---

[1] *Camb. Journal*, ii. 39 foll.

[2] For an account of this conspiracy, which included the abortive " Kaber Rigg Plot " of August 1663, *vide* W. C. Braithwaite, *Second Period of Quakerism*, pp. 29–30 and 39.

[3] *Vide* p. 56.

a close prisoner until September 1, 1666, when he was released. The accommodation was miserable, and his health suffered severely, but he made many friends, from the Governor of Scarborough to the soldiers in the guard-room. On one occasion his principle of non-resistance was put to a severe test.

" There were, amongst the prisoners, two very bad men, that often sat drinking with the officers and soldiers ; and because I would not sit and drink with them too, it made them worse against me. One time when these two prisoners were drunk, one of them (whose name was William Wilkinson, a Presbyterian, who had been a captain), came to me and challenged me to fight with him. Seeing what condition he was in, I got out of his way ; and next morning, when he was more sober, showed him, how unmanly it was in him to challenge a man to fight, whose principle he knew it was not to strike but if he was stricken on one ear to turn the other. I told him, if he had a mind to fight he should have challenged some of the soldiers, that could have answered him in his own way. But, however, seeing he had challenged me, I was now come to answer him with my hands in my pockets and (reaching my head to him) ' here,' said I, ' here is my hair, here are my cheeks, here is my back.' With that he skipped away from me and went into another room ; at which the soldiers fell a laughing ; and one of the officers said : ' You are a happy man that can bear such things.' Thus he was conquered without a blow." [1]

Rumours of this " Rising in the North " and of Quaker complicity were already current in the latter half of 1662,[2] but a much more definite alarm was given a year later. An unsigned letter to Secretary Bennet, dated July 24, 1663, tells of news from the North " that they are all ready in the four counties and Yorkshire, that they will be up in a few days, the Quakers to a man are engaged in it. . . . So far as I can learn it is a wild business and nothing formidable in it, save only that the inferior officers and disbanded soldiers who live in these parts are in it." [3]

The Quakers' case is given in a letter from Sir Thomas Gower, Governor of York, a few days later. " I had this morning some Quakers with me who do not deny that they have been solicited to join in outward things to spiritual good, and that their answer was they would use no carnal weapon." [4] They refused, however,

[1] *Journal*, p. 67.   [2] *Extracts*, pp. 150, 157-9.
[3] *Extracts*, p. 171. S.P.D., xxvii. 50.
[4] *Extracts*, p. 171. S.P.D., xxviii. 6.

to betray the conspirators. "Joseph Helling, a Quaker prisoner in Durham, who had fallen under Ranter influence . . . and was out of unity with Friends, is stated to have sent a letter to Richardson, one of the plotters, in which he regarded ' the favourable conjunction of the stars ' as hopeful for action. Richard Robinson, of Countersett, admitted knowledge of one of the arch-plotters, John Atkinson of Askrigg, the stockinger, who seems to have been something of a Quaker, as Robinson and he had been in prison at York together, and both names occur in the Fifth Monarchy Lists in Besse. Robinson himself seems to have been quite clear." [1]

Even in February 1665 an East Riding magistrate was busy taking the depositions of villagers who had heard Quakers or alleged Quakers use wild words about the sword of God.[2] When the Great Fire raged in the first week of September 1666, the guilt of the catastrophe was impartially assigned to the Catholics and the Quakers. The smoke was still rising from the ruined city when a subordinate at Grantham reported his discovery to Sir Philip Frowd, Governor of the Post Office.

"I have here enclosed some printed papers and a letter from William Talby, harness maker in St. Martin's Lane, near the Mews which was sent to John Petchell, a Quaker, in a trunk, and eight quires of them to be dispersed. If you please to communicate them to the King and Council, I shall, whenever you please to command them, send them up. They are full of sedition, and I am sure of a dangerous consequence, considering the sad condition the City and Kingdom are now in." A postscript called attention to the weighty fact that the seal of the seditious letter bore the device : "The man of sin shall fall, and Christ shall reign o'er all." [3]

In 1663 Francis Howgill assured Judge Twisden at Appleby Assizes that the Friends were clear of complicity in the rising. " If I had twenty lives I would engage them all, that the body of the Quakers will never have any hand in war, or things of that nature, that tend to the hurt of others, and if any such, whom you repute to be Quakers, be found in such things, I do before the Court here, and before all the country deny them : they are not of us." Yet,

---

[1] Braithwaite, *Second Period of Quakerism*, p. 39 note, summarizing *Extracts*, p. 178.

[2] *Extracts*, p. 236. *S.P.D.*, cxiii. 63.

[3] *Extracts*, p. 255. *S.P.D.*, clxxi. 24, date September 10, 1666.

after a remand to the next assizes, Howgill was sentenced to imprisonment for life, and in fact died in prison in 1668.[1]

Apart from these suspicions of treason, as the military system of the country was reorganized upon a settled basis, Friends inevitably came into conflict with its demands. Acts were passed levying a poll tax for the maintenance of the war against the Dutch in 1667, and of that with France in 1678. From the account book kept by Sarah Fell of Swarthmore Hall, which still survives, it is evident not only that the women of the Fell family paid the tax for some property they held jointly with other owners, but that it was also paid by, or on behalf of, their stepfather George Fox.[2]

The item reads :—

	£	s.	d.
29 May [1678] By m° paid to the Poll Money for ffather and Mother	1	2	0

An ancient document [3] in the Friends' Reference Library endorsed by Fox, " A paper concerning trebet [tribute] by g. f.," apparently refers to one of these Acts, as it is also endorsed : " This is a copy of a letter sent to some Friends concerning the Poll Act."

In it he says : " So in this thing, so doing, we can plead with Cæsar and plead with them that hath our custom and hath our tribute if they seek to hinder us from our godly and peaceable life . . . then " [if payment were not made] " might they say and plead against us, How can we defend you against foreign enemies and protect everyone in their estates and keep down thieves and murderers, that one man should not take away another's estate from him ? " This distinction between taxation by the Government and the exaction of direct military service has been accepted by most later Friends. The question of a standing army was ever in dispute between the King and the people, and Parliament saw to it that the royal guards were kept down to the smallest possible numbers. Partly, perhaps, owing to the small size of the army,

---

[1] Besse, ii. (Westmorland). Howgill received his sentence with the words : " Hard sentence for obeying the commands of Christ, but I am content, and in perfect peace with the Lord. And the Lord forgive you all."

[2] *Swarthmore Account Book*, edited Norman Penney, pp. 45, 79, 181, 209, 355, 391, 395, 443, 473, 503, for instances of payment of assessments on property for militia and naval purposes, etc.

[3] *Swarthmore MSS.*, vii. 165. Cp. Fox, *Epistles*, p. 137, quoted in Chapter IV.

there were few instances of conversions to Quakerism among professional soldiers after the Restoration.   A militia soldier in Ireland, Christopher Hilary, while serving in 1670, became " convinced of the unlawfulness of wars and fightings under the Gospel," and refused to bear arms.   He received the punishment of riding the wooden horse (of which Quakers in the Colonies endured more than their share) and was (illegally) imprisoned for a short time.[1] In 1693 the Meeting for Sufferings[2] was interested by the account of a soldier, James Predeaux, convinced at Canterbury, who, upon laying down his arms, was committed to Canterbury Gaol and much abused.   The Meeting procured his discharge from gaol and army, and he presumably joined the Society.   In 1690 there is a curious instance of Quaker pertinacity.   " Henry Hayes and three other Friends, carpenters that worked in the King's Yard at Chatham, being turned out (because they could not bear arms) without their wages, Thomas Barker is desired to assist them to get their wages." [3] Apparently the workmen in the dockyard were being drilled from fear of a French attack, and though these Quakers worked on the ships of war their scruples awoke at this further development.[4] The constant fear of the constitutional danger involved in a regular army led Parliament to entrust the defence of the country to the old institution of a county militia.   By the Act of 1662 property owners were required to furnish men, horses, and arms in proportion to the value of their property, while those of smaller means contributed to a parish rate for the same object.   In theory the militia, or " trained-bands " as they were popularly termed in some districts, were called under arms for a few weeks of every year, but in practice the levy must have been erratic, for Friends in the various counties " suffered " at irregular intervals for their refusal to serve or to send substitutes.   Besse, for example, in his two folio volumes of Friends' Sufferings, gives instances under this head in Yorkshire in 1664, Essex in 1659 and 1684, Cambridgeshire in 1669 and 1670,

---

[1] Besse, vol. ii. (Ireland).

[2] A Committee of representative Friends established in 1675 to have the oversight of all cases of suffering, whether by persecution or misfortune.

[3] *Meeting for Sufferings MSS.*   1690 and 1693 (in D.).   A case of a Friend pressed as a soldier for the Flanders War in 1692, beaten for his refusal to serve, and finally ransomed by Friends, is recorded in Beck and Ball, *London Friends' Meetings*, p. 272.

[4] In 1660 Robert Grassingham was actually travelling to his home at Harwich " with an order from the Commissioners of the Navy to refit one of the King's frigates," when he was arrested by the Sheriff of Essex as a Quaker (Besse, i. 195).

Wales in 1677, Bristol in 1681, Berkshire in 1685, and Cornwall in 1688. No doubt levies were made more frequently, and Besse's records do not claim to be exhaustive, but punishments on this count are far less common than those for ecclesiastical offences, especially for non-payment of tithes. There was also, apparently, in some Friends' minds a doubt whether records of persecution should not be limited to these latter instances. In 1675 the Morning Meeting directed that " in the several counties they that find arms, etc., be tenderly admonished about it, according to the ancient testimony of Christ Jesus." [1] The Meeting for Sufferings considered, on December 20, 1678, the cases of " Friends' sufferings on account of not bearing arms, sending out men in arms, and not gratifying the marshals or other officers "—perhaps a hint that the officials were not incorruptible. It was agreed that " sufferings by distresses of their goods or otherwise on any such accounts is a suffering for the Lord and His truth, and . . . that the respective sufferings on that account be recorded in the respective monthly meetings, and thence returned to this meeting." [2] In Kent and Sussex, where the fear of foreign invasion was ever present, and in London, whose train-bands a hundred years before John Gilpin were formed as an efficient force, the hand of the law fell most heavily on Friends. The minute-books of Kent Quarterly Meetings show only fourteen years in the period 1660 to 1702 in which there is no record of fine or imprisonment for this cause.[3] Kent Friends were evidently men of small means, for the liabilities laid upon them are curious fractions of the normal claims. They are brought before the courts for " refusing to send out three parts of an arms," " not finding arms for the quarter part of a musket," " not contributing to the quarter part of the charge of finding a musket 30 days at 2s. a day," and, strangest of all, for " not sending in half a man to a muster with a month's pay."

In the earlier years of the period prison was sometimes the penalty. John Hogbin of Dover spent nineteen weeks of the year 1661 in the Castle, " by which means his trading was spoilt to his great damage." But usually there are distraints for fines, often much in excess of the sum required. " A silver cup worth 50s.

---

[1] W. C. Braithwaite, *Second Period of Quakerism*, p. 616, quoting a Minute of May 31st.
[2] *Meeting for Sufferings*, MSS. Vol. i.
[3] *Kent Q.M. MSS. Records of Sufferings* i. 299–322. In D.

for a fine of 20s.," "One mare worth £7 for a fine of 30s.," and similar plaints are recorded. In 1690 Friends at Ashford suffered special hardship. "When William Honeywood the Colonel was about reckoning the days the bands had been out he would have fined them at the rate of 2s. a day. But the said Thomas Curtis told him if they fined them not more than so, they would not care whether they sent them out or not. So they fined some after the rate of 4s. a day, which was to the utmost rigour of their Act. And when the Constables had done their parts, and sold things for half the worth, some Friends were at 8s. a day charge." [1] The excess was occasionally returned. At Cranbrook John Colvill and his wife were hardly dealt with in 1682 and 1683, and the record unconsciously paints for us a Dutch picture of a thrifty Quaker's kitchen plenishings. In the former year, for a fine of 40s., " the said constable, searching Susannah Colvill's spice-box found there twenty shillings and sixpence of ready money which he seized in part of the said fine, and to make it up carried away thirty-nine pounds of pewter." Next year the levy was more varied.

"   14 pieces of dish pewter
      2 porringers
      1 flagon
      1 brass mortar
      1 iron dripping pan (returned)
      3 new trundle bed sheets (returned back) also in money
        eleven shillings."

The successive Clerks to the Quarterly Meeting make methodical notes of these exactions, to be forwarded to London as the Meeting for Sufferings had requested. Only once does the record diverge from a plain statement of facts, when George Girdler of Tenterden in 1667 declares that he is " refusing, not in contempt of the King or any of his officers, but in obedience to the Lord, who had showed him mercy, and had called him from carnal weapons to love enemies according to Christ's doctrine, and not to take up arms against them." In Sussex, Middlesex, and London there were frequent

---

[1] These duties in connection with the militia and with the Test oaths, were the main reason why Friends refused the office of constable, a refusal for which they incurred fines. In 1672, one Thomas Talbot, " being cunstabell or ofeser," so far forgets himself as to press men for the King's service " too fight, it being contrary to the principal of Trewth which Friends one " (*London Friends' Meetings*, p. 288).

instances of these militia distraints during the same period, and Besse gives cases in which claims were made on women property owners.[1]   But sufferings " for not bearing arms," as will be seen later, were far heavier in the Colonies, and the records of the Meeting for Sufferings and the Epistles interchanged between London Yearly Meeting and those established in the Colonies contain frequent references to these troubles.   Occasionally the Meeting for Sufferings had to take cognisance of pettier forms of persecution, as when Abram Bonifield complained in November 1692 that the Mayor of Reading had paid off an old grudge against him " by quartering great numbers of soldiers, near twenty at a time, and when spoken to he tells him he will send him more." [2]   Even meeting-houses were not exempt, for in 1686 George Whitehead and Gilbert Latey, in a personal interview with James, laid before him " the hardships which had befallen their friends in regard to their meeting-houses at the Park in Southwark and at the Savoy in the Strand."   The Park had been turned into a guard-room in May 1685, and the soldiers (as soldiers have done in all centuries) " did great spoil and damage by pulling down pales, digging up and cutting down trees, carrying away and burning them with the wainscotting and benches.   They carried away one of the outer doors, and many of the casements."   The troop was called out to camp, and Friends began to undertake the necessary repairs, but in October the soldiers returned again to take forcible possession of the whole building.   " They pulled down the galleries and made a brick wall cross the lower rooms, with many other alterations, as if they intended to have the sole and perpetual possession to themselves, having made a place for prayers (or a mass-house [3]) at one end inclosed from the rest by the said wall."   The total damage was computed at £150.   At the Savoy, Friends were debarred from the use of their meeting-house for many weeks. The representation of " the unreasonableness and illegality " of these acts made sufficient impression on the King to effect the

[1] E.g. Besse, i. 172, 708.

[2] Bonifield was soon relieved from his incubus, and the mayor so far relented as to promise that he should not suffer again. There is another instance of unfair billeting. *Meeting for Sufferings*, 1688, 3rd mo. 18.

[3] The Monmouth Rebellion had enabled James to increase his army, and he showed much favour to Catholic soldiers. At the camp at Hounslow " a wooden chapel was set up within the lines, and horse, foot, and dragoons were encouraged to attend the Mass " (Trevelyan, *England Under the Stuarts*, p. 432).

clearance of the meeting-houses from soldiers within a few weeks of the interview.[1]

As early as 1678 the Meeting for Sufferings was so much occupied by "the often sufferings of Friends by being impressed into the King's ships of war" that Daniel Lobdy of Deal was appointed to procure their discharge in such cases. Any expenses he incurred were reimbursed by the Monthly or Quarterly Meetings concerned, and he proved very serviceable in his mission. At times in the hunt for seamen the gaols were invaded and Friends lying imprisoned for tithes were carried away. In 1695 an unhappy Northerner, Gerard Sefferenson, appeals to the Meeting for help, "being kept on board by force and from his wife and child, although a Dean by nation." [2] But the hardest case perhaps was that of the Friends captured by Algerine corsairs and ransomed by the Meetings at home. In March 1701 a letter announced to the Meeting the safe arrival in the Downs of some who had been redeemed. Not only were they "very uneasy" at the crew's wicked living and "very desirous to see Friends' faces" (after fifteen or twenty years' captivity), but they also feared that they would be pressed into men-of-war before they could land. The Meeting at once appealed to the Admiralty to exempt these men, who were "redeemed at the particular charge of Friends and not at the Government charge." The danger was averted, but at least one of the captives was pressed a few months later at the outset of a voyage to Pennsylvania, and was not released until a deputation from the Meeting for Sufferings had laid the case personally before the Lords of the Admiralty.[3]

It is indeed surprising not only that Friends were so ready to cross the seas on religious visits, but that so many followed the merchant service as their profession. In times of war with France and Holland the enemy's cruisers and privateers haunted the seas on the watch for prizes,[4] and, if this danger was escaped, an English

---

[1] Besse, *Sufferings*, i. (London), p. 483.

[2] *Meeting for Sufferings*, 1695. Dean = Dane, the *ea* being then pronounced *ā*.
Cp. "And thou, great Anna, whom three realms obey,
Dost sometime counsel take, and sometimes tea."—POPE.

"Here is a great pressing seamen, and beating up for voluteers to send to France. And several shiploads are already sent to France, so that it is like to be a dismal summer" (*Swarthmore MSS.*, i. 52, Ellis Hookes to Margaret Fell, March 1671).

[3] *Meeting for Sufferings*, 1701, 1st mo. 3.

[4] In 1689 the Meeting for Sufferings had before it the case of the Quaker master and crew of a Newcastle collier taken by the French to Dunkirk. They were exchanged for French prisoners taken on the *Noisteridame* (Notre Dame or Nostridamus ?) and other vessels.

man-of-war might hold up the merchant ship to press the likeliest members of the crew. Even in days of nominal peace the Mediterranean and Levant were never safe, when swift Algerine pirate-ships swooped down to carry crew and cargo captive to the "Sally" coast. Friends, as has been already noticed, were often held in durance there. In 1682 the Meeting for Sufferings notes the formation of a new meeting "even among the captives in Algiers," and collections for the redemption of these unhappy people are a common item in the Quaker records of the time.[1] In 1689 the Meeting sent a letter of warning to the ten Friends then enslaved at "Macqueness" [Mequinez in Morocco] not to resort to weapons for their liberty—a caution which they received with great meekness, replying that it agreed with their own resolution, not to grieve the Spirit of Truth, "though in all probability there will be no redemption for them while the [pirate] King lives, without guns." Some of them have been six years as slaves in this "dismal place," and have seen many perish. If, however, the merchants to whom they have entrusted money for their freedom bestow it in guns, should that deter them from using the opportunity? The Meeting's answer is not recorded, but another letter from one of the prisoners, read a few days later, shows that the "guns" were to procure their freedom by the peaceful process of barter.

"James Ellis writes to his father from Mackarness that a bargain was made by an English merchant, one Smithson, to give 4,000 musket barrels, 500 barrels of powder, and 30 Moors for 30 Englishmen to the King. But is now made void again."[2]

Negotiations for the release of the captives were constantly renewed, sometimes with the help of the English Government and sometimes by private effort. The pirates evidently allowed their slaves to correspond with friends, or letters were smuggled, for the Meeting often received piteous appeals for money or provisions. In 1690 the captives were fed on "seven year old decayed corn made into bread and mixt with lime," and they suffer greatly

---

[1] J. W. Rowntree, *Essays and Addresses*, p. 47. "There is a pathetic entry [in the Minutes of Scarborough, Whitby, and Staintondale Monthly Meeting] in 10th month, 1681, of money returned which had been collected for the redemption of John Easton of Stockton from the Turks' captivity, as Easton was 'not to be found.' The sum was then set apart for the "redemption of Henry Strangwis from Turkish Slaverie," but two years later the money was returned again, 'both being dead.'"

[2] *Meeting for Sufferings*, 1689, 7th mo. 16 and 7th mo. 27.

from eating the unwholesome stuff. The attempts at ransom were made through various traders (although it is strange that any trader would risk his person and his ship in the lion's den of these pirate harbours), and the business, in Quaker phrase, was " continued " from month to month, while the Meeting awaited the arrival in England of a certain " Jew " and a " Dutch Counsel " [Consul ?] who left the corsairs' haunts in 1690 and reached England in October 1691.[1] Yet it was not till 1701 that half a dozen captives were released from " Sally " at a cost of £480, and all of these were men who had been " convinced " during their long captivity. Some of the original Friends of the first messages had died as prisoners, and a few had been ransomed by private effort. In 1700 the Yearly Meeting, while reminding Friends of their duty to these sufferers, added : " When the collectors shall come with the briefs to Friends' houses, we hope Friends will be inclined to extend their charity in common with their neighbours, towards the redemption of the other English captives." [2]

Two artless narratives have come down to us from this later seventeenth century, telling of the dangers and difficulties which beset the ordinary Quaker in his witness for peace and universal love. They are both self-told : one, the pressing of Richard Seller, a Scarborough fisherman, the other the later experiences of Blake's seaman, Thomas Lurting.

Seller was pressed on Scarborough Pier in 1665, and later told his story " weeping " to a friend, who took it down from his lips.[3] He refused to follow his captors and, naturally, met with much rough treatment, being hauled with a tackle aboard the vessel, which was hovering off the port to carry away the pressed men, and later, at the Nore, " haled in at a gun-port " on the ship-of-war *Royal Prince* (captain, Sir Edward Spragge).[4] Refusing either to work or to eat, he was promiscuously beaten by most of those in authority, from the boatswain's mate with a piece of the capstan to the captain with his cane, and at last put in irons for twelve days. His patient endurance, however, won him some friends, for the boatswain's mate declared he would never beat a Quaker again or anyone else for conscience' sake ("and lost his place for it "), while the car-

---

[1] *Vide Meeting for Sufferings*, vol. vii, *passim*.
[2] Quoted by Luke Howard, *The Yorkshireman*, iii. 351.
[3] It is found in full in Besse, *Sufferings*, ii. (Yorkshire).
[4] Seller always writes of him as " Sir Edward," but he was actually knighted on June 24th, after these naval actions.

penter's mate brought him food secretly, telling him that before he sailed his wife and mother had charged him to be kind to Quakers.

But the captain had to deal with this stubborn passive resister, and Seller was brought before a court-martial constituted by the captains of the Fleet at the Nore, and (whether as co-adjutor or spectator is not very clear) the Governor of Dover Castle,[1] a Judge, but a Roman Catholic, "who went to sea on pleasure." The account of the trial leaves an impression that it was intended to frighten Seller into submission. The "Judge," having a pleasant fancy in punishments, suggested rolling the recusant in a barrel of nails, but the captains thought this "too much unchristian-like," and decided to hang him. Seller, however, remained unshaken, and told his judges that he was ready for death and glad to suffer, though some on board interceded for him. For the rest of the day he was treated kindly, and at night "slept well." Next morning he was brought on deck, prepared for execution, and a curious scene followed.

"Then spake the Judge, and said : ' Sir Edward is a merciful man, that puts that heretic to no worse death than hanging.' Sir Edward turned him about to the Judge, and said : ' What saidst thou ? ' ' I say,' replied he, ' you are a merciful man, that puts him to no worse death than hanging.' ' But,' said he, ' what is the other word that thou saidst, that heretic ? ' ' I say ' (said the Commander), ' he is more a Christian than thyself ; for I do believe thou wouldst hang me, if it were in thy power.' Then said the Commander unto me : ' Come down again, I will not hurt an hair of thy head, for I cannot make one hair grow.' Then he cried, ' Silence all men ! ' and proclaimed it three times over that, ' If any man or men on board the ship, would come and give evidence, that I had done any thing that I deserved death for, I should have it, provided they were credible persons.' But nobody came, neither opened a mouth against me then. So he cried again, ' Silence all men, and hear me speak.' Then he proclaimed that ' the Quaker was as free a man as any on board the ship was.' So the men heaved up their hats, and with a loud voice cried ' God bless Sir Edward, he is a merciful man.' The shrouds, and tops, and decks being full of men, several of their hats flew overboard and were lost. Then I had great kindness showed me by all men on board, but the great kindness of the Lord exceeded all, for the day I was

---

[1] Apparently, Sir George Strode.

6

condemned to die on, was the most joyful day that ever I had in my life."

Whether Seller's life had been in serious jeopardy may be doubted, but his own calm courage was not doubtful. He was now well treated, but still kept on board. We were at war with the Dutch, and a naval action was impending in which even a Quaker might be of service. Of service, in fact, he was. A few days before the action he had a vision or presentiment that the ship would run aground on a certain spot. He had some difficulty in making the pilot pay heed to his warning, but when Seller had pointed out the direction of the danger on the compass, the other consulted his chart and found "the Sand, and the name thereof."

When the fight began, the sense of danger again pressed upon Seller, and he warned the pilot, who set two men to take soundings.

"They cried, 'Five fathom and a quarter.' Then the pilot cried, 'Starboard your helm!' Then the Commander cried, 'Larboard your helm, and bring her to.' The pilot said he would bring the King's ship no nearer, he would give over his charge. The Commander cried, 'Bring her to!' The pilot cried to the leadmen, 'Sing aloud that Sir Edward may hear' (for the outcry was very great amongst the officers and seamen, because the ship was so near aground, and the enemies upon them), so they cried, 'A quarter less five.' The Commander cried, 'We shall have our *Royal Prince* on ground! Take up your charge, pilot.' Then he cried hard, 'Starboard your helm, and see how our ship will veer,' so she did bear round up. The men at the lead cried, 'Five fathom, and a better depth.' Then the Commander cried, 'God preserve the *Royal Prince*!' Then the pilot cried, 'Be of good cheer, Commander.' They cried, 'Six fathom,' then 'Nine fathom,' then 'Fifteen fathom,' then 'Sixteen fathom.' The Hollanders then shouted and cried, 'Sir Edward runs!' Then he cried 'Bring her to again,' and the fight continued till the middle of the day was over, and it fell calm."

This was not Seller's only service, for through the fire and smoke of the engagement he saw a Dutch fire-ship making for the *Royal Prince*. He pointed out the danger to the chief gunner, and a "Chace-gun with a ball in her" did its work effectively. His own occupation was "to carry down the wounded men and to look out for fire-ships," and he proved so serviceable that the commander ingenuously remarked that it was very fortunate he had escaped the death-sentence. A young lieutenant, Sir Edward's nephew, said, " There was not a more undaunted man on board, except his Highness."

A few days later a second engagement occurred.[1] Seller again volunteered for ambulance work, and late in the fight his friend the lieutenant meeting him, asked after his wounds. Seller replied that he was unscathed. " He asked me, ' How came I to be so bloody ? ' Then I told him, ' It was with carrying down wounded men.' So he took me in his arms and kissed me ; and that was the same lieutenant that persecuted me so with irons at the first."

The English fleet retired, taking shelter at Chatham. There the commander offered Seller leave on shore.

" I asked him, if I might go on shore to recruit or go to my own Being ?[2] He said, ' I should choose, whether I would.' I told him, ' I had rather go to my own Being.' He said, I should do so. Then I told him there was one thing I requested of him yet, that he would be pleased to give me a certificate under his hand, to certify that I am not run away. He said, ' Thou shalt have one to keep thee clear at home, and also in thy fishing ' ; for he knew I was a fisherman." The certificate was prepared, and his pay as sailor offered, which he " deserved as well as any man on board," but Seller refused both this and a gift of money from the lieutenant, having, he said, what would see him home. He had a friendly parting from the commander, who desired to hear of his safe arrival home. " I told him, I would send him a letter, and so I did." But his dangers were not quite over, for in London he found his story was known to some crimps for the press-gang, who greeted him as " Sir Edward's Quaker " and begged him to come to a tavern for a welcome to shore. However, on his refusal, they let him alone, and wished him a good journey home.

Other sufferings awaited him at home in Yorkshire, but he had gone through his testing-time on this forced service in the Fleet, and he stood the test. If the narrative reveals him as a simple soul,

---

[1] The first battle was almost certainly that of Sole (or Southwold) Bay, June 2–3, 1665, in which the *Royal Prince* was engaged. There was also some fighting about ten days later. It is a strange coincidence that on June 3, 1666, the *Royal Prince* ran aground on the Galloper Sands and was burnt by the Dutch " which touched every heart in the Fleet. She was the best ship ever built, and like a castle on the sea " (*Cal. State Papers, Domestic*, 1664–5, pp. 403–9 ; 1665–6, pp. 481–2).

[2] That is, to go home. So Mr. Peggotty, a Norfolk fisherman, speaks of finding a " Bein " for Mrs. Gummidge (*David Copperfield*, ch. 51).

it also reveals honesty, courage, and an absolute trust in the guidance and protection of God.

Thomas Lurting, who had entered the merchant service when his conscience drove him out of the Navy, was also pressed several times in the early years of the Restoration and met with harsh treatment. Like Seller, he refused to eat the King's food, and neither words nor blows would make him do the King's work on a war-vessel. His captors soon grew weary of him and sent him home. He was a man of greater intellectual ability than Seller, and able to hold his own when there was opportunity for argument. To threats, indeed, he opposed his favourite principle of silence. When one captain had wearied of curses, " he said more mildly, ' Why dost thou say nothing for thyself ? ' My answer was, ' Thou sayest enough for thee and me too.' For I found it most safe to say nothing, except I had good authority for it." Another thought he had found a sharp taunt against the Quaker, who had been pressed from a ship carrying corn. The corn would feed the sailors, and the sailors would kill the Dutch. Was Lurting not an accessory to their deaths ? " I kept very still and low in my mind, and . . . said to the captain, ' I am a man that have fed and can feed my enemies, and well may I you, who pretend to be my friends.' " To which the captain could only reply, " Take him away He is a Quaker." Another captain made a serious effort to gain the services of this experienced and hardy seaman and to meet his scruples, as far as he understood them. Lurting told him he had been as great a fighter as others, but was so no more. " ' I hear so,' said the captain, ' and that thou hadst a command, and so shalt thou have here ; or else thou shalt stand by me, and I will call to thee to do so and so ; and this is not killing of a man, to haul a rope.' I answered, ' But I will not do that.' ' Then,' said he, ' thou shall be with the coopers to hand beer for them, there is great occasion for it.' I answered, ' But I will not do that.' ' Then,' said he again, ' I have an employment for thee which will be a great piece of charity, and a saving of men's lives —thou shalt be with the doctor, and when a man comes down, that has lost a leg or an arm, to hold the man, while the doctor cuts it off. That is not killing men, but saving men's lives.' I answered, ' I am in thy hand, thou mayst do with me what thou pleasest.' "

Seller readily helped the wounded : but he had already taken his stand and won recognition for his conscience. Lurting would not accept an offer which was intended to enrol him as one of the ship's company and as a part of the machinery of war.

But Lurting's most constructive and active piece of work for his faith was done in the course of his own trade. The dangerous state of the Mediterranean gave him the opportunity of putting into practice his principle of peace and goodwill to all men. He was mate of a ship under a Quaker captain, George Pattison, on the return voyage from Venice when, near the Spanish island of " May York " (Majorca), the vessel was captured by a " Turkish " (Algerine) corsair. The boat was boarded by the " Turks," who sent the master, with four men, on board their ship, leaving ten of the pirates to guard the English vessel and the rest of the crew. In this strait Lurting was supported by an inward monition that he and his fellows would be saved from captivity in Algiers, and he exerted himself to keep the crew patient and under discipline. Before long the other prisoners were sent back on board, although there still seemed little hope of deliverance. But Lurting had his plans formed.

" We being all together, except the Master, I began to reason with them, What if we should overcome the Turks and go to May York ! At which they very much rejoiced, and one said, ' I will kill one or two ' ; and another said, ' I will cut as many of their throats as you will have me.' This was our men's answer, at which I was very much troubled, and said to them, ' If I know any of you that offers to touch a Turk, I will tell the Turks myself. But,' I said to them, ' if you will be ruled, I will act for you, if not, I will be still.' Then they agreed."

Lurting's plan was to disarm suspicion by ready obedience to the pirates. He unfolded it to his captain, a " very bold-spirited man " but so averse to bloodshed that he did not approve until Lurting assured him that " I questioned not but to do it without one drop of bloodshed and I believed that the Lord would prosper it, by reason I could rather go to Algiers than kill one Turk. So at last he agreed to this, to let me do what I would, provided I killed none." A storm, which separated them from the corsair-ship, favoured the plan, and the policy of cheerful submission rendered the Turks so careless that two nights later he was able to disarm them all in their sleep and keep them below decks while the vessel's course was shaped for Majorca. Next morning one was allowed on deck, "expecting to see his own country, but it was May York." Lurting had some fear of a rising at this point, but when the Turk told his fellows, "they instead of rising, fell all to crying, for their courage was taken from them." They only begged not to be sold to the Spaniards, a promise readily given by Lurting, who hid them when the vessel entered the harbour. Unluckily, another English captain in the port, to whom they revealed the secret, had no such scruples, but offered to buy some himself, saying "they are worth two or three hundred pieces of eight each. Whereat the master and I told him, that if they would give many thousands, they should not have one, for we hoped to send them home again." The man, thinking them fools, told the Spanish authorities, who prepared to confiscate the human cargo. But Lurting and his men explained the danger to their prisoners, who helped them to get the ship under way, and they sailed off in all haste, "which pleased the Turks very well."

For a week or so they coasted about, not daring to put in at a Spanish port. When the immediate danger was over both sides grew discontented. The Englishmen grumbled at the good treatment of the Turks, to which Lurting's reply was, "They are strangers, I must treat them well"; while the Algerines feared they might be carried to England. One day they began to threaten the captain, and Lurting's account of the way in which he dealt with the incipient rising shows the ascendancy he had gained by his character and courage.

"I started up, and stamped with my foot, and our men came up, one saying, 'Where's the crow?' Another, 'Where's the axe?' I said, 'Let us have them down, we have given them too much liberty; but first lay down (said I to our men) the crow and the axe and, every man of you, what you have provided to hurt them. They are Turks and we are Englishmen; let it not be said we are afraid of them: I will lay hold on the [Turkish] captain.' So I stepped forward, and laid hold of him, and said he must go down, which he did very quietly, and all the rest."

The boat's course was turned along "the coast of Barbary," and Lurting collected volunteers for the dangerous venture of rowing the prisoners ashore. Captain Pattison was unwilling to risk his men's lives, but Lurting assured him of his confidence in Divine protection, "for I had nothing but good will in venturing my life." Before the start the sailors' hearts began to fail them, and they begged that the Turks should be bound. Lurting replied, in his common-sense way, that the attempt would only exasperate them and, being quiet, it was well to keep them so. He packed them tightly in the stern of the boat, armed himself and his men with some rough-and-ready weapons—a boat-hook, a carpenter's adze and a cooper's knife—and piled the Turks' own arms in the bow. So they started, "committing ourselves to the Lord for preservation, we being three men and a boy, and ten Turks." But the way to shore with only two rowers seemed long, and the men's courage gradually ebbed. They were but thirty yards from the shore when the man Lurting had appointed to keep a look-out raised an alarm of an ambush.

"And he speaking so positively, it seized me, so that I was possessed with fear ; and so soon as the Turks in the boat saw I was afraid, they all rose at once in the boat. And this was one of the greatest straits I ever was put to ; not for fear of the Turks in the boat, but for fear of our men killing them : for I would not have killed a Turk or caused one to be killed for the whole world. And when the Turks were risen, I caused our men to lay their oars across the boat for that was all that was betwixt us, and bid the men take up such arms as they had. Then said I to them, I would have you be as good as your word, for you promised me you would do nothing, until I said I could do no more : now I desire you to keep to that. For there was nothing lacking but my word to kill the Turks."

All this while (Lurting tells us) the Turks were standing up, and the fact that the boat was not swamped speaks well for its solid construction. After a sharp rebuke to his men for their cowardice, Lurting had recourse to his favourite method of silent meditation.

"At last all fear was taken away, and life arose and courage increased again ; and it was with me, it is better to strike a blow than to cleave a man's head or cut off an arm. Having turned the hook of the boat into my hand, I got into the middle of the boat upon the main thwarts. I struck the captain a smart blow and bid him sit down, which he did instantly, and so did all the rest, without any more blows. Then I stepped forward and said to our men, Now you see what it is to be afraid ; what shall we do now ? "

The men proposed to take back their prisoners to the ship,

but Lurting's reply showed the sympathy which was the source of his influence.

"Not so, said I, God willing, I will put them on shore ; for they will come quietly near the shore, but if we carry them on board there will be nothing but rising. For *if it were my own case,* I would rise ten times, and so will they." A suitable landing-place was chosen, a few miles from some Arab villages and fifty miles from Algiers, and the Turks disembarked, with arms and provisions. "So we parted in great love, and stayed until they had all got up the hill, and they shook their caps at us, and we at them."

A fair wind brought the ship to England, where the last scene of the story was played.

"King Charles and the Duke of York and many of his lords being at Greenwich it was told them there was a Quaker ketch coming up the river that had been taken by the Turks and had redeemed themselves, and had never a gun. And when we came near to Greenwich the King came to our ship's side, and one of his lords came in and discoursed with the master, and the King and the Duke of York stood with the entering-ropes in their hands, and asked me many questions about his men-of-war. I told him we had seen none of them. Then he asked me many questions how we cleared ourselves ; and I answered him. He said, I should have brought the Turks to him. I answered, that I thought it better for them to be in their own country ; at which they all smiled and went away."

These sea perils led many merchants and captains to arm their ships against pirates and privateers, and the step was approved by the Admiralty. Often vessels delayed their sailing until others bound for the same port were ready, and the little fleet was convoyed by ships of war through the dangers of the Channel. This practice brought the Quakers into difficulties, for the other captains were unwilling that unarmed ships which could give no help in case of attack should sail in the convoy. On December 10, 1672, Ellis Hookes, a leading London Friend, later the first Clerk to the Meeting for Sufferings, wrote to Margaret Fox that he was working in the cause of two Friends, Thomas Hutsin and James Strutt, whose ships had been stopped from sailing by command of the Duke of York. An Order in Council had been passed that "from that day forward not any vessel, little or great, shall go to sea out of any port in England, without guns ; great guns if great ships, and small guns and granadoes if small ships, and must give bond to fight, if occasion be. This Order is procured by the envious petition of some Barbadoes merchants in this city, which will tend to the great damage of many Friends, whose whole maintenance depends upon the sea trade." [1] Friends prepared to present a counter petition to the Council, and Ellis Hookes used his " utmost interest " on their behalf. On Christmas Eve he wrote again that, after much exertion, he had obtained an order for the two vessels to sail, and they were at the Downs, " which was a great satisfaction to many Friends, for nobody would believe they should be suffered to go." [2] Twenty years later a similar difficulty was caused not by Government interference, but by backsliding in the Society. In the summer of 1690 the Meeting for Sufferings was exercised by the report that a shipmaster at Liverpool " that comes among Friends " carried guns on his ships.[3] A letter was sent by the Meeting to the Liverpool Friends reminding them of their ancient testimony and " that it hath not been the practice of Friends to use or carry carnal weapons, and Friends at London have suffered much for refusing." This shipmaster may not have actually identified himself with Friends, but there was shortly after a real defection in their own ranks. For some years (since 1678) the Yearly Meeting, after its sessions were over, had circulated among the local meetings a " Paper " or " Epistle," which summarized the conclusions reached during the discussions. This Epistle, in 1692, emphatically asserts the loyalty of the Society to the newly established rule of William and Mary, " being obliged to demean ourselves not only as a grateful people but as a Christian society, to live peaceably and inoffensively under the present Government, as we have always done under the various revolutions of govern-

---

[1] *Swarthmore MSS.*, i. 76. The petition, or another to the same purpose, is preserved in the Colonial Records under date December 27, 1672. (*Vide Cal. State Papers, Colonial*, 1669–74, p. 455) ; it was as follows : " There is now going to the West Indies several considerable ships commanded by Quakers, who sail without guns. Now, if the said ships shall fall into the enemy's hands they will make considerable men-of-war against us. And also, these ships can sail much cheaper than ships of force, and by consequence get much profit to their owners, which will in time ease all ships of force of all trade. And this mischief will increase, if not by his Majesty's timely wisdom prevented."

[2] *Swarthmore MSS.*, i. 53.

[3] *Meeting for Sufferings*, 1690, 4th mo. 13.

ment, ever since we were a people, according to our ancient Christian principle and practice." [1]

But in the following year the claims of Government and Gospel were conflicting, and the question of armed merchant ships was definitely raised in the Yearly Meeting.

The Epistle gives out no uncertain voice on the matter. " A complaint being made about some shipmasters (who profess the truth and are esteemed Quakers) carrying guns in their ships, supposing thereby to defend and secure themselves and their ships, contrary to their former principle and practice, and to the endangering of their own and others' lives thereby ; also giving occasion of more severe hardships and sufferings to be inflicted on such Friends as are pressed into ships of war, who for conscience' sake, cannot fight nor destroy men's lives, it is therefore recommended to the Monthly and Quarterly Meetings whereunto such shipmasters belong, to deal with them in God's wisdom and tender love, to stir them up and awaken their consciences, that they may seriously consider how they injure their own souls in so doing, and what occasion they give to make the truth and Friends to suffer by their declension and acting contrary thereunto, through disobedience and unbelief ; placing their security in that which is altogether insecure and dangerous ; which we are really sorry for, and sincerely desire their recovery and safety from destruction, that their faith and confidence may be in the arm and power of God." [2]

After this statement of the particular difficulty, the Epistle passes on to explain the principles underlying the rebuke :—

DEAR FRIENDS,

You very well know our Christian principle and profession in this matter, both with respect to God and Cæsar, that, because we are subjects of Christ's kingdom, which is not of this world, we cannot fight (John xviii. 36) ; yet, being subjects of Cæsar's kingdom, we pay our taxes,

---

[1] With the official document, two well-known Friends, Steven Crisp and George Whitehead, circulated a letter of their own, deprecating the party spirit which had distracted the country. " Away with those upbraiding characters of Jacobites and Williamities, Jemmites and Billites, etc., so used by the world's people one against another, to make parties and divisions, and to stir up wrath and enmity. Let the spirit of enmity, strife, and contention be judged and kept out of God's heritage forever, and let us have no such upbraiding distinctions in God's camp . . . no more than of Whig and Tory, long since judged out and testified against."

[2] It is worth noting that the Minute of the Yearly Meeting upon which this passage is based is somewhat more emphatic. " Some that profess Truth and carry guns in their ships . . . should be dealt with in love and plainness."

tribute, etc., according to the example of Christ and his holy apostles, relating to Christ's kingdom and Cæsar's, wherein we are careful not to offend (Matt. xvii. 27; xxii. 20. Rom. xiii. 6, 7).

How far the trouble had spread it is not easy to judge. There was certainly a case in the North, at Shields, where the Monthly Meeting had successful dealing with Lawrence Haslam, a merchant captain of North Shields, who in earlier days had suffered imprisonment for his Quakerism. In January 1693/4, at the Monthly Meeting, it was reported that "Friends had some discourse with him about having guns in his ship, and tenderly admonished him of the evil consequences of it, and of its inconsistency with the principle of truth "; upon which the meeting decided that representative Friends "may further deal with Lawrence as in the wisdom of God they may see necessary, and give account to this meeting." These further steps were evidently successful, for in March, "Jeremiah Hunter and Lawrence Weardale having spoke to Lawrence Haslam about carrying guns does certify this meeting that he gives them an account that for the satisfaction of Friends he hath sold his guns, and is to deliver them very shortly." [1]

The Society, which had been born in the days of the Civil War, had now, as an organized body, to face again the difficulties of civil strife, first in the West during the Monmouth Rebellion, and then for three terrible years in Ireland. West Country Friends were for the most part innocent spectators, and they escaped comparatively lightly even amidst the butcheries and terrors of the Bloody Assize. Monmouth landed at Lyme Regis on June 11, 1685; his cause fell in ruin at the battle of Sedgemoor on July 6th, and for the rest of the year his hapless followers were hunted down by Colonel Kirke in the open fields and by Jeffreys in the Assize Courts.

One of the simple memoirs of this early generation of Friends gives a vivid sketch of Somersetshire under the Rebellion and under the vengeance which followed. John Whiting, the author of *Persecution Expos'd,*[2] was a small farmer of Nailsea, near Bristol, who from 1679 for more than six years suffered imprisonment in Ilchester Gaol, with many other Friends, on account of his refusal

[1] Moberly Phillips, *Forgotten Burying Grounds of the Society of Friends.* Proceedings of Newcastle Literary and Philosophical Society, November 1892.
[2] *Persecution expos'd in some memoirs relating to the Sufferings of John Whiting.* . . . 1715.

to pay tithes. The durance was not always of the harshest, depending on the caprice of the individual gaoler, and at times Whiting was allowed to make a short visit to his home. When Monmouth, in 1682, was on his triumphal progress through the West, he visited Ilchester, " with some thousands on horseback attending him, the country flocking to him and after him, the eyes of the nation being upon him and towards him, as the hope and head of the Protestant interest at that time. . . . We stood in the Friary-Gate as he rode through the town, and as he passed by, taking notice of so many Quakers together with their hats on, he stopped and put off his hat to us. And our Friend John Anderdon had a mind to speak to him and tell him, that we were prisoners for conscience' sake, but had a stop in his mind, lest there should be an ill use made of it, in applying to him and making him too popular, the Court having a watchful eye over him : however, we could not but have a respect to him for his affability, and therefore were the more concerned for him when his fall came." [1]

The gay young noble and the gentle Quaker were to meet once more, after their ways had parted widely. Whiting's imprisonment continued, but in 1685, when mercy was hoped for from the new king, " the keepers grew careless of us, and gave us pretty much liberty, in hopes to get money by us, it being reported that Liberty of conscience was in the press so long, that it became a proverb that ' Liberty of conscience was in the press,' it was so long a-coming out." [2] Whiting was allowed to attend his Monthly Meeting at Hallatrow, where, on May 29th, news reached them that the Earl of Argyle had raised an insurrection in Scotland. A fortnight later came the more startling news of Monmouth's arrival in Dorset, whereon Whiting, who was still at home, set out to return to prison, but at Wrington was stopped by the watch.

" He asked me whither I was riding ? I told him, southward which (though directly towards the Duke), without asking me any further question, he wished me a good journey, and so let me pass ; at which I could not but smile to myself, to see how easy they were to let any pass that way (for indeed the hearts of the people were towards him, if they durst have showed it). But that he might not think I was going to the Duke, I told him there was a fair at Somerton that day, and thither I was riding." [3] Near

---

[1] Whiting, pp. 32–3.   [2] *Ibid.*, p. 140.   [3] *Ibid.*, p. 141.

Somerton was the home of a " dear Friend," Sarah Hurd, afterwards Sarah Whiting, and we may forgive the young Quaker if he
turned aside from prison to visit her.   She had strange news for
him, " how some of the Duke's men had been at Ivelchester, to
free some of the Duke's friends who came down from London to
meet him and were taken up on suspicion, and imprisoned there ;
and withal, freed all they found prisoners there on account of conscience, and among the rest, some of our Friends.   But they took
little notice or advantage of it, but went in and out as at other
times." [1]

Whiting stayed a few days at Somerton, and then went over
to the Quarterly Meeting at Gregory-Stoke, at which they heard
that the Duke and his army were at Taunton, six miles away, and
" the country flocked unto him."   At the Meeting he met with
Sarah Hurd's sister, the wife of one Scott, who " dealt in horses,
expecting to make advantage of them, which proved a snare to him."
He had gone to make his profit of the Duke, and the poor woman
begged Whiting to go with her to Taunton and " get him home."
Next day the rescue party went to Taunton, putting up at the Three
Cups Inn, opposite the house where Monmouth and Lord Grey
were having a hurried meal.   They soon met Scott, but he was
so committed to his horse-dealing that he refused to come home.
The persistent wife " went over to speak with the Duke, to
desire him not to take it amiss if her husband went home, for
it was contrary to our persuasion to appear in arms, because
we could not fight ;   and had a pretty deal of discourse with
him (for she was a woman that could handle her tongue as well
as most).   The Duke seemed to take it well enough, and told her
he did not desire that any should appear with him against their
consciences."

Meanwhile Whiting waited outside the inn " observing passages " in the street, such as the fall of one of Monmouth's local
supporters into the kennel with " his great high horse," a disaster
which the young Quaker thought " a little ominous."   " But,"
he continues, " I did not go out of my way to see the army, which
lay in a field hard by the town, or any of them ;   which I account
a great preservation ;   and soon after, the Duke and Lord Grey
came forth and took horse (their horses being held in the street
all the time) and rode down the street the same way as we were

[1] Whiting, p. 141.

to go home. And two great guns were haled down before them, to plant (as they said) at the town's end, it being reported that the Duke of Albemarle (Lord-Lieutenant of the county of Devon) was coming against them. So we took horse, and rode down after, and when we came to the town's end, the street was so full of people, that I thought it impossible to get through the wood ; but asking one if we could ride by, he said, we might of one side. So I put forward till I was got into the middle of them, looking about me to see the Duke. I asked somebody, which was him, he showed me just at my right hand. So I stopped a little to take a view of him, and thought he looked very thoughtful and dejected in his countenance, and thinner than when I saw him four years before, as he passed through Ivelchester in his progress as aforesaid, that I hardly knew him again, and was sorry for him as I looked at him. I spoke a few words to him, which I do not mention out of vanity, but to show how narrowly I escaped a snare at that time, to the Lord's protecting hand of providence I ascribe it in my preservation."

The Quakers got safely away from Taunton in spite of a false alarm that the King's troops were at hand, and it is no surprise to read that "next day I went to my Friend's at Long Sutton, where, and at Somerton, I mostly stayed, till after the Duke's defeat at Sedgemoor, being a time of great exercise with her, having several relations (not Friends) out in the Duke's army, as three brothers-in-law, an uncle, and several kinsmen. And her brother Glisson, a Baptist, came and would have had me gone out also, and took up the sword till the work was over, which, if I had, I might have suffered as he did ; but through the mercy of God (whose holy name I magnify and adore in my preservation) I knew my place and principles better than so."

Even Long Sutton was not to escape the troubles of war. " There came down the Queen's Guards (as they said) under the Lord Churchill, and terror marched before them (for we could hear their horses grind the ground under their feet, almost a mile before they came), and 'twas reported, there were six houses to be burnt, of which my Friend S. H.'s was one . . . but through the Lord's mercy was preserved. For when they came to the Cross near her house, they inquired for Captain Tucker's (who was out with the Duke) and went and ransacked his house, cutting and tearing the beds, hangings, and furniture to pieces, shaking out the feathers and carrying away the bed-sticks and what else they could, letting out the beer, wine, and cider about the cellar, setting fire to a barn that joined to the dwelling house, to set that on fire also, but being a stone-tiled house it did not burn that. . . . And the seventh day before the fight came down the Earl of Pembroke, with his Wiltshire troops of horse, and made dreadful work in the parish, taking several prisoners and threatening to hang some, to the terror and affrighting of the inhabitants." [1]

But when Whiting has to describe the Terror after Sedgemoor, his indignation flames through his breathless sentences.

"Several of the country gentlemen (who hardly dared appear before) came about in pursuit of the Duke of Monmouth's men, and Sir Edward Phillips (Judge of the Sessions, as aforesaid) came to my Friend's house at Long Sutton, and sat and slept in a chair, while his men went hunting about the fields to take men. And several were brought to my Friend's door and sent to prison, sending them to prison in droves as if it had been to get their horses, for which some of them paid dear after King William came." Scott the horse-dealer had his share of trouble. He passed the night after Sedgemoor in Weston Zoyland church with many other prisoners, "in order to be hanged next day, as many were ; but he got out at the little north door, while the watch was asleep, and so escaped with his life, lying in cornfields by day and going by night till he got home, and so lay about till after the general pardon. But many were hanged in cold blood by that cruel, inhuman, bloody wretch Colonel Kirk, to the shame of mankind. And some were hung in chains naked, to the terror and shame of the country." [2]

Whiting, as a prisoner on leave, felt some delicacy in meeting Sir Edward Phillips, and so "lay innocently out in the garden" during his visit. Afterwards he regretted his action, as savouring more of caution than of courage.

His next step was eminently characteristic of the early Quaker. "And soon after, seeing our bondage returning, and that I must submit to a prison again, and that it was the safest place as things were, I thought it better to go than to be sent thither or sent for, and so returned to Ivelchester, where the keepers began to look

---

[1] Whiting, pp. 140–3.

[2] Page 144. Scott was dealt with for six years by Taunton Monthly Meeting, which received from him a full profession of repentance in 1692. He alleged "inability to write" as the chief reason for his delay (*J.F.H.S.*, xii Pt. I, p. 35).

after their prisoners again, and to inquire for us, and to be very wicked to us when we came, calling us Rebels, Rogues, etc. though ever so clear." The keepers did worse than call names, for in that sad July and August the thirty or more Quakers were all imprisoned in one small room, chained together in pairs. Whiting gives a plain-spoken account of the filth and discomfort they were forced to endure, and adds :

" Nor could we put off our clothes at night but from one arm and let them hang on the other, so that we could not turn, but lay mostly on the one side (being linked together), which was very tedious in the heat of summer. And that which troubled us much also was to answer people that came into the prison, what we were put in or hand-bolted for, thinking 'twas on the Duke of Monmouth's account." [1]

The September Assizes at Wells and Taunton, with the resulting massacres, roused his deep indignation. Some of his fellow-prisoners were carted thither. " Most of them were condemned, even by wholesale. Jeffreys making what haste he could, not regarding how he threw away men's lives, or run over them to hasten home to the King at Windsor to be made Lord Chancellor, having done the work he was sent about. . . . Many were executed, and their heads and quarters set up on trees, poles, etc. in most of the highways in this county, Dorset, and Devonshire, to the terror of travellers, being dreadful to behold ; and many transported, some wheedled out of their lives, and others terrified to confess in hopes of pardon, and then hanged." Some were hanged, he says, " for a little hay, or letting them [the rebels] have a morsel of victual."

Ilchester did not escape the Terror. " There were eight executed, quartered, and their bowels burnt in the market place, before our prison window. I went out of the way, because I would not see it, but the fire was not out when I returned." Some in the town were forced " to hale about men's quarters like horse flesh or carrion, to boil and hang them up as monuments of their cruelty and inhumanity, for the terror of others, which lost King James the hearts of many." It was not until March 10, 1686, that James proclaimed a general pardon, which freed the Quakers and saved the remnant of Monmouth's men who had been hiding in woods and ditches and " might as well have been pardoned before

[1] Pages 145–6.

winter, if some had endeavoured it as much as they did to take away their lives." [1]

The Meeting for Sufferings worked hard to protect West Country Friends. It kept in constant touch with them, and was active in procuring evidence of their innocence. In the autumn of 1685 the pages of its Minute Book are filled with copies of certificates to the King from officials or leading inhabitants of Somerset and Dorset villages, testifying to the " clearness " of Friends dwelling there during the " late rebellion." " Carried themselves very civil and peaceable," is the verdict of the constable and churchwardens of Conford. Vicars in some cases put their names to a similar testimony. In the autumn suspicion apparently spread to the eastern counties, and Suffolk and Essex Friends were forced to provide themselves with similar certificates. It was equally important to prove that some concerned in the rebellion were not attached to the Society, and twelve Friends testify that Thomas Paul of Ilminster had " deserted Friends these many years, and being of a loose, bold, drunken behaviour and conversation and derided of his companions for the same."

On August 1st the prisoners at Ilchester and other Somerset Friends send a full reply to inquiries made by the Meeting for Sufferings. They use " as much brevity as the case would well permit," but the letter can hardly be called concise. It deals with " such as did appear in James Scot's army,[2] whereof some had arms and some not ; several of them, before the said insurrection their bad conversation had manifested them to be wholly gone from our Society (though they might retain the name of Quaker), even in the judgment of such as are not friends to us, as we believe. One of them for open and frequent drunkenness testified against and denied. Another for drunkenness and card-playing, and forsaking

---

[1] pp. 152-3. On his release Whiting married his " dear Friend," and they later settled at Wrington. There his conscience was troubled by the public fasts appointed to be held in 1690 and 1691 in connection with the Irish War. Quakers, as a rule, kept their shops open on such occasions, but Whiting had to remonstrate with some in his neighbourhood who conformed and so weakened the collective testimony of the Society. He was himself accused of disloyalty " though unjustly and undeservedly, being obliged to the Government for our liberty, and wishing well to the Protestant interest all the world over, though we could not join in wars and fightings or pray for shedding of blood, being taught to love enemies. For Christ came not to destroy men's lives, but to save them " (p. 216).

[2] Monmouth had married the heiress of Buccleuch, and had the title Duke of Buccleuch. The Buccleuchs were head of the clan of Scott.

our assemblies. Another married a wife and had a child before marriage. Another left his master for reproving him for his disorderly living. Another, an unstable man and outbreaker, borrowing and not paying again. . . . There was another rode in that army who pretty long time had forsaken the Society and fellowship of the people called Quakers, because of sufferings. And another, that since he profest himself a Quaker hath been found fighting and quarrelling, and came not to meetings in time of sufferings." All these (amongst whom " brother Scott " may be included) had been testified against by Friends for their offences in time past. A Quaker blacksmith, Roger Slocombe of Long Sutton, had been arrested by the King's army on a charge of making scythe-weapons for the ill-armed rebels, but he had been able to clear himself. The most serious case was that of an undoubted Friend, Thomas Please, or Plaise, grocer and draper of Edington. It is sorrowfully confessed that he was active in " J. Scot's army " and among the " clubmen " in the Severn marshes. " Though he bore no arms, yet in some things he acted rashly and madwise to the great grief and trouble of the Quakers. . . . And as for the reason of some Friends walking in the army, we answer, some had horses taken away and some oxen pressed to draw their carriages, and so went to get them back again. And some, as they went to market or travelled about their occasions, did happen to come where the army was, and so came into it. Or sometimes when the army came near their dwellings some went out to see it. And we have not heard of any that walked in it otherwise than as before expressed." Recently the Clerk of the Western Assizes had visited Ilchester, and told the Quakers there " that on inquiry made he found but two of us amongst nine hundred, he having made inquiry at Bristol, Bath, Wells, Bridgewater, Taunton, and Exeter." One of these two was a prisoner at Ilchester, a young ship's surgeon, who had not fought but had followed his profession in the campaign. He had only frequented Friends' meetings for a few months. It is to be hoped he was not one of those so horribly done to death in Ilchester market place. The letter, in conclusion, repeats that it was entirely against Friends' will that any should concern themselves in the war, " as being contrary to our peaceable principles and profession, and was and is their grief and trouble that any such did."

On August 8th George Whitehead, on behalf of the Meeting

for Sufferings, writes to thank them for " such an ample and satisfactory account," which shows how Friends in the West realize that " Christ's Kingdom and Church must not be promoted by the arm of flesh nor built by might or armies, but by his spirit." Those concerned in the rebellion are not worthy of the name of Quakers and " by this very action of joining in this late disturbance " are a dishonour and scandal to the Society. Although Thomas Please " did not proceed so far as to take up arms," yet in many ways he had greatly offended against Friends' principles. It would be well for the Friends there to issue a paper in testimony against him and his actions in the rebellion, " as one that has thereby turned aside from the Truth professed by us, and become false to our holy profession and excluded himself from our society and rendered himself unworthy the name of Quaker." The testimony should make it clear that the Society as a whole has maintained its loyalty and peaceable behaviour, and it should be given out to magistrates and other persons of authority. On August 22nd Whitehead writes again, to acknowledge the receipt by the Meeting for Sufferings of a paper for presentation to the King and copies of local certificates of " Friends' innocency." The meeting, however, has somewhat amended the paper, making it as " general and inoffensive " as possible, their desire being " that Friends may keep as clear as they can possibly from charging particular persons by name about this late rebellion, lest we seem to be their persecutors." As to Thomas Please, " we find nothing that will clear Friends of him, before this public occasion, wherein he has *ipso facto* gone from Truth and rendered himself no real Quaker, ceasing by the same fact to be of us or in society with us." So their " very dear Friend," George Whitehead, emphatically expresses the verdict of the Meeting for Sufferings. The testimony, as " presented to authority ' in its amended form, is preserved among the Bristol and Somerset Quarterly Meeting records.[1]

It states emphatically that all Friends in the district were warned " not to concern themselves in this war," and those who took part " are wholly disowned." The Meeting for Sufferings completed the testimony by inserting a brief account of the episode at Ilchester gaol, when Friends refused to accept freedom at the hands of Monmouth's men.

[1] See *Meeting for Sufferings Minute Book*, 1685, and *Bristol MSS.* (Bristol and Somerset Q.M., 1842), vols. i. and ii. in D., for these letters and testimonies.

By this time some of the Friends concerned had reached London to bear their own testimony, and on August 28th George Whitehead reported to the Meeting that he had escorted them to the King's Secretary, in order to bring under his notice the local certificates of innocence. The Secretary promised to communicate with the King, and declared (perhaps from experience of the treachery and cowardice then rife) " that of all the people he knows in the world none has that love as Friends to each other, to cover their friends' nakedness." He did not, however, fulfil his promise, and the mission was entrusted to William Penn, whose influence with James had already won pardon for some of the unhappy West Countrymen condemned by Jeffreys. It was largely due to his efforts that many Friends were set free at the beginning of 1686. The next year came the Declaration of Indulgence, which the Quakers welcomed more heartily than the ordinary Dissenter, since they alone were willing to extend liberty of conscience to the Catholics   Whiting expresses the Quaker attitude to the Declaration :—

" It did not come forth in the way we could have wished for, viz. by King and Parliament, which would have been more acceptable than granting it by virtue of the prerogative. . . . We could do no less than accept of it now, and be thankful to God and the King for it, however granted, as that which was right in itself, and made way for the establishing of it in Parliament when King William came." [1]

The Yearly Meeting sent an address of thanks to the King. The deputation was headed by Penn, who probably was mainly responsible for the wording of the address. While expressing gratitude for the grant of toleration, it added : " We hope the good effects thereof . . . will produce such a concurrence from the Parliament as may secure it to our posterity in after times." The King replied : " Gentlemen, I thank you heartily for your address. Some of you know (I am sure you do, Mr. Penn) that it was always my principle that consciences ought not to be forced, and that all men ought to have the liberty of their consciences. And what I have promised in my declaration, I will continue to perform so long as I live. And I hope, before I die, to settle it so that after ages shall have no reason to alter it." [2]

---

[1] Whiting, p. 172, also Sewel, *History*, pp. 607–8.
[2] Quoted by Janney, *Life of Penn* (1852), p. 296.

There is no doubt that, in spite of James' earlier record as a persecutor in Scotland, Friends as a whole believed that this was a genuine expression of opinion.

It is needless here to tell again how James' one good deed led to his fall. On November 5, 1688, William of Orange landed at Tor Bay, James fled to France and, returning next year, could only find troops and subjects in Ireland, and in 1690 the Battle of the Boyne finally settled the question of the Protestant Succession. These years of war, which left so deep an impress on the political and religious life of Ireland, were a time of testing for Irish Friends.[1] They were hated as settlers of English origin by the one side, and suspected by the other for their neutrality and the shelter they gave to fugitives from both parties. In fact, their political interests and sympathies during the war must have been strangely divided. On the one hand they owed to James what liberty of conscience and worship they enjoyed. On the other the security of tenure for land held by most English Protestants in Ireland rested on the Act of Settlement of 1662, which the Catholic Irish naturally wished to repeal. The Dublin Parliament, during the war, actually ordered the restitution of estates to their original owners, but the order was only enforced in a few instances near the city.

George Story, a chaplain in the English Army, declared in his history of the war that the Irish Quakers maintained a regimen for James at their own cost.[2] The slander has been revived by modern writers. It was emphatically denied in a memorial by the Society to the Irish Parliament of 1698, and there is no evidence to support it. One definite service, according to tradition, was rendered to the Jacobite cause by Francis Randall, a Wexford Friend. James, after the Battle of the Boyne, took refuge in his house. Randall fed him, supplied him with horses, and sent his son as a guide to Duncannon Fort, where a ship was waiting to convey the King to France.

Even before the actual outbreak of war Friends suffered at the

[1] Statements in the following account for which no reference is given are due to the generous help of Isabel Grubb of Carrick-on-Suir, who put at the writer's disposal not only her published article on "Irish Friends and War" (*Friends' Quarterly Examiner*, May 1916), but also her unpublished researches into the contemporary records preserved at Eustace Street Meeting House, Dublin.

[2] George Story was a brother of Thomas Story, who became a Friend in 1691.

hands of both parties. During the war they shared to the full in the miseries of Ireland. Letters pour over to the Meeting for Sufferings in the winter of 1689–90 describing their plight. William Williamson at Ballyhagan writes in December that the English Army "take their corn, hay, oats, and provision, and pay them little for it," and the Meeting decides to lay the case before the Secretary to the "Duke of Scambergh" (Schomberg) and other persons of influence. In April they are able to assure Irish Friends that William has taken cognisance of their case, and written to "Duke Scumbergh." Rumour, however, said that Friends had provisioned James' army. Some, indeed (the Irish Friends reply), had been arrested on this charge on "Rogues' information, but so clear that they were set at liberty without examination." In the districts held by the Irish troops matters were much worse. From Lurgan William Hooper sent a gloomy account in March 1690 (read in the Meeting on March 14th). "Friends, some well and many sick and dead, and many thousands of other people and army. Blanch Holden is lately dead, and others too tedious to mention here. The face of things looks very foul here, and nothing like to be but destruction and our exercises very great several ways. Famine seems at hand, little food and very dear, and all hindrances for further supply of food is made upon the country, that cannot get their seed put in the gound. . . . We have amongst us money yet, but cannot have victuals for it. They are made so scarce by the army, so that many live poorly, and not for want of money." The Meeting for Sufferings was generous in offers of help, but Irish Friends, in their fear of further plundering, refused all money while the war continued, though they welcomed the "tender letters" sent over by the Meeting. In December 1690 the latter heard from John Workman of Cork "that after he, his wife, and children had been stripped by the Irish rebels they burnt his house down," and from Dublin come frequent reports that the "Raparees" are killing, plundering, and burning in the neighbourhood.

There are still preserved among the Dublin records many reports, pathetically primitive in style and spelling, of the losses of country Friends. Nothing was too trifling to escape the plunderers. A small farmer in Kildare wrote : "Thay dug my potatoes and took all the profit of my garding. . . . Thay distroyed in garding ten hifes of bees worth £7. . . . Thay took my gloves

and pokat hancarchar." [1] " Thay," in this case, were the followers
in the wake of the Irish army, whose depredations were especially
felt in the south and centre after the Battle of the Boyne.   In Ulster
Friends suffered heavily from the billeting of William's mercenaries ;
furniture was destroyed, grain and crops commandeered or trampled
into ruin, and stock carried away.   Losses of beds, blankets, and
linen sheets recur constantly in these lists.   One Ulster meeting-
house was turned into a brew-house by a band of Danish soldiers,
and the solid wooden forms served them for fuel.

And besides all this, at the return of the armies to winter
quarters, " the country was filled with violent sickness, which took
away many of all sorts, and several that were driven away from
their habitations, and had lost most of their substance, tho' they
yet had left wherewithal to support nature, seemed to grieve at
their losses and low estates, and so languished and died, which
Friends were greatly supported over, having an eye to the Lord
who not only gives, but takes, or suffers to be taken away." [2]

The loss of horses made travelling difficult, while contending
armies also cut off communication.   For twelve months Dublin
Friends seem to have been isolated from all intercourse with Ulster
or England.

A belated Epistle from the Dublin Half-Yearly Meeting,
written in November 1690, but not received till December 1691,
estimated the losses of Friends in Leinster alone at more than ten
thousand pounds, " besides the quarter of soldiers."   In 1692 it
was computed that the total loss of Friends through the nation was
a hundred thousand pounds.[3]   In that year Irish Friends at last
accepted the aid of their English brethren, who sent them about
£1,800, while £100 came on their behalf from the small community in Barbadoes.[4]   During these three years of suffering the
Society in Ireland organized relief for its members.   Friends driven
from home were re-established at the earliest opportunity, and in
the meantime welcomed by other groups of Friends.

---

[1] The Report of the Carnegie Commission which inquired into the conduct
of the Balkan Wars (1911–13) contains many similar peasant lists (*vide Report*,
p. 139, for both " hives " and " kitchen-garden").
[2] Wight and Rutty, *History of the Rise and Progress of the Quakers in Ireland*,
1751, p. 165.
[3] *Ibid.*, p. 158.
[4] The National (Half-Yearly) Meeting records that a letter of thanks was
sent to Barbadoes " but a French privateer took it."   A second arrived safely.

The meetings at Dublin and Cork provided houses and clothing for Friend refugees and schooling for their children. In the former meeting Friends were warned not to apply for relief from any other funds besides those raised in the Society.

There was also opportunity to help other sufferers. At Limerick, Dublin, and other places, Friends supplied the prisoners taken from William's army with food and clothing, "so that many of them said when at liberty, if the Quakers had not been there they had been starved to death."

Both at Limerick and Cork, Friends endured all the dangers and privations of the siege. Joseph Pike records that the latter city was about to be stormed when the Duke of Grafton, the leader of the attack, was killed, and later a capitulation was arranged on terms. This probably saved the lives of the Quakers for the besiegers believed that all Protestants were in prison, and intended to put to the sword everyone found in the streets and houses. "But Friends were at liberty, the Irish believing there was no danger from us." [1]

Meetings were regularly held, though Friends travelled to them over roads infested by robbers. "In worship no molestation," wrote John Burnyeat, although in many places a blank in the records shows that the business meetings were discontinued for months, and in some cases for two years. [2] When James' responsible officers were at hand Friends were in better case, "those that were in Government then seemed to favour us," and they were able to extend some protection to their fellow Protestants. Wight's *History* gives many instances, both of sufferings and of providential escapes, adding : " Tho' in those times many of the English neighbours fell by the hands of those bloody murderers, yet we know but of four, that we could own to be of our Society in all the nation, that fell by the hands of cruelty, and two of them too forwardly ventured their lives when they were lost."

Of these, the names of three have been preserved. Thomas Greer was killed by a stray shot fired into his home by night, James Waseley was killed in trying to recover his stolen cattle, and John Barnes died of wounds during the second siege of Limerick. Four Friends are known to have taken up arms. " Three of these were

---

[1] Joseph Pike, *Journal*, pp. 49–54.
[2] From T. Wight's MS. it is also clear that these meetings for discipline were very irregularly held.

officially ' condemned,' for having acted ' scandalous to the principles of truth by us professed and our known practice since we were a people.' At least one of them publicly repudiated his action afterwards, while of another it is recorded four years later that he had been ' out of unity for many years.' In the fourth case, that of a man who took a commission in the English Army, after much serious and lengthy consideration he was told he ' could not be owned ' by the Society." [1]

William Edmundson's *Journal* [2] gives the fullest picture of the hardships endured by individual Friends. Edmundson was a Westmorland man who, after leaving the Parliamentary army in 1651, migrated to Ireland, and on a visit to England in 1653 was convinced by the preaching of James Naylor. He settled as a farmer at Rosenallis, near Mountmellick, and as early as 1685 led a deputation from the district to Tyrconnell at Dublin, begging for protection from the plunder of the Irish troops, which was grudgingly granted. Edmundson's own influence was more effective : before they left for Ulster the troops begged his forgiveness, and some of their officers, with whom he made interest for Friends in the North (" for they were not in arms ") promised to protect them, and in some measure kept their promises. As the troubles increased he was constrained to take a step which some modern critics have considered involved a breach of the Quaker testimony against war. " Now calamity increased, the Raparees on one hand plundered and spoiled many of the English ; and on the other hand the army marching and quartering took what they pleased from us, and our families were their servants to make what we had ready for them, and it looked like a sudden famine, there was such great destruction. Now I considered the way to prolong time, that the English might eat part of their own, was to get a guard of Irish soldiers in that quarter which lay open to all mischief. So I went to Dublin and got an order from the Duke of Tyrconnell for one Captain Francis Dunn and his company to stay with us, and protect that quarter against thieves, Raparees, and other violence." This mended matters somewhat for the time, but when the pressure of the war led to the removal of the guard the Irish began their plundering again, and " the Protestants with us went fast to wreck in their substance."

---

[1] The quotation is from an unpublished paper by Isabel Grubb.

[2] *A Journal of the Life of . . . William Edmundson*, 1715, pp. 112-36.

It does not appear that this request for a guard went beyond the use of " the magistrates' sword," so often expressly upheld by the early Quakers. Dunn and his men were acting as police to check the excesses of their own supporters. During 1689, Edmundson more than once visited Dublin to lay the sufferings of the Protestants before James, and was, at least, received with courtesy. His own house was a city of refuge to many of his Protestant neighbours, " thinking themselves safer there than elsewhere." The turn of the tide at first brought little advantage. " At the Boyne fight, the Irish army being beaten, many of them fled our road, and plundered many in our parts. They plundered my house several times, and we were in great jeopardy of our lives. . . . Now was violence let loose and no Government to make address to ; the English army did not come near us for some time, and to look outwardly, we were exposed to the wills of cruel, bloodthirsty men."

The English troops, on their arrival, carried off five hundred head of cattle and horses, and took prisoner Captain William Dunn and his sons, including the former protector of the Edmundsons. One of the sons they prepared to hang, and the Dunn family appealed in their distress to William Edmundson, who rode after the soldiers " as swift as I could, having regard to my promise of neighbourhood." His story of the rescue throws a vivid light on the confusion of those times.

" When the Irish neighbours saw me ride after them, many followed in expectation to get their cattle and people released. I rode four miles before I overtook them. When I came near, the two captains, perceiving who it was (for they knew me before), made an halt, and met me. I reasoned the matter with them, and told them of the King's proclamation, and how it would not be the soldiers, but they who commanded that must answer the injury done, and that it was a reflection upon the King's promise, as well as a great reflection upon the English nation. . . . The two captains seemed willing to release all, if the soldiers could be prevailed on. I rode with them to the head of the party, but they were very angry, would needs have killed the Irish that followed for their cattle. Whereupon I quitted my horse, and ventured my life amongst the rude soldiers to save the Irish, and with much ado I, with the two captains' assistance, got them moderated, on condition to give them a small part of the cattle to release the rest.

Then I mounted my horse, and sought out the man whom they had stripped for hanging. When I found him, I threw him my riding-coat to put on, and desired one of the captains to assist me in finding of him that had taken his clothes. When we had found him, I reasoned the matter with the captains and soldiers, telling them, it was unmanly and not like a soldier to strip men in that manner, for I had been a soldier myself, and would have scorned such a base action. Besides it might be a precedent to the Irish to strip the English."

When the English withdrew to winter quarters, the Raparees took up the work in turn. In November 1690, Edmundson attended the Half-Yearly Meeting at Dublin, to which many Friends came, in spite of the perilous roads. " We had a heavenly, blessed, powerful meeting, and Friends were more than ordinary glad one of another in the Lord Jesus, who had preserved us alive through so many dangers, to see one another's faces again." He himself had need of all the spiritual help he received, for shortly after his return a midnight band of plunderers attacked and burnt his house, and carried him away with his two sons, all three scantily clothed to meet the rigours of a winter night. At a mock trial they were sentenced to death, although the marauders admitted that Edmundson had protected men of both parties from the wrongs of their opponents. As they prepared to blindfold him the old soldier told them it was needless, " he could look them in the face and was not afraid to die." But in this crisis a band of Irish soldiers, led by one of the Dunns, whom he had saved before, came up and rescued the three Quakers. Dunn, however, treated them harshly. They were dragged, still starving and half-clad, to Athlone, and there thrown into prison, although several of the Catholic gentry spoke in their favour. Happily, other Friends in the neighbourhood were able to supply their necessities and at last to obtain their release. When Edmundson reached home it was to find that his farm and tan-pits were ruined and his wife had suffered the very fate of which he had warned the English marauders, having been stripped and driven from home in another night attack. She died a few months later as a result of the shock and exposure.

The whole story is typical of the anarchy which ravaged Ireland in these years. It is perhaps natural that Wight's *History*, written in the reign of William III, should slur over the injuries received by Friends at the hands of the English army, but from the con-

temporary records it is clear that these were severe.   The grim touch
with which Edmundson ends his story shows how much blood had
drenched Ireland in the three years' struggle.   "Now, as soon
as the ways were opened to travel I went into the North, to visit
Friends, and some Friends accompanied me.   As we went by
Dundalk, there were many bones, and tufts of green grass that
had grown from carcasses of men, as if it had been heaps of dung."

Yet the final result of these sad times, in the view of the Society's
Irish historian, was that "Truth gained ground and Friends came
more into esteem than formerly in the minds of many, both rulers
and people, through their innocent, wise deportment in the fear of
God."   In the years immediately following the war (as is stated
in T. Wight's original MS. of 1698) Dublin Friends found such
numbers frequenting their meetings for worship that they were
constrained to build a large meeting-house in Sycamore Alley, on
the site of the present Eustace Street building.   It was probably
the characteristic, noted in the same document as "Friends keeping
their places in the midst of dangers" (displayed not for the first or
the last time in the Society's history) which drew others to seek
strength and confidence from the same source.

In England, under William III, Friends enjoyed a large measure
of toleration, and were fast settling down into quiet respectability,
although before the seventeenth century ended they had one more
opportunity of expressing their "clearness" of all rebellious designs.
In February 1695/6 a Jacobite plot for the murder of the King
was discovered.   The result was an outburst of loyalty, which took
shape in a voluntary "Association" to swear loyalty to William
and to promise him armed protection.   This oath was popularly
used as a test of loyalty, and Friends came into some difficulty.
On February 28th the Meeting for Sufferings ordered John Whitehead and George Whitehead to draw up "A Paper relating to
Friends' innocence from plots and all murderous designs."   This
was approved next month and, when printed, distributed to country
meetings.   In April "Thomas Lower reports that the paper
declaring Friends' innocency from plots, etc., was the 8th instant
delivered the King by the Friends appointed, and he returned them
thanks for the same and wished them good success in the House
of Lords.[1]   Since which they understand the King has read it,

---

[1] Where a Bill was in progress giving Quakers the right of Affirmation in
certain cases.

and expressed himself well-satisfied therewith." In the paper Friends "solemnly and sincerely declare" that they have always believed "the setting up and putting down Kings and Governments is God's peculiar prerogative, for causes best known to himself,[1] and that it is not our work or business to have any hand or continuance therein, nor to be busybodies in matters above our station. . . . And according to this, our ancient and innocent testimony, we often have given forth our testimony, and now do, against all plotting and conspiracies and contriving insurrections against the King or the Government, and against all treacherous, barbarous, or murderous designs whatsoever, as works of the devil and darkness. . . . And whereas we, the said people, are required to sign the said Association, we sincerely declare that our refusing so to do is not out of any disaffection to the King or Government, nor in opposition to his being declared rightful and lawful King of these realms, but purely because we cannot for conscience' sake fight, kill, or revenge either for ourselves or any man else.

"And we believe that the timely discovery and prevention of the late barbarous design and mischievous plot against the King and Government and the sad effects it might have had, is an eminent mercy from Almighty God, for which we and the whole nation have great cause to be humbly thankful."

William III always showed friendliness towards the Quakers, even to those, like Penn, who were openly favourable to his predecessor. Gilbert Latey, his watchmaker, a London Friend, was on intimate terms with his royal employer. On their side Friends cherished real gratitude to the first ruler who was able to establish a workable, even though incomplete, system of religious toleration. They shared to the full the joy of other Englishmen at the Peace of Ryswick, concluded in 1697, and the Yearly Meeting on this occasion addressed the King with an expression of thankfulness that God had "graciously turned the calamity of war into the desired mercy of peace."

---

[1] This became a favourite formula much employed by American Friends in the Revolutionary War.

PART II

THE GROUND OF THE PEACE TESTIMONY

THERE is a spirit, which I feel, that delights to do no evil nor to revenge any wrong, but delights to endure all things, in hope to enjoy its own to the end. Its hope is to outlive all wrath and contention, and to weary out all exaltation and cruelty, or whatever is of a nature contrary to itself. It sees to the end of all temptations : As it bears no evil in itself, so it conceives none in thought to any other : If it be betrayed, it bears it ; for its ground and spring is the mercies and forgiveness of God. Its crown is meekness, its life is everlasting love unfeigned, and [it] takes its kingdom with entreaty and not with contention, and keeps it by lowliness of mind. In God alone it can rejoice, though none else regard it or can own its life. It is conceived in sorrow and brought forth without any to pity it : nor doth it murmur at grief and oppression. It never rejoiceth but through sufferings ; for with the world's joy it is murdered. I found it alone, being forsaken : I have fellowship therein with them who lived in dens and desolate places in the earth ; who through death obtained this resurrection and eternal holy life.—*Dying Words of James Naylor*, 1660.

CHAPTER IV

EARLY APOLOGISTS FOR PEACE

1653–64

THE seventeenth century might be called the Age of Tracts. The possessor of any view on any subject, political or religious or social, felt bound to give it to the world, his opponents felt bound to combat it, and despite the intermittent censorship of the time, the result was a snowstorm of hastily written and hastily printed pamphlets which in some degree took the place, in the free expression of opinion, of the modern newspaper and review.

The Quakers contributed their full quota to the mass ; many of the weighty folio volumes entitled the "Works" of one or another early Friend consist mainly of reprinted pamphlets, and large numbers survive as separate tracts, often anonymous. Amongst those of the early period which deal with the questions of peace and war, those now to be discussed deserve consideration, either from the standing of their writers or from their own intrinsic interest, or for both reasons. They fall into three classes. Some, accepting the soldier's profession as a necessity of the time, appeal to the Army of the Parliament to use its power on the side of righteousness ; others set forth "the life and power that take away the occasion for wars" ; others explain and vindicate the Quaker attitude against the misunderstandings of suspicion or enmity. In Fox's own writings all these positions may be found. His *Epistles* are direct personal appeals to individuals or groups. As early as 1653 he issued an exhortation to "all soldiers, governors, and officers" to refrain from persecution, to follow the inner light, and to take the Baptist's words as their guide of conduct.[1] In a similar strain (probably in 1657) he addressed "George Monk and the army in Scotland."[2] But in the letters to Friends already

---

[1] *Swarthmore MSS.,* ii. 66.   [2] *Swarthmore MSS.,* ii. 75.

113

quoted, and in many others he is emphatic on the peaceable nature of true Christianity. "The Peace-maker" (he wrote in 1652) "hath the kingdom, and is in it ; and hath the dominion over the Peace-breaker, to calm him in the power of God." [1] Again, in 1657 : "For all dwelling in the light that comes from Jesus, it leads out of wars, leads out of strife, leads out of the occasion of wars, and leads out of the earth up to God, out of earthly mindedness into heavenly mindedness, and brings your minds to be in heaven." [2] At the time of the militia levies in 1659 his advice was clear. "As for the rulers, that are to keep peace, for peace's sake and the advantage of truth, give them their tribute. But to bear and carry carnal weapons to fight with, the men of peace (which live in that which takes away the occasion of wars) they cannot act in such things, under the several powers ; but have paid their tribute," and in so doing, he adds, Friends may better claim their liberty.[3] All war and persecution is a departure from allegiance to Christ. The Jews, indeed, fought against the heathen, but Christ came to put an end to the Jewish outward types. "In the apostate-Christians' times, they are crying up the outward sword again," [4] and each Church is ready to propagate its doctrines by force and to settle all disputes by war. "Forgive us as we forgive them, cry Papists, cry Episcopal, cry Presbyterians, and Baptists and Independents . . . and then, like a company of senseless men, without understanding, fall a-fighting one with another about their trespasses and debts." [5]

The Declaration of January 1660/1 is definitely addressed to the public as a vindication of the Society. In 1684, after the Insurrection Plot for which Algernon Sidney and Lord William Russell paid with their lives, the "Morning meeting" [6] reprinted the Declaration "as the unchangeable and assured testimony of Friends against all conspiracy and violence." At its first publication it was sold in the streets as a broad-sheet under the title, "A

[1] Fox, *Epistles*, p. 11.
[2] *Epistles*, p. 108, *vide* also *Swarthmore MSS.*, ii. 95.
[3] *Epistles*, p. 137.
[4] *Ibid.*, p. 103.
[5] *Epistles*, p. 132, and *Swarthmore MSS.*, ii. 103.
[6] *The Second Day Morning Meeting*, formally set up in 1673, was composed of leading Friends who were ministers, and amongst other functions acted as a censor and corrector of Friends' writings. In 1901, it was amalgamated with the *Meeting for Sufferings*. In 1684, Penn's intimacy with Sidney may have brought Friends under suspicion.

Declaration from the harmless and innocent people of God called Quakers, against all sedition, plotters, and fighters in the world : for removing the ground of jealousy and suspicion from magistrates and people concerning wars and fightings. Presented to the King upon the 21st day of the 11th month 1660." [1] The document is signed by Fox, Hubberthorn, and ten other Friends. It is lengthy and contains repetitions, but its tenor is unmistakable. Although there are frequent quotations from Scripture, the principle of peace which the writers proclaim is derived not from texts as its ultimate warrant, but from the ever-present and ever-teaching Spirit of Christ.

First they set forth their testimony. " Our principle is, and our practice always has been, to seek peace and ensue it ; to follow after righteousness and the knowledge of God ; seeking the good and welfare, and doing that which tends to the peace of all." War arises from the evil passions of man's lower self : the Friends have utterly abjured all use of outward weapons. " This is our testimony to the whole world." But the objection has been raised that this may be only a temporary opinion : if " the Spirit move," Friends (as Ranters have been in the past) may be found among plotters and fighters. The answer of the Declaration gives no uncertain sound.

" The Spirit of Christ, by which we are guided, is not change-able, so as once to command us from a thing as evil, and again to move us to it, and we certainly know and do testify to the world, that the Spirit of Christ, which leads us into all truth, will never move us to fight and war against any man with outward weapons, neither for the Kingdom of Christ nor for the kingdoms of this world."

For further proof they can point to their admitted record in the past. " This we can say to the world, we have wronged no man, we have used no force nor violence against any man : we have been found in no plots, nor guilty of sedition. When we have been wronged, we have not sought to revenge ourselves ; we have not made resistance against authority ; but whenever we could not obey for conscience sake, we have suffered the most of any people in the nation. We have been counted as sheep for the slaughter,

---

[1] There are various editions in D. of the 1660 tract, which differ somewhat from that of 1684, quoted in Ellwood's edition of Fox's *Journal*. One, D. 575, 13, is considered by Norman Penney to belong to the first (confiscated) edition. Another has a paragraph complaining of the " violent and unjust taking away the whole first impression."

persecuted and despised, beaten, stoned, wounded, stocked, whipped, imprisoned, haled out of synagogues, cast into dungeons and noisome vaults, where many have died in bonds, shut up from our friends, denied needful sustenance for many days together, with other the like cruelties." They have never resisted the violence of their opponents. " It is not an honour to manhood or nobility to run upon harmless people, who lift not up a hand against them, with arms and weapons."

The charge of treason has been brought against them under every form of Government. " Our meetings were stopped and broken up in the days of Oliver, under pretence of plotting against him ; in the days of the Committee of Safety we were looked upon as plotters to bring in King Charles ; and now our peaceable meetings are termed seditious." Yet the spirit of love breathes through the paper. " Never shall we lift up hand against any that thus use us ; but desire the Lord may have mercy upon them, that they may consider what they have done."

Fox says that the *Declaration* was drafted by Hubberthorn and himself. How much its style and coherency owed to the former may be seen from a later manuscript testimony drawn up by Fox during his imprisonment at Lancaster in 1664,[1] and afterwards signed by Margaret Fell and other imprisoned Friends. A copy sent to Colonel Kirkby, the chief of the magistrates who had committed Fox to gaol, has been preserved in the Record Office. The paper is drawn up under fifteen heads, but the testimony against war and plots and the testimony against oaths are almost inextricably entangled. Its chief interest is the very definite statement of the Quakers' political attitude. " I saw by the power of God the King was brought into the land, which brought down a great deal of that which we do declare against, and suffered by that hypocrisy. So I and we do say that he ought to have his right and all men. . . . So our allegiance lies in this that we would not have the King hurt, and we would have him have his right, and we deny all that take up arms against him, we first deny it in ourselves and then in others." Some of us, he continues, have known " a time of the spear and sword," but now they are broken. He also develops a favourite theme in the argument that the weapons and wars of the Jewish dispensation were a type of the spiritual weapons and contest described in Ephesians vi. 11–17.

[1] *Vide* Chapter III, p. 70.

This doctrine of submission to established authority, in so far as that authority did not invade the realm of conscience, was one cause of the aloofness of the majority of Quakers from political matters in days when the ruling powers of one decade were the rebels of the next. Its resemblance to the high Tory doctrine of passive obedience was only superficial, for the Quaker's obedience was given to the *de facto* Government and he never plotted on behalf of the deposed power.

Yet, in spite of this non-political bias, Quakers, like other pamphleteers, were prodigal of advice and admonition in the troubled year 1659, when the Army threatened to rule. Perhaps the words most relevant to the situation were those written by George Fox the Younger in a little tract entitled, "This is for you who are called the Commonwealth men both in the Army and Parliament to read." [1] The power of the sword, he says, was committed to them for the specific purpose of establishing the liberties and freedom of the nation and destroying tyranny, "and not to make a trade of using your swords to enrich yourselves by them. . . . This spirit if it ruled you, would make you as freely willing then to lay down your places and swords as ever any of you were made free to take them up, and then to fall upon improving the creation in the fear and wisdom of the Lord, and to be content to enjoy an equal proportion and share of the liberty (with your fellow-creatures) which you have fought for ; and if it were thus, then you might truly be called the Commonwealth men, or servants." If they desire to continue as an army, the temptation will come not to use their power to re-establish complete order and liberty "lest your trade should fail."

This sober reasoning by their old colleague may have influenced the temper of the troops ; they displayed the very spirit he desired when, upon the Restoration, they submitted to disbandment, and returned quietly to their old civilian occupations. "Of all that they had done for England's welfare and liberty nothing is more to their credit than that they voluntarily laid down their power when they perceived that they had begun to abuse it." [2]

There was a general admission on the part of early Quakers that the majority of the Commonwealth soldiers were inspired by

---

[1] In D. The writer was so-called because "younger" in the faith than George Fox, though not in years.

[2] G. M. Trevelyan, *England Under the Stuarts*, p 330.

high motives, and as many of the Society's members were recruited from the ranks of the Army they had had opportunities of judging its character.   George Fox the Younger, in another paper addressed to the Army in 1659, says : " The Lord appeared with you in the field, giving you mighty victories over your enemies, that so he might make way for his living truth to be spread, which was then stirring in his people." Again : " O Army ! In which was I several years together, in which time I saw the mighty appearance of God with thee, even in the time of the outward war, and when the war was ended I left thee in obedience to the appearance of the living God unto me, who . . . hath brought me into the life of that Truth which I, and many of you in the Army professed in words." [1]

A different and more dangerous view of the duties of the English soldier was uttered by Edward Burrough in that same year.   The episode is curious, and deserves some notice.

Edward Burrough and Samuel Fisher were two of the first Friends to carry their message across the seas.   In the spring of 1659 they visited Dunkirk, tried to hold some intercourse with the religious seminaries there, and had meetings with the English garrison.   Like Paul, Burrough's spirit was stirred within him by the sight of a city given up to what seemed to him idolatry, and at his departure he addressed the soldiers in an Epistle [2] which gave men of war a worthier place in the divine economy than other Friends allowed.   After exhorting them to observe their duty in their military station, he continued : " What do you know but the Lord may have some good work for you to do, if you be faithful to him ? . . . The Lord hath owned and honoured our English Army, and done good things for them in these nations in our age, and the Lord once armed them with the spirit of courage and zeal against many abominations, and gave them victory and dominion over much injustice and oppression and cruel laws."   But at last they were overcome by ambition and self-indulgence.   Let them recover their old spirit and take no rest " till you have visited Rome, and inquired after and sought out the innocent blood that is buried therein, and avenged the blood of the guiltless through all the dominions of the Pope : the blood of the just it cries through Italy and Spain, and the time is come that the Lord will search it, and

[1] *Writings of George Fox the Younger*, London, 1665, pp. 12 and 68–70.
[2] *Works*, pp. 537–40.

seek it out, and repay it ; and it would be to your honour to be made use of by the Lord in any degree." It was, he added, the Lord's own work to bring men into the spirit of true religion, but " yet he may work by you, to break down the briars and thorns and the rocks and hills that have set themselves against the Lord." Therefore the officers should treat their men with justice and mercy, and the men must be dutiful and obedient to their officers, that " having no sin lying upon your conscience then shall you face your enemies with courage and not fear death." The Scriptural quotations and allusions in this fervent appeal are drawn from the Apocalypse and the Prophets, rather than from the teaching of Christ and the Apostles. The preacher himself felt that the passage in which he counselled the soldiers to turn for guidance to the light of Christ within lacked congruity with the earlier part of the Epistle, for he made an attempt to reconcile reliance on the outward sword with the spiritual doctrine of the Quakers. " And yet though such a victory would be honourable unto you, yet there is a victory more honourable, to wit, the victory over sin and death and the devil in yourselves. . . . Your work hath been, and may be, honourable in its day and season, but he hath a work more honourable to work after you ; that is, to destroy the kingdom of the devil and the ground of wars." The other side of his nature, however, triumphs again in the final exhortation to seek " the glory of the Lord and the freedom of the oppressed ; and in that you will be blessed and prosper, till you have set up your standard at the gates of Rome." In this year, 1659, Fox wrote : " Friends, take heed of blending yourselves with the outward powers of the earth," and rebuked the religions that were ready to fight about religions, and " kill like the heathen about their gods." Sewel, writing his *History* a generation later, was perturbed by the martial tone of Burrough's Epistle, which he tried to explain on the ground that Burrough was anxious " not to give them too rough a brush, but to meet them somewhat in their own way," while the Quaker teaching was emphasized " lest any should think he was for the bearing of arms and not for harmlessness or non-resistance." [1]

But Burrough can hardly be cleared from a confused attempt to make the best of both worlds—to use the weapons of war while praising the gospel of peace. The attempt has been made in all ages by many professing Christians, but the inconsistency is most

[1] Sewel, *History*, Book V.

manifest in a Quaker. It is perhaps worth noting that his private
letters, preserved in the Swarthmore collection, show a fondness for
military metaphor. His fit of militarism, however, was shortlived,
for next year he stated the Quaker position with no lack of clearness.

In " A Visitation of Love to the King and those called
Royalists," [1] he readily admits that some Quakers had been soldiers
in the army of the Parliament, " and that principle, which formerly
led some in action to oppose oppression and seek after reformation
we never have denied or shall deny, but that principle is still justified,
though we are now better informed than once we were. For
though we do now more than ever oppose oppression and seek after
reformation, yet we do it not in that way of outward warring and
fighting with carnal weapons and swords, . . . never since we
were a people." And in " A Vindication of the People of God
called Quakers," [2] he answers the accusation which confounds them
with the Fifth Monarchists. " As for killing all the wicked, this
is another false charge ; for it is not our principle to war against
the persons of any men, and kill them with carnal weapons, about
Church, and ministry, and religion, as the Papists and Protestants
do one with another ; . . . we would have men's wickedness killed,
and their persons saved, and their souls delivered ; and this is the
war we make." [3]

A curious fact, not very easy to explain, is the similarity between
this Epistle of Burrough and an anonymous tract, by some attributed
to Fox, which also belongs to the year 1659. This is an eight-
page pamphlet, entitled " To the Councill of Officers of the Armie
and the Heads of the Nation, and for the inferior officers and souldiers
to read." [4] It is signed " F. G.," but the copy at the Friends'
Reference Library is endorsed in pencil in a later hand " G. F. 1659,"
and at some time in the eighteenth century it was bound up in a
volume of tracts mainly by Fox.

[1] Burrough's *Works*, 1672, p. 671.   [2] *Ibid.*, p. 748.
[3] He has courage to champion even the Anabaptists. " I cannot believe they
are of that spirit of murder and tyranny, etc., as is reputed by your informer,
though their judgment in every case, neither about civil nor spiritual things I
dare not justify." Still earlier, in 1655, he had written to the " poor desolate
soldiers " in Ireland of the Light that " reproves you in secret of violence, and will
teach you not to make war, but to preserve peace on the earth " (*Works*, p. 93).
[4] The tract is i. 56 in D. Miss Brailsford discusses it in an article in the
Contemporary Review (November 1915, " Cromwell's Quaker Soldiers "), but
attributes it to the year 1657. The allusion to New England makes this date
impossible, and the writer mentions the Quaker evictions from the Army only as
one incident of a long persecution.

Opening abruptly, " O Friends, do not rule with your own reason ! " the writer goes on to plead against oppression and persecution of all kinds. Friends have suffered " these seven or eight years " in England, and now they are enduring fresh cruelties under " the new Inquisition in New England." An animated description is given of the persecution of Friends in their worship and in private life. " And many valiant captains, soldiers, and officers have been put out of the Army by sea and land, of whom it hath been said among you, that they had rather have had one of them than seven men, and could have turned one of them to seven men, who because of their faithfulness to the Lord God, being faithful towards him, it may be for saying *Thou* to a particular [single person], and for wearing their hats have been turned out from amongst you." Then, turning to the Army, which had acted as the agent of persecution, the writer declares : " Had you been faithful to the power of the Lord God which first carried you on, you had gone into the midst of Spain . . . to require the blood of the innocent that there had been shed ; and commanded them to have offered up their inquisition to you, and gone over them as the wind, and knock't at Rome's gates before now, and trampled deceit and tyrants under, and demanded the Pope himself, and have commanded him to have offered up all his torture-houses, and the racks and Inquisition (which you should have found as black as hell), and broke up the bars and gates where all the just blood has been shed, which should have been required. . . . And then you should have sent for the Turk's Idol, the Mahomet, and plucked up idolatry, and cried up Christ, the only King and Lord. . . . And if ever you soldiers and true officers come again into the Power of God which hath been lost, never set up your standard until you come to Rome, and let it be atop of Rome, then there let your standard stand."

Yet the writer believes that the " power of the Lord " would have accomplished this without violence and bloodshed, for he says that those obedient to Christ love their enemies, and only one " out of truth, . . . will kill and compel and persecute to death, to worship." Again, in the passage immediately before the description of the standard at Rome, he says :—

" Stand in that in which there is peace, the Seed Christ, which destroyeth the Devil the author of wars, strifes, and confusion," and exhorts the soldiers to do violence to no man nor be like blind persecutors, " for persecution was always blind."

It seems impossible either to prove or disprove the authorship of Fox. The handwriting of the MS. index to the volume of tracts is apparently that of Joseph Besse, which would carry the attribution to Fox back to the early eighteenth century. It is noted under Fox's name in Joseph Smith's *Catalogue of Friends' Books*, 1867, but in this he was probably following the pencil endorsement on the tract itself. On the other hand, I have not found its title in two very careful and elaborate chronological indices to Fox's works, made either during his lifetime or immediately after his death, and now in the Friends' Reference Library. The style is not very characteristic of Fox, and in some points more resembles that of George Fox " the Younger," particularly in the elaborate conclusion :

From a Lover of peace and all souls, who stands in the election before the world began,

F. G.

One sentence almost implies that the writer was a soldier : " Thousands *of us* went in the front of *you*, and were with you in the greatest heats." The signature, " F. G.," however, is not known to have been used by George Fox the Younger, while, although rare, it does occur in some of Fox's pamphlets and letters, for instance the declaration to Cromwell in 1654. The tract has no publisher's name, and on the whole I am inclined to think it may be a résumé of recent utterances and writings by several leading Friends, made for the benefit of the army by some ardent follower (possibly George Fox the Younger ?) without their knowledge. This would explain its echoes and inconsistencies. The passages about Spain and the Pope resemble Burrough's Epistle too closely to be mere coincidence. An undoubted tract by Fox, published immediately after the Restoration, gives no countenance to wars of religion. This is the " book," *Fear God and Honour the King*, of which Fox wrote in his *Journal*, 1666, that it " did much affect soldiers and most people." From his allusion it might belong to that year, but in fact it was published in 1660, and was probably intended to establish the loyalty of Friends in the eyes of the authorities.[1] Its argument is that no one who does not live

---

[1] A word on behalf of the King, that he may see who they are that . . . Fear God and Honour the King ; . . . and also to see that Christ ends the Jews' law by which they were to kill about religion such as are contrary-minded, and he never gave out any since to do so, but to love enemies . . . and they that do so are the true Christians (1660, *Tracts*, 45, 28 in D.).

in the fear of God can truly honour the King. Fox is emphatic, and even intemperate in his denunciations of the military and civil vices of the day, but the long catalogue of sins forms a dark background against which shines out the peaceable message of the Gospel. " To love enemies, it is not to kill them and to destroy them, but to overcome them with the good. . . . Such as will fight and kill and destroy for a morsel of bread or a mess of pottage, are profane as Esau was. . . . Now the Jews who hated enemies their weapons are carnal, but they that love enemies (the Christians) their weapons were and are spiritual. So Christ ends that law of the Jews, which they thought they did God good service by, when they put to death them that were contrary minded to them ; for they could not love enemies that killed them, neither can they that love enemies now kill them. . . . And he broke down the partition wall which was between Jew and Gentile, who slew the enmity, and so of twain made one new man, and thereby came the love to enemies."

Another interesting figure in this group of early Friends was Isaac Penington. Son of a Puritan Lord Mayor of London and married to Lady Springett, widow of a Parliamentary officer, he was not likely to be looked upon favourably by the new Government. Husband and wife had been convinced of the truth of Friends' principles in 1658. In 1659, like many other Friends, he addressed " The Parliament, the Army, and all the well-affected in the Nation who have been faithful to the good old cause." [1] The pamphlet bears clear traces of his Puritan upbringing. He urged the soldiers not to become discredited by their dissensions. " The account of all the blood which hath been shed lies somewhere. Was it for a thing of naught ? Was it of no value ? Nay, it was precious in the sight of the Lord, many (yea, very many) in the singleness and simplicity of their hearts losing their lives for the cause." There had often been " a naked, honest, simple, pure thing stirring in the army," but evil persons had made it a tool for their private ends so that it did not procure the " righteous liberty and common good " at which the majority aimed. Turning to the Parliament, he warned them : " Let not the army be your confidence. Do not any one thing to please the army, much less a corrupt interest of a part of the army ; but apply yourselves to do that which is truly just and righteous in the sight of God, of

[1] Penington, *Works*, p. 135.

the army, and of all men." A few months later, when the monarchy was restored, Penington drew the moral. " It is man's way to settle himself by outward strength against outward strength, and then he thinks he is safe, not eyeing the invisible hand which turns the wheels." ¹ Next year, 1661, while lying in Aylesbury gaol on behalf of his faith, he wrote an apology for the Quaker as citizen, which shows a real effort to enter into the mind and meet the objections of the average Englishman when confronted by this unfamiliar attitude towards war. The paper is lengthy, and it has a lengthy title.²

The Weighty Question (the apology is written in the form of a catechism) is, whether Quakers " who (by the peaceableness and love which God hath wrought in their spirits, and by that law of life, mercy, good-will, and forgiveness, which God by his own finger hath written in their hearts) are taken off from fighting and cannot use a weapon destructive to any creature," have any claim on the protection of the magistrates and the laws. Penington answers that the powers of the State are intended for the benefit of the whole nation, including women, children, the sick and aged, and priests, " who have ability to fight but are exempted by their function, which is not equivalent to the exemption which God makes by the law of his Spirit in the heart." Fighting " came in by the Fall," so is it not righteous and equitable that the fighting nature should come to an end in those redeemed from the Fall, and chosen to be examples of peace ? " How can he fight with creatures in whom is love and good-will towards those creatures ? . . . Fighting is not suitable to a gospel spirit, but to the spirit of the world and the children thereof. The fighting in the gospel is turned inward against the lusts, and not outward against the creatures." This blessed state of outward peace and inward spiritual victory will, according to prophecy, some day prevail throughout the world. But it must first arise in individuals, and these peaceable folk are

---

¹ *Works*, p. 293.

² Somewhat spoken to a Weighty Question, concerning the Magistrate's protection of the Innocent, wherein is held forth the blessing and peace which Nations ought to wait for and embrace in the latter days. With some considerations for the serious and wise in heart throughout this Nation to ponder for diverting God's wrath (if possible) from breaking forth on it.

Also a brief account of what the people called Quakers desire, in reference to the Civil Government. With a few words to such as by the everlasting Arm of God's Power have been drawn and gathered out of the Apostacy, into the living Truth and Worship.

not a weakness to the State, but rather a strength. Penington presses this argument with great earnestness and animation.

"When righteousness is brought forth, and when the seed of God springs up and flourisheth, that nation grows strong; and instead of the arms and strength of man the eternal strength overspreads that nation, and that Wisdom springs up in the spirits of men, which is better than weapons of war; and the wisdom which is from above is pure and peaceable, and teacheth to make peace and to remove the cause of contentions and wars, and unites the heart to the Lord in waiting upon him for counsel, strength, and preservation in this state, who is brought into it. Now is not this much better and safer then the present estate of things in the world? First, to have the cause of wars removed, and a sweet, peaceable, righteous spirit in the stead thereof? Secondly, to have a peaceable and a righteous generation (whom the Lord hath made and preserved so) breathing to the Lord for peace, good, and prosperity to the nation and the magistrates thereof, and to stretch forth his arm to be a defence about them? Thirdly, to have the God of Heaven engaged by his power to defend that power and magistracy, which defends righteousness in general, and particularly his people in their obedience unto him, whom it is most righteous for them to obey, and for the magistrate (who claims his rule and dominion under God) to protect them in? Were not this much better both for magistrates and people than the present state?"

The imaginary questioner, passing over the ingenious plea for toleration, here objects that "this is a Utopian state, or a world in the moon." Penington replies that it is the state foretold in divine prophecy. Will it not be happy when it comes to pass? Who would hinder it? Nay, more, in the early days of Christianity this state was in "a fair forwardness," but many generations ago the true Church, the Bride of Christ, was driven out into the wilderness, and a "cruel bloody stepmother" was welcomed by the world in her place. And now, after the long night of apostasy, the spirit of Christ is awakening again and gathering men together to the true Church, making them pure and peaceable. "As the Lord does this so will it go on, and the nations, kings, princes, great ones, as this principle is raised in them, and the contrary wisdom, the earthly policy (which undoes all) brought down, so will they feel the blessings of God in themselves, and become a blessing to others." This is the only way of healing the grievously distracted nation, but man is not ready to learn it until taught in the hard school of adversity.

A new objection, however, is raised. " If all men were of this mind, and none would fight ; suppose a nation should be invaded, would not the land of necessity be ruined ? " The objection is a familiar one to-day, and Penington's answer is worth citing at some length :

" First, whensoever such a thing shall be brought forth in the world, it must have a beginning before it can grow and be perfected. And where should it begin but in some particulars [individuals] in a nation, and so spread by degrees, until it hath overspread the nation, and then from nation to nation until the whole earth be leavened ? Therefore, whoever desires to see this lovely state brought forth in the general, if he would further his own desire, must cherish it in the particular. And O that men would not spend their strength and hazard the loss of all in cherishing pretences and names of Christianity, but would pray to the Lord at length to open that eye in them which can see the loveliness of the truth, power, and virtue of Christianity, that they might cherish that tenderness of conscience wherein the truth grows and springs up in its virtue and power." Thus the conversion to a peaceable state will not be sudden and catastrophic, but gradual. But, secondly, the objection is really based on distrust of God. " It is not for a nation (coming into the gospel life and principle) to take care beforehand how they shall be preserved, but the gospel will teach a nation (if they hearken to it) as well as a particular person to trust the Lord, and to wait on him for preservation. Israel of old stood not by their strength and wisdom and preparations against their enemies, but in quietness and confidence and waiting on the Lord for direction (Isa. xxx. 15), and shall not such now, who are true Israelites, and have indeed attained to the true gospel state, follow the Lord into the peaceable life and spirit of the gospel, unless they see by rational demonstration beforehand, how they shall be preserved therein ? I speak not this against any magistrates or peoples defending themselves against foreign invasions, or making use of the sword to suppress the violent and evil-doers within their borders (for this the present state of things doth require, and a great blessing will attend the sword where it is borne uprightly to that end, and its use will be honourable ; and while there is need of a sword, the Lord will not suffer that Government or those governors to want fitting instruments under them, for the managing thereof, who wait on him in his fear to have the edge of it rightly directed) : but yet there is a better state which the Lord hath already brought some into, and which nations are to expect and travel towards. Yea, it is far better to know the Lord to be the defender, and to wait on him daily, and see the need of his strength, wisdom, and preservation, than to be never so strong and skilful in weapons of war."

Lastly, Old Testament history gives abundant proof that the power of God, and not material force, alone avails to protect and defend those that trust in Him. Is the arm of the Lord shortened ? "Will he not preserve and defend that nation, whom he first teacheth to leave off war, that they shall not be made a prey of, while he is teaching other nations the same lesson ? " As he preserved Israel of old in their obedience to him, so can he do now. "Consider this" (Penington utters his vehement appeal), "O ye great men, O ye wise men, and deep politicians ; all ye have done or can ever do in relation to overturning that God hath purposed, what are ye therein, or what has your work come to ? It is just like the small dust of the balance, it hinders not at all the weight of his power on the other hand, but he will carry on his work, bring to pass what he hath purposed in himself and promised to his people." The nation "at the bottom" longs for righteousness, and a Government of worldly wisdom and policy can never bring this forth, nor the peace that accompanies righteousness.

The arguments in the second portion of the pamphlet ("Some considerations for the serious and wise in heart throughout the nation ") are chiefly drawn from the desperate state of contemporary politics (to which Penington finds parallels in the Apocalypse) and include a reiterated assertion of divine omnipotence. "Those that fight against the Lamb must needs be overcome by Him, His invisible strength and armies being much stronger than the visible armies and all the outward strength of nations, though to the outward eye such may appear very great and invincible."

The last section, "A brief account of what the people called Quakers desire in reference to the Civil Government," contains a programme which might have saved Charles and his successor from some of their misfortunes.

"There are three things which we cannot but earnestly desire in our hearts, and pray to the Lord for, as the proper means of settling aright the spirit of this nation, as also necessary for the growth of God's pure living truth and as just and equal in themselves.

"1. Universal liberty for all sorts to worship God, according as Christ shall open men's eyes to see the truth. . . .

"2. That no laws formerly made contrary to the principle of equity and righteousmess in man, may remain in force ; nor no new ones be made but such as are manifestly agreeable thereunto. . .

"3. . . . . That no party might be bolstered up in enmity and opposition against another, but that every party might be considered, in what might be done for their ease and benefit, without detriment to any other party. And if I might be hearkened to, I would persuade those now in power, not to deal with their enemies as they formerly dealt with them, but as they would have been dealt with by them when they were in power."

He earnestly dissuades all people from plots, and begs instead their prayers for the new Government. But if its members act corruptly and selfishly, plots will be superfluous, " for the Lord God Almighty who with ease removed their enemies and made way for them can with as great ease remove them and put the power into another hand."

Much of the treatise, Penington adds, was written long since, but it is published at this juncture to show the loyalty of his Society and issued from his own place of bondage, where he prays " for the turning of the captivity of the whole creation."

Penington's incidental remark that he does not condemn magistrates or a people who defend themselves against foreign invasion hardly seems, when read in its context, to bear the weight of meaning put upon it by some critics of the Quaker position, even were it (what it is not) an official pronouncement by the Society. Penington, who is addressing the outside public, agrees that defence by force of arms is permissible to those who believe that by such methods they are fulfilling God's will, " but yet there is a better state, which the Lord hath already brought some into, and which nations are to expect and travel towards."

The next peace treatise leads us from politics to mysticism. William Smith, of Beesthorp, Notts, suffered much imprisonment for his faith.[1] His voluminous works were collected under the title *Balm in Gilead* in 1675, and include two pronouncements on peace. The first, published in 1659, was " A right Dividing and a true

[1] He had been an Independent minister and was convinced in 1658.

Discerning, showing the use of the sword, and how and where it is in its place, and what it is to be laid upon." This tract develops the favourite theme that the sword's only lawful use is in the repression of crime. "To suppress violence, to punish the evil-doers, and to rule those that are unruly, disobedient, and disorderly, this is manly, and answers the end for which the sword is put in their hands." But some have advanced further. To them " the use of the sword is not known, they are out of the place of a soldier, neither do know a soldier's place, which is under the state of a man, violently to kill and destroy each other and know not wherefore. . . . They return not to it again, they see a further thing the end of that." Soldiers, however, who become convinced of Friends' views are not to be hasty, but to consider " whether God hath set thee there." God may call some warrior like Cyrus to do his work, but that is no concern of those, the " Children of Light," who have heard the divine call to turn away from the world. " The true minister's work is to bring people to God and to Christ, and not to keep people in the world, where the tribulation, wars, and fightings is. . . . For where the Spirit of the Lord puts itself forth in any measure there will not be a killing, devouring, or taking away the lives of men, for he came not to destroy men's lives but to save them." And the pamphlet ends with a condemnation of the corrupt magistrate, who misuses the civil sword and " lets the poor be punished and the rich escape, because he can give money to free himself from punishment . . . and if he has not money he must be whipt or stockt or go to prison."

Two years later he was himself a prisoner " in Worcester County Gaol . . . for obedience to the command of Jesus Christ." There he wrote another peace tract,[1] inflamed with a glow of mystical fervour. Like many Quaker writers, Smith is too diffuse, but for beauty of thought and expression this little-known tract must take high rank in the literature of religious experience. It opens with a fervent description of the love and mercy of God and of the yearning of men's hearts towards him until " the light leads out of the earth and all earthly things and leads up to God, the fountain

---

[1] The Banner of Love under which the Royal Army is preserved and safely conducted. Being a clear and perfect way out of all wars and contentions ; with a short testimony unto the way of peace. Given forth for the edification and comfort of all that truly fear God. Written by the hand of one who bears good-will to all men.

of eternal love, in whose pure presence the fulness of joy is found."

And as men learn more of the love of God they enlist under him in the war of righteousness.

"And of the immortal seed is the Royal Army born, and they are conquerors through him that loves them and spreads his banner over them, and their weapons are love and patience, by which they overcome ; and they do not think ill to their neighbours, but love their enemies, and are ready to do good to those that are contrary minded ; and they would have all come to the love of God, that they might be saved. . . . And this is an Army that the Lord hath gathered and is gathering from amongst the earthly warriors, whose strength is in the horse and his rider, and the Lord God puts into their hands the spiritual weapon, and with it they go forth to battle, and they seek to save men's lives and not to destroy them." It is an army of peace. "The aliens' army draw their swords and kill one another ; the Royal Army have put up their swords and would have all men saved. And who need to fear such an army, whose banner is love, and their weapons good-will ? There need no horsemen and strong armies to oppose them, not prisons to quiet them, for they are marching under the Banner of Love, and in love meet their enemies and quench their fury ; and whatever can be done against them love is their Banner, and with it they are wonderfully preserved." In time the army will grow to an overwhelming strengh and "war will cease, and cruelty come to an end, and love will abound." Those who fight the Lord's battle dare not destroy the life of any, for outward weapons cannot establish a spiritual kingdom. The argument closes with a direct address to Fifth Monarchists and others who rely on force.

"Now all that are striving and warring and have it in their hearts so to do, and thereby think to set up their religion and their observations ; or such as expect a time in which Christ will appear personally upon the earth to reign, and have in their hearts to cut off and destroy the contrary minded, and so by weapons of war fight for his kingdom into his dominion, unto such sorts of people it is said, Be still and quiet, lest ye put forth your hand to do evil, and so provoke the Holy One to anger ; and in your froward minds provoke one another, and so kindle wrath and anger one in another. From which comes all wars and contentions which is not the way

in which Christ appears, nor the path in which he leads his Royal
Army." If men follow the "pure principle of light in their own
conscience" it will lead them into unity with the spirit of Christ.
In conclusion, Smith breaks out into a "Short Testimony to the
Way of Peace," a rhythmic utterance of the deepest spiritual
experience, only paralleled in Quaker writings by Thomas Story's
later rhapsodies.

"The life of Christ is sweet, it is the substance of whatever
can be spoken of : to inherit a measure of it is joy and peace, and
the desire of the simple is abundantly satisfied therein. . . . It
hath its course in the valley, and flows in the channel of lowliness ;
the humble meet it in the way, and in the pure streams they receive
their portion ; to be low and humble is the way of life, and therein
do the lambs enjoy their pasture. As it is tasted it draws still after
it, and the more it is tasted the more it is beloved ; and as it is
beloved the more it springs, and flows to that which thirsteth, and
in patience waiting the virtue of it is felt, and the mind sinks down
more into it, and the delight is in the sweet savour of it. This is
the way of the humble and this is the path of the lowly mind. . . .
There is no limitation of its breaking forth, but when and where
and in whom it pleaseth ; it prepares the vessel for its use and makes
it honourable in its own holiness. It springs and fills according
to its pleasure and the vessel must be new that doth contain it."
The love of God is "a fresh stream that cannot cease its course,
nor stop its flowing, but must shed itself abroad," and constrains
those touched by it "to behave themselves in love and tenderness
to all people ; and in the one Spirit hath the Lord gathered them ;
and in the one Spirit he hath bound them up, and they are his
people, and he is their God, and dwells amongst them, and walks
in them ; and the Prince of Peace orders them, and they are his
Royal Army in whose Love and Life they stand in unity, and give
up their bodies and spirits unto God, that his own Will may be done,
and the intents of his own Heart performed and his own Name
therein glorified."

So the gentle prisoner of Worcester Gaol ends. Little more
is known of his life, but his thoughts must have sunk deep into
Quaker minds, for the sufferings on peace grounds multiply fast
after the Restoration.

The last pamphlet of this early period which deserves notice here is a plain statement [1] of the Quaker position and a defence of it against popular misconceptions, put forth by William Bayly in 1662. Bayly was a sea-captain, convinced in 1655, and often imprisoned. He died in 1675.

The argument follows familiar lines. Friends' principle of peace, he says, is everlasting and universal, founded on God himself, and " before death, hell, strife, and wars." Being joined to Christ, they partake in some measure of the Spirit of Christ which " destroys the ground of enmity in man." [2] " We bear good-will to all people upon earth, Jew and Gentile, bond and free, barbarians, Turks, Indians, Greeks, Romans, English, or any other. God hath made us all of one blood to dwell upon the face of the earth. We are all of one blood, all the workmanship of one creator."

This principle is not " an opinion or judgment which may fail us, or in which we may be mistaken or doubt, but it is the infallible ground and unchangeable foundation of our religion (that is to say) Christ Jesus the Lord, that Spirit, Divine nature or Way of Life, which God hath raised and renewed in us, in which we walk, and in whom we delight to dwell, and cannot but worship and yield obedience to." Such a definition of Christ, laying stress rather on divine Immanence than on divine Personality, was soon to expose the Quakers to charges of heresy.

Some, remembering the extravagances of Anabaptists and Millenarians, feared lest this " spirit " should at times move the Quakers to fight. " To which we answer in the fear of God in the truth and simplicity of our hearts as it is in Jesus, that we do really and confidently believe that the Lord our God (who is that good spirit that guides us into all truth) will never move us to do that or those things again for which he hath rebuked us. . . . So that to us it seemeth as impossible for us to be found in such things (plottings, fightings, and violence) as for a good tree to bring forth evil fruit, or for one fountain to yield salt water and fresh, for we

---

[1] A Brief Declaration to all the world from the innocent people of God called Quakers, of our principles and belief concerning plottings and fightings, with carnal weapons, against any people, men, or nations upon the earth, to take away the reproach, or any jealousies out of the minds of all people concerning us in this particular and to answer that common objection whether we would not fight if the Spirit moved us (D. *Tracts*, 99, 36).

[2] So John Whitehead, an old soldier, writes of his fellow Quakers : " Being leavened through with love and mercy, it is against their very nature to revenge themselves, or use carnal weapons to kill, hurt, or destroy mankind " (*A Small Treatise*, 1661).

have felt God's rebukes because of the strong nature that dwelt in us, from whence envy, pride, wrath, malice, and heart-burnings one against another spring."

Lest this attitude of peace should lead their enemies to say, "We use them as we list without fear," Bayly warns them that God will exact an account from all persecutors. And finally he, as far as in him lies, clears the Society from any scandal brought upon it by pseudo-Quakers.

"And now if any that hath been at our meetings, or have come at any time (as many do) to see our manner, or that may be by some called a Quaker, should be (which we have never yet known among us) found in any plotting against any men or people whatsoever, to contrive mischief, danger, or hurt either to body, soul, or estate any way under any pretence whatsoever, we do utterly (in the Spirit of Jesus Christ our Lord and Saviour) deny that part or spirit in all men upon the earth, as that which our principle (the everlasting foundation of God) and our spirit have no fellowship or unity with."

CHAPTER V

ROBERT BARCLAY THE APOLOGIST

THE foregoing vindications and explanations of the Quaker principle had all been short occasional writings, called forth by some emergency. The reign of Charles II witnessed the establishment, and in some sense the recognition, of the new sect. Its message had spread, its organization had developed, and the time was ripe for a fuller and more literary statement of its belief and practice. Quakerism found its apologist in Robert Barclay, one of the comparatively few men of birth and scholarship who joined the Society in its early days. Born in 1648, at Gordonstown in Moray, he was the son of Colonel David Barclay, a Protestant soldier of fortune in the Thirty Years and Civil Wars, and of Catherine Gordon, a distant cousin of the house of Stuart.[1] Young Robert, however, was educated under a Jesuit uncle, head of the Scots Theological College in Paris, and the boy (as he wrote in later years), exposed to Calvinist teaching at home and to Catholic in his school days, kept himself " free from joining with any sort of people," noticing in all their defect in " the principle of love."

His father had been a lukewarm supporter of the Cromwellian rule, but at the Restoration he fell under suspicion, and in 1665 he was imprisoned in Edinburgh Castle. " While in London he had often heard of the Quakers, and had been attracted by the principles they taught as well as by their manner of life. He noticed that they refused to fight even those who might be called their enemies, and that they loved one another. These two facts struck him as very remarkable, and he decided that these must be the true followers of Christ upon earth, if there were any such." [2] A Quaker, John Swinton, was his fellow prisoner, and he soon converted David

---

[1] See *Robert Barclay*, by M. C. Cadbury, 1912.
[2] *Ibid.*, p. 26.

Barclay to the faith, which he upheld with constancy and courage under suffering (as Whittier's ballad [1] reminds us) for the rest of his long life.

Robert Barclay at first was allowed to visit the prison, and when the permission was withdrawn he had learnt enough from Swinton to induce him to attend the Friends' Meetings in Edinburgh, which, though proscribed, were regularly held. The result he has described in a beautiful and familiar passage. In the section of his *Apology* discussing the Quaker mode of worship, he explains, with a rare autobiographical touch, that he is speaking out of his own experience : "Who, not by strength of argument, or by a particular disquisition of each doctrine and convincement of my understanding thereby came to receive and bear witness of the truth, but by being secretly reached by this life. For when I came into the silent assemblies of God's people, I felt a secret power among them, which touched my heart, and as I gave way unto it, I found the evil weakening in me, and the good raised up, and so I became thus knit and united unto them, hungering more and more after the increase of this power and life, whereby I might feel myself perfectly redeemed." "It must be" (he added) "rather by a sensible experience than by arguments, that men can be convinced of this thing, seeing it is not enough to believe it, if they come not also to enjoy and possess it." [2]

Thus, in 1666, as a youth of eighteen, he joined the Society of Friends. The rest of his life was consecrated to preaching, defending and suffering for what, in his belief, was Divine Truth. At first he lived as a peaceful student on his father's estate at Ury, doing what he could to maintain the property, for David Barclay

---

[1] "Barclay of Ury." Alexander Barclay, an ancient Scottish poet, was claimed by the house as an ancestor. He left behind him some moral maxims, which suit well with the lives of his Quaker descendants.

> "See that thou pass not thy estate ;
> Obey duly thy magistrate ;
> Oppress not, but support the puir,
> To help the commonweal take cuire ;
> Use no deceit ; mell not with treason,
> And to all men do right and reason,
> Both unto word and deed be true ;
> All kind of wickedness eschew.
> Slay no man ; nor thereto consent ;
> Be nought cruel, but patient."

[2] Barclay, *Apology*, Proposition xi. sec. 7 (Concerning Worship). The whole section is of extraordinary force and beauty.

was not released from prison for some years. Robert Barclay's first tract in defence of Quakerism was published in 1670, the year of his most happy marriage. Of the twenty years of life before him, the next ten were the most eventful. In them he was thrice imprisoned for his faith, he published his chief works, and he made two missionary journeys to Holland and Germany. The fruit of this foreign travel was a close friendship with the learned and mystical Princess Elizabeth of the Rhine, the patroness of Descartes and cousin of Charles II. Barclay, through his mother, was a distant kinsman, but the sympathy between himself and Elizabeth was based on a community of thought, and until her death in 1679 they kept up a frequent correspondence on spiritual themes. The Princess must have had little in common with that dashing cavalier her brother Rupert, but they were on affectionate terms, and more than once she wrote urging him to influence the King to deal more leniently with Quakers, especially with Barclay and his friends. Barclay also obtained some help from the Duke of York, and their acquaintance was maintained during James' Commissionership at Holyrood, in spite of the cruel persecution of the Covenanters, which Barclay reprobated. In James' reign he was often at Court on behalf of his fellow Quakers. It was to him that the King just before his flight made the well-known remark that, according to the Whitehall weathercock, the wind was fair for William of Orange. After the Revolution he naturally fell under suspicion for Jacobitism, and was accused of being a disguised Jesuit. He wrote in reply a spirited "Vindication," [1] in which, while disclaiming all sympathy with the doctrines and practice of the Roman Church, he admitted that he had personal friends among members of that communion, and boldly declared that he had less inclination to attack Catholicism in its present adversity than in its days of power. Persecution, "the worst part of Popery," comes with an ill grace from its opponents ; "to say we are right and they are wrong, and therefore we have a right to force their consciences, but not they ours, is miserably to beg the question."

Barclay, and his father before him, had undoubtedly feelings of loyalty to the House of Stuart, and to the charge of holding aloof

---

[1] *Reliquiæ Barcleianiæ*, 1870. Vindication of Robert Barclay of Ury, being an explanation by the Apologist of circumstances connected with his intercourse with King James II, written in 1689. From an MS. formerly at Ury, (lithographed). In D.

from the change of government he replied : " I never did believe nor ever shall, that it is my duty to be active in such a change. . . . I shall always hold me by the doctrine of non-resistance and passive obedience." Of his feelings towards the fugitive King he wrote without disguise. " To do him right, I never found reason to doubt his sincerity in the matter of liberty of conscience. . . . I must own, nor will I decline to avow that I love King James, that I wish him well, that I have been and am sensibly touched with a feeling of his misfortunes, and that I cannot excuse myself from the duty of praying for him that God may bless him and sanctify this affliction to him. And if so be his will to take from him an earthly crown, he may prepare his heart and direct his steps so that he may obtain through mercy an heavenly one, which all good Christians judge the most preferable."

Holding these sentiments, he was naturally not regarded with favour under the new reign, and he spent the short remainder of his life quietly on his estate of Ury. He was not yet forty-two when he was struck down by a fatal illness. Among his last words were : " God is good still ; and though I am under a great weight of sickness and weakness as to my body, yet my peace flows." He died on October 3, 1690.

Three of Barclay's works bear directly on the subject of peace. The *Apology for the True Christian Divinity*, published in 1676, deals at length with the whole body of Quaker doctrine and practice, including the testimony against all wars. In the winter of 1676–7 he was imprisoned, with other Quakers, in the Tolbooth of Aberdeen for some months. During this time he wrote the treatise on *Universal Love*, a protest to all Christians against any form of persecution or war. The following year, 1678, he dispatched an Epistle to the representatives of the Powers assembled for peace negotiations at Nimeguen, expounding to them the " means for a firm and settled peace." Thus, in three years, a distinct advance had been made. Earlier writers had contented themselves with defending Quaker peaceableness against misunderstanding and misrepresentation in times of special crisis. Barclay first showed it in its true relation to their whole body of belief, then urged it on his fellow Christians as an essential part of Christianity, and finally he made a definite effort towards the restoration of peace to the war-ravaged countries of Europe. Had he lived longer he might have been able to share with Penn in a new development, the government of a State according to the principles of Friends. In his later years he did actually join in the colonization of East Jersey, founded, mainly by Friends, on the principle of toleration, and was appointed its nominal governor, paying a deputy. From David Barclay his son had learned much of the horrors perpetrated by all the contending parties in the Thirty Years War, and of the sufferings endured even in the milder campaigns of our own Civil War, while the Low Countries and Westphalia, during Robert Barclay's visits, bore plain traces of the devastations caused by the war between Louis XIV and the Dutch. In all his writings on the subject his position is the same. His firm conviction that war and Christianity are irreconcilable and that force is ineffectual to change opinion or belief, gives him an especial horror of the religious motive so loudly trumpeted in the wars of his day and of the action of religious leaders in fomenting war. He has a burning pity for the mass of innocent suffering created by any war, and for the great armies automatically driven to mutual slaughter at the will of a few statesmen. To him the only remedy lies in the awakening of the individual conscience and the revival of true Christianity. The Society of Friends had made this attempt, but the world had received its teaching with persecution and contumely. Thus he links together an apology for Quakerism and a plea for the abolition of war. Into the *Apology* Barclay put all the learning and power of exposition which he possessed. The foundations of his theological knowledge had been well laid at the Scots College, and the edifice was built up by years of patient study. William Penn in his writings shows a wider and more liberal culture, but in divinity Barclay had few rivals at his age, and he employs his knowledge of patristic and mediæval writers with great aptness and facility. The learned John Norris, one of the Cambridge Platonists and a weighty opponent of Quakerism, pays Barclay sincere and ungrudging compliments. " Mr. Barclay is a very great man, and were it not for that common prejudice that lies against him as being a Quaker, would be as sure not to fail of that character in the world as any of the finest wits this age has produced." Again, " That great and general contempt they lie under, does not hinder me from thinking the sect of the Quakers to be by far the most considerable of any that divide from us, in case the Quakerism that is generally held be the same with that which Mr. Barclay has delivered to the world as such ; whom I take to be so great a man, that I profess to you freely, I had rather engage against an hundred Bellarmins, Hardings, or Stapyltons, than with one Barclay." [1]

Later the *Apology* received the hearty praise of Voltaire, both for its argument and its latinity. For it was first published in the universal tongue of scholars, though it soon was translated into the chief European languages. In the business records of the Society for the next hundred years there appear many arrangements for the publication and distribution of foreign editions of the *Apology*, as the best handbook to Quaker faith and practice. The original Latin edition appeared at Amsterdam in 1676, during Barclay's travels in Holland. Two years later the first English edition was published. The book is an expansion of or commentary upon fifteen *Theses Theologicæ* published by Barclay a year or two earlier, also in Latin, and these, in their turn, are to some extent based on the order of the propositions in the Westminster Confession. Hence it comes about that War is treated of, oddly enough, under Proposition XV, "Of Salutations and Recreations." An address to the King, prefixed to the *Apology*, is couched in terms very unlike those in which authors usually presented their treatises to the favour of Charles II.

"It is far from me to use this Epistle as an engine to flatter thee, the usual design of such works, and therefore I can neither dedicate it to thee nor crave thy patronage, as if thereby I might have more confidence to present it to the world, or be more hopeful of its success. . . . But I found it upon my spirit to take occasion to present this book unto thee ; that . . . thou mayest not want a seasonable advertisement from a member of thine ancient kingdom of Scotland." If Charles can allow himself "so much time as to read this," he will discover the consonance of Friends' principles with "scripture, truth, and right reason." Addressing himself to the King as to one who had known intolerance and hardship, Barclay pleads against the persecution of the Restoration. His criticism of the Civil War is interesting : "As the vindication of liberty of conscience (which thy father . . . sought in some part to restrain) was a great occasion of the troubles and revolutions ; so the pretence of conscience was that which carried it on, and brought it to that pitch it came to. And though (no doubt) some that were engaged in that work, designed good things, at least in the beginning (albeit

---

[1] *Two Treatises Concerning the Divine Light*, by John Norris, M.A., 1692. Treatise Two. (*The Grossness of the Quakers' Principle of the Light Within*, pp. 1, 32.)

always wrong in the manner they took to accomplish it, viz. by carnal weapons) yet so soon as they had tasted of the sweet of the possessions of them they had turned out, they quickly began to do those things themselves, for which they had accused others." Charles himself was restored to his throne " without stroke of sword," by a manifest working of divine providence.

"There is no king in the world who can so experimentally testify of God's providence and goodness ; neither is there any who rules so many free people, so many true Christians : which thing renders thy government more honourable, thyself more considerable, than the accession of many nations filled with slavish and superstitious souls. Thou hast tasted of prosperity and adversity ; thou knowest what it is to be banished from thy native country, to be over-ruled as well as to rule, and sit upon the throne ; and being oppressed, thou hast reason to know how hateful the oppression is both to God and man, if after all these warnings and advertisements thou doest not turn unto the Lord with all thy heart, but forget him, who remembered thee in thy distress, and give up thyself to follow lust and vanity—surely great will be thy condemnation."

In Proposition XV Barclay asserts as a definite tenet of the Society and in so many words that " it is not lawful for Christians to resist evil, or to war or fight in any case." " Revenge and war," he writes, " are an evil as contrary to the spirit and doctrine of Christ as light to darkness. . . . The world is filled with violence, oppression, murders, ravishing of women and virgins, spoilings, depredations, burnings, devastations, and all manner of lasciviousness and cruelty." He refers to the early fathers and to mediæval commentators in proof that both oaths and war, though permitted to the Jews, were forbidden to the early Christians, and that the Church observed these prohibitions for the first three hundred years of her existence. " For it is as easy to reconcile the greatest contradictions, as these laws of our Lord Jesus Christ with the wicked, practices of wars. Whoever can reconcile this, ' Resist not evil,' with ' Resist violence by force ' ; again ' Give also thy other cheek,' with ' Strike again ' ; also ' Love thine enemies,' with ' Spoil them, make a prey of them, pursue them with fire and sword ' ; or ' Pray for them that persecute you, and those that calumniate you,' with ' Persecute them by fines, imprisonments, and death itself' ; and not only such as do not persecute you, but who heartily seek and desire your eternal and temporal welfare : Whoever, I say, can find a means to reconcile these things, may be supposed also to have found a way to reconcile God with the Devil, Christ with anti-Christ, light with darkness, and good with evil. But if this be impossible as indeed it is, so will also the others be impossible ; and men do but deceive themselves and others, while they boldly adventure to establish such absurd and impossible things." Barclay then goes on to take some of the familiar sayings of Christ and the Apostles, and to contrast them with the practices of war. For example : " Christ commands that we should ' love our enemies ' ; but war, on the contrary, teacheth us to hate and destroy them. . . Christ calls his children to ' bear his cross,' not to crucify or kill others ; to ' patience ' not to ' revenge ' : to truth and simplicity not to fraudulent stratagems of war, or to play the sycophant, which John himself forbids ; to flee the glory of this world, not to acquire it by warlike endeavour : therefore war is altogether contrary unto the law and spirit of Christ."

Barclay then meets the objections of his opponents who wish to reconcile Christianity and war. First they bring forward the familiar appeal to Old Testament precedents. His reply, in brief, is that the Old Testament dispensation has passed away in all its details, and Christ's followers have learnt a purer and more spiritual religion. Secondly, " they object that defence is of natural right, and that religion destroys not nature. I answer, Be it so ; but to obey God, and commend ourselves to him in faith and patience is not to destroy nature, but to exalt and perfect it."

A more trivial objection is based on John the Baptist's admonition to the soldiers, and Barclay treats it almost contemptuously.

" I answer, what then ? The question is not concerning John's doctrine, but Christ's, whose disciples we are, not John's. . . If it be narrowly minded, it will appear that what he proposeth to soldiers doth manifestly forbid them that employment. For he commands them ' not to do violence to any man, nor to defraud any man, but that they be content with their wages.' Consider then what he dischargeth to soldiers, viz. not to use violence or deceit against any ; which being removed, let any tell how soldiers can war. For is not craft, violence, and injustice, three properties of war, and the natural consequence of battles ? " To the instances of the devout centurions of the Gospels and the Acts, Barclay opposes the admitted practice of the Early Church. " It is as easy to obscure the sun at mid-day as to deny that the primitive Christians renounced all revenge and war." "Yet it is as well known" (he continues) "that all the modern sects live in the neglect and contempt of this law of Christ, and likewise oppress others, who in this agree not with them for conscience' sake towards God. Even as we have suffered much in our country, because we neither could ourselves bear arms, nor send others in our place, nor give our money for the buying of drums, standards, and other military attire.[1]   And lastly, because we could not hold our doors, windows, and shops close, for conscience' sake, upon such days as fasts and prayers were appointed, for to desire a blessing upon, and success for the arms of the kingdom or commonwealth under which we live, neither give thanks for the victories acquired by the effusion of much blood."

The idea of Christians in the different warring nations imploring their God for "contrary and contradictory things" always struck Barclay with peculiar horror, and here he turns aside to reproach another sect opposed to war (probably the Baptists) for its conformity on these days of prayer and thanksgiving.

The passage concerning two swords (Luke xxii. 36) is frequently cited as a proof of the lawfulness of arms.   Barclay frankly admits that its meaning is difficult and has been variously interpreted. "However" (he adds sturdily) "it is sufficient that the use of arms is unlawful under the Gospel."   The next objection raises the whole question of the rights of the State over the individual.   "They object, that the Scriptures and old fathers (so called) did only prohibit private revenge, not the use of arms for the defence of our country, body, wives, children, and goods, when the magistrate commands it, seeing the magistrate ought to be obeyed.   Therefore albeit it be not lawful for private men to do it of themselves, nevertheless they are bound to do it by the command of the magistrate."

Barclay replies that this contention presupposes that the magistrate is himself not truly Christian, and he quotes a strong passage from Vives [2] on the corruption induced by Constantine's union of Christian profession with military power : " He came into the house of Christ accompanied by the devil."   In such a case the Quaker, and those who think with him, must obey God rather than man.

---

[1] This is the " Trophy Money " ; distraints and imprisonments for its non-payment are often recorded among early " sufferings."

[2] A Spanish theologian and opponent of Scholasticism, a friend and correspondent of Erasmus.

"As to what relates to the present magistrates of the Christian world, albeit we deny them not altogether the name of Christians, because of the public profession they make of Christ's name ; yet we may boldly affirm that they are far from the perfection of the Christian religion." In this imperfect state, resembling that of the Jews, "we shall not say that war undertaken upon a just occasion is altogether unlawful to them, but for such whom Christ hath brought hither, it is not lawful to defend themselves by arms, but they ought, over all, to trust to the Lord."

The imperfect Christians who are "yet in the mixture" cannot, he quaintly says, "be undefending themselves." This very qualified permission of defensive war for the professing Christian may be contrasted with Penington's somewhat more emphatic toleration fifteen years earlier. For the Quaker, Barclay's condemnation of war is unhesitating.

"If to revenge ourselves, or to render injury, evil for evil or wound for wound, to take eye for eye, tooth for tooth ; if to fight for outward and perishing things, to go a-warring one against another whom we never saw, nor with whom we never had any contest nor anything to do ; being moreover altogether ignorant of the cause of the war, but only that the magistrates of the nations foment quarrels one against another, the causes whereof are for the most part unknown to the soldiers that fight, as well as upon whose side the right or wrong is ; and yet to be so furious and rage one against another, to destroy and spoil all that this or the other worship may be received or abolished—if to do this and much more of this kind be to fulfil the law of Christ, then are our adversaries indeed true Christians, and we miserable heretics, that suffer ourselves to be spoiled, taken, imprisoned, banished, beaten, and evilly entreated without any resistance, placing our trust only in God, that he may defend us and lead us by the way of the Cross unto his kingdom. But if it be other ways we shall receive the reward which the Lord hath promised to those that cleave to him, and in denying themselves confide in him."

The abhorrence of all attempts to propagate opinion by force, whether through war or persecution, was deep-rooted in Barclay's nature. In the *Apology* he meets the objection of those who argued that the doctrine of the divine light would lead men into anarchic frenzies like the excesses of the Munster Anabaptists by the bold reminder that "as bad, if not worse, things have been committed by those that lean to tradition, Scripture, and reason. . . . I need but mention all the tumults, seditions, and horrible bloodshed wherewith Europe hath been afflicted these divers ages ; in which Papists against Papists, Calvinists against Calvinists, Lutherans against Lutherans, and Papists assisted by Protestants against other Protestants assisted by Papists, have miserably shed one another's blood, hiring and forcing men to kill one another, who were ignorant of the quarrel and strangers to one another. All, meanwhile, pretending reason for so doing, and pleading the lawfulness of it from scripture." Barclay concludes the argument by a spirited sketch of the rival sects with their several reasons for killing their wicked and profane opponents.

His own view of the rights of the individual conscience is given in the Fourteenth Proposition of *Theses Theologicæ,* " concerning the power of the civil magistrate in matters purely religious and pertaining to the conscience."

" Since God hath assumed to himself the power and dominion of the conscience, who alone can rightly instruct and govern it ; therefore it is not lawful for any whatsoever, by virtue of any authority or principality they bear in the government of this world to force the consciences of others ; and therefore all killing, banishing, fining, imprisoning, and other such things which men are afflicted with for the alone exercise of their conscience, or difference in worship or opinion, proceedeth from the spirit of Cain, the murderer, and is contrary to the truth ; provided always, that no man, under the pretence of conscience, prejudice his neighbour in his life or estate, or do anything destructive to or inconsistent with humane society ; in which case the law is for the transgressor, and justice to be administered to all, without respect of persons."

Any Church, he contends (in the chapter of the *Apology* which expands this thesis) has the right of spiritual discipline, including the excommunication of the obstinate backslider, but " we would not have men hurt in their temporals, nor robbed of their privileges as men and members of the commonwealth, because of their inward persuasions." Bodily suffering never brings conviction ; argument, reason, and the power of God alone can do this : " not knocks and blows and suchlike things, which may well destroy the body but never can inform the soul, which is a free agent, and must either accept or reject matters of opinion as they are borne in upon it by something proportioned to its own nature." This argument is as old as Socrates and Plato, but was heretical enough to the Christian world of Barclay's day, to each section of which freedom of opinion meant freedom for its own views and suppression of those repugnant to itself. Such a policy, he reminds them, may make hypocrites, but not Christians, and in a pregnant sentence he declares that *" the ground of persecution is an unwillingness to suffer."* Men cannot hold their own belief with unshaken confidence if they expect that suffering will induce others to abandon theirs. The patient and peaceable endurance of the early Friends had already proved the most effective way of meeting persecution, since it touched the hearts of those engaged in the work, and " made their chariot wheels go very heavily." The proviso that freedom of conscience should not involve anything " destructive to or inconsistent with humane society" was seized upon by critics of the *Apology*, who argued that the refusal to bear arms is itself inimical to the safety of society. This charge has often been levelled against the Quakers, as it was, by Celsus, against the early Christians.

In 1679 Barclay wrote a short reply [1] to one John Brown, who had published a vehement attack on the *Apology* and on the whole body of Quakers. In regard to wars, " he chargeth us " (says Barclay) " with a bloody design . . . by disarming Christians [to] give up Christendom as a prey to Turks and Pagans. To which I shall only answer : that as it is obviously enough malitious, so he shall never prove it true : and therefore I wish the Lord rebuke him, and forgive him for these his evil thoughts ! " Brown's further remarks on the necessity of defensive war are " more like an atheist than a Christian, and like one who believeth nothing of a divine providence." Such arguments can never " brangle the faith " of true believers or make them think " they are less secure under the protection of the Almighty than by their guns and swords." " How men can love their enemies, and yet kill and destroy them is more than I can reach ; but if it were so, such as rather suffer than do it do surely more love them, and to do so is no injury to ourselves nor neighbours, when done out of conscience towards God." Brown believes in the prophecy of an age of universal peace and " thinks fit there should be a praying for the fulfilling of it : and what, if some believe, that (as to some) there is a beginning already of the fulfilling thereof ? " Thus Barclay virtually adopts

[1] R.B.'s *Apology for the True Christian Divinity Vindicated from John Brown's Examination.*

the position of Penington, that the conscience of the individual or the minority must often be in advance of that of the majority, and that ideal Christianity will be established by gradual stages, not by a cataclysmic conversion of humanity. His next treatise was written in his prison in the Aberdeen Tolbooth during the winter of 1676-7. It is curious to note that both Penington's peace tract and Smith's *Banner of Love* were also written in prison. The " dens " of the Stuart reigns inspired the Bedford tinker with his immortal dream, and the quantity of Quaker writings of all kinds originating from prisons shows how much of the seventeenth-century Quaker's life was spent there. No doubt the tedium and discomfort drove the more educated to the solace of composition, as it forced the more practical minded, like Thomas Ellwood, to the tailoring of red flannel waistcoats.[1]

Universal Love is "a serious inquiry how far charity may and ought to be extended towards persons of different judgments in matters of religion " by " a lover of the souls of all men." The plea for a practical application of the spirit of love among the divers sects of Christians is urged with fervour and cogency. Barclay tells how his early experience of Presbyterian and Catholic impressed him with their mutual intolerance. He brushes aside with contempt all pleas for coercion. To rob a man of life, goods, or liberty, or of " the very common and natural benefits of the creation " and to say " thou dost it for good, and out of the love thou bearest to my soul is an argument too ridiculous to be answered, unless the so doing did infallibly produce always a change in judgment : the very contrary whereof experience has abundantly shown." He again dwells with horror on the " bloody tragedy " of the Civil War, arising so largely from religious dissensions and " fomented from the very pulpits." No doubt Barclay himself in childhood had heard some of these war sermons, and in his thoughtful youth the contrast between the Gospel and its expounders struck him with unpleasant force, while he himself was gradually attaining to the conviction he here beautifully expresses, that " God being the Fountain and Author of Love, no man can extend true Christian love beyond his ; yea, the greatest and highest love of any man falls infinitely short of the love of God, even as far as a little drop of water falls short of the vast ocean." Turning to the Quakers, he claims that they, more than any other sect, attempt to practise

[1] Ellwood, *Journal.*

this universal love, and in a brief sketch of the origin of the Society (which has interesting resemblances to that in Penn's well-known essay prefixed to George Fox's *Journal*) he shows to what this characteristic should be attributed. " Friends," he says, " were not gathered together by a unity of opinion, or by a tedious and particular disquisition of notions and opinions, requiring an assent to them, and binding themselves by Leagues and Covenants thereto ; but the manner of their gathering was by a secret want, which many truly tender and serious souls in sundry sects found in themselves : which put each sect upon the search of something beyond all opinion which might satisfy their weary souls, even the revelation of God's righteous judgment in their hearts. . . . And so many came to be joined and united together in heart and spirit in this one Life of righteousness who had long been wandering in the several sects ; and by the inward unity came to be gathered in one body, from whence by degrees they came to find themselves agreed in the plain and simple doctrines of Christ. And as this inward power they longed for, and felt to give them victory over sin, and bring the peace that follows thereon, was that whereby they were brought into that unity and community together ; so they came first thence to accord in the universal preaching of this power to all, and in directing all unto it, which is their first and chiefest principle, and most agreeable to this Universal Love." One of the chief signs among Friends, he continues, of this principle of Universal Love, " which necessarily supposeth and includes love to enemies," is their refusal to reconcile Christianity with war or forcible resistance to injury. " He that will beat, kill, and every way he can destroy his enemy, does but foolishly contradict himself if he pretend to love him."

In the summer of 1677 Barclay had visited Holland and Germany in the company of Fox, Penn, and other Friends, and had seen the devastation and suffering left by war. His experience bore fruit during that autumn in an address to the plenipotentiaries who had been already negotiating terms of peace at Nimeguen for more than two years. The address in polished Latin, and the Latin edition of the *Apology*, were delivered to each Ambassador, possibly by one of the Dutch Friends, in February 1678.[1] The

---

[1] The full title is " An Epistle of Love and Friendly Advice to the Ambassadors of the several Princes of Europe, met at Nimeguen to consult the Peace of Christendom, so far as they are concerned. Wherein the True Cause of the present War is discovered, and the Right Remedy and Means for a firm and settled Peace is

war had begun in 1672, and was an attempt on the part of Louis XIV to subjugate the United Provinces. The courage and wary sagacity of William of Orange and his people eventually frustrated the scheme, but the wider questions of European policy involved had brought about curious alliances during the course of hostilities. Protestant Sweden had helped Catholic France, and Charles II had employed the English Fleet on Louis's behalf, much against the will of the English people. On the other hand, the Emperor, German rulers, Denmark, and even Spain, had taken Holland's side, or rather the side opposed to France. The Epistle opens with a graceful apology for his intervention. Let it not seem strange to them, men chosen for their wisdom and prudence, " to be addressed by one who by the world may be esteemed weak and foolish ; whose advice is not ushered unto you by the commission of any of the princes of this world, nor seconded by the recommendation of any earthly state. For since your work is that which concerns all Christians, why may not every Christian who feels himself stirred up of the Lord thereunto, contribute therein ? And if they have place to be heard in this affair, who come in the name of kings and princes, let it not seem heavy unto you to hear him that comes in the name of the Lord Jesus Christ, who in the truest sense is the Head and Governor and chief Bishop of the Church, the *Most truly Christian and Catholic King* ; many of whose subjects are concerned in this matter." Yet, though claiming this divine commission for his arguments, Barclay is content to leave the proof of their truth " to the holy and pure witness of God in all your consciences, to be received or rejected by you as it shall there be approved or not approved."

He has been, he tells the Ambassadors, under a deep sense of the sufferings of Christendom, and " being last summer in Holland and some parts of Germany the burthen thereof fell often upon me, and it several times came before me to write unto you what I then saw and felt from God of those things," but he waited until

proposed, by R. Barclay. A Lover and Traveller for the Peace of Christendom, which was delivered to them in Latin, the 23rd and 24th days of the month called February, 1677-8, and now published in English for the satisfaction of such as understand not the language (Psalms ii. 10)." A postscript gives a list of the assembled delegates, " the Ambassadors of the Emperor, of the Kings of Great Britain, Spain and France, Sweden and Denmark, of the Prince Rector Palatine, as also of the States General, and of the Dukes of Lorraine, Holstein, Luxemburg, Osnaburg, Hanover, and the Pope's Nuncio."

the call, on his return to Scotland, became clearer and more insistent. The cause of "all this mischief and confusion and desolation" originates from the "Author of all Mischief." Human designs and ambitions may be the immediate cause, and the peace settlement may attempt to meet these (on the approved principles of diplomacy) "by giving way to some and taking from others according as they are more or less formidable and considerable," but such methods can only bring about a temporary peace. "Those called Christians . . . are only such in name, and not in nature, having only a form and profession of Christianity in show and words, but are still strangers, yea, and enemies to the life and virtue of it ; owning God and Christ in words, but denying them in works." The want of Christian virtue, notably at the Courts of Christian princes ("nests of vilest vermin"), dishonours the name of Christian in the eyes of the heathen nations. And these rulers in their relations of State are equally far from true Christianity.

"Upon every slender pretext such as their own small discontents, or that they judge the present peace they have with their neighbours cannot suit with their grandeur and wordly glory, they sheath their swords in one another's bowels ; ruin, waste, and destroy whole countries ; expose to the greatest misery many thousand families ; make thousands of widows and ten thousands of orphans ; cause the banks to overflow with the blood of those for whom the Lord Jesus shed his precious blood ; and spend and destroy many of the good creatures of God. And all this while they pretend to be followers of the lamb-like Jesus, who came not to destroy men's lives but to save them, the song of whose appearance to the world was, ' Glory to God in the highest, and good will and peace to all men ' : not to kill, murder, and destroy men ; not to hire and force poor men to run upon and murder one another, merely to satisfy the lust and ambition of great men ; they being often times ignorant of the ground of the quarrel, and not having the least occasion of evil or prejudice against those their fellow Christians whom they thus kill ; amongst whom not one of a thousand perhaps ever saw one another before."

"Is it not so ?" asks Barclay, in conclusion to this spirited picture of the horrors of war. To him the position of the clergy ("for the most part the greatest promoters and advisers of these wars") is especially horrible, and their prayers and thanksgivings for the destruction of brother Christians seem nothing better than blasphemy. In the shifting tangle of alliances, all bonds of religious fellowship are broken, French Catholics and Huguenots praying for the defeat of Spanish Catholics and Dutch Protestants, and other paradoxical situations arising, of which Barclay could find examples enough and to spare in the existing war.

"The ground then of all this," he reiterates, "is the want of true Christianity—the proud, ambitious, Luciferian nature that sets princes and States at work to contrive and foment wars, and engages people to fight together, some for ambition and vain glory, and some for covetousness and hope of gain. And the same cause doth move the clergy to concur with their share in making their prayers turn and twine, and so all are out from the state of true Christianity." Yet all claim to have a truly Christian desire for peace, although the very peace they succeed in making belies their claim. "How is peace brought about ? Is it not when the weaker is forced to give way to the stronger, without respect to the equity of the cause ? Is not this known and manifest in many, if not most of the pacifications that have been made in Christendom ? "

Here Barclay turns aside for a moment to explain that he is no Anarchist or Ranter, but has a due respect for authority. "Yet nevertheless, I judge it no prejudice to magistracy nor injury to any for one that is called of the Lord Jesus to appear in this affair, for he is not a little concerned—his authority has been contemned ; his law broken ; his life oppressed ; his standard of peace pulled down and rent ; his government encroached upon : (what shall I say ?) his precious blood shed, and himself afresh crucified, and put to open shame by the murders and cruelties that have attended those wars."

Unless the negotiators bear these things in mind their efforts for a lasting peace will not avail. They may bring the warring potentates to be " good friends and dear allies," but when a pretext for war appears " all your articles will not bind them, but they will break them like straws." Strong rulers may not even trouble to find a pretext other than the assertion " that to be at peace is no longer consistent with their glory." The evil passions that are the cause of war must be quelled before peace can be established. Worldly wisdom cannot accomplish this, rather it finds its work in the incitement to war.

" Let me exhort you then seriously to examine yourselves by

the light of Jesus Christ in you, that can alone discover unto you your own hearts, and will not flatter you (as men may) whether you be fit for this work you are set about?" This divine light and peaceable spirit alone can guide them in the settlement of peace, and Barclay relates how it has led Friends in the past.

"Many of them, who have been wise according to the wisdom of the world, have learned to lay it down at the feet of Jesus, that they might receive from him of his pure and heavenly wisdom; being contented in the enjoyment of that by the world to be accounted fools. And also many of them who were fighters, and even renowned for their skill and valour in warring, have come by the influence of this pure light to beat their swords into plough-shares and their spears into pruning-hooks, and not to learn carnal war any more, being redeemed from the lusts from which the fighting comes. And there are thousands whom God hath brought here already, who see to the end of all contention and strife, and that for which the world contends, and albeit the Devil be angry at them—because he knows they strike at the very root and foundation of his kingdom in men's hearts—by a patient enduring in the spirit of Jesus, they do and shall overcome." But to clear their minds of the calumnies attached to such doctrines, Barclay sends them the *Apology*, to be read and considered by them and the princes they represent, that they may learn the principles which would bring "peace and quietness and felicity to all, both outward and inward. And so his conscience is discharged in love to their souls and for the common peace and good of Christendom."

Several treaties were concluded between the separate belligerents during the year 1678, and hostilities ceased for the time, but Barclay's predictions were more than fulfilled. Although Louis had attained much military glory, he had failed in his aim—the conquest of the Netherlands, and the latter State had not shown sufficient strength to remove the fear of a fresh attack. As for the other Powers, a modern historian writes: "The concert of Europe was partial and ill-cemented and, although peace had been made, could not be other than short-lived, in face of the jealousies of the various States, which the fear of France had temporarily united." "It was," says another, "an armed truce rather than a permanent settlement of differences." [1]

The influence of Barclay on the non-Quaker world was chiefly

[1] *Cambridge Modern History*, v. 46 and 165.

exerted through the *Apology*.   It is not too much to say that for the next hundred years inquirers into the Quaker doctrines were referred to that work for satisfaction.   Voltaire read it, apparently in the Latin version, during his residence in England, and quoted with approval from the section on War.   The strong wave of Evangelicism which passed over a portion of the Society in the early nineteenth century led to some depreciation of early Quaker writings, on the ground that their teaching as to the divinity and redemptive power of Christ was insufficiently clear.   One result was to depose the *Apology* from its quasi-authoritative position—a result not to be deplored in so far as it emphasized the truth that the Society of Friends is a living organism which gives no unquestioning allegiance either to tradition or the written word.   But Barclay's application of the religious principles of the Society to practical life, including the question of war, has always remained in harmony with the convictions of the great bulk of its members.

CHAPTER VI

WILLIAM PENN AND JOHN BELLERS

WILLIAM PENN, Oxford scholar and fine gentleman, son of Admiral Penn (who was a servant first of the Commonwealth and later of Charles II) seemed a most unlikely subject for conversion to Quakerism. Yet, even in his schoolboy and student days he had attended Friends' Meetings, where the preaching of Thomas Loe had deeply affected him and, his zeal outrunning his wisdom, some breach of University regulations led to his removal from Oxford.[1] A course of foreign travel and study was intended to cure his "notions," and he seemed in Pepys' eyes Frenchified enough when he returned to London to attend the Court and read a little law. In 1666–7 he was sent over to transact some business on his father's Irish estates. At Cork he attended a Friends' Meeting, where his old friend, Thomas Loe, spoke on the theme of "the faith that overcometh the world and the faith that is overcome by the world." As he listened the young man of twenty-two made his life's decision. It is worth noting that on this visit to Ireland he took part in an attack on some "rebels," or mutinous soldiers, and was offered a commission by the Duke of Ormonde. The one authentic portrait, which dates from this period, shows a handsome youth in a suit of armour. Prison, for attending the Cork meetings, was at once his lot, but powerful friends secured his release. He returned to England a Quaker, to meet the pathetic and puzzled opposition of his father. Soon he visited the Tower and Newgate for publishing and preaching the new heresy. The trial of Penn and Mead in 1670 is famous for its incidental establishment of the

[1] S. Janney, *Life of Penn*, is a full and trustworthy memoir. Joseph Besse wrote a valuable account of Penn, as preface to the 1726 edition of his *Works*. Principal J. W. Graham's volume, *William Penn*, deals especially fully with his early life and his writings.

right of juries to return a free verdict.[1]   In the same year his father died, after learning to respect his son's new creed.[2]   Penn's missionary tour with Barclay and Fox in Holland and Germany has already been mentioned.   The sufferings of Friends in England turned his mind to the refuge of the New World.   With Barclay and a number of other Friends, he acquired the proprietorship of New Jersey.   In 1681 he received from the Crown, in settlement of debts due to his father, the grant of wide territories further up the Delaware ;   next year he established the province of Pennsylvania, the "holy experiment" in Quaker government and liberty of conscience.   The story of Pennsylvanian policy in peace and war is told in another chapter.   After his return to England, he was a shocked and unwilling spectator of the cruelties which followed the Monmouth rebellion ;   he used his undoubted influence with James II (an old friend of the Admiral) to free his fellow Quakers from their prisons, and he supported and welcomed the Declaration of Indulgence.   The King even employed him as an emissary to William of Orange, but after the Revolution he fell (unjustly) under suspicion of conspiracy to restore James, and he was not cleared of the charge until 1694 when Pennsylvania (which had been placed under a royal deputy) was restored to him. The later years of his life were clouded by financial troubles and at times by constitutional disputes with the Pennsylvanians, aggravated by his mistaken choice of deputies.   When he and his people were able to meet, the real respect and confidence they felt towards him was strong enough to clear away misunderstandings.   He died in 1718, after several years of enfeebling illness.

Deep religious feeling, undaunted courage, wide tolerance, good sense, and enthusiasm for freedom, were Penn's main characteristics.   His most serious defect was the mistaken estimate he often formed of his subordinates, which involved him in public and private difficulties.   Freedom of conscience, with Penn as with

---

[1] Through *Bushell's Case*.   Bushell was foreman of the jury which in spite of threats from the judge, imprisonment, and starvation steadily returned a verdict of " Not Guilty," until at last they amended it to one that Penn was " Guilty of speaking in Gracechurch Street.   William Mead not guilty."   " Speaking " not being a criminal offence the judge was baffled, and in revenge fined the jury. Bushell appealed against the legality of the fine, and won his case.

[2] On his death-bed he said : " Son William, if you and your friends keep to your plain way of preaching, and keep to your plain way of living, you will make an end of the priests to the end of the world " (quoted by his son in the later editions of *No Cross, No Crown*).

Barclay, was a deep and passionate conviction. In 1678, amid the dangers and delirium of the " Popish Plot," he attended a parliamentary committee to protest against the injustice which confounded Quakers with Roman Catholics, because both refused the Test Oaths. " Yet," he continued, " we do not mean that any should take a fresh aim at them, or that they must come in our room : for we must give the liberty we ask, and cannot be false to our principles, though it were to relieve ourselves. For we have good-will to all men, and would have none suffer for a truly sober and conscientious dissent on any hand ; and I humbly take leave to add, that those methods against persons so qualified, do not seem to me convincing, or indeed adequate, to the reason of mankind ; but this I submit to your discretion."[1]

" This " was doctrine too high for Parliament for many years to come, but the speech shows us not only why Friends welcomed the Declaration of Indulgence, but also why the grotesque cry of " Papist " or " Jesuit " was raised against them. A disinterested passion for justice and fair play is, happily, not rare among our countrymen. It is the more perplexing, therefore, that when it is active in an unpopular cause, its advocates are so often accused of private and selfish interests. In a later work,[2] Penn describes instances of Protestant intolerance, which are not a reproach "against Protestancy, but very much against Protestants." In another direction Penn's thoughts were generations in advance of his time. He never accepted the social system, with its sharp divisions of wealth and poverty, as a divine ordinance. The pithy apothegms in *Fruits of Solitude* give his mature views on the taxation of luxury, the equalization of income, and other problems which have a strangely modern ring. These views had changed little since he wrote in his ardent youth : " That the sweat and tedious labour of the husbandmen, early and late, cold and hot, wet and dry, should be converted into the pleasure, ease, and pastime of a small number of men ; that the cart, the plough, the thrash, should be in that continual severity laid upon nineteen parts of the land, to feed the inordinate lusts and delicious appetites of the twentieth, is so far from the appointment of the great Governor of the world, and God of the spirits of all flesh that to imagine such horrible injustice as the effect

---

[1] *Life of Penn* : *Select Works*, p. 46. There is an interesting comment on Penn's attitude in G. M. Trevelyan, *England Under the Stuarts*, p. 436.
[2] *Good Advice to the Church of England*, 1687.

of his determinations, and not the intemperance of men, were wretched and blasphemous." [1]

On the question of outward wars and fighting, if we believe the often-quoted anecdote, he soon made up his mind. Like other young men of fashion, he wore a sword, and one day after his convincement he asked the advice of Fox about the custom, saying that once in Paris it had saved his life, as he had been able to disarm and put to flight a highwayman. Fox simply replied : " Wear it as long as thou canst." Shortly afterwards they met again, and this time Penn had no sword. [2] The story is certainly characteristic of Fox.

When, during one of his many trials, on this occasion for unlawful preaching, the oath of allegiance was offered to Penn in the form " that it is not lawful, upon any pretence whatever, to take up arms against the King," he refused on the ground " I cannot fight against any man, much less against the King," and " it is both my practice and all my friends to instil principles of peace and moderation." While in Newgate, serving his sentence, he wrote a memorial to Parliament emphasizing the submission of Friends to all lawful demands of the civil government. [3]

In his Works there are many plain assertions of the unchristian nature of war. " Even the Turks," he says, [4] " are outdone by apostate Christians ; whose practice is therefore more condemnable, because they have been better taught : they have had a master of another doctrine and example. It is true they call him Lord still, but let their ambition reign ; they love power more than one another, and to get it, kill one another, though charged by him not to strive, but to love and serve one another. . . . A very trifle is too often made a ground of quarrel here : nor can any league be so sacred or inviolable, that arts shall not be used to evade and

---

[1] *No Cross, No Crown* (1669), pp. 61–2.

[2] The original source of the story is unknown. It was first printed by Janney in his *Life of Penn* (Philadelphia, 1851). He had it from oral tradition in America.

[3] In the famous trial of Mead and Penn (September 1670), Mead (an old soldier) protested against the terms of the indictment " which is a bundle of stuff, full of lies and falsehood ; for therein I am accused that I met *vi et armis, illicité et tumultuosé*. Time was, when I had freedom to use a carnal weapon, and then I thought I feared no man ; but now I fear the living God, and dare not make use thereof, nor hurt any man ; nor do I know I demeaned myself as a tumultuous person. I say I am a peaceable man." (" The People's Ancient and Just Liberties Asserted, in the Trial of William Penn and William Mead." Penn's *Works*.)

[4] *No Cross, No Crown*, ch. viii. sects. 6 and 7.

dissolve it, to increase dominion. No matter who, nor how many are slain, made widows and orphans or lose their estates and livelihoods : what countries are ruined, what towns and cities spoiled ; if by all these things the ambitious can but arrive at their ends." And he calls as witness the bloody history of the seventeenth century. The last sixty years " will furnish us with many wars begun upon ill grounds, and ended in great desolation." Quoting the seventh Beatitude, he comments that Christ did not say " Blessed are the contentious, backbiters, tale-bearers, brawlers, fighters, and makers of war ; neither shall they be called the children of God, whatever they may call themselves."[1] In several passages he explains and defends the Quaker position. Once he says half-humorously, " they cannot kill or slay their own kind, and so are not fit for warriors," but he goes on in seriousness, " let not this people be thought useless or inconsistent with Governments, for introducing that harmless, glorious way to this distracted world (for somebody must begin it), but rather adore the providence, embrace the principle, and cherish and follow the example."[2]

In another place he says : " As this is the most Christian, so the most rational way : love and persuasion having more force than weapons of war. Nor would the worst of men easily be brought to hurt those that they really think love them. It is that love and patience which must in the end have the victory."[3] In the long and able account of the Quakers which Penn prefixed to the first edition of George Fox's *Journal* [4] he condenses their peace testimony into the phrase " not fighting, but suffering " " As truth-speaking succeeded swearing, so faith and truth succeeded fighting, in the doctrine and practice of this people. Nor ought they for this to be obnoxious to civil government, since if they cannot fight for it, neither can they fight against it ; which is no mean security to the State ; nor is it reasonable that people should be blamed for not doing more for others than they can do for themselves. And Christianity set aside, if the costs and fruits of war were well considered, peace, with its inconveniences, is generally preferable." He contributed another preface to the posthumous edition of Barclay's Works, " Truth Triumphant."

[1] *No Cross, No Crown*, ch. xx, sect. 1.
[2] " A Key opening the way to every Capacity to distinguish the Religion professed by the people called Quakers, etc." (1692, Penn's *Works*).
[3] " Primitive Christianity Revived, etc." (Penn's *Works*).   [4] In 1694.

In this he speaks with admiration of the *Epistle of Love*. It is still only too much needed. " Is not the wrath of God revealed sufficiently against us in the faction, strife, war, blood, and poverty, that we see almost all over Europe this day ? God Almighty make people sensible and weary of it, and the cause of it their sins— sins against light, against conscience and knowledge, their unfaithfulness to God and man, their scandalous immorality, and most inordinate love of the world, the ground of all contention and mischief —that so the peace of God which passeth worldly men's understanding, may fill all our hearts through repentance and conversion. Amen. I have been the longer," he adds, " in my notes upon this occasion, than I expected ; but our present condition in Europe drew it from me, that needs an olive branch, the doctrine of peace, as much as ever."

Europe, indeed, rent and distracted by the war of the League of Augsburg against Louis XIV, presented a sorry spectacle for any peace lover. Penn's three years of retirement had given him time for thought and study. On the religious side its fruits were shown in the studies of Quakerism already mentioned, on the political and practical side in the " Essay towards the present and future peace of Europe," published in the year 1693–4.[1] After Dante's dream of a Europe united under the spiritual guidance of the Pope and the temporal rule of the Empire had faded before the realities of the Reformation, a new hope arose of a federal Union of Christian nations deliberating and settling differences in a general Council, maintaining national independence and unbroken peace among themselves but presenting an impassable barrier to the tide of Turkish aggression. This scheme of federation was first mooted in the *Grand dessein* of Henry IV and Sully, as recorded by that statesman, and gained the approval of Elizabeth of England. But the assassination of Henry ended the project, and though Grotius wrote in favour of arbitration, and though the seventeenth century saw the machinery of an international congress used, at least, to terminate war in the

---

[1] An essay towards the Present and Future Peace of Europe, by the Establishment of an European Dyet, Parliament, or Estates. " *Beati Pacifici. Cedant Arma Togæ.*" The essay was included in his *Works* (2 vols., 1726), and was brought to the notice of the Peace Congress at Paris in 1851. In 1897 it was published as a pamphlet by the American Peace Society at Boston and re-published, with a preface by J. B. Braithwaite, in December 1914 by John Bellows, Gloucester. It is also included in a volume of selections from Penn in Everyman's Library, *The Peace of Europe, The Fruits of Solitude,* and other writings by William Penn, 1916.

negotiations preceding the peace of Westphalia, yet the *dessein* rusted in neglect, until Penn brought it again to light.[1] In his enforced leisure he had read Sully's *Memoirs* and Sir William Temple's *Account of the United Provinces*. The former set forth the elaborated scheme, while the latter showed the successful working of federal government in the example of Holland. Penn was fired by the ambition that England, too, might play her part in so great a work. " For this great King's example tells us it is fit to be done and Sir William Temple's *History* shows us by a surpassing instance that it may be done ; and Europe, by her incomparable miseries, makes it now necessary to be done. . . . My share is only thinking of it at this juncture and putting it into the common light for the peace and prosperity of Europe."[2]

At the outset Penn disclaims any intention of preaching a millenary doctrine. His design is a practical one, and of all reforms, this was most likely in his judgment to increase the happiness and prosperity of mankind. How was it that nations went to war when the miseries of war were so overwhelming and unmistakable ? The groaning state of Europe called for peace.

" What can we desire better than peace, but the grace to use it ? Peace preserves our possessions ; we are in no danger of invasions ; our trade is free and safe, and we rise and lie down without anxiety. The rich bring out their hoards, and employ the poor manufacturers ; buildings and divers projections, for profit and pleasure, go on : it excites industry, which brings wealth, as that gives the means of charity and hospitality, not the lowest ornaments of a kingdom or commonwealth. But war, like the frost of '83, seizes all these comforts at once, and stops the civil channel of society. The rich draw in their stock, the poor turn soldiers, or thieves, or starve ; no industry, no building, no manufactory, little hospitality or charity ; but what the peace gave, the war devours."

The explanation seems to be that men are passionate, obstinate, slow to learn, and quick to forget the lessons of experience. It is

---

[1] *Vide The Arbiter in Council*, pp. 276–90, for a summary of the *grand dessein*. Grotius published *De Jure Belli et Pacis* in 1625. In the *Nouveau Cynée* a year before, a French writer, Emeric de Crucé, pleaded for a permanent court of arbitration.

[2] The following summary is borrowed from the *Arbiter in Council*, pp. 299–305, by permission of my brother, Mr. F. W. Hirst. Some further quotations have been added.

a mark, Penn thought of the corruption of our natures that we cannot taste the benefit of health without a bout of sickness, or enjoy plenty without the instruction of want, " nor finally know the comfort of peace but by the smart and penance of the vices of war."

From the evils of war Penn passes in a second section to the means of peace. Peace can only be established and maintained by justice. " The advantage that justice has upon war is seen by the success of embassies that so often prevent war by hearing the pleas and memorials of justice in the hands and mouths of the wronged party." War on behalf of justice, i.e. where you have been wronged, and redress has been refused upon complaint, is a remedy almost always worse than the disease, " the aggressors seldom getting what they seek or performing, if they prevail, what they promised." Justice, therefore, is the true means of peace, to prevent strife between Governments, or between governors, and governed. Peace, therefore, must be maintained by justice, which is a fruit of government, " as government is from society, and society from consent." This thesis is developed and explained in a third section entitled, " Government : its rise and end under all models."

" Government is an expedient against confusion ; a restraint upon all disorder ; just weights and an even balance ; that one may not injure another, nor himself by intemperance."

The most natural and human basis of government is consent, " for that binds freely (as I may say) when men hold their liberty by true obedience to rules of their own making. No man is judge in his own cause, which ends in the confusion and blood of so many judges and executioners."[1] Penn concludes his introduction by explaining that in these three first sections he has briefly treated of Peace, Justice, and Government, " because the ways and methods by which peace is preserved in particular Governments will help those readers most concerned in my proposal to conceive with what ease as well as advantage the peace of Europe might be procured and kept ; which is the end designed by me, with all submission to those interested in this little treatise."

---

[1] " Government, then, is the prevention and cure of disorder, and the means of justice, as that is of peace ; for this cause they have sessions, terms, assizes, and parliaments, to overrule men's passions and resentments. . . . So depraved is human nature that without compulsion, some way or other, too many would not readily be brought to do what they know is right and fit, or to avoid what they are satisfied they should not do."

In his first section he had shown the desirableness of peace ; in his next the truest means of it, to wit, *justice, not war* ; and in the third, " that this justice was the fruit of good government." Then follows in section four, the proposal or design itself, which must be given in Penn's own words :

" Now, if the Soveraign Princes of Europe, who represent that society, or independent state of men that was previous to the obligations of society, would, for the same reason that engaged men first into society, viz : love of peace and order, agree to meet by their stated deputies in a general Dyet, estates, or parliament, and there establish rules of justice for sovraign princes to observe one to another ; and thus to meet yearly, or once in two or three years at farthest, or as they shall see cause, and to be stiled, the sovraign or imperial Dyet, parliament, or state of Europe ; before which sovraign assembly, should be brought all differences depending between one sovraign and another, that can not be made up by private embassies before the sessions begin ; and that if any of the sovraignties that constitute these imperial states, shall refuse to submit their claim or pretensions to them, or to abide and perform the judgment thereof, and seek their remedy by arms, or delay their compliance beyond the time prefixt in their resolutions, all the other sovraignties, united as one strength, shall compel the submission and performance of the sentence, with damages to the suffering party, and charges to the sovraignties that obliged their submission : to be sure, Europe would quietly obtain the so much desired and needed peace, to her harassed inhabitants ; no sovraignty in Europe having the power and therefore can not show the will to dispute the conclusion ; and consequently, peace would be procured, and continued in Europe."

In a fifth section Penn reviews the causes of difference and the motives that lead States or their rulers to settle such differences by war rather than by diplomacy or arbitration. The motives of war are three : namely, Defence, Recovery, Aggression. Penn imagines the warlike aggressor saying to himself : " Knowing my own strength I will be my own judge and carver." The aggressor would have no chance in the Imperial States of federated Europe ; but any State claiming protection, or the right to recover territory of which it had been deprived, would be heard whenever it chose to plead before the sovereign court of Europe and there find justice

Thus Penn (in the sixth section) is led to consider the titles by which territories may be held or claimed. A title comes by right of long succession, as in England and France, or as in Poland and the Empire by election, or by purchase, as often in Italy and Germany, or by marriage, or lastly by conquest—as the French in Lorraine, and the Turks in Christendom. What titles then are good and what bad ? These problems must be left to the sovereign States and the international court to deal with and decide in each case. But Penn was ready to show upon what principle such controversies would be decided, by an examination of titles. He decides that all are good except the last. Conquest only gives a questionable title, morally speaking, "engross'd and recorded by the point of the sword, and in bloody characters." When conquest has been confirmed by treaty it is an adopted title. "Tho' that hath not always extinguished the fire, but it lies, like ember and ashes, ready to kindle so soon as there is fit matter prepared for it." If there is to be a restitution of conquests it is a tender point where to begin. Could they go back, for instance, to the Peace of Nimeguen ?

In a seventh section Penn describes the constitution of his European Parliament. The number of delegates sent by each country should be in proportion to its wealth, revenue, and population. These would have to be accurately ascertained ; but Penn makes the following guess. He allows twelve representatives to Germany, ten to France, ten to Spain, ten to Turkey, and ten to Muscovy.[1] Italy was to have eight, England six, the Seven United Provinces of Holland, "Sweedland," and Poland four each. Venice and Portugal were to send three delegates apiece, and the smaller States in proportion. Ninety delegates in all would form the Diet. Its first session should be held in some central town ; after that the delegates would choose their place of meeting.

In the eighth section he gives some details for the regulation of his Imperial States in session. Thus, "to avoid quarrel for precedency the room may be round [as at the first Hague Conference] and have divers doors, to come in and go out at, to prevent exceptions." Members should preside by turns ; voting should be by ballot to secure independence and to prevent corruption. A majority of three-quarters should be necessary and "neutralities in debates should be no wise endured." The language used would be Latin

[1] The *grand dessein* contemplated aggressive action against Turkey and was doubtful whether to admit Russia, "almost a barbarous country," or to expel the Czar from his European territory (*Arbiter in Council*, p. 283).

or French—the first would be best for civilians, the second for men of quality.

In section nine he entertains some objections that might be advanced against his design. First it might be said that the richest and the strongest sovereignty would never agree to this " European League or Confederacy," and there would be danger of corruption if it did agree. A more plausible objection was that disuse of the trade of soldiery would lead to effeminacy, and a deficiency of soldiers, as happened in Holland to 1672. But each nation would instruct and discipline its youth as it pleased. Manliness, says Penn, depends on education. You want men to be men, not either lions or women. Teach them mechanical knowledge and natural philosophy, and the art of government, " how to be useful and serviceable, both to themselves and others : and how to save and help, not injure or destroy." No State would be allowed to keep a disproportionately large army, or one formidable to the confederacy. Another objection would be that if the trade of soldier declined, there would be no employment for the younger brothers of noble families, and further, if the poor could not enlist they must become thieves. Penn answers that the poor should be brought up to be neither thieves nor soldiers but useful citizens. Education, next to the immediate welfare of the nation, " ought of all things to be the care and skill of the government. For such as the youth of any country is bred, such is the next generation, and the government in good or bad hands." Again, it would be said : " Sovereign States will cease to be sovereign, and that they won't endure." No, for they remain just as sovereign at home as ever they were. Is there less sovereignty " because the great fish can no longer eat up the little ones ? "

Finally, Penn recounts " the real benefits that flow from this proposal about peace." (1) Not the least is that it prevents spilling much " humane " and Christian blood. " And tho' the chiefest in government are seldom personally exposed, yet it is a duty incumbent upon them to be tender of the lives of their people ; since without all doubt, they are accountable to God for the blood that is spilt in their service. So that besides the loss of so many lives, of importance to any government, both for labour and propagation, the cries of so many widows, parents, and fatherless are prevented, that cannot be very pleasant in the ears of any government, and is the natural consequence of war in all government."

(2) It will in some degree recover the reputation of Christianity

in the sight of infidels. " Here," he says, " is a wide field for the reverend clergy of Europe to act that part in . . . May they recommend and labour this pacific means I offer."

(3) It releases the funds of princes and peoples, which can go to learning, charity, manufactures, etc.

(4) Border towns and countries like Flanders and Hungary will be saved from the rage and waste of war.

(5) It will afford " ease and security of travel and traffic, an happiness never understood since the Roman Empire has been broken into so many sovereignties." We may easily conceive, he adds, the comfort and advantage of travelling through the governments of Europe by a pass from any of the sovereignties of it, which this league and state of peace will naturally make authentic. " They that have travelled Germany, where is so great a number of sovereignties, know the want and value of this privilege, by the many stops and examinations they meet with by the way ; but especially such as have made the grand tour of Europe."

(6) Europe will be secured against Turkish inroads, which have usually occurred through the carelessness or connivance of some Christian prince. But Penn looked to the inclusion of the Turk in the federation, " for the security of what he holds in Europe," and not to a Christian crusade to drive him from these possessions.

(7) It will beget friendship between princes and States ; and from communion and intercourse will spring emulation in good laws, learning, arts, and architecture.

" For princes have the curiosity of seeing the Courts and cities of other countries, as well as private men, if they could as securely and familiarly gratify their inclinations. It were a great motive to the tranquillity of the world : *that they could freely converse face to face, and personally and reciprocally give and receive marks of civility and kindness.* An hospitality that leaves these impressions behind it, will harldy let ordinary matters prevail, to mistake or quarrel one another."

In short, reciprocal hospitality and intercourse will plant peace in a deep and fruitful soil.

(8) Princes will be able to marry for love, and family affections will not be crushed by dynastic quarrels and reasons of State. Penn, probably thinking of his own happy marriage and of the embittered life of James II, declares that " the advantage of private men upon princes by their family comforts is a sufficient balance against their

greater power and glory." Thus he ends his proposal of means whereby " the same rules of justice and prudence by which parents and masters govern their families, and magistrates their cities, and estates their republics, and princes and kings their principalities and kingdoms, Europe may obtain and preserve peace among her sovereignties." According to Besse, the work was so well received by the general public that a second edition was issued in the same year.

II.

Penn's plan for a reasonable European settlement, if not un-noticed, was at least untried. The Treaty of Ryswick, 1697, only secured a brief truce until the War of the Spanish Succession brought suffering once more upon the peoples. And once more a Friend was found to plead for peace and federation. John Bellers is an interesting and unique figure in the annals of the Society.[1] He was not a child of his generation, but belongs much more to those groups of philanthropic reformers who arose in England and France in the late eighteenth or early nineteenth century and who were agents in the removal of so many abuses. Half a century later he might have received from the overseers of his meeting a gentle reproof for excessive " creaturely activity," but in Queen Anne's reign Friends listened patiently to his schemes, and in one or two instances even put them in some degree into practice. Bellers was born in 1654, the son of a prosperous Quaker grocer in the City of London. By his marriage to Frances Fettiplace, also a Friend and heiress of an old Gloucestershire family, he inherited a small estate at Coln St. Aldwyn, and he seems to have led a life of leisure and some affluence. He was a member of the Meeting for Sufferings, which relieved the necessities of Friends in prison or otherwise distressed, and he was eager in pressing upon Friends as a body and on his own local meetings their obligation to maintain and provide for the poor.

His scheme for a " College of Industry," published in 1695, influenced the Society in the foundation of a " School and work-house " at Clerkenwell seven years later, which, after various changes, has taken modern shape as a large co-education boarding school at Saffron Walden. Bellers' own proposal was in many ways a curious anticipation of Socialist theories. In 1818 Robert Owen and Francis

---

[1] There is a good account of Bellers as writer and philanthropist in Braithwaite, *Second Period of Quakerism*, pp. 571 foll.

Place reprinted the pamphlet on the "College," claiming it as a forecast of Owen's plan for an industrial commonwealth. Karl Marx has described Bellers as a "phenomenon" in the history of political economy, and in 1895 Edward Bernstein made him the subject of a very careful study, based on original research, in the large *History of Socialism* compiled by German Socialists. Throughout his life he was busied with philanthropic plans, which he urged in numerous pamphlets on Electoral Reform, Hospital Reform, Prison Reform, and other topics that are still with us to-day. He was a friend of Penn and of the celebrated physician Sir Hans Sloane, but, apart from his benevolent activities, little is known of his life, although it did not end until 1725. The peace tract, which is his chief title to notice here, was published in 1710, after the War of the Spanish Succession had for nine years consumed uncounted lives and treasure.

The tract, "Some Reasons for an European State," [1] opens with a series of dedications or addresses. The first, to Queen Anne, expresses the assurance that she at least would welcome the prospect of a rational peace since "crowns have cares sufficient in the best of times." Lest she should think the prospect of a European federation chimerical, she is reminded that "the ten Saxon, Welsh, Scotch, and Irish Kingdoms are now happily united in one Government, to the saving of much humane blood." Then, turning to "the Lords and Commons of Great Britain in Parliament assembled," Bellers points out to them that the "deluge of Christian blood and the vast treasure which have been spent to procure the expected peace, is a most powerful argument of the necessity when made that it may be perpetual if possible." The first essential step, in his view, is that England and her Allies should establish a Supreme Court "to decide their future disputes without blood." If then an invitation is extended to all the Neutral Powers to join this Court "it will draw on the peace the faster (if not made

[1] Some reasons for an European State, proposed to the Powers of Europe by an Universal Guarantee, and an Annual Congress, Senate, Dyet, or Parliament, to settle any disputes about the bounds and rights of Princes and States hereafter. With an abstract of a scheme formed by King Henry IV of France, upon the same subject. And also, a proposal for a General Council or Convocation of all the different religious persuasions in Christendom (not to dispute what they differ about, but) to settle the General Principles they agree in : by which it will appear that they may be good subjects and neighbours, though of different apprehensions of the way to Heaven. In order to prevent broils and wars at home, when foreign wars are ended (1 Peter iv. 8. London, printed Anno 1710).

before) and the more incline France itself to come into it, by which that kingdom will reap the blessings of a lasting peace, which their present King's grandfather had formerly proposed." The details of the scheme are then worked out in the body of the pamphlet.

At the opening Bellers lays stress upon the economic argument, and estimates the waste of labour and wealth by a strangely modern use of statistics.

If we suppose this war since '88 hath cost the French Crown 12 Millions Sterling a year. In 20 years it comes to... ... ... £240,000,000

For which 12 Millions a year, if reckoned at 6 per cent., the interest (compound) comes to £200,000,000

Which in all make £440,000,000

And besides that they have lost 30 thousand men a year at least, that in 20 years comes to 600 thousand, which if valued at £200 a head, which every able man and his posterity may be deemed to add to the value of the Kingdom at £10 a yr. per head at 20 years' purchase, comes to £120,000,000

And the total loss is thus £560,000,000, or, from another point of view, this £440,000,000 at 5 per cent. interest would bring in an annual revenue of £22,000,000, "which is four or five times as much as the usual revenues of the Crown of France in time of peace." And the 600,000 men lost are double or treble the number now under arms in France. And "where there are no men, there can be no money, nor women, nor children, nor kingdom, but a land without inhabitants." The other kingdoms and countries of Europe engaged in the war have been impoverished in the same way, in proportion to their expenditure of men and money. Yet what result has been gained to compensate for all this outlay? "It would be much more glorious for a prince to build palaces, hospitals, bridges, and make rivers navigable, and to increase the number of his people, than by pouring out humane blood as water, to invade his neighbours."

This leads Bellers to his main proposal. At the next peace there should be established by universal guarantee an annual Congress of all the princes and States of Europe, in one federation, "with a renouncing of all claims upon each other," which should debate under acknowledged rules of an international law "to prevent

any disputes that might otherwise raise a new war in this age or the
ages to come ; by which every prince and State will have all the
strength of Europe to protect them." It would be to the interest
of the Allies to begin the scheme among themselves, for Holland,
Switzerland, and other instances show the advantages of federation.
Bellers himself favours the plan of dividing Europe into a hundred
or more equal cantons, of such a size that every Sovereign State
shall send at least one member to the Congress. Each canton must
raise an equal proportion of soldiers or a contribution in money
or ships of the same value, and for every such contribution furnished
by a State it shall have the right to send an additional member to
the Senate or Congress. Like Penn, Bellers would include Russia
and Turkey in the Federation, and in a later passage he censures
Henry IV for shutting them out. " The Muscovites are Christians,
and the Mahometans men, and have the same faculties and reason
as other men. They only want the same opportunities and applications of their understandings to be the same men. But to beat their
brains out, to put sense into them, is a great mistake, and would
leave Europe too much in a state of war." By this arrangement
of representation in proportion to territory, the stronger States will
be willing to enter the union, and yet " the major part of the senate
not being interested in the dispute, will be the more inclined to that
side which hath most reason in it." The limitation of armaments,
too, will prevent the peace from degenerating into an armed truce,
which would crush the peoples under new expenditure in addition
to the vast charges of the debts incurred by the war. Even under
this scheme there will be no compensation for the sufferings of the
past. " There can be no righting the people that have been ruined
and destroyed by war, nor the princes they have belonged unto,
and the longer the war continues, injuries will be the more increased.
For war always ruins more people than it raiseth, and the rights
of both princes and people are best preserved in peace. Therefore,
the best expedient that can be offered, is such a settlement, as will
prevent adding more injuries by war to those irreparable ones already
past."

A third address follows, " to the Councillors and Ministers
of State " of Europe, which contains some pungent home-truths.
They are reminded that war " shakes, if not throws down those
ministers that set at helm, for whether their management be defective
or not, the people only cry them up or run them down by their

success." Bellers lays to their account the awful toll of death and bereavement during the previous nine years. "The princes of Europe," he says, "have seldon been more weary of war than at present, yet the impossibility of submission drives them on, until he that is nearest ruin must first ask for peace." But Bellers longed for peace, not only in the political, but also in the religious world. The last address, to bishops, clergy, and religious teachers, is a plea for concord and tolerance. The disunion of the churches is a reproach to Christianity, and an insuperable obstacle to the conversion of the heathen. Yet in war the different sects are able to form alliances and to act in friendship, while science and learning know no barriers of race or creed. The English Royal Society, and the French Academy "lament the obstruction that is given to their desired correspondence by the war." Bellers' views on freedom of thought can bear repetition even to-day. "If a man but lives agreeable to the public peace, his error in opinion cannot hinder a better Christian from heaven. . . . Remove but the various passions that cloud men, and then truth will be discovered by its own light. Imposing religion without reaching the understanding is not leading men to heaven. Men will not be saved against their wills." Hence, as a European Congress will harmonize the interests and desires of the several States, so let another Council of men of religion meet to discover a common basis of belief and morality among the several sects.

Next anticipating the Abbé St. Pierre,[1] Bellers gives a short summary of the *grand dessein*, drawn from Sully's *Mémoires*. In his *Conclusion* he alludes to the "small treatise" of Penn on the same theme, giving (with unusual exactness for that age) the name of its publisher. This *Conclusion* summarizes the previous arguments against war, and one statement comes to the modern reader with fresh emphasis. "War is destruction, and puts men (they think) under a necessity of doing those things, which in a time of peace they would account cruel and horrid." Bellers ends with a finely expressed prayer to God to "bless the Princes of Europe with the knowledge of Thyself . . . that the noise of war may be heard no more, and that Thy will may be done in earth as it is in heaven."

The only other Quaker writings of the eighteenth century calling for notice is a group of tracts published in 1746–7, which are of more interest as a symptom of the state of the Society

[1] *Un Projet de Paix Perpetuelle* first appeared in 1713.

than for their intrinsic merits. The War of the Austrian Succession was dragging on its inglorious course and Charles Edward had seen his Highland army shattered, and had fled to France. The shock of war, as usual, caused heart-searching among Quakers ; for the first time a Friend was found bold enough to challenge the whole peace position in a public, though anonymous, pamphlet, " The Nature and Duty of Self-Defence : Addressed to the people called Quakers, 1746."[1] The writer, Richard Finch, a London merchant, dedicates his work to that " illustrious hero," William, Duke of Cumberland. His arguments are straightforward, and more ingenuous than some advanced in later days. " Self-defence," he says, " is a natural right, and the Gospel ought not to abolish any of our natural privileges." If the command to love enemies and to forgive injuries is to be obeyed literally, then all the Sermon on the Mount must be obeyed literally. This Finch evidently considers a *reductio ad absurdum,* and he explains that the command means " to bear or pass by, as far as is *possible or convenient,* all sorts of injuries and abuses." The soldier is merely an executioner, who takes away life for the public good. Finch evidently holds the view that the other side is always the aggressor, whether " several thousands of armed villains should assemble together with full resolution to overturn that Government to which they ought to submit," or a foreign enemy comes " to disturb the quiet and repose of a people who give them no umbrage." A man may rightly refuse, he admits, to fight in an unjust cause ; but if the land is invaded in retaliation for an unjust attack, he may then take up arms " notwithstanding the first false step."

It is odd to find a spirited defence of the conscientious nature of Quaker scruples included in the pamphlet. Finch tells the following story, whose conclusion cannot be traced in the records of the Society. " There is now, while I am writing this, a particular case depending in London, viz. four soldiers, who were lately quartered at Bristol, have entered into the Society of the Quakers, refused to wear the King's clothes, receive his pay, or bear arms. They are brought to London, to be tried, as I suppose, by a court-martial, where, if this change appears to be matter of conviction and sincerity, they will doubtless meet with the same favour the rest of their Friends enjoy."

Finch was answered in several pamphlets. Joseph Besse, com-

[1] In D. *Tracts,* 339, 12.

piler of the *Sufferings*, under the pseudonym of " Irenicus," edited
Penington's tract of the "Weighty Question."[1]   In his preface
he reminds the reader that Christ calls His followers lambs and sheep.
" To imagine an army of sheep encountering the wolves, or two
armies of lambs worrying and destroying one another, would be
an absurdity in nature."

In another anonymous tract, " A modest plea on behalf of the
people called Quakers,"[2] the position taken up by Penington is re-
emphasized.   " Our arguments are urged only in behalf of those
who are brought in themsleves to the knowledge of this inward
and peaceable principle, and refusing to fight with carnal weapons,
have surrendered cheerfully their all into the hands and protection
of the Almighty.   The magistrates or any other person, not convinced of this to be their duty, may very fitly fight in defence of
life, liberty, and property, and it is even possible, if not probable,
that the outward sword thus drawn in a good cause has been secretly
blessed and prospered by the Almighty and that such an army, formed
on these principles, may have often been a bulwark and security
to those whose tender consciences would not permit them to draw
the carnal sword themselves."   The writer gives a recent and striking
instance of the distinction between civil justice and war.   The rebel
Earl of Kilmarnock, he says, at his execution expressed gratitude
that he had been given time for repentance, and had not fallen " in
the midst of his sins in the dreadful carnage at Culloden."

Another reply, also attributed to Besse, was published in 1747.[3]
Its arguments cover familiar ground, and its chief contribution
to the discussion is a renunciation of the right of self-defence.
Finch, he says, " acknowledges that war is a very terrible and
undesirable state ; but queries ' Would it not be more terrible to
remain quiet and unopposing under the horrid murders, ravages,
and devastation of execrable abandoned villains ? '   I answer that
in such a state the condition of the Patient is much to be preferred
to that of the Agent ; and suffering Innocence is far more desirable
and less terrible than insulting Wickedness."

These replies were, of course, the work of private members

---

[1] In D. *Tracts*, 214, 3. " The doctrine of the people called Quakers in relation
to bearing arms and fighting, extracted from the works of a learned and
approved writer of that persuasion—1746."

[2] *Ibid.*, 204, 11.

[3] *Ibid.*, 212. " An Enquiry into the Validity of a late Discourse," etc.

of the Society. The most interesting feature of the controversy is that nine years later Finch himself published a recantation of his own pamphlet.[1] In it he carefully explained that neither for this nor for his earlier tract was the Society in any degree responsible, and he indignantly repudiates the libel that he was hired by the Quakers to retract his opinions. On the contrary, even when he wrote his first tract his mind was uneasy and he suspected his error. At that time he dallied with sceptical opinions in religious matters. "But it pleased God . . . once more to draw me towards Himself, and afresh incline my mind to attend those religious assemblies where I had formerly enjoyed that satisfaction of mind, which I never so experienced in any other place of public worship ; which may be accounted for, when we consider that the truest method of waiting for divine strength and comfort is in this day too much derided as novelty and enthusiasm. . . . And I no sooner complied with the drawing aforementioned but I was favoured with a composure of mind to me unknown for a long season before : my book came fresh to remembrance, and the same which spread a solemnity over my mind seemed to indicate or at least it then appeared to me, that I should, or might, in due time as heartily retract as ever I wrote it, which I now do. And were I to set down all that hath since befel me, in the course of my experience, some might think it very strange, while others, more sober and considerate, would readily acknowledge a divine hand to have followed or led me along." In his repentance he had published in a London newspaper a notice of his change of view, and gave voluntarily to the Society " that satisfaction which is due from her members, who have flagrantly and publicly deviated from a fundamental doctrine."

Nevertheless he considered that some of his critics had been unfair, and he replied to them at length. He had evidently been much influenced by Isaac Penington, and was still willing to consider war for some men necessary and even honourable, though he admitted a clear distinction between it and civil justice. His indignant description of the sufferings of the ordinary soldier reaches back to Barclay and forward to Carlyle.[2]

---

[1] Second Thoughts concerning War, wherein that great subject is candidly considered, and set in a new light in answer to and by the author of a late pamphlet, entitled " The Nature and Duty of Self-Defence, addressed to the People called Quakers " (Job xlii. 3, 5, 6 ; Nottingham, 1755. In D. *Tracts*).

[2] *Vide ante*, p. 149, and Carlyle, *Sartor Resartus*.

"For in war the innocent and the guilty not only perish promiscuously ; but war drags the innocent from all quarters to butcher each other in the open field ; leaving their families to great distress, or to pine away their days in hunger and sorrow ; bereaved of their natural support, the industry of the husband or the parent. Wherefore, I think, that such as have faith enough, had better under all risks, commit themselves, soul and body and all that is theirs, to Providence, rather than be active in such dismal scenes. For men forced from the plough and the spade, from mechanics, husbandry, and their families, and pushed on by the pike or by arbitrary power to fight, kill, and destroy such as they have no quarrel with or enmity against, may surely be deemed innocent in comparison of the obdurate villain, the midnight ruffian, and murderer ; and yet so far nocent, too, that they may be laudably withstood by such as see no farther than they do (or not to the end of war) being by arbitrary power or the custom or law of their country compelled to draw the sword. I do not therefore compare the mutual slaughter of these to downright murder, and yet the destruction of these people in war (whose condition is much to be pitied) by the hands of such as believe themselves redeemed from all war, would too much resemble that black crime."

PART III

THE EIGHTEENTH CENTURY

A DRY doctrinal ministry, however sound in words, can reach but the ear, and is but a dream at the best. There is another soundness, that is soundest of all, viz. Christ the power of God. . . . Therefore, I say, for you to fall flat and formal and continue the profession, without that salt and savour by which it is come to obtain a good report among men, is not to answer God's love, nor your parents' care, nor the mind of truth in yourselves, nor in those that are without; who, though they will not obey the truth, have sight and sense enough to see if they do, that make a profession of it.—WILLIAM PENN, 1694.

CHAPTER VII

DAYS OF TRADITION

1702–55

THE first half of the eighteenth century is not a period to which any religious body in England can look back with satisfaction. In spite of much fervent individual piety the general level of spiritual life was low. The Established Church was chiefly concerned to maintain her privileges and revenues, the Dissenters feared that by any undue activity they might forfeit the toleration they had hardly won, and the Roman Catholics were fortunate if they could practise their faith by stealth and under risk of harsh penalties.

The Society of Friends did not escape the deadening influence of the time. The leaders of the early period had passed or were passing away. The business integrity of Friends had brought a temporal reward, and the new generation included many wealthy or well-to-do men, merchants, bankers, and retail traders. They felt a genuine gratitude to the rulers who had relieved them from persecution, and an equally genuine abhorrence of rebels and rioters who disturbed both their spiritual and material well-being. They were faithful to the traditional " testimonies," but they were not of the stuff of the martyrs. Most fatal change of all, they tended to think their Society as merely a sect among other sects. It is perhaps not fanciful to consider that the decline in the spiritual power of the Quakers coincides with their willingness to adopt the official description of " Protestant Dissenters." Certainly the beginnings of a revived influence coincide both in England and America with the test of war and the first organized movements against slavery. There were, of course, in the earlier eighteenth century, still Friends of the primitive type, unworldly, selfless, and courageous, but the official standpoint was one of caution. A trivial instance shows the tendency, when Anne was scarcely settled on the throne.

In December 1702 the Meeting for Sufferings had before it " a letter from John Love to William Warren," with a paper of rhymes that he published at Canterbury relating to war and bloodshed among professors of Christianity ; which Friends judge to be very unsafe, and that he ought to have shown it to Friends there before published. Also (he) sends a copy of his commitment by the Mayor of Canterbury for the same. . . . It's referred to the Correspondents to write to him to endeavour to be quiet and still, and have a care how he brings an exercise upon himself and Friends, and therefore that he endeavour to get in his paper from the magistrates again, Friends esteeming it not fit for them nor Government."

In justice to the Meeting, it must be said that its members showed more sympathy and less fear of " Government " in the many cases of Quakers pressed for the Navy who appealed to them for deliverance. The experiences of Thomas Chalkley show what a menace hung over the ports and trading-ships in time of war. In 1694, as a boy of nineteen, he was seized near his Southwark home, brought on board ship and thrown into the hold, where his physical discomfort was overshadowed by his moral shrinking from the " dark and hellish " conversation of his fellow prisoners. When the longed-for morning came and they were brought on deck, the lieutenant asked him whether he would serve the King. " I answered that I was willing to serve him in my business, and according to my conscience ; but as for war or fighting, Christ had forbid it in His excellent Sermon on the Mount ; and for that reason I could not bear arms, nor be instrumental to destroy or kill men. Then the lieutenant looked on me and on the people and said, ' Gentlemen, what shall we do with this fellow ? He swears he will not fight.' The Commander of the vessel made answer, ' No, no, he will neither swear nor fight.' Upon which they turned me on shore."[1] In 1701 Chalkley emigrated to Pennsylvania. There he became a leading minister among Friends, and made many journeys " in the cause of Truth " on the American Continent, to the West Indies, and to England. The quaint and charming pages of his *Journal* note as ordinary incidents of travel the attacks of privateers on the high seas and the raids of the press-gang in home waters. In 1719 the ship in which he was returning to the West Indies was stopped and boarded in the English Channel, and the best of the crew carried off to a

[1] Chalkley, *Journal,* p. 7.

man-of-war. Again, in 1735, he as merchant and shipowner was himself bringing a cargo from Philadelphia by the West Indies to England. It was a time " of very great pressing for seamen " (when fears of French and Spanish designs were at their height), and some of Chalkley's crew hid themsleves as they approached England. When the press-gang boarded the ship, the lieutenant asked for the missing men, and Chalkley tried some very elementary diplomacy. " I made him very little answer ; he then said he was sure I could not bring the ship from Barbadoes without hands. I told him sailors were hard to be got in Barbadoes, either for love or money, to go to London, for fear of being pressed, and I was obliged to take any I could get. He said it was in vain to talk much, but if I would say I had no more hands on board he would be satisfied (he having a belief that I would speak the truth, though he never saw me before). . . . But I made him no answer, not daring to tell a lie. ' Now I know that there is men on board,' said he. So he commanded his men to search the ship to her keel. So they stripped, and made a narrow search and sweated and fretted, but could not find them. He being civil, I made him when he went away a small present. He wished me well, and so I carried my people safe up to London."[1]

Some of Chalkley's experiences with privateers will be told in the account of West Indian Quakerism, but the North Sea and the Channel were as dangerous to quiet voyagers. The adventures of William Hornould on his return from a religious visit to Holland so impressed the Yearly Meeting of 1706 that a full account was entered in the minutes. The little lugger or fishing boat, in which Hornould was a passenger, had hardly left the Dutch shore when a privateer was sighted, but the English boat had the wind in her favour and was able to draw away. Next, two more sails appeared, but they proved to be " great ships, supposed to be Deans, and then it took off the fears of the people." The boat sailed well, and was but eight leagues from Harwich when three French privateers were seen ahead " making all the sail they could, both top and top-gallant sails, bearing down upon us, which put the people into a great consternation, and caused the commander and the master to change their course from west nor'-west to full west. . . . And there fell a dead calm, which put the people still into a greater consternation than before."

[1] Chalkley, *Journal,* pp. 100, 277.

" But," continued Hornould, " it was with me then, and also in the danger before, to encourage them all, and to desire them not to be afraid, for I did believe and was fully satisfied that they should not come near us to do us any hurt, but that we should go very safe to Harwich. And then it came into my mind to say to them, " Have you no oars ? " and they answered " Yes." " Then now," I said, " is the time to use them." Whereupon they hoisted them all out presently, and rowed (for all the men cried out they would all work that were able to work), and we rowed four men at an oar for the space of two hours, and then night came on and we had gained a great deal of them." Then a favourable wind sprang up which brought them to Harwich at dawn of the fourth day of the voyage. " After that we had fully escaped and their fright was over, they were exceeding loving to me, and I had a good time to open something of the principles of truth to them that we held. But some of them did for a time argue against our principles, but in a little time were overcome and said it would be a very good time if ever it should come to it, for all so to love one another that nobody would seek to injure or wrong one another, for then there would be no fear of privateers. Some of them answered again and said they were afraid that it would never come to that. But I told them I did not question it at all, but that the Lord would bring such a day and time over the world, according to the testimony of holy Scripture to look for such a day and time, and so in this testimony I left them."

Another stalwart for peace was Thomas Story, a Quaker preacher, whose message and comforting presence was welcomed by many scattered congregations of Friends in English villages, American backwoods, West Indian plantations, and Dutch or German cities. He was as great a traveller as Chalkley, but a man of more education and intellectual power. As a youth, even before he joined the Society in 1691, amid the turmoil of the " glorious revolution, " he was moved to pour out his soul in " Spiritual Songs," fervent strophes of rhythmic prose, whose striking beauty contrasts with the homely and ill-framed sentences in which other Friends struggled to express their message. The atmosphere of war and political strife lay heavily on him and he heard his Master reproach His erring children. " Instead of the Sceptre of Peace they have laid hold on War, and despised the words of my kingdom. . . . I commanded them to love, but behold they hated ; to forgive each other, but they hatched

Revenge. . . . I told them that my Gospel was Truth and Peace ; but behold they have chosen War and a Lie."

Story never wavered in this position, and upheld it in strange scenes and before men of all conditions. In the year 1718, with another Quaker, Dr. Heathcote, the Earl's physician, he had, by request a long interview with the Earl of Carlisle concerning the Quaker faith.[1] After some discussion the earl said : " I think you want but one thing to make you a very complete people ; that is, to bear arms. Pray, what would have become of this whole nation t'other day when the Spaniards were coming to invade us, if we had all, or greatest part, been of your religion ? No doubt we should all have been destroyed or enslaved."

Story made a long reply, in which he told the Earl that " the kingdom of Christ is not of this world, neither is it national, but spiritual. And it cannot be supposed that any one nation can ever be the Church of Christ, which is not national and so subjected to the violence of any other nation." But God has ordained government and entrusted power to rulers. " And the temporal sword, as well of civil magistracy as military force, being in the hands of Kings and rulers, to exercise as need shall be, they, and not the disciples of Christ, must apply and administer accordingly, till by degrees the kingdom of Christ, the Prince of divine Peace, have the ascendant, over all kingdoms, not by violence, for His servants can offer none. " Not by might, nor by power, but by My spirit, saith the Lord." It will not be by human force or policy, but by conviction, not by violence, but consent, that " the kingdoms of this world will become the kingdoms of God and of his Christ." Nor will the kingdoms and powers in this world ever cease (being God's ordinance in natural and civil affairs) till the reason of them cease ; that is, till all violence and injustice cease, and evil-doing come to an end." " So that " (Story continued) " this nation is not in danger of the Spaniards or of any other nation, by reason of our principle, or for want of our help in fighting, which we have not declined because we durst not, or could not use the weapons of war. For many of us have been fighters, and I myself have worn a sword and knew very well how to use it. But being convinced of the evil, by the Spirit of the Lord Jesus, working in us in conformity to the will of God, and subjecting us to Himself as subjects of His peaceable kingdom, 'tis neither cowardice in ourselves or rebellion or disloyalty in nations,

---

[1] Story, *Life*, pp. 617–23.

but conscience towards God, and obedience to His dear Son, the Prince of Peace, our Lord and Saviour Christ Jesus, which makes us decline fighting."

Such a discourse must have sounded strange in the Earl's ears, and in his reply he grasped with relief at some evident and material facts. "'Tis true, so long as you do behave peaceably, are loyal to the Government, and pay your taxes, as you do, I think ; when all's done, there is not an absolute necessity for your personal service in War, since his Majesty may always have soldiers enough for money, as he may have occasion."

Story, however, brought him back to first principles. "Without all doubt, Volunteers, of all others, are fittest for that service, where no man jeopards his life, but by his own consent, choice, and inclination, and has no man to blame but himself in the consequences of it, with respect either to body or soul, since both may be in hazard."

All Friends, however, were not as staunch. Apart from those who were tempted by commercial interest or actual danger to compromise their peace principles, there were by this time some members whose adherence to the Society was rather a matter of hereditary attachment than conviction. The introduction of "birthright membership," natural and almost inevitable as such a step was meant that many acknowledged Friends had not yet fully grasped all the implications of the Society's teaching.[1] On the theological side (although heresy hunts were still infrequent) some Friends of this period were more than suspected of Deism, or even scepticism, and others held but a wavering testimony against war. Amongst these, perhaps, was Dr. Johnson's friend, "Tom Cumming," who is mentioned several times in Boswell's *Life*. In 1783 the Doctor told Boswell that "in 1745 my friend Tom Cumming the Quaker said he would not fight, but he would drive an ammunition cart." But Thomas Cumming strayed farther from the paths of peace than by a mere hasty expression. In the *Gentleman's Magazine*, June 1774, is his obituary notice, "At Tottenham, Mr. Thomas Cumming. He formed the plan for taking Senegal and Goree in the late war." The story is told at length in Smollett's continuation of Hume's *History* under the year 1758. The French

---

[1] In 1737 a difficulty in regard to the relief of poor members of the Society led to a minute of Yearly Meeting by which, incidentally the wife and *children* of a Friend were " deemed members of the Monthly Meeting of which the husband or father is a member," not only during his life, but after his decease.

possessed important trading settlements on the West Coast of Africa, at the mouths of the rivers Gambia and Senegal and had also fortified the island of Goree. They thus had a monopoly of the valuable gum-senega, which English merchants could only buy at an exorbitant price through the medium of Dutch merchants. Hence, as Smollett says naïvely, " this consideration forwarded the plans for annexing the country to the possession of Great Britain." Even before the outbreak of the Seven Years War, Cumming, a " sensible Quaker," seems to have entertained the project. He was a London merchant and had himself made a voyage to Africa, where he met a chief " extremely well disposed " to the English. Smollett continues : " Mr. Cumming not only perceived the advantages that would result from such an exclusive privilege with regard to the gum, but foresaw many other important consequences of an extensive trade in a country which, over and above the gum-senega, contains many valuable articles, such as gold dust, elephant's teeth, hides, cotton, bees-wax, slaves, ostrich feathers, indigo, ambergris and civet. Elevated with the prospect of an acquisition so valuable to his country, this honest Quaker was equally minute and indefatigable in his inquiries touching the commerce of the coast, as well as the strength and situation of the French settlements." On his return home he pressed the scheme upon the Government, but it was not put into execution until the year 1758. A force was sent against Senegal, and a later expedition under Keppel bombarded and captured Goree. According to Smollett, Cumming declared to the Ministry that his scheme could be carried out without bloodshed, and it is implied that this was actually the case. In fact, whether he really hoped for a pacific conquest or not, the operations were those of ordinary warfare, and his plans of a British trade monopoly were also doomed to disappointment. The island and coast were handed back to France at the Peace of Paris in 1763. The tantalising part of this odd story is the obscurity in which the later history of Cumming is wrapped. The *Dictionary of National Biography* says that he explained his action to the Society of Friends, took the entire responsibility, and was not disowned, but as Smollett's account is the main source of the article these statements seem to be a mis-reading of the passage referred to above which gives his statements to the " Ministry." It would almost seem as if the writer had supposed this term to refer not to the English Government, but to the Society of Friends. The only contemporary fact about Cumming in the records of the Society is to be found in the London Burial Register, as follows : " Thomas Cumming, died 1774, 5 mon. 29. Age 59, residence Tottenham. Died of Dropsy. Monthly Meeting Gracechurch Street. Buried 1774. 6th month 2 at Bunhill Fields. Non-Member." From this it is clear that he was not a Friend at his death, and no Birth Register of the Society for the years 1714–15 contains his name. Nor does it occur in the numerous lists of representatives, committees, and signatories of official documents in the records of Yearly Meeting and the Meeting for Sufferings during the period covered by his life. The minutes of Tottenham Monthly Meeting, within the area of which his death took place, also make no mention of him. Those of Gracechurch Street were destroyed by fire in 1821 ; but it is probable that the reference to this Monthly Meeting in the Register merely means that Cumming's place of business was in that London district. If he resided there in earlier life, it would be the duty of Gracechurch Street Meeting to deal with this conduct. But the foregoing facts suggest the possibility that he was never an acknowledged member of the Society, although he may have been an adherent.

Turning from these instances of the views held by individual Friends, the question of the official attitude of the Society next claims consideration. It may be said with fair accuracy that this was expressed each year in the proceedings of Yearly Meeting, which in particular took note of delinquencies within the Society, while in the intervening months the Meeting for Sufferings guarded against persecution and misunderstanding from without.

From the establishment of the Yearly Meeting this body had requested the local meetings to keep and report " an exact account " of the spiritual and material state of the Society in their district. In the year 1682 the following three queries were framed to be answered annually by all Quarterly Meetings :

" 1. What Friends in the Ministry in their respective Counties departed this life since the last Yearly Meeting ?

" 2. What Friends, imprisoned for their testimony, have died since last Yearly Meeting ?

" 3. How the Truth has prospered among them since the last Yearly Meeting, and how Friends are in peace and unity."

Various alterations and additions were made to these queries during the next half-century ; the replies from the several meetings were regularly read in the Yearly Meeting, and after the year 1705 their substance entered upon its minutes. It is not until the year 1742 that a specific allusion to warlike activities was included among the queries, for, as has been explained, throughout this period in most parts of the country Friends endured little suffering on this account. The militia was only embodied twice, in the dangerous years of 1715 and 1745, and, with the exception of the latter year, between 1715 and 1757 no Votes for the Militia were presented to Parliament. In 1705 Kent Quarterly Meeting returned sufferings "for not bearing arms" to the amount of £17, and between that year and 1718 London returned varying amounts for "Trained Bands." A more frequent form of "suffering" is recalled by the Yearly Meeting's appointment in 1706 of a small committee (including Milton's friend, Thomas Ellwood) to read the "Act for pressing of men or better recruiting the army for one year," and the "Act for manning the fleet," and to take Counsel's opinion on them, in case any Friends should be impressed.[1]

In this and the following year the Meeting for Sufferings had actually to obtain the discharge of Friends pressed into both services. This time of war led the Yearly Meeting to repeat in the Epistle of 1709 the warning of 1693 against arming ships. After the Peace of Utrecht, the Meeting (maintaining the recognized Quaker privilege of personal access to the sovereign) presented a congratulatory address on the establishment of "so long desired a peace." This was delivered to the Queen on June 4, 1713, and "kindly received." In 1715 Friends in the north were in the track of the Jacobite rising, and the next year's Meeting received their reports. A Scottish Friend declared that "Friends in that kingdom did and do undoubtedly account the late rising and tumults against the Government was rebellion and that they have cause to bless the Lord for the defeating and disappointing of the evil purpose therein intended." In Lancashire, "Friends in general have behaved themselves inoffensively," while in Cheshire their quiet behaviour "gained them love and respect even from the very soldiers." The Meeting itself presented George I with an address upon the overthrow of the "Black Conspiracy." But, in common with other Dissenters, Quakers suffered from the attacks of disappointed Tory mobs. At Oxford damage to the amount of £55 was done to the

[1] Four manuscript "Books of Cases" preserved in D. contain, amongst other matters, many such opinions by leading lawyers, chiefly on questions of tithes or militia, from the reign of Charles II up to modern times.

meeting-house and Widow Fletcher's house adjoining. Widow Fletcher herself appeared before the Meeting for Sufferings on May 18th to tell how "the soldiers and Oxford scholars have been very abusive in Friends' Meetings," and Andrew Pitt (Voltaire's Quaker friend) was deputed to approach the Secretary of War. A fortnight later he reported that a new Colonel was in charge of the Oxford troops, and would "prevent these abuses."[1]

In 1727 the Meeting presented George II on his accession with an address couched in the florid and adulatory style of the period. Little mark of its origin appears beyond the Quaker "thee" and "thou," and a wish that the new King may "compose the differences of Europe and avert the threatened War." Three years later, at a time when war was raging on the Continent, although Walpole firmly refused to imbroil England in the conflict, the Yearly Meeting made an emphatic declaration in its Epistle.

"It hath been a weighty concern on this meeting that our ancient and honourable testimony against Friends being concerned in bearing arms or fighting may be maintained ; it being a doctrine and testimony agreeable to the nature and design of the Christian religion, and to the universal love and grace of God. This testimony, we desire, may be strictly and carefully maintained by a godly care and concern in all to stand single and clear therein ; so shall we strengthen and comfort one another." In 1742 the stress and strain of the European situation is reflected in the Epistle. "The judgments of the Lord are in the earth" : famine and the sword devour multitudes. Let Friends implore the Almighty to restore peace, and demean themselves as followers of Him who commanded men to love their enemies. The meeting appointed this year a Committee to revise and re-draft the queries. This Committee increased them to eleven, of which the eighth read as follows : —

"Do you bear a faithful and Christian testimony against the receiving or paying tithes ? And against bearing arms ? And do you admonish such as are unfaithful therein ?" Year by year answers to these queries were sent by Monthly Meetings to Quarterly

---

[1] In 1739 a Guy Fawkes Day celebration at Timahoe, Kildare, for which Friends were unjustly held responsible, led to a serious riot in which the Meeting-house was burnt. Dublin Friends applied to the Duke of Devonshire, Lord-Lieutenant, and parties of soldiers were sent down to Timahoe to protect them. Yet in 1743 at Limerick, Waterford, and Clonmel, and again in 1746–7 at Cork a "rude mob of soldiers and others" enjoyed themselves in breaking Friends' windows, on nights of illumination for victories (Rutty, *History*, p. 369).

Meetings ; each of these in turn answered them on behalf of the Monthly Meetings within its compass, and the answers were considered at the Yearly Meeting.

The summaries of replies to the eighth query entered on the minutes give a clue at any rate to the position in various localities, though obviously some meetings possessed a more tender corporate conscience than others. In 1743 for the most part they declared that Friends were " clear " in the matter of bearing arms, or, perhaps more honestly, " we are not tried " (Gloucester), or " we have no militia raised " (Norfolk). Next year there was less complacency. London feared " all are not duly careful," and Derby said quaintly " there be several among us who are the reverse in their conduct to the account above, notwithstanding the repeated admonitions received on account of their unfaithfulness."

From Bristol came a definite appeal :—

" We sorrowfully acknowledge to you that some under our profession are concerned in fitting out a privateer or privateers, and tho' we have seen it our duty to admonish such against a practice so inconsistent with the peaceable doctrines of Christ, yet, as we fear this case may not be singly confined to us, and is of such consequence to Society, we submit it to your consideration to give such further advice as in the love and wisdom of truth you may see expedient."

The Yearly Meeting responded by a cautionary minute sent down for the consideration of the local meetings. The Quaker position, it says, is " agreeable to the doctrine of our blessed Lord and Saviour Jesus Christ and His Apostles, to which our ancient Friends abundantly bore testimony, both in doctrine and practice, and suffered deeply for." The arming of ships, whether for offence or defence, was expressly condemned by the Yearly Meeting in 1693, 1709, and 1730, and Friends are " under many strong engagements to observe the same, from the particular care of Providence over such as have been faithful to this our testimony, particularly those of our Friends in Pennsylvania." Those professing Friends concerned in armed ships, letters of marque or privateers have committed " a flagrant and lamentable departure from our peaceable principle which hath always been to confide in the protection and providence of Almighty God and not in weapons of war ; which practice of theirs may be attended with injustice, barbarity, and bloodshed." " This Meeting therefore " (the minute concludes) "having taken this sorrowful and afflicting case and breach of our ancient testimony into our serious consideration, have thought it our incumbent duty to bear our testimony against such practices, and 'tis the unanimous sense of this Meeting that all Quarterly and Monthly Meetings ought speedily to deal with every person found in the practice of such things, in the spirit of truth and love, in order to bring them to a sense of their error, and to reclaim them from it, which if they cannot do, to testify against them and let them know we have no unity or fellowship with them."

This was a clear lead to the subordinate meetings to set their affairs in order, and in 1745 Yorkshire Quarterly Meeting in answering the eighth query, acknowledged that "in one or two maritime places something disagreeable hath appeared, whereunto suitable advice hath been given." Thus began the long "dealing" with Whitby and Scarborough shipowners which disturbed the peace of the Monthly and Quarterly Meetings concerned for the next half-century. The Jacobite Rising of 1745 proved a time of trial in which not all Friends were able to walk consistently. Charles landed in Scotland in July, and on the 20th of September the Meeting for Sufferings took into "serious consideration the present Rebellion in North Britian and the many obligations we lie under of allegiance and fidelity to the King and Government," and accordingly sent out an address of warning to Friends. In October they were besieged with letters from country meetings, asking advice concerning the "associations and voluntary subscriptions towards assisting in the great charge occasioned by this present Rebellion." The small committee appointed to consider the question decided that "consistent with our ancient Christian testimony and known practice" the Society could take no part in these arrangements.[1] "As we are conscious of our firm regard and affection to our rightful sovereign King George and sensible of the obligations we are under of fidelity and cheerful submission to his mild and just government, so we do trust that our principle against bearing arms is so well known that our not joining in such associations of subscriptions will be attributed to no other cause than a conscientious adherence to our Christian belief and persuasion."

[1] Yet, with the consent of Friends of that Monthly Meeting, Devonshire House Meeting-house (now the headquarters of the Society) was taken for soldiers' billets. Much damage was done during the occupation for which the meeting was never repaid (*vide* W. Beck and Ball, *London Friends' Meetings*, pp. 169–70).

But the replies from the northern counties to the Yearly Meeting of 1746 showed that in the actual seat of war there had been delinquencies or weakness among Friends. In Cumberland, the first time for many years, Trophy Money had been levied, "and the same in collecting being mixt with other taxes, could not well separate so innocently paid, . . . it being a critical conjecture in the county at that time." This last reason casts some doubt on the absolute "innocence" of the payment.

In Lancashire "many Friends have been taxed towards the maintenance of the militia and have paid the same," and in Westmorland "many of our Friends have paid Trophy Money, and some going under our name have not stood clear of bearing arms." The Quaker gift to the Army, however, which at the time created considerable interest, was apparently not made in any official way, as no trace of it can be found in the records. The *Gentleman's Magazine*, in a list of many subscriptions to buy necessities for the army, stated "the Quakers sent down ten thousand woollen waistcoats to keep them warm." Longstaffe's *History of Darlington* says that a large proportion of these garments were furnished by Friends in Darlington and the neighbourhood in four or five days, at their own expense.

According to James Ray of Whitehaven, a volunteer who wrote a personal account of the campaign, the Duke of Cumberland's army received the gift when encamped at Meriden near Coventry, on December 6th, the day the Highland army withdrew from Derby.[1]

Ray says of the Quakers that they are "a quiet, peaceable people that don't swear and fight for the King as we do," and after some exemplary remarks on the folly of profanity, he continues : "it is contrary to their principle to bear arms, yet they contribute to them that do, in paying the regular taxes due to the Government. I have not met with any . . . but what were zealous friends to the Government." He also quotes some jingling couplets extemporized by a soldier (probably himself) praising the "Friendly Waistcoats" and promising to

> Exert my utmost art, my utmost might
> And fight for those whose creed forbids to fight.

[1] *Vide Gentleman's Magazine*, 1745, p. 514 ; Boswell, *Life of Johnson*, 1783 ; J. J. Green, *Souvenir of Address to King Edward VII*, p. 75 ; and Ray, *Compleat History of the Rebellion*, quoted by Hicks, *Quakeriana*, March 1894, p. 7.

Some Friends were very vigorous in their loyalty. Luke Hinde, the Quaker printer and bookseller in 1746, published a pamphlet entitled " A summary account of the marches, behaviour, and plunders of the rebels, from the time of their coming into England, to the retaking of Carlisle by the King's forces, under the command of the Duke of Cumberland. By an Eye-witness of many of the facts herein related." Most of the stories refer to the neighbourhood of Carlisle, and the eye-witness was probably the Quaker Thomas Savage of Clifton, near Carlisle, although he discreetly veils his name. On the night of December 18th the Jacobites had planned an ambush for the Duke of Cumberland's army near Clifton. " As it pleased God T — s S — ge (a friend who lived in Clifton), hearing of their base and treacherous designs, and being very uneasy how he might give the Duke intelligence thereof, his son, with hearty goodwill (though with the hazard of his life) went privately out of his father's house," and succeeded in warning the English army. A skirmish followed, in which seventy prisoners were taken, but the main body escaped into Scotland, leaving a small garrison in Carlisle, which surrendered on December 30th. The Duke of Cumberland, the Duke of Richmond, and the Duke of Kingston quartered themselves in Savage's house, and the Quaker was filled with enthusiasm for his royal and noble guests. In this, indeed, he was not singular, for the Yearly Meeting of May 1746 presented to George II a congratulatory address signed by two hundred and eighty-six Friends, which far outdid even the rhetoric of 1727. It is hard to believe that the same body which sent out the emphatic warning to its members two years before was so dazzled by the Hanoverian throne as to pen the following phrases :—

" We humbly beg leave to approach thy Royal Presence, with united hearts, to congratulate thee upon the deliverance of these kingdoms from the late impending dangers with a joy as sincere as the occasion is signal. We beheld with grief and detestation an ungrateful and deluded people combined against thy person and government, wickedly attempting to subject a free people to the miseries of a Popish and Arbitrary power.

" As none among all thy Protestant subjects exceed us in an aversion to the tyranny, idolatry, and superstition of the Church of Rome, so none lie under more just apprehension of immediate danger from the destructive consequence, or have greater cause to be thankful to the Almighty for the interposition of his providence in our preservation. A preservation so remarkable makes it our indispensable duty also to acknowledge the King's paternal care for the safety of his people, of which he hath given the most assured pledge in permitting one of his Royal Offspring to expose himself to the greatest of dangers for their security.

" May we, and all thy faithful subjects, demonstrate the sincerity of our gratitude for this signal instance of the divine favour, by the deepest humiliation and by turning every one of us from the evil of our ways. . . . We earnestly beseech him, by whom Kings reign and Princes decree justice, that his providence may ever attend thy Royal Person and Family, and make even the efforts of thine enemies conducive to the establishment of thy throne in perfect peace, give success to thy endeavours for settling the general tranquillity of Europe on a lasting foundation, and grant that an uninterrupted race of Kings of thy Royal Progeny may perpetuate the blessings of thy reign to our posterity."

It is obvious that prosperous Friends, in common with other members of the wealthy middle class, had been badly frightened on that Black Friday when the invaders reached Derby and the Bank of England only averted a disastrous run by paying out in sixpences. But Cumberland, the " Royal Offspring," was at this time still a popular hero. The House of Commons had voted him an annuity of £25,000 and City guilds were busy enrolling him as their freeman. " As the news of the cruelties committed in Scotland filtered through to the public, a reaction of opinion manifested itself. When in July it was proposed to make him free of one of the City Companies an Alderman said aloud : ' Then let it be of the Butchers,' and ' Billy the Butcher ' was the nickname by which he was thenceforth known."[1]

A more characteristic activity of this Yearly Meeting was the arrangement for a general collection to relieve the losses sustained by Friends in the North and Midlands " in the late rebellion." The distribution of the fund was undertaken by the Meeting for Sufferings.

In 1748, the long European war was brought to a close by the Peace of Aix-la-Chapelle. The Yearly Meeting Epistle welcomed " with joy " the prospect of peace, and the Meeting for Sufferings, or rather some of its more ardent members, undertook a piece of propaganda. The translation of Barclay's *Apology* into various

[1] *Political History of England*, ix. 407.

languages and its circulation at home and abroad, had often engaged the attention of the leaders of the Society. Now, on the suggestion of Simeon Warner, it was proposed to follow Barclay's own example at the time of the Treaty of Nimeguen, and to send copies of the *Apology* to the plenipotentiaries at Aix-la-Chapelle.[1] The proposal was accepted, and a few Friends, amongst them David Barclay, the Apologist's son, were appointed to carry it into effect.

In August a letter they had drafted in English and Latin to accompany the books was approved and signed, and the consignment dispatched to a Dutch Friend, Jan Van der Werf, for personal delivery to the Ambassadors. The minutes of the Meeting for Sufferings and an abstract in the *Book of Cases* of the correspondence with Van der Werf give a clear picture of this interesting episode. Seventy-four *Apologies* were sent in Spanish, Latin, French, English, Danish, and High Dutch, and the worthy Dutch Friend was asked to take an " Intelligent Person " with him to assist in the distribution. The Memorial to the Ambassadors told those dignitaries that nearly a century before the people called Quakers had been raised up to publish to the world, " amongst other gospel truths . . . the inconsistency of wars and fighting with the example and precepts of Christ and the doctrine of his followers." They are constrained " in love to the whole race of mankind, to promote the knowledge and practice of these blessed doctrines, as they tend so manifestly to extirpate violence, injustice, and all the dreadful calamities of war." Hence they send for " candid perusal " the *Apology*, which, besides setting forth their " belief in relation to wars," also gives a view of the Christian religion in its original simplicity. The Epistle ends with a fervent hope that the negotiators may be able " to perpetuate the blessings of peace to the States you represent, and through them to the whole world."[2]

In November 1748 the Meeting received from Jan van der Werf an account of his stewardship. He had spent several days in Aix-la-Chapelle in September (his expenses and those of his companion, £30, were carefully set out and punctually defrayed by a bill from London), and on the whole received much courtesy from the Ambassadors. Although, in Quaker fashion, he kept his hat on at the interviews, none took offence, " no, not the Pope's Nuncio."

---

[1] *Meeting for Sufferings*, 5th mo. 15, 1748 and following months. *Book of Cases*, iii. 42 foll.

[2] The English version is in D. *Tracts C.* 108.

There is much that is characteristic in his report of the different Ambassadors. The French, finding the book was " about religious affairs," said he had no occasion for it, while the Prussian, after much questioning on the origin of the Quakers, said, " we should come into Prussia, where we might enjoy all freedom." The Bavarian Ambassador was churlish and would not take books which he could not buy, but the Spanish, Genose, and Swedish were all very courteous. The Spaniard offered a " Large Piece of Gold " for the books, and when that was declined, pressed a " dish of coffee or chocolate or whatsoever else we chose " upon his visitors, promising to convey one copy of the *Apology* to his King. The Nuncio, too, who was quartered in the Dominican convent, was very friendly, and although some part of the Friends' memorial " seemed to displease," he passed it over with the remark, that : " There were many Christians and many books wrote, but true and real Christianity consisted in obeying the commands of Christ," to which Van der Werf fully agreed. The Dutchman was closely questioned on the religion of his forefathers, and replied that as far as he knew they were all " believers in the Almighty God and His Son Christ Jesus and His grace to the sanctifying their consciences." " That is a good faith," said the suave ecclesiastic, " but yet there are some necessary circumstances to attend it." He then put to the Quaker the direct question : Could Catholics be saved ? " I cannot judge other men," replied Van der Werf, and pleaded the difficulty of speaking through an interpreter as an excuse for any more full answer. A few days after his return to Amsterdam came news that peace was signed. " The fruit of years of expenditure of blood and treasure," writes a modern historian, " was the *status quo ante bellum* " ; [1] yet good Van der Werf cherished the hope, as he told English Friends, " that this seed sown might be prosperous through God's blessing." The Meeting for Sufferings closed the episode in December 1748, by instructing him to distribute the surplus copies of the *Apology* among foreigners visiting Holland, especially those that might attend the Meeting-house.

The half-century of quietude was over, and soon Friends both at home and in America were forced to set their house in order and to build up again the weak places.

[1] *Political History of England*, ix. 418.

13

CHAPTER VIII

IN TIME OF WAR—ENGLAND AND IRELAND

1755–1815

THE Seven Years War opened in 1755, after the brief truce of Aix-la-Chapelle. The American War, the rise of the new Republic across the Atlantic, the French Revolution, and the long struggle between France and Europe all followed the bloody campaigns which made the names of Clive, of Wolfe and of Chatham, household words to the English people.

> Praise enough
> To fill the ambition of a private man
> That Chatham's language was his mother tongue
> And Wolfe's great name compatriot with his own.[1]

In the smaller world of the Society of Friends, also, these were years of stress. In England and in America it entered the period as a prosperous, inoffensive, and somewhat cautious body. In England, and yet more in America, it emerged after a testing time, smaller in numbers, perhaps for the time narrower in outlook, and yet with a clearer view of some of the foundation principles of the Quaker faith. It was, in particular, the emphatic testimony against war and against slavery that had stripped the Society of so many members, not a few among them Friends of standing and influence. The labours of John Woolman fall within the first half of this period, and if to any one man, then assuredly to him must be attributed the awakening of the conscience of the Society.[2] He was himself an embodied conscience, and he witnessed for complete sincerity and pureness of heart in all the relations of life. His brief visit to England in 1772, sealed by his death, left an abiding impression upon English Friends.

In 1758 and 1763 the Yearly Meeting Epistle had touched

[1] Cowper, *Task*, Book II.   [2] For John Woolman, *vide* Chapter XIII.

the question of the slave trade, but it was in the year 1772 that the Epistle opened the long series of protests against both the trade and slavery itself, which were not to cease until the crime came to an end in British possessions.[1]

Quakers did much for the cause of the slave, but the living interest created by such a cause perhaps did as much for Quakerism. The Society gained courage and independence as it learned to plead for a despised race. The term " Protestant Dissenters " quietly disappears from its memorials and addresses during the reign of George III, and with it much of the flowery style of the earlier eighteenth-century documents.

The pressure of the Seven Years War led necessarily to an increased vigilance by the Yearly Meeting over individual short-comings. In 1757 the Epistle again called attention to " that great inconsistency of being concerned in privateers, letters of Marque, or ships armed in a warlike manner," and recommended subordinate meetings to keep a watchful eye over their members. Another passage expressed the better side of eighteenth-century Quietism. " And, dear friends, as it hath pleased the Almighty to reveal unto mankind His son Jesus Christ, the peaceable Saviour, let it be our steady concern to demonstrate to the world that we are His followers by bringing forth the fruits of the Spirit, ' love, joy, peace, long-suffering, gentleness, goodness, faith, meekness, temperance.' And as we are called out of wars and fightings, so let them be as seldom as possible the subjects of our conversation ; but let a holy care rest upon us, to abide in that power which gives dominion over the hopes and fears of an unstable world."

Next year the advice against privateering was repeated, and the testimony against war was extracted from the eighth query by the Yearly Meeting, and made the subject of an independent query, the twelfth. This new query read as follows :—

" Do you bear a faithful testimony against bearing arms or paying Trophy Money, or being in any way concerned in privateers, letters of Marque, or in dealing in prize goods as such ? "

The Epistles of this period repeatedly caution Friends against in any way defrauding the revenue (the subject of another query)

[1] The subject occurs in more than half the Epistles of the sixty years from 1772 to 1833. John Woolman, in 1772, felt that English Friends were " mixed " with the slave trade, through their share in supplying manufactured goods for the cargoes of outward-bound slave ships.

and against dealing in "run" or smuggled goods. As usual, the emendation in the query resulted in an awakening of conscience among the local meetings. Bristol and Ireland both feared that there had been some dealings in prize goods, while Kent reported its "unspeakable pleasure and satisfaction" to find no instances of participation in "so iniquitous a trade." Since 1755 the Seven Years' War had been rolling across three continents, till in 1759 the tide turned against France. The Yearly Meeting was constrained to remind Friends that public rejoicing over victories was inconsistent with a refusal to take part in war. Next year the result was seen by a report from London Friends of damage "for not illuminating windows" to the extent of nearly £11.[1]

In 1760 a joint Committee of the Meeting for Sufferings and the Morning Meeting drew up a paper of Advice "to be dispersed among Friends' Families respecting the keeping their shops shut on Fast Days and the illuminating of windows on what are called rejoicing nights," of which two thousand were printed and distributed to the Monthly Meetings.[2] This "Tender Advice and Caution" referred any waverers to the light which had guided early Friends. "In this light . . . they not only saw that they must cease from outward hostility, but that their conversation and conduct must be consistent, and of a piece throughout. As they could not join with others in shedding the blood of their fellow creatures, neither could they be one with them in rejoicing for the advantages obtained by such bloodshed ; as they could not fight with the fighters, neither could they triumph with the conquerors ; and therefore they were not to be prevailed upon to make a show of conformity by placing lights in any part of the fronts of their houses ; but patiently suffered whatever violences and abuses were committed against them, for the sake of their peaceable *Christian* Testimony."

[1] Isaac Richardson (born 1707) "has left it on record that the mob of Whitby three times broke his windows and destroyed his property, because he, like other Friends, refused to illuminate his house on occasions of public rejoicing. Fifty years later . . . in Sunderland, blazing tar barrels were rolled along the streets to burn down the house of a Friend who would not illuminate on some occasion when political feeling ran high. The work had begun when a gentleman whose sympathies were with Friends, but who, not being a member of their Society, was not bound by its regulations, hurried to the barracks and appealed to the officer in command. The soldiers were soon on the spot, and the half-burned house was saved " (*Records of a Quaker Family*, by A. B. Richardson, p. 17).

[2] *Morning Meeting Book*, 2th mo. 25, 1760. I am indebted for this passage to A. Neave Brayshaw.

Their successors in the Society should not lightly abandon this testimony. " The Spirit of Truth . . . will unite us to itself, and lead us into unity one with another, baptizing us into one body, and causing us to drink of one Spirit, and doubtless would bring all to bear the same Testimony in every essential point of faith and conduct, and would ever preserve us from differing so far as to appear contrary to each other, and thereby from laying waste our ancient Testimony and, by that means, depriving the body of the strength of Unity. And though *mere uniformity* is not the essential part of religion, yet it is the indispensable duty of all to endeavour after the Unity of the Spirit, which, as it prevails, naturally produceth a consistency and harmony, both in reality and appearance, that all, being gathered into the same Spirit, may see by the same light, and may, like the primitive Church, be of one heart and of one soul. . . . Therefore let no branch of the Testimony of Truth be opposed as insignificant or treated with contempt."

The same difficulty was to recur in the Napoleonic War.

In the meantime the pressure of war had led to army re-organization and extension. In March 1756 a Militia Bill was introduced with Pitt's support, the aim of which was to establish a regularly trained army of reserve. This was passed in the Commons, but thrown out by the Lords, as tending " to make this a military country and government." In 1757 the Bill was passed into law in a modified form. It was, however, unpopular, and on the attempt to enforce it in the autumn, riots broke out in several counties.[1] Friends watched the matter anxiously through a vigilant Committee of the Meeting for Sufferings. The first Militia Bill was considered on its introduction and judged likely " to expose the Society to very grievous suffering." A deputation approached the Chairman of the House of Commons Committee, who assured them " that it could not be possible to obtain a total exemption from some expense, but that nothing of this kind was intended to be inflicted as any punishment for not complying, but as a reasonable compensation to the country." He accordingly suggested a clause by which, if the ballot fell upon a Quaker a substitute should be hired, and the expense met by distraint on the Quaker's goods. However, the fact that the Bill was " dropt in the House of Lords " prevented further action. Next year the

[1] *Vide Gentleman's Magazine*, 1757. Cowper in the *Task* (" Winter Evening," 613–58), nearly thirty years later, gave a vivid description of what seemed to him the social evils of the three years' militia training.

new Bill was passed into law, with this clause exempting Quakers from personal service. In June the Meeting for Sufferings with just pride transcribed into its records a minute of the Yearly Meeting expressing satisfaction with the " care and pains " taken by the former meeting in the matter. A new and comprehensive Militia Bill of 1762 replaced this experimental Act and remained in force for twenty-four years. Two clauses especially affected Friends. By one it was provided that if a Quaker were chosen by lot to serve and refused or neglected to appear and to take the oath or to provide a substitute, the Deputy-Lieutenants or other local authorities, " upon as reasonable terms as may be," should provide a substitute to serve for three years, and levy a distraint upon the goods of the Quaker to defray the expense. If the distraint provided more money than was required, the surplus was to be returned and the Quaker had the right of appeal should the distress seem unduly oppressive. Under another clause, when a rate for the expenses of the militia was levied upon any parish, and Quaker householders refused to contribute, the justice of the peace was authorized to recover the amount by process of distraint.

The Meeting for Sufferings was entrusted by the Yearly Meeting with the task of circulating information about the provisions of the Act. But it proved more timid than the larger body. On June 17, 1762, a sub-committee reported to the Meeting that : " We are of opinion that it will not be safe to put the advice, left by the Yearly Meeting respecting the Militia into print, inasmuch as those mistaken or malignant persons who are continually watching against the Society for evil, might make a pernicious use of them by representing Friends as taking upon them publicly to control and oppugn the acts of the legislature." Hence they recommended that manuscript copies of the said advices should be circulated among the Monthly and Quarterly Meetings, while only the special clauses of the Act relating to Friends should be printed for distribution. The advices, as they appear in the pages of the Yearly Meeting records, do not seem to the modern reader either seditious or dangerous. Probably the declaration that " it is our sense and judgment that we cannot, consistent with our well-known principles," pay the militia rates or hold offices involving the duty of their collection, was the sentence which roused the fears of the Meeting for Sufferings. But this opinion is immediately followed by a direction to the local Meetings that " Friends should be tenderly advised to avoid giving occasion of reproach by any unjustifiable endeavours to evade or elude the law, and that in all cases wherein they allege a conscientious scruple for not actively paying what may be demanded of them, that they manifest by a patient and Christian conduct under such sufferings as may attend in consequence thereof that their scruples are real and sincere."

In any case, the Society as a whole was prepared to uphold the position of the Yearly Meeting. From 1761 until 1815, these distraints for the militia and other local rates levied for war purposes are constantly recorded and reach a formidable total. They were not finally abolished until the army re-organization of 1848. The militia was included, as an occasion for peace testimony, in the twelfth query in 1761. In the following year, deputations appointed from the Yearly Meeting visited all the Monthly and Quarterly Meetings in England to strengthen and encourage them in the faith. A few delinquencies, both in regard to the hire of substitutes for the militia and also in the arming of ships were found in the North and West. In the London district " too many concur with others in giving public testimony of joy upon the devastation of war and other occasions of illuminating their windows."

When peace was concluded with France in 1763, the Yearly Meeting presented an address to the young King. Though loyal and respectful in tone, it is much less adulatory than those offered to his grandfather. " To a people " (it runs) " professing that the use of arms is to them unlawful, a people who reverence the glorious Gospel declaration of good will to men and fervently wish for the universal establishment of peace, its return must be highly acceptable. To stop the effusion of blood, to ease the burden of thy people, and terminate the calamities that affected so large a part of the globe, we are persuaded were thy motives to effect the present pacification. Motives so just in themselves, so full of benevolence and humanity, demand our united and cordial approbation. May the sovereign of the Universe, who created all nations of one blood, dispose the minds of Princes by such example, to learn other means of reconciling their jarring interests and contentions than by the ruin of countries and the destruction of mankind."

George III was not to prove an apt scholar in the art of peace, but he returned a kindly answer to the Address. Like Charles II he was amused by Quaker simplicities, and maintained a friendly, though eccentric, intercourse with individual members of the Society.

It was perhaps the knowledge of this royal interest that encouraged contemporary journalists to make considerable " copy " out of the Quakers. The *Gentleman's Magazine,* for example, between 1765 and 1810, often printed the Yearly Meeting Epistle, or extracts from it, in its pages, and allowed its correspondents much latitude in friendly and unfriendly criticism of Quaker tenets.[1] This, at any rate, made Friends' principles known, and perhaps had some influence upon public opinion.

Peace, however, did not end the militia fines, and Quarterly Meetings had to report occasional delinquencies, such as the actual enlistment of a member in Yorkshire in 1767 and next year the payment of the rate in Derbyshire by some " who plead for the same." The old trouble of the " mixed rate " (a militia rate levied as part of the poor rate) recurred, and although a Committee of the Yearly Meeting which examined the text of the Militia Act in 1770 declared that any expenditure for such purposes out of the poor rate must legally be re-imbursed by a distinct and separate rate, yet the difficulty arose year after year in various districts.

For a few years during the interval of peace the clause concerning armed vessels was dropped out of the war query (now the eleventh) but the American War made its re-introduction necessary. The outbreak of resistance naturally caused grave concern to Friends. The Meeting for Sufferings in February 1775 had the courage to address the House of Commons in protest against the Bill (one of the King's methods of conciliating his rebellious subjects) by which the fishermen of Nantucket were to be debarred for ever from the use of the Newfoundland fisheries. Of the five thousand inhabitants, nine-tenths were Quakers, and the Meeting explained (as the King and his advisers well knew) that such a prohibition meant utter ruin. In March they made an earnest effort in favour of peace, by an address to the King. The plea ran thus :—

" From the intercourse subsisting between us and our brethren abroad, for the advancement of piety and virtue, we are persuaded there are not, in the extensive dominions, subjects more loyal, and more zealously attached to thy Royal person, thy family, and Government, than in the Province of America and amongst all religious denominations. We presume not to justify the excesses committed, nor to inquire into the causes which may have produced them ; but, influenced by the principles of that

[1] *Vide J.F.H.S.,* 1916, Nos. 1 and 2. J. J. Green, *Notices Relating to Friends in the " Gentleman's Magazine."*

religion which proclaims ' Peace on earth and goodwill to men,' we heartily beseech thee to stay the sword ; that means may be tried to effect, without bloodshed, and all the evils of internecine war, a firm and lasting union with our fellow subjects in America." The task, they add, is an arduous one ; but they are confident that men can be found on both sides of the Atlantic capable of conducting such a mediation. Men, indeed, there were, some of them Friends or closely connected with Friends, who were spending themselves in the effort. Throughout December 1774 and the following January and February Dr. Fothergill and David Barclay, both well-known London Friends, were in frequent conference with Franklin, and with some of the more moderate members of the English ministry, in the attempt to find terms of settlement acceptable both to the colonists and the home Government. Franklin, with the advice and encouragement of the two Quakers, drafted these terms under the modest title, " Hints for a Conversation." They influenced Chatham's abortive proposals in the House of Lords on February 1. Fothergill, whose profession had brought him into friendly relations with leading politicians, showed them to Lord Dartmouth and the Speaker, and Barclay to Lord Hyde. With Lord Howe, Franklin was carrying on tentative and informal " conversations." There is evidence that through Hyde and through Dartmouth, the well-intentioned but weak Secretary for the Colonies, the proposals came before the Cabinet, or at least before its leading members. But the Quakers were much disappointed by the attitude of ministers ; when Franklin, in despair, sailed for America, he took with him a message from Fothergill to Philadelphia Friends : " Whatever specious pretences are offered they are all hollow. . . . Nothing very favourable is intended." [1]

[1] For some of these details, *vide Dr. John Fothergill and His Friends,* by Dr. R. Hingston Fox. There is a minute autobiographical account of the negotiations by Franklin in his *Memoir (Works,* i. 430 foll., edition 1818). See also Sir George Trevelyan, *The American Revolution,* i. c. viii. According to Franklin, Barclay was also a prime mover in the " Merchants' Petition " against the war. Fothergill was constant in advice and sympathy to American Friends until his death in 1781. Franklin always felt esteem for his two fellow workers in the attempt to avert war. On Fothergill's death he wrote from his post in Paris to Barclay :—

" I condole with you most sincerely in the loss of our dear friend, Dr. Fothergill. I hope that someone who knew him well will do justice to him by an account of his life and character. He was a great doer of good. How much might have been done, and how much evil prevented if his, your, and my joint endeavours in a certain melancholy affair had been attended to ! "

Franklin was not given to indiscriminate eulogy, least of all of his Quaker acquaintances, and this letter is good testimony to Fothergill's merits.

Although George III heard the address "favourably," he had neither the will nor the power to stay the sword. The Epistle, two months later, could only express a hope that Friends on both sides of the Atlantic might keep clear of "the present heats and commotions," and entreat members not to make them even the subject of conversation. But the mild conservatism of official Quakerdom cannot hide its bias. "We cannot consistently join with such as form combinations of an hostile nature against any, much less in opposition to those providentially placed either in sovereign or subordinate authority; nor can we unite with such as indecently asperse or revile them." Other Yearly Epistles of this war period express warm sympathy with the sufferings and privations of Friends in America, to whom (especially to those of Pennsylvania) generous contributions of relief were sent by their fellow members in England and Ireland. In 1779 the Epistle gave a plain warning against war activities and war profit-making whether by sea or land. Any who thus backslide "afford evident tokens that they either prefer the gain of a corrupt interest to the convictions of divine light in their own conscience, or that they are become insensible to them." Two years later the advice was even more emphatic. "Keep clear of touching in any respect, or dealing in those things which tend to promote the dreadful calamity of war. Let not the love of gain be put in competition with the welfare and happiness of mankind." The Epistle of 1783, which welcomed the return of peace, for the first time mentioned the militia fines as a "suffering" of Friends. The war had unmistakably tried the weak places in the Society. Some Cornish Friends in time of peace had acquired an interest in a "packet employed by the General Post Office," which, on the outbreak of war, was "equipped in a warlike manner for defence, but with no commission to take prizes, and with positive orders to avoid all other ships." The Friends tried to withdraw from the concern, but without success, and this mild-mannered mail packet eventually captured some French prizes. How these events brought a little group of French Quakers to the notice of English Friends is told in another chapter.[1]

Not only Yorkshire, but several other seaboard Meetings, had to report "deficiencies" in the matter of armed vessels in these years when Paul Jones was disturbing the boasted immunity of British shores. In 1777 the clause dealing with this branch of

[1] *Vide* Chapter XVII, p. 469.

testimony was re-inserted in the query. At Norwich in 1780 " one unguarded youth lately enlisted himself in the Army," and another joined the militia. Both were dealt with by their meeting. A Welsh Friend was concerned in privateers and letters of Marque, but in 1781 he gave in " a paper of condemnation of the practice, with an assurance of renouncing it, to the satisfaction of the meeting he belongs to." That same year, Yorkshire, besides the usual " sorrowful defection," had to lament over a few members who bought prize tobacco at the sales.

Another vessel part-owned by a Friend, John Warder, in 1781, took out letters of Marque without his knowledge, and on the voyage to New York captured a Dutch East Indiaman. His share of the prize-money was £2,000, which, on the advice of his Monthly Meeting in London (Devonshire House), he invested for the benefit of the original owners, " whensoever they might be found." He had already disposed of his share in the privateer, but when a few years later he removed to Philadelphia, his Monthly Meeting refused to grant him the usual certificate recommending him to the fellow-ship of Philadelphia Friends, on the ground that he had taken no steps to restore the money. His duty was evidently pressed upon him by his new associates, and at last, in 1799, he transferred to the London Monthly Meeting both the principal and interest to be refunded to the Dutch owners, or dealt with as Friends might think " most consistent with truth and equity." Upon this he received his certificate. The London Friends at once inserted an advertise-ment in the Dutch papers, and although investigations were hampered by the war, yet by 1818 claims amounting with interest to £7,000 had been settled. There still remained a balance of £2,000, and this was applied to the building and maintenance in Amsterdam of an infant school, one of the first of its kind, which is still doing useful work.[1] The school was named " Hollandische Welvaren " (Holland's Welfare) after the captured ship.

Bristol Friends on March 1, 1780, spent an unpleasant evening from their refusal to illuminate their houses on the news of a British victory. The mob broke windows wholesale and threatened to burn the houses, while the captain of the local militia, a magistrate, led the window-breaking with some of his soldiers. The letter in

[1] Luke Howard, *The Yorkshireman*, ii. 327. There is a full account of the episode and of the present school by Mary Willis Brown in *Bulletin of Friends' Historical Society* (Philadelphia), May 1916.

which Joseph Fry of Bristol informed the Meeting for Sufferings of the riot, naïvely adds that " if an account of another victory should arrive, we fear a repetition of the insult in a much greater degree."[1] But the course of the American War was not such as to bring much more inconvenience to the Quakers of Bristol.

The war had long been unpopular with all Englishmen except the King and some of the " King's friends," yet even so the Address of the Society to George III on the conclusion of peace contained a bold passage.

" When we reflect on the dreadful calamities and the great effusion of human blood which ever attend the prosecution of war, we deeply lament that any of the professors of the Christian religion should continue a practice so inconsistent with the doctrines of Christ the Prince of Peace." But George III, stubborn and petulant with his trusted ministers and insanely bitter against his political opponents, never took offence at Quaker plainness. " I always receive " (he replied) " with pleasure your assurance of duty and affection to my person and family, and do so particularly upon the event of peace. You may be assured of my constant protection, as your uniform attachment to my Government, and peaceable disposition are highly acceptable to me." In this same year, 1783, the first petition against the slave trade, signed by 273 Quakers, was presented by the Yearly Meeting to the House of Commons.[2] Its promoters had been well received by Fox and North, leaders of the Coalition, and Lord John Cavendish, Chancellor of the Exchequer.

In the House North, in some kindly phrases, welcomed the action of " the most benevolent Society in the Universe," but the address was allowed to lie upon the table. The Society for the Abolition of the Slave Trade was formed in 1787, with ten Quakers on the first committee of twelve members, and through weary years their help in time, influence, and money was ungrudgingly given to Clarkson and Wilberforce. One result of this intercourse was the awakening in Clarkson of a great interest in the Society, which eventually led him in 1807 to publish in three volumes a *Portraiture of Quakerism*. This work, though not free from

---

[1] *Meeting for Sufferings*, 3rd mo. 17, 1780.
[2] *Book of Cases*, iii. 197. A Friend, William Southeby, petitioned the Pennsylvania Assembly against slavery in 1712 (Sharpless, *Quakers in the Revolution*, p. 232).

inaccuracy, was in many respects a sympathetic study of Friends, and no doubt introduced a knowledge of their views and character into circles which had hitherto been prejudiced against them. In his introduction Clarkson remarks as a trait of Quaker character that " whenever they can be brought to argue upon political questions, they reason upon principles and not upon consequences " ; the long exposition of their " tenet on war," which fills nearly a hundred pages of his third volume, opens with the emphatic declaration that " there is no such character as that of a Quaker soldier. A Quaker is always able to avoid the regular army, because the circumstance of entering into it is generally a matter of choice. But where he has no such choice, as is the case in the militia, he either submits, if he has property, to distraint upon it ; or if he has not, to prison." This statement is interesting, as showing what, in the view of an onlooker, was the general practice of the Friends in regard to the militia, even at a time when Quarterly Meetings were lamenting over the " sorrowful deficiencies " among their members.

From the allusion to prison it will be seen that the hand of the law gradually tightened upon Quakers. In the earlier Militia Acts an ordinary delinquent who refused or evaded service when balloted was liable to three months' imprisonment if he proved unable to pay the costs of a substitute. The clauses relating to Friends made provision only for fine or distraint, and the case of a young apprentice, or other Friend of small means, was not considered. Occasionally a magistrate, willing to stretch the utmost rigour of the law, sent such a Friend to prison. The Book of Cases shows the vigilance of the Meeting for Sufferings in maintaining Friends' legal rights. In 1759 it obtained an opinion from Bicknell, K.C., that the Act gave no power to imprison Quakers. He added, " I apprehend that the legislature, out of tenderness towards the Quakers' religious principles or scruples, who hold it unlawful to bear arms or fight in war, did not intend to make them liable to personal punishment." Under the Act of 1762 a Friend, Daniel Massey, was imprisoned at Chester. Dunning, the great Whig lawyer, was appealed to, and considered that the sufferer had a right to apply for his discharge by a writ of Habeas Corpus. In the time of the American War two cases tested the same point of law.

Bernard Harrison was a young servant of David Barclay. In 1776 he was drawn for the militia at Standon, Hertfordshire, but had no property on which distress could be levied, " save his clothes." The Hertford magistrates in these circumstances, when he " intimated his religious objection to the bearing of arms," proposed to commit him to gaol. His master took up the matter, showing the justices copies of the legal opinions already quoted. To this they replied that these were out of date. Nothing daunted, David Barclay proposed that both sides should obtain a fresh opinion, which was done. The Deputy-Lieutenants took the case to Lloyd Kenyon, later Lord Chief Justice, who confessed that the Act " was not as explicit as one could wish," but was " inclined to think " that a justice had power to commit a Quaker. Barclay, however, was encouraged to persevere by the support of several magistrates, who (as he told the Meeting for Sufferings) " reprobated the opinion in severe terms, and said if the Society did not defend the particular privilege which Parliament had given them, they did not deserve it ; that it was a *Common Cause* and so notoriously known that an Englishman cannot legally be deprived of his Liberty without a positive direction in an Act of Parliament that there could not be a shadow of risk in defending the privilege." He applied to Thurlow, then Attorney-General, and shortly after Lord Chancellor. The reply was emphatic :—

" I am of opinion that a Quaker cannot be legally committed by virtue of the Act, and consequently that if the Commitment pursues the case, he may be discharged by Habeas Corpus."

To this the Deputy-Lieutenants submitted. Bernard Harrison was excused service, and a fresh ballot taken in Standon to fill his place. The Meeting for Sufferings took steps to inform all Quarterly and Monthly Meetings of the case, sending to them copies of Thurlow's opinion. In 1782 Thomas French of Sibford found himself in the same position, and though a fresh ballot was taken no one could be found to serve. The militia officer concerned pressed, not for imprisonment, but for the conscription of French on the ground that the former punishment was by no means adequate at a time of national danger. He rested this claim on an amending Act of 1779 (19 Geo. III, c. 72) which provided that when a person without effects declined to serve, his " name shall be entered on the bill and he shall be handed over to some proper officer of the regiment or company for which he was drawn, and be compelled to serve for the full term of three years . . . and be liable to the same punishments as if regularly enlisted. Friends claimed that this provision did not apply to members of their Society. Keynon's opinion was again invoked. In the five years' interval he had become Attorney-General and he had, seemingly, made up his mind on points of legal construction, for he replied in decisive terms :—

" It would be harsh measure if the legislature made any law pressing upon tender consciences, and if any clause affords two constructions it would be reasonable to adopt that construction which avoided so great severity." The fine, he added, levied on a Quaker was not punitive, but only sufficient to provide a substitute, " and in all this the Quaker is to be passive and not active." Another amending Act of 1778 had also threatened some unnecessary hardships to Quakers. By it, as introduced to the House of Commons, to prevent false claims no person could be accepted as a Quaker within the meaning of the Act, unless he produced a certificate of acknowledgment from two Quaker householders. If he then refused to serve and was possessed of no property, the distraint was to be levied *on the property of the certifying Quakers.* The Meeting for Sufferings, however, applied at once to Members of Parliament and to the Speaker, with the result that this latter clause was dropped. Yet another Act in 1786 (26 Geo. 3, c. 107) made a breach in the Quaker immunity from imprisonment. If a Quaker (such is the effect of the clause) has no goods upon which to distrain, although in the opinion of the Deputy-Lieutenants he is able, if willing, to pay the sum of £10, then " it shall be lawful " for them to commit him to gaol for three months, or until payment be made. The power was thus permissive and not obligatory. It was little used until war hardened the temper of the authorities, although in 1788 George Gibson, a well-known Friend of Saffron Walden, reported to the Meeting for Sufferings that John Bush, from the neighbouring town of Thaxted, was imprisoned on this account at Chelmsford, and that no relief could be obtained. Militia sufferings everywhere, as reported by the Quarterly Meetings, were heavy this year. The Yearly Meeting, becoming aware " that the practice of arming ships prevails in some trades in time of peace " (presumably those which plied near the haunts of Algerine corsairs), directed that the whole of the eleventh query should be answered every year.

In 1790 a Written Epistle was sent out by the Yearly Meeting to its subordinates in reference to the queries, the replies to which in future are no longer summarized on the minutes. It utters an

emphatic condemnation of all warlike practices, including the manufacture or sale of arms, " and as warlike preparations are making
in this country, we entreat Friends to be watchful, lest any be drawn
into loans, arming or hiring out their ships, or otherwise promoting
the destruction of the human species." The warning against loans
is evidence both of the change in the nature of military resources
and of the increasing wealth of many Friends. The war query
in 1792 in a re-arrangement of the series, returned to its old
position of eighth, and was simplified to : " Are Friends faithful
in our testimony against bearing arms, and being in any manner
concerned in the militia, in privateers, letters of Marque, or armed
vessels, and dealing in prize goods ? " In a few months war was
upon them. The Correspondence of Charles James Fox gives a
lively picture of the anxiety with which English Liberals followed
the gradual estrangement of the French and English Governments.
English Quakers, as a body, had little sympathy with the Revolution, but their horror at the catastrophe was as keen. Cobden, who
was not in the habit of making statements at random, declared at
the Manchester Peace Conference in January 1853, that " the
Society of Friends co-operated with Mr. Fox and his colleagues
in trying to prevent that most unrighteous and most unhappy war
of the French Revolution. I find that Mr. Gurney of Norwich
corresponded constantly with Mr. Fox in the House of Commons,
and that Mr. Fox corresponded with Mr. Gurney, entreating him
to get up a county meeting in Norfolk and encouraging him to get
up numerous petitions from Norwich." [1]

On January 25, 1793, the Meeting for Sufferings passed the
following minute : " This Meeting, being weightily impressed
with a sense of the calamities attendant on war, the inconsistency
thereof with Christianity, and the present prospect of such an event
taking place, concludes to adjourn to to-morrow morning at ten
to take the affair into further consideration. John Ady is directed
to summon the absent members." Next day the Meeting adopted
a strongly worded address to the King against the threatened
war.

" We cannot at this time discharge our duty to God, to thee,
and to our fellow subjects, many of whose precious lives may be the

---

[1] The speech is given in the *Herald of Peace*, February 1853, and in Cobden's
Speeches (edited Bright and Thorold Rogers, pp. 527-8), *vide* also Morley,
Life of Cobden, ch. xxi.

victims of the impending hostilities, without beseeching thee to exert thy constitutional power to prevent a measure which may consign to danger and to death thousands of our fellow countrymen." The protection of the kingdom rests with God rather than with any armed strength ; the pursuit of righteousness, and in particular the abolition of the slave trade, will give the nations favour in His sight. The address was presented by three Friends whose company was declared to be " acceptable " by a message from the Secretary of State. To them the King returned a friendly but unhopeful answer :—

" Whatever steps I may feel myself bound to take for the security of my people, I am not the less inclined to judge favourably of the motives which have led you to present this address, and you may depend upon the continuance of my protection."

The twenty-one years of war which followed were difficult ones for the Quakers, as the national resources were drawn upon with increasing rigour to meet the growing power of Napoleon. Nor was the Society entirely united. Some wealthy Friends who led a life of decorous luxury and sat loose in many respects to the generally accepted code of their fellow members, shed their peace views, or, in some cases, had none to shed. To give one instance, of Samuel Hoare the banker, it was said : " Trusting in the superiority of our Navy, and calculating the length of time which must elapse before a fleet could be raised, he never believed it possible that Buonaparte could make good a landing in this country. Educated in the principles of a sect reprobating war, he looked upon it in the present state of society as a necessary evil. Defensive war he regarded as lawful ; the nice point was determined when it became so ; for where preventive measures are not had recourse to, defence may become impossible. . . . Self-defence he considered lawful, and that it is the duty of a man to defend his country." [1]

Quakers of this type seldom gave offence by any overt act of war-like tendency, though they might gradually drift away from the Society or be disowned on other grounds. On the north-east coast Quaker shipowners and sea-captains were faced by the old dilemma. Disownments " for carrying guns on ships " were not so numerous as in the American War, but the process was more summary and less attempt was made to reclaim the delinquent. It is to this period that many of the often-repeated stories of warlike Quakers belong.

[1] *Memoirs of Samuel Hoare* (1751–1815), by his daughter and widow, 1911.

When name, place, and date are wanting, these are difficult to verify, and their details do not carry conviction.

As the war continued and was felt at home in high prices and scarcity, an attempt was made by some unscrupulous journals to divert unpopularity from the Ministry to the Quakers. A considerable number of Friends were engaged in the corn trade, either as millers or dealers, and the *Morning Advertiser* in 1799 charged them with the responsibility for the high price of corn and bread by forming a combination to monopolize the supply. The poor were starving—for two or three years past William Allen the chemist and other Friends had been maintaining a soup kitchen in Spitalfields for the relief of the worst cases of distress—and when in 1800 the price of the quartern loaf rose, first to fifteen pence and then to seventeen pence halfpenny, the more desperate among the sufferers were ready to vent their anger upon any scapegoat. There were some ugly riots in the City and East London. William Allen noted in his *Journal* that at his father's burial the Whitechapel rabble " proved very disturbing." One mob attacked Robert Howard's factory in Old Street, in the belief that stores of grain were concealed there.[1] But, though the owner would call in no assistance, his workpeople were not Quakers, and beat off the attack with their wooden stools, the only weapons at hand. Robert Howard published a brief vindication quaintly entitled, " A Few Words on Corn and Quakers," which it is unlikely that his assailants ever read. In October the Meeting for Sufferings was under " deep concern at the calumnies which Friends lie under on account of the dearness of corn," and after some discussion of the newspaper attacks a statement was drawn up for publication in the Press, declaring their abhorrence of the " wicked and baneful practices " of combination and monopoly. Some help came to them from an unimpeachable quarter. The Society for Bettering the Condition of the Poor had watched the work of Quakers in Spitalfields and elsewhere, and its Committee, meeting in December 1800, with Shute, Bishop of Durham, in the chair, passed unanimously the following resolution :—

" That it appearing to the Society that the labouring classes in this metropolis have derived the greatest benefit, during the severity of the preceding winter, from the personal labours and liberal contribu-

[1] In *John Halifax* the Quaker miller of fiction is guilty of thus holding back corn for a higher price.

tions of the Friends, commonly called Quakers, it is incumbent upon the Society to bear public testimony to these exertions and to express our desire to co-operate with them in their meritorious endeavours to diminish the distresses of their fellow subjects. *Resolved*, that this Resolution, signed by the President, be inserted in the public papers." [1]

Philanthropy, indeed, was the main refuge of the Society in those years of war and unrest. Friends took part in the struggle against slavery, and helped young Lancaster, at that time himself a Quaker, with his plans for national education. From its foundation in 1804 three Friends were on the Committee of the Bible Society ; as the war opened, William Tuke began at York his pioneer work in the treatment of insanity, and before its close Elizabeth Fry was visiting the prisoners in Newgate. None of these movements, except that against slavery, was officially adopted by the Society, which still contained many conservative members who feared that such " creaturely activity " might lead Friends astray ; but the exhortations of the Yearly Epistles throughout the war are in evident harmony with the new conception of social responsibility.

" Cultivate, with unwearied assiduity and patience, all those dispositions which make for peace," urged the Epistle of 1797 : a year later, " let all be careful not to seek or accept profit by any concern in the preparations so extensively making for war : for how reproachfully inconsistent would it be to refuse an active compliance with warlike measures, and at the same time not to hesitate to enrich ourselves by the commerce and other circumstances dependent on war." In 1802 Friends, after the Peace of Amiens, were reminded " that it peculiarly behoves us, as we are well known to have a testimony against those modes of rejoicing, even for peace itself, which are generally attended with profusion and tumult, to evince that we really rejoice at the prosperity of our country, by doing good, according to our ability to all."

In 1804, when war was renewed, the Epistle set out at length the grounds of the Society's stand against war, at the same time uttering a warning against the weakness of individuals. " Friends, it is an awful thing to stand forth to the nation as the advocates

[1] *Vide Life of William Allen*, i. 46–50. Luke Howard, *The Yorkshireman, vide* pp. 28 foll. In 1801 the Friends of Pennsylvania and New Jersey sent a contribution of £5,691 to London Friends to be used for the relief of distress. This was specifically sent in gratitude for the help of English Friends during the War of Independence.

of inviolable peace ; and our testimony loses its efficacy in proportion to the want of consistency in any." " Guard against placing
your dependence on fleets and armies " (this in 1805, the year of
Trafalgar) ; " be peaceable yourselves in words and actions ; and pray
to the Father of the Universe that he would breathe the spirit of
reconciliation into the hearts of His erring and contending creatures."
" The root of our testimony against war " (in 1809) " is no other
than Christian love." Side by side with these testimonies the
Epistles and the Yearly Meeting Records recount the heavy distraints
for the non-payment of " demands for warlike measures," which
in several years amount to two or three thousand pounds (apart
from the much larger claims in respect of tithes) [1] and (especially
in the later years of the war) the imprisonment of young Quakers
who refused to serve in the militia and were without property on
which distress could be levied to procure substitutes. In 1813 young
Joseph Sturge only escaped the imprisonment he was very ready
to endure by the loss of the flock of sheep with which his father
had stocked for him a little farm.[2] The position of Quakers in regard
to service in the militia distinctly worsened during the war as legislation increased in stringency, and the Meeting for Sufferings could
do little but notify the changes as they took place. In June 1793
it circulated among Friends the clauses of the consolidated Militia
Act of 1786 which concerned them, including that which made
the unpropertied Quaker liable to imprisonment, and particularly
warned Friends against paying the militia rate when illegally levied
as part of the poor rate.

In 1795 it petitioned the House of Commons for relief from
the Navy Bill providing that the owners of merchant ships should
provide a certain proportion of sailors to the Royal Navy, since
Friend shipowners could not supply " men for the purposes of war."
This Bill, in conjunction with the dilemma of the armed ship, made
the shipping business one almost impossible for Friends. Pitt, in
November 1796 introduced a Cavalry Act, for the supply both of
horses and riders, which in its original form inflicted the very heavy
fine of £20 per horse in case of non-compliance. In the following
January, however, an amending Act was passed, by which any

---

[1] The Yearly Meeting is more than once concerned to contradict a prevalent
report that the account kept of these " sufferings " was for the purpose of the
Society refunding their losses to individual members.

[2] *Life of Joseph Sturge*, by H. Richard, p. 23.

acknowledged Quaker was fined £1 in lieu of every horse required from him. Some Friends chose this easy way of escape, for the next Yearly Meeting expressed its concern " to find that it is in any degree necessary to declare that the said fine, and all other such fines imposed in lieu of military service, let the application be what it may, cannot be actively complied with by Friends, consistently with our principles." Taxes, imposed by the Central Government, whose application was more general than that of these war rates and fines, were usually paid by Friends, but in 1799 a special war tax was levied under the title of " an Aid and Contribution for the prosecution of the war." Of those Friends affected by it, some refused to pay and submitted to distraint, while others were " uneasy " ; when an income tax was substituted, they felt a relief which was probably not shared by their fellow citizens.[1]

Under the alarm of the projected French invasion the militia in 1802 and 1803 was thoroughly reorganized and enlarged throughout the United Kingdom. The provisions (as reported by a Committee of the Meeting for Sufferings) regarding distraint, imprisonment, and the production of certificates in proof of the genuineness of the Quaker claim, were in substance unaltered, and by sect. 10 Quakers were to be marked as such in the list of men aged from 17 to 55 liable to the militia ballot, which was to be hung upon the church door in each parish. Moreover, by sect. 20, if any Quaker holding a parish office refused to execute the Act, the justices were empowered to appoint a deputy and recover his expenses from the Quaker up to the sum of £10. This was the first English Act which in set terms exempted the Quaker as such from personal military service. In sect. 12 amongst other exceptions, " no person labouring under any infirmity rendering him incapable of military service, nor any person being one of the people called Quakers, nor any medical man practising as such and being a housekeeper, shall be liable to military service under this Act, so long only as they shall respectively continue in any of the descriptions aforesaid." It was probably the fact of this definite recognition (which did not, of course, affect the claim to provide a substitute) that led the Meeting for Sufferings, in sending out printed copies of these clauses, to comment on the lenity shown and to caution Friends " to give great heed that any scruples may be, and appear to be, the consequences of a sense of religious duty." [2]

---

[1] Luke Howard, *The Yorkshireman,* iv. 352.
[2] *Meeting for Sufferings,* 7th mo. 28, 1803.

The Epistles of Yearly Meeting also testify that in many cases the authorities treated the conscientious objector with courtesy and consideration. Nevertheless, it was not an easy time for Friends, and the records frankly state that there were backsliders. Direct payments for war purposes were discountenanced by the general opinion of the Society. In 1796 the Yearly Meeting by minute expressed its censure on " the active compliance of some members with the rate for raising men for the Navy," and directed local Friends to have such cases under their care. In 1810 another warning was given. " It is inconsistent with our known testimony against war for Friends to be in any manner aiding and assisting in the conveyance of soldiers, their baggage, arms, ammunition, and other military stores." Poverty and discontent were everywhere prevalent. Luddites attacked the machinery which, they believed, had robbed them of work, and hungry rioters terrified prosperous citizens into supplying them with food and drink. The Meeting in 1812 found that some Friends had followed their neighbours in securing armed protection for their property, upon which it expressed a " tender concern " that all Friends would trust in the divine protection. " This Meeting further feels itself engaged to caution Friends everywhere against keeping guns or arms of any kind in their houses, or on their premises, or in any manner uniting in armed associations, that so, whatever trials may take place, our Society may not by thus becoming liable to contribute to the destruction of their fellow creatures, violate our peaceable principles ; in the belief of the rectitude and safety of which we feel our minds increasingly confirmed."

The position was that Friends who joined the military forces, who manufactured munitions of war, or who armed their ships were considered to violate the peace testimony of the Society so seriously that if they persisted in their course after due remonstrance, disownment was the inevitable sequel.

Those who paid taxes and fines direct, without waiting for the process of distraint, were deemed to have acted " inconsistently," but disciplinary measures were left to the discretion of each Monthly Meeting. In waiting for a distraint to be levied the Quaker was, as Bicknell had said, " passive, not active " ; often the goods taken were such as he could ill spare and of a greater value than the sum required. The records of a rural Monthly Meeting, that of Thaxted in Essex, during the war contain many such instances. In 1797

George Gibson of Saffron Waldèn, for a Cavalry fine of £1, lost a copper boiler and meat screen worth £1 13s., and Peter Smith of Bardfield, for a Navy rate of 5s. 8d. plus a charge for distraint of 10s. 6d., had coals taken to the value of £2 13s. 9d. On another occasion Joshua Marks Green, also of Saffron Walden, had £20 worth of furniture seized for a militia fine of £12 12s.[1]

Almost every year two or three young Friends were imprisoned on account of the militia, but it was not until Windham in 1808 remodelled the militia, making it a training ground for the regular army, that the numbers became considerable. At the end of 1809 the Meeting for Sufferings made inquiry into the cases of imprisonment for that year. The returns were not quite complete, but according to them eighteen Friends and two non-members connected with the Society had been imprisoned for periods varying from a fortnight to a month, while twenty were exempted at the discretion of the magistrate. Some were " very kindly treated " during their confinement, but others were classed as ordinary offenders. Three from the London district were placed " with felons in Horsemonger Lane," and three in Wakefield gaol were put into prison dress and restricted to prison fare, although on application to the Deputy-Lieutenant this treatment was modified.[2]

After their appeal on behalf of peace at the outbreak of the war the Society took no official action on behalf of international reconciliation until 1812. In 1802, indeed, the Meeting for Sufferings had before it the proposal to address the King upon the Peace of Amiens, but in common with the rest of the nation it realized the instability of that settlement, and did not " feel its way to proceed." Ten years later the Meeting made an earnest appeal to the Regent on behalf of peace. William Allen headed the deputation, and read the address, to which the Prince listened " with marked attention."

" It is now many years " (so ran the chief passage of the address) " since war has been spreading its desolation over great part of the civilized world, and as we believe it to be an evil from which the spirit of the Gospel of Christ would wholly deliver the nations of the earth, we humbly petition thee to use the royal prerogative now placed in thy hands, to take such early measures for the putting a period to this dreadful state of devastation, as we trust the wisdom of thy Councils under divine direction will be enabled to follow."

[1] List of " Sufferings " preserved at Saffron Walden Meeting-house.
[2] *Book of Cases*, iv.

The royal answer, though kindly in tone, was not encouraging, only " a change in the views and conduct of the enemy " could put an end to " the calamities which necessarily attend a state of war." In 1815 peace at last came to exhausted Europe, and though peace alone could not cure the social and political maladies of the several States, yet they were freed from the awful drain of life and resources which had sapped their strength for twenty years. When peace was felt to be secure, the Society of Friends, looking back over the past generation, summarized its experience. The Yearly Meeting, in the Epistle for 1819, wrote : " The continuance of the blessing of peace to this nation has warmed our hearts with gratitude. Our refusal to bear arms is not only a testimony against the violence and cruelty of war, but against a confidence in what is emphatically termed in Scripture the ' arm of flesh ' ; it is a testimony to the meekness and gentleness of Christ, and a resignation to suffer, in reliance on the power, the goodness and the protection of the Almighty." The passage was probably written not so much in allusion to the minor hardships of English Friends, but in remembrance of the providence which had watched over the members of the Society in Ireland.

English Friends during the war might suffer from unpopularity and even occasionally from harsh treatment, but their principles were not put to the test of actual war   In some parts of Ireland they were exposed to all the terrors of the Rebellion of 1798, and came through confirmed in their belief that faith in God manifested by a peaceful life and good-will towards men was a surer protection than any armed force.[1] The narratives of Quaker experience during the rebellion present many curious parallels to those of the struggle a hundred years earlier, although the hostilities of 1798 covered only a few weeks and a comparatively small area. Although through the exertions of Grattan's party some of the rights of citizens had

---

[1] The earliest printed account is that of Dr. Hancock, *Principles of Peace exemplified in the Conduct of the Society of Friends in Ireland during the Rebellion of* 1798 (1825). This was compiled from manuscript narratives, but the names of the narrators were omitted to avoid stirring up ill feeling. The story of a single family is given with great vividness in *Divine Protection through Extraordinary Dangers Experienced by Jacob and Elizabeth Goff and their family through the Irish Rebellion in* 1798, by Dinah W. Goff, 1857. One of Hancock's sources, the narrative of Joseph Haughton of Ferns, has been reprinted in full by A. M. Hodgkin in a little pamphlet, *Friends in Ireland*, published by the Friends' Tract Association. The accounts are summarized by Rufus Jones, *Later Periods of Quakerism*, pp. 161-4.

been granted to the Catholics, yet poverty, high rents, and the oppression of tithes all fostered discontent, and formed a fertile soil in which French plots could germinate. The abortive French expedition to Ireland in 1796 gave an opportunity for the Government to put into force stern measures of repression. In 1797 Ulster was almost in revolt, martial law was proclaimed through the province, and, while the malcontents plundered private houses for weapons, the soldiers in their search for arms resorted to outrage and torture. " The troops," writes a modern historian, " were little better than bandits." The trouble in Ulster was largely economic, but farther south it assumed the character of a Catholic movement. In Wexford especially the rebellion, when it actually broke out, had all the characteristic ferocity of a religious war. The steps taken in Ulster had been effective, and, with the exception of outbreaks in Antrim and Down, the province remained sullenly quiet ; even in Leinster, which was the main seat of war, the rebellion which began in May was crushed, as far as regular hostilities were concerned, in July, though guerilla bands harassed the countryside for some months. Friends took their own course in the troubled times before the rebellion, when both parties were trying to requisition all weapons. In 1795 and 1796 the Quarterly and Monthly Meetings throughout Ireland recommended that all Friends who had sporting guns in their houses should destroy them, " to prevent " (as the Yearly Meeting said in confirming the recommendation) " their being made use of to the destruction of any of our fellow creatures, and more fully and clearly to support our peaceable and Christian testimony in these perilous times."

The Monthly Meetings appointed Committees to visit Friends in order to urge them to carry the suggestion. Joseph Haughton of Ferns, in his narrative of the rebellion, relates that he was one of the Committee for Wexford Monthly Meeting, and that, by way of first " cleansing his own hands," he broke his own fowling-piece in the street outside his door. On his visits he found that the majority of Friends had already destroyed their guns or were prepared to do so. " There were a few who would not be prevailed upon to make this sacrifice, but the conduct of most of them in other respects was such as to occasion disownment. A short time after this, when the Government ordered all arms to be given up to the magistrates, it was a comfortable reflection and circumstance that in a general way Friends were found clear of having any such things in their possession."[1]   When the magistrates visited Haughton's house for this purpose he was absent from home, but they remonstrated with his wife "on the supposed impropriety of having destroyed my gun instead of delivering it up to the Loyalists for the purpose of defending the Loyalists against the fomenters and plotters of rebellion and for the preservation of myself and family." In fact, Friends, though generally on good terms with their neighbours on both sides, were suspect both by the Government authorities and the leaders of the rebellion.   As they were known to abhor all plots and outrages and to profess loyalty to the throne, they were accused of cowardly shelter behind those who were willing to fight for the established Government.   On the other hand, many of the Irish Catholics were infuriated by their steady and open attendance at religious worship, which they maintained in spite of all threats of vengeance and attempts at forced conversion.

Irish Friends, as a body, seem to have been more horrified by the rebellion than by the centuries-old wrong and oppression which evoked it, though they faithfully recorded the atrocious and organized cruelty of the loyalist troops as well as the barbarity of the rebel Irish.   The narratives from different parts of the country are much the same in general outline—weeks of sickening uncertainty and disorder, towns held first by one side and then by the other, indiscriminate plunder by both, and murder and massacre as a daily event.   Yet in the midst of these horrors the Quaker households were wonderfully preserved.   They suffered in loss of property and personal possessions, but comparatively little from actual violence, and, in spite of many threats, it was believed that no Quaker house was burnt or otherwise destroyed.   So remarkable was their immunity, that Joseph Haughton noted that, after the rebellion, "strangers passing the houses of Friends and seeing them preserved with ruins on either hand, would frequently, without knowledge of the district, say they were Quaker houses."   These houses were filled with refugees and wounded men, Protestant and Catholic, often with those of both parties at one time, and no threat from either side could induce a Quaker householder to withdraw his protection from these unfortunates.   Abraham Shackleton of Ballitore

[1] John M. Douglas, an Irish Friend, who has studied the MS. records of Friends' experiences, informs me that "Some thirty or forty members were disowned for refusing to destroy their weapons.   Friends were not unanimous on passive resistance.   Some retained their weapons and were not disowned. Others obeyed out of loyalty to the Society."

in Kildare, grandson and successor of Burke's old schoolmaster, gave both his house and school as a refuge, and when a body of Protestant Militia tried to drag him with them to battle the women he sheltered pleaded for him.[1]

Joseph Haughton protected the Protestant servants of the Bishop of Ferns, gaining from him a letter of heartfelt thanks, while some of the United Irishmen and their families also quartered themselves in the house when the town was taken by the loyalists, "*supposing they would be more safe than in their own homes.*"

One Friend, who was living in West Meath, wrote afterwards of the rebel occupation : "All those in this quarter who professed principles of peace were marvellously spared from extreme suffering. . . . Through Divine aid, and that alone, was I enabled to refuse to take up arms, or to take their oaths, or join them, assigning as a reason that I could not fight nor swear *for* or *against* them. They threatened, they pondered, they debated, marvelled, and ultimately liberated me." Another Friend in County Kildare refused to give the rebels green cloth for their badges, telling them, "We could not join any party." "What," they asked ingenuously, "not the strongest ? " In this place, when the soldiers regained possession, the priest tried to disguise himself in Quaker dress, while at Enniscorthy a Protestant clergyman made the same attempt. At Antrim, on the capture of the town by the Loyalists, the soldiers began an indiscriminate massacre and sack, but the few Friends living there were spared.[2]

Joseph Haughton went through several testing times. Before the rebellion the Earl of Mount Nories demanded his store room as a guard house. Haughton felt that to plead its use as a store was "a mean reason" for refusal. "But considering this an opportunity afforded me to lift up the standard of peace and bearing my testimony against war . . . told him . . . that the purpose he wished it for was such as I could not unite with, having conscientious scruple against war and everything connected with it. He grew very angry and desired the soldiers to afford me no protection in case disturbance arose ; to which I replied I hoped I would not trust to or apply for military protection." Just before the rebellion broke out, some

---

[1] Shackleton and two other Friends—William Leadbeater and John Bewley—later mediated, between a detachment of the rebels and the loyalists, but the negotiations broke down over the choice of hostages.

[2] Hancock, *Principles of Peace*, pp. 113 foll.

suspects were arrested for not delivering up their arms. The soldiers determined to hang some and to apply the torture of pitch caps to others. Haughton's shop contained ropes and linen, and he feared that under martial law a refusal to sell might endanger him, while he was determined not to help in the torment and execution of his fellow creatures. When the military applied to him, he refused, whereupon they forcibly requisitioned the goods, offering him money, which he refused to take. This refusal, Haughton adds, became known to the rebels, and was a source of protection to himself and his family when that party occupied Ferns.

Dinah Goff was a child of fourteen at the time of the rebellion, the youngest of the family of a well-to-do Quaker landowner, settled on the estate of Horetown, in Wexford. For nearly a month they were surrounded by rebel encampments, and hundreds came daily to demand food and drink. Her vivid narrative tells how the maid-servants were at times up all night baking bread, which the rebels would carry off on the ends of their pikes. They tried to requisition the family carving-knives for weapons, but Mrs. Goff, whose courage never flagged, interposed and saw that they were " carefully locked up after meals." The daughters of the house were kept busy handing out the food demanded by these mobs, and, in return, the rebels at times entertained them by details of the cruelties they had committed. Once, after a particularly horrible description, little Dinah " could not refrain from bursting into tears, throwing down what I had in my hand, and running away into the house." The Goffs sheltered a dozen refugees of both parties, so that the mother's task was no light one. Two Roman Catholic men-servants were forced by the rebels to join them as pikemen. " On my dear mother hearing of their having these weapons, she sent to let them know she would not allow anything of the kind to be brought into the house ; so each night they left them outside the door. They behaved quietly and respectfully throughout, generally returning home at the close of the day." There can seldom have been a more incongruous picture than the bloodstained pikes leaning against the Quaker doorpost. Not far from Horetown was the dreadful barn of Scullabogue, in which on June 4th the rebels burnt alive 180 prisoners, men, women, and children. The smoke of the burning was seen from the house. Jacob Goff himself and the whole family were more than once threatened with instant death, though the mob were always restrained from actual violence. There was a general belief in Wexford, in which Friends shared, that a certain date had been fixed for a massacre of the Protestants, and that only the success of the Loyalist troops prevented the plan from being carried into effect.

Notwithstanding all these dangers and alarms, the elder daughters regularly walked to the First-day Meeting at Forrest, and were never molested. The father and mother were unable to go with them, as the family horses had been requisitioned. For the same cause, they could not attend Leinster Quarterly Meeting, held " in usual course " at Enniscorthy, two days after a battle had raged in the town. Some Friends who drove thither had to alight and clear the way for their horses by removing the corpses that lay about the streets.[1] It is easy to believe the report by the few Friends present, that the meeting was a solemn and heart-stirring occasion. Another family of Goffs, cousins of those of Horetown, were threatened by the rebels that unless they ceased to attend meeting and became Roman Catholics, they should be murdered and their house burnt down. The parents called their children together, and, after solemn prayer, laid the matter before them. The eldest son, a boy of seventeen, was spokesman, replying, " Father, rejoice that we are found worthy to suffer." They continued to attend the meeting, but the threats were never put into execution. Other Friends were carried off by the rebels to their camps at Vinegar Hill and elsewhere. There forced conversions were attempted, and sometimes they underwent mock trials, but in the end all were sent home unhurt, while their Protestant neighbours were murdered without mercy. Two young men, brothers of the name of Jones, who had some connection with the Society, were told, when they refused to conform to Catholicism, that if they could prove they were Quakers their lives would be spared. But they refused also to make this false claim, and died with great courage. At last, news came that English and Hessian troops had landed, and the Protestants awaited deliverance from one set of oppressors, with an apprehension too well justified, that they might also suffer from their helpers. On the 20th of June a battle was fought for some hours at Goff's Bridge, close to Horetown ; the house was in the line of fire and cannon-balls fell thickly around it. The rebels were routed, and, as they fled, some turned to the Goffs to have their wounds dressed. Then the victors arrived, heralded by two cavalry officers. As Jacob Goff came out to meet them, one, a German, alighted and

[1] *Journal of David Sands.*

embraced him, saying in broken English, " You be Friend—no enemy—no enemy. We have Friends in Germany." The troops bivouacked on the lawn that night. Next morning some thirty officers breakfasted with the family, " and said that we had had a marvellous escape the previous day ; the cannon having been placed on the bridge and pointed against the house to batter it down.— even the match was lighted—when a gentleman who knew my father came forward, and told them the house was inhabited by a loyal Quaker and his family. They had previously supposed it to be a rendezvous of rebels." The soldiers soon moved away from Horetown on their task of mercilessly extirpating the rebellion. After all open rebellion had been suppressed, vagrant hordes took refuge in the woods, coming out by night to plunder. Twice they visited Horetown, where they proved more terrifying than the earlier bands. On the first visit, Dinah Goff was awakened by a noise to find her father in the grasp of armed men. As the little girl looked on, they put a pistol to his head. " Seeing his situation, I threw myself on my knees on the floor, and clung with my arms round him, when the ruffians pushed me away, saying, ' You'll be killed if you stop there.' But my father drew me towards him more closely, saying, ' She would rather be hurt, if I am.' They snapped the pistol several times, which was perhaps not charged, as it did not go off." The robbers came a second time, and, after plundering the house, dragged him out of doors, asking if he had anything to say, as his last hour was come. " He said, he prayed that the Almighty might be merciful to him, and be pleased to forgive him his trespasses and sins, and also to forgive them, as he did sincerely. They said that was a good wish, and inquired if he had anything more to say. He requested them to be tender towards his wife and children ; on which they said, ' Good-night, Mr. Goff, we only wanted to rattle the mocuses out of you '—meaning guineas." The Goffs were convinced that these terrifying threats were in fact only an attempt to extract money, of which the household had by this time little enough, but there is no wonder that Jacob Goff returned home when the robbers left him, " pale and exhausted," saying he could not hold out much longer. He died in December 1798, worn out by these trials, although his gallant wife survived him for nearly twenty years.

Mary Leadbeater of Ballitore, sister of Abraham Shackleton, lived on terms of intimacy and understanding with her Irish Catholic neighbours, both rich and poor. Her *Cottage Dialogues* have been praised by high authority as a vivid picture of the Irish peasant. She passed through all the horrors which rebellion and coercion inflicted on her unhappy village with an impartial indignation at the cruelties of both sides.[1] In the searches for arms which preceded the rebellion she had seen her village friends whipped savagely to extract information about the hiding-places of the rebel pikes. " The torture," she commented, " was excessive, and the victims were long in recovering ; and in almost every case it was applied fruitlessly." When the rebels gained power, there were cruel murders in the village and the district.[2] The few Quaker families were unscathed, but the terrible scenes through which they passed left their impress on Mary Leadbeater's nerves : " For many days afterwards I thought my food tasted of blood and at night I was frequently awakened by my feelings of horror."

The speedy triumph of the Loyalist troops brought a new series of atrocities. At Carlow, near by, a row of cabins to which the insurgents had fled, was fired by the troops, and all the inmates perished—the Protestant counterpart of the barn of Scullabogue. After Shackleton's vain attempt at mediation the rebels fled from Ballitore, while the troops who occupied the village took vengeance on the peaceable inhabitants. Houses were plundered and burnt. That of the Shackletons escaped destruction, but soldiers burst into it demanding food and calling the mistress names, " which " (she says) " I had never heard before. They said I had poisoned the milk which I gave them and desired me to drink some, which I did with much indignation." At the same time her neighbours' houses went up in flames, and she was forced to listen to disgusting boasts of the cruelties committed on the rebels. No wonder that in her account of the scene, she declared that she had never been able to retain a coherent picture of those dreadful hours. Later, as the troops withdrew, she saw a soldier flogged for killing a pig. " Oh, how shocking that seemed to be ! Commanded to take the precious human life—punished for taking that of a brute ! " When the immediate danger was over, Mary Leadbeater exerted herself on behalf of her humble neighbours arrested on suspicion as rebels.

[1] The story is told in her autobiography, *Annals of Ballitore*, pp. 221 foll.

[2] Mary Leadbeater says emphatically that the rebels in their neighbourhood spared women and children and " Quakers in general," but (she adds) " woe to the oppressor of the poor, the hard landlord, the severe master, or him who was looked upon as an enemy."

For one prisoner she wrote to the officers of the court-martial. The Court saw that the letter was from a woman, and " women did not care what they said." But the Friendly date caught the eye of someone ; it was from a Quaker, and " Quakers tell the truth." Mrs. Leadbeater's plea was admitted and the suspect was set free. As at Horetown, for months after the rebellion, Ballitore was harassed by robber bands, who produced as much terror by their night raids as had been caused by the contending forces.

Dublin Yearly Meeting in 1801 sent an account of the events of the rebellion as they affected Friends, to its sister assembly in Philadelphia. In this the statement was made that amidst all the massacre and violence of the time only one member of the Society lost his life. From other sources it appears that he was a youth of twenty from the neighbourhood of Rathangan in Kildare, who was panic-stricken by the approaching danger. He urged his friends and family to take shelter with him in Rathangan, the nearest garrison town, and on their refusal he fled thither himself. He joined the local defence corps as a dispatch rider. Later, the town was stormed by rebels, who found him armed with others defending a house, and promptly shot him.[1] One or two other Friends who took up arms were disowned by their Meetings.

The Irish Government offered some compensation to those loyalists who had incurred heavy loss during the rebellion. A portion of this was offered to Jacob Goff and other Friends, but, as they had neither aided the army nor asked for its protection, they felt it would be inconsistent to accept the grant. Offers of help came from the Yearly Meetings of London and Philadelphia, the latter impelled by the remembrance of the " generous relief " sent by Irish Friends in the American War. Dublin Yearly Meeting, in returning grateful thanks, said that there was no need for such assistance. The Monthly Meetings raised nearly £4,000 to assist Friends rendered actually destitute, and the relief was administered by a committee appointed by the Yearly Meeting. The actual losses of these Friends were in money value £7,000, but it was found that the expenditure of £2,218 would set them on their feet again. In 1800 the surplus of the subscription was returned to the Monthly Meetings. Friends who had suffered loss, but still were able to support themselves and their families, neither asked for nor received any restitution.

[1] The house belonged to another Friend, who was dealt with by his Monthly Meeting for permitting it to be put to such a use.

CHAPTER IX

SOME DISOWNMENTS

1774–1815

FROM the earliest times, even when there was no recognized test of membership, Friends had exercised the power of disownment, against those who "walked disorderly." After the Monmouth Rebellion it was used against those West Country Friends who had taken any active part in the rebellion. But the process was both less summary in execution and less penal in result than some historians outside the Society have imagined. The disowned person was no longer considered a member of the Society ; he could take no part in its business, and was thus excluded from meetings for discipline ; if poor he had no claim upon its charitable funds, and the machinery of the Society would not be put in motion to rescue him from any legal difficulty. But there was no check on his attendance at meetings for worship. There were not a few disowned Friends both in England and America who constantly shared in this spiritual communion, First Day by First Day, and who at death were laid in a Friends' burial ground, where their dust now peacefully mingles with that of their judges. In many other cases, of course, the delinquent had shown by habitual absence from meeting, or by laxity of conduct, that he was no longer in sympathy with Friends, and in such instances the severance was complete. But Friends, as a rule, were not disowned until the matter had been long in the care first of the overseers, who only brought it under the notice of the Monthly Meeting when their private exhortations had produced no effect, then of the Monthly Meeting, sometimes for a period of years, and until they had been often visited and "dealt with" by a small delegation of members of the meeting, whose endeavours to reclaim the erring were patient and protracted.[1] In a small meeting the

[1] This statement does not apply to some of the American meetings in the Revolutionary War. By them enlistment in either army or any overt assistance in the conduct of the war was taken as good ground for immediate dissociation.

scandal and discomfort created by the expulsion of a well-known Friend were particularly felt, and at times the larger body of the Quarterly Meeting had to intervene to help the Monthly Meeting in its task. The final minute of disownment almost invariably contained a wish that the ex-Friend might be convinced of error and return to fellowship with the Society—a wish that was sometimes fulfilled. The general history of disownment among Friends does not concern us here. There is no doubt that in its zeal for consistency the Society at times deprived itself of valued and spiritually minded members. But even where the stated grounds of disownment seem inadequate, it is generally true that the Friend had drifted away from his old associates. It is impossible to form any idea of the total number of disownments in the eighteenth century, nor of all the causes which led to them.[1] They lie hidden in the records of the many Monthly Meetings throughout the country, and a careful study of each minute book would be necessary to discover the delinquencies which Friends themselves showed no desire to publish further. The disowned person had the right of appeal to the Quarterly and thence to the Yearly Meeting, but it was seldom exercised. When there was an appeal it was heard in private by a small committee, which reported its decision to the Quarterly or Yearly Meeting ; and this bare fact is alone entered on the minutes. There is no collected record of disownments ; and the Quarterly Meeting answers to the queries are the only guide as to the districts in which from time to time trouble arose over any point of the discipline. Thus, as no full history of disownments for breaches of the peace testimony can be given, it has seemed best to select the story of one Monthly Meeting in North Yorkshire as typical of the difficulties which might beset a whole Quaker community, and the story of an individual disownment in Birmingham by which the Society lost the adherence of a family of keen intellectual vigour.

The repeated warnings by the Yearly Meeting against any concern in armed ships show that the trials of Quaker shipowners and captains did not diminish in the eighteenth century. It was in those days little part of the duty of the fleet to defend the country's trade against the enemy. Merchantmen had to trust to themselves,

---

[1] " Marriage by a priest," that is, to a non-Friend, was probably that most frequently alleged. This disastrous policy, not amended till the middle of the nineteenth century, led to the severance of many young Friends from the Society.

and it was customary to carry at least sufficient armament to put up a fight against an ordinary privateer. It was seldom possible to man a Quaker vessel with a Quaker crew, and in war-time the unregenerate seaman often refused to sail on a defenceless ship. It was this difficulty, rather than personal fear, which led to most of the delinquencies recorded in the sea-board meetings. Durham, Yorkshire, Suffolk, Kent, Devon, Cornwall, and Bristol, all at various times suffered from this backsliding. It is the history of Whitby and Scarborough Monthly Meeting which is outlined here.[1] In the eighteenth century Whitby was a busy and prosperous port, even before the Greenland whale fishery brought it fifty years of wealth. Whitby men were hardy sailors, who not only carried on the profitable coasting trade to London, but crossed distant seas to strange lands. Captain Cook was a Whitby 'prentice, and his first voyage to the South Seas was made in a Whitby-built ship. The War of the Spanish Succession brought temptation to Whitby Friends, for in March 1713/14 the Monthly Meeting records that while it " did formerly make a minute showing their dissatisfaction that some of our friends carried guns in their ships, which thing is contrary to the principle of truth, and advised them from time to time to put them away," now, in time of peace, by the advice of the Quarterly Meeting and " the sense and desire " of this Monthly Meeting, these friends are still to be " laboured with " until they give forth a " testimony " against that practice. In conformity with this minute Joseph Linskill, a leading shipowner, and one of the seventeen Friends who signed this minute, published his own testimony.

" Whereas I have made profession and am in communion with those people who are in scorn called Quakers, whose principle and practice has been and is against all fighting with carnal weapons ; but forasmuch as I have been prevailed on by the enemy of my soul, and my own reasonings for self-preservation, to carry guns in the time of war, which did belong to a ship when I bought her and also in heat and passion did make use of them in order to defend myself with the arm of flesh, the which, when I considered it in coolness of mind, it became a great exercise, and having seen the evil consequences thereof, and in some measure tasted of the judgments of God . . . I find it my place voluntarily, for the clearing

---

[1] I have to thank J. T. Sewell of Whitby, and Allan Rowntree of Scarborough, for supplying extracts from records and other information.

our holy profession and all faithful professors thereof, to condemn
that spirit which led me, and myself for being drawn into such actions,
to wit, using guns for defence, which I am fully satisfied is contrary
to the principles of truth. And therefore I do in great humility
treat and warn all those of our profession who have been guilty
of the same transgression, that if such as the late times for use of guns
should happen again, that they take care never more to be entangled
in that deadly snare, but trust in the Lord, the great Jehovah, in
whom is everlasting strength, to defend and preserve us all if we
abide faithful."

" Times for use of guns " were not to recur until, against
Walpole's desire, a new war with Spain broke out in 1739. In
1742 the Yearly Meeting introduced the query on bearing arms
and, at the instance of Bristol, followed it up in 1744 by the strong
caution already quoted.[1] This roused the conscience of Yorkshire
Quarterly Meeting which admitted delinquencies in 1745, reported
in 1747 " some seafaring persons notwithstanding they have been
advised against it continue to carry guns on their ships," and in 1748
found this still the case in " one Monthly Meeting." The matter
dropped for a few years, but in 1756 the Quarterly Meeting reported
that it had advised the Monthly Meeting " closely to admonish
such to act more conformably to our profession." The advice is
found in the Whitby and Scarborough minute books under the
month of April

" Finding by your answers to the Yearly Meeting queries
that some masters of ships professing with us in their voyages do
carry arms for their defence contrary to our professed principles
and that Christian frame of mind that the followers of Christ have
walked in : therefore in the love of Truth we tenderly advise that
such Friends be laboured with in a spirit of love to desist from such
practices and put their trust in that arm of power that is able to
preserve beyond any contrivance of man—and we desire they would
weightily consider the distress of mind they bring upon their brethren
on account of the inconsistency that appears amongst us, as many
cannot for conscience' sake take up arms."

The Monthly Meeting, however, appears to have shelved this
letter, for the next Quarterly Meeting sent down a request that it
might be given to the " Masters and Chief Owners of ships," which
Scarborough reports has been done for all " that are at home " by

[1] Chapter VII, pp. 187-8.

October 1756 and Whitby in the following November. But in 1757 Yorkshire could report no reform, and the Yearly Meeting Epistle reiterated its advice. In 1758 Yorkshire Quarterly Meeting explained in reply to the query that the "seafaring people" who carry guns, do so "without letters of Marque or being concerned in privateering. They have been visited in behalf of the meeting of several Friends, whose advice and labour with them was well received." In 1760 both Lancashire and Yorkshire confessed the same fault, although it appears from the Whitby and Scarborough minute books that the Quarterly Meeting had again in April sent down advice against the practice.

The Yearly Meeting was sufficiently moved to send down a "Written Epistle" to the subordinate meetings. This form of communicating advice or reproof was frequently adopted in the discussion of serious and confidential matters of discipline, since the printed Epistle had a wide general circulation. The Peace of Paris brought the scandal to an end for the time, but it sprang up again at the outbreak of the American War. In 1777 Yorkshire reported to the Yearly Meeting that "some owners of ships arm them in order to their being employed in the Government service." The Yearly Meeting's recommendation that "the minutes of the Meeting under the head of Fighting in 1693, 1730, and 1740 be read in the several Quarterly and Monthly Meetings and duly observed," was followed by visits to all the Quarterly Meetings by representatives from the Yearly Meeting. Those to Yorkshire reported that "two Monthly Meetings [1] are concerned in armed vessels, but our expectation is that the cause of complaint would be removed as speedily as possible." But in 1779 a further declension appeared, when Yorkshire Quarterly Meeting was "concerned to find that some of our seafaring Friends not only carry guns on board their ships, but that some particulars are concerned in ships that have taken out letters of Marque, which afflicting case came weightily under the consideration of this Meeting, and some Friends are appointed to join the Friends there in visiting the parties and laying before them the great inconsistency of their conduct with our peaceable and benevolent principles." In April 1780 these Friends were appointed (we find from Whitby and Scarborough minute books) to meet with Friends of the Monthly Meeting at Whitby, and in November the case

---

[1] *Sic*, there were two "Particular" Meetings, i.e. Whitby and Scarborough; but possibly Hull Friends were also involved.

came up of " a Friend whose vessel carried letters of Marque and was let for a considerable time to the East India Company." This probably is the case in regard to which Yorkshire informed the Yearly Meeting of 1781 that " some steps have been taken, the other cases but very lately known. There are many others concerned, as owners of ships and shares of ships armed for defence, and divers employed as masters and mates of such vessels, to most of whom divers visits have been paid, by appointment of this Meeting and the whole is closely under our care. We request this sorrowful defection may also come closely under the consideration of the Yearly Meeting." The Epistle responded by a reference to the advices of 1757. During this year the Quarterly Meeting did take, and inspire the Monthly Meeting to take, severe action. In February the Monthly Meeting received a report from the Quarterly Meeting Committee on the matter which gave a list of Friends concerned in armed vessels, of whom " we have not sufficient grounds of hope that an alteration of conduct in these respects is likely at present to take place with any of them." The names of fourteen Whitby Friends are given, including John Walker, to whom Captain Cook had been once apprenticed. Abel Chapman, of another well-known local family, was concerned in letters of Marque. In August, at a joint meeting of the Monthly Meeting and the Quarterly Meeting Committee, Thomas Scarth was disowned for sailing under letters of Marque, and Abel Chapman's subscription was not to be received until he had disposed of his vessel. In September, Samuel Clemesha and T. Henderson, both of Scarborough, reported that they have disposed of their shares in armed vessels. It is a sign of the widespread nature of the defection that Samuel Clemesha was actually at the time Clerk to the meeting. Abel Chapman was ultimately disowned. In July 1782 a recommendation came down from the Quarterly Meeting that fifteen Scarborough and Whitby Friends (mentioned by name) who owned armed vessels should be debarred from acting in meetings for discipline, and that their subscriptions should not be received. In August and September the collections recorded in the minutes average about £1 10s. from each meeting, whereas for many years previously the amounts (sometimes taken each month, sometimes less frequently) were about £2 from Scarborough and £4 or £5 from Whitby—at that time a larger and more wealthy meeting. In April 1783 one Friend, a sea-captain, made acknowledgment of his fault :—

"Under a due sense of my own weakness in suffering myself to command where guns were carried for defence, I am now convinced I was wrong and am in hopes that Friends will overlook my weakness." In June the remaining fourteen Friends (thirteen from Whitby and Sarah Gott, a woman shipowner, of Scarborough) were disowned for "arming their vessels in defence of their property although acknowledgment was made that the practice could not be defended from the doctrine of the New Testament." It is interesting to see that the Friends who had "dealt" for six years with their erring brethren in the end based their disownment, not upon the scandal brought to the Society or upon any breach of "ancient testimony," but upon their disobedience to the teachings of Christianity. A strong minority, however, especially in Whitby, where the declension had been greatest, sympathized with the disowned members. One Friend who got access to the minute book relieved himself by the childish device of crossing out the word "not" from the foregoing minute. Possibly he was Samuel Clemesha, who was deposed from the office of Elder, "having during the sittings of the Monthly Meeting misrepresented the conduct of our last." In Whitby, John Routh, the chief schoolmaster of the town, and Clerk of the Preparative Meeting, refused to deal with the notices of his friends' disownments, and returned them to the Monthly Meeting in August unread. This Meeting, which was held at Scarborough, found "that the Preparative Meeting of Whitby is not likely at present to be held select," under which circumstances it resolved not to accept any Whitby Friends as duly appointed representatives to the Monthly Meeting, while welcoming individuals who cared to attend. The difficulty, as reported to the Monthly meeting in October, was that Whitby Friends took the line of ignoring the disownments, and carried on the business of the meeting with the disowned members. Friends were appointed to visit the meeting with the aim of restoring due church order, but it was not until December 1784 that the Monthly Meeting again assembled at Whitby. A few Friends, women for the most part, admitted their fault and applied again for membership during the years immediately following the disownment. They were welcomed back, but the Whitby Meeting, having refused to accept the disownments, now refused to read the new minutes of membership, and after some remonstrance the Monthly Meeting yielded the point. Even in 1786 Thomas Smailes was withholding his usual subscription for the services of the Society, on account of the recent disownments, but eventually he " complied with the advice of Friends." In the following year two or three of the disowned Friends gave a curious proof that they no longer considered themselves members of the Society. In 1778 English Friends had raised large sums for the relief of their brethren in Pennsylvania who had suffered from the war (and who, incidentally, were also faced with the same problem of disownment). The Monthly Meeting had contributed nearly £250, of which Whitby's share was £204. More was subscribed than was required to meet the necessities of the American Friends, and when the accounts were closed in 1787 four or five of the disowned Whitby members, who had learned this fact from the report of the committee of the fund, applied to the Monthly Meeting " to have their share of the unexpended balance returned to them," which was apparently done.

One result of this period of disownment was a change in the area of the Monthly Meeting. Scarborough and Whitby Friends had become too small a body, and they were reinforced by the adjoining inland meetings of Pickering, Kirby Moorside, and Thornton-le-dale, the first-named of which gave its title to the new Monthly Meeting. It was as Pickering Monthly Meeting that Friends of the district passed through the long years of the French War. Traditions live long in the neighbourhood, and an impression still prevails that it was during this war that disownments for armed ships were most frequent, but this is not borne out by the records, which show only six or seven disownments for breaches of peace testimony. A considerable number are for " immorality " or " drinking to excess." In those days the wide moors cut off this little corner of Yorkshire from many civilizing influences, and these delinquents had no doubt found much opportunity of stumbling in the society which surrounded them. Of the disownments for war activities, some are for being " concerned as owners of vessels armed, and let out to Government to assist in carrying forward war," others are against those who, after being pressed for the Navy, continued to serve voluntarily, " thereby laying waste our ancient Christian testimony," and there is a single case of a Friend who became " a volunteer soldier." Further north, on the confines of Durham and Yorkshire, the Quakers of Shields were faced with the same problem. There, too, some shipowners armed their vessels, and in consequence, after remonstrance and " dealing," lost their membership in the Society.

Perhaps the best-known instance of disownment from the Society in the eighteenth century is that of Samuel Galton of Birmingham for his concern in the manufacture of guns. It is interesting, not only from the position of the disowned Friend, a leading citizen of Birmingham, grandfather of Francis Galton, the eugenist, but also from the influence exercised by the Yearly Meeting upon the Monthly Meeting of Birmingham in its dealings with the delinquent.

In the first half of the eighteenth century Joseph Farmer, a " convinced " Friend, carried on the business of a gunsmith at Birmingham ; on his death it was continued by his son James, and when in 1746 Mary Farmer became the wife of Samuel Galton of Bristol, the two brothers-in-law entered into partnership, and the firm of Farmer & Galton set up a large gun factory in Steel-house Lane, which carried out important Government contracts. " But the business had much wider ramifications ; there were large transactions in Lisbon, and on one occasion £54,000 of slaves were handled in America."[1] In the year 1790 the business was in the hands of the two Samuel Galtons, father and son. In that year the Yearly Meeting, alarmed by the war upon the Continent, sent a " Written Epistle," in addition to that usually printed, to the Monthly and Quarterly Meetings in comment on their answers to the queries. One passage runs as follows :—

" Some of the accounts are not quite clear, and as the ambition of nations is ever now slaughtering its thousands, let none amongst us, whose principle is peace, be employed to prepare the means. We have been publicly charged with some under our name fabricating or selling instruments of war. We desire an inquiry may be made, and if any be found in a practice so inconsistent, *that they be treated with love, but if by this unreclaimed, that they be further dealt with as those whom we cannot own.*" This recommendation, of which the italicized portion was taken from an actual minute of Yearly Meeting, was not adopted by the Birmingham Monthly Meeting. The first distinct objection raised to the position of the Galtons was in 1792, when a collection was made towards the enlargement of the Bull Street Meeting-house. Joseph Robinson, a local Friend, then wrote to one of the committee, Joseph Gibbons,

---

[1] Karl Pearson, *Life, Letters, and Labours of Francis Galton*, p. 32.

in protest against the receipt of Samuel Galton's contribution. "So many eyes are opened to scrutinize into the several branches of the African trade, the minutest of which are likely to be weighed and exposed. The supplying of the merchants trading to the coast of Guinea with an article likely to be very hurtful to them (the natives), for I cannot think they are only made a bauble of and hung up in their houses for ornament, and if applied to birding, being so slightly proved, are a kind of snare to them, but the worst of it is many of them are used in their wars with each other, I firmly believe. And for us to receive part of the thousands that have probably been accumulated by a forty years' commerce in these articles and apply it to the use of Friends, is, I think, a matter that requires your very serious consideration."[1]

The grammatical construction of Joseph Robinson's sentence leaves much to be desired, but it is clear that he made three objections to the Galton's trade, these being its close connection with the slave trade, the poor quality of the guns, and their use in native wars. It seems doubtful whether Friends in general were aware of the Galtons' work for the Government. Still the Monthly Meeting took no official action. C. D. Sturge, in the *Notes* just quoted, mentioned a tradition that "the meeting did not actually take the case upon its minutes" until Bristol Half-Yearly Meeting refused to receive Samuel Galton as a representative. There is, however, no trace of this refusal. The Half-Year Meeting was a committee of Somertsetshire Friends for the management of charitable funds, but Galton, originally a Bristol man, may have had some connection with it. In any case the first minute (4th mo. 18, 1795) of the Monthly Meeting shows clearly that the matter had been already under discussion. "Mention having been made at this and some former sittings respecting the case of Samuel Galton and Samuel Galton, Junior, members of this Meeting, who are in the practice of fabricating and selling instruments of war, concerning which divers opportunities have been had with the parties by several Friends under the direction of the overseers and others, to some satisfaction," the meeting appoints three Friends to continue the visitation. This year the Yearly Meeting sent down a further written Epistle to the Quarterly Meeting expressing sorrow that in some places the testimony against war "is violated in divers ways

---

[1] C. D. Sturge, *Notes on Birmingham Friends*, preserved in Bevan-Naish Library, Bull Street. *Vide also*, Hicks, *Quakeriana*, No. 5, July 1894.

and sometimes for the sake of gain. We therefore desire you will be vigilant in your oversight over such of the family who may fall into these inconsistencies." The Monthly Meeting continued its care, which can be traced through the minutes of 1795.

In July " it is in degree satisfactory to this Meeting to find that Samuel Galton, the elder, has relinquished the business and declined receiving any further emolument from it. The minute as far as respects his case is therefore discontinued," but the Friends appointed are asked to pursue their dealings with Galton, the son. This minute was "continued" for the rest of the year, until in January 1796 Samuel Galton himself took action. " A letter being received from Samuel Galton, Junior, and read in this Meeting, the same is referred to further consideration." Such consideration was given in February, when the appointed Friends were desired to " inform him that we cannot admit his arguments as substantial, and 'tis matter of real concern to us that he should attempt to vindicate a practice which we conceive to be so inconsistent with our religious principles." Accordingly, the Preparative Meeting of Birmingham was directed not to receive his collection. Next month the Friends reported that Samuel Galton had informed them that " his address was not intended as an attack on our principles (as some Friends had supposed), but he still remains of the same mind in regard to the facts and opinions therein expressed, and does not give Friends any assurance of his quitting the business." Accordingly the meeting "declines to receive any further collection from him or to admit his attending our meetings for discipline, as a testimony of our decided disunity with the practice of fabricating and selling instruments of war. And feeling our minds impressed with a consideration of the desolating consequences of war, and the importance of this branch of our Christian testimony being supported by those in profession with us, we desire that the weighty advices which have at times been given by our Society on this subject may claim the serious attention of all our members, and that they will be careful, not only to avoid engaging in personal service and the fabrication of instruments of destruction, but also in any other concern whereby our testimony against war may not be supported." It is not surprising that Friends listened to Galton's lengthy letter with feelings of distress, and that it seemed to them an attack upon their principles. Opinions upon the merit of the argument differ considerably. To one Friend (Edward Hicks in *Quakeriana*) it has seemed "very able," and to Professor Karl Pearson "excellent common sense." But Morris Birkbeck,[1] who made manuscript annotations upon the copy of the letter preserved at the Friends' Reference Library in London, finds the argument in one place "corrupt and unsound," in another "illusory and inconsistent," in another "weak, foolish talk." The best point made by Galton is the undeniable fact that the business had been carried on by Friends for half a century without any official censure. But his attitude is one of resenting the interference of the meeting and of determination to pursue his own path—a "characteristic stubbornness" (to quote Professor Pearson again) which he showed in other episodes. Nevertheless, he writes with a good deal of affection for the Society and for individual members.

He believes (he tells the meeting) that it has entered on the business with reluctance and only in compliance with the Yearly Meeting minute of 1790. He is anxious that his letter should be preserved as a record for his children or future generation of "the circumstances and of the motive of my conduct," and he opens his defence with a series of "Facts" which are certainly the strongest part of his case.

"1st. The sole and entire cause alleged for this process is that I am engaged in a manufactory of arms, some of which are applicable to military purposes." On this Birkbeck comments that "the chief or principal part" are "designedly made for war."

"2nd. My grandfather—afterwards my uncle, then my father and uncle—and lastly my father and myself have been engaged in this manufactory for a period of 70 years, *without having received any animadversion on the part of the Society.*

"3rd. The trade devolved on me as if it were an inheritance, and the whole, or nearly the whole, of the fortune which I received from my father was a capital invested in the manufactory ; a part of which consists in appropriate mills, erections, and apparatus, not easily assignable or convertible to other purposes.

"4th. I have at various times during my carrying on the said business performed many acts, with the concurrence and at the instance of the Society, which alone would have constituted me a member.

"5th. I have been engaged in this business from the year 1777,

[1] 1734–1816. The copy in D. is to be found in Tracts E96.

and it was not until the year 1790 that the minute was made upon which this process against me is founded.

"6th. My engagements in the business were not a matter of choice in the first instance ; and there never has been a time when I would not have withdrawn from it could I have found a proper opportunity of transferring the concern."

Birkbeck notes that there were many other " honourable and religious " means of livelihood open, but that the opportunity for which the Galtons waited was that of selling " to more profit than continuing the manufactory." He does not defend the Monthly Meeting from the charge of negligence, but points out that the Minutes and Advices of the Society are frequently read in meetings, and that the individual is responsible for their application. " It is known that animadversions were made and private admonition given, before public labour was bestowed, which is agreeable to gospel order."

Next Galton, after having made clear that the censure was belated, passes to more dubious ground. He is convinced, he says, by his feelings and reason

" 1. That the manufacture of arms implies no approbation of offensive war ;

" 2. That the degree of responsibility that has been imputed to that manufacture does not attach ;

" 3. And that in its object or its tendencies it neither promotes war or increases its calamities."

His aim in manufacturing guns is that " which all commercial persons propose, viz. the acquisition of property. . . . In too many instances firearms are employed in offensive war, yet it ought in candour to be considered, that they are equally applicable to the purposes of defensive war, to the support of the civil power, to the prevention of war, and to the preservation of peace." Birkbeck queries : " Is defensive war, war of any sort, consistent with Christianity and Friends' principles ? . . . The distinction of offensive and defensive will not hold, as there can be no war without opposition, murder only."

If the argument against possible abuse forbids the " use and existence " of things, it may, says Galton, be carried far. The farmer, the brewer, the importer and the distiller, would be responsible for intemperance and disease. " Upon this principle, who would be innocent ? " Such an argument shows the wide difference between a Samuel Galton and a John Woolman. Birkbeck gives some proof that the Society's conscience was awakening on the matter of temperance by noting " the enormous distilleries are not clear." No reflecting person, says Galton, will contend that firearms have ever caused war, their manufacture is only a consequence of war, and even an alleviation of its horrors. " Those horrid contents, since the invention of firearms, are universally allowed to have been less sanguinary and less ferocious."

This remarkable argument is endorsed by Birkbeck, with justifiable impatience, as " weak, foolish talk."

Next Galton plunges into the war and peace texts of the New Testament, but in this argument he feels out of his depth and declares that he has no wish to explain the Scriptures much less to apologize for offensive war, " for which I profess the most decided abhorrence." He returns to the argument of Quaker precedent—his own ancestry and other Friends who manufactured munitions of war. Birbeck admits that many Quakers have carried arms " until they became too *heavy* for them."

Then, after a quotation from Penington in regard to defensive war, Galton points out the inconsistency of paying taxes and investing in loans, while refusing tithes. It is inconsistent, too, to use slave-grown products and food on which taxation is levied. " If you should be so conscientious as to abstain from all these enjoyments, I shall have no reason to complain of any partiality in applying the same strict construction of principle against me. I shall greatly admire the efficacy of your opinions, whilst I lament that the practice of your principles is not compatible with the situation in which Providence has placed us." The sting of these remarks is partly removed by the fact that for some years Friends had been cautioned by the Yearly Meeting against war loans, and in common with other Abolitionists many members of the Society did abstain from sugar and other slave-grown products. Galton himself does not wish to be taken seriously, he does not suggest an extension of the " Penal code "—" I have too sincere a respect for the right and duty of private judgment, and too strong a doubt of the compatibility of ecclesiastical censures and punishments with the genuine spirit and object of Christian discipline, not to express a most decided disapprobation of such a measure." On the contrary, he is opposed to the disownment of those who pay tithes—and presumably, like the " Free Quakers " of Philadelphia, to all dis-

ownments.[1] His "preference" of Friends before other sects will
not be altered by any measures that the meeting may feel it their
duty to carry out, or which may be imposed upon it by Yearly
Meeting. The Galton "stubbornness" breaks out again in his
concluding remark :

"I mean to give no pledge or expectation to the Society with
respect to the abandoning my business ; but to reserve to myself
a perfect independence on that head, to act as circumstances suggest.
So that whenever I may have an opportunity of withdrawing myself
from those engagements consistently with my judgment, I shall
have the satisfaction to feel that I act from spontaneous sentiment
only, and not from unworthy influence. . . . If I should be
disowned, I shall not think that I have abandoned the Society, but
that the Society have withdrawn themselves from their ancient
tolerant spirit and practice."

In spite of this plain declaration the anxiety of Midland Friends
to retain Samuel Galton in membership was evinced in April 1796,
when five Friends of the Quarterly Meeting (Warwick, Leicester,
and Rutland) were present by appointment to "visit and assist"
the Monthly Meeting, and two of them agreed to join with the
Friends already concerned in the matter in a further visit to the
delinquent. The arrangements continued for three months, but at
the July Meeting in Birmingham, again attended by Quarterly
Meeting Friends, no satisfactory report could be given. They
had had "some conversation with Galton respecting the business
alluded to and find it remains in the same state as reported to the
Monthly Meeting, and this meeting being painfully affected therewith, and our Friend William Lythall having expressed desire to
see the Party on the occasion in company with some other Friends
on the appointment, who have also expressed a willingness to see
him again, this meeting approves thereof." But a message from
the Quarterly Meeting calls the "solid attention" of Birmingham
Friends to a minute sent down from the late Yearly Meeting :
"A deficiency contained in the answer to the eighth query from the
Quarterly Meeting of Warwickshire, Leicester, and Rutland, having
again come under the notice of this meeting, it is earnestly recommended to that Quarterly Meeting that the same be brought to
a speedy and satisfactory issue, and our testimony against war and
fighting maintained inviolate."

[1] *Vide* Chapter XV, p. 412.

The issue came speedily enough. In August " one of the Friends appointed to visit Samuel Galton, Junior, reports that on having further conversation with him respecting his business, he stated the continuance of the impracticability of his relinquishing that part of the concern which had given Friends uneasiness. This meeting, therefore, in order for the clearing of our Society from an imputation of a practice so inconsistent as that of fabricating instruments for the destruction of mankind, thinks it incumbent upon us (after the great labour that has been bestowed) to declare him not in unity with Friends, and hereby disowns him as a Member of our religious Society ; nevertheless we sincerely desire he may experience such a conviction of the rectitude of our principles and a practice correspondent therewith as may induce Friends to restore him again into unity with them."

As Galton had foretold, he disregarded the disownment and, with his wife, continued to attend the worship of Friends. Of course he could take no part in business meetings. On his death in 1832 he was buried in the Bull Street graveyard. In religion, as Professor Karl Pearson says, he was practically a Deist ; he was a close friend of Dr. Priestley and showed his courage by offering him hospitality after the riots of 1791.

In 1802–3 Galton gave up the gun business, converting it into a bank in 1804. In 1803 the meeting accepted from him a donation towards the enlargement of the Friends' burial-ground.[1] Possibly this was to ensure for his wife and himself a grave, and it may also have been accepted with the knowledge of his change of business.

[1] *Francis Galton*, p. 45.

PART IV

THE NINETEENTH CENTURY

THE early history of the Friends is one long record of invincible fortitude displayed in the presence of atrocious malevolence and unsparing ridicule. Theirs was a courage that the world calls passive and not active; the distinction is an idle one, for nobody who has seen the Friends working in the thick of a famine or a fever, directing the operations of the life brigade on a stormy sea coast or immersed in the heat and turmoil of a contested election, will ever doubt that they are potentially the keenest of fighters. —SIR GEORGE TREVELYAN, *The American Revolution.*

CHAPTER X

PEACE AND WAR

1815–99

THE end of the struggle with Napoleon left a world weary of war. In all the belligerent countries a heavy load of taxation pressed upon the citizens, and among the working classes distress was acute. In addition, the political reaction and continued suppression of popular rights disappointed idealists, who had hoped that when the menace of a French despotism was removed, the nations might have opportunity for internal reforms. These influences reinforced the natural horror with which humane and thoughtful men regarded the bloodshed and devastation of the long years of war. In England, at least, the sentiment in favour of peace was stronger and more widespread than ever before, and the opportunity arose for an organized movement to promote international good-will. This movement had its origin within the Society of Friends. In June 1814 (6th mo. 7) William Allen noted in his journal "a meeting to consider of a new Society to spread tracts, etc., against war." [1]

But though the meeting was held at his house in Plough Court, Lombard Street, and Allen was thus one of the first founders of the Peace Society, the idea actually originated with another Friend, Joseph Tregelles Price, an ironmaster of Neath Abbey. He had been so impressed by the considerate treatment an unarmed trading vessel owned by him had received from an enemy ship, that he felt it his duty to spread abroad the doctrines of peace which he professed. [2] Although the formation of the Peace Society was discussed in 1814,

---

[1] *Life of William Allen*, i. 191.

[2] The vessel was a collier, the *Clifton Union*, bound from Neath for Falmouth. The French captor asked why it was unarmed. The captain replied that it belonged to men " who believed that all war was forbidden by Christianity." The Frenchman at once left the ship and allowed it to return home (*Herald of Peace*, 1853, p. 175, a letter from Price himself).

it was not actually established until 1816, after the final Peace of Paris. The original members, in number ten, were not all Friends, but included Churchmen and Nonconformists.[1] Its basis was religious (" war is inconsistent with the spirit of Christianty and the true interests of mankind ") but unsectarian, as it admitted as members all " desirous of the promotion of peace on earth and good-will towards men." The first American Peace Society was founded independently in 1815 ; in 1819, largely through the influence of Tregelles Price, a French *Société de Morale Chrétienne* was established, which had for one of its objects the promotion of peace.

For many years the peace movement in England and, to a large extent, on the Continent was inspired and organized by the Peace Society. It met with abundant ridicule and some angry opposition, but its leaders, many of them Friends, persevered, doing all in their power, by speech, pen, and influence, to uphold their cause. The programme of the Peace Society from the first included the substitution of arbitration for war, a general reduction of armaments, and the institution of an International Court for the settlement of disputes. This is not the place to relate its history in detail, but Friends played an active part in the pioneer efforts towards International Peace Congresses held between the years 1848 and 1851 at Brussels, Paris, Frankfort, and London.[2] Tregelles Price was a leader of the movement till his death, and it may be said that he died in peace harness, for he had come to London in the cold December of 1854 to join in the Peace Society's protest against the Crimean War.

Thus a channel was found for the peace activities of Friends in co-operation with others. Their personal convictions against military service were not severely tried in time of peace. In 1814 and again in 1815 it was reported to the Yearly Meeting that ten young Quakers were in prison for refusal to serve, but after these dates very few instances appear. Although Militia distraints recur

[1] Among them were Thomas Clarkson, the Abolitionist, and Joseph Hall.
[2] Among these Friends were Joseph Crosfield, Joseph Sturge, and Edmund Fry. Cobden, though not a Friend, was a leading speaker at the Congresses. In 1843 an International Peace Convention held in London addressed a plea for arbitration to all the civilized Governments, which was forwarded to each by deputations or through their Ambassadors. In 1844 the Massachusetts Legislature declared in favour of arbitration, and recommended it to the Congress of the United States. In 1849 Cobden introduced the proposal to the House of Commons, where he had seventy-nine supporters.

in the pages of the Yearly Meeting records until the suspension of the Militia Ballot in 1860, yet they are more sporadic in occurrence and much less serious in amount than the "sufferings" for Church rates and tithes. They mainly arose from rates levied to defray the expenses of the annual exercising of the militia, which was reduced to such small numbers that it became practically a volunteer body, the ballot being seldom put into force. Even when drawn, the authorities did not always require a Friend to provide a substitute, and if they thus dismissed the case, he escaped further inconvenience. If, however, they demanded a substitute the law of 1802–3 still stood, under which the propertied Quaker was distrained upon, and the unpropertied sent to prison for default.[1]

In 1846 and again in 1848, at the instance of Lord John Russell, the Government introduced Bills for the increase and embodiment of the militia. These proposals were in response to the anti-French agitation of the time, but on each occasion they roused so hearty a counter-agitation that they were hastily withdrawn. A proposed increase of the income tax, which was combined with the Militia Bill of 1848, added to its unpopularity. Large meetings of protest were held in the great towns ; Joseph Sturge, who had helped to organize that in Birmingham, received a letter from Douglas Jerrold promising the help of *Punch* and the *Daily News* against the war-fever. He added, " the fact of an anti-war meeting taking place in what may be called the arsenal of England is, indeed, encouraging."[2] In January 1848 the Meeting for Sufferings presented the Premier (Russell) with a grave remonstrance on the perils of increased military preparations. " We cannot but regard military preparations, even when undertaken by a nation on the ground of defence against apprehended or possible aggression, as calculated to irritate the inhabitants of other countries, and as therefore practically tending to precipitate the very events against which they profess to guard." Lord John Russell received this cogent appeal in a " kind and friendly manner," but it did not deter him from introducing his Militia

---

[1] The *British Friend*, January 1846, gives a clear statement of the law. This paper and the *Friend* (both founded as monthlies in 1843) during the troublous years 1846–8 of Chartist agitation, contain much discussion on the consistency or otherwise of a Friend acting as special constable. The editorial opinion, and that of many correspondents was clearly favourable, but there were instances where Friends refused the office and were fined in consequence (*British Friend*, November 1848).

[2] *Life of Joseph Sturge* (H. Richard), p. 406.

Bill.[1] It was in reference to the meetings in opposition to this, and to those a few months later in favour of his arbitration proposals, that Cobden wrote to Sturge : " You peace people seem to be the only men who have courage just now to call a public meeting. I always say that there is more real pluck in the ranks of the Quakers than in all our regiments of redcoats."[2] The comparative ease with which the Militia Act of 1852 (15 & 16 Vic., c. 50) was passed, was due to the rise of Louis Napoleon to power, and to the sedulous panic-mongering by the Press and by military and naval experts. By the Act, Friends without property were specifically exempted from imprisonment. This concession, however, did not check their opposition to the Bill, under which 80,000 men were to be embodied in time of peace to be raised to 120,000 at an alarm of invasion. A strong petition against the Bill, drafted by the Meeting for Sufferings, was adopted by the Yearly Meeting. The latter body, in its Epistle commenting on the proposals, declared that : " The whole system of war is so directly at variance not only with the plain precepts of our Lord, but with the whole spirit of his gospel, that any attempt to bring under its influence those who are engaged in the ordinary peaceful occupations of life cannot but awaken painful apprehensions."

The Bill was passed, but the great growth of volunteer rifle clubs led to the official recognition of the Volunteers in 1859, while in the next year the Militia Ballot Act authorized the suspension of the ballot for one year. This Act was annually renewed by Parliament, by which means the compulsory powers of the Government in regard to home defence were kept in a state of suspended animation until the year 1916. It is characteristic of English methods that the Act was entitled " An Act to amend the laws relating to the ballots for the Militia in England, and to suspend the making of lists and ballots for the Militia of the United Kingdom," and that the majority of the clauses were occupied with elaborate arrangements for the ballot which was suspended by the remainder of the law. Amongst other provisions, the exemption from personal service granted in the Act of George III was continued to those " who become, or *but for being Quakers*, would become liable in the rotation " for the militia. Thus the Quaker claim was again specifically recognized, although for fifty-six years to come England, with her voluntarily recruited Army and Navy and volunteer

---

[1] Report in *British Friend* March 1848.   [2] *Life of Sturge*, p. 424.

auxiliaries, was free from the shadow of conscription, even for home defence.

The change in the legal position of Friends was partly responsible for the alterations in the " war query," during the nineteenth century. The query of 1792 stood unchanged (with the exception of the omission of the words " letters of Marque ") until 1859. But in that year the whole list of queries was thoroughly revised, and in its new form approved by the Yearly Meeting of 1860 After the legislation of the past year, it was no longer necessary to inquire whether Friends were concerned in the militia. The new query, sweeping all details on one side, recognized a general principle of action. " Are Friends," it asked, " faithful in maintaining our Christian testimony against all war ? " In 1875 the practice of requiring written answers to these queries from the subordinate meetings was dropped by the Yearly Meeting. Since that date they have been regularly read both in meetings for worship and in those for Church business, but they are left to the consideration of the individual conscience. To a newcomer into the Society there is perhaps nothing more impressive than the reading by the Clerk of the meeting of one of these queries, followed by a short pause for reflection and self-examination. Since 1875 the war query has been the eighth in order, and reads :—

" Are you faithful in maintaining our Christian testimony against all war, as inconsistent with the precepts and spirit of the gospel ? "

Thus " the testimony against all war " for more than fifty years has been accepted by the members of the Society as an accurate description of the Quaker attitude.[1] There have been, undoubtedly, in time of peace always a small number of Friends who have openly criticized or silently disagreed with this article of the " Doctrine." In time of war these dissentients become more articulate and are reinforced by others who honestly believe the war of the day to be one waged on their country's side with much greater justification

---

[1] Dublin Yearly Meeting also adopted the revised queries. The phrase " testimony against all war," or its equivalent, had been used on many earlier occasions, e.g. in the Declaration of 1660, and by American Friends in the War of Independence. See also London Yearly Meeting Epistles, 1779, 1781, 1806, 1809, 1839, 1861, etc. The Society's *Book of Christian Discipline* in a section " Peace among the Nations " gathers together some of the most typical declarations of the testimony. This section was reprinted in 1915 as a pamphlet, with the addition of further documents issued during the war.

than any with which they are acquainted through the cold medium of history. Curiously enough, however, the line of attack on these occasions is not usually an appeal to the Society to abandon a traditional but untenable position, but an attempt to prove that the peace testimony is a comparatively new development, not in the orthodox line of Quakerism.

Yet the most intellectual Quaker writer of the early nineteenth century unhesitatingly proclaimed the "testimony" as an integral part of his Society's ethics. Jonathan Dymond's *Essays on the Principles of Morality* won the praise of Southey and Bright, and still find readers and admirers.[1] Born in Exeter of an old Quaker family in 1796, Dymond grew into a delicate and thoughtful youth, something of a poet and nature-lover, who exercised his mind by wide reading and (after the fashion of the day) by membership of an Essay Society. The contest with Napoleon, which overshadowed his boyhood, helped to strengthen his hereditary opposition to war. As early as 1819 he contributed discussions on war to his Essay Society; in 1823 he published a more elaborate treatise, *An Inquiry into the Accordancy of War with the Principles of Christianity and an Examination of the Philosophical Reasoning by which it is Defended.* This brought him into some repute among his own religious body and the supporters of the Peace Society, of which he became an active member. But a severe illness in 1826 caused the almost complete loss of his voice, an affliction which he bore with exemplary patience and resolution. He worked steadily at his more ambitious treatise on *The Principles of Morality*, and at his death in 1828 this was left in manuscript practically complete. It was published in the following year, with an explanatory note stating that the author had been dissatisfied with existing text-books of moral philosophy, in particular with the utilitarianism of Paley, and had attempted to correct them by a system of morality based upon the revealed Will of God.

His editor calls this a "code of *scripture* ethics," but such a definition is too narrow, since Dymond devotes a long chapter to a discussion of "the immediate communication of the will of God," or, in other words, the doctrine of the Light Within. In fact, consciously or unconsciously, the work is an attempt to give a logical

---

[1] The ninth edition was published in 1894. Bright had contributed a preface to the eighth, nine years earlier. The *Essay on War* was published separately by the Friends' Peace Committee in 1915.

basis of the faith and practice of Friends. The deeper questions raised in philosophical and metaphysical studies are not touched, but the chapters range over a wide field of practical ethics. Here there is no need to consider the general merits of the book. Southey's verdict at the time was that it had "such ability and (was) so excellently intended, as well as well executed, that those who differ most widely from some of its conclusions, must regard the writer with the greatest respect and look upon his early death as a public loss." [1]

While Southey wrote in strong approval of the moral principles laid down by Dymond, he could not refrain from some gentle censure of the section upon political morality. A Quaker, he remarked, was necessarily a "leveller," and thus held "political opinions which are not harmless when brought into action, because they strike at the roots of the British constitution." Indeed, Dymond's offence seems to have been that he considered the British Constitution, as it existed in the year 1829, was capable of further improvement. To the modern reader his remarks on elective monarchies, the advantages of a democratic Government, of an extended franchise and electoral reform, and on Catholic relief, are neither startling nor revolutionary.

Southey criticizes these portions of the book at such length that he has no space to consider the chapter on war, and dismisses it with the comment that if the young author had lived to middle age, " he might have retained his persuasion of the unlawfulness of war ; but he would have seen reason to be thankful that fleets and armies protect the British Quakers against foreign enemies, and that penal laws protect them against violence at home." [2]

The chapter on war in the *Principles* is in substance the same as the earlier essay, though it is revised and amplified. Dymond had felt and thought deeply on the subject. He had written (in a private letter of the year 1826), " I am inclined to hope that (after

[1] *Quarterly Review*, January 1831, pp. 83-120.

[2] Southey might have found it difficult to discuss the argument, as Dymond had included him among a list of " acute and enlightened men " convinced of the unlawfulness of war, quoting in support the following passage from the *History of Brazil* (1810-19). " There is but one community of Christians in the world, and that, unhappily, of all communities one of the smallest, enlightened enough to understand the prohibition of war by our Divine Master, in its plain, literal, and undeniable sense, and conscientious enough to obey it, subduing the very instinct of nature to obedience." He might have added the familiar lines on " The Battle of Blenheim " in further testimony.

the approaching day is passed when slavery shall be abolished) the attention and the labours of Friends will be more conspicuously and publicly directed than they have hitherto been to the question of war—an evil before which, in my estimation, slavery sinks into insignificance." " I doubt not " (he added) " that now is the time for anti-slavery exertion. The time *will* come for anti-war exertion."[1]

His own clear statement of the case against war has served as material for much later " anti-war exertion," and need not be dealt with here at length. He summarized his arguments in a few short propositions, of which the two following practically cover the ground :

" That the general character of Christianity is wholly incongruous with war, and that its general duties are incompatible with it. . . .

" That those who have refused to engage in war, in consequence of their belief of its inconsistency with Christianity, have found that providence has protected them."

This latter proposition perhaps accounts for his most notable omission from a statement of the causes of war, in which he does not mention wars of liberation undertaken on behalf of an oppressed people, or by that people against their rulers. Already, in a chapter on " Civil Obedience," he had expressed the belief that even in such cases a policy of " resolute non-compliance " would attain the desired end more effectually, and at the cost of less suffering than any warlike measures. He was at any rate consistent, for he applied the same rule to the individual in his discussions of the rights of self-defence and of the death penalty, maintaining that though forms of coercion to prevent crime were lawful, yet neither the advantage of the individual nor the community could justify the taking of life. His arguments, however, were not confined to moral and religious considerations. In a powerful section he stated the social and political evils involved—the suffering, bereavement, and poverty which follow in the train of war. The supposed justification of war from the practices of the Old Testament he treated with unconcealed contempt. At the very outset of his work he had remarked that in questions of morality " an appeal to the Hebrew Scriptures is frequently made when the precepts of Christianity would be too rigid for our purpose. He who insists upon a pure morality applies to the New Testament :

[1] *Memoir* by C. W. Dymond.

he who desires a little more indulgence, defends himself by arguments from the Old." This attitude is in rcmarakable contrast to that of another Friend, Joseph John Gurney, who in an almost contemporary account of Quakerism, is put to sore straits in the chapter on War,[1] by his attempt to maintain at once the unchristian character of modern wars and the uplifting and purifying influence of those waged by the Jews. Dymond's last words on war were addressed to those already convinced of the truth of his thesis. "What then are the duties of a subject who believes that all war is incompatible with his religion, but whose governors engage in a war and deemand his service ? We answer explicitly : *It is his duty mildly and temperately, yet firmly, to refuse to serve.* Let such as these remember that an honourable and an awful duty is laid upon them. It is upon their fidelity, so far as human agency is concerned, that the cause of peace is suspended. Let them then be willing to avow their opinions and to defend them. Neither let them be contented with words, if more than words, if suffering also, is required."

John Bright was an admiring student of Dymond's book, and the courageous and fervid eloquence with which he opposed later wars drew its material to some extent from the more prosaic, though equally sincere utterances of his fellow Quaker. But for many years to come Friends, in England at least, had little opportunity to seal their peace principles by suffering. On the other hand, in this half-century, they made peculiarly their own the task of relieving the sufferings which war leaves behind it.[2] William Allen in 1822, on his way to plead the cause of the slave to the diplomatists assembled at Verona, saw at Vienna the piteous state of Greek refugees escaped from the "massacre of Scio," and other Turkish outrages. Returning to England, he stirred up his fellow-members ; the Meeting for Sufferings raised a fund of £8,000, which was disbursed by competent agents among the refugees collected at

[1] J. J. Gurney, *Observations on . . . the Society of Friends*, 1834. Gurney's arguments were probably meant as a reply not only to the rationalistic attitude of Elias Hicks and his followers, which led to the Separation of 1828 in America, but also to the views of Abraham Shackleton and other Irish Friends, for which they were disowned in the beginning of the nineteenth century. Shackleton's difficulty "lay in the supposed divine command . . . enjoining the children of Israel to wage wars of extermination against Canaanite peoples " (R. Jones, *Later Periods of Quakerism*, p. 293). This was also a count in the charge of unsound teaching brought against Hannah Barnard, a visiting Friend from America, by some English leaders in 1802 (*op. cit.* 302–3).

[2] This field of service was not new ; a noteworthy instance was the relief work of American Friends round Boston in 1775–6 (*vide* Chapter XV, p. 392).

Trieste, Ancona, Leghorn, Odessa, Malta, Marseilles, and other points.

The relief work carried out by the Society during the years of the Irish famine is better known to their countrymen, through Cobden's eloquent tribute,[1] and its reproduction in Lord Morley's *Life* of that statesman. Cobden argued that the courage and devotion displayed in war may be turned into nobler fields of social service and reform.

" A famine fell upon nearly one half of a great nation. The whole world hastened to contribute money and food. But a few courageous men left their homes in Middlesex and Surrey, and penetrated to the remotest glens and bogs of the west coast of the stricken island, to administer relief with their own hands. To say that they found themselves in the valley of the shadow of death would be but an imperfect image ; they were in the charnel house of a nation. Never since the fourteenth century did Pestilence, the gaunt handmaid of Famine, glean so rich a harvest. In the midst of a scene, which no field of battle ever equalled in danger, in the number of its slain, or the sufferings of the surviving, these brave men moved as calm and undismayed as though they had been in their own homes. The population sank so fast that the living could not bury the dead ; half-interred bodies protruded from the gaping graves ; often the wife died in the midst of her starving children, whilst her husband lay a festering corpse by her side. Into the midst of these horrors did our heroes penetrate, dragging the dead from the living with their own hands, raising the head of famishing infancy, and pouring nourishment into parched lips from which shot fever flames more deadly than a volley of musketry. Here was courage. No music strung the nerves ; no smoke obscured the imminent danger ; no thunder of artillery deadened the senses. It was cool self-possession and resolute will—calculating risk and heroic resignation. And who were these brave men ? To what gallant corps did they belong ? Were they of the horse, foot, or artillery force ? They were Quakers from Clapham and Kingston ! If you would know what heroic actions they performed, you must inquire from those who witnessed them. You will not find them in the volume of reports published by themselves—for Quakers write no bulletins of their victories."

[1] *Political Writings of Richard Cobden*, ii. 378 (1793 and 1853). *Life of Cobden*, ch. xxi.

In his geographical limitations Cobden did less than justice to those he praised so liberally. The reports he mentioned [1] show that the work was carried out by a large number of English and Irish Friends, and are scrupulously careful to explain that their organization was only one branch of the measures of relief attempted by a conscience-stricken Government and nation. There was a Central Friends' Committee in Dublin, with auxiliaries in the provinces, and a sister Committee in London. These bodies raised nearly £200,000, of which more than half came as food from America, not only or mainly from Friends, though they were responsible for the organization of the shipments. Among the English Friends who personally worked at the distribution of relief in the stricken districts were William Forster, his son (the Education Minister of 1870), James Hack Tuke, and Joseph Crosfield. There were also, of course, many Irish Friends engaged in the work. Besides the immediate distribution of food, some constructive relief was undertaken—seed corn was provided for the farmers and small-holders, and grants made to fishermen who in their poverty had been forced to pawn their nets.

Many Friends also worked vigorously for Free Trade and Franchise Reform—among them, to name only two, Joseph Sturge and John Bright. But, with the important exception of the anti-slavery movement, the official bodies of the Society were very chary of identifying it with public causes during this period. " Study to be quiet " was the advice pressed upon young and impetuous

[1] *Transactions Relating to the Famine in Ireland,* 1846–7 (Dublin) (see also the Lives of the Friends named, particularly that of James Hack Tuke, by Sir E. Fry). The following reminiscence of Quaker experience during the abortive Rebellion of 1848, is contributed by J. Ernest Grubb of Carrick-on-Suir, County Waterford. This district was a centre of the Rebellion, and most of the Protestant inhabitants of the little town fled in alarm to the garrison at Waterford, to England, or even to America. J. Ernest Grubb, however, recalls that his father and mother remained with their three young children (of whom he was one) quietly at their home. " My father was engaged in the iron trade and sold steel which was in considerable demand for making pikes. However, when the disturbances began he refused to sell steel of the sizes and quality needed for pikes. . . . My mother took us children our usual walks without hindrance " (although the rebels under Smith O'Brien were encamped four miles to the north while the town and district were alive with soldiers, who searched every house for arms), and the family went regularly each Sunday the fourteen miles drive to Meeting at Clonmel. A few miles away, Curraghmore, the seat of the Marquis of Waterford, was guarded by cannon and a strong body of armed men ; the young Marquis went about fully armed and his beautiful wife was not allowed out of sight of the windows (Augustus Hare, *Story of Two Noble Lives,* i. 304–13).

members. Even active work for peace was carried on through the channels of the Peace Society. Yet the genuine spiritual revival in Quakerism, after the formalism of the mid-eighteenth century, overflowed in many individual Friends into channels of social reform and international friendship. The work of John Bright is described in a separate chapter. Here another Friend may be taken as typical of the " universal spirit " which was beginning to stir the Society to new life.

Joseph Sturge was born in 1793, of a family which had belonged to the Society of Friends since the days of George Fox. In 1813, as already mentioned, he refused militia service. Next year he entered the corn trade, and his firm soon became one of high standing in that business. In 1822 he settled in Birmingham. The abolition of slavery, franchise reform, free trade, temperance, the adult school movement were all causes into each of which he threw enough of his energy and resources to satisfy the conscience of any ordinary man. But peace and freedom were the nearest to his heart. His friend, the American peace advocate, Elihu Burritt, wrote of him that it was a happy coincidence for the people of Birmingham to place his memorial statue at " The Five Ways," where Edgbaston and Birmingham meet, since " Freedom, Peace, Temperance, Charity, and Godliness were the five ways of his good and beautiful life."

In 1818 he founded, at Worcester, one of the earliest branches of the Peace Society, and nine years later another at Birmingham. In 1839 he took active part in the opposition to the Chinese War and to the opium traffic from which it sprang. From a visit to the United States in 1841 he returned a warm supporter of Jay's proposal for the insertion of an arbitration clause in all treaties. For the next twenty years he was the soul of the Peace movement, helping in the conventions and congresses organized by the Peace Society, but more especially throwing all his personal and public influence into the promotion of good relations between his own countrymen and the peoples of the United States and France. The boundary disputes with the former country and the English mistrust, first of the Orleans dynasty and then of Louis Napoleon, made this work one of pressing necessity.

Henry Richard, his biographer, wrote well of Sturge's peace belief, that it was " something far more than one of the dogmas of an hereditary creed. In proportion, as his own spirit was brought under the power of the gospel, did this tradition which he had received from the fathers deepen into a profound personal conviction. His belief, like that of most of those who share his views, rested not, as is generally but mistakenly represented, upon a literal interpretation of a few isolated passages of scripture, but upon what he felt to be an essential and irreconcilable antagonism in principle, spirit, and tendency between a religion of charity and brotherly love and the whole system of malignity and violence which war inevitably engenders."

But Sturge held his views in charity to all men. " It is a mystery " (he once wrote in a private letter to a friend) " which I cannot fathom, why those who are equally anxious to act up to the directions and spirit of the New Testament see so differently as to what these require. Nothing, for instance, has surprised and grieved me more than to witness the views entertained by many on the subject of war, who, I cannot doubt, have made much further advances in the Christian life than I have. But it seems to be the will of Him who is infinite in wisdom that light upon great subjects should first arise and be gradually spread, through the faithfulness of *individuals* in acting up to their own convictions." and he instanced the work of John Woolman against slavery.[1]

There were three occasions on which Sturge was able to take practical, though not in every case successful, steps to forward international peace. These were : an attempted mediation between Denmark and the Duchies of Schleswig-Holstein in 1850, the peace deputation to the Czar in January 1854, and the mission of relief to Finland at the close of the Crimean War.

The vexed question of Schleswig-Holstein, which in 1864 gave Bismarck his first opportunity to increase the power of Prussia, had led in 1848 to an attempt by the German majority in the Duchies

---

[1] *Life of Sturge*, pp. 414-15. It was during the anti-French panic of 1853 that Cobden who, though a courageous advocate of peace, never committed himself to a condemnation of all war and military defence, made this interesting comment on the advantages and drawbacks of an alliance with the Quakers. " The soul of the Peace movement is the Quaker sentiment against all war. Without the stubborn zeal of the Friends there could be no Peace Society and no Peace Conference. But the enemy takes good care to turn us all into Quakers, because the non-resistance principle puts us out of court as practical politicians of the present day. Our opponents insist on it that we wish to totally disarm, and leave ourselves at the mercy of Louis Napoleon and the French ; nay, they say we actually invite them to come and invade us " (Letter quoted in Morley, *Life of Cobden*, ch. xxi).

to free them from Danish sovereignty. At first supported by other German States, the Duchies were hard pressed after Prussia had concluded a separate peace with Denmark in July 1850. In August the Peace Congress held its sittings at Frankfort, and Dr. Bodenstedt of Berlin appealed to that body to urge the belligerents to make use of arbitration. Under the rules of its constitution the Congress was unable to intervene, but Joseph Sturge, Frederick Wheeler (another Friend), Elihu Burritt, and Dr. Varrantrap, the German Secretary of the Congress, resolved to make the attempt as an unofficial deputation. They were received by representatives both of the *de facto* Government of the Duchies, and that of Denmark, and reminded them that an old treaty between Denmark and the Duchies made provision for the settlement of disputes by arbitration. In response to the suggestion " the two Governments had gone so far as to appoint a sort of unofficial negotiator on each side . . . to confer as to the character and constitution of the proposed court of arbitration. At that time Chevalier Bunsen, who was Prussian Ambassador in this country, told Mr. Cobden that he had a stronger hope of adjustment of the matter in dispute from that pacific embassy than from all that had been done before by the professional diplomatists of Europe."[1] These latter, however, interposed at the critical moment, and by the authority of Great Britain, France, Norway, Russia and Austria, the unwilling Duchies were restored to Denmark.

The opening of the Great Exhibition in 1851 was the stimulus to the expression of a good deal of rather evanescent peace sentiment. The tried advocates of peace, however, certainly did not share the view that an era of unbroken good-will had set in. Had they done so, they would soon have been undeceived. The *coup d'état* of December 1851 increased the popular prejudice against Louis Napoleon, and men like Bright and Sturge had much to do in combating the rising tide of fear and ill-will. Yet with startling suddenness the tide suddenly changed its direction. English politicians joined with the hated Napoleon to oppose the claims of Russia in the Near East. As the menace of war grew nearer, the thought came to Sturge that possibly the Society of Friends had the duty laid upon it of pleading with the Czar on behalf of peace. The intercourse between Alexander the First and the Quakers of his day might give modern Friends some right to claim a hearing ;

[1] *Life of Sturge*, p. 454.

they were known to be impartial in their advocacy, and to be inspired not by political but religious motives. And while public opinion in England was unmistakably bellicose, and it was a weary task to convert millions of angry and ill-informed voters, there was at least the chance that the individual mind of the absolute ruler might be more open to pacific appeals. With arguments such as these Sturge brought his "concern" before the Meeting for Sufferings, and on January 17, 1854, it was approved by that body in the following minute : "This Meeting has been introduced into much religious concern in contemplating the apparent probability of war between some of the nations of Europe. Deeply impressed with the enormous amount of evil that invariably attends the prosecution of war, and with the utter inconsistency of all war with the spirit of Christianity and the precepts of its divine Founder as set forth in the New Testament, this meeting has concluded, under a strong sense of religious duty, to present an address to Nicholas, Emperor of Russia, on this momentous question ; and it also concludes to appoint Joseph Sturge, Robert Charleton, and Henry Pease to be the bearers of this address, and if the opportunity for so doing be afforded, to present the same in person.

"In committing this service to our dear brethren, we crave for them, in the prosecution of it, the help and guidance of that wisdom which is from above ; and we commend them, as well as the cause entrusted to them, to the blessing of Almighty God."[1]

The deputation left England on the 20th of January. It was no light impulse which moved three men of more than middle age to brace all the rigours of a long journey through a northern winter to a country which at any moment might be at war with their own. When they reached St. Petersburg their personal reception was all that was kind and courteous. After they had held private interviews with Nesselrode, the Foreign Minister, and other high officials, the Czar and Nesselrode received them for the presentation of the Address.[2]

---

[1] *The Times* and other contemporary publications (as Kinglake, the historian of the war) persistently declared that this deputation was sent by the Peace Society. The first assertion was made in *The Times* of January 23rd, and though it was contradicted and corrected in next morning's issue by the Secretary of the Peace Society, the leader-writers ignored the correction and continued to repeat the mis-statement.

[2] For the Address, *vide* Appendix D. Cornelius Jansen, a Mennonite, translated and widely distributed the Address in Russia.

This was followed by a speech from Joseph Sturge, leaving the political question on one side, but pressing the moral and religious arguments against war. " Among the multitudes who would be the victims in the event of a European war, the greatest sufferers would probably be not those who had caused the war, but innocent men with their wives and children." He ended with a hearty expression of good-will towards the Emperor.[1] The latter seemed affected even to tears, and the Empress, with whom the visitors had afterwards a most friendly conversation, told them that this was the case. The three Friends were fully convinced of the Czar's sincerity, and believed that he intended to make some further proposals for peace, since they were asked to stay a day or two beyond the date originally fixed for their return. But on that date (February 14th) a sudden chill appeared in the attitude of their Russian acquaintances. " Nor," said Charleton, " were we at a loss to account for this change. *The Mail from England had arrived*, with newspapers giving an account of the opening of Parliament and of the intensely warlike speeches in the House of Commons."[2]

The mission was loudly denounced by the war party in England. The *Times*, indeed, on February 21st, was contemptuously friendly. "We must not deny to the gentlemen engaged in this piece of enthusiastic folly the praise of sincerity." It was " unfitting to ridicule " their " well-meant admonition," even to a " half-crazy monarch." But two days later the leader-writer changed his mind, and poured a flood of ridicule upon the " mischievous " deputation. " Every principle," he announced, " is mischievous which leads men to place reliance upon visionary hopes and feelings," a condemnation which would involve most systems of religion.[3] The deputation also gained the notice of a slighting and inaccurate page in Kinglake's *Invasion of the Crimea*. But the historian's assertion

---

[1] From an account by Robert Charleton quoted in the *Life of Sturge*.
[2] *Life of Sturge*, p. 480. War was declared by England on March 28, 1854.
[3] *The Times* was always unsympathetic to the peace cause. It even sent a special correspondent to Frankfort in 1850, for the purpose of turning the Peace Congress into ridicule, and on August 29, 1850, followed this by a leading article taunting the Congress with having done nothing to stop the war in Schleswig. Yet if the writer had known of Sturge's attempt at mediation, he would probably have ridiculed it as he did in 1854. But *The Times*' conversion, as regards the Crimean War, was comparatively rapid. "Never," it wrote in 1860, " was so great an effort made for so worthless an object. . . . It is with no small reluctance we admit a gigantic effort and an infinite sacrifice, to have been made in vain " (August 16, 1860).

that the Czar afterwards cherished a bitter grudge against his visitors, accusing them of misleading him about English sentiment, is supported by no evidence, and was certainly not borne out by the widowed Empress' later intercourse with other Friends, to whom she mentioned the mission " in a very different tone from what we should have expected had she been aware that the remembrance of it had driven the Emperor to the transport of wrath described by Mr. Kinglake."[1]   At the Yearly Meeting of 1854 Bright was emphatic in his approval of the enterprise.

The two Quaker weeklies took a strong line against the war, and there seems to have been great unanimity in the Society in its condemnation.   A few years before, the question had been raised in Yearly Meeting whether Friends could consistently supply clothing to the Army, when the Clerk " gave it as the judgment of the Society that the supplying of such articles was clearly a violation of our testimony."[2]   In the winter of 1854–5 some criticisms were made by zealous Friends of a transaction between the War Office and a firm of Quaker leather merchants.   The firm (C. & J. Clark of Street) defended their action in a letter to the *British Friend*.[3] They explained that, when the War Office began to take tardy measures for the protection of the troops against the Crimean winter, it tried to make a provision of sheepskin coats.   An application was made to the Clarks, who held almost the only stock of suitable skins, but they refused to accept an army contract.   As the winter advanced and the sufferings of the troops increased, a fresh appeal was made. This time the firm accepted the contract, but the partners determined to gain no advantage from it.   The entire profits, about £300, were used as the nucleus of a fund for a new school-building in the village.   An anonymous Friend, indeed, wrote next month to the journal that the Clarks were guilty of the death of many Russians, since by their supplies English soldiers were kept alive to kill the enemy, but his logic was not echoed by his fellow members.

In December 1854 the Meeting for Sufferings resolved to circulate an appeal against the continuance of the war, although, as the minute remarked, " at this critical juncture, and under the excited state of public feeling, the adoption of this course has been

---

[1] *Life of Sturge*, p. 482.   For Kinglake, *vide Invasion of Crimea*, i. ch. xxiii. 402, and iv. ch. ii. 46.
[2] *British Friend*, 1851, p. 69.
[3] *Ibid.*, January 1855.

felt to be truly serious, and warranted only by a strong apprehension of religious duty." Under the title : " A Christian Appeal from the Society of Friends to their fellow countrymen on the present war,"[1] about 50,000 copies were circulated. The language was uncompromising enough. War between Christian nations, it asserted, involved the adoption of a heathen standard by them. " That which is morally and religiously wrong cannot be politically right."

Sturge had his full share of the unpopularity which fell to the opponents of the war. Even in Birmingham he was shouted down at a public meeting, and the more ignorant charged him with responsibility for the high price of corn. Cobden consoled him with the reminder that Quaker corn-merchants endured the same accusation in the Napoleonic War. From across the Atlantic his friend, Judge Jay, wrote : " You Quakers and those who act with you are the real heroes of the war." He was not deterred from doing what he could in the interests of peace and humanity. When the war ended in 1856, the standing Committee of the Peace Congress waited on the Prime Minister urging that the negotiators at Paris should include among their recommendations the settlement of future disputes by arbitration. With Palmerston they made little way, but when it was suggested that a direct appeal to the Plenipotentiaries might be more effective, Sturge at once agreed to join in a small deputation to Paris. There they found warm sympathy from Lord Clarendon, and unexpected support from the French and Prussian Plenipotentiaries. Clarendon introduced the question in the sittings of the Congress, when his colleagues (as Gladstone said later) expressed " at least a qualified disapproval of a resort to war, and asserted the supremacy of reason, of justice, humanity, and religion."[2]

[1] In D. (Tracts G 112).

[2] Protocol No. 23. " The Plenipotentiaries do not hesitate to express in the name of their Governments, the wish that States, between which any serious misunderstandings may arrive, should, before resorting to arms, have recourse so far as circumstances might allow, to the good offices of a friendly Power. The Plenipotentiaries hope that the Governments not represented at the Congress will unite in the sentiment which has inspired the wish recorded in the present protocol." Another deputation, this time of Friends from the Meeting for Sufferings, visited all the Plenipotentiaries (excepting England, but including Turkey) with a " plea on behalf of liberty of conscience." They were courteously treated by all, but found that only Cavour had any real conception of religious tolerance (Report in *Book of Cases*, iv. 190). When Robert Charleton and two other Friends visited the Northern Governments on the same errand in 1858 Prince Gortschakoff told them frankly that the circulation of the document in Russia

The war was over, but the sufferings caused by the war continued, and Sturge still had work to do. In 1854 the coast of Finland had been ravaged by the British fleet, to the great loss, and indeed ruin, of many non-combatants. Timber stores, merchants' warehouses, and shipyards were burnt down, stock carried away from the farms, and even the fishermen's boats and nets destroyed. " One shriek of woe sounds throughout Finland," wrote *The Times* correspondent.[1] At the time nothing could be done. Sir James Graham answered a Parliamentary criticism of the Baltic operations in true Governmental style. " The officers had only obeyed their instructions and were open to no criticism whatever. . . . Every effort had been made to distinguish between public and private property, but the difficulty of doing so was one of the unhappy incidents of war. . . . It will be hard, indeed, if at the commencement of a war involving immense difficulties and sacrifices, it shall be related to our gallant officers and seamen that the first notice taken of their conduct in the British House of Commons partook of the character of censure."[2]

But some Englishmen did not forget the Finns. In September 1856 Joseph Sturge and Thomas Harvey (one of a Quaker family well known in Leeds) journeyed to make inquiries on the spot. They found the sufferers moderate in their statements of losses, but still heavily straitened by them (and by a serious failure of the harvest), and pathetically bewildered by such action on the part of England, to whom they had looked with reverence as the land of progress and liberty. " We can't think of the English as before," said one to Sturge. A merchant told them that " the printing by the British and Foreign Bible Society of the New Testament and the Psalms in their own language had made a deep impression on the Finnish people ; but after the ravages committed on the property of unarmed and unoffending fishermen and peasants during the war, the cry was, ' Can these be the English :—our friends ? ' to which

could not be allowed. On the other hand, the Danish and Swedish Governments were friendly, and the " Plea " was published at length in the leading newspapers. A Baptist pastor of Copenhagen told the Friends that the liberty of conscience existing in Denmark was largely due to the visit of J. J. Gurney and Elizabeth Fry in 1841, and their intercession with the King for some Baptists imprisoned for their religion (*Life of Charleton*, pp. 111–31).

[1] June 23, 1854.

[2] Hansard, June 29, 1854. The critic was Milner Gibson. Some naval commanders behaved well. Admirals Napier and Dundas later censured some of the wanton destruction and pillage.

he sometimes replied : 'The English who send you the Bible are not the same persons as the English who carry on the war.'" [1] The two Friends made careful inquiry into the real needs of the people, and after forming a local committee, they returned to lay the matter before the Meeting for Sufferings. Nearly £9,000 was raised in England, chiefly by Friends, Sturge and his brother opening the fund with £1,000. This was expended by the local committee on food, clothing, the provision of seed-corn, the replacement of fishing-nets, and the like practical help. The Czar sent his personal thanks to the Mission, through Baron Nicolay, Secretary to the Embassy in London, but it was more grateful to Sturge and Harvey to hear from two younger Friends who visited Finland in 1857 that they found the feeling among the people much softened. Whittier singled out this as one of his friend's most Christlike works in his memorial verses on Sturge's death, and in some earlier lines on the " Conquest of Finland."

> Out spake the ancient Amtman,
> At the gate of Helsingfors :
> " Why comes this ship a-spying
> In the track of England's wars ? "
>
> " Each wasted town and hamlet
> She visits to restore ;
> To roof the shattered cabin,
> And feed the starving poor.
>
> The sunken boats of fishers,
> The foraged beeves and grain,
> The spoil of flake and storehouse
> The good ship brings again.
>
> And so to Finland's sorrow
> The sweet amend is made.
> As if the healing hand of Christ
> Upon her wounds were laid ! "
>
> Then said the grey old Amtman,
> " The will of God be done !
> The battle lost by England's hate
> By England's love is won ! "

It is not strange that in 1859 the news of Joseph Sturge's death spread sorrow in Finland. In these last three years of life he was instrumental in founding the *Morning Star* as a paper to spread

[1] *Life of Sturge*, p. 512.

progressive and pacific views, and in forwarding the return of Bright for Birmingham. Lifelong opponent of slavery as he was, he refused to join in a remonstrance to the United States in 1857 on the ground that to an American such a plea from members of a nation engaged in the Chinese War would seem mere hypocrisy and cant. His horror at the Indian Mutiny was profound, yet he could not regard it as an unprovoked crime. " Had we acted," he wrote, " on Christian principles in the Government of India, even though we obtained much of it by robbery, the present state of things would not have existed, and yet the advocates of war are ready enough to ask the friends of peace how *they* would now get out of a position in which they would never have placed themselves." The spirit of the knight-errant in forlorn causes still burned in him. He volunteered to the Peace Society to lead a mission of inquiry to India, to study on the spot the needs of the natives and our future policy. His friends felt that for a man of sixty-five, with shaken health, such an enterprise was too hazardous, and there was little probability of being allowed sufficient freedom of travel and intercourse to make the attempt profitable.

In 1859 he resigned from the Birmingham Chamber of Commerce because that body petitioned for the recognition of Sir James Brooke's rule in Sarawak by making the country a British protectorate. Sturge had denounced the sanguinary wars with Dyaks and Chinese by which Brooke won his power, and to him the suggestion seemed an encouragement of " filibusterism and piracy." He died almost without warning in May 1859, three days before the Annual Meeting of the Peace Society, of which he was the president. At his funeral Birmingham was a city of mourning, the roads thronged " in crowds amid the pouring rain " by the working people, who knew him for their friend and helper.

Few Friends had worked more untiringly for peace than Joseph Sturge, but his fellow members recognized such work as in harmony with the fundamental principles of the Society. Occasionally, indeed, some Friend might raise the question whether the peace policy was a practicable one, whether any logical limit could be put on the exercise of force, or whether a less sweeping condemnation of war might not be more effective.[1]

[1] See, for example, letters by Dr. Edward Ash in the *Friend* of 1871–2. Dr. Ash had left the Society for a time, but was re-admitted after a short sojourn in the Church of England. His views were controverted by Robert Charleton, by the Editor of the *Friend*, and other correspondents.

But these suggestions met with no acceptance, and whenever the official voice of the Society was raised in the nineteenth century on this subject, it maintained the old testimony. Instances have already been mentioned. The wars in India and China, in the early part of the Queen's reign, were wholly repugnant to Friends. The Epistle of 1840 contained some very plain words on the unchristian policy of Christian nations in the East. This was followed in 1842 by a memorial to the Queen, which, admitting the many difficulties connected with the administration of the Empire, nevertheless urged that the war might be brought to a close. The strained relations between England and America over the Oregon boundary question in 1845–6 led the Yearly Meeting to a specific recommendation of arbitration as a substitute for war. A deputation from the Meeting for Sufferings had already, in January, interviewed Peel, the Premier, and Aberdeen, the Foreign Secretary. The former " spoke strongly of the Earl of Aberdeen's peaceable policy in regard to Europe as well as America," and asked whether Friends in the United States could not use their influence with their Government. To this the deputation replied that they were in correspondence.[1]

In 1848, "amidst the rumours of wars prevailing around us, we continue to feel the value of the testimony which has been given us to bear against the use of arms and against all war, defensive as well as offensive. But in making this declaration we are not unmindful of the difference between bearing this testimony in a season of peace and in a time of actual war or civil outbreak ! " Four years later the Epistle, in protesting against the Militia Bill, reminded Friends of the only sure foundation for their principles. " Our testimony against the bearing of arms being grounded upon the supreme authority of the Lord Jesus, we have had afresh to feel that in maintaining it, our strength and safety consist in drawing very near unto Him, and in seeking to live under the government of His Spirit." The Crimean War, as already said, found Friends as a body united in opposition. " We feel bound explicitly," said the Epistle of 1854, " to avow our continued unshaken persuasion that all war is utterly incompatible with the plain precepts of our Divine Lord and Lawgiver, and with the whole spirit and tenor of His Gospel ; and that no plea of necessity or policy, however

---

[1] *Vide* also Yearly Meeting Epistles, 1834, 1839, 1840, 1847. A deputation from the Indiana Meeting for Sufferings memorialized Congress on the matter in April 1846. The account of the deputation to Peel is in the *Book of Cases*, iv. 169.

urgent or peculiar, can avail to release either individuals or nations from the paramount allegiance which they owe unto Him who hath said ' Love your enemies.' " In 1856 the Meeting welcomed " with reverent thankfulness " the return of peace. The outbreak of the Continental war in 1859 was sorrowfully commented on, and, while the pacific course of the English Government was gratefully recognized, the Epistle added :—

" We cannot reflect without sorrow upon the contagious tendency of war, and upon the symptoms so widely prevalent of a spirit prompt both to take and to give offence ; which no professions of international amity, however sincere, can counteract. If war is to be prevented the spirit from which war proceeds must be excluded. As with individuals, so with nations, the beginnings of strife must be watchfully guarded against. To give occasions of offence or jealousy to the Governments or to the inhabitants of other countries, whether by imputing evil motives, by needless alarms of invasion, or by anything approaching to a hostile attitude, is inconsistent alike with Christian duty and with true patriotism. We ought, as Englishmen, to remember that the feelings of our neighbours are as sensitive and as much entitled to consideration as our own ; and if our words or our actions tend to irritate and offend them, we can hardly hope for the continuance of peace."

A warning to young Friends against joining the Volunteer Rifle Clubs ("the object of which is to acquire dexterity and certainty in the destruction of human life ") implies that some had done so and, in fact, the summarized replies to the queries of this period mention one or two instances. Friends, however, do not seem to have realized at first the significance of the Volunteer movement and of the suspension of the Militia ballot in keeping the country for so many years clear of the tide of Continental militarism. During the Civil War the Epistles (as well as those directly addressed to American Yearly Meetings) offer deep sympathy to American Friends both in the trials of war and " the unfaithfulness of their own members." In December 1861, when peace between England and America was threatened by the *Trent* affair, Friends in both countries worked hard to maintain good relations, and English Friends in 1866, " opposed as we are on Christian grounds both to war and slavery," welcomed the United States deliverance from both.

The Franco-Prussian War of 1870 was perhaps the first to cause in the public mind an uneasy feeling that such bloodshed and destruction were out of harmony with modern civilization and religious thought. The *Illustrated London News* even expressed a pious hope that the military inventions of the day were fast making war impossible.[1] But the dreadful effectiveness of the German military machine soon aroused an interest in the technical details of military operations, and also a certain fear for the safety of England as the supposed " preparedness " of France crumbled into ruins. In reference to this fear the *Friend* in September 1870 commented on a " panic " leading article in *The Times* (" we are the only unarmed people in the world ") that " the two most *prepared* nations of Europe are now those engaged in the deadliest strife." Early in 1871 the Meeting for Sufferings published in the daily press and otherwise circulated an earnest " Appeal " to its fellow countrymen to discountenance the war spirit in their midst.

The Society, however, was not content with mere words. As news came through of the sufferings and privations of non-combatants in the districts over which hostilities had passed, the heart of England was stirred to pity. Individual Friends felt the call to service. At the end of October 1870 Samuel J. Capper, from personal experience in France, endorsed the appeal (in the *Daily News*, October 21st) of the Maires of the Arrondissement of Briey, between Metz and Sedan, " not for aid to enable us to destroy life, but for aid to maintain human life " in their famine-stricken district. In the same (November) issue of the *Friend* appeared another appeal, dated October 27th, and signed by eight Friends attending the Social Science Congress at Newcastle, for a fund to be raised by Friends and expended under the care of the Meeting for Sufferings for the benefit of the victims of the war. These appeals were the starting-point of the two funds, the " *Daily News* Fund " and the " Friends' War Victims Relief Fund," which in the next nine months brought untold comfort to these unhappy people. The Meeting for Sufferings took up the " concern," issuing an appeal of its own and appointing a committee which included John Bright and other Quaker members of Parliament, to arrange for the raising and distribution of the Relief Fund. The final Report on the administration of the fund accounted for its expenditure as follows [2] :—

---

[1] " The war just commenced so recklessly will, perhaps, make a large contribution towards permanent peace by showing that in these latter days it can only be prosecuted under conditions too horrible, both in their certainty and in their severity, for men to accept. This is the only solace we can discover in it—namely, a possibility that war may die by its own hands " (July 23, 1870).

[2] *Rapport de la Répartition des Secours*, by James Long, M.A.

Relief to Agriculturists.

	Francs.
Seed corn of various kinds	2,611,630
Agricultural implements	82,947
Cattle	102,000

Relief to the Poor.

Houses and furniture	13,750
Food, medicine, and fuel	257,250
Organization of the work for the unemployed, wages, etc.	50,525

Gifts in Money.

To various localities	167,625
To 69 Communes round Paris	536,375

This relief at the current exchange in France at the time amounted to 4,055,071 francs, or about £162,000, and there were in addition large gifts of clothing. The fund was greatly helped by sympathizers outside the Society : as the need grew, public meetings were held on its behalf in many towns. About forty workers, nearly all Friends, were engaged for a whole or part of the period in organizing the relief in France, besides a number occupied at the London Office.[1]

[1] The names of the workers in France were : Henry J. Allen, William Jones (later Secretary of the Peace Society), Thomas Whitwell, Robert Spence Watson (President of the National Liberal Federation 1890–1902), Eliot Howard, William Pumphrey, Daniel Hack, John Bellows, Elizabeth Ann Barclay, J. Augusta Fry, Richenda E. Reynolds, Amelia de Bunsen, Samuel Gurney, John Henry Gurney, Junior, Charles Elcock, Henry Tuke Mennell, Theodore Nield, John Dunning, Joseph Smith, Thomas Snowdon, Thomas D. Nicholson, Samuel J. Capper, Charles Wing Gray, Joseph Crosfield, Edmund Pace, William Beck, William B. Norcott, Walter Rigley, Ellen Jackson, Ernest Beck, William Dyne, James Hack Tuke (worker in the Irish Famine), James Long, John Burnett Taylor, Arthur Albright, Wilson Sturge, J. Fyfe Stewart. Many accounts of the work have been published. Besides the official *Rapport* presented to the French Government, mentioned above, reference may be made to the privately printed Reports of the Committee, or to the Report to the Yearly Meeting (*Proceedings of the Yearly Meeting*, 1871), articles by Henry Tuke Mennell in the *Friend*, January–September 1871, three contemporary publications by relief workers ; S. J. Capper, *Wanderings in War Time* ; Spence Watson, *The Villages round Metz* ; John Bellows, *The Track of the War round Metz* ; also William Jones, *Quaker Campaigns in Peace and War*, 1899, and P. Corder, *Life of Robert Spence-Watson*, ch. iv ; also reminiscences in the *Friends' Quarterly Examiner* by two of the workers (Eliot Howard in 1913 and H. T. Mennell in 1915). The official certificate, granted as credentials to each worker on behalf of the Yearly Meeting, described Friends as believing " all war to be contrary to the will and spirit of our Heavenly Father as shown in the New Testament, but moved by Christian love we desire to alleviate, as far as may be in our power, the misery of non-combatants irrespective of nationalities—remembering that all are children of one Father, and that one Saviour died for all."

The first two workers, William Jones and Henry J. Allen, on their way to investigate the conditions in the devastated area, were advised by the British Minister at Brussels to adopt some distinguishing device other than the Red Cross brassard, which had for the moment been discredited by unauthorized use. Their choice fell upon a red and black star, which, as badge and brassard, has ever since been the device of the Friends' War Victims Relief organizations in different wars, and has become known in many scenes of misery.

The scope of the work may be gathered from the financial statement already quoted, and it has been described at length in the books and papers mentioned in the note on the preceding page. At first, in its strict neutrality, the Committee offered relief to the German villages in the Saar Valley, which had suffered severely from the passage and quartering of troops, and to some extent from actual hostilities. The offer, however, was politely declined by the authorities, and the Commissioners found from a visit that German organizations had supplied all the help required. The case of France was, of course, far otherwise. An arrangement was made with the *Daily News* and other relief funds by which overlapping was as far as possible avoided, and the Commissioners started work in the wide district round Metz, which had been the scene of some of the bloodiest battles of the opening campaign, had supported vast hordes of the soldiers of both armies, and much of which, after the fall of Metz, was administered by the Germans as a conquered province. Here, in many cases, the villages had been dependent upon their conquerors for food, and when the army moved on, they were left utterly destitute. To these unhappy people the Friends brought regular supplies of food, medical treatment, and supplies, fuel for the winter, and later on—what was almost more valuable as a provision of present work, hope for the future, and the means of life—ample stocks of seed-corn and the steam ploughs with which to prepare the ground. In the early spring, when the Loire district was clear of the contending armies, work was begun there. There the long hostilities had resulted in the almost entire destruction of crops and farm stock. The chief work of the Friends was the provision of seed-corn and milch-cattle. Of the latter, several hundred of good quality with bulls, calves, and goats were purchased by James Long in Spain, and apportioned among the various Communes, the authorities of which agreed to maintain in perpetuity cattle,

to the number granted, for the benefit of the inhabitants. These
" Quakers " (as the cattle were branded) supplied an urgent need.[1]
As soon as the armistice was signed and it was possible to reach Paris,
a deputation proceeded thither to investigate the needs of the surrounding district.   After conferences with the local authorities
and the representatives of other relief societies, it was arranged that
the whole of the relief in the Department of the Seine, outside Paris
and St. Denis, should be undertaken by the Friends.   The district
and its needs was thus described by one of the investigators :—

"The Department forms a narrow belt or girdle round Paris
varying in width from two to six miles.   It embraces all the district
which has been actually desolated by the operations of the siege,
and its condition is a most deplorable one.   The suburban district
immediately outside the walls of Paris has not greatly suffered by
actual bombardment ; but the inhabitants having been compelled to
leave it during the siege, it has been occupied by the French Mobiles,
who have completely wrecked it, tearing up the floors and all the
woodwork of the houses for firewood, and inflicting every possible
injury and damage upon it.   Outside this belt are the villages
occupied by the advanced posts of either army, and the space between
them, which was untenable by either.   In this zone there is nothing
but ruin and desolation ; a sadder scene of destruction it is impossible
to imagine.   Outside this belt are the villages held by the Prussian
Army, which have suffered severely and are greatly injured, but not
to the same extent as those which I have described."[2]

On March 3rd, the day of the Prussian occupation of Paris,
three Friends, Joseph Crosfield, Robert Spence Watson, and Ernest
Beck, left London to administer the relief, joining W. B. Norcott,
who had remained in Paris to secure offices and make preliminary
arrangements.   By these friends and others who followed them
(including James Hack Tuke, who brought with him the experience
gained in the Irish Famine), the sum of £20,000, a quantity of
clothing, and a grant of £1,000 of vegetable seeds from the
Mansion House Fund, were distributed among 62 Communes
containing about 300,000 inhabitants.   Yet the Committee, in
reporting this relief to the Yearly Meeting, spoke of it as but " a
drop in the bucket," in comparison with the immense losses of the
people.

[1] *Friend*, February 1871.
[2] *Ibid.*, March 1871 (H. T. Mennell).

The work in all the districts was carried on at no inconsiderable risk to the Commissioners. More than one, on leaving England, was told by men just returned from the scene of hostilities that nothing could be done in regions infested with *francs-tireurs* and robbers without the protection of pistols. Yet no Friend travelled armed. At first they were constantly suspected of being French or German spies, and had uncomfortable experiences in consequence, but they soon won the confidence of the authorities on both sides. Round Metz their greatest enemy was the pestilential air from the battle-fields. Here many workers were laid aside by illness. Five suffered from small-pox, of whom one, Ellen Allen, died.

In Paris those workers who remained until the outbreak of the Communists also suffered considerable risk. Indeed, the mere routine work of investigation and relief in a devastated country under military occupation in mid-winter was no light or easy task. From both Government and people there was a warm expression of gratitude : decorations were pressed on individual Friends, which they steadily refused. Finally the Minister of Agriculture and Commerce sent the following letter, in November 1871, to the official representatives of the Society of Friends :—

"Je suis autorisé par Monsieur le Président de la République et par la Conseil des Ministres, à transmettre à la Société Anglaise des Amis l'expression des sentiments du peuple et du Gouvernement Français. Puisse le souvenir de notre profonde reconnaisance vivre chez vous aussi longtemps que vivra chez nous le souvenir de vos généreux efforts."[1]

At the close of the war some other Friends engaged earnestly in Christian mission work in Paris and other parts of France. This led to the establishment of a mission for women and girls under Justine Dalencourt, a French Catholic who had been brought into touch with Friends while a refugee in London and later joined the Society. She is still continuing her work. The miseries they saw burnt in upon many of the workers a personal and intimate horror of war and its accompaniments. "How the remembrance" (wrote William Jones of the villages round Metz) "of homes like this in which happiness will never again be known on this side of the grave

[1] Quoted by William Jones, *Quaker Campaigns*, p. 83. The Society was also gratefully mentioned in the *Journal Officiel* of the French Republic, and the *Journal Mensuel* of the Society of Agriculture. In 1873 Robert Spence Watson was unexpectedly presented by the French Government with a gold medal specially struck in recognition of his "eminent services."

crowds on the mind, and utterly tarnishes and blots out all that men call *glory* in successful war, and leaves behind nought but its cold reality in the unspeakable misery and sorrow of its wretched victims."[1]

In a similar strain Spence Watson wrote home :

" I wish I could tell you how I loathe this war. It is too horrible. The misery which it brings with it is altogether incredible. I begin now to dream of it all night, for it has become a terrible reality. Bad I always thought it, but I never dreamed that it could be so bad. I am glad I have seen what I have ; it is a great lesson, and I wish all the editors in England could just see Bazaine's army ; we should hear less of the glory of war for some years to come."[2]

In 1876 two of the Commissioners, James Long and William Jones, were sent out again by Friends to distribute relief, this time to Bulgaria and Macedonia, to the scenes of the atrocious massacres and cruelties which led to the intervention of Russia and the liberation of so much of the Balkans from the Turkish yoke. In 1892 other Friends, one of them, John Bellows, also a former Commissioner, devoted themselves to the relief of the famine-stricken districts of Russia, distributing a fund of £40,000. At the end of the century Russia again claimed their interest. The accounts of the persecuted Doukhobors brought to England by Tolstoyans perhaps over-emphasized that sect's points of resemblance to Friends ; the latter, however, particularly interested by the Doukhobors' refusal of military service, took up their cause warmly. It was largely through the financial help and organization of a Committee of Friends, that seven thousand of the sect were transported to Canada in the autumn of 1899 ; and other Friends, particularly women teachers, helped them through the first difficulties of their settlement in communal villages there.[3]

The Czar's call of the Governments of the civilized world to a Hague Conference to consider the reduction of armaments and the establishment of an International Court of Arbitration, was warmly welcomed by Friends. The Yearly Meeting of 1899 sent a deputation to The Hague with a message of congratulation and

[1] William Jones, *Quaker Campaigns*, etc., p. 93.

[2] Corder, *Life of Spence Watson*, p. 104, quoted from *The Villages around Metz*.

[3] The Committee at first hoped to settle the Doukhobors in Cyprus, but the island proved an unsuitable home, and the thousand who reached it eventually were removed to Canada. *Vide* Aylmer Maude, *A Peculiar People—The Doukhobors*.

prayerful good wishes to the various Ambassadors assembled there. But soon these hopes of a brighter dawn for the coming century were overshadowed by the Transvaal War.

Apart from these activities, the last thirty years of the nineteenth century were not marked by any new departure in the peace work of the Society, unless the revival of the National Peace Congress as an annual event, in which many Friends assisted, may be thus described. In 1877 and again in 1885 the Yearly Meeting Epistle expressed the thankfulness of Friends that threatened wars between England and Russia had been averted, and in 1884 it recorded their " sorrow and distress at the bloodshed which has taken place in Egypt and the Soudan in the course of the last two years." When in 1897 English sympathizers began to work for the relief and protection of the Armenians, Friends joined heartily in the effort, in which they continue to take an active part. But the Epistle of that year rejected the plea that war in this case was the only remedy. " Our sympathy with the persecuted and oppressed in Armenia, Crete, and elsewhere, does not lessen our conviction that even on their behalf it is wrong to take the sword, and that all war, defensive as well as offensive, is incompatible with true loyalty to the Prince of Peace." Such a declaration might seem to be an easy one, made at the expense of others, but as the nineteenth century closed, it was repeated in the midst of a war in which England was involved. " We fail to see " (was the declaration of the Yearly Meeting of 1900) " how any war can be waged in the Spirit of Jesus Christ."

CHAPTER XI

JOHN BRIGHT

WE feel that Mr. Bright is entitled to a higher eulogy than any that could be due to intellect or any that could be due to success. Of mere success he was indeed a conspicuous example; in intellect he may lay claim to a most distinguished place; but the character of the man lay deeper than his intellect, deeper than his eloquence, deeper than anything that can be described or seen on the surface, and the supreme eulogy which is his due I apprehend to be this, that he elevated political life to a higher elevation and a loftier standard, and that he has thereby bequeathed to his country the character of a statesman which can be made the subject not only of admiration and not only of gratitude, but of reverential contemplation. —Mr. Gladstone in the House of Commons, March 29, 1889.

AFTER the year 1756, when the Quaker deputies retired from the Assembly of Pennsylvania, for almost a century the Society of Friends had little representation in the political world. It is true that the agitation against the slave trade, both in England and America, originated among the Quakers, but their interest in it was primarily philanthropic, and the actual political leadership of the movement was in other hands. William Penn and John Bright—the list of Quaker statesmen is short but noteworthy. Of the two it is the modern Friend for whom the higher place must be claimed, on the ground of a complete and consistent life. He was not like Penn, the ruler of a great territory or the adviser of a king, but his empire was in the hearts of the working people, and his highest reward was their unbounded trust in him. Palmerston could say, during the Crimean War fever, that he did not " reckon Cobden, Bright and Co. for anything," and in 1859 the Queen refused a suggestion that Bright should be given a Privy Councillorship on the ground that " it would be impossible to allege any service Mr. Bright has rendered "—this fourteen years after the Repeal of the Corn Laws ! Yet in the Home Rule crisis of 1886–7 his influence, more even

18

than his arguments, told heavily against the Government. " Every word," wrote Lord Morley, " seemed to weigh a pound."[1]

This is not the place in which to sketch once more Bright's career, the touching and romantic comradeship with Cobden in so many righteous causes, the struggle for the enfranchisement of the people, the attacks on privilege and tyranny. But his work for peace was so much a part of his life that biographical detail will occasionally be necessary. First, it may be well to clear up a misunderstanding. It has been hinted by some that although Bright was a Quaker by birth and upbringing, he was not in full sympathy with the views of Friends. Nothing could be less true. Throughout his life he faithfully attended Friends' Meetings for worship, and took at times an active part in their Meetings for business. His household worship of " reading " and " silence " impressed Lord Morley with its purity and fervour. Yet Bright felt himself a lack of power to give public utterance to his deepest spiritual experience. In 1875, at the age of sixty-four, he refused to take up the office of Elder, on these grounds : " The labours of my life have taken me out of the way of service for our little Church, and have, to a large extent, unfitted me for it. I feel that there is nothing above the humblest office—shall I say that of doorkeeper ?—which I could properly undertake. . . . I feel humbled by the proposition made to me, and that I am so far from the state in which it would or might seem possible for me to consider it." [2]

" He always remained a Friend both in his heart and in his life," writes Mr. Trevelyan,[3] basing his verdict on the testimony of those nearest to Bright. Yet it is true that at the opening of his political career he was regarded with some distrust by elderly and conservative Friends, who, influenced by a tradition from the old days of revolution and conspiracy in which the Society suffered unjust persecution, shrank from any form of political activity. Mrs. Boyce, in Records of a Quaker Family,[4] describes how Bright's defence of himself and the Anti-Corn Law League from a veiled censure in the Yearly Meeting of 1843 was rewarded by " a slight tapping noise " from those quiet benches as he resumed his seat. Surely this gentle applause,

---

[1] Morley, Life of Gladstone, ii. 582.
[2] No doubt Bright's words carry an allusion to Psalm lxxxiv, but in the larger Friends' Meetings there are actual " doorkeepers."
[3] Life of John Bright, p. 414.
[4] The Richardsons of Cleveland.

against all Quaker precedent, was the greatest triumph of John Bright's golden oratory.

Of late years, when the great peace advocate is no longer here to answer for himself, some critics have gone further and have tried to prove that his opposition to war would have given way before the circumstances of some particular war (waged since his death), and that he would have supported and approved the arbitrament of force in such a case. In this argument they rely on the admitted fact that Bright carefully and explicitly met the advocates of each war on their own ground, and showed that even on their principles it was to be condemned. As was said once, he always argued the question on a Blue-book basis.[1] In two instances, as will be seen, he admitted that on those principles one party to the struggle was justified in meeting war by war, but even so he was unsparing in his condemnation of the crimes and errors which had plunged the combatants into so terrible a catastrophe.

However honestly he believed that his opposition was confined to the circumstances of each case, there is scarcely a speech in which his personal abhorrence to war is not manifest, and more than once he alludes specifically to the principles of Friends. For example, at a Peace Conference in Manchester in the year 1853, in a remarkable passage, he distinguished his personal convictions upon war from the arguments, political and economic, which he employed in public controversy.

" I shall not read the Sermon on the Mount to men who do not acknowledge its authority, nor shall I insist on my reading of the New Testament to men who take a different view of it ; nor shall I ask the members of a Church whose Articles especially justify the bearing of arms to join in any movement which shall be founded upon what are called abstract Christian peace doctrines. But I will argue this question on the ground which our opponents admit, which not professing Christians only, but Mahomedans and heathen and every man of intelligence and common sense and common humanity will admit. I will argue it upon this ground, that war is probably the greatest of all human calamities." [2]

Again, in his great speech in the House of Commons on the declaration of war against Russia (March 31, 1854) he declines to discuss the war, " on the abstract principle of peace at any price,

[1] *Friend*, 1889, p. 101.
[2] Report of Conference in the *Herald of Peace*, February 1853, p. 182.

as it is termed, which is held by a small minority of persons in this country, founded on religious opinions which are not generally received." Many years later, at Manchester (October 2, 1876), he definitely attributed his opposition to the Crimean War to his Quaker upbringing.

" I do not know why I differed from other people so much, but sometimes I have thought it happened from the education I had received in the religious sect with which I am connected. We have no creed which monarchs and statesmen and high priests have written out for us. Our creed, so far as we comprehend it, comes pure and direct from the New Testament. We have no 37th Article to declare that it is lawful for Christian men, at the command of the civil magistrate, to wear weapons and to serve in wars—which means, of course, and was intended to mean, that it is lawful for Christian men to engage in any part of the world, in any cause, at the command of a monarch, or of a prime minister, or of a Parliament, or of a commander-in-chief, in the slaughter of his fellow-men, whom he might never have seen before and from whom he had not received the smallest injury, and against whom he had no reason to feel the smallest touch of anger or resentment. Now, my having been brought up as I was would lead me naturally to think that . . . the war with Russia in the Crimea was a matter that required very distinct evidence to show that it was lawful, or that it was in any way politic or reasonable."

In the great speech for peace at Edinburgh, in October 1853, Bright defined war in no uncertain terms.

" What is war ? I believe that half the people that talk about war have not the slightest idea of what it is. In a short sentence it may be summed up to be the combination and concentration of all the horrors, crimes, and sufferings of which human nature is capable."

In 1879 a Mr. Urquhart of Manchester was moved by Bright's strenuous opposition to the war policy of the Conservative Government to write to him with the question whether he was prepared to condemn all war and abolish all means of military defence. Bright made the following reply [1] :—

" I have not time to write fully upon the question. It is one on which men should make up their minds as to their own personal duty. So far men have defended war as if it were a natural condition

[1] *Public Letters*, p. 238.

of things which must always continue. It might be true that war could not always be avoided, and that in some cases it might be justifiable, and yet, granting this, it might be shown that nineteen out of every twenty wars which have been waged ought to have been avoided, and were criminal in the highest degree. I believe that all our wars since the time and accession of William III might have been avoided on principles which do not require the absolute condemnation of war in every possible case that may be suggested or imagined. We need not discuss the question as you put it. We shall change the policy and the aspect of our country and of the world, if we leave the demon of war to the cases in which there seems to Christian and rational men no escape from the miseries he inflicts upon mankind. I would advise you not to trouble yourself with the abstract question. The practical question is the one which presses, and when we have settled that, there will remain very little of the mischief to contend about or to get rid of. If you wish to know the best argument against war, I would recommend you to read Jonathan Dymond's *Essays on the Principles of Morality*, or his *Essay on War*."

The recommendation of Dymond's uncompromisingly Quaker Essay shows plainly where Bright's own opinion rested, in spite of the careful phrasing of the letter.[1] A few months before, at Manchester,[2] he had described the essentially unchristian character of war in language which may have inspired Mr. Urquhart's question.

"We may differ upon many points of Articles in Churches, but we are all agreed on this : that if there be anything definite

[1] In 1885 Bright contributed a short introduction to Dymond's *Essay*, which included some of the strongest phrases from his own utterances. " I think (he wrote) every man must make up his own mind on that abstract [Quaker] principle, and I would recommend him, if he wants to know a book that says a good deal about it, to study the New Testament, and make up his mind from that source. . . . If we may presume to ask ourselves what, in the eye of the Supreme Ruler, is the greatest crime which His creatures commit, I think we may almost with certainty conclude that it is the crime of war." The one specific case in which Bright thought arbitration impossible was that of the issue between the Turkish Government of 1876 and its persecuted Christian dependencies (speech at Birmingham, December 4, 1876).
" I do not in any case, as you know, stand forward as a defender of those sanguinary struggles which continually or at times take place among the nations ; but I know not how in some cases they are to be avoided. There can be no arbitration unless the parties to the dispute are willing. There can be no arbitration between a Government such as that which reigns at Constantinople and the suffering peoples of whom we have lately heard so much."
[2] April 30, 1878, Robertson, *Life of John Bright*, ii. 201.

and distinct in the teachings of the New Testament, it is that which would lead to amity among people and to love and justice and mercy and peace on the whole of God's earth upon which His sun shines. If then we are agreed upon this, let us, if it be possible to throw off the hypocrite in this matter—let us get rid of our Christianity, or get rid of our tendency and willingness to go to war. War is a game which, if their subjects were wise, kings would not be able to play at ; and be they kings or queens, be they statesmen of this or that colour or party, never let any man go headlong into any policy that points direct for war until he has thoroughly examined the question by his own best intellect, brought it to bear on his own Christian conscience, and decided it for himself as if he were asked to pull the trigger or to use the sword."

Such was the careful and considered language of John Bright, both in the maturity of his political life and in later years. It is impossible to resist the conclusion that his opponents were right in their belief that his opposition to war was primarily based on moral and religious convictions, though they were wholly wrong in seizing upon this fact as an excuse for neglecting the weighty political arguments which he marshalled against each war or project of war in its turn.

A brief account of these particular episodes must complete this study of Bright as a man of peace. He won his spurs as an orator in scenes which fitly illustrate the favourite thesis of Friends, that peace is an active virtue different in quality from the passiveness of non-resistance, and that wrong may be effectively resisted without resort to physical force. The struggle against Church rates in Rochdale was only the preliminary to the greater struggle against the Corn Laws. And it must not be forgotten that both in the Corn Law agitation and in the longer agitation, not yet ended, for reform of the franchise and the land laws, Bright was attacking evils which he believed in each case to be largely the result of our last great Continental war.

" The knowledge of what that war had meant to the mass of the people while it lasted, and the legacy of misery and degradation that it left behind, was burnt into the soul of Bright, and reinforced by its modern example the faith of his peace-loving forefathers. His view of the unnecessary character of the war begun in 1793 may be wrong—or it may be right ; but his grasp on the fact that war, though sometimes sport to the rich, is always death to the poor, was to stand England in good stead in coming years."[1] The repeal of the Corn Laws and the introduction of Free Trade was at once the triumph and the justification of the peaceful agitation of the League with its weapons of argument and persuasion. Later generations have forgotten the strong tide of discontent and disorder which surged through the working classes during the thirty years of misery and hunger after Waterloo, finding vent in the abortive Chartist Movement and in many serious local riots. It was the considered judgment of careful observers that England's immunity from the revolutionary upheaval which shook down the continental thrones in the year 1848 was very largely due to the improvement in the condition and temper of the people brought about by Free Trade.

The next campaign of Bright and Cobden was one in which, instead of acting as the leaders of strong and enthusiastic forces, they were more and more isolated in what was, at the time, a losing battle. It was no thanks to Palmerston that England was not continuously at war during the two decades before his death in 1865. In his spirited foreign policy he employed a dual method, treating all strong Powers as our natural enemies, to be met by large armaments and bullying diplomacy, and the weaker Powers as our natural inferiors, to be reformed and scolded and generally set in their proper places. This intervention and admonition was often on behalf of the oppressed (although they seldom gained much benefit from their champion), but sometimes, as in the famous case of Don Pacifico and the mischievous Chinese War of 1857, for less worthy objects.

In the great Don Pacifico debate of June 1850 Bright did not speak, giving way to Cobden, but he had to defend even his vote against a nominally Liberal and really Whig Government to his Manchester constituents, which he did on the grounds that Palmerston's policy " necessarily leads to irritation, and to quarrels with other nations, and may lead even to war ; and that it involves the necessity of maintaining greater armaments and a heavier taxation."[2] Next year, when Kossuth visited England, Bright, while joining warmly in the popular welcome, made clear his distrust of any movement for intervention abroad. He wrote to Cobden (November 4, 1851) : " I am expected to be at the meeting in the Free Trade Hall [Manchester] and to speak. I am in a desperate puzzle what to do, but certainly if I speak I shall go against

---

[1] Trevelyan, *Life*, p. 47.   [2] Trevelyan, *Life*, p. 192.

any notion of *fighting* for Hungary or any other country. . . . I am very apprehensive that this Hungarian sympathy will breed a spirit which we have hoped was subsiding, and will tend to fill the people's heart with pride and self-conceit, and with a notion that it is our mission to become knight-errants in the cause of freedom to other nations, whilst we are forgetting how much we have to do at home." In his speech (November 11, 1851) he emphasized the moral force of public opinion as opposed to the material pressure of armaments. " There are men who say : ' Why, what is the use of your sympathy if you have no regiments and no ships ? Well, I shall take another line of argument, and ask you whether there be any force in opinion, in opinion acting upon the nation. Why, let me ask you where are you assembled ? Recollect when this hall was built, recollect by whom it was built, recollect from this platform and this hall went forth the voices which generated opinion in England, which concentrated it, which gathered it little by little, until it became a power before which huge majorities in both Houses of Parliament became impotent minorities—and the most august and powerful aristocracy of the world had to succumb, and finally, through that opinion we struck down for ever the most gigantic tyranny that was ever practised."[1]

But the star of Lord Palmerston was in the ascendant. In 1852, dismissed from office by the influence of the Court, he regained power by the defeat of Lord John Russell's Militia Bill, and at the beginning of 1853 there broke out one of those mysterious " panics "—or agitations for larger armaments—which attack the political world with, apparently, the same periodicity as those which shake the financial world. An ill-defined distrust of Napoleon III, which Palmerston shared with a large number of his countrymen, blossomed, under careful nurture by Press and politicians, into a full-blown " invasion " panic. Cobden and Bright used all the resources of eloquence and satire to show the baseless nature of such fears, and Bright described the disastrous results of a war between two great and civilized nations, undeterred by the readiness of his enemies to declare that he judged all things by the touchstone of commercial interest.

" I draw no picture," he said,[2] " of blood and crime, of battles by sea and land ; they are common to every war, and nature

[1] Robertson, *Life*, ii. 10, 11.
[2] Manchester, January 27, 1853, Robertson, ii. 14.

shudders at the enormities of man ; but I see before me a vast
commerce collapsed, a mighty industry paralysed, and a people
impoverished and exhausted, with ever-increasing burdens and a
gathering discontent."

In the autumn he repeated the picture : " War will brutalize
our people, increase our taxes, destroy our industry, postpone the
promised Parliamentary reform, it may be many years."[1] But the
threatened war of October 1853 was not the threatened war of the
previous January. France was no longer the enemy waiting to
invade our coasts, but the ally with whom we were to rescue the
helpless Turk from Russian intrigue. At Edinburgh in that month
a Peace Congress was held at which Admiral Sir Charles Napier
vigorously expressed the views of the war party. Bright's reply
has become a classic, which may be read with profit to-day. In it
he alluded to the objection that the time was inopportune to speak
of peace.

" The right time to oppose the errors and prejudices of the
people never comes in the eyes of those writers in the public Press
who pander to those prejudices. They say : ' We must not do so-and-
so, we shall embarrass the Government.' . . . We wish to protest
against the maintenance of great armaments in time of peace. We
wish to protest against the spirit which is not only willing for war,
but eager for war ; and we wish to protest, with all the emphasis
of which we are capable, against the mischievous policy pursued
so long by this country of interfering with the internal affairs of
other countries, and thereby leading to disputes, and often to
disastrous wars."

The peroration of the speech was an appeal to the moral sense
of his countrymen.

" . . . You profess to be a Christian nation. You make it
your boast even—though boasting is somewhat out of place in such
questions—you make it your boast that you are a Protestant people,
and that you draw your rule of doctrine and practice as from a
well pure and undefiled, from the living oracles of God and from the
direct revelation of the Omnipotent. . . .

" Is this a reality ? or is your Christianity a romance ? is your
profession a dream ? No, I am sure that your Christianity is not
a romance, and I am equally sure that your profession is not a

[1] Letter to a public meeting at the Manchester Athenæum, October 6, 1853,
Robertson, ii. 27.

dream. It is because I believe this that I appeal to you with confidence and that I have hope and faith in the future. I believe that we shall see, and at no very distant time, sound economic principles spreading much more widely amongst the people ; a sense of justice growing up in a soil which hitherto has been deemed unfruitful ; and which will be better than all—the Churches of the United Kingdom—the Churches of Britain awaking, as it were, from their slumbers, and girding their loins to more glorious work, when they shall not only accept and believe in the prophecy, but labour earnestly for its fulfilment, that there shall come a time—a blessed time—a time that shall last for ever—when ' nation shall not lift up sword against nation, neither shall they learn war any more.' "

The hope at the moment was doomed to disappointment, for the Churches gave no help to the small, but weighty minority which opposed the Crimean War.[1] Bright and Cobden were left almost alone, branded as traitors and refused a hearing in the country, though never in the House of Commons. The eloquence of Bright's speeches and letters upon the war was even then frankly admitted, and few are now prepared to controvert his arguments, but eloquence and reason could not save him from execration and defeat. As Mr. Gladstone[2] finely said of him, at that crisis he laid his popularity as a sacrifice upon the altar of his duty. The chapters upon the war in Mr. Trevelyan's *Life* deal fully with the political side of his opposition. Here there is only space for some quotations which

---

[1] Years later (Birmingham, January 13, 1878), Bright diagnosed the war-fever of the nation. "At that time the public mind was filled with falsehoods, and it was in a state which we might describe by saying that it became almost drunk with passion. With regard to Russia, you recollect, many of you, what was said of her power, of her designs, of the despotism which ruled in Russia, of the danger which hung over all the freedom of all the countries of Europe. And the error was not confined to a particular class. It spread from the cottage to all classes above, and it did not even spare those who were within the precincts of the throne. It was not adopted by the clergy of the Church of England only, but by the ministers of the Nonconformist bodies also. The poison had spread everywhere. The delusion was all-pervading. The mischief seemed universal, and, as I know to my cost, it was scarcely worth while to utter an argument or bring forth a fact against it." Many, of course, recognized the folly and futility of the war, but had not the courage to be unpopular. Walter, proprietor of *The Times*, said to Bright : " When the country would go to war, it was not worth while to oppose it, hurting themselves, and doing no good." Sir James Graham said in later years : " You were entirely right about the Crimean War ; we were entirely wrong."

[2] At Birmingham, June 1, 1877.

characteristically reveal the moral impulse which urged him to that opposition. It is true that, as Mr. Trevelyan says, Bright definitely claimed to oppose the war as " contrary to the national interests and the principles professed and avowed by the nation, and on no other ground,"[1] but it is equally true that his opponents disregarded the claim, and branded him as a " peace-at-any-price " man. Their policy was unfair in itself, and cowardly, inasmuch as on this plea they escaped the necessity of answering his unanswerable attacks, but their instinctive feeling that whole moral continents divided his view of any war from theirs was well founded. Even Palmerston's ill-bred taunt to " the honourable and reverend gentleman " serves to remind us of the moral indignation which linked Bright's speeches with the utterances of the Hebrew prophets. As Dr. Johnson's old friend confided to him that he had tried in his time to be a philosopher, but " cheerfulness was always breaking in," so we may say of Bright's speeches that he tried to be a politician, but Christianity was always breaking in. In the very speech (March 31, 1854) in which he claimed to discuss the war on admitted principles of English policy are two passages which reveal the distance which separated him from many of his countrymen. He had sympathy, he said, for the oppressed everywhere, " but it is not on a question of sympathy that I dare involve this country, or any country, in a war which must cost an incalculable amount of treasure and of blood. It is not my duty to make this country the knight-errant of the human race." And, as was his wont, he translated the cost of war into terms of individual and national happiness—a calculation which, half a century later, would have drawn upon him the name of " Little Englander."

". . . I believe if this country, seventy years ago, had adopted the principle of non-intervention in every case where her interests were not directly and obviously assailed, that she would have been saved from much of the pauperism and brutal crimes by which our Government and people have alike been disgraced. This country might have been a garden, every dwelling might have been of marble, and every person who treads its soil might have been sufficiently educated. We should, indeed, have had less of military glory. We might have had neither Trafalgar nor Waterloo ; but we should have set the high example of a Christian nation, free in its institutions, courteous and just in its policy towards all foreign States, and

[1] Letter to Joseph Sturge, September 1857.

resting its policy on the unchangeable foundation of Christian morality."

The famous peroration of December 22, 1854, opening : " I am not, nor did I ever pretend, to be a statesman," closes with the hope of maintaining " to the last moment of my existence the priceless consolation that no word of mine has tended to promote the squandering of my country's treasure, or the spilling of one single drop of my country's blood." Palmerston and his followers were ready enough to label such an aspiration as " peace-at-any-price." Part of the price of war Bright described in his grave rebuke to Palmerston in debate on the Vote of Censure in July 1855 : " The noble Lord seems to me to be insensible to the fact that clouds are gathering round the horizon of this country ; he appears not to know that his policy is the doom of death to thousands upon thousands, carrying desolation to millions of hearts. He may perchance never see that which comes often to my vision—the interminable ghastly procession of our slaughtered countrymen, to which every day fresh lists of victims are added."

It was this sense of the desolation and destruction of war, far more than any pain arising from isolation or misunderstanding, that finally broke down Bright's strength and endurance and withdrew him, in 1856, from public life. He had in especial measure the emotion Wordsworth describes as,

> Due abhorrence of their guilt
> For whose dire ends tears flow and blood is spilt.

While he was seeking health in Italy, there came in February 1857 the dramatic overthrow of Palmerston by Cobden's Vote of Censure on the Chinese War. But at the General Election Palmerston swept the country on a wave of Jingoism, and every member of the " Manchester "—or peace—party lost his seat. Bright heard at Florence that he was placed at the foot of the poll in Manchester, on the express ground of his opposition to the Crimean and Chinese Wars. In the wise and courageous letter which he sent to Cobden[1] he made two prophecies, both fulfilled even more rapidly than he foretold.

" Ten years hence, those who live so long may see a complete change on the questions on which the public mind has recently been so active and so much mistaken. . . . We have taught what

[1] April 10, 1857.

was true in our ' School,' but the discipline was a little too severe for the scholars.   Disraeli will say he was right ; we are hardly of the English type, and success, political and personal success, cannot afford to reject the use which may be made of ignorance and prejudice among a people.   This is his doctrine and, with his views, it is true ; but, as we did not seek for personal objects, it is not true of us.   If we are rejected for peace and for truth, we stand higher before the world and for the future than if we mingled with the patient mediocrities which compose the present Cabinet."

In August 1857 a movement was set on foot among Birmingham Radicals to secure Bright for their vacant seat.   The one question in doubt was his attitude to the Indian Mutiny, news of which was just then filling England with horror and panic.   An urgent telegram to Scotland received a satisfactory reply, which he expanded in his election address.   In the latter (August 8, 1857) he said :—

" The success of the insurrection would involve anarchy in India unless some great man, emerging from the chaos, should build up a new empire based on and defended by military power. I am not prepared to defend the steps by which England has obtained dominion in the East but, looking to the interests of India and of England, I cannot oppose such measures as may be deemed necessary to suppress the existing disorder.   To restore order to India is mercy to India, but heavy will be the guilt of our countrymen should we neglect hereafter any measures which would contribute to the welfare of its hundred millions of population.   I hope the acts of the Government will be free from that vindictive and sanguinary spirit which is shown in many of the letters which appear in the newspapers, and that when the present crisis is over, all that exists of statesmanship in England will combine to work what good is possible out of so much evil."

To this position he steadily adhered.   As Mr. Trevelyan comments, his Quaker training freed him from the colour prejudice so deeply rooted amongst Englishmen, and he condemned in unsparing terms the blind passion of revenge which found vent in barbaric acts in India and wild words at home.   Some Friends felt that this pronouncement was a surrender to the war spirit, and it was to meet their objection that Bright wrote to Joseph Sturge (in the letter already quoted).

" Does our friend Southall think our Government should rest

quiet and allow every Englishman in India to be murdered ? I don't think so. They must act on their principles, seeing they admit no others. I have never advocated the extreme non-resistance principle in public or in private. I don't know whether I would logically maintain it." But whether Bright exposed himself to criticism from pacifist or from militarist, Birmingham welcomed him gladly and returned him unopposed, even though for some months more he could take no active part in politics. It was not until the autumn of 1858 that he was able to deliver the first of his great addresses to his constituents, which were to be the pride and delight of the city for many years to come. This speech on foreign policy, made on October 29th, is throughout entirely characteristic in its moral fervour, its passionate earnestness, and its touches of homely humour. In the opening sentences he met the charge of want of patriotism.

" How, indeed, can I, any more than any of you, be un-English and anti-national ? Was I not born upon the same soil ? Do I not come of the same English stock ? " and, after a scathing description of the confused policy which led to our past wars for the " balance of power " and of the tangle of treaties which still hampered our international relations, he uttered the magnificent *apologia* for his own attitude, which, familiar as it is, must be quoted once more here.

" I believe there is no permanent greatness to a nation except it be based upon morality. I do not care for military greatness or military renown. I care for the condition of the people among whom I live. There is no man in England who is less likely to speak irreverently of the Crown and Monarchy of England than I am ; but crowns, coronets, mitres, military display, the pomp of war, wide colonies and a huge Empire, are, in my view, all trifles, light as air, and not worth considering, unless with them you can have a fair share of comfort, contentment, and happiness among the great body of the people. . . .

" I have not, as you have observed, pleaded that this country should remain without adequate and scientific means of defence. I acknowledge it to be the duty of your statesmen, acting upon the known opinions and principles of ninety-nine out of every hundred persons in the country, at all times, with all possible moderation, but with all possible efficiency to take steps which shall preserve order within and on the confines of your kingdom.

But I shall repudiate and denounce the expenditure of every shilling, the engagement of every man, the employment of every ship, which has no object but intermeddling in the affairs of other countries, and endeavouring to extend the boundaries of an Empire which is already large enough to satisfy the greatest ambition, and I fear is much too large for the highest statesmanship to which any man has yet attained."

It was in this very speech that Bright emphasized the solemn sense of responsibility which should weigh upon all political orators, and it is surely his right that this careful statement of his peace position should be accepted at its full value.

In the next summer Bright would only give his support to the Palmerston–Russell Government, then in process of formation, in return for a pledge of non-intervention in the war raging in Northern Italy. Russell gave it readily, for, as he said, the chief fear was lest distrust of Napoleon III should lead us to intervene on the Austrian side, and his and Palmerston's Italian sympathies were directed to the preservation of an attitude of benevolent neutrality. This was the first-fruits of Bright's teaching, a greater triumph was secured when we remained at peace through the American and Danish Wars, and by that time we had learnt the lesson sufficiently well to pass through the Austro-Prussian and Franco-Prussian Wars without a hint that our interests were involved or our intervention necessary.

Yet distrust of the Emperor of the French swept Palmerston and the hotter heads of the nation into a " French panic " in the years 1859 to 1861. Cobden and Bright strove, in speeches and writings, to dissipate the atmosphere of mutual mistrust and suspicion. The French Commercial Treaty, carried through by Cobden in 1860, was intended to counteract the war preparations ; it was a favourite thesis of the two great Free Traders that protective tariffs and other hindrances to international trade were a frequent incentive to war. At this time Bright was much exercised by the rapid growth of armaments in Europe. He wrote to Cobden [1] (October 10, 1860) : " The greatest mechanical intellects of our time are absorbed in the question how to complete instruments of defence and destruction, and there seems no limit to their discoveries or projects, so long as France and England shall lead in great armaments and in the attempt to dominate over the world."

[1] Trevelyan, p. 292.

In January 1861 he proposed to Gladstone that the Government should allow Cobden to supplement his treaty success of the previous year by negotiating with the French Emperor for a mutual reduction of armarments. " At least fifteen millions a year might be saved to the two countries at once by such an arrangement as I speak of, besides the increasing peril of war from these frightful preparations and this incessant military excitement." Bright had reason to believe that the Emperor (who, as President, had made such a suggestion in 1849 only for it to be rejected by Palmerston) would favour the plan, while in England it had the support of Disraeli as leader of the Opposition, but it was not taken up by the Palmerston Government, which thus threw away a precious opportunity. Within five years the rivalry in armaments was transferred to Prussia and France, and the dreaded conflagration soon followed.

But before that time Bright had to pass through a crisis which tried him more keenly than any other episode of his life, excepting the dark years of the Crimean War. In the summer of 1861 the smouldering trouble between North and South in the United States burst into flame, and for four years the great Republic was torn by civil war. Bright in his private business life suffered severely from the cotton famine induced by the Northern blockade, but his sympathies never wavered. To him the cause of the North was the cause of liberation against slavery, and of constitutional order against rebellion.[1] He steadfastly opposed the attempts made in England to recognize the Confederate Government as an independent State, and his great speeches did much to instruct public opinion on the merits of the struggle. Even at the opening of the war he defended the Federal Government—with a significant proviso. He said : " No man is more in favour of peace than I am ; no man has denounced war more than I have, probably, in this country ; few men in their public life have suffered more obloquy—I had almost said more indignity—in consequence of it. But I cannot for the life of me see upon any of those principles upon which States are governed now—I say nothing of the literal words of the New Testament—I cannot see how the state of affairs in America with regard to the United States Government could have been different from what it is at this moment."

In his private letters to Sumner he expressed himself more freely, blaming the North for mistakes of policy in the past and for their

[1] For another view *vide* Goldwin Smith, *The United States*, p. 249.

" foolish tariff " which alienated English opinion. Indeed, while denouncing the Southern leaders as " traitors to human nature itself," he was at first doubtful whether the war could be brought to a successful issue and feared the brutalizing effects of the struggle on the America which he loved and admired. In the autumn of 1861 he wrote to Sumner : " Many who cavil at you now say, ' If the war were for liberating the slave, then we could see something worth fighting for, and we could sympathize with the North.' I cannot urge you to such a course, the remedy for slavery would be almost worse than the disease, and yet how can such a disease be got rid of without some desperate remedy ? "

During the *Trent* crisis of 1861 Bright was one of the most strenuous workers for peace,[1] his letters to Sumner urging moderation on the American side were read in the Lincoln Cabinet, and received the more attention because at the same time Bright was making some of his most effective speeches on behalf of the Northern cause. In the *Alabama* difficulty he was equally earnest that England should be ready to submit the case to arbitration. At Rochdale (December 4, 1861) he pleaded for the same benevolent neutrality towards the North that we had exercised towards Italy in 1859, and a few days later in the same town (December 21st) he spoke out boldly against the criticisms that *The Times* directed against the North : " I hope it is equally averse to fratricidal strife in other districts ; for if it be true that God has made of one blood all the families of man to dwell on the face of all the earth, it must be fratricidal strife whether we are slaughtering Russians in the Crimea or bombarding towns on the sea-coast of the United States.

" Now, no one will expect that I should stand forward as the advocate of war, or as the defender of that great sum of all crimes which is involved in war. But when we are discussing a question of this nature, it is only fair that we should discuss it upon principles which are acknowledged not only in the country where the strife is being carried on, but are universally acknowledged in this country. When I discussed the Russian War, seven or eight years ago, I always condemned it on principles which were accepted by the Government and people of England, and I took my facts from the Blue-book presented to Parliament. I take the liberty, then, of doing that in

[1] On December 9th, when war seemed imminent, he wrote to Cobden : " I look for a retirement from Parliament if war actually takes place. I will not kill myself with proving it wicked, as I nearly did seven years ago."

this case ; and I say that, looking at the principles avowed in England, and at its policy, there is no man, who is not absolutely a non-resistant in every sense, who can fairly challenge the conduct of the American Government in this war. It would be a curious thing to find that the party in this country which on every public question affecting England is in favour of war at any cost, when they come to speak of the duty of the Government of the United States, is in favour of ' peace-at-any-price.' "

Next year at Birmingham (December 18, 1862) he spoke in condemnation of all forms of excessive nationalism, " whether from an Englishman who professes to be strictly English, or from an American strictly American, or from a Frenchman strictly French —whether it asserts in arrogant strains that Britannia rules the waves, or speak of ' manifest destiny' and the supremacy of the ' Stars and Stripes,' or boasts that the Eagles of one nation, having once overrun Europe, may possibly repeat the experiment." In the same speech he expressed the opinion that only a miracle could have averted this " measureless calamity " of war, and brought about the abolition of slavery by peaceful means. " Is not this war the penalty which inexorable justice exacts from America, North and South, for the enormous guilt of cherishing that frightful iniquity of slavery for the last eighty years ? " In a similar strain he wrote to Whittier : [1] " It seems as if a peaceable termination of the great evil of slavery was impossible—the blindness, the pride, and the passion of men made it impossible. War was and is the only way out of the desperate difficulty of your country, and fearful as the path is, it cannot be escaped. I only hope there may be virtue enough in the North, notwithstanding the terrible working of the poison of slavery, to throw off the coil and to permit of a renovated and restored nation."

This letter has been described as one " in support of the American Civil War." It is rather one of gloomy submission to a terrible evil. That Bright supported the *ideals* represented by the North against those of the South is indisputable and, when Lincoln had once made Emancipation a plain issue, he felt that no peace could be admitted which involved any recognition of slavery. Perhaps his most emphatic expression of this is found in a letter to Villiers (August 5, 1863).

" I want no end of the war, and no compromise, and no reunion

[1] February 27, 1863, Pickard, *Life of Whittier*, ii. 451.

till the negro is made free beyond all chance of failure." This language is strong enough, but it must be remembered that it was used by a neutral to a neutral, and not addressed to the warring North. His other letters of the time show that he feared the North was winning too easily and had not yet paid her share of the "penalty" for maintaining slavery. A week before he had written, also to Villiers (July 29, 1863): "It needs as many plagues as Pharaoh suffered to force the corrupt portion of the Northern people to let the negro go."[1]

Mr. Trevelyan, in his praise of Bright's attitude, describes him as "swallowing" the peace formula by such a declaration, but the peace "formula" does not include a desire for the victory of the worse cause and the lower civilization. Bright deliberately refrained from urging the North into war on behalf of the slave,[2] but when that battle-cry had been adopted, he naturally desired that it should prove no false claim. Peace principles do not involve a neutrality which apportions equal condemnation to every belligerent, any more than religious toleration involves the view that all doctrines are equally false.[3]

When the war ended, he wrote in his journal: "The friends of freedom everywhere should thank God and take courage."

The eighteen years from the Peace of Paris in 1856 to the fall of Mr. Gladstone's Government in 1874 were, as Mr. Trevelyan says,[4] a time in which Bright's principles of foreign policy gradually won their way in England, until even in the Cabinet itself they supplanted the evil old superstition of the "balance of power," so long honoured by statesmen at the expense of the peoples of Europe. In 1859 sympathy for Italy and distrust of Napoleon III were counteracting forces which ensured our neutrality.[5] In 1861 a few wise men on both sides of the Atlantic had restrained the rasher and more sensitive spirits in each nation. In 1864 a more dangerous crisis arose over the question of Schleswig-Holstein. Palmerston and Russell had expressed their sympathy for Denmark in terms

---

[1] Trevelyan, *Life*, p. 319.   [2] *Vide ante*, p. 289.

[3] It may, perhaps, be noted that Bright seldom spent his eloquence in denouncing the actual conduct of hostilities by a belligerent, as distinct from the policy which led to war and the moral and economic evils which resulted from it. In 1861 he dissociated himself from Cobden's objection to the methods of the Northern blockade. "*War* is *barbarous*, and this is but an act of war" (to Sumner, December 21, 1861).   [4] Trevelyan, *Life*, p. 417.

[5] See Bright's Speech at Birmingham, January 29, 1864.

which were interpreted by the Danes as pledges of intervention on their behalf. But the Cabinet and the country were resolutely against a new Continental war, and the "two aged ministers," as Bright called them, had to retreat with considerable loss of prestige from their original position. Bright, of course, spoke against intervention,[1] pointing out that England had no concern in the question of the Duchies, and adding : " If there be a Government possible in our day that will plunge this country into war under the pretence of maintaining the balance of power in Europe and sustaining any kingdom there, be it little or great, I say that Government not only is not worthy of the confidence of the people of England, but deserves our execration and abhorrence."

But for the time the lesson had been learnt. We were content to remain spectators in the duel between Austria and Prussia in 1866,[2] and in the greater and more sanguinary duel of France and Germany in 1870. In 1873 we swallowed the somewhat nauseous medicine of the *Alabama* award without excessive complaint. Bright's influence had had some effect in inducing American statesmen to modify the less tenable of the claims for compensation. This period, though saddened by the death of Cobden, must have been, politically, the most serene of Bright's life. Both in home and foreign policy Conservative and Liberal Governments alike bore witness to the impress of his teaching.[3] In December 1868, with much searching of heart, he joined the Gladstone Government, just fourteen years after he had been burnt in effigy, and nine years after he had been excluded, by Court and aristocratic influence, from the Whig Government of 1859.

In the same year he had received the freedom of Edinburgh, and at his visit[4] delivered two fine speeches, one of which, to a deputation of working men, condensed into a few pungent paragraphs his teaching and his aspiration. After telling them that past wars had saddled the country with a debt on which they were then paying out of taxation £26,000,000 as interest, that they were spending

---

[1] In 1858 (October 29th), Bright had protested against the " networks and complications of our treaty system," including the treaty which " invites us, enables us, and perhaps, if we acted fully up to our duty with regard to it, would compel us to interfere in the question between Denmark and the Duchies."

[2] Even *The Times*, in reviewing the events of that year, spoke of " the recent English policy of withdrawing as much as possible from foreign complications " as being " common ground to both parties " (Trevelyan, *Life*, p. 417).

[3] E.g. in Franchise, Land, and Irish legislation.

[4] November 5, 1868.

a similar sum on military and naval preparations, in spite of the
discredit under which " the ancient theory of the balance of power "
then laboured, he continued :

" I do not know whether it is a dream, or a vision, or the foresight of a future reality that sometimes passes across my mind—I
like to dwell upon it—but I frequently think the time may come
when the maritime nations of Europe—this renowned country of
which we are citizens, France, Prussia, Russia, resuscitated Spain,
Italy—and the United States of America may see that those vast
fleets are of no use ; that they are grand inventions by which the
blood is withdrawn from the veins of the people to feed their
ulcers ; and that they may come to this wise conclusion—they will
combine at their joint expense, and under some joint management,
to supply the sea with a sufficient sailing and armed police, which
may be necessary to keep the peace on all parts of the watery surface
of the globe, and that those great instruments of war and oppression
shall no longer be upheld. This, of course, by many will be thought
to be a dream or a vision, not the foresight of what they call a
statesman. Still, I have faith that it will not be for ever that we
shall read of what Wilberforce called the noxious race of heroes
and conquerors ; that what Christianity points to will one day
be achieved, and that the nations throughout the world will live
in peace with one another."

When the catastrophe of the Franco-Prussian War convulsed
Europe in July 1870, Bright was suffering from serious illness,
and unable to take his share in Cabinet deliberations. He roused
himself, however, sufficiently to protest against the Government's
action in regard to Belgium. The secret draft treaty suggested
by France to Prussia in 1867 under which France was to annex
Belgium, had just been published by *The Times*. Mr. Gladstone
wrote to Bright (August 1, 1870), that this revelation, " has thrown
upon us the necessity either of doing something fresh to secure
Belgium, or else of saying that under no circumstances would we
take any step to secure her from absorption. . . . Neither do
we think it would be right, even if it were safe, to announce that
we would in any case stand by with folded arms, and see actions done
which would amount to a total extinction of public right in Europe."[1]
The step taken was a treaty, by which England engaged to join with
either belligerent in the defence of Belgium, should the other violate

[1] Morley, *Life of Gladstone*, i, 341.

its neutrality. Bright was alarmed, and replied (August 3), " I differ from the Cabinet, and cannot sanction our entering into any new engagement for the military defence of Belgium, nor can I consent to ask Parliament to raise men and money for supporting the independence of any foreign State. To adopt the policy of the Cabinet would be for me to abandon principles which I have held and advocated during all my public life."[1] Accordingly, though with great regret, he pressed his resignation upon his chief. " I am consoled by the belief that I have never taken a step more clearly loyal to the Sovereign, and more faithful to the true interests of the people. I cannot consent to spend English blood and treasure for purposes which I do not deem to be English." Bright's objection was, in fact, primarily to the original treaty of 1831, as it is usually interpreted, and then to its renewal or re-emphasis under very different conditions.[2]

Mr. Gladstone replied with an assurance that the step had been taken in the interests of peace, and that the annexation of Belgium by France would be a public crime, which might be averted by such a warning as the renewal of the treaty. He urged his colleague not to act hastily, but to await events, and this suggestion Bright adopted, being " very anxious to do no harm at so critical a time."

He wrote more than once to Gladstone during the autumn, expressing grave misgivings over the question of Alsace-Lorraine. " We ought strongly to urge " (September 11, 1870) " the folly of retaining French territory, for to annex any part of France would be to sow the seeds of another war at no distant date. Europe has a right, at least by argument and advice, to endeavour to bring about such a settlement as shall leave no needless grievance in the minds of the French people." Again (October 3rd), while considering Gladstone's proposal for a plebiscite of the provinces impracticable, he wrote, " the true objection is that peace will be less secure in future if territory be taken from France, and should Prussia be at war with Austria or Russia, she may calculate on an attack from the country she is now seeking to despoil. . . . I had hoped that Germany would have been content with the demolition of the frontier fortresses,

---

[1] For permission to quote from these letters I am indebted to the kindness of Mrs. W. S. Clark and Mr. John Albert Bright.

[2] In 1858, in his criticism of the multifarious treaties which hampered our foreign policy, he had said : " If I mistake not, we have a treaty which binds us down to the maintenance of the little kingdom of Belgium, as established after its separation from Holland."

and the payment of the expenses of the war—but the conqueror is seldom generous or just—and if the temper of the Germans is like that of the English during the Crimean War, there is no hope of good from any appeal to them. I suspect neither Russia nor Austria would quite approve of a protest on the ground of the indisposition of the population to the transfer to Germany. They have not been accustomed to pay much attention to the popular will. The more broad objection, which I call European, would perhaps suit them better, and I think it would have quite as much weight with Germany. . . . France, under her military Government, has been a constant source of disquiet to Europe, and she will now suffer the more on that account. I grieve over the troubles of her peoples—yet, from the standpoint of Germany, I am not surprised at the determination of the Germans to disable her for the future."

In the previous letter he had described the triumph of Germany and the downfall of France as "a great gain for liberty and peace" —words which seem now unduly hopeful, but which have some justification, if we compare the condition of Europe during the twenty years of the Third Empire with the twenty years from the siege of Paris to the cession of Heligoland.

When, in November 1870, Russia took advantage of the change in the European situation to shake off the restrictions imposed on her in the Black Sea by the Treaty of Paris, Bright again urged the Government to exercise restraint. "Forgive me," he wrote to Gladstone (November 18th), "for supposing there was danger of your becoming too much involved in the Russian question. But there are people who seem always to hunger for war, and Governments are too often moved by them, and drift on to positions from which there seems no honourable retreat. . . . When I remember the treatment of Russia by England and France in 1854, I am not much surprised that, when France is *down*, and England almost helpless in the matter, Russia should speak in uncivil tones."

The peaceful settlement of the *Alabama* question by the award of 1873 gave much satisfaction to Bright. He wrote to Granville :

"I believe if the English Government had shown the same wise and just disposition in time past, almost all wars with European Powers since the days of William III might have been avoided."

But he was still able to take little active part in politics, and his chief utterances on the peace question during these years are to be found in a few public letters.

To a working man's conference held at Leeds amid the war alarms of 1878 he declares that if the trade unions " would speak out for peace, there would be no war. There are men and classes to whom war is sometimes gain ; to the working men it is only loss."[1]

In 1874 the Gladstone Government had been succeeded by that of Disraeli, the first to adopt deliberately the watchword of " Imperialism," and the policy of aggression on the borders of the British Empire. This, and the threat of intervention in the Russo-Turkish quarrel, involved the country in wars and dangers of war, which finally led to a reaction in favour of peace and a change of ministry.

Bright did much, though less, indeed, than Gladstone, to bring about the change. In 1870 he had expressed the hope that, on the question of foreign policy, "I may yet have strength given me to speak at least one speech to my countrymen—for their blindness upon it has been their bane, and it may be their ruin."[2] The wish was more than fulfilled. In 1877–8 he was able to make several strong and strongly reasoned speeches against the threatened Russian War. One of the best, delivered at Birmingham on January 13, 1878, has several passages which have now gained a fresh significance. He reminded his hearers that in 1839 "some people had really so nearly approached a condition fit for Bedlam that they believed the Russians were likely to come through the Baltic and invade the east coast of England," and then he went on to draw a parallel between conditions in 1854–5 and 1877–8.

" But still, we cannot disguise from ourselves the fact that there is something of a war party in this country, and that it has free access to some, and indeed to not a few, of the newspapers of the London Press. If there is any man here who thinks the question of our policy doubtful, if there is any man in the country who shall read what I say now who is in doubt, I ask him to look back to the policy of twenty-three years ago and to see how it was then tried, and how it succeeded or how it failed. The arguments were the same then exactly as they are now. The falsehoods were the same. The screechings and howlings of a portion of the Press were just about the same. But the nation now—and if nations learned nothing, how long could they be sustained ?—has learned something—and it has risen above this. I am persuaded that there is a great difference of opinion as to Russian policy in the main, or Turkish policy in this

---

[1] *Public Letters*, p. 213.   [2] To Gladstone, December 14, 1870.

war, and men may pity especially the suffering on the one side or the suffering on the other—for my share I pity the sufferings on both sides—and whatever may be our differences of opinion, I think it is conclusively proved that the vast bulk of all the opinion that is influential in this country upon this question leads to this : that the nation is for a strict and rigid neutrality throughout this war.

"It is a painful and terrible thing to think how easy it is to stir up a nation to war. Take up any decent history of this country from the time of William III until now—for two centuries, or nearly so—and you will find that wars are always supported by a class of arguments which after the war is over, people find were arguments they should not have listened to. It is just so now, for unfortunately there still remains the disposition to be excited on these questions. Some poet—I forget which it is—has said :

> Religion, freedom, vengeance, what you will,
> A word's enough to raise mankind to kill;
> Some cunning phrase by faction caught and spread,
> That guilt may reign, and wolves and worms be fed.

'Some cunning phrase by faction caught and spread' like the cunning phrase of the 'balance of power,' which has been described as the ghastly phantom which the Government of this country has been pursuing for more than two centuries, and has never yet overtaken. 'Some cunning phrase' like that we have now of 'British interests.' Lord Derby has said the wisest thing that has been uttered by any member of the Administration during the discussion on this war, when he said that the greatest of British interests is peace. And a hundred, far more than a hundred, public meetings have lately said the same, and millions of households of men and women have thought the same."

Happily the war party of 1878 had less power than its forerunner of 1855. But its passions were as easily inflamed and as reckless. A jingo mob broke Mr. Gladstone's windows. Bright was attacked and roughly handled on leaving a peace-meeting at the Free Trade Hall, Manchester, on April 30th. A fortnight later his wife died, and he took no further active part in the peace campaign, although he watched its progress anxiously. Next year, in his annual speech to his constituents,[1] he denounced "this unpleasant business" of the Afghan War then in progress, as one "deformed by falseness

[1] Birmingham, April 1 1879.

and dishonour." This judgment he reiterated in the following
year, with fuller information.[1]

" It was a war begun in the dark, carried on in secret by a
diplomacy which was denied in both Houses of Parliament, and
falsely denied. It was begun against the evidence and opinion . . .
of all the sensible and just men who have heretofore been thought
the greatest authorities upon Indian matters. . . . Our Government, by its policy, has carried anarchy, and war, and slaughter,
and fire throughout the whole of that country."

These wars upon native races always aroused Bright's deep
indignation, and in this election campaign of 1880 he had for text
not only the Afghan, but the Zulu War. In allusion to both he said,[2]
" I believe all wars are savage and cruel—but I mean harsh and cruel
wars on uncivilized or half-civilized men. When I read of transactions of that kind something always puts to me this question : ' What
is it that makes, if anything makes, this needless and terrible slaughter
different in its nature from those transactions which we call murder ? '
. . . At most, in regard to either of these people, the case was one
of suspicion ; but was it right, upon a mere suspicion, that a country
like this should send in the one case 20,000 and in the other 40,000
troops to invade territories, and to put to death not less perhaps
than 20,000 men engaged in the defence of their own country,
which in our case we considered honourable and needful ? "
Again : " You hear of the hanging of scores of men, you hear of
villages burnt, of women and children turned out into the snow
and the cold of this inclement season, and all done at the command
of a Government and a people professing to be wiser, more intelligent,
more humane, and more Christian than those upon whom those
attacks are made. . . . Take down, at any rate, your Ten Commandments from inside your churches, and say no longer that you
read, or believe in, or regard, the Sermon on the Mount. Abandon
your Christian pretensions, or else abandon your savage and heathen
practices." He had the courage on a later occasion to describe the
Zulu warriors as men " who, if they had been of our nation, would
have had songs written in their honour, and magnificent orations
delivered in their praise, and their leading men who fell would have
found no doubt a home for their bones and a tablet in Westminster
Abbey."[3]

[1] March 28, 1880.   [2] January 22, 1880.
    [3] Birmingham, March 28, 1880.

In this speech one passage is peculiarly characteristic of the tenderness which always underlay his abhorrence of war and oppression. It may be compared with the description of his little children, which occurs in the midst of his great speech on America (June 30, 1863). Next to children, Bright loved animals, and his eloquence made the sufferings of the army camels an item in the indictment of the Disraeli Government.

" You know something of the untold miseries which war brings upon men and women and little children ; but there is one point that nobody, so far as I know, has ever touched upon, that which has always had a certain interest for me, and which has excited my sympathy. I have seen in some of the narratives of the Afghan War that all the region round had been swept for camels as beasts of burden for the forces. What became of the camels ? The least number I have heard it put at was 30,000—it has been reckoned as high as 40,000 or 50,000 camels—who have perished in these expeditions. One of our greatest poets in a beautiful stanza has one line where he says, ' Mute the camel labours with the heaviest load,' and though the camel is not able by any voice of his to make protest or complaint, yet the burdened, overdriven, exhausted, dying beast—I cannot but believe that even the cruelties inflicted on him will be found written upon imperishable tablets by the recording angel."

The General Election of 1880 ended in a decisive victory for the Liberals. Bright again entered the Cabinet, but his tenure of office was not to be long. With his colleagues he became involved in the deplorable South African policy, and cannot be acquitted of a share of responsibility for the errors and delays which culminated in the disaster of Majuba Hill. But when he awoke to the facts he was one of the strongest influences for peace and conciliation. Indeed, if hostilities had been continued, the Cabinet would in all probability have lost both Bright and Chamberlain. Even before the matter was finally adjusted he replied to a deputation that " the conflict is one in which England can gain nothing, not even military glory, which is the poorest kind of glory in my view which men and nations strive for."[1] The discoveries of the mistakes of this year had probably aroused his vigilance, for he became a strong opponent of the Cabinet's Egyptian policy, although in this struggle he stood alone. When the bombardment of Alexandria took place,

---

[1] *Public Letters*, p. 250.

he resigned. The only wonder is that he delayed so long, but Gladstone had repeatedly assured him that the negotiations would have a peaceful end, and he was very reluctant to embarrass a Government to some of whose members he was bound by ties of old and intimate friendship. On July 12th he wrote to Gladstone announcing his resignation and explaining it by " the doctrines connected with foreign policy which I have preached and defended during forty years of my public life." Gladstone urged reconsideration, but Bright was inflexible. " I cannot allow the country " (he wrote next day) " to assume that I have supported, or do support, a policy the results of which are so dreadful, and to which I have been opposed." Again, on July 15th :

" I should ruin myself in the estimation of all those who have been influenced by my teaching on what should be our foreign policy, and on the moral code by which we ought to be, and by which I feel myself, bound. There is nothing the world can offer me which would make amends for the remorse I should feel if I were associated with the policy in which the Cabinet is involved. . . . From your conversation to-day, and from your letter or memorandum, I am driven to the conclusion that there is a wide gulf, wider than I had supposed, between your views and mine."

Although Bright refrained from a campaign against the Egyptian War on the lines of his speeches in the Crimean War, his condemnation of it never wavered. In his short speech to the House of Commons explaining his resignation, he described the bombardment as " a manifest breach not only of international law, but also of the moral law." His other public utterance at the time took the form of a reply [1] to the Reverend Thomas Rippon, who had drawn his attention to a criticism by the *Spectator*.

" The *Spectator* and other supporters of this war answer me by saying that I oppose the war because I condemn all war. The same thing was said during the Crimean War.

" I have not opposed any war on the ground that all war is unlawful and immoral. I have never expressed such an opinion. I have discussed these questions of war, Chinese, Crimean, Afghan, Zulu, Egyptian, on grounds common to and admitted by all thoughtful men, and have condemned them with arguments which I believe have never been answered.

" I will not discuss the abstract question. I shall be content

[1] *Public Letters*, p. 273.

when we reach the point at which all Christian men will condemn war when it is unnecesssary, unjust, and leading to no useful or good result. We are far from that point now, but we make some way towards it.

" But of this war I may say this, that it has no better justification than other wars which have gone before it and that, doubtless, when the blood is shed, and the cost paid, and the results seen and weighed, we shall be generally of that opinion. Perhaps the bond-holders and those who have made money by it, and those who have got promotion and titles and pensions, will defend it, but thoughtful and Christian men will condemn it." In 1883, at a meeting of the Liberation Society, he attacked in scathing language a thanks-giving for the campaign promulgated by one Bishop in his diocese in which was the phrase, " Teach us to see that Thy hand hath done it." " It proves " (said Bright) " the indestructible quality that there is in the Christian faith that it should so long have survived the treason of those who pretend to teach it."

Later, in his opposition to the Home Rule Bill, he alluded to the bombardment as " a great blunder, and I am afraid nationally a great crime."

Except in this opposition to the Home Rule Bill, which was partly based on his detestation of the disorder and violence by which the Nationalist agitation had been defaced, Bright in his last years took little part in politics. He watched with apprehension the growth of the militarist spirit in both political parties—a growth which led to Mr. Gladstone's resignation of leadership a few years later, and he found no politician willing to take up his mantle and go forth as a prophet of peace.

What then had he accomplished in the cause of peace during almost fifty years of political activity ? Throughout his life he had stood firmly for principles of foreign policy, which were profoundly unpopular when he first advocated them, yet became the admitted maxims of the British Government for many years of the nineteenth century. He denounced secret diplomacy and entangling treaties, and the heedless spirit which goes to war for prestige or intervenes in quarrels where the country's interests are not involved. With Cobden's help, he taught the nations to know one another better and showed them the folly of the panic-breeding competition in armaments. When Lord Derby, in 1878, declared that " the greatest of British interests is peace," he showed himself a pupil in the school

of Bright and Cobden. But it needed less wisdom to draw this moral
after the object lesson of the Crimean War and the convulsions
of Europe during the 'sixties and 'seventies. Bright had the courage
and insight to teach the principles of peace in the midst of the fury
and madness of war. As Mr. Trevelyan says, he " showed the
world how a war can be patriotically denounced, with permanent
effects upon opinion in favour of keeping peace."[1]   Yet eloquence
and patriotism had inspired the leaders of the opposition to the
American and French Wars, but they did not stand as remote from
all suspicion of personal or party advantage as did Bright and Cobden,
who manfully risked (and incurred) the loss of political prospects
and popular influence to uphold what they believed to be right
in itself and for the true interests of their country.

> Amongst innumerable false, unmov'd,
> Unshaken, unseduc'd, unterrified,
> His loyalty he kept, his love, his zeal ;
> Nor number, nor example, with him wrought
> To swerve from truth, or change his constant mind.

Bright was equally ready to give up office itself for the sake of
principle, but this was a lesser sacrifice than those he underwent
during the Crimean War. He was devoid of the personal ambition
which finds its reward in political power and patronage, and he
was always more ready to leave than to enter a Ministry. His
countrymen felt assured that the moral principles which he advocated
in his political speeches were the same in kind as those guiding his
individual conduct. This, rather than his eloquence, gave him
his unequalled hold upon the affections of the working people.
Dr. Dale of Birmingham said (on the " silver wedding " of Bright's
representation of the city) : " The man is greater than the eloquence,
the man is nobler than his service. . . . I believe he has elevated
the national ideal of political morality."

It was a common sneer of their opponents (even echoed by
Tennyson) that Bright and Cobden's advocacy of peace was based
on the fear of the mere monetary and commercial losses of war.
Bright had lived through the years following Waterloo, and he
had seen the abject wretchedness of the mass of the people, due to
the pressure of war debt and war taxation. As he said, he cared
for the condition of the people among whom he lived, and the

[1] Trevelyan, p. 218.

impulse of pity and indignation inspired his opposition to the Corn Laws and to war. In his old age he wrote : " In war the working men find the main portion of the blood which is shed, and on them fall the poverty and misery which are occasioned by the increase of taxes and damage to industry."[1] The economic arguments against war are neither ignoble nor unpatriotic, and Bright never shrank from employing them. But the moral argument fills and colours every speech which he made. One of his finest perorations is typical of many other passages.[2]

" The most ancient of profane historians has told us that the Scythians of his time were a very warlike people, and that they elevated an old cimeter upon a platform as a symbol of Mars, for to Mars alone, I believe, they built altars and offered sacrifices. To this cimeter they offered sacrifices of horses and cattle, the main wealth of the country, and more costly sacrifices than to all the rest of their gods ; I often ask myself whether we are at all advanced in one respect beyond those Scythians. What are our contributions to charity, to education, to morality, to religion, to justice, and to civil government, when compared with the wealth we expend in sacrifice to the old cimeter ? . . . I do most devoutly believe that the moral law was not written for men alone in their individual character, but that it was written as well for nations, and for nations great as this of which we are citizens. If nations reject and deride that moral law, there is a penalty which will inevitably follow. It may not come at once, it may not come in our lifetime ; but, rely upon it, the great Italian poet is not a poet only, but a prophet when he says :

> The sword of heaven is not in haste to smite
> Nor yet doth linger.

We have experience, we have beacons, we have landmarks enough. We know what the past has cost us, we know how much and how far we have wandered, but we are not left without a guide. It is true we have not, as an ancient people had, Urim and Thummim —those oraculous gems on Aaron's breast—from which to take counsel, but we have the unchangeable and eternal principles of the moral law to guide us, and only so far as we walk by that guidance, can we be permanently a great nation or our people a happy people."

[1] *Public Letters*, p. 293.
[2] On foreign policy, Birmingham, October 29, 1858.

PART V

FRIENDS ABROAD

LET all nations hear the sound by word or writing. Spare no place, spare no tongue nor pen; but be obedient to the Lord God; go through the work; be valiant for the truth upon earth; and tread and trample upon all that is contrary. . . . This is the word of the Lord God to you all, and a charge to you all in the presence of the living God; be patterns, be examples in all countries, places, islands, nations, wherever you come; that your carriage and life may preach among all sorts of people, and to them; then you will come to walk cheerfully over the world, answering that of God in everyone; whereby in them ye may be a blessing, and make the witness of God in them to bless you. . . . Go through your work faithfully, and in the strength and power of the Lord; and be obedient to the power; for that will save you out of the hands of unreasonable men, and preserve you over the world to himself.—*Letter of George Fox in Launceston Gaol*, 1656.

CHAPTER XII

THE WEST INDIES

THE West Indian Islands, occupied by England in the days of Charles I and the Commonwealth, were soon invaded by Quaker missionaries on their way to the American continent. Two women, Mary Fisher and Ann Austin, were the first visitors in Barbadoes in 1655, and in a few years' time there were settlements of Friends on that island, Jamaica, Antigua, Nevis, and Bermuda. At the high-water mark of Quakerism in Barbadoes there were five meeting-houses there, seating some 1,200 worshippers, and in the year 1700 the number of Friends in Jamaica was reckoned at 9,000. The two women made but a short stay. In 1657 John Bowron of Durham travelled in Surinam and spoke frequently to the natives through an interpreter. They greeted him as " a good man come from far to preach the white man's God," and he seems to have been the first Quaker to give his message to men of another race.[1]

In the same year the Governor of Jamaica[2] wrote home for instructions how to deal with two Quaker visitors who appeared " people of an unblameable life," although he learnt from " prints " (English news letters) that their leaders at home were conspiring against the Government. Bermuda received the Quaker message in 1660. In Barbadoes a wealthy planter, Lieutenant-Colonel Rous and his son John became Friends and leaders of the Society in the island. John Rous, with other Barbadian Quakers, visited New England as a preacher in 1657. There he suffered cruel floggings and the loss of an ear by order of what Friends at home called bitterly " the new Inquisition in New England." Later he settled in England and married the eldest daughter of Margaret Fell, and in 1671 he returned to the West Indies with his father-in-law, George

[1] *Piety Promoted*, i. 234.
[2] Thurloe, *State Papers*, vi. 834. *Vide* Rufus Jones, *Quakers in American Colonies*, p. 43.

Fox, and ten other English Quakers. They spent some strenuous months there before visiting North America, and during his stay Fox wrote an often-quoted letter to the Governor of Barbadoes defending Quakers against charges of heresy, and showing that they held orthodox views concerning the person and work of Christ.

The islands, however, for Quakers were scarcely

> a grassy stage
> Safe from the storm and prelates' rage,[1]

for much emigration thither was involuntary. Cromwell began the bad practice of transporting prisoners of war as servants to the plantations, and it was soon extended to other persons of inconvenient views whom the home Government wished to keep at a safe distance. The most notorious instance of this practice was the wholesale exportation from the West Country after the Monmouth Rebellion, but even in 1677 the Governor of Nevis in an Act forbidding Friends to land on the island specifically excepted from the order " all such Quakers as are sent hither by his Majesty's special command."[2] There are frequent complaints in the colonial records that these Quakers, after their term of service, enjoyed what their neighbours considered an undue share of prosperity as merchants, planters, or shopkeepers.

The rapid growth of Quakerism, as also the sensitiveness of its leaders to moral issues, is shown in an epistle sent by Fox in 1657 to " Friends beyond the seas that have Blacks and Indian Slaves."[3] " In this he points out that God hath made all nations of one blood, and that the gospel is preached to every creature under heaven. And so, he says, ' ye are to have the mind of Christ, and to be merciful as your heavenly Father is merciful.' "[4] In his letter to the Governor of Barbadoes in 1671 he defended the practice of the Quakers there in giving moral and religious instruction to their negroes. The Governor feared that this instruction implied " teaching negroes to rebel," and his fear was probably not allayed by Fox's explanation :

" As to their blacks or negroes, I desired them to endeavour to train them up in the fear of God, those that were bought, and those born in their families.

. . That they would cause their overseers to deal mildly and

---

[1] Andrew Marvell.   [2] Besse, ii. 362.   [3] Fox, *Epistles*, p. 153.
[4] *Quakers in the American Colonies*, p. 44.

gently with their negroes, and not use cruelty towards them, as the manner of some hath been and is ; and that after certain years of servitude they would make them free."

Thus the first seeds of the anti-slavery movement were scattered, to grow and spread for a century and a half until the evil was overthrown.

It was not to be expected that the Quaker peace testimony would meet with much sympathy in the West Indies. The islands belonged to several of the chief European States—Spain, France, Holland and Great Britain—and were swept into the whirlpool of each European war in turn, while yet their position was so isolated that they had mainly to depend on their own resources for defence.[1]

In these wars there were temporary conquests, during which the conquered islands suffered from fire and sword, only to be handed back to their original owners when peace was made. The appearance of an enemy's fleet to bombard the shores was terrifying enough, but still more serious was the menace to trade from robbers on the high seas, who called themselves privateers in war-time, but were unabashed pirates in peace. The West India merchant ships made their voyages armed like men-of-war, and even so their rich cargoes often fell a prey to these adventurers. In addition, on some islands, there were still tribes of the wild Carib Indians who could be bribed or incited by Spain or France to make war on the English settlers, and there was the ever-present danger of a slave rebellion.

Under these conditions, in most of the islands, both Friends and magistrates had to undergo considerable exercise of mind before they were able to reach a *modus vivendi*. In Barbadoes, for example, the Governor and Council met in June 1660 to consider measures for the safety of the island. The latest news from England showed that the restoration of Charles II was imminent, and it was feared that the King of France might claim some colonies from him in return for all the French aid given to the Stuarts in their necessity. The Council had before it some " Reasons against the being and sect of the Quakers within this island " as follows :

" 1. For that they correspond not in the civil and military services and duties of this island equal with the other inhabitants.

" 2. For that their principles and practice is against the funda-

---

[1] In 1650, Barbadoes declared for the Royalist cause, proclaiming Charles II as King, and the island was able to hold out until 1652.

mentals of the Christian faith, constitution, and laws of the Commonwealth.

" 3. For that they daily seduce multitudes to be their proselytes and consequently weaken the island's defence."

For these reasons the Council was advised to pass an Act against all refusing to serve in the militia, fining them " five hundred pounds of sugar for the first offence, one thousand pounds of sugar for the second, and a thousand pounds for every default after the second, and to be committed (to gaol) until the same be paid."

With a promptness that might arouse envy in modern Ministries hampered by constitutional restraints, the advice was followed : "an Act was passed this day, and entered in the book of Acts." [1] Besse, in his chapter on Barbadoes,[2] gives the sequel. Between 1659 and 1669 the Quakers were fined to the amount of 111,000 pounds of sugar, of which all but 22,000 pounds was on account of the militia, and several members of the Society suffered imprisonment. In the last-named year they petitioned the Governor and Council to relieve their sufferings, " for not bearing or sending in to arms, and for not sending help to build and repair forts ; we witnessing in measure that prophecy fulfilled, ' not to learn war any more,' and it is according to Christ's own words, where he saith ' My kingdom is not of this world, therefore My servants do not fight,' and it is likewise according to Christ's precept, to ' love enemies.' "

The hearts of the authorities were not softened, and fines increased. In the five years from 1669 to 1674 they amounted (for the militia) to nearly 118,000 pounds of sugar. In 1674 the Quakers petitioned once more, though, indeed, " petition " is hardly the appropriate word for their challenge. " So be it known unto all people, that from henceforward we are resolved to fight under no other commander but the Lord Jesus Christ. . . . We cannot, directly, nor indirectly, war, fight against, kill, nor destroy men's persons, neither be aiding nor assisting them therein ; but if we must suffer from men for obeying our Commander, we must bear it with patience until he shall arise to plead our cause." They meet the familiar taunt " that if all were of your mind, our enemies would come and take the island from us," by the reply that if all were of a mind to obey God's commandments they would escape his judgments " one

[1] *Calendar State Papers Am. and West Indies*, 1574–1660, p. 483. *Colonial Entry Book*, xi. 12, C.O. 31/1. [2] Besse, *Sufferings*, ii. ch. vi.

whereof is war." A year earlier the Governor and Council had written to the home authorities that the weakness of the militia was due to the number of islanders with physical or mental defects, " in which quality we deem the Quakers." [1] Hence the reply to this declaration was a more severe Militia Act in 1675, which was reinforced in 1677. The steady increase in fines was due partly to the fall in the price of sugar and partly to an increase in the efficiency of the militia, " there being," Besse says, " every month a general exercising in the island." Some brutal punishments are recorded. Young Richard Andrews, aged eighteen, was taken for the militia out of his master's shop. [2] He refused to bear arms, saying: " He durst not break Christ's command," and a few days later he was sent to a fort, and there one Sunday " tied neck and heels for an hour," beaten, and kept at the fort for a week, " his lodging being mostly on the cold stones." He came home ill and wretched, but a fortnight later he suffered the same punishment, " tied so strait that he could hardly speak," till even the soldiers pitied him. In a few days he was struck down by dysentery, and before his death he expressed " great satisfaction of mind for having stood faithful to his testimony against fighting."

Charles had appointed a Committee for Trade and Plantations, a body which was to develop into the Colonial Office. To it in 1680 Sir Jonathan Atkins, the Governor, more than once referred for instructions about his Quaker subjects. The Committee had advised him not to administer oaths to them, but to govern in some other way. " What that other way is," replied the poor Governor, " I am to seek. . . . To the great discontent of the people, to their own great ease and advantage, they neither will serve upon juries, find arms, or send to the militia, nor bear any office, shifting it off with their constant tricks ' they cannot swear,' when profit is the end they aim at. And the King's faithful and dutiful subjects are forced to bear their burden, when by an Act of Parliament of England they were proscribed . . . and condemned to be transported to this and other of his Majesty's Plantations foreign ; of which they have made so good use as to put themselves into a better condition than they could be elsewhere." Later in the year he repeated this complaint against " Anabaptists, Quakers, and other Dissenters." [3]

[1] *Col. Papers*, xxx. 40, C.O. 1. [2] Besse, ii. ch. vi.
[3] *Col. Entry Book*, vi. 318 ; vii. 89-100, C.O. 29/2 and 3. *Calendar*, 1677-80, pp. 503-4.

Even in smaller matters the knight was inconvenienced by Quaker scruples. On May 21, 1680, he told the Commissioners that he was sending to them a map of the island. " But I cannot much commend it to your Lordships. It cost the fellow a good sum of money to get it perfected, for he was forced to send it to London. But that it is true in all particulars I cannot affirm, but there is none here that ever undertook it but himself. He is a Quaker, as your Lordships may perceive by his not mentioning the churches, nor expressing the fortifications, of both of which they make great scruple."[1]

The reign of James II at first witnessed an increase of trouble for Barbadian Quakers. A Militia Act with even stiffer penalties was passed in 1685. The records of the Colonial Office and of the Meeting for Sufferings show that for some years there was a brisk correspondence on the matter between England and the colony. After a vain appeal to the Governor the Quakers twice petitioned the King, once before the new Act had received his signature, and again when it had passed into law. They complained that the fines imposed showed undue discrimination against Quakers, and that the method of levy was changed. Up to this time the fine had always been in sugar, but now " the price being low, they levy their executions upon our most serviceable negroes, both men, women, and children, taking away, parting and selling husbands, wives, and children one from another, to the great grief, lamentation, and distraction of our negro families." Cattle, too, and horses had been seized, and whereas in the towns formerly one member only of a household had been liable to service, now both master and apprentice were required to appear in arms. Hence Quaker tradesmen were forced to carry on their business without apprentices, and " the young people go off the island to their own hurt and parents' grief." [2]

Steady pressure on the Committee for Plantations by the Meeting for Sufferings (a deputation from which presented the Petition) and possibly Penn's influence with James induced both King and Committee to write to the island authorities. The Committee reminded them that " his Majesty, having lately extended his favour to those people here, may be inclined to continue the same towards them in this particular " and that the Governor should do his best to give them some ease. These are excellent sentiments in a docu-

---

[1] *Col. Entry Book*, vii. 19, C.O. 29/3. *Calendar*, 1677–80, p. 536.
[2] *Col. Papers*, lvii. 111, C.O. 1/59. *Calendar*, 1685–8, p. 208.

ment whose first signatory is " Jeffrys, Chancellor." James himself
wrote to the Governor that as he had already received the Declaration of Indulgence, he should put it into force towards Quakers
both in respect of liberty of worship and of admission to office without
an oath. " And in case any of them scruple or make difficulty to
perform my service or take any employment upon them either civil
or military, our will and pleasure is that no fine or fines be imposed
upon them exceeding the usual value for the hire of another person
to discharge the duty or service required." The Governor in reply
made many professions of willingness to administer the Act with
leniency, but there were " very few supernumerary people to be
hired on the island." The Quakers themselves did not keep enough
white servants ; in fact, the general tendency of all employers was
to replace " Christians " by negroes, who were cheaper and more
profitable. The prosperity of the Quakers was such that " they
ought to make one regiment on the island," and the lack of this
might prove a danger in time of war.[1] In spite of the Governor's
promises, the Meeting for Sufferings received constant complaints
of his severity. Even in March 1689, when James was a fugitive,
heavy fines were inflicted " in King James's name, but no notice
taken of what he sent in favour of Friends there." The Meeting
for Sufferings petitioned William and Mary, and the trouble must
have ceased with the removal of the Jacobite governor, for in the
autumn of 1690 Barbadian Friends sent £100 to the relief of the
sufferers in Ireland. In 1693 the French war and fears of a negro
rising led to the passing of an Act that all travellers in the island
should ride armed. The Governor, as Friends wrote plaintively,
" let the Militia Act loose upon them," vowing that he would hang
all the Quakers at first sight of the French fleet. Some of his
subordinates went beyond threats. A Quaker pleaded conscience
as a reason for not bearing arms, and " the Major replied, ' God
damn your conscience, if I cannot make your conscience bow,
I'll make your stubborn dog's back to bend,' and so tied him neck
and heels with his own hands in such a manner it almost deprived
him of his life."[2] Quakers at home obtained letters of intercession
from the Duke of Bedford and the Earl of Rochester to the Governor.
These proved so effective that next year London Friends sent an

---

[1] *Col. Entry Book*, cviii. 286 ; vii. 379, 459, 463, C.O. 391/5. *Calendar*,
1685–8, pp. 213, 219, 477, 516.

[2] Besse, ii. 351. *Meeting for Sufferings*, 1693. Barbadoes, 10th mo. 8.

official letter of thanks to the same Governor for his "kindness" to their brethren. Another difficulty in 1696 (when Friends were ready to ride on patrol duty if they might go unarmed) was met in the same way by an application to Admiral Russell, whose brother was the recently appointed Governor, and this seems to have been the last trouble of the kind. Besse reprints the careful record compiled by Friends on the island of the distraints and fines (mainly for the militia) suffered by their small body. Between 1658 and 1690 the value of these fines in money and sugar amounted to £118,000. In the eighteenth century the number of Friends gradually dwindled away. The last letter received by the English Friends was in 1764 from John Luke, and in it he writes that the only meeting regularly held, at Bridgetown, seldom numbered more than a dozen worshippers.[1]

Jamaica records also show a gradual tightening of the laws against Friends. A Proclamation of 1662 granted to them freedom of worship and trade, with the promise that they "shall not be forced in their own persons to bear arms, provided they shall contribute for the same," and also be prepared to reveal to the Governor any "foreign designs, invasions, conspiracies, or plots" that come to their knowledge. This compromise did not succeed, for two years later Sir Thomas Moddyford and his Council resolved that any Quaker "not appearing in the field at the several muster days should receive due punishment." But in 1668 it was necessary to pass a reasoned Ordinance "Whereas no Government can subsist" unless its subjects are willing to execute the military and civil duties assigned to them, and the Quakers' refusal "may prove, if many others should follow such evil example, the ruin and destruction of this Government," therefore, all recalcitrants are to be committed to gaol until they pay the due fine. In 1670 Governor and Council had to own themselves beaten. "Whereas [a] few of the people called Quakers, living at Port Royal, have represented to the Governor and Council that they cannot against their consciences bear arms and have given several reasons for the same, by which they seem to the Council very obstinate in that matter, and although the Governor and Council look on the said reasons as weak and frivolous, and on that opinion as dangerous and destructive to all government : yet, out of pity and compassion to those poor misled people in that particular" (and also to help the

[1] In D. *Epistles Received.*

" gentlemen and merchants," who were ordered to guard the town
every night in person) the Quakers were excused on condition of
paying to the commander of the guards sufficient to hire *three*
soldiers in each place.[1]

The fines cannot have been very strictly enforced. Besse only
gives a few instances for a somewhat later period (1683–91) and
the story of the maltreatment of one unfortunate, Peter Dashwood,
who in 1687, for refusing military service, had twice " to ride the
wooden horse with a musket at each leg." In the more northern
group of the Leeward Islands, Friends also suffered for their faith.
The Quakers' first visits to Nevis were between 1656 and 1658.
Humphrey Highwood, who welcomed them and embraced their
principles, was imprisoned for not warning the authorities of the
arrival of these suspects. " In process of time," says Besse, " being
more perfectly convinced of the doctrine by them professed, he
declined to bear arms or to serve in the militia, things which he
had not formerly scrupled to do," and in consequence he endured
many imprisonments and fines.[2] In 1671 two of the English Quakers
who came with Fox to the West Indies, William Edmundson and
Thomas Briggs, sailed to Nevis, but they were forbidden to land
by the Governor, although the island Friends came on board ship
for a meeting. The captain was forced to give £1,000 security
that he would take back the two Quakers at once to Antigua.
William Edmundson, with his accustomed courage, told the authorities " it was very hard usage that we being Englishmen and coming
so far as we had done to visit our countrymen, could not be admitted
to come on shore, to refresh ourselves within King Charles's
dominions after such a long voyage." Colonel Stapleton (Governor
of Montserrat) said it was true. " But " (said he) " we hear that
since your coming to the Caribbee Islands there are seven hundred
of our militia turned Quakers, and the Quakers will not fight,
and we have need of men to fight, being surrounded with enemies,
and that is the very reason why Governor Wheeler will not suffer
you to land."[3] Even these quarantine measures could not check
the spread of Quakerism, and in the next few years imprisonments
were frequent. In 1674 ten Quakers sent from gaol a touching
letter to the Governor. " It is now twelve days since we were confined

[1] *Col. Entry Books*, xxxiv. 53–60, 126, 180, 203, C.O. 140/1. *Calendar*,
1661–8, pp. 111, 287, 597 ; 1669–74, p. 84.   [2] Besse, ii. 352.
[3] *Journal of the Life . . . of William Edmundson*, p. 55. Besse, ii. 353.

here, and there are some of us who have wives and children, and have nothing to maintain them but our labours. Now, General, the reason why we are thus imprisoned we do not well understand, unless for keeping the commandment of Christ, which we dare not disobey, for here we do declare that it is not of stubbornness nor of wilfulness, but in obedience of Christ Jesus. . . . We desire that He would order thy heart that thou mightest discern betwixt us, who are in scorn called Quakers, a peaceable people, who fear God and make conscience of our ways, and those who run wilfully on their own heads and disobey thee."[1] The Governor relented, for these men were released within a week, and next year there was some attempt at a compromise, if we may judge from a letter of George Fox. The Epistle " to Friends at Nevis and the Caribbee Islands concerning Watching "[2] was sent from Swarthmore Hall in November 1675. Fox mentions that he was unwell at the time, and the letter is confused with many repetitions, but its importance is sufficient to justify a full summary here. He had heard that there was " some scruple concerning watching, or sending forth watchmen in your own way," that is, unarmed, and possibly also not under military command. Fox is not inclined to uphold this scruple. " It is a great mercy of the Lord to subject the Governor's mind so much by his power and truth that he will permit you to watch in your own way, without carrying arms, which is a very civil thing, and to be taken notice of." Friends in Jamaica and Barbadoes would welcome such a concession, and indeed they had offered to watch " against the Spaniards," but because they refused to bear arms they had been severely punished and fined. Fox adds, " So where Friends has the Government, as in Rhode Island, . . . Friends was willing to watch in their own way, and they made a law that none should be compelled to take arms."[3] Friends, he continues, watch in their plantations against robbers, and they have no scruples concerning the town watch against housebreakers and fire-raisers. They even go before the magistrates about the wrongs they have suffered. " You are not to be the revenger, but he is the revenger ; . . . we must be subject to that power, and own that power, not only for wrath, but for conscience' sake ; which is for the punishment of the evildoers and the praise of them that do well. For

---

[1] Besse, ii. 353.
[2] *Epistles*, No. 319. The letter was approved by the Six Weeks Meeting.
[3] *Vide* ch. xiii. p. 331.

if any should come to burn your house or rob you, or come to ravish your wives and daughters, or a company should come to fire a city or town, or come to kill people ; don't you watch against all such actions ? And won't you watch against such evil things in the power of God in your own way ? You cannot but discover such things to the magistrates, who are to punish such things . . . and if he does it not, he bears the sword in vain." " You know," he adds, " that masters of ships, and Friends, have their watches all night long, and they watch to preserve the ship, and to prevent any enemy or hurts that might come to the ship by passengers or otherwise." Here Fox quotes some New Testament passages concerning watching, and then quaintly spiritualizes them. " So here is the goodman watching against sin and evil without, and the spoiler and thief without . . . and here is also a watching against sin and evil within, and a waiting to receive Christ at His coming. And as there is a shutting the outward doors to keep out the murderers and the thieves, and a bolting and locking of them out, so there is a shutting up and locking the doors of the heart." Therefore, if Indians come, " let them come from home or come from abroad," it is the duty of Friends to watch. " Neither judge one another about such things, but live in love which doth edify."

It is clear that Fox in his peaceable English county, far enough even from the Dutch guns which ten years before had echoed up the Thames, did not realize the atmosphere of war and alarms amid which Friends lived in the West Indies. Or, if he realized it, he did not face the difficulty. It was not the only time in the history of the Society that the " unplumb'd, salt, estranging sea " of the Atlantic bred misunderstanding or want of sympathy. The West Indian Friends knew from their own experience of the barbarous revenge the white man was wont to take in answer to the barbarous cruelties of Indian attack or negro rising. It was not the actual advice given by Fox, but his commentary upon it, which seemed to open the way to an almost unlimited share by Friends in services auxiliary to war. Curiously enough, with the exception of another time of difficulty in the West Indies, to be mentioned later, this Epistle has seldom been used as a weapon of argument in the perennial controversy between Friends and the military authority. If the Nevis Quakers followed the advice of Fox, apparently the compromise was not accepted. A few months later Governor Stapleton reported to the Committee at home that " the Quakers' singularity and obstinancy have given me more trouble than any others. Not contenting themselves with a peaceable enjoyment of what they profess in their families, as others are well satisfied therewith, the Quakers do meet, and have once disturbed a minister, for which they were imprisoned and fined by due course of law, since [then] they have been quiet. They will neither watch nor ward, not so much as against the Carib Indians, whose secret, treacherous, and most barbarous inroads, committing murders, rapes, and all other enormities, discourages the planters in the Leeward Islands more than any one thing, knowing how they have been made use of in the last war by our neighbours."[1]

There were, in fact, sixteen Quakers imprisoned on account of the militia in 1676, and the year 1677 saw the passage of an Act to prevent the landing of Quakers on the island, " that are not satisfied with the enjoyment of the liberty of their conscience and of his Majesty's laws, but are daily seducing others of the King's subjects from their allegiance, by persuading them not to bear arms for the defence of the rights of his Majesty and subjects, contrary to all laws." The Friends indignantly replied that they were loyal subjects, and never seduced any from allegiance. " But if any are convicted by the Spirit of God in their own hearts, that fighting with any carnal weapon to the destroying of any man, although their greatest enemy, be sin, then to him it is sin, if he do it."[2] Next year " Friends at Nevis in America " (sic) wrote an account of their troubles to the Meeting for Sufferings, and simultaneously the Governor bewailed to the Committee for Plantations the defenceless state of the islands. While the Spaniards protected their possessions with a squadron of thirteen ships of war, at Nevis, " for naval strength, there is nothing but the Quaker ketch," and even that in a few weeks' time had sailed for home. It is not clear whether the Quaker boat had been commandeered by Government from its original owners, or whether Colonel Stapleton intended to seize and arm it in case of need. But after this date there are few records of fine or imprisonment. Either succeeding Governors proved more lenient, or the majority of eligible Quakers had left the island. Antigua was captured by the French in 1664. The commander forced the inhabitants to take an oath of allegiance to Louis XIV, under threat of deporting the men, and leaving their families to the

---

[1] *Col. Entry Book*, xlvi. 185. *Cal.*, 1675–6, p. 502.
[2] Besse, ii. 362–3.

mercy of the Indian. There were four Quaker householders on the island, and these men refused to swear. The English Governor, Colonel Buckley, who had himself taken the oath argued with them, " but they stood firm, saying they could not swear, what suffering so ever might follow." At length the French Governor himself came to them and said, " I believe you are honest men, and if you will promise not to fight against the King my master, during this war, I will take your words." To which one of them replied : " We desire to be rightly understood in this our promise, for we can freely promise not to fight against the King of France nor for him ; nor indeed against the King of England, nor for him ; for we can act no more for the one than the other in matters of war. Only, as the King of England is our natural prince, we must own allegiance to him." [1] The Governor was satisfied by this explanation, but when Antigua was restored to the English at the peace of Breda, in 1667, Friends again endured the familiar round of fines, imprisonment, and even beatings. A certain Colonel Mallet was the chief persecutor, going to such lengths that at times the Governor intervened. On one occasion, when he was trying to force some Quakers to perform drill, his lieutenant refused to assist him, saying that he could not judge of a man's conscience, and was unwilling to meddle with them. Bermudian Quakers, also, in this Restoration period, suffered under the local Militia Acts. But after 1688, as the British possessions gradually settled under the Protestant Succession, Friends in the West Indies enjoyed greater liberty of conscience.

Yet the islands can never have proved a very congenial home for them. The journals of Thomas Story and Thomas Chalkley, both well-known Quaker ministers, draw lively pictures of the danger and excitement of a voyage in the West Indies during the early eighteenth century. In 1709, after four false alarms of French privateers,[2] the vessel in which Story was returning from Jamaica to America, was actually captured and taken to Hispaniola, where Story, with the help of his schoolboy Latin, was able to hold friendly

[1] Besse, ii. 370 foll.
[2] On the voyage from Antigua to Barbadoes the Captain at sight of a suspicious vessel " made ready for defence ; having twelve men, thirty guns, and suitable ammunition. They knew I would not be active in such defence, but desired me to keep with the doctor and make him what help I could, if any should be wounded, which I was very free to have done." Night fell, however, and they lost sight of the other ship.

intercourse with the French officials and a Jesuit priest. The latter, "a good old man," even devoted a Sunday sermon to the Quakers, saying (as it was reported to Story) "that we were an innocent religious people, differing in many points, both of doctrine and practice, from all other Protestants, and seemed to have a right faith in Christ ; only we seemed too diffident concerning the Saints, our duty to them, the Church's power, and the like. But, in the end, exhorted his people to keep firm in their own religion, and, as this people were thus cast among them, to show their Christianity and respect to them. And so they generally did, more than could have been expected ; and several of them said, though too lightly, ' The Quaker preacher had converted their minister.' "

The French Governor, Le Sieur de Laurens, invited Story to Sunday evening supper at his house and listened with great interest to an account of Pennsylvania, wishing for peace and an opportunity to visit the State. The wish moved Story to a short discourse on peace and war, well fortified with New Testament quotations. The Governor answered that " it was not they that desired the war, for they were generally much hurt by it, but the King, and that as God had set a king over them, they were bound in conscience to obey him ; who was answerable for all the evil, if any, and not they." This theory of passive obedience reminded Story of the doctrine preached in England in a " former reign." He met it with a reference to Nebuchadnezzar and his Hebrew ministers, but the Governor replied, " That was a heathen King, who commanded idolatry, but ours a Christian, and gave only Christian commands, so ought to be obeyed." To this Story made the obvious retort that the Christianity of the command depended rather on its character than on the religion of the King. The Huguenots, for example, had felt it a Christian duty to resist his laws " to the loss and sacrifice of many of their lives, and others were fled, and many thousands of them in the Queen of Great Britain's dominions to the great depopulating and weakening of his kingdom." The Governor bore no malice for this home thrust, but admitted that liberty of conscience was " no unreasonable thing," and showed his Quaker guest the *Confessions of St. Augustine* and the *Imitation of Christ*, in both of which Story found " many good sayings." Eventually the Englishmen were taken by the privateers to Martinique and Guadaloupe. There they were freed under a flag of truce after about three months' captivity.[1]

[1] *Life of Thomas Story*, 1747, pp. 441 foll.

Thomas Chalkley made several visits to the West Indies, showing himself as true to his peace principles there as in Pennsylvania. In 1707, while the Quaker-owned ship in which he travelled was being chased off Barbadoes by a French privateer, the seamen "cursed the Quakers, wishing all their vessels might be taken by the enemy, because they did not carry guns in them : at which I was grieved and began to expostulate with them : ' Do you know the worth of a man's life ? ' ' Lives ! ' said they, ' we had rather lose our lives than go to France.' ' But,' said I, ' that is not the matter : had you rather go to hell than go to France ? ' They, being guilty of great sins and wickedness, and convicted in their own consciences, held their peace, and said no more about the poor Quakers." [1]

Later, in a similar strait off Jamaica, this time on an armed vessel, Chalkley was jeeringly asked what he thought of Quaker principles now. He quietly replied that he was as willing to go to heaven as his questioners, and that he would pray for the souls of the crew. In the midst of the noise and hurry he prayed earnestly for a favourable wind, " that we might be delivered from the enemy without shedding blood." The wind did change, and they sped far out of sight of the privateer.

Twenty years afterwards, when he visited Barbadoes, he met an old acquaintance, not a Friend, who reminded him of a peace argument on his former visit. After Chalkley had given " Love enemies " and other Scriptural grounds for his own belief and practice, his hearer had asked " If one came to kill you, would you not kill rather than be killed ? " I told him, " No ; so far as I knew my own heart I had rather be killed than kill." He said, " That was strange," and desired to know what reason I could give for it. I told him, " that I being innocent, if I were killed in my body, my soul might be happy ; but if I killed him, he dying in his wickedness would consequently be unhappy ; and if I were killed, he might live to repent ; but if I killed him, he would have no time to repent. So that, if he killed me, I should have much the better, both in respect of myself and to him." This reasoning, which is entirely characteristic of Chalkley, and has been amplified at times by later Friends,[2] made a deep impression on the listener, who, as he now told the Quaker, as a result left off the sword he wore " and his business also,'

[1] Chalkley, *Works*, p. 55.
[2] *Vide* the reply of Joseph Hoag to the American General, p. 419.

which was presumably connected with weapons of war. "When we parted," Chalkley writes, "we embraced each other in open arms of Christian love, far from that which would hurt or destroy."[1]

On another visit in 1734 Chalkley lodged with a Dutchman at St. John's. His two sons had lately been killed in a negro rising, " for which their mother and sisters were in bitter mourning," and Chalkley was filled with silent horror at " the bloodshed and vast destitution which war makes in the world." [2]

Even in the early part of the eighteenth century, however, the number of Friends in the West Indies had much diminished. The story of their decline can be traced through the bulky manuscript volumes of *Epistles Sent* and *Epistles Received*, which contain the annual intercourse between London Yearly Meeting (or its permanent Committee, the Meeting for Sufferings) and the brethren across the seas. From Bermuda in 1703 John Richardson wrote " there is few Friends here, but two men," and the last letter from Jamaica in 1708 also bewails their small number. In 1705–6 Antigua sent a vivid account of the alarm of a French fleet, which passed them by, but cruelly ravaged Nevis and St. Kitts, and in 1707 the few Friends left on Nevis wrote a last letter to London in grateful acknowledgment for gifts in relief of " our great suffering by the French." Letters on both sides in those unsettled days often miscarried, and the isolated Friends had a hard struggle. Misfortunes in trade and moral delinquencies brought scandal at times upon the Society, particularly in Tortola, whence the final Epistle in 1763 reaches the depths of gloom. For many years Barbadoes remained the chief centre of the Society and was even prosperous enough to send at times substantial contributions to the charitable funds administered by English or Pennsylvanian Friends. The attraction of the mainland amid the troubles of continuous wars seems to have proved irresistible. A great drought in 1713, and epidemics of smallpox and yellow fever also played their part in driving Friends away from the West Indies. The Society in Antigua, during its last days, passed through one crisis which developed out of the perennial difficulty in reconciling the claims of the State with the Quaker interpretation of the teachings of Christianity. The appearance of the French fleet in 1705 had evidently frightened the authorities of the island into active prepara-

[1] Chalkley, *Works*, p. 207.   [2] *Ibid.*, p. 265.

tions for defence, but they honestly tried to respect the scruples of Friends by assigning them not to direct service in the militia, but to subsidiary work. Hereupon there arose a division of opinion in the Society. The older Friends, remembering bygone days of persecution, advised the acceptance of this compromise, while some young men declared that the work was inconsistent with their principles. Another difficulty concerned the payment of a church rate included in the general poor rate, and the dispute was so sharp that in 1708 two Epistles to London crossed the Atlantic, one signed by the Clerk of the Meeting, Jonas Langford, and the other by the dissentient young men Friends.[1]

The official document sets forth that the alternative service offered to Friends, in view of bearing arms or building forts, was " the public service of the island, that is to say, building of watch-houses, clearing common roads, making bridges, digging ponds. . . . Also they are willing to accept of us without arms only appearing at their training place, and also that we should go messages from place to place in the island, in case of danger by an enemy. These things they require of us, and we have performed them, for which we have been excused from bearing arms." But now these young Friends say that such work is " all one " with actual military service. The same kind of scruple had arisen a generation before, when Friends hesitated about " planting potatoes for them that watched and builded the forts," and the matter was referred to " dear George Fox and the Meeting in London for advice . . . and their advice was they were innocent things and might be safely done." It was on this occasion that Fox sent his letter to Nevis Friends, to which Langford and his party have referred for guidance. In any case (they conclude, after explaining the poor-rate dilemma) they would welcome a ruling from London, as these scruples have produced more strife and contention in the Meeting than has been known in the past forty years.

The Epistle from the younger Friends, which follows, is a remarkable and interesting declaration. They, too, they explain, would welcome a decision on these points, which to them are matters of conscience. They then state very clearly the actual nature of the " public service " imposed on them.

" Whereas it is often ordered by the Government that fortifica-tions are to be built, for the accomplishments whereof ponds for

[1] In D. *Epistles Received*, ii. 65 foll.

holding water (for the use of these persons who defend these places and inhabit them) are also to be dug, now the same Friends do think that if the Government will excuse them from carrying of great guns to these places, and digging of trenches, building of bulwarks, and such warlike things, and instead thereof employ them in digging these ponds, building of bridges, repairing of highways, building of guard-houses, and such things, they can freely do them, yet we do think that in such a case to dig ponds or the like to be excused from carrying of guns, etc., is not bearing a faithful testimony against such things, but below the nobility of that holy principle whereof we make profession, and (at best) but doing a lawful thing upon an unlawful account and bottom. Yet we are very willing to dig ponds, repair highways, and build bridges, or such convenient things when they are done for the general service of the island and other people at work therein equal with us, and not to balance those things which for conscience' sake we cannot do."

On the question of appearing unarmed at the militia muster, one Monthly Meeting has agreed with them that the practice is inconsistent with Friends' principles. " And as concerning alarms or invasion of an enemy, we are free to give notice to the magistrate of any approaching danger or be serviceable as far as we can at such times, in going to see what vessels may be off or giving them information in such things, though as to carrying of permits for vessels of war ' quietly to pass ' such and such forts, when we are sensible their commissions are to kill, sink, burn, and destroy the enemy, we are scrupulous and not free in that case. And as concerning watching, we are free to do it in our own way, " that is, unarmed, as Fox had recommended to the Friends of Nevis. The signatures to the letter are " John Brennan, John Darlow, junior, Henry Hodge, William Haige, John Butler, John Fallowfield."

The answer returned by the Meeting for Sufferings in 1709 [1] is instinct with that spirit of timidity and caution, combined with a genuine loyalty to the tolerant English Government, which marked Quaker leadership in the first half of the eighteenth century. The writer (possibly John Askew, who is the first name among the signatures) barely mentions the receipt of the young Friends' letter, while he speaks warmly of "our ancient worthy Friend Jonas Langford." A wish that "condescension in the spirit of love" may reconcile the disputants, is followed by approval of " the intentions

[1] In D. *Epistles Sent,* ii. 122.

of love and favour granted by the magistrates" of Antigua. In its view of what military works are possible for the Quaker conscience the Epistle goes beyond the concessions of the elder Antiguan Friends. "As for digging ditches and trenches and making walls, they are of like use with doors, locks, bolts, and pales, to keep out bloody wicked and destructive men and beasts ; and to give warning and to awake our neighbours by messengers or otherwise to prevent their being destroyed, robbed, or burnt, doubtless is as we would desire should in the like nature be done and performed to us."

The most serious feature of the Epistle is its general inaccuracy of reference. It gives in inverted commas, as if a direct quotation, a summary of Fox's Nevis letter, which, whether intentionally or not, almost stiffens it into an argument for military defence against attack, and while referring to the services rendered by Seller and other pressed Friends in naval battles, omits to describe their stead-fast resistance to any compromise of principle. An account of the help given by Hornould in rowing, when the boat in which he was passenger escaped an enemy ship, ends : "the relation whereof the Friend gave in our Yearly Meeting and was well liked by Friends." There is no hint that the "relation" included an account of the peace meeting which Hornould held with the crew and his fellow passengers.[1] It should be Friends' aim to show themselves to Governors and magistrates, not as "a self-willed and stubborn people," but ready to do the will of the authorities in anything "that is not an evil in its own nature, but service and benefit to our neighbours."

The question of the poor rate is handled with greater sympathy, possibly because the same dilemma was already pressing upon them in England. Among the names appended to this temporizing document are those of George Whitehead and of Fox's son-in-law, Thomas Lower. How the advice was received in Antigua cannot be known, for intercourse seems to have been broken off for some reason, and the next letter from the island is dated 1718. In it John Brennan wrote sadly of "a poor handful of people dispersed in a dark and barren island." Smallpox and the great drought had driven Friends away, among them Henry Hodge and his family to Pennsylvania, and William Hague and his family to Carolina. Ten years later the few remaining Friends "are inclinable to leave this island on account of the sickliness of the place," and after 1728 London

[1] *Ante*, p. 179–80.

hears no more from Antigua. If the Quaker records of the island had been preserved, we might have known whether the conscientious objectors agreed to work on " trenches and bulwarks," or whether it was a recurrence of the old difficulty that drove Henry Hodge and William Hague from their homes.

CHAPTER XIII

THE AMERICAN COLONIES

THE first Quaker visitors to America were the two women, Mary Fisher and Ann Austin, who came in 1656 to Barbadoes and thence to Boston. The Puritan officials and ministers, who had already heard ill reports from England of the new movement, seized the women, imprisoned them under the harshest conditions for five weeks, burned their books by the public hangman, and at last shipped them back to Barbadoes. In spite of this welcome and the most stringent laws against the entrance of Quakers to Massachusetts, they continued to come and to suffer under the "new Inquisition," as it was bitterly called by Fox and others, until in the years 1659 and 1660 three men and one woman were hanged under a law recently passed, making it a capital offence for Quakers once banished to return to the colony. Edward Burrough and other English Friends appealed to Charles II to stop this "vein of innocent blood." In response he issued an order to the Governor of Massachusetts, under which many Friends were released from prison, and one saved from the death sentence. It was not until 1681, however, that the savage laws against Quakers were formally suspended. Massachusetts was their cruellest persecutor, but in the other Puritan colonies, in aristocratic Virginia, and even in tolerant Maryland, they were almost as unwelcome. The Dutch colonies of the New Netherlands also promulgated harsh laws against them, until in 1663 the colonial officials were rebuked by a wise and far-sighted letter from the Directors of the West India Company in Amsterdam. In this they reminded their deputies that Holland's tradition of religious liberty had made her a refuge for all nationalities and that her colonies should follow the same path. "The consciences of men, at least, ought ever to remain free and unshackled." There was little opportunity to try the new policy, for in 1664 the colony passed into English hands as the provinces of New York and New Jersey. In spite of hostile legislation, Quakerism made its way. During Charles II's reign Meetings were settled in all these colonies, and before the end of the seventeenth century the organization into Monthly, Quarterly, and Yearly Meetings was fully adopted.[1]

In one colony Friends found not merely tolerance, but a congenial home. Rhode Island, both on the mainland and on the island itself, was tenanted by exiles for conscience' sake, who founded their settlements on principles of absolute religious freedom. Roger Williams, driven in 1635 from Salem for preaching against persecution, established Providence to be "a shelter for persons of distressed conscience." Two years later a settlement was founded on the island of "Aquiday" (now Rhode Island) by the so-called "Antinomians" or "Hutchinsonians," who had revolted against the strict Calvinism of New England, and as they gradually formed an organized Government, the assembly of citizens in 1641 passed the memorable law "that none be accounted a delinquent for doctrine." Roger Williams, though the enemy of all persecution, was no friend to Quaker doctrine, but some of the settlers seem, even thus early, to have held views very near to those preached later by Fox and his followers. They "would not wear any arms," opposed an ordained ministry, and in Portsmouth, at least, met together to "teach one another, and call it prophesie."[2]

When, in 1657, a small band of English Quakers visited the island, these men and women accepted their teaching at once, and many of the leading citizens of the colony were among its first Quakers. From the New England authorities came requests that Rhode Island should follow their example and stamp out the contagion of the new doctrines, but both Governor and Assembly steadily refused to violate liberty of conscience. "Freedom of *different* consciences," the Assembly stated in its reply, "was the principal ground of our charter." If the Quakers should refuse to submit to the duties required of citizens, "as training, watching, and such other engagements as are upon members of civil societies, for the preservation of the same in justice and peace," then the Assembly

---

[1] Rhode Island Yearly Meeting, 1661 (later New England Yearly Meeting) ; Baltimore Yearly Meeting, 1672 ; Virginia Yearly Meeting, 1673 ; Burlington (New Jersey) Yearly Meeting, 1681 (later Philadelphia Yearly Meeting) ; New York Yearly Meeting, 1696 ; North Carolina Yearly Meeting, 1698.

[2] *Vide* authorities quoted in Rufus Jones, *Quakers in the American Colonies,* pp. 21–5.

would refer for advice to the "supreme authority in England," by whom, they understood, the sect had been tolerated. This was a rebuff to New England, which was forced to watch the hated people growing in power, and even holding high office in Rhode Island. A Quaker was first chosen Governor in 1672, after which for many years the control of the colony was in Quaker hands.

In 1674 the proprietors of New Jersey sold half of that colony, afterwards known as West New Jersey, to two Friends who soon transferred it to William Penn and others of the Society. The new proprietors drew up a constitution which ensured full liberty of conscience, and, as Penn said, "put the power in the people." There was a definite intention that this thinly populated province should prove a new home for persecuted Quakers from England. The proprietors did all in their power to encourage emigration, and before 1681 fourteen hundred Friends had settled there. In 1680 East Jersey was for sale, and was purchased by Penn and other Friends, who included Robert Barclay, and some leading Scots. The latter were anxious to find a place of refuge for the persecuted Covenanters, and this division of the province was less markedly Quaker than West Jersey. In 1702 the proprietors surrendered the government of the united colony to Queen Anne. In the decade between 1670 and 1680 Carolina was twice visited by William Edmundson and once by George Fox. Among its scattered settlers there was little religious organization ; they welcomed the teaching of these travelling missionaries, and before long Meetings were established. A Friend, John Archdale, played an important part as Governor of the Colony. Lastly, in 1681, the Royal grant of Pennsylvania and the "counties upon Delaware" (the modern State) to William Penn gave him a better opportunity than he had had in the Jerseys for his "holy experiment" of a Quaker Commonwealth.

From this brief summary it will be seen how the position of Friends varied in the several colonies, from a persecuted minority in some to a powerful majority in others. Where they were in a minority, they suffered for their refusal of military service as they did for other nonconformity to the practices of the society which surrounded them. It was, no doubt, partly this refusal which for so long shut out the Quakers in New England from all exercise of the franchise or holding of public office. The current of policy at home in England at times embroiled the provinces in war with their French or Dutch neighbours, while in the debatable land between Indian settlements and colonial outposts the fires of savage warfare ever smouldered. These spasmodic outbreaks of war were always the signal 'for the enforcement of fines and imprisonments upon the Quakers, who would neither train nor fight ; in the intervals of peace the punitive clauses of the militia laws were sometimes allowed to lie unused.

In the provinces where Friends had political power, their trials were of a different character. There was no question of persecution for the holder of conscientious scruples against war, the problem was rather that of the limits of compromise—how far one part of the British dominions was bound to shape its policy in accordance with that of sister colonies or of the home Government, and how far a Quaker Government must conform to a demand for war preparations.

In Rhode Island this latter difficulty was raised in an acute form, since there Quakerism as the predominant form of belief was grafted upon the existing Government, and many of its chief officers joined the Society. The result was that the individual Quaker conscience was unmolested, and that the Quaker influence in the administration and Assembly was always exerted on the side of peace, but that, when military preparations were imposed upon them by the demands of the home Government, a Quaker, if he happened to be Governor, did not refuse to take such steps. This compliance was the price which they paid for the charter granted in 1663. It was not a very dignified or consistent position, and it gradually became untenable, but the frequent re-election of Quaker Governors shows that the citizens on the whole were not dissatisfied. Nicholas Easton, one of the original " Hutchinsonians," who became a Friend about 1657, was first Deputy-Governor and then Governor in the years between 1666 and 1674, a period which covered the two wars between England and Holland.

Rhode Island was uncomfortably near New York, and it was feared that the Dutch (during their brief re-conquest in 1673) would stir up Indian tribes against the settlements in the mainland. Both in 1672 and 1673 the Quaker Governor and his mainly Quaker Council passed Acts, in obedience to orders from England, putting the colony into "a posture of defence." These were followed by a law making provision for the support of maimed soldiers, and those " whose dependency was on such as are slain," and another for the relief of the conscientious objector—the first of its kind. Much of this Act of 1673 is a long statement of the scriptural and other arguments against war, which comes oddly from men busied with military preparations. As the inhabitants of the colony stand for liberty of conscience, they must needs forbear " to compel their equal neighbours against their consciences to train to fight and to kill." The crucial paragraph reads as follows :—

" Be it therefore enacted, and hereby it is enacted by his Majesty's authority, that no person (within this colony) that is or hereafter shall be persuaded in his conscience that he cannot or ought not to train, to learn to fight, nor to war, nor kill any person or persons, shall at any time be compelled against his judgment and conscience to train, arm, or fight, to kill any person or persons by reason of or at the command of any officer in this colony, civil nor military, nor by reason of any by-law here past or formerly enacted ; nor shall suffer any punishment, fine, distraint penalty, nor imprisonment, who cannot in conscience train, fight, nor kill any person nor persons for the aforesaid reasons." But the exempted were not to be idle. Another clause empowered the magistrate to require of them civil duties, such as the evacuation of the sick and aged and valuable property from threatened districts, the keeping watch and ward unarmed, and similar pieces of work.[1]

All other militia laws, even in the Revolution, exempted Friends, with the exception of one passed in 1677 under a reaction from Quaker government, which stated that " some under pretence of conscience hath taken liberty to act contrary, and make void the power, strength, and authority of the military, so necessary to be maintained." The warlike party, however, only held office for a year, and thereafter until 1685 the power was continuously in Quaker hands. The cause of the reaction had been the sufferings of the colonists on the mainland round Narragansett Bay, during " King Philip's War," the fierce Indian rising which terrified New England from 1675 to 1677. " Left to themselves the Rhode Island colonists could have maintained peace, for their Indian policy was wise, humane, and enlightened, and gained for them the confidence and love of their Indian neighbours."[2] But, in addition to the inevitable discontent engendered as the white men's settle-

[1] *Rhode Island Colony Records*, ii. 495 ; see also Arnold, *History of Rhode Island*.
[2] Jones, *Quakers in the American Colonies*, p. 175.

ments expanded over the Indian territories, acts of real injustice
and the treatment of the Indians as an inferior race by the New
England settlers had inflamed their proud and revengeful tempers.
Nevertheless, the Rhode Island Government, while disclaiming
all responsibility for the war, made an effort to avert it. John Easton,
the Deputy-Governor, son of Nicholas Easton, and four other
Quakers, came unarmed to the quarters of " King Philip," the great
Indian chief, on Narragansett Bay, and spent a day pleading with
him and his warrior council for a settlement.[1] The Indians gave
them a catalogue of their grievances against the English, such as
the unrestricted sale of spirits, and the rejection of Indian evidence
in cases where the white man was the aggressor. " We told them
that our desire was that the quarrel might be rightly decided in the
best way, not as dogs decide their quarrels. . . . They owned
that fighting was the worst way, but they inquired how right might
take place without fighting. We said by arbitration. They said
that by arbitration the English agreed against them, and by arbitration they had much wrong.

"... We said they might choose an Indian king, and the
English might choose the Governor of New York ; that neither
had cause to say that either were parties to the difference. They
said they had not heard of this way. We were persuaded that if
this way had been tendered, they would have accepted." But the
deputation from Rhode Island could not satisfy the Indians that
the rest of New England was willing to adopt such a course, and
there was no result from the visit except an assurance by the Indians
of their friendly feeling towards the Island. A few days afterwards,
June 1675, war broke out. The Rhode Island Government took
up the attitude that it was an unjust and unnecessary conflict for
which they were in no way responsible. They refused to assist the
other colonies, or even at first to send an armed force to their own
settlements on the mainland ; but urged the inhabitants of those
towns to take refuge on the island, where they would be supported
during the war. The other New England Governments had joined
in a " compact " to crush the Indian menace, and bitterly reproached
Rhode Island for holding aloof. When the war was over, the
General Court of Plymouth sent home a complaint to Charles II.
" The truth is the authorities of Rhode Island, being all the time
of the war in the hands of the Quakers, they scarcely showed an

[1] Narrative of Easton quoted in *Quakers in the American Colonies*, pp. 182–3.

English spirit either in assisting us their distressed neighbours or relieving their own plantations on the main. But when by God's blessing upon our forces the enemy was routed and almost subdued, they took in many of our enemies that were flying before us, thereby making profit of our expense of blood and treasure."[1]

What "profit" the Rhode Islanders made is not clear, for while some of the Indian leaders were court-martialled and shot at Newport, the Assembly refused to sell the other captive Indians on their territory into life-long slavery, which was the policy of the other colonies towards those whose lives were spared.[2] One real service was rendered by the Rhode Island authorities to the Colonial troops. After a bloody battle on Narragansett Bay, in the winter of 1675, the colonial wounded, one hundred and fifty, were brought across to the island, where Governor Coddington, a Friend, made arrangements for their treatment, although some "churlish Quakers" objected even to this connection with the war.[3] This encouraged the New England authorities to ask again for military help. Coddington replied in a short letter and a long "postscript." The letter ran thus :—

"The Governor and Council of the Massachusetts and Committee of the United Colonies writing to us do give us thanks for transporting their soldiers and provisions, and that sloops transported their wounded, and desired us to let out a hundred or two hundred soldiers, we answered you denying so to do, and gave you our grounds."

The postscript calls attention to a recent "day of humiliation" in Boston for the sins which had called down the war upon the colonists. One was, the neglect to suppress the Quakers and their meetings, and "a law was simultaneously passed imposing a fine of five pounds upon every person who should attend a Quaker Meeting, with imprisonment at hard labour upon bread and water."[4] No wonder that the Quaker Governor of the colony where none was "accounted a delinquent for doctrine" commented :—

---

[1] *Colonial Papers,* xli. 16. C.O. i. 41. *Calendar of State Papers (Colonial),* 1677–80, p. 115.

[2] Kelsey, *Friends and the Indians,* p. 56. By a vote of the Assembly in 1676, indentured Indian labour for a term of years and under various restrictions was sanctioned " as if they had been countrymen not in war."

[3] Authorities in *Quakers in American Colonies,* p. 186.

[4] Jones, *Quakers in the American Colonies,* p. 187. *Colony Records of Massachusetts,* v. 59.

"You say you have apostated from the Lord with a great backsliding : to which I do consent ; so great (as) hardly to be paralleled, all things considered. . . . Our houses are open to receive your wounded and all in distress, we have prepared a hospital for yours, but you a house of correction for all that repair to our Meetings. Your ministers with us have not been molested, ours with you have been persecuted. Is this a time for you to set up iniquity by a law ?"[1]

The appeals of the settlers at Providence, Warwick, and the other mainland towns were harder to resist. The towns were desolated by the war, and the refugees in Newport could not look with calm on the destruction of their homesteads across the water, while those who refused to flee were in still worse plight. The Assembly decided in April 1676 that "there appears absolute necessity for the defence and safety of this colony." John Cranston, a non-member though connected with Friends, was chosen to organize the militia and "to kill, expulse, take and destroy all and every the enemies of his Majesty's colony."[2] The commission was given by Governor Coddington and at the same time a garrison of eight men sent to help Providence. Yet Walter Clarke, a Quaker who had been most stubborn in resisting the pleas from the mainland, was chosen Governor this year, just before the war ended with the death of King Philip. William Edmundson, who was travelling among American Friends this year, found at Newport that "great troubles attended Friends by reason of the war, which lay very heavy on places belonging to that quarter without the island, the Indians killing and burning all before them ; and the people who were not Friends were outrageous to fight. But the Governor, being a Friend (one Walter Clarke), would not give commissions to kill and destroy men."[3]

It was in 1677, when the war was over, and the full extent of its ravages became apparent, that the elections went against the

---

[1] Easton's *Narrative*, Appendix.

[2] A curious report to the English authorities in April 1675 gave an optimistic account of the excellence of the Rhode Island Militia, with their " buff-coats, pistols, hangers, and crosslets." " All men that are able bear arms except some few Anabaptists and the Quakers, who will not bear any " (*Col. Papers*, xxxiv. iv. 66. C.O., i. 34. *Calendar*, 1675-6, p. 221).

[3] Edmundson, *Journal*, p. 82. During this year of 1676, Edmundson travelled through regions where the Indian war was raging. He says : " I committed my life to God who gave it, and took my journey," even holding peaceful intercourse with a band of Indians in full war-paint.

Quakers and the new Assembly passed the Militia Bill, already mentioned. Yet the reaction was short-lived. From 1678 to 1714 Quakers were almost continuously in office, except during an attempt from 1686 to 1689 by James II to annul the charter, annex the colony to Massachusetts, and govern both by one of his creatures, Sir Edward Andros. Throughout these years the local authorities opposed a quiet but firm resistance to the demands of Andros, refusing to give up their charter, and organizing self-government for the towns, when the General Assembly was dissolved. The Quakers of the colony in 1686 sent an earnest plea to James that the conscientious scruples to "bear arms or learn war any more" might be respected.[1] There is no evidence that they were molested. Under William and Mary the colony returned to its old privileges, and its succession of Quaker governors. In the term of one of these, John Easton, King Philip's friend, a fleet of French ships seven in number appeared off the Narragansett coast and were bombarding the shore (it was at the time of the war between William and Louis) when two Rhode Island sloops made a spirited attack upon them and drove them off in much disorder.

During these latter years of Quaker government there were animated disputes with the Governors of New York and Massachusetts over the colony's right to control its militia, and with the English Home Office over matters of trade and navigation. All these questions, the authorities of the colony maintained, were by the charter left in their own decision and control. On the other hand, charges were made to the home authorities that Rhode Island was unwilling to take punitive measures against the pirates who infested American waters at the end of the seventeenth century. The Quaker politicians were even accused of a corrupt and profitable alliance with the pirates, but no proof was ever brought forward of this. As the population of the island grew in the eighteenth century, the Quaker influence waned, although several members of the Wanton family held the office of Governor. Their ancestor Edward Wanton had been converted to the faith by witnessing the martyrdom of the Quakers on Boston Common in 1659.[2] He must have been a youth at the time, for his son, John, was born

[1] *Col. Papers*, lviiii. 36. C.O., i. 60. *Cal.*, 1685–8, p. 232.

[2] The tradition was that he was a member of the guard, and " came home from the execution, greatly changed, saying, as he unbuckled his sword : ' Mother, we have been murdering the Lord's people, and I will never put a sword on again ' " (Jones, *Quakers in American Colonies*, p. 201).

in 1672 and was Governor of Rhode Island from 1733 to his death in 1741. During his last term of office the " War of Jenkin's Ear " broke out between England and Spain, which involved the Spanish and English settlements in the West Indies and on the American continent. John Wanton, although a leading Friend, had to carry out many military duties, which alarmed the corporate conscience of his Society. A Committee was appointed to " deal " with him, but he maintained that as Governor he had no choice except to fulfil his legal obligations. " I have endeavoured," he added, " on all previous occasions, as on this, to do my whole duty to God and to my fellow men, without doing violence to the law of my conscience."[1] As he died during this year, it is not certain whether the Meeting would have taken any further action in the case. Some of the Friends of Rhode Island were leaders in the struggle against the taxation claims of the English Crown and Parliament in the decade before the outbreak of the Revolution. Stephen Hopkins, the most distinguished of these men, was nine times Governor and a signatory of the Declaration of Independence. But during the same years, stirred up by John Woolman, the Rhode Island Yearly Meeting (representative of all New England Friends) was setting itself to free the Society from the reproach of slave-holding. In 1773 it resolved " *that we do no more claim property in the human race.*" Stephen Hopkins was the owner of one slave, whom he steadily refused to free, and in this year he was, in consequence, disowned. Yet, when in 1774, the Yearly Meeting appointed a Committee to secure anti-slavery legislation from the assembly, Stephen Hopkins brought in and carried the required Act.

In the New England colonies, amid all their other sufferings, Friends did not escape those for refusal to bear arms. Indian raids on the outskirts of the settled territory were a constant menace, and Indian wars were frequent. The Puritan pioneers could not understand neighbours who went about unarmed, who even in war-time often refused the protection of a " garrison," and who would take no part in measures of retaliation. It did not add to the popularity of a Quaker settler that he was able to establish amicable relations with the red men, and that he could live in his cabin unmolested, while his neighbour's home went up in flames and the neighbour's life was worth nothing if he strayed outside the garrison. These " garrisons " were houses or groups of houses

[1] Quoted in *Quakers in American Colonies*, p. 204.

roughly prepared for defence, surrounded by a loopholed palisade, at which stood ever an armed guard. Here the old men, women, and children took refuge on the first alarm, while the majority of the able-bodied sallied out from it for punitive expeditions. The early Epistles to London from Rhode Island Yearly Meeting often speak of the troubles due to the " barbarious Indians." From Thomas Chalkley and Thomas Story we gain more intimate accounts of their own personal experiences in these wars.

In 1699 Story was travelling on religious visits through New England, at a time of especially ferocious warfare. He kept a close watch on the conduct of New England Friends under the test : " I did not hear of any of our Friends that carried arms when abroad or in their business, but two, and these the Indians had killed, but most went into garrisons to lodge in the nights, and some not, but trusted in the Lord ; and we kept clear of all garrisons, always lodging without their bounds and protection of their guns and arms."[1] Another Indian war broke out in 1703–4. Anne and her Government had been drawn into the war of the Spanish Succession, and in revenge the French stirred up their native allies against the English colonists. Story, on his travels through Massachusetts, found the countryside panic-stricken. " It was a dismal time indeed in those parts ; for no man knew, in an ordinary way, when the sun set, that ever it would arise upon him any more ; or, lying down to sleep, but his first waking might be in eternity, by a salutation in the face with a hatchet, or a bullet from the gun of a merciless savage, who from wrongs received (as they too justly say) from the professors of Christ in New England, are to this day enraged, as bears bereaved of their cubs, sparing neither age nor sex."[2] As in 1699, some Friends took refuge in the garrisons, and some even carried arms, but the " faithful and true " remained quietly in their homes. Story, though he visited the most disturbed parts, would never lodge in a garrison. At first he doubted whether to hold meetings in places to which Friends must travel by dangerous paths. But by an " invisible Power " he was encouraged to continue his work, the meetings were held to the great comfort of those who attended, and no lives were lost on the journeys. He found that the more timid Friends, who sheltered in garrisons and carried arms, " to the dishonour of Truth," were trying to justify themselves by condemning those who remained faithful in their

---

[1] *Life of Thomas Story*, 1747, p. 197. [2] *Ibid.*, p. 315.

principles. Story, therefore, who was always ready to preach a peaceable gospel, " had much to say in every meeting on that subject," and no doubt used the fate of some of these waverers as a text. The facts are told both by Story and Chalkley. The latter wrote in his *Journal* for this year, on the subject of the Indian wars :—

" Among the many hundreds that were slain, I heard but of two or three of our Friends being killed, whose destruction was very remarkable, as I was informed (the one was a woman, the other two were men). The men used to go to their labour without any weapons, and trusted to the Almighty, and depended on His provision to protect them, it being their principle not to use weapons of war to offend others or to defend themselves. But a spirit of distrust taking place in their minds, they took weapons of war to defend themselves ; and the Indians, who had seen them several times without them, and let them alone, saying, *They were peaceable people and hurt nobody, therefore they would not hurt them*, now seeing them to have guns and supposing they designed to kill the Indians, they therefore shot the men dead." Story tells of a similar, but apparently distinct, case where two young Friends were walking together, one with a gun and one without. " The Indians shot him who had the gun, but hurt not the other. And when they knew the young man they had killed was a Friend, they seemed sorry for it, but blamed him for carrying a gun : for they knew the Quakers would not fight nor do them any harm, and therefore, by carrying a gun, they took him for an enemy."[1] The woman already mentioned was killed on the same day as this young man. She had lived in a lonely spot with her daughter, son-in-law, and their family. At first she remained quietly there during the danger, but in time what Chalkley called " a slavish fear " so preyed upon her mind that she induced them to move with her to a neighbouring town, Hampton, where there was a " garrison " in which they could take refuge in case of a sudden attack. The daughter, Mary Doe, left an account of the whole episode in a quaint and touching letter to her children, which Chalkley quotes in full. In it she told them that, in the neighbourhood of the garrison, " my dear mother . . . found herself not at all easy, but, as she often said to many, that she felt herself in a beclouded condition, and more shut from counsel than she had been since she knew the Truth, and, being uneasy, went to move to a Friend's house that lived in the neighbourhood ; and

[1] Story, *Life*, p. 316.

as she was moving, the bloody cruel Indians lay by the way and killed her. O, then, how did I lament moving!" Thereafter the daughter persuaded her husband to return to the lonely dwelling, but he was uneasy in his mind "till our dear friend Thomas Story came and told him, he did not see that I could have a greater revelation than I had. And (this) satisfied my husband so well that he never asked me more to go, but was very well contented to stay all the wars; and then things were made more easy, and we saw abundance of the wonderful works and of the mighty power of the Lord, in keeping and preserving of us, when the Indians were at our doors and windows, and at other times; and how the Lord put courage in you, my dear children. Don't you forget it, and don't think that as you were so young, and because you knew little, so you feared nothing; but often consider how you staid at home alone, when we went to Meetings, and how the Lord preserved you and kept you, so that no hurt came upon you."[1]

Of this, the home of Henry Dow, or Doe, Story said it was "a place of as much seeming danger as any being within pistol-shot of a great swamp or thicket, where Indians formerly inhabited, and there I lodged, where there was neither gun nor sword, nor any weapon of war, but Truth, faith, the fear of God, and love, in a humble and resigned mind, and there I rested with consolation."

Another Friend in this district told Chalkley that he was working in his field when some Indians called him, and *he went to them*. They told him that they had no quarrel with the Quakers, for they were a quiet, peaceable people and hurt nobody, and that therefore none should hurt them. But they complained bitterly of the Presbyterians who "had taken away their lands and some of their lives." Chalkley, after recounting the barbarous revenge the Indians took for these wrongs, adds: "But we travelled the country and had large meetings, and God was with us abundantly, and we had great inward joy in the Holy Ghost in our outward jeopardy and travels. The people generally rode and went to their worship armed, but Friends went to their meetings without sword or gun, having their trust and confidence in God."

This Indian war was a by-product of the struggle with France, in which the Government of New England was bearing its part by an invasion of Canada. To recruit this expeditionary force they passed a draft law, under which any defaulters were to be fined,

---

[1] Chalkley, *Journal*, pp. 41-6.

" and refusing to pay the fine, should be imprisoned, and sold or bound to some of the Queen's subjects within that colony, for so long a time as by their work they might pay their fines and charges." This law at once brought some young Quakers into prison, and revived the old New England bitterness against them. One preacher gave a fast-day sermon on the three judgments of God, which were : the Indian war, the failure of the crops, and the increase of Quakerism ! Two young men of Bristol, Massachusetts—John Smith and Thomas Maccamore—were conscripted under this law, fined five pounds, and imprisoned for its non-payment.[1] They had already been in prison some two months when Thomas Story, who was on a religious visit to Rhode Island, took occasion to cross the bay with other Friends and hold a meeting with them in the prison. The meeting was held again a fortnight later, when the company " were favoured with a good time in the Presence and Love of God together." But Story was anxious to obtain for them material relief as well as spiritual comfort, and his negotiations show that the conscientious objector was an inconvenient phenomenon to the colonial officials of Queen Anne's day. With Thomas Cornwell, a Friend from Rhode Island, Story visited Colonel Nathaniel Byfield, one of the magistrates. At first they had an uncomfortable reception. " He was very boisterous, reproaching Friends in general as a sort of people not worthy to live upon the earth, particularly those of Rhode Island and New England, who would not go out nor pay their money to others to fight against a common enemy so barbarous as are the Indians ; wishing us all in the front of the battle until we had learned bettter ; charging us with many errors and heresies in religion by the lump, instancing only in refusing to fight, and believing in sinless perfection in this life." The Friends took up the challenge, and the Colonel soon grew weary of the argument, for he " flounced " about the room, saying : " He could not stay, for there were a hundred men waiting for him, and he must be going." He calmed down, however, and invited the Friends to dine with him, to continue the discussion. As he repeated his condemnation of those who would not fight, Story asked, " seeing he was so keen of war, why was he not among the rest in the expedition then on foot against the Indians ; for, if he had courage to his stature, he might do something more than merely talk against the infidels." He had no commission, he said ; but Story retorted that,

[1] Story, *Life*, pp. 266–311.

doubtless, he could have one for the asking. The Colonel took
the quip good-naturedly, and after the meal the three walked back
to Bristol together. As they went, the harassed official declared
that " it might be well if we (Friends) were all settled in a place
by ourselves, where we could not be troublesome unto others by
our contradictious ways." But Story, with something of the sublime
confidence of Fox, replied that even so, " more would spring up
in our places. For what would the world do if it should lose its
salt and leaven ? " Their companion was not unnaturally "a little
surprised " at the answer, but turned the subject by telling them
the young men were to be sent to Boston to labour at the fort until
they had worked off their fines. The Friends argued that this
was not the penalty assigned by the law, but the Colonel's mind
was made up and he left them. " After this " (adds Story) " we
went to the prison to see the young men, and acquainted them that
we could find little ground to expect any favour ; at which they
seemed altogether unconcerned, being much resigned to the will
of God at that time." Next day the trial began, with a revival of
the old hat controversy. When this was settled by their headgear
being taken from the Quakers, the judge (Colonel Byfield again)
said humorously that : " If he thought there were any religion
in a hat, he would have the largest he could purchase for money."
Then he asked the prisoners the reason of their obstinancy.

" The young men modestly replied, It was not obstinacy, but
duty to God, according to their consciences and religious persuasions,
which prevailed with them to refuse to bear arms or learn war.
But the judge would not, by any means, seem to admit there was
any conscience in it, but ignorance and a perverse nature ;
accounting it very irreligious in any who were personally able, and
legally required, to refuse their help now in time of war against
enemies so potent, and so barbarous as the French and Indians."
Then he charged the Society with inconsistency in paying taxes,
and refusing fines. This brought Story to his feet, with a request
to be allowed to explain the distinction, which was granted.
Beginning " with the example of Christ himself," he distinguished
a general tax from " a law that directly and principally affects the
person." But the judge interrupted with the remark that Story
was preaching a sermon. The court postponed its decision, and the
elder Friends made acknowledgment of the courtesy they had received.
" Our hats being delivered us, we accompanied the young men back

to the prison, where, being set down together, the Presence of the
Lord was sensibly with us, and I had some things to say concerning
faithfulness unto God, and the great reward of it here and
hereafter."

The sentence was as foretold, and Story, with other Friends,
went to Boston to lay the case before the Governor, Colonel
Dudley. He was courteous, saying (in reply to Story's explanation
of the peace position—" those who are in wars are not in the life
nor doctrine of Christ ") that " he was no disputant about religion,"
but that, in the existing state of public opinion, he could not override
the Justice's decision. But, said Story, the decision was against
the law, and the Governor on that ground should release the men.
" The country " (he replied) " would be about his ears if he should
do that ; but it is a harmless thing to work at the castle ; they need
not fight there." They cannot work at it, Story answered, for it
is an " erection for war." The Friends were forced to leave
unsatisfied, but eventually, though the young men were taken to
Boston, they were not sent to the Castle, but left at liberty " to
be ready upon call." Story had several other opportunities during
this visit to New England of stating his views on war. He recounts
at great length a dispute on war in the island of Canonicut with
a Baptist teacher who had informed him " with some ostentation "
that his two sons were serving in the expedition to Canada. The
argument ranged over the whole field, the distinction between the
civil and the military power, the contradiction of war with the
spirit of Christ—" the whole tenor of his doctrine and example
of life was for peace and love, and in that love and the power and
divine virtue of it he yielded up his life "—and the necessity that
individuals must begin the practice of peace before the whole world
is convinced of their principles.[1] " And as for us, who do not fight
with carnal weapons, we meddle not with you who do, otherwise
than to persuade you to leave that off and be enlisted under the saving
banner of the Prince of Peace ; to believe in the divine light of
the Son of God ; to come out of the Spirit of this world, in which
is all trouble, into the Spirit and Kingdom of Christ, in whom there

[1] One of Story's arguments, apparently a favourite one, as he repeated it on
another occasion, was that the Jews crucified Christ in the fear that if his teaching
spread they could raise no forces for a patriotic struggle against the Romans.
He based this theory on John xi. 48, which more naturally refers to the people's
belief in Christ as " King of the Jews " and the dread of a sudden rising on behalf
of such a pretender.

is perfect peace ; which if ye will not do, we must leave you to fight one with another, until you are weary." His opponent could find little to answer, and they " parted friendly," which, Story says, was his aim in every dispute, as he wished to produce conviction, or at least understanding, rather than conquest.[1]

The New England law still remained severe, and the Epistles to London frequently mention sufferings for the " Malisa." In 1710 the Governor of Boston was " kind," and discharged several prisoners. Next year there was another expedition to Canada, and the Yearly Meeting of 1712 recorded the imprisonment of four young men who refused to serve. Two, who were in confinement for three months, seem to have been forced to accompany the expedition, but were " not abused during the time of their voyage."[2] The other two were imprisoned in Boston Castle, and thence forced on board a transport, where they underwent such hard usage that one of them, John Terry, afterwards died. This same Yearly Meeting informed English Friends that although the " barbarious Indians " had murdered many that past year in the eastern parts of New England, yet not one Friend had fallen a victim.[3] In the Seven Years War, and especially at the time of the Louisburg Expedition in 1758, Friends endured heavy distraints owing to their refusal to hire substitutes for the campaign. In certain cases the sums charged were so excessive that the legislature, on a petition from the sufferers, examined the matter and in the end returned to them the money illegally exacted.

In the colony of New York, Friends also had their full share of suffering for " not learning war," as they phrased it in a letter to London in 1706. The respectful protest the Friends at Flushing forwarded in 1672 to the Governor of New York is especially interesting from its description of the refusal of all part in warlike activities as a long-standing principle of Friends. " Whereas it was desired of the country that all who would willingly contribute towards repairing the fort of New York would give in their names

---

[1] Story, *Life*, pp. 364-7.

[2] Minutes of Rhode Island (New England) Yearly Meeting, 1712. Quoted in *Quakers in the American Colonies*, p. 150.

[3] About 1725 . . . there are records in the minutes of Philadelphia Yearly Meeting of a collection of nearly a thousand dollars taken up for John Hanson " of the eastern part of New England, whose wife, four children, and a servant were carried off by the Indians and he had to ransom them at a great price " (Kelsey, *Friends and the Indians*, p. 73)

and sums, and we whose names are underwritten not being found on the list, it was since desired by the High Sheriff that we would give our reasons unto the Governor, how willing and ready we have been to pay our customs, as country rates and needful town charges, and how we have behaved ourselves peaceably and quietly amongst our neighbours, and are ready to be serviceable in anything which doth not infringe upon our tender consciences, but being in a measure redeemed of wars and stripes we cannot for conscience' sake be concerned in upholding things of that nature as you yourselves well know. It hath not been our practice in old England since we were a people." [1]

While New Jersey was under its Quaker proprietorship there was naturally no trouble for tender consciences, and even under Queen Anne, Friends were exempted from the militia training, if certified as recognized members of the Society. It was a time of sudden alarms of a French invasion, and four young men of Burlington Meeting had to confess they had gone out with arms to search for some escaped prisoners, although their intentions were not bloodthirsty. " It seemed best for those that had guns to take them, not with a design to hurt, much less to kill man, woman, or child ; but we thought that if we could meet these runaways, the sight of the guns might fear them."[2] In war-time New Jersey Quakers suffered like other Friends from imprisonments and distraints, while their comrades of the same Yearly Meeting, across the borders of Pennsylvania, were, of course, immune.

Quakerism in New Jersey during the eighteenth century was adorned by the life of John Woolman, one of the uncalendared saints of the Christian Church. This " serene and beautiful spirit," to quote Whittier's discerning eulogy, was the chief instrument in the gradual process by which the Society of Friends cleared itself from the reproach of slave-holding and slave-dealing. By this time the practice of buying *imported* slaves was generally condemned in the Society, at all events, among Northern Friends, but the well-to-do held slaves as a matter of course. They were treated as human beings rather than chattels, and in many cases given religious teaching ; slavery was in its mildest form in a Quaker household ; but none the less it was slavery. John Woolman was a humble tradesman of Mount Holly in New Jersey. Being somewhat better

---

[1] Quoted in *Quakers in the American Colonies*, p. 250.
[2] Quoted by A. M. Gummere in *Quakers of the American Colonies*, p. 393.

educated than his neighbours he was employed by them to write their legal documents, and it was his refusal to do this in cases relating to the transfer of slaves that marked the opening of his life-long battle for the oppressed. This was in 1742. In 1746 he first visited Friends in Virginia and Carolina, where he was greatly affected by what he saw of the evils of Southern slavery. It was largely through his earnest pleading that the Philadelphia Yearly Meeting of 1758 adopted a minute condemning slavery, and urging that Friends should "steadily observe the injunction of our Lord and Master : ' To do unto others as we would they should do unto us,' which it now appears to this Meeting would induce such Friends who have any slaves to set them at liberty—making a Christian provision for them according to their ages." This minute practically made slave-holding an offence against the corporate morality of the Society. But persuasion and entreaty were tried before discipline. John Woolman and others who felt with him gave themselves up to the task of visiting and pleading with slave-holding Friends. Few could resist his gentle eloquence. In twenty years' time the Philadelphia Yearly Meeting had no slave-holding members. The Yearly Meetings of the other States also had their consciences awakened, partly through the labours of John Woolman. By the end of the Revolutionary War slavery had practically vanished from the Society of Friends. In almost all cases members had willingly freed their slaves, and the total number of disownments was very small.

To Woolman not only slavery, but conduct as a whole and in detail, was to be judged by what he called the "pure reason." Society ideally was a harmony, and each individual was responsible for the discords which marred it. Selfishness and greed lay at the roots, not only of slavery, but of the inequalities of wealth and poverty, of war, and of all other social evils. " To labour " (he wrote towards the end of his life) " for a perfect redemption from this spirit of oppression is the great business of the whole family of Christ Jesus in this world."[1] In a striking passage he pressed home his argument with regard to war. " When that spirit works which loves riches, and in its working gathers wealth and cleaves to customs which have their root in self-pleasing, whatever name it hath, it still desires to defend the treasures thus gotten. This is like a chain in which the end of one link encloseth the end of another. The rising up of a desire to obtain wealth is the beginning ; this

[1] *A Word of Remembrance to the Rich,* sect. xii.

desire being cherished, moves to action ; and riches thus gotten please self ; and while self has a life in them it desires to have them defended. Wealth is attended with power, by which bargains and proceedings contrary to universal righteousness are supported ; and hence oppression carried on with worldly policy and order, clothes itself with the name of justice and becomes like a seed of discord in the soul. And as a spirit which wanders from the pure habitation prevails, so the seeds of war swell and sprout and grow and become strong until much fruit is ripened. Then cometh the harvest spoken of by the prophet which ' is an heap in the day of grief and desperate sorrows.' Oh that we who declare against wars and acknowledge our trust to be in God only, may walk in the light, and therein examine our foundation and motives in holding great estates ! May we look upon our treasures, the furniture of our houses, and our garments, and try whether the seeds of war have nourishment in these our possessions." [1] This was written towards the close of his life ; in earlier years he had faced the question of the direct responsibility for war as it affected him. At the time of the French and Indian campaigns of the Seven Years War he decided, after much heart-searching, that he could not pay the taxes which went to their support.[2] " To refuse the active payment of a tax which our Society generally paid was exceedingly disagreeable, but to do a thing contrary to my conscience appeared yet more dreadful." Woolman devotes some pages of his *Journal* to a gentle explanation why he felt constrained to differ even from the early Friends in this matter. " From the steady opposition which faithful Friends in early times made to wrong things then approved, they were hated and persecuted by men living in the spirit of this world and, suffering with firmness, they were made a blessing to the Church and the work prospered. It equally concerns men in every age to take heed to their own spirits ; and in comparing their situation with ours, to me it appears that there was less danger of their being infected with the spirit of this world in paying such taxes than is the case with us now." In eighteenth-century America, particularly in Pennsylvania, Friends held civil office which might at times involve the performance of duties connected with war. If they saw other Friends contentedly paying war taxes, their own scruples in regard to these duties might be allayed. " Thus, by small degrees,

[1] *A Word of Remembrance to the Rich*, sect. ix.
[2] John Woolman, *Journal*.

we might approach so near to fighting that the distinction would be little else than the name of a peaceable people." Twice again during the war he had to meet a time of trial. In August 1757 the militia of his county, Burlington, was called out, and a force sent to relieve the English holding Fort William Henry, New York. Soon orders came to draft another force of men, to be held under marching orders. A considerable number of Friends were called up. John Woolman at this time was just thirty-seven, and it is not clear from his account whether he was liable to service, but he certainly was in close touch with the conscripts.[1] Some, he says, went away to avoid service, others agreed to serve ; " others appeared to have a real tender scruple in their minds against joining in wars, and were much humbled under the apprehension of a trial so near." These latter informed the captain that they could neither serve nor hire substitutes, and they were allowed for the time to return home, although he would not release them from their obligation to service. They were not, however, called up, since the fort had fallen and the French, after destroying it, had marched away before the first draft could be of service. With his innate fairness of mind Woolman was struck by the difficulty which the conscientious objector presented to the military authorities. Some officers, he wrote, felt it painful to trouble sincere and upright men on account of scruples of conscience, and were willing to treat them with consideration. " But where men profess to be so meek and heavenly minded and to have their trust so firmly settled in God that they cannot join in wars, and yet by their spirit and conduct in common life manifest a contrary disposition, their difficulties are great at such a time. When officers who are anxiously endeavouring to get troops to answer the demands of their superiors, see men who are insincere pretend scruple of conscience in hopes of being excused from a dangerous employment it is likely they will be roughly handled." From this Woolman drew the moral of " the advantage of living in the real substance of religion, where practice doth harmonize with principle."

A few months later (April 1758) troops were billeted at Mount Holly, and Woolman was required to accommodate two soldiers. " The case being new and unexpected, I made no answer suddenly, but sat a time silent, my mind being inward. I was fully convinced

---

[1] He says : " This was such a time as I had not seen before ; and yet I may say, with thankfulness to the Lord, that I believe the trial was intended for our good—and I was favoured with resignation to Him." This seems to imply that he was in the draft.

that the proceedings in wars are inconsistent with the purity of the Christian religion ; and to be hired to entertain men who were then under pay as soldiers was a difficulty with me. I expected they had legal authority for what they did ; and after a short time I said to the officers, if the men are sent here for entertainment, I believe I shall not refuse to admit them into my house, but the nature of the case is such that I expect I cannot keep them on hire ; one of the men intimated that he thought I might do it consistently with my religious principles. To which I made no reply, believing silence at that time best for me. Though they spake of two, there came only one, who tarried at my house about two weeks, and behaved himself civilly. When the officer came to pay me, I told him I could not take pay, having admitted him into my house in a passive obedience to authority. I was on horseback when he spake to me, and as I turned from him, he said he was obliged to me— to which I said nothing ; but, thinking on the expression, I grew uneasy ; and afterwards, being near where he lived, I went and told him on what grounds I refused taking pay for keeping a soldier."

In Virginia the legislature had early to deal with the Quaker objection. Finding that "divers refractory persons" refused to attend the Militia exercises, they passed a law in 1666 inflicting a fine of an hundred pounds of tobacco for each offence.[1] The Epistles from Virginia Yearly Meeting to London, and the records of the Monthly Meetings show that in many cases Friends underwent heavy distraints in lieu of these fines. In 1711 they wrote to England that some of their number had been "imprest to make fortifications," and were in prison for their refusal. This was an attempt on the part of Governor Spotswood to force those whom he considered shirkers and cowards to serve the State in some way. A few did help to build the forts, but the Yearly Meeting of Virginia declared that these "had given away their testimony," and must make amends to their Monthly Meetings. In 1726/7 William Pigott, an English Friend, held some meetings in Virginia, to one of which "came a justice, who had never been at a Friends' Meeting before. . . . We parted lovingly, and next day a Friend was set at liberty who had been imprisoned for not appearing in arms." Samuel Bownas, another English Friend, found prisoners on the

---

[1] Hening, *Statutes at Large of Virginia*, ii. 246. See Weeks, *Southern Quakers and Slavery*, pp. 170 foll. For the Epistles to London, see *Epistles Received* (in D.), for example, 1693, 1704, 1711, 1727.

same account in Virginia, when he visited the colony a few months later.[1] In 1738 there was an attempt at a relieving Act, by which Friends were exempted from personal service if they produced a substitute or paid a fine.[2] But the consciences of most Friends did not allow them to take advantage of the provision. Next year the Yearly Meeting reported the sufferings as " very considerable," including several cases of imprisonment. So matters went on for twenty years, although in 1742 the Meeting declared that many of those who administered the Act showed as much lenity " as we can reasonably expect." But at the time of the Canadian and Indian Wars, which were the colonial share of the world struggle between France and England, the Assembly passed a series of Militia laws, followed in 1755 by a " draft " (or conscription) law for single men. In 1756 this was made more stringent. Every twentieth man eligible for the militia (or his substitute) was sent to fight on the frontier under " Colonel Washington." [3] Under this Act seven young men of the Society were forced into the army and carried to the frontier, but they did not waver in their testimony, and in a few months' time they were released. This was Washington's first encounter with the Quakers in war-time ; he was to find them a source of greater difficulty twenty years later. It is evident from the warnings given out by the Yearly Meeting that some Friends paid fines, and this is implied in the report given to the London Yearly Meeting in 1759. John Hunt had gone out to Pennsylvania in 1756 to advise Friends there in their political difficulties ; after their settlement he had travelled in the other colonies. " In Virginia, particularly, he gives sorrowful accounts of the state of Friends, who are much degenerated from the primitive practices of the Society in many respects, and who, in his judgment, have suffered much from the keeping of negroes, and letting fall their Christian discipline ; but that in some places, especially in the back parts of that country, there was a virtuous, sober, and religious body of Friends who could not comply with their military preparations."

In 1766 Friends petitioned the Assembly for relief from the repeated militia fines. This they gained in some measure by an Act which exempted them entirely from training or the provision of arms in time of peace, though it maintained the old liability to

---

[1] For the accounts of these Friends, see (London) Yearly Meeting MS., 1728–9.
[2] Hening, iii. 336.　　　　　　　　　　　　[3] Ibid., vii. 9.

service or fine in time of war. Thus they had a brief respite until the outbreak of the Revolution.

Carolina made her first law to enforce military service in 1680, while the leaders of the " Culpepper Rebellion " were in power. Friends had held aloof from this movement, the aim of which was mainly to free the colony from the strict control of the English proprietors. In retaliation, the *de facto* Government enacted that those who refused to appear in arms at the muster should be fined " at the pleasure of the Court." In this year, however, John Archdale became, by purchase, one of the proprietors of the colony, where he resided from 1683 to 1686. This remarkable man was a native of Wycombe, Bucks, and according to its then vicar " the chief gentleman of the village." During the early part of Charles II's reign, he was Deputy-Governor of Maine, but on his return home (about the year 1671) he was greatly influenced by the preaching of Fox and became a Quaker. During the latter part of his residence in Carolina, he was Acting-Governor, carrying out his duties with great acceptance. Naturally at this time the Quakers were unmolested, but he had hardly returned to England when, in July 1687, the Meeting for Sufferings had under consideration a letter from Friends in Carolina detailing their troubles under a new Militia Act. " John Archdale gives account he has taken some care to get them relieved," and other Friends were appointed to join him in a deputation to his fellow proprietors to see what further steps could be taken. The fantastic constitution devised by Locke was breaking down under the strain of actual working, and the trouble was increased by friction between the two divisions of the colony—North and South Carolina, which had been established in 1688. In a good hour the proprietors chose Archdale in 1694 to be Governor and " Admirall, Captain Generall and Commander-in-Chief of all the forces raised or to be raised both by sea and land within our said province." The new Governor did not make much use of these mighty naval and military establishments, and his one piece of military legislation is characteristic. " While administering a general military law, he secured a special Act passed March 15, 1695/6, exempting Quakers from its provisions."[1] In all other ways his Government won general approbation ; he settled local quarrels, harmonized the claims of proprietors and colonists, established a just policy towards the Indians, and prepared the way for the

[1] Weeks, *Southern Quakers*, p. 59.

naturalization of a body of French Huguenots who had taken refuge in Carolina. When he returned to England in 1696, the thanks of all the colonists followed him. " By your wisdom, patience, and labour," wrote the Assembly, " you have laid a firm foundation for a most glorious superstructure." Soon after his departure the Assembly carried on the good work by granting liberty of conscience to all " except only Papists "—an exception which Archdale would not have approved. On taking his seat as Governor he had been allowed to affirm " according to the form of his profession," but after his return to England and his election as member for Wycombe in 1698 he was excluded from the House because he would not take an oath.[1]

The peaceful settlement, however, did not last long. Both in North and South Carolina, after the accession of Anne, Governors were appointed who were in strong sympathy with the desire of the English clergy, sent out by the Society for the Propagation of the Gospel, to establish the Episcopal Church in the colony. As one-half of the Assembly in North Carolina were Quakers, according to the Governor's estimate in 1703, this was not an easy task, but an Act of the home Government in 1704 imposing the oath of allegiance on all office holders was a timely aid. The Quakers were ousted in each colony from the Assembly and Council, and the political power passed into the hands of the Church. At the same time other concessions were revoked. A South Carolina law of 1703 enacted that all inhabitants between the ages of sixteen and sixty were to be armed and regularly drilled, and fines were imposed. Until 1711 the Friends and other Dissenters of South Carolina struggled to regain their old rights. In 1710 a new Governor was sent out to enforce the laws in favour of the Establishment. The Acting-Governor, John Cary, Archdale's son-in-law, and some others, rose in rebellion, which was soon suppressed. The only Friend known to have been concerned in it was one Emmanuel Lowe, also Archdale's son-in-law.

The Yearly Meeting of 1711 appointed a Committee to deal with Lowe for " stirring up a parcel of men in arms and going . . . in a barkentine with men and force of arms, contrary to our holy

---

[1] Rufus Jones, *Quakers in American Colonies*, pp. 340–50 ; Braithwaite, *Second Period of Quakerism*, pp. 412–14 ; John Archdale, *A New Description of Carolina . . . With Several Remarkable Passages of Divine Providence during my time*, London, 1707.

principle." As a result, he was no longer counted eligible to represent the Society in its business meetings, "having acted divers things contrary to our ways and principles."[1] Friends, however, were identified by the Government with the rebellious party, and their political influence was entirely lost. The militia laws in both colonies seem to have been leniently administered, though Friends underwent some suffering for their refusal to fight in the Indian war of 1711—13. In North Carolina they tried to gain exemption at the outbreak of the Indian troubles in 1755. All those eligible for the militia were required to furnish their weapons, and the Council made the interesting suggestion that the Quakers should produce instead the tools of the pioneer settler—axe, spade, and hoe. This does not seem to have been adopted, for in 1758 Friends again petitioned for relief. Legally this was not obtained till 1771, when any Quakers called upon to serve were required to produce their certificates as members of the Society. In South Carolina during the late 'sixties the records show that some thirty members were disowned for taking part in the so-called "War of the Regulation," organized by Hermon Husband, an ex-Quaker. This "war" was a spirited resistance, led by the "Regulators," to some unjust and illegal methods of taxation. One Friend repented and gave his meeting a written condemnation of his error in "aiding with a gun."

The episode was one of the first warnings of the coming struggle between the King and his colonial subjects.

---

[1] Weeks, *Southern Quakers and Slavery*, p. 166.

CHAPTER XIV

PENNSYLVANIA

THE persecution which Friends underwent in England after the Restoration naturally turned the thoughts of some to emigration. Yet, with the exception of little Rhode Island, the English colonies promised no safer resting place than the homeland. As a youth at Oxford, William Penn had dreamt of a future in the American settlements and, as has been seen, he took the opportunity offered by the sale of the Jerseys to experiment in a free commonwealth where men might govern themselves and worship as their conscience bade them. But the Jerseys were already partly settled, and the development of Penn's ideas was hampered by existing claims and obligations. In 1681 a greater opportunity came before him, which he eagerly accepted.

His father, Admiral Penn, at his death was a considerable creditor to the Crown (always embarrassed under Charles II) both for arrears of pay and for loans made to the Navy. In time, with the accumulated interest, the debt amounted to £16,000. James, Duke of York, was a friend of the Penns. He knew of Penn's desire to find a home for his fellow-sufferers and of his experiments in the Jerseys. To Charles this suggested an ideal solution of the debt difficulty. By granting a large tract of wild territory in the New World he would at once clear his debt without the disagreeable expedient of parting with ready money, he would please Penn, and he would undoubtedly get rid of a considerable number of inconvenient subjects. Penn's letters of the time show how seriously he took the grant. It was an age of constitution-making and of Utopias across the Atlantic. Locke tried his hand in Carolina with little success. Penn wished to found, not a mere asylum for the persecuted, but a free and self-governing State. "The nations," he wrote, "want a precedent—and because I have been somewhat exercised about the nature and end of government among men, it is reasonable to expect that I should endeavour to establish a just and righteous one in this province, that others may take example by it—truly this my heart desires." Again : " I eyed the Lord in obtaining it. . . . There may be room there, though not here, for such an holy experiment."[1]

Masses of records remain among the " Penn MSS." of the Library of the Historical Society of Pennsylvania, showing the zeal with which the founder worked at his " experiment." These draft schemes are known to have been criticized by Algernon Sidney, the Republican, and Benjamin Furly, a Friend in Holland. In its final shape the " Frame of Government " consisted of twenty-four articles, the first of which granted liberty of conscience and worship to all " who confess and acknowledge the one Almighty and Eternal God to be the Creator, Upholder, and Ruler of the World, and that hold themselves obliged in conscience to live justly and peaceably in civil society."[2] The mildest code of penal laws and prison discipline conceived up to that time, under which treason and murder alone were subject to the death penalty (and these by an express reservation in the Royal Charter), the encouragement of arbitration rather than litigation, and the protection of Indian rights—these were the first-fruits of the deliberations of Penn and his Assembly.

Peace and liberty were the foundation-stones of his constitution, and in regard to the former it is interesting to see the essential difference between his conceptions and those of the home Government. This cleavage of opinion was eventually to become so acute on the question of war that it led to the overthrow of Quaker control in Pennsylvania. Before the territory was granted to Penn the laws in force over such portions of it as were inhabited were those promulgated by Governor Nicholls on Long Island in 1664, after the acquisition of the New Netherlands from the Dutch. These were known as the " Duke of York's Laws," and contained very

---

[1] Janney, *Life of Penn*, p. 175, letter to James Harrison.

[2] Penn's *Frame* confined office-holding to those " who profess to believe in Jesus Christ." After 1692 a test was imposed, by order of the Crown, which excluded Catholics, though liberty of worship was maintained for all. Penn more than once tried to restore his more liberal provision, but in vain. In the year of his death the law of capital punishment was assimilated to that of England, and thus about twelve more crimes were added to the list, but this reactionary proceeding was repudiated by the colonists when they gained their independence in 1776. The alteration in 1718 had been due to a political bargain ; in return for the extension of capital punishment, the right of Friends to affirm was recognized.

specific military provisions.[1]   Every male person above sixteen (except justices, constables, schoolmasters, ministers, physicians, masters of ships, " constant herdsmen," and the infirm) was liable under penalty to a short annual period of military training. Forts and ammunition were to be maintained.   No man was to be compelled " to go out of this jurisdiction upon any offensive wars, but only upon vindicative and defensive wars." From service in these none could be exempt.

By the grant to Penn these laws, of course, ceased to run in his province.   But the Charter granted by Charles II made all due provision for the contingencies which, judging by the previous experience of English colonists, were only too likely to occur. After forbidding Penn or any inhabitant of the province to make war upon any State in friendly relations with England, it proceeded thus :—

" And because in so remote a country and situate near many barbarous nations, the incursions as well of the savages themselves as of other enemies, pirates, and robbers may probably be feared, therefore we . . . do give power by these presents, unto the said William Penn . . . to levy, muster, and train all sorts of men, of what condition or whatsoever born, in the said province of Pennsylvania, for the time being, and to make war and pursue the enemies and robbers aforesaid, as well by sea as by land, yea, even without the limits of the said province and, by God's assistance, to vanquish and take them, and being taken, to put them to death by the law of war, or to save them at their pleasure, and to do all and every other act and thing, which to the charges and office of a Captain-General of an army belongeth, as fully and freely as any Captain-General of an army hath ever had the same." The cautious Crown lawyers who framed the Charter could not foresee a State which was able to live in peace and amity even with " barbarous nations," but Penn had his policy clear in his mind and in his own " Frame of Government " the wordy particulars of this provision are represented by a simple clause.   " Ninth. That the Governor and Provincial Council shall at all times have the care of the peace and safety of the province, and that nothing be by any person attempted to the subversion of this frame of government." It is characteristic of seventeenth-century Quakerism that rebellion is specifically

---

[1] *Charter and Laws of Pennsylvania*, edited by George, Nead & McCamant, Harrisburg, 1879, pp. 30–42.

guarded against whilst war is ignored. In *Some Account of the Province of Pennsylvania*, written in 1681 to attract intending settlers, Penn summarizes the charter for their benefit. It grants " the power of safety and defence in such way and manner as to the said William Penn, etc., seems meet "—a pretty clear indication to those who knew him that William Penn was not intending, " with God's assistance," to enter upon the functions of a Captain-General.

From 1682 to 1684 he was resident in his province, and when the boundary dispute with Maryland and the sufferings of Quakers in England called him back he left the power in the hands of a council with Thomas Lloyd, a Quaker, as President.[1] This arrangement lasted until 1688, and thus for the first seven years the conscience of the Quaker colonists was not put to any test. The three counties of Pennsylvania proper were mainly colonized by English Quakers, German Mennonites, and other peace-loving sects in sympathy with them.[2] In the Delaware district the original Dutch and Swedish settlers were preponderant. But from 1682 to 1756 there was always a large Quaker majority in the Assembly, which was increased when, in 1703, the Delaware counties, after long friction, set up an independent legislature. In the Governor's Council the Quaker element was also in the majority. The difficulty came when the authorities in England demanded military aid and military preparations from the province. The position of Penn and other Friends was briefly that, while they considered all such preparations unnecessary, they would not interfere with, for example, the formation of a militia by those who were not principled against it. While James II was on the throne Penn was left with a free hand,[3]

---

[1] For Lloyd and other Quaker politicians, *vide* Sharpless, *Political Leaders of Provincial Pennsylvania*, 1919.

[2] A band of German Quakers from the Palatinate, where they had been convinced by a missionary visit from William Ames, reached Pennsylvania in 1683 under the leadership of Daniel Pastorius and settled in a district (now a suburb of Philadelphia) which acquired the name of Germantown. To them belongs the eternal credit of making, in 1688, the first clear protest to the Society against the inconsistency of Christian slave-holding. " Ah ! do consider well this thing, you who do it, if you would be done in this manner, and if it is done according to Christianity ? " (*vide* Appendix E. for the whole document).

William Edmundson, a few years earlier, had protested as an individual against slavery in an Epistle to Friends in Maryland and Virginia.

[3] Sharpless, *A Quaker Experiment*, p. 194. Penn's cousin, Markham, his first deputy, was not a Quaker, but at that date (1681) Penn certainly hoped to reside permanently in the province.

but under the new rulers his position was more delicate. In 1688 he began the practice of sending out a non-Quaker as Deputy-Governor, and Blackwell, an honest old Cromwellian soldier, was selected to fill the post. In 1689 the first trouble arose. There was fear of a French attack on the American colonies, and William III suggested that Pennsylvania should form a militia. Blackwell and the non-Quaker members of the Council urged this course, but the five Quaker members refused to sanction it. " They told the Governor that if he desired a militia, he had power to create one and they would not interfere if it did not offend any consciences." ¹ John Simcock saw " no danger but from bears and wolves. . . . For my part I am against it clearly." Samuel Carpenter, the richest man in the province, was as explicit. " I am not against those that will put themselves into defence, but it being contrary to the judgment of a great part of the people, and my own too, I cannot advise the thing, nor express my liking for it. The King of England knows the judgment of Quakers in this case before Governor Penn had his patent. If we must be forced to it I suppose we shall rather choose to suffer than to do it, as we have done formerly."² After a private conference they decided : " We would not tie others' hands, but we cannot act." Samuel Carpenter added : " I had rather be ruined than violate my conscience in this case." The French alarm passed away, and Blackwell was soon recalled by Penn, as in other respects he and the Council were at variance.

At home Penn fell under suspicion of treason and conspiracy, though nothing was proved against him beyond his friendship for James II, which he frankly acknowledged. It does not seem that William III ever entertained serious doubts of his passive loyalty, but during the King's absence abroad, in March 1692-3, Mary was prevailed upon to deprive him of his province, annexing it to that of New York under the government of Colonel Fletcher. The ostensible reasons for the change were (as given in Fletcher's commission) that the affairs of the province were in disorder owing to Penn's absence in England, and that there was no provision for defence, " whereby the province and adjacent colonies were in danger of being lost to the Crown."³

---

¹ Sharpless, *A Quaker Experiment,* pp. 194–5.
² Carpenter had formerly lived in Barbadoes and endured heavy distraints for his refusal to bear arms (Besse, *Sufferings,* vol. ii).
³ *Charter and Laws,* p. 539.

The Council and Assembly remained loyal to Penn and showed little willingness to meet the requests of the new Governor, who entered Philadelphia with the unwonted sight of a military escort. Fletcher at once asked the Assembly, on behalf of the Crown, for a grant to defend the frontiers of New York against the French and Canadian Indians. After a long discussion money was voted for general purposes, on the understanding that it should not be " dipt in blood." " They conceived," they said, " that this administration, though it suspended that of William Penn, was not to be at variance with the fundamental principles of the latter." The Governor, in great dissatisfaction, wrote to the King, setting forth the impossibility of obtaining a war vote from the Quakers of Pennsylvania and urging the propriety of forming the colony together with New York, the Jerseys, and Connecticut into one province, as the only way to outvote Friends and to obtain the desired supplies. The Privy Council directed the Attorney-General to scrutinize the patent of William Penn, in the hope that some flaw might be found in it sufficient to make it void.[1]

Early in 1694 Fletcher again applied to the Assembly, not for a war grant, but for one to supply the frontier Indians with gifts of food and clothing " to influence their continued friendship." Even this was not granted, though the members offered a tax to defray some of the expenses of government. Fletcher dissolved the Assembly, denying its right to make its own appropriations. This dispute was more a matter of privilege than of principle, and Penn himself thought the grant should be made. In August the government was restored to Penn, who appointed his cousin Markham (not a Quaker) as his deputy. Fletcher still, however, sent demands from New York for grants of men and money towards the common defence of the frontier, and in 1696 the Assembly struck a bargain by which in return for a vote of money to Indian necessities they obtained the old Penn constitution.

The parliamentary principle that redress of grievances should precede supply was very firmly grasped by the Pennsylvania Assembly-men, and these demands by successive Governors gave them opportunities which they used to the full. But on the restoration of his proprietorship in 1694 Penn had given, or was understood to have given, a pledge which committed both himself and the

<hr />

[1] Bowden, *Friends in America*, ii. 133 (*New York State Papers*, September 15, 1693).

Assemblies more deeply than they were prepared to go. The Committee on Trade and Plantations at Whitehall, August 1 and 3, 1694, records that it had an interview with

" Mr. Penn, who, having declared to their Lordships, that if their Majesties shall be graciously pleased to restore him to the Proprietary, according to the said grants, he intends with all convenient speed to repair hither, and take care of the government and provide for the safety and security thereof all that in him lies. And to that end he will carefully transmit to the Council and Assembly there all such orders as shall be given by their Majesties in that behalf ; and he doubts not but they will at all times dutifully comply with and yield obedience thereunto, and to all such orders and directions as their Majesties shall from time to time think fit to send, for the supplying such quota of men, or the defraying their part of such charges as their Majesties shall think necessary for the safety and preservation of their Majesties' dominions in that part of America."

" Yield in circumstantials to preserve essentials " was Penn's advice once to the Assembly in reference to another matter. But the question of war and warlike preparations both to him and to the majority of the Assembly and Council, was an " essential " which they were not prepared to yield. It is true that the new patent granted to him made no mention of this proviso, and a promise to " transmit " requests pledged neither himself or the Assembly to grant them. But if the clause " he doubts not " is correctly reported (and there is no evidence to the contrary), Penn went further than this. President Sharpless, no harsh judge of the founder of Pennsylvania, comments : " It looks as if he intended to promise a course of action for the future, and then unload this promise upon a body which would not redeem it."[1] It is the least satisfactory moment of Penn's career, due probably to his desire to regain control of the " holy experiment," and to save it from the rough handling of unsympathetic Governors.

From 1699 to 1701 he was in residence in his province, and during that time he had himself to " transmit " a request from the English Crown for a quota of £350 towards the fortifications upon the New York frontier. The Assembly was " paralysed " by the

[1] Sharpless, *A Quaker Experiment*, p. 194. In a reply to Colonel Quarry's charges some years later, Penn, however, expressly says in regard to military provision : " It is a mistake that I had my government restored to me upon those terms. Let the royal instrument be consulted " (*Memoirs of Hist. Soc. Pennsylvania*, ix. 27).

request, and begged for a copy of Penn's speech, which was simply a reproduction of the royal message. He remained obstinately non-committal, and after a state of "unpleasant parley" for four days [1] the Pennsylvania delegates sent a formal refusal, pleading that, though loyal, the province was heavily burdened, and they believed that neighbouring colonies had as yet done nothing in the matter. They added that they wished the King to know of "our readiness (according to our abilities) to acquiesce with and answer his commands *so far as our religious persuasions shall permit.*" The members from Delaware (where the Swedes had no objection to the principle of military defence) pointed out that as they had not been able to build defences at home, it was unreasonable to ask them to build "forts abroad." The harvest (always a convenient plea for the Assembly when it wished to postpone business) led to an adjournment. A month later Penn commended the matter to "their serious thought and care," but they unanimously refused the grant.

The home Government had appointed Colonel Quarry as Admiralty representative in the province. He was independent of the proprietor, and became the leader of the "Church" party, which gradually gained in strength as the province advanced in prosperity and immigrants flocked to it. It was apparently about this time he sent home bitter complaints of the military weakness of the Government. "There is neither any militia established nor any provision made of arms or ammunition, but the country is left defenceless, and exposed to all hazards both by land and sea." Of this, he added, the Delaware representatives had often complained to Penn. Penn replied to the charge with the plain fact that, "There is as much (military provision) as there was in Colonel Fletcher's time." It is an "imposition" to say that a militia is necessary, "since by land there is none to annoy it and by sea . . . a small vessel of war would, under God's providence be the best security." [2] This was a spirited *tu quoque* to the Admiralty representative, but when the war of the Spanish Succession broke out in 1701 the home Government were sufficiently alarmed about the defence of America to consider a plan for annexing all the proprietary Governments to the Crown. Penn gave up his cherished dream of ending his days in Pennsylvania and returned home to defend it from this danger.

[1] These phrases are used by Clarkson, *Life of Penn*, p. 248.
[2] *Memoirs of Pennsylvania Historical Society*, ii. part i. (1827), pp. 193-7.

He left behind him a faithful representative of his interests in his secretary, James Logan, and a well-intentioned Governor, Colonel Hamilton, who, however, died within a few months and was succeeded by John Evans, than whom Penn could hardly have made a worse choice. The full and frequent correspondence which Logan kept up with Penn gives a lively picture of Pennsylvanian politics. Logan had become Penn's confidential secretary in 1699, at the age of twenty-five, and served his master and his heirs faithfully for nearly fifty years, filling high office in the colony and acting in 1731 as Deputy-Governor. He was an accomplished scholar and a man of great integrity, but he was harsh and unconciliatory in his attitude towards the popular party in the Province. Altnough born and bred a Friend, he was, especially in later years, an advocate of defence, and thus had not much influence in his religious body.

Both Hamilton and Evans made attempts to form a volunteer militia from the non-Quaker portion of the population, but it was never a success, partly, according to Logan, because the Church party worked against it in the hope that its failure would be another count in the indictment against Penn, and partly because the " most ignorant " believed " that if they 'listed they would be forced to march towards Canada."[1] The rumours of a French alliance with the Iroquois caused much alarm to Logan, who wrote in a very warlike strain that an Indian danger must be resisted by an Indian alliance. " All Cæsar's army would not cope with a few of them without the assistance of some of their own nation and mode of warfare."[2] Fear breeds cruelty, but a bookish Quaker's longing for the Indian " mode of warfare " is a strange manifestation of panic. There is a curious letter of September 1703, in which Logan seems to be arguing out the Quaker view with himself before his final abandonment of it. " I wish," he says, " thee could find more to say for our lying so naked and defenceless. I always used the best argument I could, and when I pleaded that we were a peaceable people, had wholly renounced war and the spirit of it, that we were willing to commit ourselves to the protection of God alone, in an assurance that the sword can neither be drawn nor sheathed, but by His direction, that the desolations made by it are the declaration of His wrath alone, and that those who will not the sword, but by an entire resignation commit themselves to His all-powerful provi-

---

[1] *Historical Society of Pennsylvania*, ix. (1870). *Penn-Logan Correspondence*, i. 124, 147. [2] *Ibid.*, i. 88.

dence, shall never need it, but be safe under a more sure defence than any worldly arm—when I pleaded this, I really spoke my sentiments, but this will not answer in English Government, not the methods of this reign. Their answer is that should we lose our lives only, it would be little to the Crown, seeing 'tis our doing, but others are involved with us, and should the enemy make themselves master of the country it would too sensibly touch England in the rest of her colonies."[1]

Evans, however, was not the man to convert the Quaker Assembly to war views. He did not disguise his contempt for their principles, while the steady Quakers and their German neighbours were shocked by his loose life. In 1706 he tried to frighten them into military preparations by a false alarm. A messenger rode headlong into Philadelphia with the news that a French fleet was off the mouth of the Delaware. Evans, apparently in the greatest alarm, rode through the city with drawn sword calling on the inhabitants to arm. Logan gives a lively description of the panic that prevailed. Some buried their valuables, others fled to the forest, women fainted, and about three hundred citizens appeared in arms. " Friends were generally the quietest, yet many of them fled, but were miserably insulted and menaced by those that bore arms." From other sources it appears that the majority of Friends (then about half the population of the city) were quiet enough to hold their regular week-day meeting. Isaac Norris, a leading member of the Assembly, declared that " not a Friend of any note but behaved as becomes our profession."[2] Only four Friends were among the three hundred who took up arms ; the views of the Assembly were unaltered, and the effect of the trick was to discredit Evans. A few months later he induced the Delaware territory (which by this time had a separate Assembly) to build a fort at New Castle at the mouth of the river and to exact a tax for its maintenance (or " powder money ") from all incoming vessels, while those out- ward bound were challenged as they passed. This tax was both obnoxious in its application and a direct violation of the charter which granted " free and undisturbed use of the ports." After vain remonstrance Richard Hill and two other wealthy Friends ran a ship past the fort under fire from its guns, and when the commander put after them in a sloop, they allowed him to board,

[1] *Historical Society of Pennsylvania,* i. 227.
[2] *Penn-Logan Correspondence,* ii. 122.

and then making full speed carried him to New Jersey and handed him over as prisoner to Lord Cornbury the Governor. Cornbury, who also claimed rights over the river, gave the unfortunate officer a rough reception, and did not let him return without a promise to abandon the tax. After this, it was not possible for Governor and colonists to work together. The Assembly in 1707 petitioned Penn for his recall. The letter crossed with a very stern rebuke from the Proprietor to his deputy for several irregularities, and in particular for the attempt to extort fines in lieu of bearing arms from the Friends in the Delaware counties. " A thing that touches my conscience as well as honour—' He must be a silly shoe-maker that hath not a last for his own foot '—that any Friends should not be secure and easy under me, in those points that regard our very characteristics."[1]

In 1709 Evans was replaced by Gookin, an elder, and more experienced man. He did not, however, escape difficulties with the Assembly, both on military and other questions. The Queen sent a demand for quotas of men to be furnished and maintained by the various colonies towards an expeditionary force to Canada. Pennsylvania's share was a hundred and fifty men. Gookin, remembering the troubles of his predecessor, suggested as a satis-factory solution that instead of voting the men they should grant £4,000 to cover expenses. " Perhaps it may seem difficult to raise such a number of men in a country where most of the inhabitants are of such principles as will not allow them the use of arms ; but if you will raise the sum for the support of government, I don't doubt getting the number of men desired whose principles will allow the use of arms."[2]

The Assembly refused to adopt this compromise or evasion, but some of its Quaker members met their brethren of the Council for consultation. The latter, Logan and others, were of opinion that though they could not vote money for war they might testify their loyalty to the Queen by a special grant to her. The Assembly agreed to grant £500 to be " put into a safe hand till they were satisfied from England it should not be employed for the use of war."

[1] *Penn-Logan Correspondence*, ii. 220. Throughout this period there were occasional alarms from pirates and privateers, who were said to find hiding-places along the undefended coasts. In 1709 a French privateer made a descent on Lewes. In 1747, the Assembly declined to fit out vessels to guard the Delaware River against pirates (*Pennsylvania Magazine*, x. 290).

[2] *Colonial Records*, ii. 740.

The Governor refused this proposal, and the House adjourned. Gookin sent home a graphic account of his dilemma. The Assembly, " being all Quakers, after much delay resolved, *nullo contradicente*, that it was contrary to their principles to hire men to kill one another. I told some of them the Queen did not hire men to kill one another, but to destroy her enemies. One of them answered, the Assembly understood English." He " tried all ways to bring them to reason," but in vain.[1]

Logan says that the Jersey Assembly, in which Quakers were in the majority, also rejected the demand, " 'Tis said upon some advices from hence," that is from Philadelphia, and that Gookin had suggested that the money granted should be spent on provisions to be sent to Boston.[2]

It was at this time that Logan made his most querulous attacks upon his Quaker opponents in politics. " If Friends," he wrote to Penn,[3] " after such a profession of denying the world, living out of it, and acting in opposition to its depraved ways, to which they have borne a testimony by the most distinguishing characters from any other people, cannot be satisfied, but must involve themselves in affairs of Government, under another power and administration, which administration in many of its necessary points is altogether inconsistent with this profession—I say, if this be the case, I cannot see why it should not be accounted singularly just in providence to deal to their portion crosses, vexations, and disappointments, to convince them of their mistakes and inconsistency. I write freely as I think, and as I have often been obliged to express myself, tho' thou well knows I am no very pretender that way."

Before the next requisition came, in 1711, there had been a General Election, under which the party loyal to their Governor and his representative gained a sweeping victory, due mainly to the reaction after bitter attacks on Penn and Logan. None of the old Assembly were re-elected, but even the new members who represented the moderate and " weighty " Friends felt considerable repugnance to a war vote. Finally, they granted £2,000 " for the

[1] *Historical Collections Relating to the American Colonial Church, Pennsylvania*, p. 51. Quoted by Sharpless, *Quaker Experiment*, p. 201.
[2] *Penn-Logan Correspondence*, ii. 350. The dispute dragged on for several months.
[3] *Memoirs of Historical Society of Pennsylvania*, x. (*Penn-Logan Correspondence*, ii. 351). The letter is dated 4th mo. 14, 1709.

Queen's use." "We did not see it," said Isaac Norris, "to be inconsistent with our principles to give the Queen money, notwithstanding any use she might put it to ; *that* not being our part, but hers."[1] In fact, it was used by a later Governor not for war but for his personal expenses.

At this time Penn was considering the transfer of his province to the Crown, under strict safeguards of his subjects' charter rights, but he was struck down by paralysis before the arrangement was completed. He lingered on till 1718. During his illness and the minority of his sons, i.e. till 1725, Hannah Penn managed the affairs of the province with great wisdom, with the help of James Logan. For thirty years an "era of good feeling" prevailed. As far as military matters were concerned, the long peace prevented trouble. The Governor occasionally raised a volunteer militia, but there were no calls for war aids.

"But, beginning with 1737, the gradual alienation of the Indian tribes made a disturbed frontier ready to be dangerous at the first outbreak of war, and new conditions prevailed."[2] At the same time the population in the province was rapidly increasing (in 1741 it was estimated at 100,000) while the proportion of Friends decreased. Persecution had ceased in England and the new immigrants were largely Lutherans from the devastated Palatinate, who became the "Pennsylvania Dutch" of to-day, and Ulster Presbyterians who were driven from home by civil disabilities, and by the crushing of Irish industry by English legislation. The Lutherans for the most part raised no objection to the Quaker control, but the Ulstermen reinforced the old "Church" party of opposition, and "Quaker" and "Presbyterian" in the Assembly gradually became the titles of two political parties.

Until the young Penns assumed control of the province there had been no friction between Indian and white man. Penn's most earnest efforts were directed towards the maintenance of good relations. In the admirable letter which he dispatched to the natives in 1681 by his first deputy Markham, he informed them that his King had granted him territory : "But I desire to enjoy it with your love and consent that we may always live together as neighbour and friends, else what would the great God do to us, who hath made us, not to devour and destroy one another, but to live soberly

---

[1] *Penn-Logan Correspondence,* ii. 436.
[2] Sharpless, *Quaker Experiment,* p. 203.

and kindly together in the world ? Now I would have you well observe that I am very sensible of the unkindness and injustice that have been too much exercised towards you by the people of these parts of the world, who have sought themselves, and to make great advantages by you. . . . But I am not such a man, as is well known in my own country. I have great love and regard towards you and desire to win and gain your love and friendship by a kind, just and peaceable life ; and the people I send are of the same mind, and shall, in all things behave themselves accordingly ; and if in anything any shall offend you or your people, you shall have a full and speedy satisfaction for the same, by an equal number of just men on both sides."[1]

Markham was charged to meet the Indian chiefs in conference, to buy land for settlement from them by free bargaining, and at what they considered a fair rate of barter, and to explain that Penn had no wish to eject them from their hunting-grounds and that they were to enjoy the same protection at law as a white settler. There is little wonder that the Indians, in repeated treaties, declared that they would " live in peace with Onas and his children as long as the sun and the moon shall endure." Even before Penn left England he gave proof of his care for Indian interests. He was offered £6,000 for a monopoly of the Indian trade, and refused. " I truly believe," wrote one of the would-be monopolists, " he does aim more at justice and righteousness and spreading of truth than at his own particular gain." Penn's own comment was : " I did refuse a great temptation last Second Day . . . but I would not defile what came to me clean."[2]

Through Penn's lifetime he gradually acquired south-eastern Pennsylvania, buying strips as the population increased, and fresh settlements were required. Bowden says that he paid, in all, the equivalent of £20,000.[3] The practice of buying Indian rights was not new. The Dutch and Swedes had always done so, and many settlements in New England, though not all, had followed the practice. Rhode Island and New Jersey were acquired by purchase. In the southern colonies purchase was less frequent and trouble with the Indians had resulted from the omission.

It was the acknowledged fairness of the methods adopted by

[1] Bowden, *Friends in America*, ii. 58.
[2] Hazard, *Annals of Pennsylvania*, p. 522.   *Pennsylvania Magazine*, x. 189.
[3] Bowden, *Friends in America*, ii. 72.

Penn and his settlers that marked them out from earlier intercourse (with the possible exception of Rhode Island). Care was taken not only to purchase, but to purchase from all who claimed rights in the territory. The Indians were not cheated in any way, in smaller transactions, such as the purchase of furs or game, they were given payment which contented them. Complaints by the settlers against Indians for theft or trespass were referred to the jurisdiction of the chiefs; complaints by Indians against white men were fully investigated, and those guilty punished. The famous "treaty," probably made at Shackamaxon in June 1683 was only a type of the general relations between Quaker and Indians for the first six years of the settlement. It was not, as Voltaire said, "the only treaty," but one of a series of agreements "never confirmed by an oath and never broken." The Indians lived in peace and friendship with their neighbours, and in return the Friends tried, with little success, to bring them to Christianity, and to keep them from the vices and follies of civilization.

In 1701 the Assembly prohibited the selling of rum to the Indians, but the Yearly Meeting had pronounced its opinion on the matter years before. "It is not consistent with the honour of truth" (1685) "a thing contrary to the mind of the Lord, and great grief and burthen to his people, and a great reflection and dishonour to the truth" (1687). In 1719 it was made a disciplinary offence. The Indians appreciated the care of their friends. At an early conference in New Jersey one chief said the Dutch and Swedes who sold liquor to them were "blind, they had no eyes, they did not see it to be hurtful for us to drink it, although we knew it to be hurtful to us; but if people will sell it to us we are so in love with it we cannot forbear it. . . . But now there is a people come to live among us that have eyes; they see it to be for our hurt, they are willing to deny themselves the profit of it for our good. These people have eyes. We are glad such a people are come among us."[1]

From 1681 to 1755 there was no conflict and no bloodshed between Pennsylvanians and Indians. There were often rumours that the tribes would be stirred up by their over-lords under French instigation to raid the settlements, and at such times a growing minority of non-Quaker settlers complained bitterly of their defence-less condition. But in actual fact the good relations were never disturbed. "Without any carnal weapon," wrote a Friend in early

[1] Janney, *Life of Penn* (1852), p. 123.

days, " we entered the land and inhabited therein as safe as if there had been thousands of garrisons, for the Most High preserved us from harm, both man and beast." In 1688 a mysterious report arose that five hundred Indian warriors had assembled at an Indian " town," and were preparing to march on Philadelphia to massacre all the immigrants. The rumour was so persistent and alarming that the Council took cognizance of it, whereupon one of its members, Caleb Pusey, a leading Friend, offered to visit the alleged rendezvous, with five others, all unarmed. When the deputation reached the town, they found an old chief surrounded by women and children. The men were out on a hunting expedition, and the only ill-feeling shown was by the chief against the authors of the report, who, he declared, should be " burnt to death."[1]

After Penn's death, James Logan managed the relations with the Indians in the spirit of his old master, and he was fully supported by the Assembly. But two new factors were at work which he was unable to control. The Ulstermen and Germans naturally pressed forward to take up unoccupied lands. These newcomers cared little for Indian rights and settled where they chose. Even when Logan made them move, or paid for their holdings, friction had been caused ; and the whole attitude of these new frontiersmen was the Puritan one of contempt and dislike for the savage. The Lord had given them the land, and they were eager to smite the Amalekite. In any case, as the population grew, the difficulty of maintaining Indian hunting-grounds increased. But a more serious trouble was the avarice and chicanery of the proprietors. Penn's children had early left their father's sect, and with it they seemed to have left his policy of justice. Their aim was to extinguish all the Indian rights to the province, and between 1737 and 1754 this was practically accomplished by means that do not stand investigation. Old deeds were examined, and their titles strained, chiefs were made drunk and induced to sign away their rights, the Iroquois, the feudal overlords of the Pennsylvania Indians, were called in to threaten and coerce the malcontents, and a whole series

---

[1] Proud, *History of Pennsylvania*, i. 337. In one of Penn's early reports from the colony (" A Further Account of Pennsylvania ") he alludes to a false report of a massacre by Indians circulated in England. " The dead people were alive at our last advices." He adds : " Our humanity obliges them (the Indians) so far that they generally leave their guns at home, when they come to our settlements. . . . Justice gains and awes them " (*Pennsylvania Magazine,* ix. 79).

of misdeeds, of which the "Walking Purchase" was one of the earliest and most flagrant, were perpetrated. The "Walking Purchase" was based on an old agreement, never enforced, conveying land in a certain district to Penn, as far as a man could walk in a day and a half. Thomas Penn produced this deed, and sent to take the "walk" two trained runners who covered in the time more than sixty miles, and included land in Indian occupation which by no possibility could have been intended in the old agreement. Finally, in 1754, the Proprietors bought from the New York Iroquois, without consulting the majority of the Pennsylvania tribes, all the remaining territory in western Pennsylvania. The Delaware and Shawnee tribes were left with a sense of rank injustice, and as the French, after winning over most of the tribes on the Canadian frontier, approached the chiefs of Pennsylvania, they found ready listeners.

The Assembly, and the Quakers as a body, had no power to check the proprietors, but they were guiltless of these wrongs. The Assembly did what it could, refusing to enforce the "Walking Purchase," and when the Penns, in alarm at the growing alienation of the Indians, tried to buy their good-will with gifts, the Assembly made grants on their own account for the same purpose, amounting to some £8,000 between 1733 and 1751.[1]

But, as the long peace showed signs of breaking up, the position of the Quakers in the Assembly grew more difficult. For years they held the majority of seats there and, under Hannah Penn, in the Council, while the Quaker body was gradually becoming a minority of the population, which in 1740 numbered about 100,000. This was partly due to the fact that after the Delaware counties had established a separate legislature, the three original Pennsylvania counties increased their representation in the Assembly, and as the new counties were added, these latter were considerably under-represented. But it is also true that the German element in the population voted steadily for the Quakers. The numbers of the Assembly were 36 : in 1740, 33 were Quakers ; in 1755, when their policy was fiercely assailed both in the province and in England, and when they were preparing to give up political power, 28 were returned at the election. The questions at issue were not confined to defence. The Assembly represented the democratic party, which took its stand on the rights of the charter, resisting any arbitrary

[1] Sharpless, *The Quakers in the Revolution*, p. 22.

24

encroachment by the Crown or the proprietors, and in this position the majority of the province were in hearty agreement with them. The old " Church " party naturally supported the Proprietors and were bitter against the Assembly, and in the later years of the period the Ulstermen on the frontier clamoured for expeditions against the Indians.

Up to 1739, however, the " golden age " of Pennsylvania still flourished. " Between 1710 and 1740 there was hardly a ripple of discontent, but everyone throve under, and rejoiced in the beneficent charter. Immigration was active, trade grew, peace was secure, taxes were practically unfelt, and the powers of the Assembly were unquestioned. But during the latter year the first serious demands were made for men and money for wars against England's enemies—demands which grew greater with the succeeding years—causing great uneasiness among the peace men of the province, and stirring up disputes as to the methods to be employed in raising the money. These troubles gradually but manifestly changed Pennsylvania from a colony remarkably free, prosperous, and unburdened, to one disunited and struggling under a heavy load of expenditure and consequent taxes." [1]

In 1739 the first trouble began. England was at war with Spain, and Governor Thomas asked for a money grant and for the establishment of a militia, pointing out the defenceless state of the colony. In a series of long papers Governor and Assembly argued out the question.[2] The Assembly began :

" As very many of the inhabitants of this province are of the people called Quakers, who, though they do not as the world is now circumstanced condemn the use of arms in others, yet are principled against it themselves, and to make any law against their consciences to bear arms would not only be to violate a fundamental in our constitution and be a direct breach of our charter of privileges, but would also in effect be to commence persecution against all that part of the inhabitants of the province, and should a law be made which should compel others to bear arms and exempt that part of the inhabitants, as the greater number in the Assembly are of like principles, would be an inconsistency with themselves and partial with respect to others "—therefore they cannot accede to the Governor's request. The Governor replied that the Assembly

---

[1] Sharpless, *Quakers in the Revolution,* p. 16.
[2] *Colonial Records,* iv. 366 foll.

represented the whole province, not a sect, and it was their duty to arrange for its defence, not leaving the matter entirely to providence. He also emphasized the inconsistency of maintaining capital punishment, while objecting to war. To this the Assembly replied that the soldier fights " in obedience to the commands of his sovereign, and may possibly think himself in the discharge of his duty," while the burglar or other criminal " must know at the time of the commission of the act that it was a violation of laws, human and divine, and that he thereby justly rendered himself obnoxious to the punishment which ensued." The Governor asked them in despair : " Is it a calumny to say your principles are inconsistent with the ends of government ? "

The dispute culminated in a letter from the Governor to the home authorities advising that Quakers should be excluded from the Assembly. The Assembly learned of this and indignation ran high in the next election, during which there was a street fight between the Governor's party and the German supporters of the Assembly. The Assembly was re-elected, and withheld the Governor's salary until he came to terms with them. Evidently there was much ill-feeling, and Dr. Fothergill, who from England followed the affairs of the province with intelligence and sympathy, wrote a letter of gentle rebuke to his friend Israel Pemberton, one of the leaders of the Assembly :

" If I may be permitted to give my opinion of the management of your controversy with the Governor I can scarcely upon the whole forbear to take his side. Your cause is undoubtedly good, but I am afraid you discover a little more warmth than is quite consistent with the moderation we profess. . . . Be pleased to remember that a deference is due to a magistrate in some sense though a wicked one." Pennsylvania Friends had asked the help of London Friends in this threat to their liberties, and Fothergill was one of a Committee of the Meeting for Sufferings which sat often on the matter. Petitions were presented and groups of Friends appeared before the Board of Trade in 1742 and the Committee of Council in 1743.[1]

The French War followed the Spanish, and in 1744 Thomas was able (with the active help of Benjamin Franklin) to raise a volunteer militia of ten thousand men. Next year, after the fall of Louisburg, the Assembly was called upon to provide men and

[1] Dr. Hingston Fox, *Dr. John Fothergill and his Friends*, p. 301.

arms. Again they protested that they could not vote munitions of war, but as "tribute to Cæsar," granted £4,000 for "bread, beef, pork, flour, wheat, or other grain." Franklin says that the Governor spent the money on gunpowder, declaring that that was the "other grain" intended. During the next ten years there were several calls for military aid, and on each occasion the Assembly granted money "for the King's use." But, as the grants were always used for war, the position of the Quakers in the Assembly was becoming very difficult, and the crisis was hastened by pressure both within the Society and by their enemies without. In the Society itself there were by this time three fairly clear divisions. A certain number followed James Logan in justifying defensive war and warlike preparations. At this time they were much under Franklin's influence, who supported the "Quaker party" in the Assembly in their resistance to the claims of the Crown and the Proprietors, though he had no sympathy with their peace views. Franklin had formed a volunteer fire brigade of thirty members in Philadelphia, of whom twenty-two were Quakers. In 1744–5 he proposed that the brigade funds should be invested in a lottery which he had started to provide a battery on the river. Franklin and his seven friends met to consider the proposal and one Quaker to oppose it. "We carried the resolution eight to one ; and as of the twenty-two Quakers, eight were ready to vote with us, and thirteen, by their absence, manifested that they were not inclined to oppose the measure, I afterwards estimated the proportion of Quakers sincerely opposed to defence as one to twenty-one only." Excessive scrupulousness was never one of Franklin's failings, and this remarkable calculation neglects to consider that, as the stricter Quakers had considerable mistrust of his principles, they were not likely to have joined his brigade.[1] On the next page of his *Autobiography* he contradicts his own assertion by saying of the second division of the Friends—those who were members of the legislature—that in regard to war votes, "they were unwilling to offend Government, on the one hand, by

[1] Samuel Fothergill, brother of the Doctor, and himself a famous Quaker minister, paid a long visit to America from 1754 to 1756. In the spring of the latter year he wrote of a disrespectful address from the Assembly to the Governor : " It is altogether imputed to B. Franklin, their principal penman, who, I have sometimes thought, intended to render the Assembly contemptible, and subject our religious Society to the imputation of want of respect for authority, as a factious sort of people and I fear he has gained his point " (Sharpless, *Quaker Experiment*, p. 248). Franklin himself, in his *Autobiography*, admits the disrespect of these addresses.

a direct refusal ; and their friends, the *body of the Quakers*, on the other, by a compliance contrary to their principles."

These Quaker Assemblymen, as has been said, ultimately found themselves on the horns of a dilemma. While Penn was in control they could confide in his support, and in the twenty years of peace after his death they managed the affairs of the province without qualms of conscience. But from 1739 to 1756 they progressed along a slippery path of compromise. The Proprietors were unsympathetic, and the English Government was warlike, and eventually the Assembly was forced to provide the financial means for war. On the other hand, they were able to maintain the rights of the charter, and to ward off the imposition of compulsory military service. At last the policy broke down. It was too pacific for the war party, and too warlike for the Yearly Meeting, and the two currents of opposition swept over the Assembly in the same year, 1755/6.

Before 1739 the Yearly Meeting had no occasion to concern itself with any danger to the peace principle of Friends. In that year it issued a paper urging its members to keep clear of any warlike preparations, and " to demonstrate to the world that our practices, when we are put to the trial, correspond to our principles." From this time onward both the Yearly Meeting and Philadelphia Quarterly Meeting keep in close touch with the London Meeting for Sufferings, sending that body full information of the situation in Pennsylvania, and receiving in return advice and help in putting the Quaker case before the English authorities.

In 1741, during the Assembly's dispute with Governor Thomas, James Logan made an attempt to influence the views of the Yearly Meeting. He sent a letter to them in which, while admitting that Friends held as a principle the unlawfulness of all war (though he himself believed in defensive war), yet as they now constituted only a third of the population, he considered they had no right to impose their views on others. Hence he urged that Friends should not offer themselves as candidates at the coming General Election. In accordance with its usual practice the Yearly Meeting handed the letter unopened to a small committee, who retired to consider it, and reported that it " related to the civil and military affairs of the Government, and in their opinion was unfit to be read in this meeting." A contemporary letter-writer (not a Friend), in telling the story, adds a graphic touch. One Friend rose to advocate the reading of Logan's paper, as a token of respect to him, "but John Bringhouse plucked him by the coat, and told him with a sharp tone of voice, ' Sit thee down, Robert, thou art single in the opinion.' " [1]

Although the majority of Friends dissented from Logan's general argument, there had always been an appreciable number who held the same conclusion—that Friends should not engage in politics. This view, however (which it is evident from Logan's letters to Penn was held even at the beginning of the century) [2] was based not on expediency, but on religious grounds. It was felt that there was danger both of inconsistency and of spiritual loss for those members who were preoccupied with affairs of State. The attitude of the Assembly during these years of war strengthened this conviction among the general body of Friends, and the events of the years 1755 and 1756 hastened the final decision.

In 1754, when the first alarm of the French and Indian troubles arose, the Governor, at the urgent request of the Penns, tried to induce the Assembly to establish a compulsory militia and, failing in this, he wrote home angrily of the "absurdity" of the Pennsylvania constitution and of Quaker principles. The evil policy of the Proprietors towards the Indians now bore its fruit, and the frontier Indians were in undoubted league with the French. Panic prevailed, and as Braddock led his expedition through the province, he received much private support (Franklin working indefatigably for him), and the Assembly voted grants for provisioning the army and for presents to the Indian tribes, in the hope of buying their friendship. Braddock's defeat loosed the pent-up tide of Indian passion, and for the first time the Pennsylvania settlers on the frontier experienced the atrocities which for generations had been sadly familiar to other colonists.

---

[1] *Vide* Franklin, *Autobiography; Philadelphia Yearly Meeting Records*, 1741 ; *Pennsylvania Magazine*, vi. 403, which gives the text of Logan's letter.

[2] E.g. in 1702 he writes that " the most knowing " Friends think Government ill-fitted to their principles (*Penn-Logan Correspondence*, i. 147). So also in 1708 (letter published in *Bulletin of Friends' Historical Society* (Philadelphia), May, 1916). In 1757, Lord Loudoun, Commander-in-Chief in America, wrote home to Pitt, after an attempt to raise men and money in the Jerseys, " Altho' I have been a great favourer of the Quakers, I am thoroughly convinced since I came to this country that they are very unfit to be employed in any public employment " (Gummere, *Quaker in the Forum*, p. 147).

Some writers, notably the American historians, Parkman and Fiske,[1] have argued that the Delaware and Shawnee Indians of Pennsylvania, being subject to their Iroquois overlords, were a poor-spirited race, and that Pennsylvania's immunity from trouble had been due to this rather than to Penn's policy. But now it was not only the fiercer tribes, but Penn's old allies, who scalped and tomahawked their victims. An English Friend, Samuel Fothergill, who was in Pennsylvania at this time, noted in his letters home, of the land wrested from the Delawares in 1742, that " it is pretty much in this land, and land fraudulently obtained, that the barbarities are committed." There is other evidence that settlers in regularly purchased land felt themselves comparatively safe. Kelsey, *Friends and the Indians*, while admitting that Friends generally lived in the earlier-settled and safer districts, adds : " Yet it seems very clear from the records that at the opening of the war there were Friends in the outlying settlements exposed to the Indians. . . . In 1756 the Meeting for Sufferings was established, chiefly because of the disturbances on the frontier, and its first duty was ' to Hear and Consider the Cases of any Friends under Sufferings, especially such as suffer from the Indians or other Enemies.' " He also quotes a letter of Israel Pemberton in 1758 : " In all the desolation on our frontiers, not one Friend we have heard of has been slain or carried captive, and we have reason to think, both from their conduct in places where Friends were as much exposed as others and from their declarations to us, they (the Indians) would never hurt Friends if they knew us to be such."[2] Philadelphia, however, was filled with refugees, whose tales of horror roused strong feeling against the Assembly. Scenes like the following, which John Woolman saw a few months later, were common : " The corpse of one so slain (by the Indians) was brought in a wagon, and taken through the streets of the city in his bloody garments, to alarm the people and rouse them to war."[3]

Nevertheless, in spite of the feeling in Philadelphia, the country Germans, who were more exposed to the danger, voted steadily for the Quakers. In the Assembly of 1755 twenty-eight of the thirty-six members were Friends, or closely connected with the

[1] Parkman in *Conspiracy of Pontiac*, i. 80–5, and Fiske in *The Dutch and Quaker Colonies*, ii. 164 foll., and elsewhere.

[2] Kelsey, *Friends and the Indians*, pp. 74–6. Letter of Pemberton printed in Philadelphia *Friend*, 1873, p. 187

[3] Woolman, *Journal.*

body. In a long letter to the London Meeting for Sufferings, defending the Quaker members of the Assembly, the Quarterly Meeting of Philadelphia says : [1]

" Our former representatives were at our last election chosen throughout the province by the greatest majority ever known. . . . And it is remarkable that for sixteen years successively, more than half of which was a time of war, a set of men conscientiously principled against warlike measures have been chosen by those of whom the majority were not in that particular of the same principle ; and this we apprehend may be chiefly attributed to the repeated testimonies we have constantly given of our sincere and ready disposition to provide for the exigencies of the Government . . . in such manner as we can do with peace and satisfaction of mind." The main ground of the defence was the service rendered by the Assemblies in maintaining the constitution against " arbitrary and oppressive measures."

But the new Assembly was soon to prove too warlike for Friends, while still not satisfying its enemies ; £55,000 was voted for the relief of loyal Indians and " other purposes," and was immediately applied to the erection of a chain of forts upon the frontier. In the autumn the first Militia law of Pennsylvania was passed :

" Whereas this province was first settled by (and a majority of the Assemblies have ever since been of) the people called Quakers . . . yet forasmuch as by the general toleration and equity of our laws, great numbers of people of other religious denominations are come amongst us, . . . some of whom have been disciplined in the art of war, and conscientiously think it their duty to fight in defence of their country, their wives, their families, and their estates, and such have an equal right to liberty of conscience with others," and had petitioned for the right to form a militia, accordingly provisions were made for this step, with due exemptions for those " conscientiously scrupulous of bearing arms."[2] The legislature for the Delaware counties introduced an Act without such exemptions. At this time John Woolman, attending the Yearly Meeting, found some Friends shared his scruples against paying the new taxes obviously intended for war, while others saw no objection. The

---

[1] 5th mo. 5, 1755.
[2] The text of the Act was reproduced in the *Gentleman's Magazine* for 1756, p. 53, as well as a dialogue in its favour (p. 122). The latter was written by Franklin, and in his *Autobiography* he claims most of the credit for the Act.

Yearly Meeting finally left the matter to the individual conscience of Friends, many of whom during the next few years refused to pay and suffered distraint, though James Pemberton admitted that the majority " not only comply with it, but censure those who do not."

During the Yearly Meeting, and at the time of the passing of the Militia bill (November 1755) a deputation of some of the leaders of the Society, Israel and John Pemberton, Anthony Benezet, and others, approached the Assembly with a protest against the war taxes, a warning that they personally would not pay them, and a plea that the representatives might pursue " measures consistent with our peaceable principles, and then we trust we may continue humbly to confide in the protection of that Almighty Power whose providence hath hitherto been as walls and bulwarks about us." This was practically a censure on the Quaker members of the Assembly, and the majority showed their resentment by describing the address as " unadvised and indiscreet." But the Yearly Meeting was anxious to clear itself of all suspicion of compromise. In its 1756 Epistle to London it urged Friends at home to draw a clear distinction " between the acts and resolutions of the Assembly of this province, though the majority of them are our brethren in profession, and our acts as a religious Society." Samuel Fothergill, who was in touch with all the currents of opinion among Pennsylvania Friends, wrote bluntly : " The Assembly have sold their testimony as Friends to the people's fears, and not gone far enough to satisfy them."

The matter was complicated by financial disputes with the Governor and the Penns. The latter were more anxious to secure for their great estates exemption from the war taxes than even to arrange for the defence of the colony, while the people and the Assembly were determined that they should share the burden. Complaints from Governor and Proprietors of factious opposition, and a petition from leading Philadelphians protesting against the weakness of the colony's defences, due to the Quaker tenets of the Assembly, reached the English Ministry.

In February 1756 counsel for these petitioners were heard in London before the Board of Trade and Plantations.[1]

[1] *Vide Pennsylvania Magazine*, x. 283 foll. (" Attitude of the Quakers in the Provincial Wars," by C. J. Stillé). This is an interesting and impartial investigation, although Dr. Stillé tends to look upon the Assembly as thoroughly representative of the Society of Friends.

Their main requests to the English Government were two—to exclude all Quakers from the Assembly and, inconsistently enough, to veto the Militia Bill passed by the Assembly in the previous November. This was nominally on the ground that such a Bill was a usurpation of the rights of the Crown. In fact, as Dr. Stillé remarks, it was from fear that the measures taken would leave them without reasonable ground of complaint against the existing Assembly. " The chain of forts so effectually protected the province that from the time they were established no English or French invaders ever came through them."[1] The speech for the petitioners was unscrupulous in its misrepresentations, and in particular in its entire identification of the Society of Friends and the Assembly, at a time when the breach between them was most acute. For example, it alleged that, " the Quakers in Pennsylvania have, upon every application, for sixteen years now passed, refused to raise a militia, refused to put the country in a posture of defence, refused to raise men or money for the King's service, declared themselves principled against all military measures and, at length, declared even self-defence to be unlawful and that, at a time when the Indians and enemy were in the heart of their country, burning and destroying the inhabitants with unheard-of cruelties and barbarities." The Assembly had just passed a Defence Bill and voted £55,000 for military purposes, as was admitted by the petitioners themselves. The " canting Quakers," went on the lawyer, had settled themselves out of danger (in " the heart of the country," perhaps), and it was evident from the " insolent address " presented to the Assembly, that that body was " led by the nose by that illegal cabal, called their Yearly Meeting and their Quarterly Meeting." Yet this very address had been sharply rebuked by the Assembly. The Militia Bill, through its conscience clause, was none other than a Bill to make " Quaker proselytes," and " when persons in power declare as these do, we cannot, we will not, defend, the bond and first principle of society and of nature itself is broke and dissolved, and they ought not to govern."

The Board of Trade heard the defence of the Assembly from Richard Partridge, a Friend and the London representative of Pennsylvanian interests, but its final reply was ominous. It declared that the " measures taken by the Assembly for the defence of the province were improper, inadequate, and ineffectual, and

[1] *Vide Pennsylvania Magazine*, p. 302.

that there was no cause to hope for other measures while the majority of the Assembly consisted of persons whose avowed principles were against military service."

The London Meeting for Sufferings, which included men such as Dr. Fothergill and David Barclay, in close touch with members of the Court and Ministry, discovered that the home Government was seriously considering the exclusion of Quakers from all legislative and civil office, not only in Pennsylvania, but throughout America, by the imposition of an oath. The Meetings' records during the spring and summer of 1756 show the time, care, and anxiety expended by the " Committee on Pennsylvania," led by Fothergill, in averting this crisis.[1] A " Nobleman in high station " assured them of " the general and strong prepossession " against Quakers, excited by garbled accounts from Pennsylvania. He strongly urged that the Quaker members of the Assembly should voluntarily retire from office, resigning " a trust which under present circumstances they could not discharge." " Other persons in high stations " concurred in this advice, which the Committee accepted, believing that the majority of the members only held their seats from a sense of duty, and would readily resign if that course seemed best. The Meeting for Sufferings agreed to the report and decided not only to write in that sense to the Quarterly Meeting of Philadelphia, but also to send over a deputation of two Friends to support the advice in person. The letter earnestly pressed resignation upon the Assembly members, " as your own immediate interest, the preservation of your charter, and our reputation jointly require it." Fothergill also sent a personal letter to James Pemberton, urging the necessity of the step. Everyone, he said, had told him that " you accept of a public trust which at the same time you cannot discharge. You owe the people protection and yet withhold them from protecting themselves." What answer, he adds, can we make ? Samuel Fothergill, in Philadelphia, also used all his influence to the same end.[2]

The Exclusion Bill was only held in abeyance by the Meeting's assurance that Friends would voluntarily give up office. Before the deputation arrived matters had already moved in the desired direction. In April 1756, as the raids of the Delaware Indians

---

[1] *Meeting for Sufferings*, 1756 ; 4th mo. 9 ; 6th mo. 18 ; 7th mo. 9 ; 8th mo. 6.

[2] Dr. Hingston Fox, *Dr. John Fothergill and his Friends*, p. 308.

continued, " after full consideration and debate, all the Council (except Mr. Logan, who desired his dissent might be entered on the minutes) agreed that the Governor ought not to delay declaring war against the enemy Indians. The bounties for prisoners and scalps were then considered and agreed to." [1]

So opened Pennsylvania's first Indian war, after more than seventy years of peace. Mr. Logan was William, son of James Logan, and himself a Friend. Earlier in the debate he had supported an address presented by Friends to the Governor, begging that further efforts should be made towards peace, since they believed that by presents and negotiations these tribes could be won back to their old friendship. But when the war began, when bands of friendly Indians and of frontier settlers wreaked fierce retaliation for their past sufferings, sending in to Philadelphia the scalps of Indian men and women, then the Quaker members of the Assembly had to choose between active support or open condemnation of these measures. In June, six resigned, led by James Pemberton, making this statement :

" As many of our constituents seem of opinion that the present situation of public affairs calls upon us for services in a military way, which from a conviction of judgment after mature deliberation we cannot comply with, we conclude it most conducive to the peace of our minds and the reputation of our religious profession to persist in our resolution of resigning our seats." [2] At the election in the autumn other Friends refused to stand and many of the Society abstained from voting, in the hope of preventing the election of any fellow members. But through the efforts of the " war " Quakers and the democratic party, some sixteen, in close connection with the Society, were chosen. At this point the English delegation arrived, and through their labours and those of a committeee of the Yearly Meeting four more members resigned their seats, while twelve Quakers or nominal Quakers remained. " Several of these are not acknowledged by us as members of the Society," Philadelphia Friends explained in a letter to London, December 1756.

So ended the Quaker predominance in Pennsylvanian government. It had lasted for seventy-five years and had broken down

[1] *Colonial Records,* viii. 84. The Council consisted of ten members, four of whom were Quakers or of Quaker origin (Howard Jenkins, *Pennsylvania, Colonial and Federal History,* p. 452).

[2] *Votes of (Pennsylvania) Assembly,* iv. 564.

under pressure from external forces. Pennsylvania was never an independent State, at all times it was subject to the interferences of the home authorities, and after the death of Penn the Proprietors were in sympathy with the demands of the Crown rather than with the charter rights of the original settlers. It was not the policy of the colony itself, but the clash of French and English interests, which put the Quaker legislators to the hard necessity of voting monies to the Crown, which they knew would be used in warfare. While Penn's policy towards the Indians was maintained no breath of trouble stirred between settler and red man ; had it been continued by his children and adopted by the other colonies the danger from the French in Canada would have been almost negligible. But it is impossible to inflict a succession of wrongs on a proud and savage race without reaping, in due course, a bloody retribution. It was the unfair dealing of the younger Penns that mainly brought about the failure. Divided responsibility and opposing policies were sure, in the end, to spell disaster. A second cause, which worked concurrently with the former, was due, ironically enough, to the success of another of Penn's ideals. A State founded on universal toleration attracted to it an amazing number of immigrants and, as its prosperity increased, many entered who had no sympathy with its foundation principles. If Quakerism had retained the white heat of its early convictions, the newcomers might have been convinced of the truth, not of an isolated principle, but of the whole body of Quaker doctrine. That they were not is additional evidence of the fact that (to quote Samuel Fothergill) "the salt had lost its savor." The Quaker legislators were upright and conscientious men, but, as preceding pages have shown, they were timorous, and fumbled long at compromises before they realized their untenable position. The religious leaders of the Society were men of proved holiness and sincerity, but they had largely lost the missionary zeal of the first generation and were more concerned to repair breaches in the traditional faith than to spread their message far and wide. This judgment is not true without important qualifications as regards individuals,[1] but the swamping of the Quaker by the non-Quaker element in the province after the middle of the eighteenth century, attests its general accuracy. The influence of European war, the alienation of the Indians, the warlike tendencies of the new immigrants—such were the external causes of the change of control.

[1] For example, Thomas Story, Anthony Benezet, and John Woolman.

The extent and influence of an internal cause—the loss of spiritual power within the Society—could only be gauged by a very close study of the records and religious biographies of the time, but contemporary allusions show that it certainly must be taken into account. President Sharpless raises the question what might have happened if the members of the Assembly had retained both their principles and their places, maintaining the same policy in government as their brethren did in Indian raid or Irish rebellion, not evading danger but calmly facing it.[1] They certainly never lost in the country districts the confidence of the voters, who were only too anxious to choose Quaker representatives in the twenty years before the Revolution. Later events seem to show that they could have won back the Indians to alliance. On the other hand, a steady though passive resistance to English demands might have hastened the breach between Crown and colonies. It is more relevant to the discussion to recall the many successes of Penn's " holy experiment," in spite of all obstacles. In regard to peace, it is true that for seventy years there was neither war nor rebellion, the frontiers were secure without forts, and the harbours without men-of-war. " Peace and justice were for two generations found available defences for a successful State. . . . As long as exact justice prevailed, peace existed, and this is the lesson of Pennsylvania."[2]

[1] Sharpless, *A Quaker Experiment*, p. 260.   [2] *Ibid.*, pp. 275–6.

CHAPTER XV

THE WAR OF INDEPENDENCE

ALTHOUGH the Quaker control of the Pennsylvania Assembly ended in 1756, the colonists continued to return representatives who, except in regard to defence, maintained the old policy. Up to the Revolution the majority of the Assembly was known to its opponents as the " Quaker " party. Isaac Norris, the younger, remained Speaker until his death in 1764, and signed various Bills for war purposes. His father had been a close friend of James Logan. But the influence of the Society was strongly against the entrance of Friends into the legislature. The Philadelphia Meeting for Sufferings—the first in America—was established in 1756 partly to meet the troubles due to the Delaware Militia Bill and the Pennsylvania war taxes.[1] Both it and the Yearly Meeting issued repeated cautions to Friends against taking any active part in politics. When peace came, however, some Friends felt that their scruples were allayed, especially as the Assembly disbanded the military forces, leaving only one hundred and fifty men in the State militia. For some years after 1765 even James Pemberton resumed his seat, although he resigned again before the troubles with England became acute. But the efforts of the official bodies always kept the actual Quaker element in the Assembly small.

The real activity of the Society was displayed not in the legislature, but in some important, though unofficial, negotiations with the Indians. The Quaker Memorial to the Governor in April 1756, before the declaration of war, while pleading for another attempt to preserve peace, had added :

[1] The New York Meeting for Sufferings was founded in 1759, also as a result of the war with France. The fullest account of Pennsylvania Quakerism between the Seven Years' and the Revolutionary Wars is found in Sharpless, *Quakers in the Revolution*, chaps i–v.

" We hope to demonstrate by our conduct that every occasion of assisting and relieving the distressed, and contributing towards the obtaining of peace in a manner consistent with our peaceable profession, will be cheerfully improved by us, and even though a much larger part of our estates should be necesssary than the heaviest taxes of a war can be expected to require, we shall cheerfully, by voluntary presents, evidence our sincerity therein."

Not only did they contribute liberally to the relief of the refugee settlers from the frontiers, but " The Friendly Association for Gaining and Preserving Peace with the Indians by Pacific Means " was formed under the leadership of such Friends as Israel Pemberton and Anthony Benezet, who had been foremost in opposition to the Quaker membership of the Assembly. These friends went out again and again beyond the frontier, at the peril of their lives to confer with the Indians, and none of the " children of Onas " (Penn) as the Indians called them came to any harm. With some of the German peace sects, they raised between five and six thousand pounds, which was partly applied to the ransom of prisoners, but mainly to an attempt to win back by gifts the Pennsylvania Indians to their old friendship. They believed, rightly as it proved, that these tribes were not irretrievably alienated, and that by a full and frank discussion of grievances, the situation might be cleared up. Between 1756 and 1758 several conferences were held by the Governor and delegates from the legislature with these tribes, which representatives of the Friendly Association attended at the express request of the Indians, to ensure fair treatment, though their presence was not always welcomed by the colonial officials. Tedyuscung, chief of the Delawares, showed considerable skill in setting forth the old grievances of his people at the fraudulent dealings of the past, and in the end the wronged tribes received, in addition to the Quaker gifts, some compensation for their lost lands, while the former treaties of friendship were renewed. The Friendly Association was bitterly reproached by the " Presbyterian " party for its share in the negotiations, but there is no doubt that Israel Pemberton stated their true motives :

" If we can but be instrumental to restore peace to our country and retrieve the credit of it with our former kind neighbours, but of late bloody enemies, we shall have all the reward we desire. The name of a Quaker of the same spirit as William Penn is still in the highest estimation among their old men."[1]

The frontier war flared out again in 1764 after the conspiracy of Pontiac, this time, however, mainly with the Algonquin and Iroquois Indians, and the Friendly Association again worked for peace.[2]

But in the interval another Indian trouble brought deep concern and even division to the Philadelphia Quakers. Some twenty friendly Indians, mainly women and children, the last remnants of the once powerful Conestoga tribe, were murdered in December 1763 by a lynching party of Irish Presbyterians from Paxton. The crime was inspired partly by the general principle that the only good Indian was a dead Indian, partly by the wish to avenge the frontier's sufferings at the hands of more warlike tribes, and partly by an unfounded suspicion of treachery. The whole tribe was extirpated, some were killed at their homes, and others in Lancaster gaol, where they had been placed for safety. The province as a whole was indignant, but the border settlers supported the " Paxton boys," who were never brought to justice. Growing bolder, they marched with two or three hundred sympathizers towards Philadelphia, declaring that they would destroy not only a band of Moravian Christian

[1] Quoted in *Friend* (Philadelphia), xlvi. 187. See also Charles Thomson, *The Alienation of the Delaware and Shawnese Indians*. Thomson, as a young man, acted as secretary for Tedyuscung at some of the Conferences. In the Revolutionary War he was Secretary to the Continental Congress. *The Gentleman's Magazine* (1757, p. 474 and 1759, p. 109) gives brief reports of some of these negotiations. One of the current slanders of the time against the Quakers was revived in the correspondence columns of the *Spectator* (February 26, 1916), in the quotation of an official report containing the allegations of an Indian chief against the Friendly Association. He stated that some Quakers had urged the Iroquois chiefs of the Six Nations to spare the Pennsylvania settlers, " but, if you incline to carry on a war against any nation, we have everything fit to kill men in plenty, such as guns, swords, hatchets, powder, lead, clothing, and provisions, which we are ready to furnish you with. . . . You must kill the soldiers only, and not us. . . . You may kill men enough in other parts of the country without coming here." This remarkable statement was sent by the officer who received it in 1757 to Lord Loudoun, Commander-in-Chief of the forces in America, and in the following year to Abercromby, his successor. Loudoun paid no attention to it, Abercromby forwarded it to the military commander in Philadelphia, who took no action. The work of the Friendly Association was carried on in the most open way, and it is incredible that any episode so flagrantly inconsistent with its professed aims and the principles of its leaders, should not have been trumpeted abroad by their opponents, if it had had any foundation in fact.

[2] The New Jersey Indians were also involved in these negotiations, and Friends of that province formed a similar association for their benefit. In 1763, John Woolman paid a religious visit to the Indians of the Susquehanna Valley.

Indians, who had been sent for shelter to the city, but the Quakers who had taken the lead in the Friendly Association. This was in February 1764. When these frontiersmen appeared in threatening array at Germantown on the outskirts of Philadelphia, the citizens armed themselves to resist and to defend their helpless clients. But force was not needed. The settlers had brought with them a statement of grievances, and through Franklin's negotiations they were induced to lay these before the Governor (Richard Penn) and to return home. They did not obtain their most legitimate demand for an increased representation in the Assembly, but they were placated by the Governor's offer of a reward for the scalps of hostile Indians, which turned their activities into that channel. They had left behind them trouble among the Friends. Many of the younger men had rushed to arms to defend the Indians and their elders, and had even used the meeting-house as a shelter for themselves and their weapons on that stormy February day. James Pemberton wrote of them to Dr. Fothergill :

" It was matter of sorrowful observation to behold so many under our name (it is supposed about two hundred) acting so contrary to the ancient and well-grounded principle of our profession, the testimony whereof suffered greatly on this occasion, and furnished our adversaries with a subject of rejoicing, who will make no allowance for the instability of youth ; they who take up arms being mostly such who could scarcely be expected to stand firm to the testimony upon a time of so sudden and uncommon a trial, or such who do not make much profession."

Many of these young men belonged to that section of the Society in Philadelphia which had supported Franklin's defensive measures and which was to take active part in the Revolution. In March, their Monthly Meetings, through a committee, began to labour with them. From the committee's periodical reports it appears that a considerable number at once acknowledged their error, some thirty or more of whom " were in their minority, and appeared much unacquainted with the grounds of Friends' testimony herein." Some justified their action as the defence of the helpless against lawless violence and a few maintained the lawfulness of defensive war. The work of the committee went on until 1767, by which time many had made public acknowledgment of their fault to their meeting. A few were still convinced that they had acted rightly, but even these promised to be more circumspect in future. With this the meetings appeared satisfied, for no member was disowned. Samuel Wetherill, one of the " fighting Quakers " of the Revolutionary War, declared years afterwards that during the alarm " not an individual of the Society appeared to discountenance the thing." This statement is not borne out by contemporary letters and records ; probably the judgment of an English Friend represented the general view. It was, he admitted, " a very singular and extraordinary case," being to oppose an armed band of murderers, yet the full maintenance of the peace testimony was " of very great importance to the whole Society."

In their petitions to the Governor the frontiersmen had included bitter complaints against the Quakers, who had (they said) showered presents upon the Indians, while refusing to help the distressed settlers. They even accused the Friendly Association, and in particular Israel Pemberton, of keeping up a private and treacherous correspondence with tribes in time of war. These charges were the signal for the opening of an angry pamphlet controversy between the " Presbyterian " and the " Quaker " parties on the general question of the responsibility of the Quaker Assembly for the outbreak of the Indian wars. The writers on both sides were violent and, as far as is known, Friends themselves took no part in the quarrel, except for one statement to the Governor drawn up by the Meeting for Sufferings in answer to the charges of the Paxton rioters. This document, which was presented to Richard Penn in the spring of 1764, reminded him that their past history both in England and America showed the clearness of Friends from all plots and conspiracies, and defended the action of the Friendly Association in its efforts to promote peace with the Indians. Friends had willingly subscribed considerable sums to the relief of sufferers on the frontiers, but the £5,000 raised for the work of Indian reconciliation had also been for their benefit. " The chief part thereof hath been since expended in presents given at the public treaties (when they were sometimes delivered by the Governors of the province and at other times with their privity and permission) for promoting the salutary measures of gaining and confirming peace with the Indians and procuring the release of our countrymen in captivity." The Proprietors had approved of this policy. As for the accusation of usurping political power the Meeting for Sufferings replied with truth that on the contrary it had dissuaded Friends from office. " We are not conscious that as Englishmen and dutiful subjects we have ever forfeited our right of electing or being elected ; but because we could serve no longer in these stations with satisfaction to ourselves, many of us have chosen to forbear the exercise of these rights." [1]

As the dispute between England and the American colonies passed first into resistance to the financial claims of the home Government, and then into a movement for independence and open war, the position of Friends in all the colonies was peculiarly difficult. In the years from 1765 to 1773 many, as leading citizens of their provinces and towns, took an active part by writings, speeches, and deeds in the opposition to any encroachment on colonial rights, thus carrying on the policy of the earlier Quaker colonists.[2]

Stephen Hopkins and Moses Brown in Rhode Island, John Dickinson, the Pembertons, and others in Philadelphia, all were concerned in these preliminary measures of resistance.[3] Many Quakers were prosperous merchants, and so were specially affected by the Navigation Acts and the other attempts of England to restrict and control American trade.

But as events moved irresistibly towards war, Friends had to reconsider their position. John Dickinson, whose *Farmer's Letters* of 1768 formed the best early statement of the American claims, and who wrote many state papers for the Continental Congress, refused to sign the Declaration of Independence. He believed that it was premature, and that the questions then in dispute could have

---

[1] The petition of the rioters to the Governor was reprinted as a pamphlet, *A Declaration and Remonstrance of the Distressed and Bleeding Frontier Inhabitants of the Province of Pennsylvania*, etc. (in D. 39). The reply of the Meeting for Sufferings is given in full, in Sharpless, *Quakers in the Revolution*, p. 59. It may be noted that the petition, while charging Pemberton and his friends in the past with making private treaties with the Indians and encouraging them in their belief that they had lost their lands by fraud, says nothing of the allegation that they had promised weapons to the Six Nations. There is no doubt that such a charge would have been eagerly utilized by the petitioners if it had had the slightest chance of obtaining credit. One argument advanced in defence of the massacre is that in time of Indian war all Indians, even if professedly friendly, must be viewed as potential enemies, and interned or put to death.

[2] Fifty Friends were among the signatories to one of the non-importation agreements in 1765 (Thomas, *History of Friends in America*, p. 117).

[3] These men were all of-Quaker origin or connection, but not all in membership. Stephen Hopkins was disowned for slave-holding in 1773, though he continued to worship with Friends throughout his life. He was one of the signers of the Declaration of Independence. In 1774 Moses Brown joined the Society, previously freeing his slaves. John Dickinson seems never to have been in actual membership ; but for this question, see *Quakers in American Colonies*, pp. 559 foll., and Sharpless, *Political Leaders of Provincial Pennsylvania*, pp. 236 foll.

been solved by some method short of actual war. He fought, however, in the Revolution. Friends, as a body, had to make their choice. On the one side were the claims of liberty and justice. On the other was the testimony against war, and the old tradition of loyalty to the established Government. These were reinforced by the feeling which had grown during the past half-century that spiritual life was hindered by an active share in political movements.

Of those who actively supported the war the majority naturally were on the Revolutionary side. They were disowned by their Monthly Meetings, when in membership—for it must be remembered that many " Quakers" were only called so by the public from their social connection with Friends or their attendance at religious meetings. Those who joined the British cause were dealt with in the same way, but their numbers were very small. The majority of Friends maintained a quiet opposition not only to all military activity, but to all active support of the Revolutionary government. | This attitude gave rise to the general opinion that Friends were traitors and " Tories " (that is, Loyalists). Traitors they were not, for they gave no aid to the British. Loyalists the leading Friends in Philadelphia and New York undoubtedly were, though they were scrupulous in their abstention from all complicity with the war. Probably the majority of the New England Friends, and of the country Friends elsewhere, sympathized with the American cause. But they all united in a conscientious opposition to warlike measures, and a refusal to share in them.

Dr. Fothergill, who from across the Atlantic had watched the development of the American crisis with an understanding which was wanting among his Majesty's ministers, urged Pennsylvania Friends to accept the decision for national independence, and to support the liberties of America, by submitting to the general voice of the colonists, while firmly and calmly maintaining their opposition to war.[1] Possibly their position would have been easier had they taken this course, though in the heat of war, Governments are not very ready to enter into nice distinctions ; but, in giving this advice, Fothergill was more American than many of the Americans themselves. Actually Friends tried to maintain a policy of neutrality, and as a general rule they suffered equally at the hands of both contending parties. Their houses and farms were plundered, their meeting-houses were commandeered for troops or for the wounded.

[1] *Vide* Letters quoted in Sharpless, *Quakers in the Revolution*, p. 118.

Personally they endured heavy distraints, in some cases imprisonment, and in a few actual maltreatment, while hardest of all to bear was the general odium which fell upon the sect and the wrench of separation from fellow members they held in high esteem.[1] Yet they kept steadily on the course they had chosen, maintained their meetings and their discipline, and helped their members both by advice and by material assistance. Whenever possible, during this time of war, representatives from New England and the Southern States attended Philadelphia Yearly Meeting, and this no doubt helped Friends throughout the States in the maintenance of a consistent policy. They also kept up an affectionate intercourse by official Epistles and private correspondence with English Friends. The misunderstandings which for so many years after the peace continued to subsist between the two great English-speaking countries found no place within the Society. The English and Irish bodies sent generous gifts to the sufferers from the war, which were gratefully remembered and returned in later times of need by American Friends.

Intercourse between the different Meetings was greatly hampered. Overstrained military officers were apt to mistake harmless " ministering Friends " for British spies, and more than once the lives of such travellers were in imminent danger, yet by quiet faith and courage they were often allowed to pass where way seemed impossible. Even some missionary visits to Indian tribes were carried out. The English Government had adopted the bad expedient of employing Indian auxiliaries against the Americans, but on the most disturbed frontiers Friends were unmolested, a fact which their enemies took as clear proof of their treacherous collusion with the British forces. An incident recorded by George Dillwyn illustrates this Quaker immunity. The neighbourhood of Easton on the New York frontier was so harassed by raids from both armies that the American Government had advised the inhabitants to evacuate the districts. The Friends, however, remained and kept up their religious meetings. At one week-day meeting they were sitting with open doors in silent worship when an Indian came and peeped in at them. Seeing Friends sitting quietly together, he slipped inside the door,

---

[1] Not all, however, who were disowned fell under this description. Some whose conduct had long been a matter of concern took this opportunity of leaving the Society on a more respectable pretext, while others were merely " birthright members " who cared little for the connection with Friends.

followed by a company of his countrymen. They placed their weapons in a corner of the room, and took seats. When the meeting closed, Zebulon Hoxie, one of the Friends present, invited them to his house to refresh themselves, which invitation they accepted, and having partaken of his provisions quietly departed. Before going, however, the chief warrior, who could speak French, had a communication in that language with Robert Nesbitt, in which he told him they had come to the house intending to destroy all who were in it. Adding : "When we saw you sitting with your door open without weapons of defence, we had no disposition to hurt you, we would have fought for you." Yet this party had scalps with them.[1]

The difficulties of consistent conduct, and the divisions of opinion which harassed all Friends in North America, were intensified in the case of those in Pennsylvania, where they were still an important body, and where memories of their political control survived. But before describing their experiences a brief account may be given of the position of Friends during the war in the other provinces.

New Jersey Friends in 1777 were forbidden by the American military authorities to attend their Yearly Meeting at Philadelphia, owing to the British occupation of the city. More than once during the war their meeting-houses were taken for barracks and hospitals, and they suffered particularly heavy losses by distraints and requisitions. Friends in Pennsylvania relieved them to the best of their ability, and at the close of the war English Friends sent generous help. A careful student of New Jersey Quakerism has written of this period :

" Many young men yielded to the impulse, which also drew away some of the older ones, to enlist in the cause of the Americans. . . . Despite trials consequent upon a position of neutrality among people alive with the spirit of warfare, they steadily maintained their principles and profession, although at the expense, in many cases, of goods and property. To all inquiries they replied, as one meeting stated in a special minute :

" ' We, the people called Quakers, ever since we were distinguished as a Society, have declared to the world our belief in the peaceable tendency of the Gospel of Christ, and that, consistent

---

[1] The story is given in the *British Friend*, 1851, p. 290, *vide* also L.V. Hodgkin's version " Fierce Feathers " in *A Book of Quaker Saints*. The date is given as 1777 in *The Journal of Rufus Hall* (an eye-witness) in D.

therewith, we could not bear arms, nor be concerned in warlike preparations.' "[1]

When in 1775 the Committee of Safety of New York asked for a return of all male Quakers between the ages of sixteen and sixty, the Meeting for Sufferings refused to comply, on the grounds of a " truly conscientious scruple." Later in the year, when the city had been evacuated by many of the inhabitants through fear of bombardment by English ships, William Rickman, master of the Friends' School, and a few other Friends remained, doing service in the meeting-house, which was used as a hospital. After its capture, Tryon, the British Governor of New York, applied to the Meeting for Sufferings for funds to provide stockings and other comforts for the troops, on the ground that some Quakers had been " too busy and active in the present commotions." The Meeting acknowledged with regret the " deviation " of some members, but firmly declined to make the proposed gift, as " manifestly contrary to our religious testimony against war and fightings."[2]

New England Friends maintained their peace principles very firmly during the war. At its outbreak the New England Meeting for Sufferings was formed, and it soon found work to do in the relief of distress in the town and neighbourhood of Boston during its siege by the English in the winter of 1775-6. Help came from England, while the Philadelphia Meeting for Sufferings sent £2,540, mostly in gold, to the New England committee of relief. This committee, under the leadership of Moses Brown, of Rhode Island, visited Howe and Washington, the generals of the opposing armies, explaining that they wished to relieve civilian distress, without distinction of parties. They were not allowed to pass through the lines of the besiegers, but they were permitted to send part of their funds to be distributed by Boston Friends, and the remainder they themselves apportioned to three thousand families in the adjacent towns and villages. " It was a sort of school to us," wrote Moses Brown, " for we never saw poverty to compare." In 1775 and again in 1776 the town of Salem, where the early Quakers had endured cruel persecution, publicly recorded its thanks to Friends for their generous help. " Through these towns—many of them towns through which Quakers had been whipped—working in company

---

[1] *Quakers in American Colonies*, pp. 411-12 (chapter by A. M. Gummere).
[2] *Ibid.*, pp. 259-60.

with the Selectmen—the Friends, with personal painstaking care, dispensed their gifts of love." [1]

What proved to be the most noteworthy of New England disownments on account of warlike activities, was that of Nathanael Greene, of Rhode Island, later Washington's most trusted general. Though the Quaker farmer, his father, had brought him up with Puritan strictness, young Greene early showed an un-Quakerly fondness for dancing and for military science and practice. In both he was handicapped by lameness, but he pursued both with zest. His separation from Friends took place before the war. In July 1773 he and his brother came under the notice of their Monthly Meeting for visiting " a place in Connecticut of public resort, where they had no proper business." In other words, they had attended a militia training camp. In September they were both disowned, and two years later the Rhode Island Assembly elected Nathanael Greene as their brigadier-general. There is a tradition that he was the third choice, two other men of more experience having refused, and that when the result of the voting was announced, he rose and said : " Since the Episcopalian and the Congregationalist won't, I suppose the Quaker must." Another tradition gives him a Spartan mother, who dismissed him with the assurance that, though her grief at his choice of a soldier's life was very great, it would be deeper if she were ever to hear that he had turned his back to the enemy.[2] What is certain is that, although at times he spoke bitterly of the narrowness of his early education, he always showed confidence in Friends. After the bloody battle of Guildford Court House, North Carolina, before his retreat he placed the wounded of both armies in the Friends' meeting-house, and wrote to neighbouring Friends reminding them that he had been brought up in their Society, and appealing to them to help the sufferers, which they did by furnishing hospital supplies.

In 1781 Abel Thomas and another Friend, through many difficulties and dangers, paid a visit of religious consolation to their brethren in Virginia and South Carolina. After narrowly missing death as spies from one section of the American Army and losing

---

[1] *Quakers in American Colonies*, p. 152 ; *Annals of Salem*, ii. 399. Moses Brown's contemporary account was first published in the *Pennsylvania Magazine of Politics and History*, i. 168.

[2] G. W. Greene, *Life of Nathanael Greene*, i. 69, 80, etc. There is a delightful account of Greene as a man and a soldier in Sir George Trevelyan's *George III and Charles Fox*, vol. ii. ch. 16.

their horses at the hands of robbers, they still did not feel " free " (in Quaker language) to leave the district, and applied to General Greene for a pass. His answer dated June 7, 1781, was as follows :

" From the good opinion I have of the people of your profession, being bred and educated among them, I am persuaded your visit is purely religious, and in this persuasion have granted you a pass, and I shall be happy if your ministry shall contribute to the establishment of morality and brotherly kindness among the people, than which no country ever wanted it more. I am sensible your principles and professions are opposed to war, but I know you are fond of both political and religious liberty. . . . In this laudable endeavour I expect at least to have the good wishes of your people, as well for their own sakes as for ours, who wish to serve them upon all occasions, not inconsistent with the public good." Armed with the permit the Friends finished their mission, though in its course they had to pass close to a battle.

Other Rhode Island Friends were more peaceable than Greene. From the *Journal of Job Scott*, one of their members, it appears that early in the war the Deputy-Governor ordered the inhabitants to produce all their fowling-pieces and small arms at the Court House, that the military resources of the district might be known. The Friends sent a written refusal to attend, stating their opposition to all war. The Deputy-Governor was satisfied, remarking that he wished all consciences to be free. The records of the New England Yearly Meeting at Providence, however, contain many " sufferings " of Friends during the war, from distraints of cattle and property and other losses. Job Scott himself was much exercised over the use of the Continental paper currency. At last he refused it and enjoyed " peace of mind," although he found life difficult since practically no other money was in circulation. When the British forces occupied Rhode Island, many people fled with their valuables from Providence. The Friends of the town, meeting together, decided to remain, and to do nothing to increase the panic. They were " preserved in the stability of the unchangeable Truth." [1]

The inhabitants of Nantucket suffered almost as severely as those of any district not actually ravaged by the war. An embargo was laid on their cod-fishing by the English Government, their whalers were captured by the enemy, and at times they were in danger of starvation, since the Americans refused to send them

[1] *Journal of Job Scott.*

provisions, on the pretext that they supplied the British. William Rotch, a Quaker, was a large ship-owner and the chief proprietor of the island's whaling fleet.[1] He had taken a large stock of muskets and bayonets in payment of a debt. The muskets he sold as fowling-pieces to his whalers to shoot game and sea fowl in their coasting voyages. The bayonets he refused to sell. At the outbreak of the war both British and Americans wished to get hold of his stock. The American authorities sent over to requisition them, but Rotch refused :—

" The time had now come to support our testimony against war or forever abandon it. . . . My reasons for not furnishing the bayonets were demanded, and I answered : ' As this instrument is purposely made and used for the destruction of mankind and I cannot put into one man's hand to destroy another that which I cannot use myself in the same way, I refuse to comply with thy demand.' " This made, he said, a great noise in the neighbourhood, and his life was threatened. As for the bayonets—" I would gladly have beaten them into pruning hooks. As it was, I took an early opportunity of throwing them into the sea." For his refusal, he was summoned before a court-martial, where he explained his position. " The chairman of the committee, one Major Hawley, a worthy character, then addressed the committee, and said : ' I believe Mr. Rotch has given us a candid account of the affair, and every man has a right to act consistently with his religious principles. But I am sorry we cannot have the bayonets for we want them very much.' The Major was desirous of knowing more of our Friends' principles, on which I informed him as far as he inquired. One of the committee (Judge Parr), in a pert manner, observed : ' Then your principles are passive obedience and non-resistance.' I replied : ' No, my friend, our principles are active obedience and passive suffering.' I passed through no small trial on account of my bayonets." Later on William Rotch was to prove as faithful to his principles in the French Revolution as he had been in the American.

The Revolution brought much trouble to Friends in the South.[2]

---

[1] *Vide Memorandum Written by William Rotch in the Eightieth Year of His Age* (printed by Houghton Mifflin Co., Boston and New York, 1916). The three ships which brought the famous cargo of tea to Boston in 1773 were all owned by Rotch.

[2] The following facts are mainly taken from S. B. Weeks, *Southern Quakers and Slavery*.

In Virginia, Washington's own State, the official attitude of the Society was uncompromisingly opposed to any breach with the established Government. Those who took part in the war on either side, by enlistment or otherwise, were disowned yet, during this period, many joined the Society. Historians suggest that these were shirkers trying to avoid military service. But the treatment accorded to Friends and the active campaign against slave-holding which they carried on during the war were not inducements for the unconvinced and unscrupulous to enter their ranks. It is true that in Virginia the earlier " draft " laws of the war exempted Quakers and Mennonites (this sect had been migrating southward from Pennsylvania during the last quarter of a century), but they endured heavy distraints, and their general refusal to use the Continental paper money or to pay war taxes involved them in great difficulty. Later an attempt was made to force them to serve. In 1777 fourteen Friends were drafted under the Militia law and taken from home. They steadily refused either to handle a musket or to eat the army provisions, but they were dragged on with the regiment until some fell ill under their hardships and were sent home. The others were brought to Washington's camp at Valley Forge, with their muskets tied on their backs. Washington had ex-Quakers among his officers, and he had had some experience of Quaker scruples in the campaign of 1756. As soon as he heard of the arrival of the conscripts, he ordered them to be discharged and allowed them to go home.[1] Another Friend was mercilessly flogged for refusing to act as guard over Burgoyne's army, after its surrender in Virginia.

In 1777 an oath or affirmation of allegiance to the State was imposed, the penalty of refusal being the confiscation of all weapons and the loss of the franchise and other civil rights. The minutes of the next Virginia Yearly Meeting showed that this stringent penalty had drawn some to conform. Local meetings were directed to caution their members " not to join with or engage in any measures which may be carried on by war and bloodshed, or take any test that may bind them to join with either party while the contest subsists."

The Yearly Meeting of North Carolina (including South Carolina and Georgia) in its Epistle of 1776 denounced all insurrections as " works of darkness." War taxes were left a matter for the individual conscience, and many paid. But all paid involuntarily

[1] Gilpin, *Exiles in Virginia*, p. 181.

to the support of both armies. Neither side, when in occupation of this territory, spared the well-filled barns and store-houses of Quaker farmers and merchants. The Georgia draft law exempted acknowledged Quakers, but in both Carolinas they were liable to very heavy fines—in one year the record amounts to £4,000 and in another to £2,152, both presumably not reckoned in Continental currency, but in " hard money." The penalty for refusing the test of allegiance was even more severe in these States than in Virginia. In both it was expulsion, but in South Carolina the exile who returned was liable to death. This provision was, however, too strong for public opinion, and after a few months it was assimilated to the Virginia law. In 1777 the Quakers of North Carolina addressed a reasoned statement to the Assembly, explaining why they could not declare their allegiance to the Revolutionary government.

" As we have always declared that we believed it to be unlawful for us to be active in war and fighting with carnal weapons, and as we conceive that the proposed affirmation approves of the present measures, which are carried on and supported by military force, we cannot engage in or join with either party therein, being bound by our principles to believe that the setting up and pulling down Kings and Governments is God's peculiar prerogative, for causes best known to himself ; and that it is not our work or business to have any hand or contrivance therein, nor to be busybodies in matters above our station ; so that, as we cannot be active either for or against any power that is permitted or set over us in the above respects, we hope that you will consider our principles a much stronger security to any state than any test that can be required of us. As we now are, and shall be, innocent and peaceable in our several stations and conditions under this present state, and for conscience' sake are submissive to the laws, in whatever they may justly require, or by peaceably suffering what is or may be inflicted upon us, in matters in which we cannot be active for conscience' sake." [1]

This argument had its effect, for in 1780 the Assembly went so far as to pass an Act securing Quakers in the possession of their landed property, since malicious persons had attempted to oust them, on the plea that by refusing allegiance they had lost the protection of the law. After this there seems to have been no further trouble. When peace came in 1783 the Yearly Meeting told its members that, though it had dissuaded them from taking any test " to either

[1] Weeks, *Southern Quakers and Slavery,* p. 191.

of the powers while contending," they were now left " to the freedom of their own minds." In other words, the Government was now again established, and while Friends would not take part in war they accepted its verdict. Under the new authorities Quakers were either specifically or tacitly exempted from all military service in the Carolinas and Georgia, and in Virginia the penalties were comparatively light until the outbreak of the second war with England.

The difficulties which harassed Friends during the war were intensified in the case of the Quakers of Pennsylvania. The numbers of the Society were still large—they were estimated at 30,000 at this period—and it was natural that those who mistrusted their intentions should fear the influence of so important and compact a body. At first, as has been said, the Quaker merchants of Philadelphia united with the other leaders of the province in resistance of the claims of the home Government. Fifty, including the Pembertons and Whartons, were among the four hundred merchants who signed the non-importation agreement evoked by the Stamp Act of 1765. A letter was sent to the London Meeting for Sufferings explaining their reasons for this course. In 1766 they wrote again to inform English Friends that in Pennsylvania and New Jersey the rejoicings on the repeal of the Act were accompanied by less riotous proceedings than in the other States, " to which the conduct and conversation of Friends hath in some measure tended." The " tea-party," also, which Philadelphia held in 1773, was of a milder and more decorous character than the renowned one at Boston. The tea had been consigned to the Quaker firms of Wharton and Drinker, but the pressure of public opinion prevented its unloading, and the ship had to put about and return to England. The Whartons advanced to the captain sufficient money to cover the expenses of his unexpected and unprofitable voyage.

As the situation grew more acute, the cleavage of opinion widened. Philadelphia had always possessed many Friends of the Logan type, wealthy, well-educated, public-spirited, not principled against defensive war, and taking little active part in the religious life of the Society. Among these Friends were those who had refused to leave the Assembly in 1756, who had supported its war policy, and had encouraged the resort to arms against the " Paxton boys." Now they prepared to cast in their lot with the Americans. Three men of Quaker connection were among the chief organizers of the

Continental Congress of 1774, held in Philadelphia. They were Charles Thomson, not himself a Friend, but formerly master of the Friends' School and clerk to Tedyuscung at the Indian Conferences, John Dickinson, whose membership in the Society is dubious, and Thomas Mifflin, an undoubted Friend. Of the three Charles Thomson became Secretary to the Congress, Dickinson was one of its leading spirits until the actual decision for war, and Mifflin won fame as a Revolutionary general and later as Governor of the State. They were all moderates in policy, and through their influence it was hoped to win over the " Quaker party," and even the Society itself. But as the movement for independence grew, the " Presbyterians " gained power and support in the Pennsylvania legislature. Under their influence in 1776 the constitution of Pennsylvania and Penn's ancient charter were annulled and replaced by a Republican Government. This extreme course frightened back many of the moderates into Toryism (or support of England) and alienated the whole body of Friends, who wrote regretfully of " the happy constitution under which we and others long enjoyed tranquillity and peace." [1]

For some time Friends were in a balance of opinion, but as the movement in America became more violent, they fell back upon their old testimony against revolution. As early as June 1774 the Meeting for Sufferings was advising Friends to abstain from the excitements of public meetings, and in September the Yearly Meeting followed this up by an address to all Friends in America, reminding them that the experience of their forefathers in the Civil War had led them to the conviction of the unlawfulness of all wars and fightings. The Meeting reiterated the advice of Fox in 1685 :

" Whatever bustlings or troubles or tumults or outrages should rise in the world, keep out of them ; but keep in the Lord's power, and in the peaceable truth that is over all, in which power you seek the peace and good of all men, and live in the love which God has shed abroad in your hearts, through Jesus Christ, in which love

[1] *Meeting for Sufferings*, 12th mo. 20, 1776. It was Dickinson who wrote the " Liberty Song," a line of which gave the new Republic its motto—" By uniting we stand, by dividing we fail." But he had tried to carry on negotiations in the spirit of another of his aphorisms— ' The cause of liberty is a cause of too much dignity to be sullied by turbulence and tumult "—and as the tide of passion rose the control of affairs was swept out of his hands. It has been said that " his life was typical of Quaker influence (in Pennsylvania), potent to the very outbreak of war, suddenly and strikingly impotent after it becomes a fact " (*Quakers in American Colonies*, p. 560).

nothing is able to separate you from God and Christ."[1]   Three
months later the Meeting for Sufferings recorded a minute (December 15, 1774) regretting that the Pennsylvania Assembly had
approved the proceedings of the Continental Congress.   " Which
contain divers resolutions very contrary to our Christian profession
and principles.   And as there are several members of our religious
society who are members of that assembly, some of whom we have
reason to apprehend, have either agreed to the late resolves, which
are declared to be unanimous, or not manifested their dissent in such
a manner as a regard to our Christian testimony would require of
them, there being a danger of such being drawn into further inconsistencies of conduct in their public stations, the following Friends
are desired to take an opportunity of informing them of the trouble
and sorrow they brought on their brethren, who are concerned
to maintain our principles on the ancient foundations, and to excite
them to greater watchfulness, etc., to avoid agreeing to proposals,
resolutions, or measures so inconsistent with the testimony of
truth."[2]

In January 1775 the Meeting urged members (who " some of
them without their consent or knowledge ") had been nominated
to public offices to withdraw, and Monthly Meetings were asked
to deal with all inconsistencies of conduct.   Throughout this and
the following winter meetings were kept busy at the work.
President Sharpless, who made a careful study of this period, estimated
that of the thirty thousand Friends in Pennsylvania four or five
hundred asserted themselves openly in the American cause, and
five or six individuals are known to have joined the British forces.
All these were disowned.   Thomas Mifflin was the first to go,
followed by a host of less prominent men.   They gave cause for their
disownment, for John Adams wrote from Philadelphia in 1775
that it was a ludicrous sight " to see whole companies of armed
Quakers in uniform going through the manual."[3] This is confirmed
by James Pemberton's account to Fothergill in May of that year.
" A military spirit prevails, the people are taken off from employment,
intent on instructing themselves in the art of war, and many younger
members of our Society are daily joining with them."   At least an

---

[1] Bowden, *History of Friends in America*, ii. 298.   There are various copies of
the letter in D., e.g. *Tracts*, C. 147.
[2] Sharpless, *Quakers in the Revolution*, p. 107.
[3] Justin Winsor, *Narrative and Critical History of America*, vi. 131.

hundred and forty were dealt with and disowned by two Monthly Meetings in the city of Philadelphia for such causes as the following : " Acting as soldier in the American Army." " Joining the British Army " (one case). " Fitting out an armed vessel which may prove the cause of shedding human blood." " Paying fines in lieu of military service." " Making weapons of war for the destruction of his fellow-men." " Being in an engagement where many were slain." " Holding a commission for furnishing supplies to one of the belligerents." [1]

At the same time there were a considerable number of disownments for slave-holding. The influence of the most spiritually minded and most honoured members of the Society was unflinchingly set against slavery and war. Among these leaders was Anthony Benezet, already mentioned in connection with the events of 1755 and 1756. Born in 1713, of a French Huguenot family, he was only two years old when his parents fled with him to England to escape persecution. In 1727 he joined Friends, and four years later he emigrated to Pennsylvania. There he devoted the rest of his long life to the interests of the Society and of his fellow-men, working by personal influence and his pen on behalf of the slaves and the oppressed. His *Historical Account of Guinea*, read by Clarkson in 1785 when working for a University prize, gave him the impulse to his campaign against the slave-trade. Benezet had some of Woolman's transparent simplicity and benevolence, though he was a man of more education. For some years he was master of a Friends' school in the city.

In 1755, after the hapless Acadians were banished from their homes by the British Government, he was single-handed a relief committee for the five hundred quartered in Philadelphia.[2] He built them houses, collected clothing and money, and found them employment. In fact, his sympathy for these men of his old race impelled him to such efforts for their welfare that one refugee feared that this benevolence could not be disinterested, but that their helper intended to sell them as slaves.

He was a leading member of the Friendly Association, and until his death in 1784 worked untiringly for the Indians. But above all he worked for peace. His hatred of war was intense. According to his first biographer, Vaux, he once addressed an

---

[1] Sharpless, *Quakers in the Revolution*, pp. 132–4.
[2] The story of the Acadians is familiar from Longfellow's *Evangeline*.

" energetic and pathetic " letter to Frederick the Great, remonstrating with him for his share in the miseries inflicted by conquest, but this address does not seem to have survived. He used all his endeavours towards a peaceful solution of the dispute with England, and even after hostilities had broken out, published pamphlets expounding his peaceable gospel to his warring countrymen. In one he wrote : " Let us all sincerely ask our common Father for help to pray— not for the destruction of our enemies, who are still our brethren, but for an agreement with them."

In 1774 he visited many of the deputies to the Continental Congress, pleading with them for the abolition of slavery and the maintenance of peace. Among them was Patrick Henry, but he (as Benezet recorded the interview) at last remarked that " it was strange to him to find some of the Quakers manifesting a disposition so different from that I had described. I reminded him that many of these had no other claim to our principles than as they were children or grandchildren of those who professed those principles. I suppose his remark principally arose from the violent spirit which some under our name are apt to show, more particularly in the Congress."[1] This was a fair enough description of many of those disowned on account of the war. The minute of disownment generally stated that by the acts enumerated the member had " separated himself from religious fellowship with us," and expressed a hope for his future restoration. This was fulfilled in several cases. Owen Biddle, a leading Friend, repented and applied for reinstatement, giving out a " testimony of denial," or acknowledgment of his fault. The same course was followed by two young men, Peter and Mordecai Yarnall, who later became well-known ministers in the Society. Peter Yarnall had acted as assistant surgeon in the Revolutionary Army, and had also gained money by a share in a privateer. In 1780 he was reconverted to Quakerism by the preaching of Samuel Emlen at a funeral he attended. He showed his sincerity by relinquishing his privateering profits and trying to restore them to the rightful owners ; he also gave a public testimony of repentance to his former Monthly Meeting, which reinstated him.[2] There were other instances, but, of course, the majority of the disowned Friends were permanently lost to the Society.

Meanwhile, as the leaders of the Revolution had established

[1] Vaux, *Memoirs of Anthony Benezet*, p. 64.
[2] *British Friend*, 1850, pp. 63, 91.

an independent Government in the several States, Friends had to decide on their course. The one adopted was neither popular nor easy, but it seems to have been accepted without hesitation by the majority of the members, on whichever side their sympathies might lie.

Friends were to take no part in warlike measures, and to give no assistance to either side, but they were also as far as possible to maintain a quiet testimony against revolution, by a refusal to acknowledge the powers of the *de facto* Government. In January 1775 the Meeting for Sufferings had thrown down the gauntlet by publishing a "Testimony," which stated that the principles of Friends were "to discountenance and avoid every measure tending to excite disaffection to the King as supreme magistrate, or to the legal authority of his government." "We are therefore," the document continued, "incited by a sincere concern for the peace and welfare of our country publicly to declare against every usurpation of power and authority in opposition to the laws and Government, and against all combinations, insurrections, conspiracies, and illegal assemblies ; and as we are restrained from them by the conscientious discharge of our duty to Almighty God, ' by whom Kings reign and Princes decree justice,' we hope through his assistance and favour to be enabled to maintain our testimony against any requisition which may be made of us, inconsistent with our religious principles, and the fidelity we owe to the King and his government."

Dr. Fothergill, in England, was an acute critic of the royal policy, and had even told the Speaker of the House of Commons, in conversation, that England had been unjust to America and "ought to bear the consequences and alter her conduct," or the "empire would be divided and ruined." To him this address seemed too unquestioning in its loyalty. Yet the language was not warmer than that used by the Continental Congress six months later. Even after Lexington and Bunker's Hill, that body on July 6th declared : "We mean not to dissolve that union (with England) . . . which we sincerely wish to see restored," and on the 8th it adopted an address to the King couched in the most loyal terms.[1]

---

[1] This account of Pennsylvania Quakerism during the Revolution is mainly based on Bowden, *Friends in America*, vol. ii. ; Gilpin, *Exiles in Virginia* ; Sharpless, *Quakers in the Revolution*, and his chapter on the same subject in *Quakers in the American Colonies*. Dickinson was largely responsible for the drafting of the early congressional documents.

But, when in 1776, Congress had resolved on the dissolution of the Union, the Friends still maintained their old position. The Meeting for Sufferings on January 20, 1776, issued a fresh "Testimony," which next year served as one of the chief counts in the indictment against leading Philadelphia Quakers. It was headed : "The Ancient Testimony of the people called Quakers, renewed with respect to the King and Government ; and touching the commotions now prevailing in these and other parts of America, addressed to the people in general." It opened with a strong plea for peace, and for the maintenance of the "happy connexion we have heretofore enjoyed with the kingdom of Great Britain, and our just and necessary subordination to the King and those who are lawfully placed in authority under him," and encouraged Friends firmly to maintain their principles.

The document was signed by James Pemberton, as was the later pronouncement of December 1776, already quoted. The Yearly Meeting of 1776 counselled a policy which amounted to neutrality. Friends were to keep out of public office and the "present commotions," to be prompt in relief of sufferers "not only of our own, but of every other society and denomination," to be quietly loyal to the King, and to be patient under suffering. This "meek but invincible ill-will" (as Sir George Trevelyan has described the official Quaker attitude to the Revolution) [1] brought the whole sect into disfavour. Thomas Paine (later author of the *Rights of Man*), one of the chief pamphleteers on the American side, in a fierce rejoinder, printed as an appendix to his famous *Common Sense*, advised Friends to proclaim such doctrines to the enemy, rather than to those who were fighting for freedom.[2] As has been said, it is impossible to calculate the exact balance of opinion within the Society. President Sharpless says : "In one sense they were Loyalists, and it is quite probable that the personal sympathies of many of them were with the British cause. But they were innocuous Loyalists ; they were neither spies on American movements, nor did they flee for protection to British headquarters."[3] On the other hand, many, besides those who openly came out on the American side and in consequence lost their membership, must have been in secret sympathy with the Revolution. On the vexed question of the Continental

[1] *American Revolution*, iii. 59.
[2] Paine's father was an English Quaker.
[3] Sharpless, *Quakers in Revolution*, p. 131.

money the Yearly Meeting refused to give any decision, though some Friends felt that the testimony against Revolution (perhaps mingled with a natural reluctance on the part of solid business men to handle any currency so wildly inflated) forced them to refuse it.[1]

In June 1777 the Pennsylvania legislature passed a law ordering all the inhabitants to take an oath or affirmation of allegiance to the State of Pennsylvania and the United States, and to abjure for ever all connection with the King and Government of Great Britain. The majority of the Quakers stood firm, but the refusal to side with the new Government told heavily against them during the anxieties of the following autumn.

In September, Philadelphia was occupied by the British army under General Howe. A minute of the Monthly Meeting records the conduct of Friends in this crisis : " On the 29th of the 9th month 1777, being the day in course for holding our Monthly Meeting, a number of Friends met, when the present situation of things being considered, and it appearing that the King's army are near entering the city, at which time it may be proper the inhabitants should generally be at their habitations in order to preserve as much as possible peace and good order on this solemn occasion, it is therefore proposed to adjourn this Monthly Meeting."[2]

As Howe approached Philadelphia, the Continental Congress, which was preparing to remove to Lancaster, recommended the disarmament and arrest of all persons suspected of British leanings. Moreover, " the several testimonies which have been published since the commencement of the present contest between Great Britain and America, and the uniform tenor of the conduct and conversation of a number of persons of considerable wealth, who profess themselves to belong to the Society of people commonly called Quakers, render it certain and notorious that these persons are, with much rancour and bitterness, disaffected to the American cause ; that, as these persons will have it in their power, so there is no doubt it will be their inclination to communicate intelligence

[1] " In the later years of the war the Government paper was at a discount of three hundred, seven hundred, and at last of a thousand to one " (Sir G. Trevelyan, *George the Third and Charles Fox*, i. 301). The passage gives a vivid account of the evils of depreciation.

[2] " The Quakers alone gave no sign of perturbation and calmly pursued their ordinary avocations, amidst the general panic and flurry. It seemed (said an American writer) as if, in their aversion to all military operations, they regarded even running away, that very material part of battle, as opposed to the principles of their Society " (Trevelyan, *American Revolution*, iv. 368).

to the enemy, and in various other ways, to injure the counsels and arms of America." In accordance with this resolution, about forty leading Quakers and Episcopalians were arrested, and their houses and private papers searched for evidence of treason. The records of the Meeting for Sufferings were also confiscated to be examined by Congress for matter of a political nature. Parole was offered to the suspects, on condition that they remained within their houses. All the Quakers, and some others, refused the offer. "They said they had committed no offence, and that it was an outrage to throw citizens into jail without a charge and present a test to them as if they had ever been guilty of misconduct."[1]

Among those arrested were Israel and James Pemberton, Samuel Fisher, Henry Drinker, Thomas Gilpin, and John Hunt. The last-named was one of the two English Friends sent out by the London Meeting for Sufferings to advise in the Assembly difficulties of 1756, who subsequently settled in Philadelphia. In the charges levelled against the Quakers, Congress relied mainly on the publications of the Yearly Meeting and the Meeting for Sufferings, particularly that of December 1776, which was interpreted as preaching sedition. These papers were published by order of Congress over the signature of Charles Thomson, Secretary, and with them another document, always afterwards known among Friends as the "Spanktown forgery." This, it was said, had been found by General Sullivan among the British baggage captured on Staten Island ; it consisted of notes on the disposition of the American troops, headed, "Information from Jersey, 19th August, 1777," and signed, "Spanktown Yearly Meeting." The paper was claimed by the more violent revolutionaries as proof positive of a treasonable connection between the British forces and official Quakerism. Its origin was never discovered, but Friends had no difficulty in showing it to be a clumsy fabrication. It mentioned the landing of General Howe, which did not take place until August 22nd, three days after the supposed date of the information, and the signature, "Spanktown Yearly Meeting," was unlike that of any official document of Friends. Moreover, there was no such body as "Spanktown" Yearly Meeting, although a Quarterly Meeting was held at Rahway, part of which town was sometimes known as Spanktown.

But it was much less easy for the suspects to regain their

[1] Sharpless, *Quakers in the Revolution*, p. 154.

liberty. The responsibility for the arrest seemed to be divided between Congress and the Supreme Council of Pennsylvania. To both bodies the prisoners as a whole, and the Quakers in particular, addressed remonstrances. Another was sent to the Council signed on behalf of the Yearly Meeting by more than a hundred Friends. In this they declared : " We are led out of all wars and fightings by the principles of grace and truth in our own minds by which we are restrained either as private members of society, or in any of our meetings, from holding a correspondence with either army, but are concerned to spread the testimony of truth and peaceable doctrines of Jesus Christ, . . . and we deny in general terms all charges and insinuations which in any degree clash with this our profession." The prisoners were equally emphatic. James Pemberton, Clerk of the Meeting for Sufferings, one of those on whom suspicion fell most heavily, wrote later to Robert Morris : " I have never had at any time the least correspondence with General Howe or any British commander or others concerned in the military operations against America, nor do I intend to have." In an " Address to the people of Pennsylvania," the prisoners defended the Meeting for Sufferings document of December 1776 : " The testimony of the Quakers is against all wars and fightings, and against entering into military engagements of any kind ; surely, then, it was the right of the representatives of that Society to caution their members from engaging in anything contrary to their religious principles."

The Council, however, ordered those arrested to take an oath or affirmation of allegiance to the State and, in the event of their refusal, to be deported to Winchester, Virginia. In spite of the protests of the prisoners, their families, and friends, no trial was held, no evidence offered, and no formal accusation brought against them. They were hurried away ; but with indomitable perseverance they applied to Chief Justice McKean for writs of Habeas Corpus. These were granted by him and served during the journey on the military escort, but the latter refused to obey. The exiles aptly quoted a sentence from an address by Congress to the British nation in 1774 : " We hold it essential to English liberty that no man be condemned unheard, or punished for a supposed offence without having an opportunity of making his defence."

In all, twenty suspected " Loyalists " were deported, of whom seventeen were Quakers. They kept a careful and methodical diary of their experiences, from which and from the artless pages of

Elizabeth Drinker's *Journal* (she, the wife of one exiled Friend, was forced to stay in Philadelphia) a vivid impression can be gathered of their fluctuating hopes and fears. On the whole, after the first illegal haste, they were well treated, given a fairly wide parole, allowed to worship with local Friends and, at their own expense, to choose their lodgings. But they were hurried away without sufficient preparations to meet the winter. In March 1778 Thomas Gilpin, an elderly man, died of pneumonia, and soon afterwards John Hunt succumbed to blood-poisoning. The authorities relented, and in April the remaining Friends were allowed to return. Though the Council decided that " the whole expenses of arresting and confining the prisoners sent to Virginia, the expenses of their journey, and all other incidental charges, be paid by the said prisoners," yet a half-apology was made, inasmuch as the escort was ordered to treat them " with that polite attention and care which is due from men who act on the purest motives to gentlemen whose stations in life entitle them to respect, however much they may differ in political sentiment from those in whose power they are."

Their friends in Pennsylvania had been working hard for their release. After the battle of Germantown in October 1777, a committee appointed by Yearly Meeting visited both armies to explain to Washington and General Howe the basis of their testimony for peace. They were well received, and convinced Washington that the Spanktown document was a forgery and that they were innocent of any treasonable intent. Years later, when Washington was President, he met again one of the deputation, Warner Mifflin, cousin of his general, and inquired : " Mr. Mifflin, will you now please tell me on what principle you were opposed to the Revolution ? " " Yes, Friend Washington, upon the principle that I should be opposed to a change in the present Government. All that was ever secured by Revolution is not an adequate compensation for the poor mangled soldiers, and for the loss of life and limb." " I honour your sentiments," replied Washington, " for there is more in them than mankind has generally considered." In fact, Washington's treatment of Friends was invariably courteous and considerate, and on their part was repaid by esteem. When four of the prisoners' wives visited Valley Forge, to plead for their husbands, they had nothing but praise to give to their reception by the general and his wife, while he, in private letters to his subordinates, secured concessions for the anxious women. " Humanity," he wrote, " pleads strongly on their behalf."

Meanwhile the lot of Friends in Pennsylvania had been far from comfortable. If the Loyalists of Philadelphia had welcomed the advent of the British troops, the views of the quiet Quakers, at any rate, were soon changed by their behaviour. The soldiers were drunken and riotous, and the officers introduced a rout of balls, theatres, and card-playing which transformed the city and, as the meetings sorrowfully admitted, led away some of their own younger members. In the country districts, still held by the Americans, Friends endured many fines and imprisonments for their refusal to take part in the war.

When in the late spring the British Army withdrew and the American troops under Benedict Arnold entered the city, political power was seized by extremists, mostly of the old " Presbyterian " party. Moderate men, even those as deeply attached to the American cause as General Mifflin and Robert Morris, were insulted and molested, while their old enemies set to work to make life as uncomfortable as possible to any Quaker. It was not surprising that in times of rejoicing for victory their unlighted windows were broken, or that in times of anxiety the mob threatened to hang all Quakers and Tories. But those in power went further than this. Two Friends who were undoubtedly guilty of overt acts against the Government were hung on the charge of high treason, as scapegoats for more dangerous men who had followed the British into safety.

One, Abraham Carlisle, a carpenter, had been employed by the British to give out passes through the military lines between the city and the countryside. It was admitted that he had discharged his business well and he claimed that he had undertaken it in the hope of in some degree alleviating the sufferings of war. The other, John Roberts, a country miller, had been deeply stirred by the treatment of the Virginia exiles. He was so carried away by indignation that he went to the British headquarters and entreated Howe to send out a rescue party to intercept the prisoners on their journey to Virginia. The proposal was not accepted, but, having thus burnt his boats, Roberts took shelter with the British and was accused of acting as guide to their foraging parties. Both cases aroused much sympathy ; petitions for reprieve were sent in signed by many citizens, even by the judges and jurors concerned in the trials.

Friends had officially warned both men against their course of action, and they were considered to have lost their membership by disregarding the warning. The Meeting for Sufferings, therefore, did not intervene on their behalf, but Friends paid frequent visits to them in prison before their execution. They were found to be in a resigned and religious frame of mind, admitting the errors of their conduct. There were other more innocent sufferers. Not only were houses and farms plundered and laid waste, but in addition to the distraints for war purposes the test of allegiance imposed in 1778 weighed heavily on Friends. " Shortly after the return of the exiles, they themselves largely participating, the Meeting for Sufferings issued another minute, not less objectionable from the patriotic standpoint than any which had preceded it, urging Friends to subscribe to no tests, and to give no aid to the war."[1]

The test was exacted of all teachers, with the consequence that Friends' schools were seriously crippled. In spite of a petition from the Meeting for Sufferings, that the Assembly should respect the old tradition under which Pennsylvania had been an " asylum for tender consciences," several Friends were imprisoned for nearly a year in Lancaster gaol on account of these tests. The most flagrant case was that of a little company of Friends on the frontier at Catawissa. The district was harassed by Indian raids stirred up by the British, but the Quakers were unmolested. This was considered clear proof of guilty collusion with the Indians. The two settlers, Moses Roberts and Job Hughes, were arrested and taken in irons to Lancaster, where for months they lay imprisoned, while their wives and families were evicted from the farms and reduced to hard straits. Yet, on the other hand, another Quaker frontiersman, old Benjamin Gilbert and his family, were carried off as prisoners by a tribe of Indians fighting for the British. After enduring excessive hardships they were brought to Montreal, and exchanged, but the old man succumbed to the treatment he had undergone.[2] The

---

[1] *Quakers in the Revolution*, p. 177.

[2] To this instance of Indian troubles and those given in earlier chapters, may be added the following : " Just prior to the Revolutionary War the Quaker frontier in Georgia began to waver somewhat on account of the Indian troubles, and meetings were held irregularly. The climax came when Tamar Kirk Mendenhall and her eldest son were killed by the Indians and the youngest son held in captivity for about two years. It is probable, however, that in this case also that these Friends did not uphold the usual Quaker testimony of fearlessness and

repeated protests by the Meeting for Sufferings concerning the harsh treatment meted out to many Friends at last stirred the Assembly's Committee of Grievances to take up the matter. A set of test questions on the views of Friends as to the authority of the American Government was sent to the Meeting for answer, and it was asked to supply the Committee with copies of all published Epistles and Testimonies during the past seven years. The Meeting, in a written reply, declined to answer the questions on the ground that, as their gatherings were not political, such matters could not be discussed in them. Friends always, however, maintained a testimony against war, and on that account could not join actively in " measures which tend to create or promote disturbances or commotions in the government under which we are placed ; and many of our brethren, from a conviction that war is so opposite to the nature and spirit of the Gospel, apprehend it their duty to refrain in any degree from voluntarily contributing to its support." Such a reply was unlikely to conciliate governmental opinion in their favour, unless by its very candour.

Meanwhile the Society went steadily on in the maintenance of its testimonies, and disowned those who, in any way, fell below its standard, whether for laxity of conduct, for slave-holding, or for warlike activities. Among the disowned were some who still clung to the Quaker doctrines and Quaker modes of worship, and who could not feel at home in any other Church. But they had separated themselves too deeply from the Society and with too full a conviction of justification to return.

" They served actively in the armies on the American side, they appeared in the Committee of Public Safety, they were seated in the legislature, they were concerned in the printing of the Continental money."[1]

Samuel Wetherill, for instance, a minister among Friends, in 1778 not only took the oath of allegiance, but supplied Washington's destitute army at Valley Forge with a much-needed consignment

---

trust, as they had retreated from their homesteads earlier in the year, and had returned to gather the ripened grain. . . . It would seem . . . that the safety of Friends lay in the consistent attitude of peace, that set them apart in the eyes of the savages " (Kelsey, *Friends and the Indians*, p. 73).

[1] *History of the Religious Society of Friends, Called by some the Free Quakers,* by Charles Wetherill (Philadelphia, 1894, privately printed). This is a spirited vindication by the descendant of one of the original " Fighting Quakers " of the action of his ancestor and his associates.

of cloth from his own factory. He was disowned in 1779. In 1780 he and others of the disowned Friends formed themselves into a little Society, meeting for worship at the houses of its members. Among these were Timothy Matlock, a member of the Committee of Public Safety, one of the few disowned Quakers who used his influence in public life openly against his orthodox brethren, Colonel Clement Biddle, Gates' quartermaster at Valley Forge, Peter Thomson, printer of the Continental money, Lydia Darragh, who during the British occupation of Philadelphia warned Washington of a projected sortie by the enemy, and Betsy Ross (later Claypole), a needlewoman, to whom tradition points as the maker of the first Stars and Stripes. The little body, which claimed to be the true Society of Friends, but which was generally known as the " Free Quakers," drew up a constitution or discipline of more than Quaker simplicity. There was to be no creed, no testimonies, no heresies ; " no one who believed in God should be excommunicated or disowned for any cause whatever," moral or theological. Self-defence, and military service in " defensive war," were expressly permitted. A few other small meetings in Chester County, Maryland, and Massachusetts, were affiliated to the main body. When this handful of about a hundred persons claimed, on the grounds of its essential Quakerism, an equal share in the use of the Philadelphia meeting-houses and burial grounds, a difficult situation arose. From 1781 to 1783 the Free Quakers made several applications to the legislature, asking it to intervene in the matter, and charging their old Society with treason. The Assembly was not unsympathetic, but the whole procedure of Friends in the disownments had been so regular that there was no pretext for intervention. The Meeting for Sufferings in February 1782 explained to the Assembly that the Society had " power to accept or reject particular members according to the suitableness or the unsuitableness of their conduct with its doctrines and rules . . . nor are any prohibited from assembling with us in our meetings for public worship which, it is well known, are held openly and free to all sober people." Any member, on the other hand, was equally at liberty to leave them and join himself to any other people. Some of the disowned themselves addressed the Assembly, explaining that they acquiesced in the justice of their disownments and wished for no interference with Friends. Nicholas Waln, formerly an acute lawyer, but by this time a pillar of the Society, did it good service before the Commission of Inquiry. When some of the malcontents entered the room, he turned to one with the question : "What wast thou disowned for ? " The ex-Friend, whose difference of opinion had arisen on the question of cock-fighting, hesitated and would not reply. The process was gone through in the case of one or two others disowned on similar grounds, and the Commissioners were able to infer that the petitioners had not all left the Society from motives of pure patriotism.

Disappointed in this attempt, the Free Quakers raised funds to build a meeting-house, to which both Washington and Franklin subscribed. It is still standing at the corner of Fifth and Arch Streets, Philadelphia, with an inscription stating that it was built " in the year of the Empire 8," because, as one of its founders prophesied, " our country is destined to be the great empire over all this world." But gradually the first impulse died away ; some of the original members repented and again joined Friends, other died, others moved out of the city, and the meeting dwindled rapidly. After the death of Samuel Wetherhill, its Clerk, in 1816, it had little vitality. His grandson, John Price Wetherhill, " after worshipping almost alone for several years, closed the Meeting." The building was let on lease, and to this day the descendants of its founders meet once a year to apportion its revenue to religious and charitable uses.

The Revolutionary War left a deep mark on American character and manners, and the Society of Friends could not go unchanged through the ordeal. A recent historian says that Philadelphia Yearly Meeting came out of the struggle " more moral internally, more devoted to moral reforms, more conservative of ancient tradition, custom, and doctrine, more separate from the world, more introversive in spirit."[1] The testimonies against war and slavery had gained in fearlessness and decision, and added to these was a new and growing interest in temperance and in the religious education of their children. On the other hand, the unpopularity of the Quaker position had thrown the body, as it were, back upon itself. For years after the war they had little intercourse with other denominations, and the unhappy divisions which occurred in the Society in America during the earlier nineteenth century may have been intensified by this exclusiveness. Yet the troubles of the period had left some gains behind. To quote again from the same writer : " They undoubtedly felt that though they had suffered much in popular esteem they

[1] Sharpless in *Quakers in American Colonies*, p. 579.

had steered through a very troubled sea of war and confusion on a straight line of principle. . . . The years following the war were the years of the greatest increase in the number of meetings, and probably of members, which had been seen in Pennsylvania since the early years of the settlement."[1]

The Society never by word or deed repented of the course it had taken. In fact, even in their formal reconciliation with the new Government, the Friends re-asserted their position, and its chief magistrate, while regretting, accepted it. This *apologia* was made in 1789, when Washington was President. The Yearly Meeting, under Nicholas Waln as Clerk, presented him with an address of respectful congratulation on his election as President, expressing gratitude for the free toleration of religious opinion under the new Government, and adding, " we feel our hearts affectionately drawn towards thee." As for themselves, " with a full persuasion that the divine principle we profess leads into harmony and concord, we can take no part in any warlike measures on any occasion or under any power, but we are bound in conscience to lead quiet and peaceable lives in godliness and honesty among men, contributing freely our proportion to the indigencies of the poor and to the necessary support of civil government." Washington's reply was one of courteous thanks for their good wishes. Liberty of conscience, he declared, he had always considered a right, not a privilege. " Your principles and conducts are well known to me, and it is doing the people called Quakers no more than justice to say that (except their declining to share with others in the burdens of common defence) there is no denomination among us who are more exemplary and useful citizens. I assure you very especially that in my opinion the conscientious scruples of all men should be treated with great delicacy and tenderness ; and it is my wish and desire that the laws may always be extensively accommodated to them as a due regard to the protection and essential interest of the nation may justify."

Washington was not in the habit of using empty phrases, and the sincerity of this judgment is confirmed from another source. Brissot de Warville, later one of the most idealistic of the Girondins, spent the years 1783 to 1789 in America in the interests of " Les Amis des Noirs," the French opponents of the slave-trade. He was naturally thrown much among the Philadelphia Quakers, whose virtues and eccentricities he described in enthusiastic but slightly

[1] *Quakers in the Revolution*, pp. 203-4.

inaccurate detail. On one occasion Washington discussed the sect with him. " He declared to me that, in the course of the war, he had entertained an ill opinion of this Society ; he knew but little of them, as at that time there were but few of that sect in Virginia, and he had attributed to their political sentiments the effect of their religious principles. He told me that having since known them better he acquired an esteem for them ; and that, considering the simplicity of their manners, the purity of their morals, their exemplary economy, and their attachment to the constitution, he considered this Society as one of the best supports of the new government."[1]

A patriotism which satisfied Washington is not in urgent need of defence.

[1] Brissot de Warville, *New Travels in America* (English edition, 1794), p. 357.

CHAPTER XVI

THE UNITED STATES

THE first half of the nineteenth century was a time of trial for American Friends. The separation between " Orthodox " and " Hicksite " Friends in 1827–8 was followed by minor secessions, and much of the energy of the Society was expended in discussions of theology and Church organization. In Ohio, the separation, which took place at the Yearly Meeting of 1828, was attended by scenes of disorder and even violence, due mainly to non-Friends partisans of the " Hicksites " (described by the Orthodox as " a rude rabble ") who forced their way into the meeting.[1] These separations not only split the Society into smaller and weaker bodies, but acted (in the strong words of a group of American Friends) as " a moral blight," which made " ineffective and apparently insincere our peace efforts. . . . If we would preach peace, harmony, and unity among the nations, we must be able to answer the query that love and unity are maintained among us.[2]

Another difficulty during the same period was the steady westward emigration of Friends from the east and south. Those from slave States especially were attracted to the new lands, and sometimes whole meetings migrated in a body. " About two-thirds of all the Friends in the world are in the United States, west of the Alleghanies."[3] Friends had cleared themselves of the reproach of slaveholding and, though the official bodies continued to petition legislatures, and individuals did much for the slave, the political abolition movement was looked on at first with disfavour. Neverthe-

---

[1] For the history of these divisions *vide* Thomas, *History of Friends in America*, ch. v ; E. Grubb, *Separations : Their Causes and Effects*, 1914 ; Rufus Jones, *Later Periods of Quakerism*, chaps. xii and xiii. The names are given to the two bodies by popular usage, but are not adopted by them.

[2] *Conference of All Friends*, 1920, Report of (American) Commission V. 30.

[3] Thomas, *History of Friends in America*, p. 195.

less many Friends, among them Whittier, worked unceasingly and courageously in the cause.[1]

In another direction Friends maintained their old work. The burden of Indian welfare lay heavy on their hearts, and by negotiations in the cruel wars between Indian and white man, by settlements of Friends among the various tribes to give them religious teaching and to instruct them in farming and handicrafts, and by the foundation of schools they did what they could to reconcile the red man to the new civilization which was overwhelming him. Practically all the Yearly Meetings formed committees for this purpose. Gradually, as the control of Indian affairs passed into the hands of the Government, these Committees had often to approach the President and Executive on behalf of their clients, and eventually this intercourse led to a wider development of the Quaker work.[2]

For many years there was comparatively little opportunity for Quaker testimony against war. Since 1784, in several States, Quakers had been specifically exempted from serving in the militia, but after the war of 1812, in Virginia at least, the old penalties of fine and imprisonment for not bearing arms were re-imposed. The Yearly Meeting of Virginia in 1816 sent up a protest to the State legislature, drawn up and signed by Benjamin Bates, clerk to the Meeting. He also sent a letter to Hay, a member of the legislature. Both these were reproduced in *Niles' Register* (a Baltimore weekly) in November 1816, with the remark that they were a body of " the ablest arguments that have ever appeared in defence of certain principles held by this people."[3] This particular law was amended, but heavy distraints are recorded by Virginia Friends in many subsequent years, until their union with Baltimore Yearly Meeting in 1844. In North Carolina a Militia law of 1830 tried to exact a fine from Quakers, in lieu of military service, the proceeds of which were to be used for education. The Friends objected that they were willing to be taxed for the State schools, but this was " a groundless and oppressive demand. It is a muster tax in disguise and violates

[1] For details *vide* Rufus Jones, *Later Periods*, ch. xv.

[2] A full account is found in Kelsey, *Friends and the Indians* (published by the Associated Executive Committee of Friends on Indian Affairs, Philadelphia, 1917).

[3] *Vide* Weeks, *Southern Quakers*, p. 196 ; *Friends' Miscellany*, vii. In the *Memorial* the Virginia Friends declare that they " ask permission only to practise the doctrines of Jesus Christ." An Indiana Monthly Meeting memorialized the State Legislature in 1810, but Friends suffered from distraints during the war (R. Jones, *Later Periods*, p. 423).

the very principle which it seems to respect." In 1832 the law was repealed, and as at this period several States abolished militia drills and practically disbanded the State militia, the position of Friends was distinctly eased. During Indian troubles in the years from 1810 to 1813 the Friend pioneers in Ohio and Indiana took strict measures against violations of the peace testimony. Many were disowned for training in the militia, paying fines, or providing substitutes. In Indiana a man was disowned who went into a fort for protection and, after " dealing," was " not inclined to condemn his conduct."[1]

The reaction from the war of 1812 and from the greater war in Europe, of which it was an offshoot, led, almost at the time when the English Peace Society was founded, to the independent formation of similar Societies in America.[2]   But, as at all times of the Society's history, the quiet personal testimony of individual Friends to their trust in the way of peace did most to convince the world of their sincerity. The *Journal* of Joseph Hoag, a Vermont Friend in 1812, contains an instance of such testimony which recalls the quaint simplicity of Chalkley, a hundred years earlier. There was war not only with the British, but with the Indians, and Hoag was travelling in Tennessee when the frontier of the State was enduring attack. At Knoxville the traveller, in his unmistakable Quaker garb, breakfasted in the public room of the hotel in company with a number of officers, among them a General. The story is told in his own words :

" The sergeants made their returns to the General, that they had warned every man that the law required to do military duty, Quakers and all, and there had not one Quaker appeared on the ground. In the meantime the General looked sharply at me, as I was walking the room, and said : ' Well, we have lost a number of our frontier inhabitants, and some of our soldiers ; and a people who would not defend the frontier inhabitants when the savages were destroying and scalping them, could not be considered friends to their country, and should have no favour from him.' He then said : ' How do you like this doctrine, stranger ? ' I answered, ' It is no doctrine for me ; I have little or no opinion of it.' " The

    [1] Rufus Jones, *Later Periods*, pp. 423 foll., 721.
    [2] Channing was a protagonist in the movement. The New York Peace Society and that of Ohio were founded in 1815, those of Massachusetts and Philadelphia in the following year. The American Peace Society was established in 1828.

General, unused to such opposition, asked : 'Why?' And Hoag explained that the Quaker position was taken up in obedience to the commands of Christ, to whom they owed supreme allegiance.

"The General sat down, but soon rose with these words : ' I am not going to give up the argument so ; I see by the look of your eye that you are no coward ; you are a soldier ; and if an Indian were to come into your house to kill your wife and children, you would fight.' I answered : ' As for cowardice, I ever despised it,' but, pointing toward the guns standing in the house, with bayonets on them, and looking him full in the face, added : ' General, it would take twelve such men as thou art—and then you would not do it—to make me take hold of a gun or pistol to take the life of a fellow creature.'

"He turned and sat down, but not long, and said : ' I will bring you to the point. If an Indian were to come into your house, with his knife and tomahawk, and you knew he would kill you, your wife, and children, and you knew you could kill him and save all your lives, you would kill him ; if you did not, you would be guilty of the death of the whole.'

"I thought it time to look for a close, and told him . . . I should keep him to the Christian platform or creed laid down by Jesus Christ ; and that he would not deny that a Christian was fit to live or die. I then told him I would give the subject a fair statement, and he might judge. I proceeded thus : I shall state that myself and wife are true Christians and our children are in their minority —and thou knowest it is natural for children to believe what their parents teach them—and therefore we are all true Christians, as far as our several capacities enable us to be. And now the question lies here : ' Which is most like the precepts and example of our King—the Author of the Christian religion—to lay down our lives and all go to heaven together, or kill that Indian and send him into *eternity*, for he must be wicked to kill a family that would not hurt him ? General, it is a serious thing to take the lives of those who are not prepared to die ; they have no chance to come back and mend their ways, and thou dost not know but that if that Indian was spared, he might feel remorse enough to make him repent so as to find forgiveness.[1] . . . And that is not all, General : when I killed that Indian, I embrued my hands in human blood. . . . Canst thou make thyself believe that I stand as good a chance to get

[1] Cp. Chalkley's argument, p. 321.

to heaven as to die when my hands were clean and I innocent of human blood ? And, General, we find Jesus Christ had one soldier among his followers, who drew his sword and fought like a valiant for his Lord. But what then said his Lord ? " Put up again thy sword into his place : for all they that take the sword shall perish with the sword." General, thou wilt do well to remember that saying ; it is the word of a King.'

" The General made no answer, but sat and hung his head for some time. One of the company at length replied : ' Well, stranger, if all the world was of your mind, I would turn and follow after.' I replied : ' So then thou hast a mind to be the last man in the world to be good. I have a mind to be one of the first, and set the rest the example.' This made the General smile. . . . After a little discourse, the General said : ' Well, stranger, there are a great many of your sort of people in this State.' I answered : ' Yes, and I hope thou finds them an honest, industrious, peaceable people ; good inhabitants to populate and clear up a new country and make it valuable.'

" He said, ' Yes, they are an industrious, harmless people.' We were both on our feet ; I turned and looked him full in the face, and spoke with some emphasis : ' General, canst thou say then an honest, industrious people, who will harm nobody, are enemies to their country ? '

" He paused awhile and said : ' No ; and they shall have my protection, and you have the word of a General for it.'

" I then felt easy that all was done that could be done. I had the same man's word who *had said* : ' No favour should be shown to the Quakers ' *now* pledge his honour to protect them.

" After some more conversation we parted very pleasantly."

Hoag is remembered as the author of two remarkable predictions or visions of the Civil War. Of their authenticity there is no doubt, as they were both recorded years before their fulfilment. In 1820 he was riding with a friend in Pennsylvania when he reined his horse and, looking at the ground, exclaimed : " My horse's feet are wading in blood, even to the fetlocks." They were riding across the ground on which his countrymen poured out their blood at Gettysburg, forty-three years later. The other vision, which came to him in 1803,[1] was more elaborate. He saw a spirit of separation

---

[1] It was circulated in manuscript many years before it was first printed in 1854, *vide Friends' Intelligencer*, 1915, p. 741.

and schism disturbing all the Churches, including his own Society—
as was actually the case in 1827. Next, the spirit " entered politics
throughout the United States, and produced a civil war, and an
abundance of human blood was shed in the course of the combat.
The Southern States lost their power, and slavery was annihilated
from their borders." So far the prediction was striking enough,
but the conclusion of the vision, in which Hoag saw his country
under the power of a monarch and an established church, still shows
no signs of fulfilment.

Another episode, which made some stir, was the election of
a Quaker to the Major-Generalship of the Maine militia. Eli Jones
was returned in 1854 to the Maine Assembly. The position was
uncongenial, and though he fulfilled his duties faithfully, he never
spoke in the House. His fellow legislators, who respected him
as a man of character and ability, determined to force a speech from
him. The Maine militia was a body which had been in existence
some twenty years, but had never seen service—in fact, it was a
standing joke in the State. When the office of Major-General fell
vacant in 1855, it seemed that to elect a Quaker to the position
would put a fresh edge on the jest. Whether Eli Jones accepted
or declined nomination, he must speak, and a large audience of
his fellow members and of the public assembled to hear him. But
the Quaker was equal to the occasion. He opened in a strain of
good-humoured banter, saying that his election was one of the
phenomena of a phenomenal year. He continued, with an undercurrent of serious meaning :

" It is generally understood that I entertain peculiar views in
respect of the policy of war. If, however, I am an exponent of the
views of the legislature on that subject, I will cheerfully undertake
to serve the State in the capacity indicated. I shall stand before the
militia and give such orders as I think best. The first would be :
' Ground arms.' The second would be : ' Right about face ;
beat your swords into ploughshares, and your spears into pruning
hooks, and learn war no more.' I should then dismiss every man
to his farm and to his merchandise, with an admonition to read daily
at his fireside the New Testament, and ponder upon its tidings
of Peace on Earth, Good Will towards men." But, he added, he
felt that his election was in advance of the times. " With pleasure
I now surrender to the House this trust and the honour, and retire
to private life."

The speech was reprinted widely in the American, and even in the English Press. Such incidents served to remind men that the Quaker still held his ancient faith, but for nearly half a century these convictions were untested. The Mexican War of 1846–8 was fought by the regular army and by volunteers, and though Friends, in common with some of the United States' best citizens, viewed it with abhorrence as a campaign of conquest against a weak and semi-civilized race, yet they could do nothing more than put their protest upon record.[1]

In the years 1855 and 1856 Friends joined with other opponents of slavery in the migrations to Kansas, which aimed at securing that great territory as a free State. These settlers were harassed and terrorized by raiders from the bordering slave States. One Friend (William H. Coffin) has left us a candid account of his weakness before the prospect of a murderous attack. " My education was such I could not with conscience kill a man ; but when I got to reasoning with myself about my duty in the protection of my family, my faith gave way. I had an excellent double-barrelled gun, and I took it outdoors and loaded it heavily with buckshot. . . . I barred the door and set my gun handy, . . . but I could get no sleep. . . . Finally, towards midnight I got up, wife and children peacefully sleeping, drew the loads from my gun and put it away ; and then, on my knees, I told the Lord all about it and asked his protection, . . . went to bed, was soon asleep, and slept till sun-up next morning."[2] The raiders, meanwhile, met with resistance elsewhere which diverted their route, and the house was not attacked.

John Brown was one of the anti-slavery leaders in these Kansas struggles. He was on terms of friendship with some Kansas Quakers and others in Springfield, Iowa, and in the final scene at Harper's Ferry, Virginia, in 1859, two Quaker brothers, Edwin and Barclay Coppoc, from Iowa, were members of his band. Edwin had already been disowned for warlike activities ; he was executed for his share in the expedition. Barclay was later disowned because " he has neglected the attendance of our religious meetings and is in the practice of bearing arms."[3]

---

[1] The view of the opponents of the war was put with incomparable wit and indignant force by Lowell in the *Biglow Papers*. The Philadelphia and New England Meetings for Sufferings both memorialized Congress against the war, and the Quaker journals expressed vigorous condemnation of it.

[2] Kansas Historical Collections, vii. 334–5, quoted in *Later Periods of Quakerism*, p. 848.   [3] *Later Periods of Quakerism*, p. 852.

The Civil War shook the nation to its very foundations. Here we must only consider that great and bloody struggle—the most costly in men and money known to modern civilization until the recent European catastrophe—in its effect on the Society of Friends. The sufferings of Friends in the Confederate territory require separate notice. The pages immediately following only refer to the position of Quakers in the Northern States.

What has been written of John Bright in an earlier chapter may be applied with little modification to the attitude of American Friends of all branches. They ardently desired the extinction of slavery, and on the constitutional question the majority also naturally upheld the North. But it must not be forgotten that for nearly two years the Northern Government did not declare openly for abolition, and many feared that even victory and the restoration of the Union would involve the maintenance of the " peculiar institution " in the South. Whittier's poems give expression to this fear. In one, *A Word for the Hour*, he uttered the feeling of many Friends that a fratricidal war was too great a price to pay for re-union, and that it were better to leave the slave States to struggle with their own burden.

> They break the links of Union : shall we light
> The fires of hell to weld anew the chain
> On that red anvil where each blow is pain ?
> Draw we not even now a freer breath
> As from our shoulders falls a load of death,
>
> .   .   .   .   .   .
>
> Why take we up the accursed thing again ?

When the issue was definitely taken, Whittier, with other Friends, rejoiced that even by such means freedom came, and their long prayers were granted.

> Not as we hoped, in calm of prayer,
> The message of deliverance comes,
> But heralded by roll of drums
> On waves of battle-troubled air.
>
> Not as we hoped ;—but what are we ?
> Above our broken dreams and plans
> God lays, with wiser hand than man's,
> The corner-stone of liberty.[1]

[1] *Astræa at the Capitol.*

So, too, in the exultant *Laus Deo !* and *The Peace Autumn*
he hailed the work of those " who died to make the slave a man."
It was this hereditary passion for freedom, added to the natural
forces of patriotism and public opinion, which produced once more
groups of " Fighting Quakers." A considerable number of young
Friends joined the Northern army, and some of their elders were
concerned with military supplies and other war activities.   A
" Hicksite " Friend, James Sloan Gibbons, wrote one of the war-
songs of the North : " We are coming, Father Abraham," and the
15th Pennsylvania Regiment, led by a " Hicksite " Friend, Colonel
Palmer, was known as the " Quaker " regiment, since most of the
officers and a proportion of the privates belonged to their leader's
sect.   In the North-West and Middle-West the Quaker meetings
were largely made up of emigrants from the Slave States and their
children.   It was from those newly settled meetings that the largest
proportion enlisted during the war. Of the actual numbers throughout all the Yearly Meetings there is no quite certain estimate.   It
was said of the Quakers of Indiana, that in proportion to their numbers
they had more soldiers in the war for the Union than any other
religious denomination.   Yet, in fact, at Indiana Yearly Meeting
of 1862, five Monthly Meetings reported that a hundred of their
members had volunteered, and the remaining ten meetings had
" a considerable number " serving. If this number even reached
two hundred, the total would only be three hundred soldiers out
of a membership of twenty thousand.[1]   In other Yearly Meetings
the records show much fewer instances, " very few volunteers
appearing in rural sections, and more in city meetings." [2]   For

---

[1] The remark was made by Senator G. W. Julian, of Indiana, in 1895 (Weekes,
Southern Quakers, p. 306).   Recently it has been reasserted as if applying to all
Friends in America. Dr. Rufus Jones comments :   " There is no historical
evidence whatever to justify such a statement. The ' deviations ' from the
historical testimony were more numerous than one would have expected in a
conservative body which made the testimony an absolutely essential feature of its
faith.   But even so . . . the total number appears small " (*Later Periods of
Quakerism,* pp. 736–7).
[2] Rufus Jones, *Later Periods of Quakerism*, p. 729, also pp. 737–9 (a careful
study of the replies of Monthly Meetings during the war to the Yearly Meeting
query about compliance with military requisitions).   A good deal of information
about " Hicksite " Friends in the Civil War may be found in the *Friends'
Intelligencer* since 1909, in articles and notes by Thaddeus Kenderdine and George
D. John, both army veterans (*vide,* especially, *Intelligencer,* 1911, pp. 394, 446 ;
1913, p. 439).   Cartland, *Southern Heroes,* p. 129, remarks that " H. W.
Halleck, at one time General-in-Chief of the Armies, remained a member of the

example, New York City Monthly Meeting reported eleven volunteers in 1863, but two rural Monthly Meetings in the State, only two and three, respectively. One young Quaker officer, who lost his life near Washington, was James Parnell Jones, the son of Eli Jones, the peace advocate. In spite of such instances, however, two modern historians of American Quakerism, well qualified to give a verdict, have written [1] :

" Much has been said about the number of Friends in the army, but more than the occasion warrants. The peculiar custom which grew up of admitting the children of Friends as full members by right of birth, with all its undeniable advantages, had this drawback, that many who had never made any Christian profession were counted as Friends, and when these enlisted it was considered that they had forsaken their position, when in reality many of them had nothing but a traditional position on the subject. In many cases those who enlisted were disowned by their meetings, in many others their acknowledgment of regret was accepted, and in others no action was taken. On the other hand there were numerous instances of persons who were faithful to their testimony for peace amid much that was painful." The general impression of all who have inquired into the question of disownment for war activities is that, in the East the " Hicksite " Friends were on the whole lenient and the " Orthodox " stringent. At Philadelphia Yearly Meeting (Hicksite) in 1911 twenty veterans were present. In the West there was very little disownment by either body.[2]

meeting at Newport, Rhode Island, during the war, by an oversight caused by his removal to the West." If this was so the oversight must have been one of long standing, for Halleck had graduated from West Point in 1839, and had served with distinction in the army for many years. But the story was not accepted by Allen C. Thomas. " I feel sure it is an error," he wrote (October 1916) to Norman Penney, then Librarian of the Friends' Reference Library, Devonshire House, London.

[1] A. C. and R. H. Thomas, *History of Friends in America*, p. 177.

[2] As in England, the fact that disownment was by the Monthly Meetings, makes it almost impossible to collect full data. For confirmation of the foregoing statements, *vide Friends' Intelligencer*, 1911, p. 394 (T. Kenderdine). R. Jones, *Later Periods of Quakerism*, p. 730, says, more particularly of the Orthodox branch, that those who volunteered or paid commutation money under the draft were usually disowned " though meetings were generally lenient where the individual expressed regret for his course and desired to be reinstated." *All Friends' Peace Conference*, Report of Commission I (American), 1920, p 40, gives an instance of disownment in 1866 by New York City Monthly Meeting of a Friend volunteer " who had no regrets . . . feeling he had only done his duty."

Some of these young volunteers who remained in the Society were afterwards strong peace advocates. Like many others in the Civil War, they were of the type of citizen-soldier described by Whittier in his *Lexington* [1] :

> Their feet had trodden peaceful ways,
> They loved not strife, they dreaded pain ;
> They saw not, what to us is plain,
> That God would make man's wrath His praise.
>
> .   .   .   .   .   .
>
> They went where duty seemed to call,
> They scarcely asked the reason why ;
> They only knew they could but die,
> And death was not the worst of all !

There is no doubt that a majority of Friends, and a large majority of those in active membership, maintained a firm stand. There is no ambiguity in the utterances of the Yearly Meetings or of the representative bodies (Meetings for Sufferings) or in the editorials of the Quaker journals during the years of the war.[2] The Philadelphia Meeting for Sufferings in January 1862 published a lengthy paper repeating many of the Society's ancient " Advices " against war, and reminding Friends that " whatever peculiar circumstances attach to the war which is now waging in our land . . . the testimony of our religious Society has ever been against all wars and fightings without distinction," as being incompatible with Christianity. So New York Meeting for Sufferings declared : " The foundation of our well-known testimony against war rests

---

[1] *Lexington* was Whittier's contribution to the Centennial Celebrations of American Independence. He refused to write on Bunker's Hill, saying : " I stretched my Quakerism to the full extent of its drab in writing about the Lexington folk who were shot and did not shoot back. I cannot say anything about those who did shoot to some purpose on Bunker's Hill." Whittier's hatred of war was as deep as his enthusiasm for the heroic as revealed in war or peace. " I thank God," he wrote as a young man in 1833, " that he has given me a deep and invincible horror of human butchery," and years later : " It is only . . . when Truth and Freedom, in their mistaken zeal, and distrustful of their own powers, put on battle-harness, that I can feel any sympathy with merely physical daring." *Vide* " Whittier's Attitude towards War," by A. T. Murray in *Present Day Papers*, July 1915.

[2] These journals were *The Friend* (Philadelphia) and the *Friends' Review* (both " Orthodox "), and the *Friends' Intelligencer* (" Hicksite "). *The Friend* in 1863 exhorted the young Quakers " to confess Christ before men, saying in both language and conduct, as did the primitive believers : ' We are Christians, and therefore cannot fight.' "

upon the plain, undeniable injunctions and precepts of our Saviour, as well as the entire Spirit of the Gospel."[1]

As soon as the evil fell upon them, Friends showed a loyal desire to serve the country and to relieve the sufferings of war. In June 1861 Whittier, who held a peculiar position of influence and esteem among them, issued a circular letter " To members of the Society of Friends," in which he sounded a clear call of duty. " We have no right," he said, " to ask or expect an exemption from the chastisement which the Divine Providence is inflicting upon the nation. Steadily and faithfully maintaining our testimony against war, we owe it to the cause of truth to show that exalted heroism and generous self-sacrifice are not incompatible with our pacific principles. Our mission is, at this time, to mitigate the sufferings of our countrymen, to visit and aid the sick and wounded, to relieve the necessities of the widow and the orphan, and to practise economy for the sake of charity. . . . Our Society is rich, and of those to whom much is given, much will be required in this hour of proving and trial."[2] He repeated the appeal two years later in his fine "Anniversary Poem," written when conscription was pressing on the country.

Many Quakers, both men and women, helped in the hospitals, and even in the medical service of the battlefields, but the work they made peculiarly their own was the care of the freedmen and coloured refugees. Thousands of these had been taken prisoners by the Northern armies, and by a kindly legal fiction ser into free territory as " contraband of war," since they had bee ₁ employed by the Confederates on military works. They were temporarily settled in large camps, where Friends found a wide field of helpfulness in providing clothing, medical aid, and organizing employment and instruction.

In the dark days of December 1861, when it seemed as if England and America must be drawn into war, members of the Society put all their influence on the side of peace. The London Meeting for Sufferings forwarded a copy of its address to the British Government to the representative body of Baltimore Yearly Meeting for presentation to Lincoln. Francis T. King, one of the deputation, related afterwards that in the course of the interview the name of John Bright was mentioned.

[1] New York Meeting for Sufferings (Orthodox), 1861, quoted *All Friends' Conference*, Report of (American) Commission I, p. 24.

[2] Pickard, *Life of Whittier*, ii. 441.

" The President's countenance lighted up . . . and he said : 'Sherman, did you know that John Bright was a Quaker ? ' ' Oh, yes ! ' ' Well, I did not before. I read all his speeches, and he knows more of American politics than most of the men at the other end of the avenue (pointing to the Capitol). I appreciate his great work for us in our struggle at home.' Turning again to us, he said : ' Give me your address and I will send you an acknowledgment of the appeal. These are the first words of cheer and encouragement we have had from across the water.' " [1] In a private letter Lincoln wrote : " Engaged as I am in a great war, I fear it will be difficult for the world to understand how fully I appreciate the principles of peace inculcated in this letter and everywhere by the Society of Friends." [2] Indeed, in all his intercourse with them, Lincoln showed himself sincere and sympathetic. It is said that he never refused to receive their frequent deputations, saying : " I know *they* are not seeking office." He was himself of Quaker descent, and the mother of his War Secretary, Stanton, was an Ohio Friend. On this account, and from their leniency towards the conscientious scruples of Friends, they were dubbed by their enemies " The Quaker War Cabinet."

On more than one occasion Lincoln admitted, and indeed welcomed, a " religious visit " of prayer and exhortation from earnest Friends. One, from Eliza Gurney, widow of the English Friend Joseph John Gurney, left a deep impression on his mind. A letter which she afterwards wrote to him was found in his breast-pocket when he was assassinated nearly two years later. His reply to this letter (dated September 4, 1864) throws light on his own deepest convictions, and shows his respect for principles sincerely held.

My ESTEEMED FRIEND,

I have not forgotten—probably never shall forget—the very impressive occasion when yourself and Friends visited me on a Sabbath afternoon two years ago. Nor has your kind letter, written nearly a year later, ever been forgotten. In all it has been your purpose to strengthen my reliance upon God. I am much indebted to the good Christian people of the country for their constant prayers and consolations, and to no one of them more than yourself.

The purposes of the Almighty are perfect and must prevail, though we erring mortals may fail to accurately perceive them in advance. We

---

[1] Account quoted in Cartland, *Southern Heroes*, pp. 6–9.
[2] Nicolay and Hay, *Life of Lincoln*, vi. 328. Letter to S. B. Tobey, March 19, 1862.

hoped for a happy termination to this terrible war long before this, but God knows best and has ruled otherwise. We shall yet acknowledge His wisdom and our own error therein, and in the meantime we must work earnestly in the best light He gives us, trusting that so working still conduces to the great ends He ordains. Surely He intends some good to follow this mighty convulsion, which no mortal could make and no mortal could stay.

Your people, the Friends, have had and are having a very great trial. On principle and faith, opposed to both war and oppression, they can only practically oppose oppression by war. In this dilemma some have chosen one horn of the dilemma and some the other. For those appealing to me on conscientious grounds I have done, and shall do, what I could and can in my own conscience under my oath to the law. That you believe this I doubt not, and believing it, I shall still receive for our country and myself your earnest prayers to our Father in Heaven.

> Your sincere friend,
> A. LINCOLN.[1]

In her answer Eliza Gurney refused to admit that true Friends could choose the second horn of the dilemma. " The Saviour," she wrote, " has commanded them to love their enemies ; therefore they dare not fight them. The only victory which they as followers of the Prince of Peace can with consistency rejoice in is that which is obtained through the transforming power of the grace of God." Nevertheless, she added: " I think I may venture to say that Friends are not the less loyal for the leniency with which their honest convictions are treated, and I believe there are very few among us who would not lament to see any other than Abraham Lincoln fill the Presidential Chair, at least at the next election."

Elizabeth Comstock, an English Friend settled in the States, devoted herself to working among the negroes, the wounded of both armies, and soldiers in army prisons. On one occasion some army chaplains wished to prevent her work. She appealed direct to Lincoln, and at once received the following order : " Give Mrs. Comstock access to all hospitals, and to all inmates with whom she desires to hold religious services."

All Lincoln's good-will, however, could not entirely relieve Friends from the pressure of the " draft " or conscription. They were, indeed, at first exempted on payment of three hundred dollars, but Congress, on the ground of fairness to others, would not continue this as the need for men increased, nor was the payment officially

[1] The letter is given in facsimile in *Memoir and Correspondence of E. P. Gurney*, p. 318.

sanctioned by Friends. The Draft Act of March 1863 was enforced by Federal officials, and made all citizens between the ages of twenty and forty-five liable to service. The various bodies of Friends at once stated their position, and individual Friends, when drafted, claimed exemption. Baltimore Meeting for Sufferings took the lead on behalf of the "Orthodox" Friends (except those of Philadelphia Yearly Meeting, which conducted its own negotiations). In February 1863 it presented a brief but emphatic memorial to Congress, stating the reasons why they would neither serve nor voluntarily pay for exemption. Friends, no doubt, were indirectly protected by the general and extreme unpopularity of the drafts which led to bloody riots in New York and serious trouble in other districts. Lincoln was compelled to give orders that in these areas the draft should not be enforced, and thus, as the law was in any case laxly administered, the leniency shown to Friends was less noticed. Concurrently with the draft, recruiting with high bounties to volunteers was carried on so actively that some States were able to make up their quotas from this source. Yet, even under a lenient Government, some Friends came into the hands of the military. The Philadelphia Yearly Meeting of 1864 reported that some Friends in the past year had been arrested and imprisoned for several weeks, but eventually released on parole. Another was sent to the Army and roughly handled. Application, however, had been made to the Secretary for War, whereupon he was at once discharged and the officer responsible for his treatment punished.[1]

Perhaps the hardest experiences were those of five young New Englanders, Edward Holway and Charles Austin of Massachusetts, and Peter Dakin, Linley Macombe, and Cyrus Pringle of Vermont. The last-named kept a simple and singularly unimpassioned journal of his experiences.[2]

The three Vermont youths were drafted for service in July 1863. Peter Dakin was supported in his stand for peace by a strong minute from his Monthly Meeting : " This has been the belief of our

---

[1] *Extracts from Philadelphia Yearly Meeting Minutes*, 1864, p. 4.

[2] " The United States *versus* Pringle, The Record of a Quaker Conscience " (*The Atlantic Monthly*, February 1913). The names of the other conscripts are given in the *Friend* (Philadelphia), 1864, p. 21. This diary has been reprinted in book form, *The Record of a Quaker Conscience*, with Introduction by Rufus M. Jones. (The Macmillan Co., 1918.) Pringle had joined Friends in 1862, and apparently left them in later life. He died in 1911, after a career of some distinction as a botanist, *vide* also Ethan Foster, *Conscript Quakers*, 1883.

Society, and for its consistent maintenance for over two hundred years our members have been sufferers in different parts of the world."[1] Pringle's uncle was willing to pay for a substitute, but the young Quaker steadily refused. They were given a month's leave. "All these days we were urged by our acquaintances to pay our commutation money ; by some through well-meant kindness and sympathy ; by others through interest in the war ; by others still through a belief they entertained it was our duty." The parole expired on August 24, when, with other conscripts, they were taken to the guardroom at Brattleboro' Camp. The night before young Pringle wrote a simple expression of his faith :

> I go to-morrow where the din
> Of war is in the sulphurous air.
> I go the Prince of Peace to serve,
> His cross of suffering to bear.

After three days of confinement with fellow conscripts of a very different type they were transferred to Camp Vermont, Boston Harbour. On the journey they were marched under guard through Boston, two of the Quakers " like convicts (and feeling very much like such) " leading the company. In the camp they were not ill-treated, but their steady refusal to carry out military orders caused the officers much perplexity. The Major transferred them to the hospital tents, but they were no more willing to work there. Meanwhile their friends had been interceding for them, but could only report on September 13th that " the President, though sympathizing with those in our situation, felt bound by the Conscription Act, and felt liberty in view of his oath to execute the laws to do no more than detail us from active service to hospital duty or to the charge of the coloured refugees." The young Friends were unwilling to accept the concession, as such work was still under military control. This naturally hardened the authorities against them. They were transferred from one camp to another. At Culpepper the Colonel, who was unwilling to treat them harshly, urged them to work in the hospital tents. The boys were shaken and perplexed by his arguments ; Cyrus Pringle's own words are a typical expression of the mind of those who conscientiously object to any service under military control, and who thus present a Government with a problem not easy to solve. " Regarding the work as one of mercy and benevolence, we asked

---

[1] Rufus Jones, *Later Periods of Quakerism*, p. 734.

if we had any right to refuse its performance : and questioned whether we could do more good by endeavouring to bear to the end a clear testimony against war, than by labouring by word and deed among the needy in the hospitals and camps. We saw around us a rich field of usefulness in which there were scarce any labourers and towards whose work our hands had often started involuntarily and unbidden. At last we consented to a trial."

But after an honest attempt, the three Friends found the position impossible. Pringle writes, with unwonted strength of language, that they were " days of going down into sin." " I have received a new proof, . . . that no Friend who is really such, desiring to keep himself clear of all complicity with this system of war, and to bear a perfect testimony against it, can lawfully perform service in the hospitals of the army in lieu of bearing arms."

After their refusal to continue the hospital duty the Colonel said he would make no more effort to relieve them, adding that " a man who would not fight for his country did not deserve to live." Next day the lieutenant in charge ordered Pringle to clean a gun.

" I replied to him that I could not comply with military requisitions, and felt resigned to the consequences. ' I do not ask about your feelings ; I want to know if you are going to clean that gun.' ' I cannot do it,' was my answer. He went away, saying : ' Very well,' and I crawled into the tent again. Two sergeants soon called for me and, taking me a little aside, bid me lie down on my back, and stretching my limbs apart tied cords to my wrists and ankles, and to these four stakes driven into the ground, somewhat in the form of an X.

" I was very quiet in my mind as I lay there on the ground [soaked] with the rain of the previous day, exposed to the heat of the sun, and suffering cruelly from the cords binding my wrists and straining my muscles. And, if I dared the presumption, I should say that I caught a glimpse of heavenly pity. I wept, not so much from my own suffering, as from sorrow that such things should be in our own country, where Justice and Freedom and Liberty of Conscience have been the annual boast of Fourth-of-July orators so many years. It seemed that our forefathers in the faith had wrought and suffered in vain, when the privileges they so dearly bought were so soon set aside. And I was sad, that one endeavouring to follow our dear Master should be so generally regarded as a despicable and stubborn culprit."

After an hour of endurance, he was again asked to clean the gun and, again refusing, was left for a second hour, and then released. The sergeants threatened him with worse in the future. At this point, however, the situation changed. The three Friends, on October 6th, were summoned to report to Washington, where Isaac Newton, a Friend and an official in the department of Agriculture, had undertaken their case. He told them that both Lincoln and Stanton were anxious to prevent any further suffering. " There appeared one door of relief open—that was to parole us and allow us to go home, but subject to their call again ostensibly, though this they neither wished nor proposed to do." Until this could be arranged they were assigned to duty in a hospital, where the nursing staff were civilians and there was no question of releasing others for the fighting line. " It was hoped and expressly requested that we would consent to remain quiet and acquiesce if possible, in whatever might be required of us. . . . These requirements being so much less objectionable than we feared, we felt relief and consented to them." Surely never before did the leaders of a nation make such humble entreaty to recalcitrant citizens. But even in hospital the situation was not easy. At last Isaac Newton was able to bring their case directly before the President,[1] who immediately said : " I want you to go and tell Stanton that it is my wish all these young men be sent home at once." Newton hurried to the War Office and, while he was urging Stanton, the President entered. " It is my urgent wish," he said. The Secretary yielded and the paroles were given on November 7th. It was none too soon for Pringle, who was seriously ill. Another Friend, Henry D. Swift, of Massachusetts, refused service, except in the camp hospital. " Finally he was . . . made to witness the execution of a man, threatened with death himself, tried by court-martial and sentenced to be shot." Here, too, Lincoln intervened, and he was sent home on parole.[2]

These experiences roused Friends to take further action. On

---

[1] There was a slight delay due to an episode in which Lincoln played a characteristic part. One day when Newton had an appointment with him, he found a distracted woman trying to gain admittance. Her son, a boy of fifteen, had been enticed into the army, had deserted, and was to be shot next day. She had been told it was impossible to see the President, but Newton, postponing the claims of Pringle and the rest, carried her story to him. " That must not be," cried Lincoln, " I must look into that case before they shoot that boy," and he telegraphed to suspend the sentence.

[2] Rufus Jones, *Later Periods*, p. 735.

November 21, 1863, the Baltimore Committee reported to the Meeting for Sufferings their interview with Stanton, the Secretary for War.[1] This interview and the negotiations which followed threw into clear light the difficulties of an acceptable compromise even between Friends sincerely anxious to support the Government and a Government sincerely anxious to meet the case of Friends and other conscientious objectors. Stanton described " with much feeling and stress the embarrassment which our position caused the Government and our own Society, as well as himself personally, in his efforts to grant us exemption unconditionally, for which he had no law." He suggested a general conference by Friends to consider his proposal for their relief. This was to create a special fund for the benefit of the freedmen and to exempt Friends from military service upon the payment of $300 into this fund. The payment was not to be made, like ordinary military fines, to the local military authority, but direct to Washington, and he suggested that Friends should undertake the management and expenditure of the fund. The committee agreed to call the conference. It assembled at Baltimore on December 7, 1863, and consisted of representatives from the Meetings for Sufferings of six " Orthodox " Yearly Meetings (New England, New York, Baltimore, Ohio, Indiana, and Western). Iowa was unable to send delegates, and Philadelphia conducted its negotiations independently. The conference adopted the following minute as a clear statement of principle : " As faithful representatives of those who have appointed us, we believe it right for us first to record our united sense and judgment that Friends continue to be solemnly bound unswervingly to maintain our ancient faith and belief, that war is forbidden in the Gospel, and that as followers of the Prince of Peace we cannot contribute to its support or in any way participate in its spirit. That to render our service as an equivalent or in lieu of the requisition for military purposes is a compromise of a vital principle which we feel conscientiously bound to support under all circumstances, and notwithstanding any trials to which we may be subjected. . . . We gratefully appreciate the kindness evinced at all times by the President and Secretary for War, when we have applied to them for relief from suffering for conscience' sake, and honour them for their charity and

---

[1] The Reports (from the records of Baltimore Meeting for Sufferings) were printed in the *Bulletin of the Friends' Historical Society* (Philadelphia), March 1911, pp. 15 foll.

manifested regard for religious liberty. We have ever believed, and do without any reservation believe, in the necessity of civil government ; that it is a divine ordinance and that it is our duty to sustain it by all the influence we may exert, both by word and deed, subject to the paramount law of Christ ; and in this day of fearful strife, when so many of our fellow citizens are brought into suffering, we have no desire to shrink from the discharge of all our duty, nor from contributing to the relief of distress by every means in our power. . . . In special manner Friends have long believed it their duty to labour for the relief and freedom of the bondman. . . . In this way, and by many other means, Friends can discharge the duties of good citizenship without infringing upon our principles of peace." A small deputation was sent to Washington to interview Secretary Stanton. These Friends explained to him the opposition of the Society to any form of money commutation in lieu of military service, and added that, while its members were already working for the freemen and the wounded, they " did these things as a matter of Christian duty, and should do them whether relieved from military service or not." They added an expression of gratitude for the Secretary's own exertions in the matter. To this Stanton replied, in very plain terms :

" That he stood only as an officer to execute the laws and had nothing to do with making them ; that if their liberality released them from the drafts, the same cause would release nearly everyone, and no soldiers could be found ; that all sects and denominations, and people of every class, had shown an extended liberality, and if Friends had done more than others, it was because they were better able to do it. But he had great respect for their conscientious scruples, and should be very sorry to oppress them." He then repeated the proposal he had already made that Friends on stating to the military authorities their conscientious objections to military service should be released on payment of $300 for the freedmen's fund. " In this war there were two duties to perform by the Government, one to destroy the rebellion and the other to feed the hungry and clothe the naked freedmen. That last being a work of mercy and not of destruction might be done by Friends." The deputation told him that such a payment would be considered as infringing on the rights of conscience. To this he replied : " He could understand no such abstraction as that—that it was a work of mercy, and in accordance with the commands of Christ, and if our members did not choose to accept so liberal an offer, he could do no more for them, the law would have to take its effect. . . . If any meeting or body of Friends chose to place funds in his hands in advance, to a greater amount than would be requisite to cover all their members who would be likely to be drafted, he would receive their funds and release all such as should be drafted, and apply the funds as previously proposed. Any meeting or individual Friend might avail themselves of it." The deputation reported to the conference that the Secretary, while showing great courtesy and kindness, also spoke with much firmness. The conference did not come to any decision beyond assuring young Friends of their sympathy and urging them not to act hastily.

On the last day of the year the Meetings for Sufferings of Baltimore, New York, New England, and Ohio memorialized Congress on the Enrolment Bill, then under consideration, asking for complete exemption. Copies of the memorials were presented to every member and read both in the Senate and the House of Representatives. They were referred in each House to its Committee on Military Affairs, with which the four Quaker deputations held long interviews. " Deep interest was manifested by these Committees on our views upon war, and in the arguments and appeals for liberty of conscience and unconditional exemption from military service which were presented to them." Congress, in the hope of meeting their scruples, adopted a clause classing "members of religious denominations, who shall, by oath or affirmation, declare that they are conscientiously opposed to the bearing of arms, and who are prohibited from doing so by the rules and articles of faith and practice of such religious denominations,"[1] as non-combatants, assigning them to hospitals or freedmen's service, or exempting them upon the payment of $300 into a fund for the relief of the sick and wounded. The clause met with some vicissitudes in committee, but was finally adopted. " We feel satisfied," reported the Baltimore deputation, " that a majority of both Houses would have granted Friends unconditional exemption from military service, had they not believed it would embarrass the Government, when the draft was seriously resisted in several parts of the country."

The question of exemption and alternative service was fully debated in the Meetings and in the Quaker journals.[2] Though

[1] The text is quoted in *The Friend* (Philadelphia) 1864, p. 86.
[2] E.g. *Friend* (Philadelphia) 1864, pp. 86 foll. ; *Friends' Review*, October 1864, and *Friends' Intelligencer*, xxi. 456.

opinion was divided there was a strong body in favour of this service, and many accepted it—or, indeed, continued the work they had voluntarily assumed. Some paid the commutation, or, in the case of poorer Friends, it was paid for them by sympathizers, but this way of escape, at all events in the East, was not approved. Philadelphia Yearly Meeting in 1866 reported that during the last year of the war one hundred and fifty of its members had been drafted, of whom thirty were physically unfit and were dismissed on those grounds, and twenty-four, who had paid the commutation, had " made acknowledgment of error." The remainder had been paroled, for, as has been seen, Lincoln had found a solution of the problem of the extremists by paroling them " until called for."[1] Thus he went to the extreme limit of the law in aid of Friends, and in return Friends were profoundly grateful to him. They were among the sincerest mourners for his irreparable loss.

Thus in the North, Friends had passed through the national crisis, helped by the Government's recognition of their sincerity and by its genuine reluctance to enter upon any course of persecution. The words in which the Hicksite Quakers of Philadelphia Yearly Meeting described the past history of Friends, may be borrowed to summarize their attitude in these years. " Notwithstanding," they said, " there have been numerous cases of individual unfaithfulness, as a body they have maintained a uniform testimony against war." [2] The popular opinion of the Quaker as a man of peace was still held by their fellow citizens.

In the Confederate States their lot was far harder, and in many cases scruples of conscience were met with brutal maltreatment and persecution.[3] There was more than one reason for the difference in the attitude of the Federal and Confederate Governments. In the first place the South, hampered by its large negro population, was in desperate need of men. Its first Conscription Act of 1862 involved every man between the ages of eighteen and thirty-five. New Acts in swift succession extended either limit until before the

---

[1] *Friend* (Philadelphia), 1864, p. 124 ; 1866, p. 288. Cartland, *Southern Heroes*, p. 136.

[2] *Friends' Intelligencer*, xx., " Memorial to Pennsylvania Government."

[3] *Southern Heroes*, by F. G. Cartland, 1895, gives a full history of Southern Friends during the Civil War, and has been largely used in the following pages. Of earlier date is the *Account of the Sufferings of Friends of North Carolina Yearly Meeting* (Philadelphia), 1868 ; also *Friends' Quarterly Examiner*, 1869, p. 29 ; and *Memoirs* of Stanley Pumphrey.

end of the war all male citizens from sixteen to sixty were serving, and younger boys and older men were at times called upon for home defence. When the net was spread so wide there was little hope of escape, and the Friends were unlikely to meet with especial leniency, for they had long been identified by Southern politicians with the hated abolitionists. Many were known to have left the South for the West in order to escape from the slave atmosphere, and the small groups who remained were all classed as sympathizers with the Union and potential traitors. In fact, the majority of the population of North Carolina and eastern Tennessee, including the Quakers, voted against secession, but these districts were forced out of the Union by the pressure of their political leaders and the action of their neighbours, South Carolina and Virginia. Virginian Friends were few in number and lived in the northern part of the State, which became one of the chief battle-grounds of the war. They suffered almost equally from requisitions by the Confederate troops and destructive raids by Sheridan's forces, as also from the suspicions and inquisitorial visits of Confederate officials. At the opening of the war Friends were, indeed, able to gain some concessions from the Confederate Congress. But Jefferson Davis was not Lincoln, and his subordinates were left unchecked to pursue their own devices. How fiendish these devices could be is shown both in the narratives of these Quaker conscripts and in the horrible story of the prison camps at Andersonville and Salisbury, which have left an indelible stain on the honour and humanity of the Southern Government. The explanation, though not the excuse, of these cruelties lay partly in the fact that most men of character and courage were at the fighting line, and those left at the base camps included the worst elements of the Confederate army.

In December 1861 the Legislature of North Carolina considered a proposal by which all male inhabitants were required publicly to " renounce all allegiance to the Government of the United States, and also to agree to support, maintain, and defend the independent Government of the Confederate States. The alternative was banishment within thirty days."[1] A deputation of Friends appealed to some leading members of the legislature who took up their cause in the debate, pointing out that the proposal turned every Friend into a soldier or an exile. One speaker, Graham, declared : " It would amount to a decree of wholesale expatriation of the Quakers,

---

[1] Cartland, *Southern Heroes*, p. 124.

and on the expulsion of such a people from among our amidst the whole civilized world would cry ' shame.' " The Bill was not passed, and at first North Carolina Friends were not much harassed by the State drafts. In 1862, however, the Confederate Congress passed the first general Conscription Act, to be enforced by the several States. Friends petitioned the State legislatures for relief, and deputations journeyed to Richmond to appeal to Congress. The Senate Committee before which they appeared was in favour of entire exemption, but the final result was an amendment exempting " Friends, Dunkards, Nazarenes and Mennonites," duly certified to be members of these sects in October 1862, from the draft on furnishing a substitute or paying a commutation of five hundred dollars.[1] The State legislatures also imposed smaller fines. The attitude of Friends towards the concession was well stated by a minute of North Carolina Yearly Meeting held in the autumn : [2] " We cannot conscientiously pay the specified tax, it being imposed upon us on account of our principles, as the price exacted of us for religious liberty. Yet we do appreciate the good intentions of those members of Congress who had it in their hearts to do something for our relief ; and we recommend that those parents who, moved by sympathy, or those young men who, dreading the evils of a military camp, have availed themselves of this law, shall be treated in a tender manner by their Monthly Meetings." In other words such payment was not to be deemed an offence requiring disown-ment. Sooner or later a number of young men did pay, some after a severe experience of the hardships of resistance. A few accepted alternative service—usually in the salt works—which was occasion-ally offered by lenient officials. Others fled over the State boundaries to the West or, in the wilder districts, took to the woods and hills, where they led an outlaw's life for the remainder of the war. These " bush-whackers " (as they were called) included many other than Friends who wished to avoid service, and as the need for men grew more urgent, they were hunted like wild beasts by bands of soldiers

---

[1] As the value of the Confederate currency dwindled to vanishing point, the temptation to gain exemption by this payment increased. J. J. Neave and a companion in the winter of 1864 paid seventy dollars for a night's lodging, " ten dollars each for our beds, twenty for our breakfast, and five for cleaning our boots. . . . I bought all the Confederate paper money, which was the legal tender, that I needed for 3½ cents per dollar "—having brought gold with him (*Leaves from the Journal of Joseph James Neave*, 1911, p. 46).

[2] *Southern Heroes*, pp. 140–1.

under the provost-marshals. Both in North Carolina and Tennessee sympathetic Quaker farmers, at great risk to themselves, found hiding places for the fugitives, whether Friends or not. Some for a year or more kept fifteen or twenty men in concealment and fed them by night.[1] The real trial, however, fell upon those Friends who would neither buy exemption nor evade punishment, and on many who, though holding Friends' views, were not in actual membership at the date required by law. Some had worshipped with Friends for many years, while others were drawn to them during the war by a sympathy of principles. Writers have been found to sneer at " war-Quakers," but (as an account published by North Carolina Friends quietly remarks) " such a step did not allow of much hope of escape from suffering."[2]

After describing the outbreak of war, the account continues :

" It was in the midst of such commotions that many were led to very serious thoughts upon the inconsistency of war and fighting with the loving and quiet spirit of a disciple of Jesus. Decided first upon this point, and then led on to the consideration of others, many sought admission to our Society. The whole number of these, including those members of their families who were often received with them, was about six hundred. . . . Thus, it fell out that the storm burst with the greater violence upon some who were in many ways the least prepared to meet it. By their old associates those who had adopted such views were regarded as lacking the excuse of early training, and in their family circles the sufferings they endured had often to be shared more or less by those who did not partake of the convictions that occasioned it. . . . In the great multitude that swelled the two vast armies arrayed against each other, there could not have been found instances of more lofty heroism, of calmer courage, and of more fearless unshrinking endurance of death and agonies beyond those of death, than were exhibited

---

[1] Near Holly Springs, North Carolina, the home guard imprisoned the parents and wives of missing conscripts in an old schoolhouse where they tortured them to find out the men's hiding-places. At times the fugitives, who were lurking in the neighbourhood, would surrender to save their parents. " The soldiers placed the hands and fingers of the aged men and women between the lower rails of the fence, and with its crushing weight upon them would wait to be told what they wished. . . . They would sometimes tie a rope around the waist of the women and hang them to a tree " (*Southern Heroes*, pp. 184–5, where the names of Quaker witnesses to these brutalities are given).

[2] *Account of the Sufferings of Friends of North Carolina Yearly Meeting*, quoted in *Southern Heroes*, pp. 152–3.

by that little band who made up another army and followed as their only captain, the Prince of Peace." The pages of the pamphlet and of Cartland's fuller history, *Southern Heroes*, give, in matter-of-fact language, sufficient justification for this verdict.[1] The narratives come from the conscripts themselves, or from eye-witnesses of their sufferings, and they are a monotonous record of brutal military punishments met by patient endurance. The sufferers were mostly men of humble rank and little influence, small farmers, or artisans, with quaint Old Testament prenomens, telling of simple Bible-reading parents.

As was natural, they fared worse towards the end of the war, when the South was in desperate plight, but some of the earlier conscripts were for years in the hands of the army. Jesse Buckner, for example, was a Baptist colonel in a military company, who, at the outbreak of war, was surprised by Friends' unwillingness to serve. As he showed them some leniency he lost his post and gained the conviction that "war is contrary to the Gospel." Journeying one night, he was lost in the woods, where he took shelter on the steps of an isolated Friends' meeting-house. "There alone in the darkness of the night, meditating upon Friends' principles, the serious condition of the country, and the awfulness of war, he became satisfied that it was his duty to unite himself with the people who worshipped in that house." At first he evaded the draft, but he soon felt this to be an unworthy course, and for nearly three years he was driven from camp to camp, "often at the point of the bayonet," enduring much for his refusal to bear arms, until the end of the war set him free.[2] In some cases, however, the steadfastness of the sufferers won the respect of their guards. Solomon Frazier, after going through a week of tortures, was relieved by the visit of

[1] An analysis of Cartland's book produces the following statistics in regard to Friends of North Carolina, Tennessee, and Virginia. His allusions to those who obtained exemption or escaped are only incidental, and probably many more cases were unrecorded, but the number of conscripts is approximately accurate. There is a slight overlapping in the figures, as some Friends fall under more than one head, those e.g. who paid exemption after an experience of conscription : Conscripted and maltreated, 50 ; Died from this treatment, 5 ; Accepted non-military service, 27 ; Escaped into hiding, 23 ; Paid exemption, 140. An enrolling officer at Raleigh in April 1863 told two Friend-conscripts that over $20,000 had been paid him for exemption by Quakers (*Southern Heroes*, p. 256). If this were the Government fine, it would imply that forty Quakers appeared before this one officer. As far as is known only two Friends yielded and joined the army (*Friend*, 1866, p. 112).

[2] *Southern Heroes*, pp. 146-9.

an older Friend, who explained Quaker principles to the officials. " Hearing this, they concluded it was useless to try to make a soldier of him, and ceased to persecute him, though he was retained as a prisoner until the surrender of Salisbury, four months afterwards."[1] Four other young Friends, Thomas and Amos Hinshaw, and their cousins, Cyrus and Nathan Barker, were a problem to the soldiers of their camp, who urged them to solve it by running away. After four months they were given a fortnight's leave, the papers being endorsed : " These men are no manner of use in the army." At home they were much urged to pay the exemption tax, which, as one of them recalled afterwards, " was a great temptation to us, dreading as we did to return to the camp. On the second of the third month, 1863, we again took leave of our dear families and friends at home, which, I think, was as hard a trial as we have had ever to experience. The officers and men all seemed glad to see us, and gave us a cordial welcome. No military duty was required of us, not even to answer a roll-call."[2]

But such leniency was a rare exception. Gideon Macon, for instance, on his refusal to serve or do the work of the camp kitchen, was " bucked down " for an hour—a punishment which seems to have been a survival from the " tying neck and heels," undergone by earlier Friends. " The man . . . is made to sit down on the ground ; his wrists are firmly bound together by strong cords or withes ; drawing up the knees, his arms are pressed over them until a stout stick can be thrust over the elbows, under the knees, and thus the man's feet and hands are rendered useless for the time being. He can neither crawl nor creep."[3] The regiment was in retreat before the army of the North ; the commander threatened to get rid of this useless soldier by hanging him, but in the end he was sent to Petersburg, one of the miserable army prisons, where he dragged out weeks of endurance, until set free by the surrender of Lee at Appomattox. His brother, Ahijah, after serving early in the war as a volunteer, became convinced of Friends' principles, and joined the Society, too late, of course, to benefit by the exemption. He was conscripted, " hurried to Richmond, and immediately required to take a gun and fight. But he was in no mood for fighting, so they put him under guard, and for food gave him only cane-seed meal. This was followed by severe illness, and he was removed

[1] *Southern Heroes*, pp. 201–4.   [2] *Ibid.*, p. 199.
[3] *Ibid.*, p. 186.

to a hospital in Richmond, where he soon passed away."[1]   A third brother, Isaiah, also became a Friend after the passing of the exemption law. He was conscripted, not being allowed to see his wife and children, and was sent to the army a day or two before the battle of Winchester. When the action began, an officer ordered him to the front line, "to stop bullets," if he would not fight. He remained there through the battle in "plain citizen's dress," but escaped all injury though his comrades fell around him. When the retreat began, as he did not join in it, he was captured by the Northern army, and in a few days he died, from the shock and strain of his experiences

Seth Loflin, another North Carolinan, was sent in 1864 to the camp near Petersburg, Virginia. On his refusal to take a gun, on the grounds of Christian principle, "first they kept him without sleep for thirty-six hours, a soldier standing by with a bayonet, to pierce him, should he fall asleep. Finding that this did not overcome his scruples, they proceeded for three hours each day to buck him down. He was then suspended by his thumbs for an hour and a half.[2] This terrible ordeal was passed through each day for a week. Then, thinking him conquered, they offered him a gun," but he still refused. He was court-martialled, sentenced to be shot, and the regiments drawn up to witness the execution. "Seth Loflin, as calm as any man of the immense number surrounding him, asked time for prayer. . . . He prayed, not for himself, but for his enemies, ' Father, forgive them, for they know not what they do.' " Upon this, the firing party, in defiance of all discipline, declared that they would not shoot. The officers, too, were softened, and revoked the sentence to one of imprisonment. In the military prison he underwent severe punishment for weeks until at last his physical powers gave way. He died in hospital after a long illness. One of the officers, who had learnt to know him, wrote to his wife :

"It is my painful duty to inform you that Seth W. Loflin died at Windsor Hospital at Richmond on the 8th of December, 1864. He died, as he had lived, a true, humble, and devoted Christian ; true to his faith and religion. . . We pitied and sympathized with him."[3]

---

[1] Cartland, *Southern Heroes*, pp. 189–91.
[2] "If I had the Hon. Member for Hanley in my company at the front, he would be strung up by the thumbs before he had been there half-an-hour " (Captain D. Campbell, in House of Commons, January 10, 1916).
[3] *Southern Heroes*, pp. 211–13.

The two other Friends who died from their sufferings were Jesse Osborn and Edward Harris. Many more underwent persecution of the same nature and intensity as that already described. Lewis Caudle was sent into battle with a gun tied on to him, but escaped all injury. He was left on the battlefield in the retreat, where he slept among the dead and dying, and at dawn found his way to his home at Deep River. As this was near the end of the war he was unmolested. William Hockett, like Loflin, was brought before a firing party, when his prayer for his executioners so touched their hearts that he was reprieved. He was dragged along with the regiment till the battle of Gettysburg, where he saw the horrible sufferings of the wounded. A day or two later he was captured by a detachment of Union Cavalry. Northern Friends interested themselves in his case and that of other captured Friends, but an *impasse* appeared when the commander at Fort Delaware offered them oaths of allegiance to the Union, as a preliminary to release. On their refusal, " he said we professed to be a law-abiding people. We told him we were, . . . but if the law required things of us that came into conflict with our religious feelings, we peaceably submitted to the penalty, if it was death, rather than wound our consciences." The commander then took their affirmations, merely binding them not to go into or correspond with the South without permission from the Secretary of War. " Tenderly bidding us farewell, he said, ' Don't be too late for the cars.' We were on time." Till the end of the war they remained among Northern Friends, who gave them liberal hospitality and help.[1] The story of Hockett's brothers, Himelius and Jesse, was told by them later with a *naïveté* which bears the stamp of truth.[2] In the draft of 1862 they were not ill-treated, and soon discharged. Next year they were again conscripted, when a determined attempt was made to break their wills. The General offered then military service, employment at the salt works, or payment of the tax, and shut them up in prison without food or drink to make the decision. " We were impressed," said Himelius, " that it would be right to make a full surrender, and to trust wholly to a kind Providence, so we told the captain of the guard we had some cakes and cheese in our valises, that had been furnished us by our wives at home. . . . 'Oh !' he said, ' I guess you might keep that,' and he seemed very tender, but, looking at the guards, who were looking at him, there seemed no way for him to evade."

---

[1] *Southern Heroes*, pp. 231–49.   [2] *Ibid.*, pp. 254–84.

One night during the imprisonment, during a heavy shower of rain, Hockett could have drunk water trickling from the eaves, "but I felt restrained from taking any of it. Arousing my brother, who had fallen asleep, I asked him about it, and he said he thought we had better not. So we went to sleep again." After five days of starvation, some of the officers and people of the town who had heard of their plight, appealed to the Governor, who revoked the sentence At first they were too weak to eat, except in carefully doled-out portions ; but when they had recovered, they were sent to hard labour in a military prison. After some weeks Himelius Hockett was court-martialled. "On the third of eighth month I was called out on dress parade to receive with others the sentence of the court-martial. For desertion some were to have the letter D branded indelibly on their bodies, three inches broad. This was done in my presence with a hot iron, accompanied by the screams of the unhappy victims. . . . I was sentenced to six months' hard labour in one of the military forts, bound with heavy ball and chain." He learned that the officers of the court-martial had wished to discharge him, but that Jefferson Davis, the President, had insisted on some punishment. A few days later "we were ordered to assist in unloading ordnance cars, and the officers ordered that we should be pierced four inches deep with bayonets if we refused. On declining to do this service, my brother was pierced cruelly with bayonets, while I was hung up by the thumbs almost clear of the ground. After I had remained in this suffering position for some time, the corporal was told that he had no orders to tie up either of us, but to pierce us with bayonets, and that he had better obey orders. So I was untied and pierced with a bayonet, though slightly, perhaps on account of having already suffered unauthorized punishment."[1] After a week at a military fort, where, apart from the ball and chain punishment, he was kindly treated, he was summoned back, and with his brother moved from centre to centre. Now that their sincerity was proved, they met with considerable

---

[1] This was a favourite form of punishment. In one case a boy of eighteen (Tilghman Vestal of Tennessee) endured it. In reply to a remonstrance from his relatives, the major of the regiment wrote suavely that "compulsory means were used on the occasion referred to . . . and he was pricked with bayonets, but not to an extent to unfit him for duty. This proceeding was probably irregular." After a repeated experience of "this proceeding," which did not make him yield, the boy was sent to the filth and misery of Salisbury prison, but after six weeks his friends succeeding in obtaining his release (*Southern Heroes*, p. 317).

kindness and, as he ingenuously says, they had so much intercourse with officers and men, including the prisoners of both armies, that it was " more like opening a mission-field than being in a military prison." At last they were discharged and returned home to find that their wives had been courageously working on their little farms to support themselves and their children. In the record of Quaker sufferings, the patient endurance of the conscripts' families must not be forgotten. It was William Hockett's wife who encouraged him to meet the draft by saying : " Be faithful, William, for I would rather hear of thy dying a martyr for Christ's sake than that thou shouldest sin against him by staying with me." Friends in Virginia, who were few in number, formed part of Baltimore Yearly Meetings (" Hicksite " and " Orthodox "), but throughout the war they were practically cut off from intercourse with their fellow members. Some lived near Richmond, the Confederate capital, and others round Winchester, in the north of the State, in a district which was in constant occupation by one or other of the contending armies. Winchester itself is said to have changed hands more than seventy times in the course of the war. Friends' meeting-houses were occupied by Federal and Confederate troops in turn, some as barracks and others as hospitals. The same fate overtook the buildings of other denominations and the few schools, so that throughout these years public worship and education were in abeyance. After the war, Baltimore Meeting for Sufferings published an account of the conditions which had prevailed in this district " to show some of the horrors of civil war in the disregard of the peace, rights, and liberty of the individual citizen."[1] It told of arbitrary arrests and imprisonments of Friends suspected of Union sympathies, of domiciliary visits and confiscation of property. One " Hicksite " Friend, Job Throckmorton, died from his sufferings under military arrest.[2] The Federal Government ultimately paid compensation for a proportion of the loss caused by the raids of Union troops in Virginia and North Carolina, but many sufferers were brought to the verge of ruin. Some of the young Friends subject to the conscription escaped to the Northern States ; yet the few Friends of any influence in Virginia had much to do in helping their own members and those of other peace sects who were called up under the draft. John B. Crenshaw, of Richmond, took a leading

---

[1] *Southern Heroes*, pp. 363 foll., also *Southern Quakers*, p. 303.
[2] Rufus Jones, *Later Periods of Quakerism*, p. 741.

part in this work and in the delegations of Southern Friends to the Confederate Government. His father had fought in the war of 1812, after which, becoming an ardent supporter of peace and opponent of slavery, he joined the Society of Friends. A young English Friend, Joseph James Neave, who was drawn to visit the South on a mission of love and sympathy, described John Crenshaw as a man " who stood for truth and peace and righteousness " in those dark days.

Throughout the winter of 1864–5, J. J. Neave travelled among the Friends of the South, bringing them the sympathy of English Friends. Occasionally the military authorities were suspicious of his journeys, but they were disarmed by his simple statement that " Friends were one people the world over, that we were opposed to all war, and lived at peace among ourselves and with all men . . . and I felt it my duty to come if I could help them or do them any good." [1] He saw the miseries which war brings to the non-combatant, and it was partly his reports as an eye-witness which stirred up Friends in the North and in England to send aid to their fellow members as soon as the way was open. Immediately after Lee's surrender the " Baltimore Association of Friends " was formed as an agency to distribute their gifts. The work included the distribution of food and clothing, the restocking of farms, the rebuilding of Meeting-houses, and help towards the education of the children. For some years after the war this " reconstruction " claimed a large share of the thought and attention of Northern Friends.[2] Amid all the bitterness which the struggle and the settlement left behind, the love and friendship of Quakers North and South was a source of wonder to their more warlike neighbours. In the autumn of 1866 a Peace Conference of delegates from seven " Orthodox " Yearly Meetings, held at Baltimore, reaffirmed the peace position. In the eyes of most Friends, and indeed of many other thoughtful citizens, the war and its resultant evils were a terrible price to pay even for the destruction of slavery and the preservation of the Union, and the real cost of the war has been often used since to emphasize the argument for peace. The mere loss of life and expenditure of money was appalling and unprecedented. " We lost six hundred and fifty-six thousand men, or about one-sixth as many as there were slaves, and three billions and seven hundred millions

[1] *Leaves from the Journal of J. J. Neave*, pp. 26–84.
[2] *Southern Heroes*, pp. 425 foll. Also Quaker periodicals (English and American) of the years after the war.

of dollars, not including the loss of the labour and industry of the vast armies, North and South, during the four years of war. The valuation set on the slaves at the request of Abraham Lincoln, in 1862, by members of Congress from the border States, was three hundred dollars each, and assuming the number at four millions, which is an over-estimate, the value of all the slaves in the United States was one billion and two hundred millions of dollars, or less than one-third of the money cost of the war."[1]

After the close of the struggle, for fifty years American Friends were free from the trials of war and conscription, but in these quieter days they maintained their testimony for peace. It is rash for a writer in another country to make a general statement about communities with a total membership of some one hundred and twenty thousand, but on the whole it appears that the Yearly Meetings of the Eastern States have taken the lead in this branch of Friends' work. Apart from this, many individual Friends have been leaders and organizers in the general peace movement of the United States. To mention only two : for many years the late Dr. Benjamin Trueblood, of Boston (of the "Orthodox" branch) was the Secretary of the American Peace Society, and since 1895 Albert Smiley, an "Orthodox" Friend, organized yearly at Lake Mohonk, New York State, a conference on International Arbitration attended by jurists and peace workers of all lands, which was maintained after his death until the outbreak of war.

In one direction the peace work of Friends met with striking recognition from the National Government. In the year 1869 Philadelphia Yearly Meeting was urged by Thomas Wistar, an active and devoted helper of the Indians, to appeal to Congress and the executive on behalf both of those tribes living on reservations and those with whom the United States had just waged a bloody war. A delegation, led by Wistar, presented this memorial to the legislature and to the President-elect, Ulysses S. Grant, the hero of the Civil War. A similar memorial had been presented on behalf of some bodies of "Liberal" Friends in 1867, and by seven

---

[1] From *War Unnecessary and Unchristian*, an essay of Augustine Jones, published by the American Peace Society. In 1880, the Secretary for the Treasury declared the expenses of the war on account of the Northern army 1861–79 were $6,796,798,508, or sufficient to have purchased every slave at five times his market value. The Continental and American billion = one thousand millions (Cartland, *Southern Heroes*, p. 13).

·· Orthodox " Yearly Meetings, almost simultaneously with that from Philadelphia.[1] The impression made upon his mind was reflected in his first message to Congress. In this, after reference to the Indian problem and to the ill-success of past dealings with them, he continued :—

" I have attempted a new policy towards these wards of the nation (they cannot be regarded in any other light than as wards) with fair results so far as tried, which I hope will be attended ultimately with great success. The Society of Friends is well known as having succeeded in living in peace with the Indians in the early settlement of Pennsylvania, while their white neighbours of other sects in other sections were constantly embroiled. They are also known for their opposition to all strife, violence, and war, and are generally noted for their strict integrity and fair dealings. These considerations induced me to give the management of a few reservations of Indians to them, and to lay the burden of the selection of agents upon the Society itself." Thus, two hundred years later, an attempt was made to revert to the old policy of William Penn.[2] For some fifteen years the various branches of the Society continued to work on the stations entrusted to them, although after Grant's second term expired in 1877, his policy was considerably modified by the new heads of the Indian Department. Kelsey [3] says that under President Hayes the new Commissioner of Indian Affairs began to thwart the work of Friends, accusing them of inefficiency and dishonesty. He removed some from their posts, and in May 1879 the Associated Committee (of " Orthodox " Friends), in a formal note to the President, resigned all further responsibility for Indian affairs. The " Liberal " Friends were also similarly hampered in their work. " It should be said that the Commissioner of Indian Affairs who assailed the ability and integrity of Friends was peremptorily removed from his position early in 1880 under charges of gross malfeasance in office." Kelsey relates several instances of the tact and courage of Friend agents in their dealings with dangerous and malcontent Indians. The last of the Friends' agents was withdrawn in 1895, but the control of the work had practically passed out of Quaker hands in 1887. Friends continued, however, to

[1] Kelsey, *Friends and the Indians*, pp. 166–7.
[2] Next year Grant gave the remaining agencies to other denominations with missions among the Indians.
[3] *Friends and the Indians*, p. 185.

carry on missionary and educational work among the Indians :
the " Associated Committee on Indian Affairs," which was formed
by the " Orthodox" Yearly Meetings, to carry on the Government
work, is still active in this unofficial service, and other Yearly
Meetings of both branches have their own committees for the
purpose. After the acquisition of Alaska by the United States,
Friends from Oregon, Kansas, and Wilmington Yearly Meetings
carried on pioneer missionary work in that untilled field, but at
last handed their stations to the Presbyterians, also engaged in the
work there.

One effect of the hostilities with Spain in 1898 and the
" war of pacification " which followed in the Philippines was to
draw Friends of all branches closer together in their common
work for peace. The bitterness which followed the separations of
the earlier part of the nineteenth century had largely died away,
but certain difficulties in the way of " correspondence " and
" recognition " remained (and still remain). Until recently these
have tended to prevent full co-operation even in matters of practical
Christianity on which all were at one.[1] But now this isolation may
be regarded as a thing of the past in the Eastern States. An
" American Friends' Peace Conference " was held in Philadelphia
from December 12th to 14th, 1901. For the first time since the
separation in 1827 members of all the Quaker bodies met together
to take counsel one with another. The conference, which was well
attended, sat for some seven hours daily, listening to short papers
by leading Friends on various aspects of the peace question and
taking part in discussion upon them.[2]

Towards the end of the proceedings a " Declaration " was
adopted, which included a statement that " this conference of
members of the different bodies of Friends in America is convinced
that lapse of time has not made necessary any change in the position
which the Friends have always taken on the subject of war. . . .
War in its spirit, its deeds, the persistent animosities which it
generates, the individual and social degeneration produced by it is
the antithesis of Christianity, and the negation, for the time being,
of the moral order of the world."

---

[1] Thomas, *History of Friends in America*, pp. 149–54, 169, gives a clear statement of what is meant by these terms.

[2] A full report was published by the conference under the title, *The American
Friends' Peace Conference* . . . 1901 (Philadelphia, 1902), 234 pages.

The existing wars in South Africa and the Philippines, though not named, were unmistakably condemned. "We deplore the fact that nations making high profession of Christianity are at present engaged in war with less civilized and enlightened peoples, and we believe the time has fully come when the voice of enlightened humanity should make itself heard, calling for the adjustment of the matters at issue by the Christian methods which have . . . proved themselves as practical as they are reasonable and humane." Probably the most fruitful result of the conference was the establishment of the habit of co-operation in peace activities between the different branches, and this has continued. There is not space here to give a full account of the peace work of American Friends during the past twenty years. In nature and scope it did not differ widely from that carried on in England. The "Five Years' Meeting" (an official quinquennial conference of delegates of the majority of the "Orthodox" Yearly Meetings[1]) in 1903, through one of its committees, the Board on Legislation, was largely instrumental in securing an amendment to the National Militia Law exempting Friends and members of other peace sects.[2] "Provided that nothing in this Act shall be construed to require or compel any member of any well-recognized religious sect or organization at present organized and existing, whose creed forbids its members to participate in war in any form and whose religious convictions are against war or participation therein, in accordance with the creed of the said religious organization, to serve in the militia or any other armed or volunteer force under the jurisdiction of and authority of the United States."

This exemption, as will be seen, took no account of the peace convictions of individuals outside these particular sects.

[1] *Vide*, Thomas, *Friends in America*, pp. 24–6, 215 foll.
[2] *Congressional Record*, xxxvi. 780.

CHAPTER XVII

FRIENDS IN EUROPE

THE records of the first generation of Friends contain many
instances of their journeyings to distant lands, whither they
penetrated, undeterred by difficulties of travel and intercourse, and
by the persecution which often awaited them. " England is as a family
of prophets which must spread over all nations," declared the Epistle
of the General Meeting of Friends, held at Skipton in 1660. One
Friend, George Robinson, had already visited Jerusalem, and in that
very year a woman, Mary Fisher, found her way on foot and alone
to the Sultan, then encamped in the midst of his troops at Adrianople.
He marvelled at her safe passage through so many dangers, listened
gravely to her " message from the Great God," saying at the close
" it was truth," and offered her an escort back to the Franks. This
she declined, returning as she came, without guard or guide. Two
other women endured a long imprisonment in the dungeons of the
Inquisition at Malta, and a similar fate befell Friends both in France
and Italy. In Rome, indeed, one died in prison, and another,
John Perrott, returned half-crazed by his sufferings, to bring a disturbing element into the affairs of the Church at home. John Philly
and Thomas Moore, travelling in Austria in 1662, visited a Huterite
colony near Pressburg. This sect had many resemblances to that
of the Mennonites, including the refusal to bear arms. The two
Friends found sympathy and kindness amongst them, but as they
passed on to visit another settlement, they were seized at Comora
on a charge of heresy. They were sent from prison to prison, enduring
at times severe torture, and the worse trial (in a strange land) of
separation from one another. Their peace views must have been
one count in the accusation against them, perhaps inferred from
their association with the Huterites. In one prison, says Moore,
" the jailer did try me many ways, for he would have me learn to

shoot, and hath tied match about my fingers, and hath struck to make me hold the musket, but I was like a fool. And they made themselves sport with me, and several times would put pistols in my hands, and bid me shoot sometimes in seeming earnest and sometimes to make sport before strangers." Eventually both Moore and Philly were released, finding their way by diverse routes back to England.[1] In none of these countries, however, did any growth of native Quakerism spring up in the wake of these brief visits. In Holland and Germany Friends met with more success, which was due to several causes. Throughout the seventeenth century, both in theology and trade, there was much intercourse between English and " Dutch " (using the latter term to cover the " High Dutch " of Germany). To each the national characteristics and modes of religious thought of the other were comparatively familiar. The development of Nonconformity in England had been largely influenced by emigrants from these lands in the days of persecution, and now, in their turn, the Friends crossed the sea with their contribution to a more spiritual interpretation of Christianity. Among the existing religious bodies were some from whom they could receive a sympathetic welcome. In both countries the Mennonites and the followers of Schwenkfeld, and in Holland the Collegiants (the little community which befriended Spinoza after his excommunication by the Amsterdam Synagogue) and the Labadists had various points of contact with Friends.[2] It is probable that the majority of " convincements " were drawn from these sects. An " Account of the first settlement of Friends in Holland and places adjacent " presented to the Yearly Meeting of 1771, by a deputation of English Friends who had

[1] Besse, *Sufferings*, ii. ch. xiv., gives a full account of these episodes. A picturesque story tells how Hester Biddle (or Bidley) in the reign of Wiliam and Mary approached the Queen to tell of her grief " as a woman and a Christian," that " so great and tedious a war was waged between Christians." Next she crossed to France, and after many difficulties was admitted to the audience chamber at Versailles. There she addressed Louis XIV in the same strain, to which he replied : " But, woman, I desire peace, and would have peace, and tell the Prince of Orange so." Unfortunately, there is no authoritative source for the tale. It is first related by the Dutchman, Gerald Croese, in his Latin *General History of the Quakers* (English translation 1696, Part II. p. 267). This work is quite unreliable in details. Friends at the time rejected the story, *vide* the *Letter* of George Keith printed with the English edition of Croese.

[2] For these sects, and for the religious connection between Holland and Germany *vide* Robert Barclay, *Inner Life of the Religious Societies of the Commonwealth*, 1879 ; Rufus Jones, *Spiritual Reformers in the Sixteenth and Seventeenth Centuries*, 1914.

visited Holland and North Germany in the preceding year, gives thirteen names of Meetings settled between the years 1656 and 1679. They were : Amsterdam, Rotterdam, Haarlem, Alkmaar, Lansmeer in Waterland, Leeuwarden, Harlingen, Danzig, Hamburg, Friedrichstadt (in Holstein), Emden, Groningen, and Crefeld. In 1679 a Yearly Meeting was established for Holland, and in 1683 for Germany. This expansion was due to the missionary work of three Friends : William Caton, William Ames, and John Stubbs, between 1656 and 1660. Of these, Ames and Stubbs had been Baptists before they were Friends. It was through William Ames that Jacob Sewel, the father of the first historian of Quakerism, became a Friend, and later Ames' preaching won over the little company of Baptists at Kriesheim in the Palatinate, who, after their migration to Pennsylvania, were pioneers in the protest against slavery.

These Dutch and German Friends were strengthened by frequent visits from English leaders of the first generation of the Society. Fox, Penn, Barclay, and Stephen Crisp were among their helpers. It is possible that Penn and Barclay's intercourse with Elizabeth, Princess Palatine, and the high esteem in which they were held by her, had some influence in obtaining recognition in Holland for Friends as a religious body, for there they soon enjoyed full liberty of conscience.[1] In the various German cities their case was harder. The Friends of Friedrichstadt, indeed, were unmolested until the close of the seventeenth century, but in Danzig (then Polish territory) and Emden, they soon came into collision with the authorities. Fox was active in writing on their behalf to the magistrates and rulers of these city states. His appeals, usually turned into Latin by some more scholarly Friend, pressed home the utter inconsistency of persecution by professors of religion. In 1689 he wrote to the magistrates of Danzig, who had banished some Friends merely for meeting to worship :

" Are not you worse than the Turks, who let many religions be in their country, yea Christians, and to meet peaceably ? Yea, the Turkish patroons let our Friends that were captives meet together at Algiers, and said, ' it was good so to do.' . . . I pray you, what scripture have you for this practice ? It is good for you to be humble, to do justly and love mercy, call home your banished ones and love and cherish them. Yea, though they were your enemies, you are to obey the command of Christ and love them. I wonder

[1] *Vide* Chapter V.

how you and your wives and families can sleep quietly in your beds, that do such cruel actions." [1]

After Fox's death the care of these foreign Friends passed into the hands of the Meeting for Sufferings. Beyond sending letters of sympathy and gifts of money they could do little to relieve their German brethren from the persecution they endured " for not bearing arms," or in general, " for truth and their testimony thereto."[2] It is evident from a curious letter preserved in the *Book of Cases*,[3] that in 1700, in Danzig at least, courage had nearly failed. On the 18th of Eighth Month (October) correspondents from the Meeting for Sufferings write to John Clause, of that city, with reference to the proposal of Danzig Friends to emigrate to Holland or England : " which our said meeting and Friends here are sorry for and much dissatisfied with," since they have " so long borne a testimony for Truth through their sufferings." Their plea that they are reluctant to live on charity must be dismissed, since English Friends have shown no weariness in helping them. Nor has the injunction to the Apostles to flee into another city any application in this case. " We do not find that the Church of Thessalonica, nor any other Church of the primitive Christians, were required to flee from their respective cities or places under persecution, but to be faithful unto death that they might receive a crown of life." So the letter runs, from the comfortable security of London, but a postscript, added as an afterthought, may have proved more cheering to the Danzig readers than this vicarious heroism.

" There hath been endeavours used with the King of England on the Friends' behalf in Dantzic, and the King was pleased to take so much notice thereof as to give orders to the Secretary of State here to advise Sir William Browne, merchant in Dantzic, and lately gone from this city to use his influence with the magistrates of that city for the ease and relief of Friends."[4]

---

[1] *Journal* (8th edition), ii. 485.
[2] Epistles of London Yearly Meeting 1697 and 1706.
[3] *Book of Cases*, vol. ii.
[4] In 1694, William had addressed a letter to the Count Palatine of the Rhine on behalf of the persecuted " Menists " (Mennonites) in his dominions, a copy of which the Meeting for Sufferings preserved in the *Book of Cases*, ii. 53, probably for use as a precedent. William spoke in high terms of his Mennonite subjects in Holland as peaceable and industrious folk. In 1709 the Meeting interested itself again in these Mennonites, who had left the Palatinate on account of " general poverty and misery." Friends supplied their immediate wants, furnished them with Quaker books in " High Dutch," and offered them £50 when about " to export themselves beyond the seas," to Pennsylvania.

In the same year Friedrichstadt Friends were in trouble from their refusal to observe the appointed fast-days by shutting their shops. They had appealed to the Duke of Holstein and to his Lieutenant-General Bannian. The latter they presented with French copies of Barclay's *Apology* and Penn's *No Cross, No Crown,* " which he took very kindly, and inquired after the good man William Penn and where he now was, and promised to assist them." This promise he must have performed, since an order came from the Duke to the magistrates to " let your arbitrary punishments alone."[1]

The Friedrichstadt Friends maintained their struggle for religious liberty. In 1712 worse evils overtook them and their fellow-countrymen through the campaigns waged in Holstein by Peter the Great and the Danes against Charles XII of Sweden and the Duke of Holstein. Jacob Hagen, a Hamburg Quaker, wrote to London a doleful account of his visit to Friedrichstadt, the " seat of warr " : [2] " The Zaer is there with his generals, and about four thousand men are quartered upon the inhabitants of that place, from ten, twenty, to thirty men in a family, and one or two officers and some less. They quarter themselves as they please and use great insolence, and are also a great burden to the inhabitants, hardly bearable with the charge of maintaining them with provisions, etc., which is very dear—one pound of butter, 10d. and 12d. to 14d., and hardly to be had, 20 eggs 20d. to 24d., and no fireing to be had for money, which causeth great uneasiness. The city so dirty that there is hardly passing the streets without boots. The horses are kept in the lower rooms of the house, and above stairs is full of people and their baggage. The country people are mostly ruined and destitute, houses and lands spoiled, horses and cattle taken away. The miserable state is hardly to be written as it is in reality. The war is like to be continued longer than was expected, now the Swedes have entered the city Tonengen (Töning), but the King of Denmark hath seized the whole dukedom besides." In a letter of March 7 he continued the sad story : " The Muscovites . . . are extreme cruel and turbulent, and what adds thereto, is their being of a different language, which makes their conversation very uneasy. They use great exaction on the country people, and many are so misused, even some of my acquaintance, that with wife and children

---

[1] *Book of Cases*, ii.
[2] *Ibid.*, ii. 195. This letter is dated 24, 12 mo. (Feb.) 1712.

have left their habitations, having nothing left, and the longer the Swedes continue in Tonengen the worse it will be for the country and inhabitants. They demand of Frederickstadt a contribution of 30,000 rixdollars, and now they are fallen to 20,000, but neither the first nor yet the last is possible to be complied with. . . . Most of the horses and cattle are ruined or drove away, and it is impossible to write the miserable state and sore visitation which is over those places." Matters had not improved by the next autumn, when the Friends wrote, in response to a letter of sympathy from London, that " few people account anything they have their own," houses in the country districts are " laid in ruins," and " the land lieth unplowed." Yet, in the midst of all this desolation, they could testify to a very real experience of the love of God. Friends in London did not sympathize in words alone, for they remitted fifty pounds through Hamburg to their distressed brethren. Probably it was in part due to the poverty caused by this disastrous invasion that the meetings dwindled so rapidly.[1]

No doubt the Friends joined in the stream of German emigrants which set so strongly towards Pennsylvania and other American colonies during the first thirty years of the eighteenth century. The English deputation of 1771 already mentioned, found only one meeting remaining in Holland and North Germany—that of Amsterdam. In Holland, as far as Friends could be traced, they had joined the Mennonites. There the decay of the Society was probably hastened by the lack of any spiritual fervour or missionary zeal among the English body during the earlier Hanoverian period.

The Russian occupation of Friedrichstadt led to one curious episode in which Peter the Great was a leading figure. He had already come into touch with Friends during his English visit of inquiry and self-education in 1697. When the arrival in London of this ruler from a distant Empire was known, Thomas Story and Gilbert Mollison waited on him to urge that he should allow liberty of conscience in his dominions. The young Czar, learning the principles of Friends, inquired : " Of what use can you be in any kingdom or Government, seeing you will not fight ? " Story answered : " Many of us had borne arms in times past, and been in many battles, and fought with courage and magnanimity, and thought it

---

[1] It is a curious fact that the empty meeting-house at Friedrichstadt, built by donations from English Friends, remained in their hands and was not sold till 1860 (*Proceedings of Yearly Meeting*, 1873, p. 43).

lawful and a duty then, in days of ignorance ; and I myself have worn a sword and other arms and knew how to use them. But . . . He that commanded that we should love our enemies, hath left us no right to fight and destroy, but to convert them. And yet we are of use and helpful in any kingdom or Government," as an industrious, quiet people who readily pay taxes, after New Testament example, " to Cæsar, who, of right, hath the direction and application of them to the various ends of government, to peace or war, as it pleaseth him, or as need may be, according to the constitution or laws of his kingdom ; and in which we, as subjects, have no direction or share. For it is Cæsar's part to rule, in justice and truth ; but ours to be subject, and mind our own business, and not to meddle with his." The Czar was not converted by this reasoning, nor by a visit from William Penn, George Whitehead, and other Friends, although Penn was able to hold conversation with him in German. and presented him with some Friends' books translated into that tongue.[1] Yet he was sufficiently interested in the strange new sect to attend their meetings occasionally, both at Gracechurch Street, and also at Deptford, where he worked in the shipyard. As a fellow worshipper, he proved " very social ; changing seats, standing or sitting, as occasion might be, to accommodate others as well as himself." He certainly kept these meetings in remembrance, as he proved at Friedrichstadt in 1712. Jacob Hagen told the story in the letter already quoted :

" Last First Day the Zaar acquainted our friends he was desirous to come to their meeting, but they replied, the meeting-house was taken up with twenty or thirty soldiers, who had made it like a stable. We desired that it might be evacuated, then we could keep our meeting. So he immediately gave orders for them to go out, and he came in the afternoon with about six or seven of his Princes and Generals, and sat with us still and it seemed with much patience. (Philip de Weer had a few words) and he stayed with us about an hour, to the admiration of many." Story, who in 1715 heard the tale by word of mouth from Jacob Hagen, adds the touch that the Czar translated what was said in the meeting to his Staff. The meeting-house was kept free of soldiers by the Czar's orders. In gratitude he and his suite were presented by Friends with some books, and as the Russians asked for the *Apology*, copies of this were obtained from Holland. " Friends, as well as others," added Hagen, " have

[1] Story, *Journal*, p. 123 ; Whitehead, *Christian Progress*, pp. 669–72.

their full freedom, and the Muscovites make no difference (if they get their bellies full) among whom they are quartered." The next great Czar, Alexander I, a hundred years later, also took a real interest in Friends. When the Allied rulers visited London in June 1814 the Meeting for Sufferings presented addresses to both the Czar and the King of Prussia. This was done at the instance of one of the most interesting and influential Friends of the day Etienne de Grellet (1773–1855) was the son of a French porcelain manufacturer, ennobled by Louis XVI. Well educated and wealthy, the youth had no sympathy with the Revolution. With his brothers he joined the Royalist army, although he never saw actual service In 1793 he emigrated first to the South, and later to North America. During this time Grellet had passed from Roman Catholicism to atheism, but now, by a series of striking religious experiences, he was led into the Society of Friends. At Philadelphia, where he had settled, he was admitted a member in 1796 under the name of Stephen Grellet. He soon proved a powerful preacher, and travelled widely in the service of his religion in America and Europe. Early in his career he had a narrow escape from a gruesome death. During an epidemic of yellow fever in Philadelphia, in 1798, he had worked untiringly among the sufferers. He caught the disease and was found by the police apparently dead. His name was entered in the burial lists as " a French Quaker," and his coffin was ordered. Yet he revived, to live to the age of 82, to cross the Atlantic on four visits to Europe, to cheer many struggling souls, and to hold solemn, yet friendly, interviews with Kings, Emperors, and the Pope.[1]

It was in 1814, during his second Continental tour, that, as he writes : " I was brought under deep exercise for suffering humanity on account of the cruel scourge of war, such as I have so awfully beheld during my late engagements in France and Germany. My soul was poured forth with supplication to the Lord that he might open a door for me to plead with the Kings and rulers of the nations, that if possible a return of such a calamity might be averted." He laid the " concern " before the London Yearly Meeting of 1814, who adopted it and entrusted its execution to the Meeting for Sufferings, a deputation from which approached both rulers. Alexander, who at this time was under strong influence of a pietist character, had already come into contact with Friends through

---

[1] Pope Pius VII. For this remarkable interview, *vide Memoirs of Stephen Grellet*, ii. 60, ch. xxxviii.

the foundation of the Russian Bible Society. The "respectful and affectionate" address is remarkably warm in tone. It invokes on the Czar the blessings promised to "the merciful and the peace-maker," gives a short sketch of Friends' early sufferings, by which they had learned "to feel for those in all parts of the world who may be conscientiously obliged to decline practices which they believe to be inconsistent with the Spirit of the Gospel," and thus leads up to a plea for religious liberty in Russia. A similar plea was the main theme of the address to Frederick William of Prussia, to which he returned a courteous reply, but added that "war was necessary to procure peace." There is a tradition that, on seeing some drab coats among the crowds witnessing the entrance of the Sovereigns of London, the King exclaimed : "Quakers are very good subjects ; I wish I had more of them in my kingdom."[1] If the story is true, he was assuredly an adept at dissembling his love, as the little band of Quakers which had gathered at Minden since 1790 found to their cost.

Alexander, on the other hand, not only held affecting private interviews with William Allen, Stephen Grellet, and other Quakers, but, to the gaping astonishment of London Society, drove one Sunday with his sister, the Duchess of Oldenburg, to Westminster meeting-house. The Imperial visitors arrived in the midst of the worship, but they sat "with great seriousness" through the time remaining. Two days later William Allen, Stephen Grellet, and John Wilkinson waited on the Czar to present the address. A long conversation on religion and the principles of Friends ensued in which, records Stephen Grellet, "we entered fully on the subject of our testimony against war, to which he fully assented." The Czar, indeed, was all friendliness, urged the advantages of a Quaker settlement in Russia, promised such settlers full religious liberty and, in taking leave, remarked, "I part from you as friends and brethren."[2]

Three years later, when the Emperor planned the draining and reclamation of the swamps and waste land around St. Petersburg, he sought for an Englishman, if possible a Friend, to superintend

---

[1] Mrs. Boyce, *Records of a Quaker Family*, p. 146.

[2] For these episodes, *vide Meeting for Sufferings*, 6th mo. 1814 ; *Life of William Allen*, ii. 192 fol. ; *Memoirs of Stephen Grellet*, i. 241 fol. The Czar also expressed a wish that "crowned heads" would settled their differences by arbitration rather than by the sword. Four years later at St. Petersburg he repeated this desire to Stephen Grellet, explaining that his longing that "war and bloodshed might cease from the earth," had led him to form the Holy Alliance.

the work. The post was given to Daniel Wheeler, who removed to Russia with his wife and family. For fourteen years the little group did useful work in agriculture, and enjoyed the full confidence of the Emperor.[1]

As a sect, they took no root in Russia, where many of their tenets and practices resembled those of other bodies of dissenters from the Orthodox Church. When Stephen Grellet and William Allen travelled in Russia in 1819 during their long " religious visit " to the Continent, they had dealings with many of these people, the German Mennonites, who had settled in Russia on Catherine the Second's invitation, the Molokans or " Spiritual Christians," and the Doukhobors. The last-named, even at that date, the two Friends found vague in doctrine and unruly in practice. Grellet and Allen were warmly greeted by the Emperor, with whom they had meetings for prayer. Alexander seems to have had real and hearty esteem for both men. It was at this time that he offered William Allen the exclusive supply of drugs and medicines to the Russian Army, an offer which was, of course, declined. But Allen did not hesitate to use his friendship with the Emperor for the benefit of others. In 1822 he travelled to Vienna and Verona for the express purpose of influencing him, if possible, to take action at the Congress against the slave-trade, on behalf of religious toleration, and in favour of the unhappy Greeks. At Verona he found Wellington the most sympathetic of the delegates, and he did not leave the city until he knew that the slave-trade, at least, had been condemned. But his friend the Emperor had by this time fallen under the influence

[1] Daniel Wheeler as a youth had been a midshipman in the Navy, and then in 1792 enlisted as a private, serving first in Ireland and then in Hanover, where he suffered great hardships. In 1795, on his regiment's voyage to the West Indies, his whole character was changed by the experience of a terrific storm. He said later : " I was at this time convinced of Friends' principles, they being neither more nor less in my estimation, than pure Christianity. . . . No human means were made use of ; it was altogether the work of the Holy Spirit upon my heart." Feeling that war was utterly unchristian he procured his discharge, and returned home to find that his sister had married a Friend and joined the Society. He soon followed her example. After some years as a farmer and seed-merchant, he undertook the work in Russia, which he surrendered in 1832 for a long and arduous missionary visit to Australasia and the islands of the South Pacific. He died on a visit to New York in 1840. Thomas Dimsdale, a well-known eighteenth-century physician, was the son of a Quaker. He received large rewards, and the title of Baron of the Russian Empire for his services at various times in inoculating the Empress Catherine and other members of the Imperial House, including Alexander himself as a child. Dimsdale was not himself a Friend, but Alexander may have gained his first knowledge of the Society from him.

of Metternich and other reactionaries. The various revolutions, in Spain, Greece, and Naples against established but abominable Governments, filled him with horror, which blotted out the last remains of his earlier liberal principles. When Allen learned of the course of reaction and oppression, both at home and abroad, sanctioned by Alexander, he dispatched (April 29, 1823) a very plain-spoken letter of remonstrance. " It is said that the Emperor of Russia, who had so publicly patronized the Societies in America and England for the promotion of universal peace, had now become the secret and open abettor of war." But, continued Allen, the policy of non-intervention in the internal affairs of another State, is the only one compatible with justice, for the peoples themselves are the best judges of their own interests. He added a strong plea for political and social reform.[1] This was a strange document to journey from a London tradesman to the Czar of all the Russias. It does not appear that any answer was returned. Later intercourse with Russia on the part of Friends (with the important exception of the Peace Mission in 1854) was mainly confined to persecuted sects, such as the Mennonites and Doukhobors, and to relief work in some of the great famines.

In France, as has been remarked, the early Quaker missionaries produced little effect. Yet, curiously enough, the Society, during its first century of existence, received a good deal of notice from French writers on English characteristics or on contemporary religious phenomena.[2]

---

[1] Life of William Allen, vide ii. 340.

[2] M. Gustave Lanson in his critical edition of Voltaire's Lettres Philosophiques gives a list of such works. Among them may be mentioned : Phil. Nandé, Historie Abrégée . . . de Kouakerisme, 1692 ; Henri Misson, Memoires et Observations faites par un voyageur en Angleterre, La Haye, 1698 ; Le Sage, Remarques sur l'Angleterre, Amsterdam, 1715, and P. Catrou, Histoire des Trembleurs, 1733. The works of Misson and Le Sage are in the British Museum Library ; from them a few obiter dicta may be quoted upon the Quakers : Misson, p. 359. " Les Quacres sont de grand Fanatique. Il paroit en eux quelque chose de louable ; il semble qu'ils soient doux, simples a tous égards, sobres, modestes, paisibles. Ils ont même la reputation d'être fidèles, et cela est souvent vrai. Mais il ne faut pas s'y tromper, car il y a souvent aussi bien du fard dans tout cet extérieur." Le Sage, pp. 28-9. " Ils font profession de ne point résister au mal. . . . Dans les carosses de voyages l'on les trouve de bonne humeur et pleins d'histoires plaisantes. . . . Ils refusent d'aller au guerre, mais l'on rapporte plusieurs exemples de Capitaines des vaisseaux marchands de cette religion, que se font bien défendus contre les Corsaires." Had Le Sage heard and misunderstood some version of Lurting's exploit ? For the Quaker in the stage coach, cp. the Spectator, No. 132 (1711).

These accounts are not always friendly, and very seldom accurate, since they often were based on the fantasies of Gerald Croese, but they have some importance from their share in awakening in Voltaire that interest in Quakers which led to his notable description of them.

From 1725 to 1729 Voltaire was in practical exile in England, where he gathered materials for his *Lettres sur les Anglais*, in which he contrasted the intellectual, political, and social freedom of England with the evils of privilege and restriction in France. The treatment was superficial, but there was an undercurrent of serious argument. Lord Morley has well described how Voltaire's imagination was struck by a sect which regarded Christianity as the religion of Christ. " It is impossible to say how much of the kindliness with which he speaks of them is due to real admiration of their simple, dignified and pacific life, and how much to a mischievous desire to make their praise a handle for the dispraise of overweening competitors. On the whole, there is a sincerity and heartiness of interest in his long account of this sect which persuades one that he was moved by a genuine sympathy with a religion that could enjoin the humane and peaceful and spiritual precepts of Christ, while putting away baptism, ceremonial communion, and hierophantic orders. . . . Above all, Voltaire, who was nowhere more veritably modern or better entitled to our veneration than by reason of his steadfast hatred of war, revered a sect so far removed from the brutality of the military regime as to hold peace for a first principle of the Christian faith and religious practice."[1]

In later writings, the *Dictionnaire Philosophique* and his contributions to the *Encyclopédie*, Voltaire again described the Quakers, but these *Letters* are his most elaborate treatment of the subject. An English translation was published in 1733, and the French original appeared (professedly against Voltaire's wish) in 1734. During part of his stay in England he was the guest at Wandsworth of a rich London merchant, Edward Falkener. There he had English lessons from Edward Higginson, a young usher in a Quaker school in that suburb, who left a curious account of their intercourse, published a century later. For practice in English, Voltaire " would translate the *Apology* of Robert Barclay, commending the same so far as to acknowledge it to be the finest or purest Church Latin he knew. In his translating his Epistle to King Charles II, instead

[1] Morley, *Voltaire*, pp. 82-5.

of using the word *thou* or *thee* he would write *you*, which made it to my ear seem harsh."[1]

Voltaire studied the *Apology* to some effect, making extensive use of it in the *Letters*. Another Quaker acquaintance was Andrew Pitt of Hampstead, a London merchant, who corresponded with Voltaire on philosophical subjects, after his return to France. Pitt undoubtedly figures as the Quaker informant quoted by Voltaire in the *Letters*. The first four letters of the series describe the Quakers, and in the first there is an uncompromising statement of their attitude to war, largely borrowed from Barclay, though the passage here quoted is pure Voltaire. " Our God . . . has no mind that we should cross the sea to cut the throats of our brothers, because murderers in red coats and hats two feet high enlist our fellow citizens, making a noise with two little sticks on a drum of ass's skin. And when after victories won, all London blazes with illuminations, the sky is aflame with rockets and the air resounds with the din of thanksgiving, bells, organ, cannon, we mourn in silence over the murders that cause the public delight." In the second letter are described with touches of flippancy the Quaker mode of worship, and the doctrine of immediate revelation. The third gives an account of Fox and the growth of the Society. Fox, says Voltaire, " went from village to village, preaching against war and the clergy." At Derby he was brought before the magistrates and when struck by a sergeant, turned the other cheek. He converted some soldiers, who quitted the army, for " Cromwell had no use for a sect that did not fight." These inaccuracies are perhaps due to a hasty study of Croese's *History*. Letter Four is devoted to Penn and Pennsylvania. Incidentally, in a reference to Penn's German travels, Voltaire explains the " small harvest reaped from the seed sown in Germany " by the suggestion that men who had constantly to use such terms as " Highness " and " Excellency " would not relish the Quaker *tutoiement*. The eloquent description of Penn's dealings with the Indians is sufficiently well known. His government, says Voltaire, was a true Golden Age. " A Government without priests, a people without weapons, citizens on an equality, and neighbours free from envy and suspicion."

[1] Luke Howard, *The Yorkshireman*, i. 167–9 (1832–3), also Churton Collins, *Voltaire . . . in England*, p. 15 (1908). Voltaire quoted Barclay's dedication in the *Letters*, using, however, the singular pronoun. In a letter of later date he remarks on the Quaker practice, " Le *tu* est le langage de la verité et le *vous* le langage du compliment " (*Œuvres*, edited by Moland, xxxiii. 378).

Brissot, who visited Philadelphia fifty years later, unkindly declared that Voltaire would have been sadly bored in his ideal state. " He would have yawned in their assemblies and been mortified to see his epigrams pass without applause."[1] Though Voltaire came into contact with the Society at what is generally admitted to be a period of inertia and timidity, yet it made on him an impression of sincerity and idealism. At a later date he summed up his opinion of the Quakers in the *Encyclopédie.*

" Apres cela qu'on range tant qu'on voudra les Quakers parmi les fanatiques ; ce sont toujours des fanatiques bien estimables. Je ne puis m'empêcher de déclarer, que je les estime un peuple vraiment grand, vertueux, plein d'industrie, d'intelligence, et de sagesse. Ce sont des gens animés des principes les plus étendus de beneficence, qu'il y ait jamais eu sur la terre. . . . Enfin, c'est peut-être le seul parti chez les Chrétiens, dont la pratique du corps entier reponde constamment a ses principes. Je n'ai point de honte d'avouer que j'ai lu et relu avec un plaisir singulier *l'Apologie du Quakerisme* par Robert Barclay ; il m'a convaincu que c'est, tout calculé, le système le plus raisonable et le plus parfait qu'on ait encore imaginé."[2]

Many of the French intellectuals and reformers of the eighteenth century were strongly influenced by Voltaire's enthusiasm. Montesquieu and the Abbé Raynal echoed his praises of Penn's constitution.[3] Brissot de Warville, in his pre-Revolutionary days, in *New Travels in America*, 1783-9, gave a disproportionate space to the virtues of Friends, and particularly to their philanthropic work in Philadelphia. He also combated the slanders of other French travellers who visited America during the war, when Quakers were unpopular. But Brissot, while blaming their neutrality in the struggle, equally blames their persecutors. His account is another testimony to the general belief in the peace views of Friends.

" This people believe that example is more powerful than

---

[1] Brissot, *New Travels* (English translation), p. 265.

[2] Some of Voltaire's flippancies and inaccuracies did not pass uncorrected at the time. In 1741, Josiah Martin published *A Letter from one of the people called Quakers to Francis de Voltaire,* explaining that it had been sent to Voltaire in September 1733, after the publication of the English *Letters,* but that the French edition has since appeared without modification. Martin does not criticize the remarks on war.

[3] Montesquieu, *Esprit des Lois,* Book IV ; Raynal, *Histoire des Indes,* Book XVIII. In this he speaks inaccurately of Pennsylvania as entirely undefended.

words ; that kings will always find the secret of perpetrating wars as long as they can hire men to murder each other, and that it is their duty as a Society, to resolve never to take arms or to contribute to the expenses of any war. They have been tormented, robbed, imprisoned, and martyred ; they have suffered everything ; till tyranny itself, wearied with their perseverance, has exempted them from military service, and has been driven to indirect measures to force contributions from their hands."[1]

In a second edition (1790) Brissot added a curious postscript comparing the principles of Friends with those of the Revolutionists. The only difference he can find is that while both love liberty, the French fight for it. " But notwithstanding this ardour in the French to arm themselves in so holy a cause, they do not less respect the religious opinions of the Quakers, which forbid them to spill the blood of their enemies. This error of theirs is so charming that it is almost as good as a truth. We are all striving for the same object— universal fraternity ; the Quakers by gentleness, we by resistance. Their means are those of a society, ours those of a powerful nation." [2] Three years later, when Brissot died by the guillotine, he found that French " ardour " was not the most direct road to universal brotherhood.

During his brief period of power, he had been able to give some help to the Quakers in France. For, before the close of the nineteenth century, there were two Quaker groups in that country. One was a band of temporary immigrants. William Rotch of Nantucket, whose troubles during the War of Independence have already been related,[3] migrated with other members of his family to Dunkirk in 1785, to carry on thence the whaling business, which had been ruined in Nantucket by British restrictions. From 1790 to 1793 he was himself in residence at Dunkirk. Before settling there he had applied to the Government for " a full and free enjoyment of our religion according to the principles of the people called Quakers, and an entire exemption from military requisitions of every kind." Both requests were granted, the latter on the express ground that the immigrants were " a peaceable people, and meddle not with

---

[1] *New Travels* (English edition 1794), p. 354. He is severe on the Marquis de Chastellux who had published *Travels in North America in* 1780.

[2] *New Travels*, p. 360.

[3] *Vide* Chapter XV. The references there given are also the sources of the following account.

the quarrels of princes, neither internal nor external." After the outbreak of war in 1792 the Dunkirk authorities became alarmed for the safety of the Quakers, who steadily refused to illuminate for the reported victories over Austria. At last the Mayor remarked : " Your houses are your own : the streets are ours," and arranged an ingenious framework of lamps in front of his own house and that of each Quaker. The Dunkirkers admired the new style in illumination, and the Rotch family was unmolested. When some malicious person complained to some Commissioners from Paris, visiting the town on public business, of the Quaker pecularities, they received the reply that the French Government was being established on the principles of Pennsylvania and it would be unfitting to persecute Quakers. The argument must have been supplied by Brissot.

In 1791 William Rotch and his son Benjamin appeared with Jean de Marsillac before the National Assembly in support of the petition of the French Quakers of Congénies for the recognition of their worship and for exemption from the oath of loyalty to the Republic and from military service. Brissot and other Girondins sympathized with them, assisting them in the presentation of their case. The petition was read before a full house on February 10, 1791.[1] It reminded the Assembly that France had recently set an example to the world by an edict of universal toleration. " One of our principles has drawn down on us severe persecution, but Providence has enabled us to overcome them without recourse to violence. It is the principle which forbids us to take up arms to kill man on any pretext. This harmonizes with the holy Scriptures in which Christ has said : Do not render evil for evil, but do good to all men." The French have recognized this doctrine of universal brotherhood in their oath never to undertake a war of conquest. " This course will lead you and the whole world towards universal peace. Do not then look askance on men who by their example are hastening this peace." Pennsylvania had shown that their policy is practical, and their scruples had been tolerated in England and the United States.

Mirabeau, as President of the Assembly, made a friendly reply. The various religious privileges asked for were granted. As for non-resistance, it was " un beau principe philosophique," but impracticable. In Pennsylvania (according to Mirabeau) the Quakers were " eloignés des sauvages," but if put to the test, they would

<hr />

[1] *Petition à l'Assemblée Nationale* in D. Tracts, vol. ccxii, No. 18.

have fought in defence of their wives and children. He ended :
" Si jamais je recontre un Quaker, je lui dirai. Mon frère, si tu
as le droit d'être libre tu as le droit d'empêcher qu'on te fasse
esclave. Puisque tu aimes ton semblable, ne le laisse pas égorger
par la tyrannie. Ce feroit le tuer toi-même."

The French Friends, who were the promoters of the petition,
had existed for about a century as a body quite independent of the
Society in England, to whom they had only just become known.
After the Revocation of the Edict of Nantes in 1685, the Protestants
in the South of France, when they did not escape to England and
America, for the most part adopted a policy of desperate resistance
to persecution. The mutual cruelties of the Catholic soldiers and
the " Camisards " of the Cevennes form a bloody page in history.
Yet among these Protestants a small body arose, or had survived
from Waldensian times, which believed that earthly weapons were
unlawful in a spiritual cause and that ecclesiastical ordinances were
a hindrance to spiritual life. Their origin is obscure ; according
to some they were at first led by one of the " prophetesses," who
were a feature of the Camisard movement. Others again point to
a stirring letter attributed to a " prophet," Daniel Raoul, who wrote
it, while awaiting execution, to protest against the use of the sword
in answer to persecution. Probably the parents of Antony Benezet,
before they fled from France, belonged to this sect which met secretly
at Fontanes and neighbouring villages. In 1769 Paul Codognan
of Congénies, a member, visited Holland. Here he learnt of the
existence of the English Friends, and proceeded to London. His
English was scanty, and though he became acquainted with Friends,
it does not seem that they realized his position as a member of a
kindred body. However, he was welcomed as a sympathizer, attended
Yearly Meeting, and returned to Congénies, bringing with him
French copies of two works by Penn, *No Cross, No Crown*, and
The Rise and Progress of the People called Quakers.

A few years later the little community received an important
accession. Jean de Marsillac, a young officer, first heard of Quakers
from a colleague who had served in the United States. After a
study of Barclay's *Apology* and the article upon the sect in the
Encyclopédie, he resigned his commission. This was in 1777 ; in
1783 he settled with the Friends at Congénies.[1] Next year another

---

[1] For Marsillac's later history, *vide J.F.H.S.*, vols. xv, xvi, xviii. He became
a physician, migrated to Philadelphia in 1795, and was admitted to membership by Friends there. But in 1797, the shock of a serious carriage accident,

turn of the wheel brought them again into contact with English Friends. During the war with America and France two Cornish packets, part owned by Dr. Joseph Fox, of Fowey, were fitted out as privateers and took some French ships as prizes in the Channel. The Doctor did not refuse his share of the prize, but invested it for the benefit of the original owners. As soon as the war ended, his son, Edward Long Fox, went to Paris to advertise for these owners in the official *Gazette*. But he met with an unexpected hindrance. The Comte de Vergennes, then Foreign Minister, could not believe that such an object was genuine, and was with difficulty persuaded to allow the advertisement to appear. In all £1,500 was refunded, before the war with France put a stop to intercourse. After the Peace of 1815 the balance of £600 was invested for the benefit of disabled seamen in the French mercantile marine.

The Quaker mission made some stir in France. It came to the notice of the Congénies " Quakers," from whom, in April 1785, young Fox received a letter of greeting. Thus communication was established. Marsillac visited England with an address signed by forty-five of his fellow members explaining their position. In 1788 they were visited by English and American Friends, who did much to help their organization into a religious body, although they insisted on details of " plainness " in dress and manner uncongenial to the French mind.[1] But the advice, support, and financial help of the English Society were of great value. In 1787-8 the French body negotiated with Vergennes, Louis' minister, for inclusion among the Protestants, to whom it was proposed to grant civil rights.

During the Revolution the majority stood firm in refusal to comply with the law of 1792 concerning the National Guard, and they were allowed to escape service. The war with England next year cut off all personal intercourse, though there was frequent

---

in which his companion was killed, seems to have caused in him a reaction from Quakerism. He returned to France, where he adopted fashionable dress and pursued the ordinary amusements of society. He is said to have served as a doctor under Napoleon, but our only further information comes from an affectionate letter he sent in 1815 to an English Friend. At that time he had held high office in Paris hospitals.

[1] The French Quakers printed their first *Précis des règles de discipline Chrétienne* in 1785 (D. Tracts, 214.10). A summary of Friends' history and teaching was translated in 1790 (D. Tracts, 212.15).

correspondence.[1] Stephen Grellet, as an American, in spite of difficulties and dangers, was able to visit them twice, in 1807 and 1811, to their great help and comfort. He grieved for them and for his native France under the crushing burden of conscription, and tried in vain to reach and plead with Napoleon himself. The Quakers were in a hard case. One of the first communications they received from England in 1815 was a censure upon those who had taken up arms. To this the French Friends replied with some spirit that those who yielded rather deserved compassion ; they were for the most part dragged from their homes by force. " Yet not one of our members has to blush for having done violence to any. We think ourselves happy in having never been concerned in any plot, in having never been engaged in any action where blood was spilt."[2] But the hard pressure of the law gradually drove the majority of young men into emigration. Those who remained either suffered periodic imprisonment or were forced to hire substitutes at exorbitant rates. The list of membership in 1822 showed two hundred names, of whom ninety belonged to the Congénies Meeting and the remainder to Nîmes, Fontanes, and St. Gilles. But the numbers gradually dwindled. In the war of 1870 the Friends took no part. One member, Jean Benezet, underwent severe trials for his refusal to train as a National Guard, but they felt (as they reported to English Friends) that they had not been faithful in bearing their testimony against war " with sufficient publicity."[3] Under the Third Empire the prevailing corruption had led to laxity in the enforcement of service, but now the pressure was renewed, and was followed by renewed emigration. At Congénies two elderly women are the last survivors of these French " Friends."

The story of Friends in Germany has some points of resemblance to that of their brethren in France. The old German Meetings died out early in the eighteenth century, but in 1790 English and American Friends visited many towns, holding meetings with groups

---

[1] For fuller details of these French Friends *vide* C. Tylor, *The Camisards,* pp. 431 foll. ; Jaulmes, *Les Quakers Français* ; *The Friend,* 1848, p. 51 etc. ; also MS. correspondence with Congénies in a collection of *Casual Correspondence* in D. After 1817 the Reports of the Continental Committee of the Meeting for Sufferings contain information ; the first French " Discipline " was adopted at Congénies in 1785.

[2] *Casual Correspondence,* 1815.

[3] *Friend,* 1870, p. 264 ; *Proceedings of Yearly Meeting,* 1872, p. 36 (Report of Continental Committee). For the present position in France, *vide* p. 499.

of religiously minded persons.[1] At Minden, a garrison town, the capital of Westphalia, and at Pyrmont, a health resort in Waldeck, these groups were found ready to accept the general principles and practice of Friends.[2] In 1794-5 John Pemberton, one of the three Philadelphia brothers, paid a similar visit to Germany. But the hardships of travel told heavily on a man of sixty-seven. After some weeks of earnest service at Pyrmont, he died there, leaving on the newly formed Meeting a deep impression of self-sacrifice and devotion.

The Meetings were organized and Meeting-houses built, at the suggestion and with the financial help of English Friends though, during the war, visits could only be made by Americans. Waldeck was a small independent principality ; its ruler was friendly, and the Pyrmont Meeting enjoyed toleration from the outset. Minden, which was in the Prussian jurisdiction, fared very differently. Friends there soon came into collision with the authorities. From 1798 to 1800 their Meeting-house was sealed up by order of the Government, because of objection taken to addresses delivered there by visiting American Friends.[3] In 1799 a deputation of Minden and Pyrmont Friends appealed to the King himself on behalf of the former Meeting. The King replied (June 2, 1799) :

" His royal majesty the King of Prussia holds sacred the liberty of conscience in matters of faith of all his subjects. But civil institutions, and especially the fulfilment of those civil duties without which were the dispensation general, the State itself could not exist, have nothing in common with this. No religious sect like that of the Quakers, whose confession of faith excludes its followers from the most important civil duties in an independent State, can therefore

---

[1] They were Robert and Sarah Grubb of England, and George and Sarah Dillwyn of America. They had already visited Congénies. For Pyrmont and Minden Friends, see *Proceedings of Yearly Meeting* 1868 (Historical Account of Friends in Germany), pp. 80 foll. Also articles in *The Friend*, 1845-6, taken from an account by F. Schmidt, a Minden Friend, written in 1823.

[2] The summary of Friends' History and Teaching translated for the French Quakers in 1790, was translated into German in 1792.

[3] A curious later parallel may be quoted : " A good many years ago " Professor Vinogradoff visited a settlement of Old Ritualists in Moscow. After a service in the outer chapel, " we were conducted towards the inner chapel of the altar. It was closed and seals were affixed to the gates : they were seals of different Public Departments put on because the Government, though tolerating ordinary functions in the Church, did not allow the Old Ritualists to celebrate High Mass for fear of their making converts among the adherents of the Established Church " Vinogradoff, *Self-Government in Russia*, 1915, p. 13).

lay claim to the right of the public exercise of their religion. Even to tolerate them is a favour which must not be extended too far, lest the State should suffer by it. . . ."

Thus he confirmed the decision of the Minden authorities. In February 1800 the Friends made a fresh appeal, by which they obtained a partial measure of toleration for the six families then composing the Meeting. This was granted by a royal decree (February 23, 1800) which gave them freedom of worship, the use of their form of marriage, exemption from oaths, and permission to educate their children, while " on their refusal to comply with civil regulations in essential points " (i.e. military service) their fines should be levied by legal process of distraint. These favours were shown on the express ground that the Friends " have not increased since the year 1790." They were forbidden to marry members of other sects or to acquire landed property. Finally, they were warned that, " they shall on the first admission of a new member be deprived of the toleration now granted to them. That such member, if a stranger shall, without any indulgence, be immediately passed beyond our frontiers, or, if our subject, be compelled by the successive steps of legal coercion, to submit to our civil order."

In 1801 the Friends were again solemnly warned against making proselytes, but defended themselves courageously before the Minden court, declaring that their meetings were open to all and that they had nothing to conceal. In practice the Edict was so interpreted that, while the original Friends were not deprived of toleration on the accession of new members, these latter did not share in any of the exemptions granted by the decree. During the fifteen years of war which followed, the Meeting suffered more from the weakness of its own members than from outside interference. But, though some at this time entered military service, the majority established their claim to exemption, with the result that in December 1813 (after the " War of Liberation ") a Royal Cabinet Order exempted Friends, Mennonites, and Anabaptists, on payment of a contribution to military requirements, from all forms of military service, because such service was against their religious principles. In 1814 the Friends paid the contribution not (so they ingenuously explained afterwards) as a contribution towards the war, but as a token of gratitude for the toleration they had of late enjoyed. This year a visit from Stephen Grellet brough fresh power and courage to Minden Friends, while the intercourse of Frederick William with Allen and Grellet in

London may have had its effect in preserving them at first from the operation of a new law of universal military service, beyond the levying by distraints of the usual fines, amounting to three per cent. of the Friends' income.

In 1817 the Meeting for Sufferings appointed a standing Continental committee to correspond with Friends abroad. This committee soon found work to do on behalf of Minden Friends. From 1818 onwards Christian Peitsmeyer of Eidinghausen, near Minden, was summoned each year to military service. A memorial sent by the Meeting for Sufferings to the King of Prussia in January 1826 describes what followed.

" On being called upon to serve as a soldier, he could not, from a conscientious scruple against all war, comply with the requisition ; whereupon he was stripped, and beaten with swords and sticks, he was then kicked, and when he could not stand any longer, he was tied to a stake and again cruelly treated."

The Friends at Minden protested to the Government, quoting the exemption order of 1813. To this the Government replied that the order had applied only to the existing war, and that now " Separatists " would be compelled to serve. In 1822 came the turn of his brother Ernst. He (said the memorial) " was called up and as he informed the court he could not without violence to his conscience take the military oath and bear arms, he was committed to prison for six weeks : at length a process of confiscation of property was instituted against him, but he was freed from this by the first court of magistrate, and not considered as contumacious ; because the law applied only to those who left their country on refusing to bear arms, and not to one who refused on Christian principle. But the fiscal officer of the regiment appealed against the decision, and the second court reversed it, and condemned him to the loss of all his little property, as well as his right of inheritance, and has disqualified him from conducting any business ; the court considering him of the same class with those who leave the country."

Thomas Shillitoe and Thomas Christy, who were then visiting Germany, appealed to the King for protection, reminding him that he had once declared conscience to be a sacred thing, to which he replied : " It is so, and the young man shall not suffer." He intervened to secure the remission of the sentence.[1] In some neighbouring villages there were by this time small groups of Friends

[1] *Journal of Thomas Shillitoe*, ii. 23-40.

in connection with the Minden meeting. One of these, Eidinghausen, was the home of the Peitsmeyers, and of another young man, Henry Schmidt, described in the memorial as an " adherent," though not an actual member. In 1825 he became liable to service, and, on his refusal, arrested. He was then, the memorial asserted, " stripped of his clothes and dressed in military garments, arms were bound upon his back, and he was led to the place of exercise ; but, as he still did not comply, he was again committed to prison and kept for three days and three nights in succession upon the laths (Latten), and this dreadful punishment was, it appears, repeated at different times, nothing being given him for his sustenance but a piece of bread and a bottle of water.¹ A representation was then made on his behalf to the Major, whereupon he was on the following day released from this part of his punishment, and after four weeks' imprisonment, he was set at liberty, with a warning that, if he persisted, the process of confiscation would be instituted against him."

Three English Friends (Thomas Christy, George Stacey, and Samuel Gurney) personally approached the King with this memorial. He at once condemned the action of the military authorities as " contrary to law and in opposition to the royal views," but said that the cases must be left to the decision of the Privy Supreme Tribunal (the highest court of appeal). He also directed that " the legal rights of Quakers at present residing in his dominions or who may at any future time settle therein, in particular reference to their connection with the State shall be more closely investigated and established and the result speedily made known to them."²

" The result " was not unduly favourable to Friends : although there were few cases of gross brutality in later times, the policy of imprisonment, fines, or restriction of civil rights continued for all except members of the six privileged families. Yet " difficulties fostered rather than checked religious zeal."³ Between 1814 and 1840 eighteen Friends had joined the Minden Meeting, while the

---

¹ The *Latten* was a cage or cell, floored with triangular planks of oak, sharp edge uppermost, into which the prisoner was put naked and barefoot, so that he could neither stand nor lie with comfort. According to an editorial note to Frederick Schmidt's *Account of Minden Friends*, this punishment was introduced to the garrison at Minden by Napoleon, when he made the town capital of his new kingdom of Westphalia (*Friend*, 1846, p. 88).

² Account of Meeting for Sufferings.

³ *Proceedings of Yearly Meeting*, 1868 (History of Friends in Germany).

more secure body at Pyrmont could only report five. On the other hand, the steady pressure of the conscription law drove the majority of the young men and some whole families to emigration. In 1839 the history of Danzig was repeated. The Minden Meeting suggested a complete emigration, and the London Friends dissuaded them. But piecemeal emigration continued ; children were sent to school in England, sometimes by the generosity of English Friends, or later at their parents' expense, as the German Friends prospered in trade. Some of these children settled in England and America ; [1] a few, on their return to Germany, undertook military service and were disowned. After the establishment of the Empire the same influences were in force at Pyrmont. Yet it is remarkable that in several instances the poorer Friends, who could not escape, were treated with considera-tion. The authorities tried to avoid conflict with the conscientious objector by dismissing him on various pretexts, generally that of health.[2] On one occasion a young Friend from Obernkirchen, near Minden, was put back into a lower age group, and when he came back at the appointed time the officers in dismay asked : " Why had he come ?—they would not have sent for him."

Before 1870 the Pyrmont Friends were reduced to a mere handful, but the Minden Meeting continued, in gradually decreasing numbers, until very recent times.

The last body, or rather bodies, of Friends to be noticed are those in Norway and Denmark. These Scandinavian Friends had an interesting origin.[3] During the early eighteenth century a Danish pastor, Christopher Meidel, was engaged at the Lutheran Mission to Sailors in London. Here he studied the writings of Friends, and before 1705 had joined the Society, for whose principles he suffered imprisonment at Chelmsford, and later in Denmark. Translations of various Friends' works into Danish were made by him for the Society. When in the next century Denmark became involved in the Continental war a considerable number of Danes and Norwegians serving in her Navy were captured by England and

---

[1] One of these, Benjamin Seebohm, became a leading minister among Friends.
[2] *Proceedings of Yearly Meeting* 1870 (Report of Continental Committee, p. 33). *Vide* p. 499 for recent work in Germany.
[3] *Vide* George Richardson, *Rise and Progress of the Society of Friends in Norway* 1849, and also *Proceedings of Yearly Meeting*, 1887, p. 72 (Report of the Continental Committee). At that time the number of Norwegians in actual membership was about 150, and of Danes, 90. The numbers had been larger, but were constantly reduced by emigration.

imprisoned on ships of war in the Medway. Friends were active in sending tracts and religious works in various languages to the prisoners of war. In 1814 one of these, Meidel's translation of Barclay's *Apology*, fell into the hands of a young Norwegian who, with some of his friends, had already begun to worship together in captivity much after the manner of a Friends' meeting. Finding that a religious Society already existed, and that some were living at Rochester, he wrote to them with the help of an English dictionary. Rochester Friends visited the little group, held meetings with them, and instructed them in doctrine until the peace, when some thirty Norwegian and Danish Friends returned home. Frequent visits were paid to those in Norway by English Friends, but until the year 1845 they suffered severely both for worshipping apart from the State Church and for refusal of military service. In 1845, after an appeal from the Meeting for Sufferings, the Norwegian Storthing passed a fairly liberal measure of religious toleration. This, however, did not secure any exemption from military service, as the Norwegian law did not recognize the conscientious objector.

In Denmark the returned prisoners of war did not keep up their connection with Friends. About the year 1866 a small body of persons in sympathy with Friends arose who soon were acknowledged as members of the Society. This branch of Friends was organized after visits from English Friends in 1877, and has been maintained up to the present day, in the face of many difficulties, not least of which is the law of compulsory service. Both in Norway and Denmark, throughout the nineteenth century, young men Friends suffered repeated terms of imprisonment on this account, in spite of remonstrances by their own body and appeals from the Meeting for Sufferings. There were frequent emigrations to America, and in the West, Iowa for example, there are some meetings composed wholly of Scandinavian Friends. In 1901 an attempt was made in Norway to arrange alternative service in civil occupations for Friends and others with a religious objection to war, and a few years later the same question arose in Denmark. Apparently, in both cases, non-combatant military work would have been granted to Friends as Friends, but they desired that the alternative employment should be civilian, and that the conscientious objectors outside their own body, who were also making a stand against the law, should be recognised.

In Norway the majority of the Friends are settled round

Stavanger. In Denmark they are scattered, and in no one place is there a group sufficiently large to require a meeting-house. But quite recently there has been an addition of several new members.

From the foregoing account it will be evident that on the Continent of Europe, even in a Protestant environment, Friends have held no secure place. No doubt the foundation of Pennsylvania had much to do with the emigration of the earlier bodies, many of them impelled by persecution at home. But in the nineteenth century the operation of conscription has been clearly one of the main causes of decay. The young life of these small Meetings was forced to choose between change of country and change of creed— or, at least, of practice. Had these Friends possessed the immense enthusiasm and devotion of the early Quaker preachers they might have gathered a band of adherents with whom even Governments would have had to reckon. But they had not the same missionary spirit, nor, indeed, was the world around them as ready to receive the message as seventeenth-century England and America. The growth of the modern missionary movement among English and American Friends dates from the middle of the nineteenth century. Its story has been told recently in a volume written to commemorate the fiftieth anniversary of the Friends' Foreign Mission Association.[1]

At the present time English Friends have mission fields in India, Madagascar, Syria, China, Pemba, and Constantinople, though the last is not actually under the Friends' Foreign Mission Association. During the war the Syrian missionaries were forced to suspend their work, but while on furlough some devoted themselves to the care of refugee Armenians in Egypt. Both in China and India, Friends have found that the war between Christian nations is a source of great perplexity to the converts, and even to non-Christians, who have some idea of the teachings of the New Testament. The position of Friends in regard to war is better understood than that of other missionaries.

An American Friend who travelled on peace work in Europe during 1915 found both in neutral and enemy countries friendliness towards Quakers. In Russia, memories remained of the Peace Deputation of 1854, and of famine relief work ; in Holland it was taken " as a matter of course " that English Friends should come over to help the Belgian refugees.

" But by far the warmest understanding for Friends was expressed

[1] *Friends Beyond Seas*, by Dr. Henry T. Hodgkin (Headley Bros., 1916).

by the Grand Duchess Luise of Baden, aunt of Kaiser William II, who has been acquainted for years with members of the Society. In a recent interview she compared the Society of Friends to the sower in the parable, and she laid stress on the fact that the sower had the courage to go forth and sow his seed ; and thus it is the duty of the comparatively small group of Friends to keep sowing the seeds of their views as to the settlement of international difficulties. . . . In every country " (added the writer) " and in nearly every interview my being a Friend, or a Quaker, as they usually say, was a source of added hospitality and of helpfulness in my work."[1] In the next chapter it will be shown how the recent work of Friends has led to a new growth of Quakerism at several centres on the Continent.

[1] Dr. Benjamin F. Battin of Swarthmore College in the *Friends' Intelligencer* (American), 1915, p. 807.

PART VI
CONCLUSION

CHAPTER XVIII

THE TWENTIETH CENTURY

IF, as seems most probable, the coming struggle between the forces of the world and the living spirit of Christ centres round the use or disuse of the anarchic barbarism of war as a fundamental institution of Christendom, then undoubtedly a time of suffering lies ahead for those who take their stand with the Prince of Peace on behalf of the Kingdom which calls for more courage, more divine and wholehearted devotion than any soldiering of man's creation. It is well to count the cost before the battle joins. All men will certainly cease to speak well of us; trade relationships may be crippled; children may be disqualified from some auspicious career. On the other hand, if we give way before the storm and our witness perish, no doubt deliverance will still come to humanity in another way and from another place, but "who knoweth whether we are not come to the Kingdom for such a time as this?"—JOSHUA ROWNTREE, *Brute Force* versus *Brotherhood*, 1913.

THE events of the last quarter of a century in the history both of the little Society of Friends and the great world are still too near to us to allow either a detailed or an impartial description. The present chapter can be nothing more than a summary.

The Yearly Meeting of 1900 uttered emphatic condemnation (quoted in an earlier chapter) of the war in South Africa under the shadow of which the nineteenth century ended and the twentieth began. Many Friends, in common with other Englishmen, had watched with anxiety the growth of friction and distrust between the Government of the Transvaal, on the one side and, on the other, the British settlers on the Rand and their sympathizers in our South African colonies. While the negotiations in the autumn of 1899 were proceeding, the Meeting for Sufferings addressed the English Government, expressing a fervent hope for a peaceful termination. War (on an ultimatum from President Kruger) broke out in October 1899. Public opinion here was by no means united

481

on the justice and inevitability of the war, especially when it developed into an undisguised war of conquest. The Labour Party and an important minority of the Liberal Party (including its official leader, Sir Henry Campbell-Bannerman, Mr. John Morley (now Viscount), and Robert Spence Watson (President of the National Liberal Federation) were keenly critical of the management of the negotiations, of certain harsh features in the conduct of the war itself, and especially of the policy of " unconditional surrender." Friends, as a whole, may be said to have ranged themselves on this side. What division of opinion there was mainly followed political lines. Since the rise of the Home Rule problem some members, few in numbers, but important from their wealth and influence, had become Unionists. Several of these, as was natural, gradually and almost unconsciously adopted the general views of the party to which they had become attached. These Friends, while deploring the war, considered that the Government were justified in undertaking it, and even that the prospect of better government in South Africa and better treatment of the natives should induce the Society to consider this war an exception to the rule expressed in the Eighth Query. One or two among them contributed letters on these lines to the *Friend* and the *British Friend*, but they did not press their views in the gatherings of the Society, and they certainly did not represent its general opinion.

On the other hand, Friends took a large share in the work of the " South African Conciliation Committees " formed in many centres to bring about an understanding between the contending races, and, like their fellow-workers, received the title of " pro-Boer " from the Jingo Press. At several meetings there was a good deal of mob violence, notably at Birmingham, where Mr. Lloyd George had to escape in disguise from the Town Hall. One of the worst instances was at Scarborough. The Rowntree family there had been Quakers from the first days of the Society. Joshua Rowntree, a solicitor and once Liberal member for the borough, was Chairman of the local Conciliation Committee, which in March 1900 arranged a private meeting for Mr. Cronwright-Schreiner of Cape Colony, who was visiting England in the interests of peace. The building was soon surrounded by an angry crowd, and on the advice of the Chief Constable the guests dispersed, finding both difficulty and danger in reaching their homes. For some hours that night the town was in the hands of the mob, who attacked the homes and business establishments of members of the committee, smashing windows and doing much damage.

This riot figured prominently in a debate in the House of Commons (March 15) on these disturbances. What had been done at Scarborough found few defenders, though the Premier (Mr. Balfour) declared that "those who call these meetings should be careful lest they ask more of human nature than all history shows that human nature is capable of bearing." It was replied that in many cases, as at Scarborough, these were private gatherings for intercourse and information, and did not involve a public demonstration.

On behalf of those who had suffered loss Joshua Rowntree sent a letter to the Press : " It is our desire that the sores arising from the recent visit of Mr. Cronwright-Schreiner to Scarborough may speedily be healed. As one contribution to this end, we wish to state that it is not our intention to make any claim against the Borough Fund for property damaged or destroyed during the riot which occurred on the night of the ' Reception.'[1] . . . We respectfully submit to our fellow townsmen of all creeds and parties, that the wrecking of buildings, and especially midnight assaults on the homes of women, children, and aged persons, are acts of cruel lawlessness which nothing can justify. . . . We are all at one in desiring the honour and greatness of our country ; we are intensely anxious for the good name of the British Empire amongst the nations of the earth. But we hold that the fostering of prejudice and enmity, even against our foes, is in the long run hurtful to ourselves, and that injustice to strangers never leads to justice to our own people.

" Our convictions on some great questions are, we know, different from those of the majority of our fellow countrymen ; but for these convictions we must render our account, not to men but to God.

" If we are wrong, resort to lynch law will not set us right, while it inflicts serious injury on the whole community."

This statement was received with respect and appreciation, even from men whose views on the war differed widely from those of the writer and signatories. The late Alfred Lyttelton, soon to be

---

[1] Sir Edward Carson, whose opinion had been taken, considered that they were clearly entitled to an indemnity out of the Borough Fund for the damage sustained.

Colonial Secretary in the " Khaki Government," said of it : " That was real Christianity, and must do a great deal of good."[1]

The official bodies of the Society did what in them lay to combat the war spirit. Early in 1900 the Meeting for Sufferings re-issued with necessary alterations the " Christian Appeal . . . on the Present War " of Crimean days. Of this 200,000 copies were circulated. Dissatisfied with the expedient of re-publishing an old document, the Yearly Meeting in May issued another on " Christianity and War," from which a few sentences may be quoted :

"Acquiescence in the action of the nation, whether right or wrong, is commonly regarded as the only true patriotism. . . . It is not the soldier's heroism, but the work in which he is engaged that we believe to be repugnant to the teaching and life of Christ. . . . Our position with respect to peace cannot be isolated without loss from the rest of our faith. . . . Our witness is not narrow and negative, but far-reaching in its scope and intensely positive in the active service for Christ's peaceable Kingdom to which it calls us."

The methods adopted to bring the war to a speedy close shocked many Englishmen. The Society of Friends was among the first to protest ; in December 1900 it presented to the Government a memorial against farm-burning, which appeared in *The Times* and elsewhere. These methods of warfare intensified the sufferings of the Boer women and children. It is easy to issue documents, and bodies of Friends are sometimes too prolific of the written and printed word, but, at least, they are also ready to act as living epistles of help and good-will to those who suffer. Throughout the war money was collected for its victims, and women Friends worked diligently to make and collect garments for the destitute. Through this relief fund Joshua Rowntree did further service for South Africa. His brother-in-law, John Edward Ellis, a Friend and Member of Parliament, was greatly disturbed by reports of the operation of martial law in Cape Colony and the conquered territory ; also, in common with many other Friends, he was anxious to find out how material aid could be given to the sufferers from the war.

---

[1] *Life of Joshua Rowntree,* by S. E. Robson, is the source for most of the above details. The book also tells (p. 114) that a workman " who holds widely differing political views from the Rowntrees, but who is now a strong peace advocate . . . dates his adherence to the cause from that night. ' It was what made me first think about peace.' "

At his request, and with the hearty approval of the Meeting for Sufferings, Joshua and Isabella Rowntree, with their nephew, Harold Ellis, sailed to South Africa on this mission. The journey was one of difficulty and hardship, and on their arrival the travellers were only allowed to visit the concentration camps in Cape Colony and Natal. Conditions there were sad enough. The camps had in their origin been an attempt by the military authorities to provide shelter for the women and children taken prisoner, especially those whose homes had been destroyed by the farm-burning policy. But little care had been taken to provide against the inevitable dangers of herding together a miscellaneous congeries of people.

"The sight of the women and children, crowded into hurriedly prepared huts or tents, surrounded by fences of barbed wire, often with barely sufficient food—their homes destroyed and their goods confiscated, their children dying at an average rate of 271 per 1,000 —burnt itself into Joshua Rowntree's heart." [1]

His description of the conditions in these camps confirmed the independent report of Miss Hobhouse. It was effectively quoted in Parliament on June 17, 1901, when Mr. Lloyd George referred to him as "a former member of this House—and everyone who knows him will be convinced of the accuracy of every statement he makes. His word is as good as his oath." After this visit to South Africa, Friends and others were allowed to distribute clothing, nourishing foods, and medical stores in the camps. Some help was also given to the English refugees from the Transvaal. When the authorities had realized the conditions, they took steps to remedy the worst evils, but the discovery of these evils was due to the reports of Miss Hobhouse and Joshua Rowntree, which were loudly denounced at the time as unpatriotic. Later on others continued the work of relief, and women Friends were among those who helped Miss Hobhouse in her work of reconstruction, teaching weaving and other home industries to the Boer women. One piece of work, the restoration of Boer family Bibles lost or destroyed in the war, had the especial sympathy of Lord Roberts, who issued an appeal to the soldiers to give up any which were in their possession. Where possible the original Bibles were returned and, failing that, new ones given in their place. The discovery that there were English men and women ready to befriend them in their hour of need helped to soften the natural bitterness of the Boers toward their conquerors.

[1] *Life of Joshua Rowntree*, p. 118.

The twelve years between the Peace of Vereeniging in 1902 and the outbreak of the European War in 1914, was a time of considerable growth and development in the Society. Younger Friends, in particular, began to take a large share in its activities and deliberations. Friends collectively and individually helped in the protest against the increase in all countries of vast and provocative armaments.[1] Lord Haldane's organization of a volunteer Territorial army, expressly for home defence, was carried through under the Liberal Government in 1910 ; a few young men who were birthright members of the Society joined this force. Their numbers were very small, but their action and, in one or two cases, resignation of their membership, caused some stir. The matter was under discussion in the Yearly Meeting of 1911, when the Peace Committee of the Meeting for Sufferings was commissioned to prepare a statement on " Our Testimony for Peace," which was brought before the next Yearly Meeting, approved, and circulated. During 1911 and 1912 a lively correspondence was carried on in the *Friend* on the question of joining the Territorials, the writers being almost unanimous in considering the step an impossible one for a consistent Friend. The activities of the National Service League in pressing for the adoption of compulsory military service by this country naturally called out vigorous opposition from Friends. In November 1913 the organ of the League (*National Service League Notes*) published an article, " The Quakers' Point of View," in which, by a quotation from Fox on the " Sword of Justice," and the one from Penington on defence against invasion, it was implied that the early Quakers were not opposed to war. The Peace Committee had no difficulty in bringing forward evidence to the contrary.[2] Friends especially resented the assumption that the only national service which deserved the name was that rendered by soldiers. The Yearly Meeting of 1914 made a specific declaration on this point :—

" We desire to reaffirm our sense of the responsibility for true national service which attaches to citizenship in a civilized State.

---

[1] In a memorial concerning the increased naval estimates, addressed to the Prime Minister in February 1909, the Meeting for Sufferings declared : " We regard any such increase at this juncture as calculated to bring about similar increases on the part of other nations, with whom we are now manifestly being drawn into more friendly relations."

[2] *Quakers and War : The National Service League*, by G. K. Hibbert (leaflet published by the Peace Committee of the Society of Friends).

Our conviction of the unlawfulness of war to the Christian, which prevents us from giving to our country the military service willingly rendered by many, should specially call us to voluntary service in other ways, even at the cost of much personal sacrifice. Those who devote themselves with public spirit to the building of national character, the shaping of righteous policy at home or abroad, or the manifold tasks of local or central government, are doing work of high value for the Kingdom of God. . . . It is our conviction that compulsory military training of any kind is an invasion of the rights of conscience, the right of every man to be free to follow where the truth leads him. There is to-day no more truly national service than the replacing of mutual suspicion between nations by mutual trust and helpfulness."

During these years, while Europe as a whole was happily free from war, Macedonia was never at peace. The stories which reached England of the plight of the non-combatant populations in the Balkan War led the Meeting for Sufferings to appoint a new War Victims' Relief Committee in November 1912. Three Friends, as its agents, spent nearly five months distributing relief in Macedonia and Bulgaria, through local committees, in the districts where distress was greatest. During the same winter the Friends' Mission in Constantinople (under Ann Burgess) was aided by funds from the Committee for the relief of the thousands of Moslem refugees who had taken refuge in the city. In all some £12,000 was raised by the Committee. The second miserable war in which Bulgaria struggled against her former allies and, in the end, also against Turkey and Roumania, led to the reappointment of the Committee. Four thousand five hundred pounds was raised and mainly expended in the purchase of warm clothing, of which the Bulgarian refugees were in urgent need. This was sent out to a Bulgarian who had been associated with Friends in the earlier relief efforts and distributed by him.

In the meantime, on the other side of the globe, Friends found themselves under the operation of a law to which their conscience was opposed. In 1909-10 Australia and New Zealand each adopted a scheme of defence which involved the compulsory military training of boys. In the former country all between the ages of 14 and 25 were liable, in New Zealand all between 12 and 21. Under the Australian Act the conscientious objector was to be exempt " upon such conditions as may be prescribed." This the Defence Department explained to mean, not exemption from training, but in the case of "well-known denominations, such as Friends" training in ambulance and other non-combatant duties. Twenty-four years earlier the Editor of the *Friend* had commented on a case in the Channel Islands (where by law Friends were exempted from Militia service), when two conscientious objectors outside the body were imprisoned for refusal to serve. "Is our Society satisfied with its exemption from such penalties? Will it refuse any longer to pose as a specially favoured denomination? So long as this iniquitous military system exists will it be willing to share with all others of like mind in the suffering for conscience' sake which it involves? Would it not thereby greatly increase its power in protesting against this terrible evil?"[1]

This was the problem that now faced Australasian Friends. They were very small bodies (664 members in Australia and 143 in New Zealand), but their attitude throughout the struggle never wavered.[2] Only a handful of their members were affected, but they stood by all other conscientious objectors and, as far as they could, with those who opposed the Acts as an infringement of political liberty. The Australian General Meeting of 1910 considered the proposed conscience clause, and decided that it did not in any way meet the position. "Therefore, as those who desire to remain law-abiding citizens of the Commonwealth, we are reluctantly compelled to declare that if these proposals are passed into law we shall be bound by our Christian conscience to refuse to yield them obedience." But a deputation to the Federal Premier and Defence Minister received no concession : the latter minister told them that any boy over fourteen would be arrested and detained as a prisoner as long as he refused to comply with the Act. The Acts came into force in 1911, and in both countries Friends generally filled up the registration forms for their sons, adding a note to explain their objection to service. One or two Friends declined to register their boys, as by this refusal in the first instance they, and not their children, came into conflict with the law.

[1] *Friend*, 1886, p. 115.
[2] The fullest account of the relation of Friends to the Defence Acts is in the *Australian* (later *Australasian*) *Friend* for the years since 1910. The *Friend* and *British Friend* gave much space to the question and occasionally gave additional details from private correspondence. In 1913–14 the *Manchester Guardian* and *Yorkshire Post* opened their correspondence columns to a discussion of the Defence Acts, in which both sides were fairly represented.

By this time English Friends were alive to the situation. (Technically the Australian and New Zealand Friends are considered a part of London Yearly Meeting.) The Meeting for Sufferings, which for the first time for many years had a prospect of duties towards members of the Society appropriate to its old name, appointed a Committee, later merged in the Australasian Committee, to watch the operation of the Acts and consult with Friends in the colonies, and messages of sympathy and encouragement poured over from England and America. One of these was from the Yearly Meeting of North Carolina, reminding them that " in the late Civil War, many of our Friends suffered for a like testimony. Some of these are still living at a great age and are present at this Yearly Meeting."[1] They were followed by deputations of Friends from England, anxious to share more closely in the burden of their fellow members, who did valuable work both in making clear to the authorities the attitude of Friends on the whole peace question, and in uniting the many sections of opinion in the colonies opposed to the Acts. One Friend was the founder of the political movement against the Act, later known as the Australian Freedom League.

In the summer of 1911 the Acts began to operate, and their actual working caused much moderate opinion to decide against the compulsory clauses. This was due not merely to the treatment of the conscientious objectors, who were comparatively few in numbers, but to the hardships and inequalities revealed in many other cases. Boys of the upper and middle classes could put in their drills at school with the minimum of inconvenience, while working lads, after a hard day's labour, had to travel long distances to attend. When the prosecutions of the so-called " shirkers " began, the penalties inflicted were harsh. In New Zealand youths who refused to drill could be deprived of their civil rights for any period up to ten years ; if the lighter penalty of a fine were inflicted, their employers were empowered to deduct the amount from their wages. In the case of younger boys still at school the Education Department intervened and deprived them of free places and scholarships. The New Zealand Minister for Education was also the Minister of Defence : in an interview he declared that this deprivation of educational facilities was " a punishment no greater, nor indeed so great, as that of being disfranchised. . . . I cannot imagine anyone who desires educational advantages refusing to comply with

[1] *Australian Friend*, April 1914.

the law of the land."[1] Nevertheless, both in Australia and New Zealand the prosecutions rapidly increased, and a serious proportion of the youths liable to training evaded it.

It is certain that neither Government wished to come into conflict with the objector on religious grounds. At Hobart, Tasmania, there is a large Friends' school. In it the authorities never enforced the provision for military drill in the case of Friend pupils, and allowed the others to perform it at a centre independent of the school. An early deputation of New Zealand Friends (July 1911), which told the Minister for Education that under the existing Act they saw no resort but emigration, was assured by him that " if he could manage to have their attitude met without breaking down the system, he would do so." As Friends saw the Acts in operation, however, they became convinced that no conscience clause, but only the repeal of compulsion, could meet the situation.[2] The General Meeting of New Zealand Friends in 1912, after declaring Friends' loyalty to the peace principles, " held by our Society for over two hundred and fifty years," continued, " after careful deliberation, they see no other way of consistently upholding their testimony than by declining to undertake any duty that will bring them under military control or the operation of the Defence Act. Nor can they define any duties that, whilst meeting the consciences of some, may violate those of others." In the same year the Australian General Meeting described the Commonwealth Defence Act, " with its disregard of conscience and its denial of parental rights, as subversive of religious and civil liberty."

Friends, however, were at the same time reminded that the testimony against war was a deeper thing than opposition to any specific Act of Parliament, and were warned not to let it degenerate into a purely political agitation. It was not until the winter of 1912–13 that any Friends came under the Act. Francis Hopkins, Rockhampton, Queensland, was fined for omitting to register his grandson. In the spring William Ingle, who had recently emigrated from Yorkshire, was convicted in Adelaide of the same offence, and underwent fourteen days' imprisonment, as he refused to pay

---

[1] *Herald* (New Zealand), June 25, 1913.

[2] A warning by London Yearly Meeting in 1911 against " undertaking services auxiliary to warfare in positions where they would be under military orders," was included in the *Book of Discipline* as revised in 1912. This was directly due to the Australasian situation.

a fine. His son was registered by the "area officer" in control of the cadets, without his parents' consent, and on his refusal to drill he was imprisoned by the military for fourteen days, during which time for two days he was on a bread and water diet. Sidney Crosland, aged eighteen, was prosecuted at Newcastle, New South Wales, for refusing to drill. At the trial the magistrate remarked to the "area officer," who acted as prosecutor : "It seems to me that to you the most important thing in the world is the military test, while to the defendant religious principles are highest." Crosland served three weeks' imprisonment (out of a sentence of fifty-three days) in military barracks. He was offered non-combatant clerical work, but refused it, and though after his release he still abstained from drills, he was not again prosecuted. In August a Melbourne Friend, Christopher Flinn, was fined and distrained upon for failure to register his son, aged fourteen.

After these experiences the Australian General Meeting held that autumn, definitely recommended Friends not to register their children, as by this abstention the parent had at least an opportunity of stating his views. In October 1913 another young Friend, Douglas Allen of Melbourne, was prosecuted ; at the first hearing of the case the magistrate definitely stated that the Act made no allowance for conscientious objectors. Later, Allen was sentenced to twenty days' detention in a fortress. A deputation of Australian Friends in March 1914 waited upon the Premier and Minister for Defence with a remonstrance from the London Meeting for Sufferings. The Premier replied that the Act would be administered without discrimination, though as leniently as possible, and Friends could not be exempted. "The law cannot be altered."

A few months later, in June, another boy, Thomas Roberts, aged sixteen, of Brighton, Victoria, was sentenced to twenty-one days' imprisonment in Queenscliff Fortress. "On the third day, for continued refusal to drill, he was court-martialled, and sentenced to seven days' solitary confinement. This was in a cell ten feet by ten feet, and unlighted except by a grating. He had a wooden stretcher with mattress and blankets, which were only allowed him at night. He had two half-hours' exercise daily, was placed on half-diet, and was not permitted to read or write."[1] The boy had recently been ill, when he endured this penalty, one usually reserved for refractory criminals. The case aroused so much public indignation that the

[1] *Friend* (London), July 31, 1914.

Government had to announce that no more solitary confinement would be inflicted.

The question of alternative service was discussed again at their Meetings this year by both Australian and New Zealand Friends. The Australian Meeting, which was held after the outbreak of the European War, passed a minute that, as the only alternative service suggested was in connection with the Defence Act, " We regret, from the point of view of those who desire to be and to remain law-abiding citizens, that we cannot see our way to recommend to Friends the acceptance of any form of service under its direction. We recognize, however, that the final decision must rest with the individual conscience." The New Zealand General Meeting of 1915 declared that " war, which involves the wilful infliction of sorrow and suffering upon our fellows, is the very negation of Christ's spirit." New Zealand Friends, however, had not suffered from the Defence Act. In a debate on the question of exemption in the Australian Federal Senate (June 10, 1914), the Minister for Defence was asked what course the New Zealand authorities had adopted, and replied : " What they attempted to do in New Zealand was nothing, and they did it most successfully. I have it from one of the highest authorities there that although Parliament passed a law, that law is not being carried out, and the result is that the Dominion is drifting into a system which . . . is very much of a voluntary system."[1] The imprisonment and solitary confinement of some boys (not Friends) in Ripa Island Fortress, New Zealand, in June and July 1913, led to protests by Labour organizations and their release. The position of Australasian Friends during the war is described later in this chapter.

In England the outbreak of war in 1914 was as appalling and unexpected to Friends as to the majority of their fellow countrymen. It is true that in the peace discussions at the Yearly Meeting for some years past speaker after speaker had emphasized the imminent danger to civilization in the rival armaments and incompatible claims of the Great Powers, but the liabilities assumed by England were unknown to most people, and it was believed that she stood free from the European complication. The Yearly Meeting Epistle of 1913 could say : " With thankfulness we note an advance in the Peace Movement. We are probably nearer to a complete understanding with Germany than has been the case for many years.

[1] Quoted in *Friend* (London), August 14, 1914.

The forces that make for arbitration and international good-will are gaining in strength and confidence." It is true that the document continued : "Never was there greater need. Not only the great European nations, but the hitherto peaceful peoples also, are being sucked into the vortex of military preparations. The Church of to-day needs to discover its Lord as the Prince of Peace," and added that, in view of the strength of the National Service Movement, "the time may not be distant when we too shall be called upon to defend our principles at heavy cost."

In less than three years that time had arrived. In the Yearly Meeting of 1914, held at the end of May, the grave situation in Ireland caused more concern than any anticipated danger of war abroad. An international peace convention of members of Christian Churches was actually being held in Constance at the beginning of August. Some Friends and other English delegates were able to journey home in comparative comfort owing to the exertions of the Dowager Grand Duchess of Baden, and others in high position, on their behalf. They reached England just as our country entered the war, and at the Meeting for Sufferings held on August 7th these Friends brought forward a message, "To men and women of good-will in the British Empire," which was published by the Meeting. Critics described the document as "too lengthy, too optimistic, premature in some of its propositions, and lacking in a sense of practicalness."[1] But it met with a remarkable welcome, and its call "to be courageous in the cause of love and in the hate of hate . . . in time of war let all men of good-will prepare for peace," sounded a note little heard in those fevered days of August. It was printed in full as an advertisement in many papers, read in some churches and chapels in place of a sermon, and sent out in large quantities in answer to requests for distribution. Nearly 475,000 copies were circulated in England, and 50,000 in America ; it was translated into Dutch, Danish, Italian, and Chinese and received friendly notice in various foreign papers. "An English copy of the message which was sent to Germany was also translated there, and circulated amongst ministers of religion throughout the country, the cost being borne in Germany."[2]

At this Meeting for Sufferings the first suggestions were made of work to be undertaken by Friends in war-time, and one, the help of

[1] *Friend,* August 14, 1914.
[2] *Proceedings of Yearly Meeting,* 1915.

destitute Germans and Austrians in England, took definite shape. During the war, three special branches of service were pursued by Friends, apart from the work in hospitals, in canteens, among Belgian refugees and the like, in which they joined in movements organized by the nation at large. The three branches were : " The Emergency Committee for the Assistance of Germans, Austrians, Hungarians, and Turks in Distress," " The War Victims' Relief Committee," and " The Friends' Ambulance Unit."[1] The Emergency Committee was the first formed, in the early days of August 1914.[2] Begun by Friends, it was warmly welcomed by many others (among the distinguished men and women who gave their names in support of its appeal was the Archbishop of Canterbury), and it was in close touch with the Home Office and the American Embassy, to which the interests of alien enemies had been committed. With a central office in London and branch committees and representatives in the provinces, it was almost entirely staffed by voluntary workers, many of them not Friends. Later on the Committee experienced the curious inconsistencies of a state of war. Under the Military Service Act, 1916, its first chairman, Stephen Hobhouse, and several other workers, were imprisoned, while, under the administration of the same Act, the Committee received workers through the Home Service section of the Friends' Ambulance Unit (described later in this chapter) on the ground that its work was of " national importance." The work was, of course, unpopular with a large section of the newspaper Press and its readers, but the Committee avoided many difficulties by the care with which it kept in touch with the Home Office and the police authorities. Under the War Charities Act, 1916, it was registered as an approved war relief agency. The underlying motive of the Committee was to pursue peace even in the midst of war. " It seemed the easiest and simplest way of carrying out the command to ' love our enemies ' and to ' do good ' to those that hate us."[3]

At first there was acute distress among the families of Germans and Austrians (in many of which the wife was English and the

---

[1] In November 1914, the Meeting for Sufferings circulated to all Meetings a " Declaration on the War " which, while reaffirming the Quaker faith urged members " to contribute our lives to the cause of love, in helping our country to a more Christ-like idea of service," and to join in measures of war relief.

[2] *St. Stephen's House*, by Anna B. Thomas, 1921, gives a full account of the seven years' work of the committee. The title is the name of its first headquarters.

[3] *Ibid.*, p. 20.

children English-born) when the breadwinner was thrown out of work, and in most cases interned. Later some small Government provision was made, by the English Government, where the wife was English, and by the German and Austrian Governments for women of those nationalities, but, as the cost of living increased, supplementary help was urgently needed.[1] This was given by the Committee mainly in the form of milk, fuel, and clothing. During the later years of the war nearly two thousand ailing or delicate children were sent for country holidays of a month or more, and a rest home gave renewed strength to many over-strained mothers. The visitors to these families sent reports of them to the interned men, while the visitors to the internment camps reported on the health of the husbands and fathers there. These visitors (who went under Government permits) were mainly occupied in organizing industries among the prisoners, providing tools and equipment, and advancing the materials for work, while the articles made were disposed of through the Committee. American Y.M.C.A. workers and Dr. Markel's committee (organized by the representative in England of the German Red Cross) aimed at meeting other needs of the camps, so that the Emergency visitors concentrated on this industrial work among interned civilians. A Canadian Friend devoted his whole time for three years to travelling from camp to camp getting into personal touch with the men, and an English Friend, an experienced teacher of handicrafts, also gave full-time service. The occupation provided was a godsend to men suffering from long confinement and enforced idleness, but in addition there was the moral effect of " Englishmen, representing many others, coming into the camp in pure friendship. It was a pledge that the spirit of hatred and the fever of war did not possess the whole land. It was the link, so much needed, with the common feelings of humanity and sympathy that were still ruling in simple hearts all over the world." [2]

Another branch of the work was concerned with the repatriation of women, children, and a few elderly men, allowed by the Government to return to their native land. Among these were the German missionaries and their families, expelled from their stations in India

---

[1] The scale of relief (which was administered by Boards of Guardians) was first fixed, in November 1914, at 10s. a week for the wife and 1s. 6d. for each child under fourteen years of age. It was gradually raised and stood in 1917 at 12s. 6d. for the wife and 3s. for each child. The scale in the provinces was lower, as was that granted by the enemy Governments (*St. Stephen's House*, p. 86).

[2] *St. Stephen's House*, p. 74.

and Africa, and brought to England with scanty provision for a northern winter. After many hardships the families were repatriated, and the ordained missionaries allowed to join them after a few months' internment, but the laymen were kept in England till the end of the war. An American Friend, Dr. Henrietta Thomas, was permitted during the earlier part of the war to travel several times to Germany and Austria in charge of parties of women and children and to bring back similar groups of English people to England.[1] Later the work done in this way had to be limited to arranging the details of travel and escorting the parties to Tilbury. There milk was provided for the children, and the travellers helped through the intricacies of the official examination before going on to the boat. A hostel was also provided in London to accommodate parties from the country, who often had to spend some days there completing the necessary formalities, before they could start. In one sudden and tragic emergency, the Committee's help was swift to meet an urgent need ; at the time of the *Lusitania* riots a number of families whose houses had been wrecked were sheltered for some weeks in a Friends' meeting-house in London.

Dr. Thomas's visits to Germany brought her into touch with a Berlin Committee to help alien enemies. Its members were chiefly men and women who had taken active part in the Anglo-German Friendship movement. At the outbreak of war they began to do what they could to help those stranded in an enemy country, but the news brought by returning Germans of the work in England encouraged them in November 1914 to establish a formal organization. The first appeal to the public stated : " The task is laid upon us by our own desire to render friendly service in these times of hatred to those who now find it so difficult to obtain help. Even in war-time whoever needs our help is our neighbour, and love of their enemies remains the distinguishing mark of those who are loyal to our Lord." [2] The main work of the Committee was the relief of distressed civilians, in particular the families of the interned men. A very large proportion of those helped were Russians, who for many reasons found it more difficult to return home, and who were often people of very small means. German ladies also acted as escorts to neutral countries, whence they could return to their families, of many French and

---

[1] Dr. Thomas wore out her strength in this Emergency work and later in help to conscientious objectors. She died in 1919.

[2] Quoted in *The Friend*, December 18, 1914.

Belgian children who were either at school in the occupied areas or had been separated from their parents by some misadventure.

The chief work for the interned was done by the American Y.M.C.A., but the Committee was able to send food and clothing to some camps. It was supported by people of influence—in June 1916 a meeting on its behalf was held at the house of Prince Lichnowsky, the late Ambassador in London—and it was active in making known the help given to aliens in England by the Emergency Committee. The *Berliner Tageblatt*, in particular, published several articles on the subject, some by repatriated Germans, and others by Dr. Elisabeth Rotten, secretary of the Berlin Committee and formerly lecturer at the Women's Colleges in Cambridge. The chief defect of these articles is a tendency to represent the English work as due to Friends alone, whereas about half the Committee were not Friends, and a great part of the funds came from outside sources.

Even with the armistice the work of the Emergency Committee was still required. Its employment bureau was occupied with the aliens allowed to remain in England, and early in 1919 a "Foreign Fund" was established, which, under Government sanction, sent food, clothing, and nursing comforts to mothers and infants in Germany and Austria who were suffering pitiably from the food blockade. This led in May 1919 to a request by the Board of Trade that the Committee would also organize the supply and transport of food parcels from individuals here to friends or relations in Central Europe. The difficulties of transport caused long delays in the delivery of these parcels, but comparatively few went entirely astray. The natural outcome of this work was the amalgamation of the Emergency Committee with the War Victims' Committee in 1920. Up to that time the former body had expended about £100,000 in its work in England, and had had the help of two hundred and forty workers in London besides those in the provinces.

The War Victims' Relief Committee was a little later in the field than either the Emergency Committee or the Friends' Ambulance Unit, for during the first weeks of the war the advance of the German armies in Belgium and north-eastern France made it impossible to help non-combatant sufferers. When that advance was checked, and at last pushed back, it was clear that in the areas over which fighting had taken place, there was not only terrible devastation and poverty, but grave risk of epidemic disease. The call for help was brought before the Meeting for Sufferings on September 4th by Dr. Hilda Clark and other Friends. The Meeting appointed the War Victims' Relief Committee, which early in November sent out the first band of thirty-three volunteer workers to the districts round Châlons, Vitry, and Sermaize. Among the members were doctors, nurses, architects, and sanitary engineers, who undertook, in addition to various forms of relief, the work of reconstruction, medical help, sanitation, and the revival of agriculture. Some of the damaged houses were rebuilt and many more temporary ones erected out of the timber given by the French Government. These were made in workshops and construction camps, and furnished through the help of the " Bon Gîte " and other French relief societies.[1] A Maternity Hospital was opened at Châlons, where many mothers had the rest and care they sorely needed after their harrowing experiences.[2] Other small hospitals and dispensaries were established at different centres, and a much-needed scheme of district nursing was carried out. Informal schools were provided for the children, who were running wild, and workrooms for the girls and women. They were taught simple embroidery in bright colours, and their gay productions sold readily in Paris, England, and America.

Most important of all, much was done for agriculture in a district mainly dependent on that oldest of industries. Agricultural machinery and tools were provided, and in the hay and harvest seasons young Quaker farmers helped the women and old men left on the land to save their crops, while distributions of seeds and of rabbits and poultry, from stock reared by the relief-workers, were also made. The work had its peculiar difficulties and dangers ; the most hazardous task was the removal to other districts of children from the bombarded areas, and from Rheims in particular, which was frequently undertaken. In 1918, owing to violent bombardment and air-raids, the Châlons hospital was temporarily abandoned, mothers, babies, and nursing staff being conveyed to a refuge forty

---

[1] Later on the Emergency Committee supplied some furniture made in the internment camp workshops, and clothing made by unemployed alien tailors and by women whose husbands were interned. Thus representatives of three combatant countries were united in a work of relief (St. Stephen's House, pp. 73, 133).

[2] Since the war this Hospital has been established in a permanent building endowed by the contributions of English and American Friends, and controlled by a local committee.

miles away. The relief work was appreciated by the French authorities, national and local, and on the whole the workers were trusted by the military commanders, but the necessary regulations and limitations of work in a military area were often irksome. After the coming of conscription men workers of military age had a very uncertain tenure. " In the spring of 1918, at a moment of great military anxiety, new workers leaving England and old workers returning from furlough were compelled by the authorities to sign a statement that they would not, while absent from England, take part in propaganda of any kind. Had it not been for the urgency of the work already undertaken, and the fact that the work itself was a true witness to our faith, many workers certainly would have felt unable to take this pledge. The embargo was continued for some time after the armistice and then withdrawn."[1]

In 1917, at the request of the French, the work was extended into the devastated Somme area, after Hindenburg's retreat, but in April 1918, during the last German advance, workers and inhabitants had again to evacuate this region. After the armistice the large " Verdun " area on the Meuse was handed over to the Friends for reconstruction. Military restrictions were relaxed, and " a wonderful opportunity of service came through daily contact with the large number of German prisoners who for many months worked in the neighbourhood of our different centres, many of them assisting in our task of rebuilding as well as in housework and transport. Some had grave misgivings as to the consistency of the Mission's making use of prisoners' labour, but for the prisoners themselves there was no doubt. It was not merely that they were able thus to have good food or welcome clothing and comforts ; they were treated like men and made to feel that they were among friends. " Heute ist mir wie Himmel gewesen," said one such prisoner, after a hard day's work unloading timber.[2] In the autumn of 1919 three of the Mission spent some months in Germany visiting the families of these prisoners and taking to them a gift of twenty marks for every day's labour with the Mission. This message of love and friendship was warmly welcomed by hundreds of German households.

In the summer of 1917 the first detachment of American workers sent over by the American Friends' Service Committee, was the

[1] T. E. Harvey in *All Friends' Conference*, 1920, Report of English Commission VII. 27–8.
[2] T. E. Harvey, *op. cit.* p. 28.

beginning of a continuous stream of helpers. These American Friends greatly increased the scope and usefulness of the Mission : they took full share in the organization and carrying out of all its activities, and soon became the largest contingent in the field.

Another branch of the work grew up in Holland among the great camps of Belgian refugees in that hospitable land. Industries were started to occupy the compulsorily idle, and some hut-building provided home life and privacy for those who most felt the loss. The workers in Holland, at the request of the English Government, also cared for parties of English civilians, released from Germany, on the journey from the frontier to Flushing. Relief work in Serbia was planned, and though the progress of the Austro-German invasion made this impossible, yet the Friends who went out were able to work under the Serbian Relief Fund in helping the refugees on their arrival in Albania and at Salonika, and on their further journeyings to Corsica and southern France.

Later, again, another band of medical and relief workers went out in July and August 1916 to an area of some seven hundred square miles in the Buzuluk district of south-east Russia, which had added twenty thousand Polish refugees to its population of seventy or eighty thousand souls. There was no resident doctor in the whole area. Both before and after the Revolution medical service was rendered to the whole district, and various forms of relief carried on, but in 1918 the unsettlement due to civil war forced the Mission to withdraw. In 1919 work began in Poland among the returned refugees—some of them old friends from Buzuluk—who had come back to a country devastated early in the war by both armies. Their homes were destroyed and their land desolate and out of cultivation. The Friends' Unit fought the typhus epidemic brought back by the refugees and fostered by the conditions under which they had to live, and then helped in the work of reconstruction. It lent horses for ploughing and for hauling wood to build houses, provided seeds, tools, and clothing, and revived embroidery and other industries. In 1920 the work in Russia was resumed ; since then the Mission has been working in the large famine area round Buzuluk. In the worst scarcity it fed 260,000 people daily. In Russia and Poland the danger from typhus was great, the disease attacked several of the Mission workers, Friends and others, of whom three died.

In July 1919 four representatives of the War Relief and Emergency Committees, with an American woman Friend, visited

Germany and Austria. The suffering they saw as a result of the Allied blockade and the depreciated currencies impelled them to help, though relief seemed only to touch the fringe of the misery. This help, in both countries, took the form of meals for school children and students, milk for infants and mothers, and (particularly in Vienna) employment for starving artists and craftsmen. The Vienna Mission imported nearly two thousand cows for farmers round Vienna. These were paid for in milk, which was distributed to hospitals and delicate children. In all these activities, especially after the armistice, Friends were helped by the contributions and service of sympathizers outside the Society. Up to the end of 1919 the money received from England and America, from Friends and non-Friends, amounted to more than £500,000, and about seven hundred and fifty English men and women had taken part in the work. Later resources were largely increased by relief grants from the Government and from the " Save the Children Fund." The united War Relief and Emergency Committee still continues its work in Austria, Poland, and Russia, and the final chapter of its story has yet to be written. Its work, and the very important service of American Friends (described later), have called out in Europe an interest in the religion which led men and women in time of war to help allies and " enemies " alike. One result has been the creation of small " Quaker embassies "—centres of Friends' work and worship in Paris, Geneva, and in various Austrian and German cities. This work, and the care of the groups of Friends which have grown up round these centres and elsewhere, is undertaken by the Council for International Service of London and Dublin Yearly Meetings.

This summary has not touched on the relief undertaken by Friends, under non-Quaker agencies or as individuals, in other areas suffering from the war. Work was also done by local Meetings. Yorkshire Quarterly Meeting, for example, maintained and staffed for nearly two years a seaside home in Holland, where underfed German children were brought back to normal health.

The Friends' Ambulance Unit, the third important activity of Friends, arose from the desire of many young men to serve in the war zone, where their countrymen were in hourly danger. In September 1914 sixty of these men went through a strenuous course of ambulance training, while a Committee of elder Friends, under the chairmanship of Sir George Newman, tried to find a sphere for their work. Their aim was " to render voluntary non-military service in relief of the suffering and distress resulting from war," and in October an opportunity offered itself in Dunkirk. There, in the dressing-sheds, the Unit had the care of six thousand badly wounded men. After this first emergency the work developed widely. The history of the Unit has been summarized by its chairman : " It began with forty-three men, it ended with over six hundred in France and Flanders alone ; it began with a donation of £100, it received ultimately in voluntary contributions £138,000 ; it began not knowing whither it went or what were to be its duties, it finished having been responsible for a comprehensive organization of ambulance and hospital service in many fields. It had the working of a dozen hospitals, the majority of which it actually established and managed—at Dunkirk, Ypres, Poperinghe, Hazebrouck, and elsewhere in Flanders . . . and at York, Birmingham, London, and Richmond at home. At the Queen Alexandra Hospital at Dunkirk 12,000 in-patients were treated, and a still larger total number at the other centres ; 27,000 inoculations against typhoid fever were made in Belgium and thus the ravages of this disease were stayed and the armies protected ; 15,000 Belgian refugees were fed, and a vast quantity of clothing was distributed ; lace-making centres were created, temporary schools and orphanages were established, provision was made for milk distribution and for water purification in Belgium ; tens of thousands of soldiers were received at the three recreation huts at Dunkirk ; the two hospital ships transported overseas 33,000 cases ; the ambulance convoys ran more than two and a half million kilometres and carried over 260,000 sick or wounded soldiers of all nations ; and the four ambulance trains conveyed 520,000 patients. This work was done by an *unenlisted* and *unpaid* band of young men, providing through the support of their friends their own staff, equipment, and expenditure. Twenty of these peace-lovers made the supreme sacrifice ; many others were wounded or invalided, and ninety-six were awarded the *Croix de Guerre*, or other decorations for valour."[1] Of the twenty members who lost their lives nine were killed by shell-fire or in air raids, and the others died from illness contracted on service. Besides the six hundred men (mainly Friends) and ninety women in France and Flanders, there were at one time more than four hundred men employed as orderlies in the English hospitals, apart from the General Service

[1] *The Friends' Ambulance Unit*, by M. Tatham and J. E. Miles (Introduction, pp. ix-x). This book gives a full account of the work and position of the Unit.

section, described later. Some of the workers, including the Unit's first leader, Philip Baker, afterwards served in Mr. G. M. Trevelyan's British-Italian Ambulance Unit, but this gallant body had no direct connection with Friends.

From its inception, however, some Friends considered that the Unit's work was too closely akin to ordinary war medical service, and these criticisms increased after the introduction of conscription, when the position of the Unit became, as will appear, somewhat ambiguous. On April 7, 1916, Sir George Newman, in the *Friend*, described the Unit as " voluntary, unpaid, unenlisted, and non-military. It is not a part of the R.A.M.C. or of the Non-combatant Corps. Its members do not take the military oath or bear arms, or undertake military duties." These principles led the Committee to withdraw its workers from a military hospital in London, and, after some months' service, from two hospital ships, on the decision of the authorities (during the height of the submarine activity) to remove them from the protection of the Red Cross and to put guns on board.

Out of the 20,000 Friends of Great Britain,[1] only a small proportion was able to take this active personal share in relieving the miseries of war. Those at home gave money help according to their power to these organizations and to the many other forms of suffering and distress which claimed help. A considerable number worked among the Belgian refugees and in the voluntary Red Cross hospitals, or in the Y.M.C.A., and other canteens established in the military centres. Others devoted themselves more earnestly than before to various forms of social and public work, which were losing support among the new and urgent needs created by the war. Work on behalf of peace and international reconciliation was still carried on, and met, on the whole, with a less hostile reception than in the days of the Boer War. Friends were numerous among the supporters of organizations which were popularly called by the rather clumsy term " pacifist," but there was also much peace work within the Society itself, whether in the form of conferences and open meetings, or in the publication and distribution of books and pamphlets.

But from the very opening of the war, it was clear that a section

---

[1] The numbers in London Yearly Meeting were 20,007, of whom 834 were in Australia and New Zealand. A pamphlet, *Friends' Service in War Time*, by E. Fox Howard, describes these and other activities.

of the Society felt that this war was one waged on behalf of a wronged and helpless nation and against an unscrupulous and powerful enemy, and demanded the active support of Friends and the temporary or permanent abandonment of what they described as the " traditional testimony " against war. A few went farther, trying to prove that the testimony was not even traditional, and had never been held by the majority of the Society, but in these efforts they were not very successful. The correspondence columns of the *Friend* during the first eighteen months of the war contained many letters in the foregoing sense. One reply described them as coming from those " whose active interest in the Society seems to date from the time when the outbreak of the present war disclosed their wide divergence from the position of Friends as held through long years of trial, and as stated in our official documents."[1] The description was true in many cases—some even were no longer members of the Society —but a few active and honoured Friends also took this view. Friends gathered for the Yearly Meeting in May 1915, in a state of uncertainty. It was known that some under the name of Friends had enlisted, that others were busy in recruiting or in the manufacture of munitions and military supplies, and no one was certain what proportion of the whole membership was in agreement with these actions.

Day after day the large meeting-house at Devonshire House was crowded to the doors, and while those who wished to modify the position of Friends stated their case with force and fervour, it soon became clear that the " sense of the meeting," to use the Quaker phrase, was that the peace principles held by Friends were a vital part of the Society's faith and could not be abandoned.[2] On the other hand, it was equally clear that on the question of Friends who actively supported the war the Meeting did not feel that disciplinary action should be taken at once. A report was presented to the Meeting by a Committee appointed from the Meeting for Sufferings to consider the enlistment of Friends, which was summarized as follows :

" Fifty-eight out of sixty-eight Monthly Meeting clerks had replied to the questions sent down, from which replies it appeared that about two hundred and fifteen young men Friends had joined the Army or Navy, forty-three of them as members of

[1] *Friend*, December 17, 1915.
[2] A full report was given in the *Friend*, May 28, 1915.

the R.A.M.C. In addition, about thirty had joined Citizens' Guards or similar voluntary organizations, and fifteen Friends were known to be on recruiting committees or actively engaged in recruiting.[1] Of those on active service two had already lost their lives. Some of these Friends were regular attenders at Meetings, and a few were actively engaged in the work of the Meeting, but the larger number were only nominal Friends. About fifty resignations of membership had been sent in by those who had joined the Army or their sympathizers ; thirty of these had been accepted. The Committee pointed out the following facts : . . .

" 1. There is no question as to the principles of the Society, as expressed and revised from time to time in the Book of Discipline. This maintains an unequivocal testimony against all war.

" 2. The men who have joined the Army have done so, in almost every case, until the termination of the war. There is no machinery for freeing themselves before the end of the war from the obligation they have entered upon.

" 3. According to our discipline full responsibility for membership rests with the Monthly Meeting. The Yearly Meeting can, of course, advise on general principles, but it cannot intervene in a question of discipline, except in the case of an appeal. Questions are referred to the Yearly Meeting by minute of the Monthly Meeting through the Quarterly Meeting.

" 4. Monthly Meetings have the right to remove from their membership, either by dissociation or disownment. They may dissociate members who make little or no profession with Friends and do not attend Meetings for worship. They may ' issue a testimony of disownment ' in respect of one ' who walks disorderly,' who ' commits an offence,' after he has been patiently dealt with. There are not other methods for removing a name from the list, unless the member himself decides to relinquish his membership. A member cannot be forced to resign."

In the short discussion which followed it was evident that most Friends considered that there were strong reasons for postponement of any decision. The Monthly Meetings with whom action lay had not raised the question. Many of the Friends concerned were absent in the army, and the whole matter of birthright membership was likely to come up for consideration in the near future. Some felt that a difficulty was shirked, but the general opinion was that

[1] *Vide* also Appendix F, Statistics of Enlistment.

no good could come of prolonged discussion at the moment. A very large share of the ensuing meetings was devoted to peace. The conclusion, as expressed in one of the " minutes " presented by the Clerk, and accepted without dissent by the Meeting, was that the peace testimony " has been clear and unmistakable from the earliest days of our history to the present, and we have rejoiced to hear it renewed to-day not only by those of maturer years, but particularly by our younger men. We have also been deeply impressed by the outspoken willingness of women Friends to accept all the consequences that may arise from a complete adherence to our peace testimony.[1]

" This testimony is one which comes welling up from within. It springs from the very heart of our faith. We recognize humbly that it has not been as influentially and effectively presented as it should have been and that there is an urgent call to be more faithful and to meet fearlessly the unprecedented challenge of to-day." An intense interest was taken in the Epistle sent out by the Yearly Meeting. The document was drawn up by a small group of Friends chosen at a " Large Committee " (open to all Friends), submitted by them for criticism and correction to the same Committee, and finally read and signed by the Clerk at the concluding session of the Yearly Meeting. This year the Committee was crowded to the doors, and at its second meeting the draft was minutely considered, sentence by sentence, yet in the end accepted thankfully almost as it stood. Those present will never forget the solemnity and beauty with which the last words of the Epistle rang through the crowded meeting-house at the final sitting of the Yearly Meeting.

" The world can only be won for Christ as men are possessed by the infinite power which we call the love of God—the love that will not let men go—the love that ' beareth all things, believeth all things, hopeth all things, endureth all things,' and that never faileth—the love that is Divine Omnipotence."

The Meeting ended with the familiar formula, used from early

---

[1] A group of young women Friends at a conference at Manchester some weeks earlier, had sent the following message to the young men Friends in separate session : " We ask you not to use force to defend us, where you would not use it for any other reason, but to trust God with us and for us. We did not feel we could lightly ask this of you until we had faced it for ourselves. . . . We realize that trust in God is no passive looking-on, but an intensely active thing. It often seems to fall to a woman's lot to have to trust while she sees others suffer. It may be that our men may have to share in this. And we realize that to ask you to be willing to do this is a very great thing to ask." This was read in the Yearly Meeting, and endorsed by subsequent women speakers.

days of Quakerism : " The business of this Yearly Meeting being concluded, we separate, intending to meet again in London at the appointed time next year, if the Lord permit." But instead of ending there, as usual, a sentence was added pointing to a possible re-summons of the present Meeting in case of any sudden emergency before the full year had elapsed.

This emergency arose. In August 1915 the National Register was taken, in November the Derby scheme of " groups " and " attestations " was adopted, and in January 1916 the first Bill for Compulsory Military Service was introduced, which to most clear-sighted persons seemed the obvious sequel of the methods used in these previous governmental activities. Friends for the most part followed the practice of their fellow members in Australasia, and filled up the register, many adding a declaration that they could not give any military service. A very few attested, but most of those likely to do so were among the three hundred who had already enlisted. In November 1915 the Meeting for Sufferings considered the action of the Society in the event of conscription. Emigration, a course suggested by one Friend, found no support, and it was felt that the Society had a duty to help not only its own members, but also others with a conscientious objection to military service.

The Yearly Meeting had appointed a " Friends' Service Committee," which consisted at first mainly of young men of military age. It became the chief agent of the Society in matters concerning conscription. In January 1916 the Meeting for Sufferings approved a letter to the Prime Minister, drafted by the Peace Committee, and the Friends' Service Committee, which, while recognizing that the Government wished to meet the case of the conscientious objector, explained that in the Bill it was, in fact, not met.

" We know that a large number of conscientious objectors are not prepared to accept compulsory service, whether combatant or otherwise, under military authorities. To attempt to compel persons holding these views to accept service required by the military authorities for the successful prosecution of the war would, in our opinion, be a violation of freedom of conscience."

This Meeting decided that the adjourned Yearly Meeting should be held, and it was summoned for January 28–30. Meanwhile Friends who had been brought into close touch with other conscientious objectors—three Friends were on the National

Committee of the No-Conscription Fellowship [1]—felt it was impossible for the Quaker objectors to stand apart from the rest. The adjourned Meeting was even more crowded than that of May 1915 ; the numbers at some sessions were computed at about twelve hundred, of whom young men formed a large proportion. These men of military age held two separate sessions to consider their own problems, and in particular the vexed question of alternative service. They reported that the strongest body of opinion was against the acceptance of this, and the matter was left by the Yearly Meeting to the individual decision of Friends when they appeared before the tribunals administering the Act. After long and prayerful discussion and consideration, in which a wide range of opinion was expressed, from those who thought that all ought to accept alternative service to those who felt that none should contemplate it, a public statement was issued in the name of the Meeting.

"We take this our earliest opportunity of reaffirming our entire opposition to compulsory military service, and our desire for the repeal of the Act. . . .

"We regard the central conception of the Act as imperilling the liberty of the individual conscience, which is the main hope of human progress—and as entrenching more deeply that militarism from which we all desire the world to be freed. . . .

"We consider that young men may do important service by going before the tribunals, claiming exemption, and making clear their reasons for doing so. At the same time we cannot admit that a human tribunal is an adequate judge of any man's conscience . . .

"Our lives should prove that compulsion is unnecessary and impolitic. . . . We pray that in steadfast conformity to the path of duty we may be set free to serve—to give to the community the

---

[1] This Committee was prosecuted in May 1916 for the publication of a leaflet, *Repeal the Act*, and each member was fined £100, in default two months' imprisonment. The sentence was confirmed on appeal, and five members, two of them Friends, went to prison. Three (one an older Friend) paid the fine. It was at this trial that the Crown Prosecutor (Mr. Bodkin) said that : " War would become impossible, if the view that war was wrong and that it was wrong to support the carrying on of war, was held generally " (*Manchester Guardian*, May 18, 1916). For trying to circulate this statement as a poster a peace propagandist was afterwards heavily fined. Two women peace-workers (one a Friend) in the summer of 1916 served nearly three months' imprisonment (in lieu of a £50 fine), for distributing leaflets against war. These activities were, of course, undertaken by the Friends concerned as individuals.

fullest service of which we are capable—each one in the way of God's appointing."

In March the earlier of the two Military Service Acts began to operate, and those Friends who had hoped that the provisions of the Act and Regulations, if wisely administered, would be compatible with liberty of conscience, were grievously disappointed as they watched the proceedings of the tribunals. An editorial in the *Friend*, on March 10th, had put forward the various forms of national service in which Friends might well engage : " Red Cross work, sanitary and hospital service, poor relief, education, constructive social work, industrial welfare work, assistance of disabled soldiers, interned aliens or prisoners, work on the land, and so forth." The writer had not anticipated that many tribunals would sweep most of his catalogue, notably education, on one side as " not of national importance." Many tribunals honestly tried to do the work assigned to them, but the injustices and inconsistencies of others roused widespread indignation in the country, and their treatment of the conscientious objector in particular was an open scandal. Friends, indeed, fared better than others, and there was an obvious disinclination to admit that a conscientious objection to war could exist outside the Society, but even Friends fared well or ill according to the accident of locality. One would receive absolute exemption, another would be sent into the Army, a third exempted on the ground of his relief work in France, while a fourth was refused permission to return to the same work. One, not trained to teach, might be sent to a school from which an experienced teacher was ordered to agricultural work. Some were urged to work at munitions, and others called hypocrites because firms in which they were employed had some more or less remote connection with Army work. Some were " old enough to know better," others " too young to have a conscience "—the anomalies were endless.

Exactly two months after the editorial just mentioned, the *Friend* framed a strong indictment of the tribunals for their lack of knowledge and understanding of the Act they administered, for their deplorable delay and confusion in arranging work of " national importance " for those who would undertake it, for their lack in many cases of simple justice, and their failure to understand any religious objection to war, a failure which sometimes passed into open contempt and mockery.

In the case of Friends the changed position of the Friends'

Ambulance Unit occasioned considerable difficulty and friction with the tribunals.[1] At the suggestion of the military authorities the Committee of the Unit had undertaken to provide ambulance work or other service of national importance for Friends and others closely connected with Friends, if they were absolutely willing of their own accord to take up the work. A Government Committee, under the Hon. T. W. H. Pelham, was intended to meet the case of other conscientious objectors. Unfortunately the voluntary proviso was ignored by many tribunals, and on May 12th the Committee of the Unit had to record in the *Friend* its strong objection to "attempts of the tribunals or military representatives to offer or appear to offer service with the Unit as an alternative to absolute exemption." In fact, some tribunals only offered exemption conditionally on joining the Unit, and some went further, insisting that the appellant must enter the ambulance section. The men who had already volunteered for the Unit, and those employed abroad on war relief, strongly resented this attempt to force all Friends' service into one mould.[2]

The Editor of the *Friend* wrote on May 19th : "We are not willing, though differing in method, to be pitted against each other. *We decline to be divided.* Some Friends undertake one form of service and some another, each according to his conscience, but all forms of true service spring from a common source, and may be inspired by one and the same spirit." Some young Friends even resigned from the Unit and came home to share the lot of those not sheltered by their work. The difficulty was added to by criticism of the Unit's relation to the Army, on the lines already sketched ; in August, a Committee of the Meeting for Sufferings, appointed to inquire into the whole matter, reported as follows :— [3]

"After recognizing the great help given by the F.A.U. to many of our young men, it was pointed out that the Unit was an independent organization, not answerable to the Meeting for Sufferings, but that it was by outsiders generally regarded as officially under the care of Friends. Abroad it formed part of the organization

---

[1] *Friend,* March 31st, April 7th, August 18, 1916 (statements by members of the Committee), and July 14th, August 11th (discussions in the Meeting for Sufferings).

[2] *Vide Friend,* April 7th (statement by some members of the F.A.U.) ; *Proceedings of Yearly Meeting* 1916, p. 37 (letter from men of the Friends' War Victims' Relief Expedition).

[3] *Friend,* August 11, 1916.

that serves the Army, though not under Army control. Captain Maxwell [1] has an honorary commission in the Army, and the close touch with both officers and privates has given rise to a code of behaviour closely approximating to that of the Army. There is an understanding with members abroad that they should not undertake peace propaganda, and members at home, belonging to the general section are expected not to come into opposition to the Defence of the Realm Act. Men drafted from the Army into Reserve W and sent to report to the Unit cease to belong to the Army on being received into the Unit. The Committee brought up against the essential difficulty of conducting a Quaker organization in co-operation with the military authorities engaged in actual warfare or with machinery set up by the Government in administering the Military Service Acts, was not able to offer any satisfactory solution."

In the discussion the splendid work of the ambulance men was fully recognized, as also the fact that the Committee of the Unit had no wish to be used in the interests of compulsion. The General Service Section was, however, criticized because it created a distinction between Friends accepting and refusing service in it, and between Friends and other objectors ; secondly, because in fact, though not in the intention of its organizers, it was adopted by the tribunals as part of the machinery for working the Acts, to which most Friends were utterly opposed. The Section consisted of Friends, or those closely connected with Friends, exempted conditionally by the tribunals and referred to the Unit, who were either physically unfit for ambulance service or unwilling to enter work so closely connected with the war. They were mostly placed in agriculture, though a few found openings in education, Y.M.C.A. work, or under the War Relief and Emergency Committees. By the end of the war the membership of the Section was four hundred and forty-two. [2]

There were, however, enough incompetent tribunals to bring about the result that, during the first six months of their administration, more than 2,500 conscientious objectors had been assigned to combatant or non-combatant duties in the Army, arrested and handed

---

[1] The commander of the Unit abroad, who was not a Friend. He took command after the Friend who was its original founder passed to the British-Italian Unit.

[2] For statements of the Unit's position and the status of the General Service Section *vide The Friends' Ambulance Unit*, pp. 186 foll., 245 foll.

over to the military authorities. A small number were Friends, or Attenders at Friends' meetings. Of these some half-dozen were among the conscientious objectors sent in May 1916 to Harwich Redoubt, where they were put in irons ("rigid handcuffs") and kept on a bread and water diet for disobedience to military orders. Later in the month they were among the forty sent to France. There, being in the war zone, they were sentenced to twenty-eight days of "Field Punishment No. 1," usually given to men on active service who sleep or are drunk on guard. For three days out of every four they were fastened for two separate hours to a fixed object. "They are either fastened to a gun-wheel, or handcuffed, and their arms fastened above the level of their heads to an iron bar. They can move up and down for the length of the bar, but, of course, their arms are kept in the same position."[1] At Boulogne, four objectors were court-martialled, and on June 15th, "on the top of a high hill overlooking the sea" they received sentence "to suffer death by being shot," which was at once commuted to ten years' penal servitude.[2] Similar sentences were pronounced on June 19th on thirty more. This was after repeated assurances in Parliament that the death sentence would not be pronounced on conscientious objectors.[3]

[1] *Friend*, May 26, 1916, cp. the "tying neck and heels" and "bucking-down" of Chapters XII, XVI. The punishment was abolished in 1923.

[2] *Friend*, June 30th and July 7, 1916. The Friends and Attenders sentenced were Howard Marten, Cornelius Barritt, Harry E. Stanton, Adam Priestly, and J. F. Murfin. Rendel Wyatt was sentenced to one year's hard labour. All were transferred to civil prisons.

[3] "House of Commons, June 22, 1916. *Mr. Barnes* said a report was current in the Lobbies that four conscientious objectors in France had been sentenced to death, and there was a very general feeling of resentment that such a report should be abroad after the many statements from the Front Bench in regard to the treatment of these men, and after the promises which had been made that they would be transferred to the civil power, and the assurances which had been given that they would not be sent to France at all. He could not believe the report to be true, and he raised the question in order to give the Under-Secretary for War an opportunity to deny it.

The Under-Secretary of State for War (*Mr. Tennant*) said many rumours with regard to the treatment of conscientious objectors had been circulated, and the great majority of them were untrue. He assumed the present rumour was one of these. He had no information on the subject, but he would investigate it and give full information to the House. . . . I can assure my Right Hon. Friend who has put the question that there is no intention of dealing with them in any way harshly, and that there will be no question of their being sentenced to death.

House of Commons, June 26, 1916. *Mr. Tennant*, in reply to questions by Mr. Morrell, Mr. T. E. Harvey, Mr. Whitehouse, Mr. Snowden, and Sir W.

By this time so many were under military detention or in civil prisons that the Government began tardily to arrange for a re-hearing of their cases and for the provision of some form of alternative service. By what was known as the "Home Office Scheme," work was offered under conditions midway between free employment and convict labour, and up to the end of October accepted by about five hundred and fifty of the men concerned. Some were sent to camps for quarrying, road-making and forestry, others, unfit for such labour, to "deprisoned" gaols, where they were employed on mail-bag making and other forms of what is usually prison labour.

The Yearly Meeting at the end of May, knowing that Friends were in France in the hands of the military, but closing before news of the courts-martial had been received, put the existing situation on record :

" Throughout our Yearly Meeting we have had continually in mind the fact that some of our members are in prison, or otherwise suffering for loyalty to conscience in respect of the peace testimony which has been ours from the earliest days of the Society.

" God has honoured us by counting these our dear Friends worthy to suffer shame for His name. We assure them of our loving remembrance and prayers that they may receive the Divine support in this their hour of trial."

This Yearly Meeting also reaffirmed the entire opposition of its members to compulsory military service, and their desire for the repeal of the Acts. At the suggestion of a Friend the Clerk stated in plain terms for the information of the public that the Yearly Meeting was the body representing the whole 20,000 Friends in its membership.

Much time and thought was given to the discussion of war in its relations to the social order. The Epistle (sent "To Friends the World over and all who seek the Way of Life") declared :

" There is warfare for all of us in this world, but against whom and to what end ? It is not our brother men who are our enemies,

Byles, said it was the case that courts-martial held in France had sentenced certain men professing conscientious objections to death for offences punishable by death under the Army Act. In all these thirty-four cases the sentence had been commuted to penal servitude by the Commander-in-Chief in France."

Vide also Hansard (Parliamentary Reports, House of Commons), January 18th, May 11th, May 15th, May 30th, June 1st, June 20, 1916.

but the germs of disease that destroy men's bodies and the false ideas and evil passions that destroy their souls. We strive for a state of society in which the good of all may be achieved by the self-denying labour of each. . . . The most real and abiding force in human affairs was seen in operation in the life, death, and rising again of Jesus Christ. That force we call the Love of God."

The "absolutist" conscientious objectors were gradually transferred to civil prisons, where Quakers were allowed to act as " chaplains," visiting those who asked for them (not only Friends) and holding meetings for worship. In April 1919 (five months after the armistice) those who had served two or more years' hard labour were released, and by the end of July all conscientious objectors were out of prison. Several, Friends and others, have since devoted themselves to the cause of prison reform.

Towards the end of 1917 Friends found that their convictions brought them again into conflict with war-time administration. A new Regulation (27 C) had been introduced under the Defence of the Realm Act, which made it illegal to print, publish, or distribute any leaflet about the war or the making of peace which had not been submitted to the Official Press Bureau. The Meeting for Sufferings on December 7, 1917, after considering the matter, embodied its decision in the following minute :

" The executive body of the Society of Friends, after serious consideration, desires to place on record its conviction that the portion of the recent regulations requiring the submission to the censor of all leaflets dealing with the present war and the making of peace is a grave danger to the national welfare. The duty of every good citizen to express his thoughts on the affairs of his country is hereby endangered, and further, we believe that Christianity requires the toleration of opinions not our own, lest we should unwittingly hinder the workings of the Spirit of God.

" Beyond this there is a deeper issue involved. It is for Christians a paramount duty to be free to obey and to act and speak in accord with the law of God, a law higher than that of any State, and no Government official can release men from this duty.

"We realize the rarity of the occasions on which a body of citizens find their sense of duty to be in conflict with the law, and it is with a sense of the gravity of the decision that the Society of Friends must, on this occasion, act contrary to the regulation, and continue to issue literature on war and peace without submitting it to the censor. It is convinced that in thus standing for spiritual liberty it is acting in the best interests of the nation."

The various Friends' Committees continued to publish pamphlets, and finally the chairman and secretaries of the Friends' Service Committee were prosecuted for a leaflet, "A Challenge to Militarism," on the subject of the imprisoned conscientious objectors. The trial took place at the Guildhall in May 1918 while the Yearly Meeting was sitting. The Meeting passed a minute in support of the Meeting for Sufferings and the committee, and on the second day of the trial adjourned its sitting in order that the Clerk might give evidence and other Friends attend. "While the Alderman was out of court the Quakers, who filled the plain little room, were invited to engage in silent prayer, and for a time the police court was a Quakers' Meeting."[1] The two men defendants (Harrison Barrow and Arthur Watts) were sentenced to six months' imprisonment, Edith M. Ellis to £100 fine and fifty guineas costs, or three months' imprisonment. Their appeal a month later was dismissed, and all three went to prison. At the close of the appeal a barrister, on behalf of a few Friends who supported the war, expressed their personal disapproval of the attitude of the Meeting for Sufferings and the Friends' Service Committee.

In Australia and New Zealand, at the outbreak of war, the authorities suspended the penalty of imprisonment for refusal to train, although prosecutions and fines continued. In response, the Freedom League and other anti-militarist associations gave up active propaganda. The small bodies of Friends were anxious to join in war service. Seventeen young men came over to join in the relief and ambulance work in France and Belgium, some of them working their passage across. A few in membership enlisted, and at least two did so (in the Army Medical Corps) because their means did not allow them to join the Friends' ambulance work, and the funds raised by Friends in Australia were not sufficient to help all those anxious to share in it.[2] Australian Friends also visited the aliens in internment camps, and gave some help to their families. The General Meeting of September 1915 published a

[1] *Manchester Guardian*, May 24, 1918.
[2] An estimate of Friends who enlisted, given in the *Friend*, January 29, 1915, said that there were eleven cases "in the colonies," i.e. not only in Australasia. Some of the Friends who returned to do relief work later suffered under the Military Service Acts.

minute urging the claims of war relief, and clearly explaining the standpoint of Friends.

"While we fully concede the claims of our country to the highest service we can render, we do not allow that for us this can be of a military character, or such as opposes itself to the claims of humanity in general. . . . There are many other forms of service having no connection with work for war victims, and perhaps hardly to be designated national, which are not the less commendable on that account. There is much need for sympathy and for practical help all around us : harvests have to be gathered in, and the common work of the world to be done, and not least of all does the world need to be put in train for such a settlement when the war shall end as will be reasonable, just, and abiding."

In both the Commonwealth and Dominion a "War Census" was taken in 1915. As in England, Friends filled up the form, adding a statement that for conscientious reasons they could not undertake military service. In New Zealand, in November 1915, Egerton Gill, a Friend and Secretary of the local "Freedom League," was fined £50 (under the War Regulations Act) for "publishing matter likely to interfere with recruiting." He had issued a circular to members of the League and sympathizers suggesting the above course in filling the registration form, and had sent copies of a resolution of the branch to Members of Parliament. The advice was identical with that issued by English and Australian Friends living under similar war legislation. The fine was confirmed on appeal, and his office was raided by the military and the papers of the League seized. The house of an English Friend visiting New Zealand was also raided in her absence, but the papers confiscated, which included the minute books of the meeting, were later returned to her.

In the summer of 1916 a Military Service Act was passed in New Zealand compulsorily enrolling all men aged from 20 to 46 years in the Reserve. The Act was supported by severe penalties. A conscience-clause exempted, from combatant service only, adherents of a Church whose tenets forbid military service. Friends protested against this privileged and qualified exemption ; out of the small body twenty-one Members and Attenders served terms of imprisonment, eleven were exempted on medical grounds, and twelve served in the R.A.M.C. Australia maintained its voluntary army through the war. Since then Australasian Friends have not suffered from any rigorous enforcement of the Defence Acts, although refusal to train entails a disqualification for Government appointments.

During the first three years of the war American Friends were outside its main current, though many were roused to a deeper interest in the peace testimony and a keener examination of its bearings. A Peace Conference was held at Winona Lake in July 1915, called by a group of young Friends representing the chief branches of the Society. They adopted a statement of peace principles, which, though not the utterance of an official body, was the first important statement by American Friends during the war. A Continuation Committee appointed by this Conference did good service in strengthening the peace feeling of Friends throughout the country, and in securing the appointment of the American Friends' Service Committee when the United States entered the war in April 1917.[1] " Friends as a whole were definitely and often quite actively upon the side of that great body of public opinion which favoured American neutrality."[2] Soon after the declaration of war the Five Years' Meeting (representing thirteen " Orthodox " Yearly Meetings) reaffirmed Friends' views on peace. Careful inquiry led the late Dr. Allen C. Thomas to the conclusion that " no meeting of those calling themselves Friends, and certainly no Yearly Meeting, failed to uphold the ancient testimony of Friends." He added, however, " notwithstanding the supreme devotion of some and an unchanged official attitude, the trial found many with uninformed convictions and inability to see the vital issues involved."[3]

When compulsion was introduced, the Government hoped to meet the case of the conscientious objector by a clause in the Selective Service Act granting exemption, from combatant service only, to any member of religious sects such as Mennonites, Dunkards, and Friends, whose own personal convictions were in agreement with the principles of his Church, " but no person so exempted shall be exempted from service in any capacity that the President shall

[1] Rufus Jones, *A Service of Love in War Time* (The Macmillan Co., 1920), describes the war work and suffering of American Friends. *Vide* also Thomas, *History of Friends in America*, 1919 edition.

[2] *All Friends' Conference*, 1920. Report of Commission VII. (American), p. 7.

[3] Thomas, *History of Friends in America* 1919, pp. 245, 253. The latest returns give the number of Friends in the United States as " Orthodox " 97,000, " Hicksite " 18,000, " Conservative " 3,600. Philadelphia Yearly Meeting (4,460) is included in the " Orthodox " return, but does not belong to the Five Years' Meeting.

declare to be non-combatant." The President's ruling included under non-combatant service, medical, " quarter-master " (i.e. Army Service) and engineering work. About two-thirds of the six thousand conscientious objectors conscripted accepted this compromise, and according to one estimate the same proportion of Friends to whom the choice was offered. The solution was not acceptable, however, " to the mass of the membership of some meetings, many of the young men who had been drafted, the leaders and spokesmen of most of the Yearly Meetings, and the American Friends' Service Committee."[1]

This Committee, under the chairmanship of Dr. Rufus Jones, consisted of representatives of Philadelphia Yearly Meeting, of the " Hicksite " body, of the Five Years' Meeting, and later of the " Wilburite " Friends and of the Mennonite Church. Before the draft law came into force the Committee sent a letter to the young men Friends affected, expressing the hope that " you are so deeply grounded in the principles of Friends that your conscience will lead you to act consistently with these principles." At the same time the Committee bent its energies to provide some form of war service which a sincere Friend could undertake, an aim already adopted by the Philadelphia Young Friends' Committee. The first idea, the formation of an Ambulance Unit, proved impossible, and a plan of co-operation with the English War Relief Committee and the civilian section of the American Red Cross was developed. The Service Committee resolved to recruit and train one hundred men to serve as relief workers under the general control of the Red Cross. A call for volunteers sent out in June, quickly resulted in about two hundred applications. In July one hundred men assembled to train at Haverford College, and between September and November they sailed on various boats to France. Six women Friends had already gone, at the end of June, to Russia to join the English Friends at Buzuluk. This international service from the first was necessarily affected by the conscription laws. As the drafts were progressive, nearly two hundred Friends who had gone to the work in France were afterwards drafted, and many were put on the deserters' list. Many others who had volunteered and trained for relief were called up before they could start.

The Friends' Service Committee acted as an intermediary with

[1] *All Friends' Conference,* Report of (American) Commission V. p. 9. Another estimate (Commission VII. p. 13) was that one half of the Friends who claimed exemption accepted non-combatant service. But all calculations are only approximate.

the War Department on behalf of these cases. They procured exemptions for the Friends already in France, and finally the Department agreed "that all drafted Friends who were conscientious objectors should be allowed to serve in a civilian capacity under the Friends' Service Committee. The first Friends were released for this service just about a year after the proposition was first made, and nine months after the promise of the Secretary for War that such a plan should be worked out. The confidence and responsibility placed in the Friends' Committee was much broader than that originally contemplated, in that all conscientious objectors were to be turned over to the Friends' Committee up to the number which that committee would be willing to accept. An extensive programme of farm work in the United States, for men not needed for service abroad, was planned, but the armistice rendered it unnecessary."[1]

In all two hundred conscientious objectors were offered by the Government to the Friends' Service Committee for reconstruction service in France, of whom ninety-nine were actually released from the military camps in which they were confined. Some others were given farm furlough at home. Of the ninety-nine, fifty-four were Friends and about fifty more, discharged after the armistice, also went to France. Out of five hundred and twenty-seven sentenced to military prisons only thirteen were Friends. Commission VII of the All Friends' Conference made an effort to compile statistics of the Friends subject to conscription, of those who served in the Army and Navy, of those exempted on various grounds, and of those who were conscientious objectors, but it found that complete figures could not be obtained. As the majority of the Society lived in rural areas, many young Friends received " deferred classification " for agriculture. The Commission felt that any attempt to compare the action of English and American Friends would be misleading. " Not only were the circumstances leading to war and to conscription in the two countries quite different, but the provisions for partial or complete exemption in the two Military Acts were far from parallel."[2] It must not be forgotten that there were members above military age who accepted war contracts or subscribed to war loans. In the opinion of this Commission the Mennonites of the United States held more uniformly to the peace testimony and suffered more for it than did the Society of Friends. Dr. Rufus Jones also

[1] *All Friends' Conference,* Report of (American) Commission VII. pp. 15–16.
[2] *Ibid.,* Commission V. p. 10.

pays a warm tribute to the Mennonites. " Their young men," he says,[1] " stood the test of the camps with insight and with much bravery. They had the backing of their Church and they were conscious that they were its standard-bearers. They became closely united in fellowship with our men in the camps, . . . nearly sixty of their members went abroad under our Committee. They were excellent workers, and they brought a fine spirit of devotion and co-operation to the Mission. They merged with the Friends with a natural grace, and we always thought of them as a part of ourselves. The Mennonites in every part of America contributed with liberality to the work, sending a total of more than 200,000 dollars."

Very few conscientious objectors on religious grounds took up the " absolutist " position. The Friends in military camps had mostly already been accepted by the Friends' Service Committee, and were only waiting to be released. The few Friends, and the considerable number of Mennonites in military prisons, reached them mainly through maladministration of the Act by subordinate officers. They were sentenced to terms of imprisonment varying from five to forty years, most being over twenty years. Both in camps and in prisons there were shocking instances of ill-treatment.[2] In the spring and summer of 1919 a Board of Inquiry, appointed by the Government, visited the camps, and through its means most of the Quakers were released on relief furlough. There were not more than one or two " absolutists " in the English sense. This was partly because the work offered as alternative service was of real value, and also of an adventurous and attractive character, partly because there was no national anti-conscription movement, and because American Friends, as a rule, are more widely separated from Socialists (who provided most of the " absolutist " objectors) than those in England.

The establishment by the Government of compulsory military training—the " Student Army Training Corps "—in all universities and colleges presented another problem to Friends. Of the ten Quaker colleges only one—Swarthmore—under pressure from its Board of Managers, but not without protest, established a corps, but as many students were not Friends, the other colleges, especially Haverford, had to face the loss of those who went elsewhere for training.

[1] *A Service of Love in War-time*, p. 124.
[2] For fuller description, *vide A Service of Love*, pp. 85 foll. ; *History of Friends in America*, p. 249 ; Graham, *Conscription and Conscience*, pp. 376 foll.

The War Relief work in France was carried out in the fullest sense as a joint effort, both by the English and American Committees and by the workers of both nationalities in the field. Its character has already been described. About four hundred and seventy-five American Friends (including twenty-five women) and sixty Mennonites were engaged in it during the last year of the war and the period after the armistice. Large contributions of money and clothing were made by Friends of all branches and by the Mennonite body. In 1919 American Friends undertook varied relief work in Serbia—rebuilding, agriculture, medical aid, and the care of war orphans. In Poland and Russia they co-operated with the English Missions ; in the autumn of 1919, at the request of Mr. Hoover, they undertook the responsibility for child-feeding throughout Germany, as the agents of the American Relief Commission. They were chosen partly because of their previous experience, but also on the express ground that the Quakers had won the confidence of all sides in their relief activities. Later similar work was carried on in the famine areas of Russia.

The better knowledge of one another gained by English and American Friends from their fellowship in joint effort led, during the war, to the proposal that an international Friends' peace conference should be held at its close. The plan was warmly welcomed, careful preparations were made, and from August 12 to 20, 1920, there met at Devonshire House, Bishopsgate, the old headquarters of the Society in London, the first " All Friends' Conference, to consider the nature and basis of our peace testimony, and its application to the needs of the world to-day." More than a thousand Friends were present, from England, Scotland, Ireland, the United States, Canada, Australia, New Zealand, South Africa, Jamaica, China, Japan, India, Syria, Madagascar, France, Germany, Austria, Switzerland, Norway, and Denmark. In the previous two years Commissions of Friends in England and America had prepared an historical sketch and parallel reports on six aspects of the peace testimony : the Fundamental Basis ; National Life and International Relations ; Personal Life and Society ; Problems of Education ; the Life of the Society of Friends, and Methods of Propaganda.

These reports, and the public " Swarthmore Lecture " by Dr. Rufus Jones on " The Nature and Authority of Conscience," which opened the Conference, formed the basis of the discussions.

The truth and vitality of the peace message and the importance of its implications in personal and national as well as international life, were reaffirmed by speaker after speaker. But more helpful than the opinions uttered or the conclusions reached was the stimulus of association between men and women of varied types and nationalities united in a common endeavour to seek truth in the light granted by the Spirit of God.

With the All Friends' Conference this account must close. It may serve to show that from the early days of the Society the peace testimony has been held as an integral part of its religious belief and practice. It was not based merely on the recorded teaching of the New Testament, although in full harmony with this, but it grew inevitably out of the conception of the inward light, the divine Spirit in the souls of men, that lighteth every man that cometh into the world. That Spirit, the Spirit of Christ, which leads into all truth, could never, if faithfully followed, lead men into hatred, revenge, deceit, cruelty, bloodshed, devastation, and all the host of evils bound up in war. Nor could its followers destroy their fellow men, children of the same Father, in each of whom there was a measure of the same Spirit. Nor again could the gloss of a theologian, nor the command of rulers and magistrates, stand against this inner conviction of the soul. The different testimonies were, to the early Friends, inter-related and all essential to the practice of true religion. Barclay, writing of the two against oaths and against war, says :

" There is so great a connection between these two precepts of Christ that as they were uttered and commanded by him at one and the same time, so the same way they were received by men of all ages, not only in the first promulgation by the little number of the disciples, but also, after the Christians increased, in the first three hundred years. Even so in the apostasy, the one was not left and rejected without the other ; and now again in the restitution and renewed practice of the Eternal Gospel, they are acknowledged as eternal unchangeable laws, properly belonging to the evangelical state and perfection thereof, from which, if any withdraw, he falls short of the perfection of a Christian man."

In words already quoted William Bayly declared that the peace testimony was " not an opinion or judgment which may fail us, or in which we may be mistaken or doubt, but the infallible ground and unchangeable foundation of our religion (that is to say) Christ Jesus the Lord, that Spirit, Divine Nature or Way of Life, which God hath raised and renewed in us, in which we walk and in whom we delight to dwell."

Apart from the constant exposition in Epistles and other documents of the official bodies of Friends, the same testimony is borne by a host of individuals in the later generation of the Society. Thomas Chalkley, Thomas Story, John Bellers, John Woolman, Anthony Benezet, William Allen, Stephen Grellet, Jonathan Dymond, Joseph Sturge, Robert Spence Watson and Joshua Rowntree—these are only a few of the names that rise to memory in such a context. But more eloquent and convincing than any written or spoken word is the patient faithfulness of humble men and women who have lived unterrified in the midst of danger without resort to arms, and have undergone loss, imprisonment, shame, suffering, and death itself rather than forswear the principle of peace. The " conscientious objector " is no new phenomenon. In England and Ireland, the West Indies, the American colonies, the United States, and Australasia, for two and a half centuries he has baffled all attempts at coercion, whether by legal penalties or brutal violence.

In the face of this record of profession and practice some would maintain that the peace testimony is a mere individual preference to be held or abandoned by Friends at their pleasure, or would even condemn it as a modern error thrust among our accepted beliefs. To the latter position this book is intended as a reply. Those who uphold the former bring forward two or three inconsistencies of statement among early Friends, of which that of Isaac Penington is the most notable. (Penington, as has been explained, firmly maintained that Friends, owning obedience to the law of love, could not themselves bear arms or take part in war.) There are also the inconsistencies of action by Rhode Island and Pennsylvanian Friends holding office in time of war, and the address of 1746 congratulating George II on the defeat of the Jacobite Rebellion. This is the solitary instance of *official* inconsistency in the records of London Yearly Meeting ; three years later the Meeting for Sufferings clearly indentified itself with the peace views of Barclay's *Apology*. In various wars a greater or smaller number of Friends in England or America have abandoned the peace position, but only in one case did the dissentients claim to represent the accepted doctrine of the Society, and these—the body of " Free Quakers " in the war of the Revolution—soon melted away. Up to the present time in England no effort has been made to modify the Queries and the

Discipline, on the not infrequent occasions of their revision, in the direction of a less emphatic pronouncement on peace. The section, " Peace among the Nations," in the Book of Discipline, is clear and unmistakable in its teaching, and for sixty years the Eighth Query has reminded Friends of the duty of faithfulness to the Christian testimony against all war.

It is sometimes suggested that in the last century Friends have shifted from the original ground of the testimony, and now base it rather on humanitarian and philanthropic arguments. No doubt the influences of the period of the Revolution and of Napoleon, from the diverse sources of evangelical Christianity and humanitarian philosophy, did largely affect the thought of Friends. But from the earliest period the two golden threads of love towards God and love towards man intertwine in the web of their belief and practice. There is much humanitarian sentiment in Barclay, much philanthropy in Bellers and Benezet. John Woolman combines a most purely spiritual basis for his condemnation of war with a most deeply humanitarian sympathy for those who sin or suffer in its toils.

On the other hand, recent statements, whether by collective bodies of Friends or by individual conscientious objectors explaining their convictions to tribunal or court-martial, lay the main emphasis on spiritual and religious considerations so far as these can be separated from those of humanity and brotherly love. London Yearly Meeting in 1915 recalled in one of its minutes the basis of the testimony :

" It is not enough to be satisfied with a barren negative witness, a mere proclamation of non-resistance. We must search for a positive, vital, constructive message. Such a message, a message of supreme love, we find in the life and death of our Lord Jesus Christ. We find it in the doctrine of the indwelling Christ, that rediscovery of the early Friends, leading as it does to a recognition of the brotherhood of all men. Of this doctrine our testimony as to war and peace is a necessary outcome, and if we understand the doctrine aright, and follow it in its wide implications, we shall find that it calls to the peaceable spirit and the rule of love in all the broad and manifold relations of life."

The call was re-echoed in 1920 by the All Friends' Conference in its " Message to Friends and Fellow-Seekers."

" The roots of war can be taken away from all our lives, as they were long ago in Francis of Assisi and John Woolman. Day by day let us seek out and remove every seed of hatred and of greed, of resentment and of grudging in our own selves and in the social structure about us. Christ's way of freedom replaces slavish obedience by fellowship. Instead of an external compulsion he gives an inward authority. Instead of self-seeking we must put sacrifice ; instead of domination, co-operation. Fear and suspicion must give place to trust and the spirit of understanding. Thus shall we more and more become friends to all men and our lives will be filled with the joy which true friendship never fails to bring. Surely this is the way in which Christ calls us to overcome the barriers of race and class and thus to make of all humanity a society of friends."

APPENDICES

APPENDIX A

LIST OF SOLDIERS AND SAILORS WHO BECAME FRIENDS BEFORE THE YEAR 1660

(Including ex-Soldiers and Sailors.)

Date.	Name.	Reference.
—	Abell, Richard	Joseph Smith's *Catalogue of Friends' Books.*
1655.	Ames, William (Royalist) ...	Braithwaite, *Beg. of Quakerism.*
1656.	Anonymous, Gunner on *Mermaid*	*Cal. State Pap., Dom.*, 1656/7, p. 441.
1651.	Anonymous, Trooper after Battle of Worcester	Fox, *Journal.*
1656.	Bacon, Christopher (Royalist) ...	Sewell, *History*, p. 682.
1658.	Baker, Daniel (Navy)	*Cal. State Pap., Dom.*, 1658/9, p. 139
1655.	Bancroft, Major William ...	Besse, *Sufferings* (Ireland).
—	Barber, Captain William ...	*First Publishers of Truth*, p. 171.
—	Barnardiston, Giles	Sewell, p. 386.
—	Barwick, Cornet Robert... ...	*F.P.T.*, p. 294.
—	Beal, Thomas	*Declaration of Suffering*, p. 8, in D. 76, 20.
1652.	Benson, Colonel	*F.P.T.*, p. 242.
—	Billing, Edward	
—	Bishop, Captain George... ...	Fox, *Journal.*
1656.	Braford, Edward	Besse, (Ireland).
—	Bradford, Captain William ...	Fox, *Journal.*
—	Brown, James	Fox, *Journal.*
—	Cary, John	*F.P.T.*, p. 294.
—	Clibborn, John	*Select Miscellanies*, i. 197.
—	Cook, Cornet Edward	Besse (Ireland).
—	Corbett, William (Royalist) ...	Besse.
—	Crisp, Stephen	
—	Crook, John, " Captain " ...	Lyon Turner, *Orig. Records of Nonconformity*, i. 84.
—	Curtis, Thomas	Sewell, *History.*

Date.	Name.	Reference.
1657.	Davenport, Capt.-Lieut....	*Clarke Papers*, iii. 122.
1659.	Davies, Quartermaster Daniel	*Cal. State Pap., Dom.*, 1659.
1657/8.	Dell, Jonas	Smith's *Catalogue*.
1651.	Dewsbury, William	Dewsbury, *Works*, pp. 45 foll.
1653.	Edmundson, William	*Journal* of W. Edmundson.
1657.	Foster, Lieut. Matthew ...	*Swarth. MSS.*, iv. 237.
1655.	Fox, George, the Younger	His own *Works*.
—	Fuce, Ensign Joseph	*F.P.T.*, p. 162.
—	Gibson, William...	Sewell, *History*, p. 682.
—	Gilpin, Thomas ...	G. Lyon Turner, *Orig. Records*, iii. 824.
—	Graham, John ...	*F.P.T.*, p. 294.
—	Hobman, Samuel	*F.P.T.*, p. 294.
—	Holmes, Captain	Besse.
—	Hubberthorn, Richard ...	Besse.
1659.	Jones, Quartermaster Daniel	*Cal. State Pap., Dom.*, 1659.
1656.	Killo, Ananias ...	Besse (Ireland).
1656/7.	Knowlman, Richard (Navy)	*Cal. State Pap., Dom.*, 1656/7, p. 326.
1657.	Langdall, Jonas ...	*Swarth. MSS.*, iv. 237.
—	Lawrence, Capt. John	*F.P.T.*, p. 171.
1658.	Levenes, John ...	*Cal. State Pap., Dom.*, 1658/9, p. 139.
1655.	Lilburne, John ...	Sewell, *History*.
1657.	Lurting, Thomas (Navy)	Lurting, *The Fighting Sailor*, etc.
—	Luxford, Thomas	*F.P.T.*, p. 265.
1655.	Malines, Robert...	Besse (Ireland).
1656.	Marcy, Daniel ...	Besse (Ireland).
—	Mason, John	George Whitehead, *Life*.
—	Mead, William...	William Penn, *The People's Ancient and Just Liberties*, etc.
1618.	Milledge, Capt. Antony (Navy)...	*Cal. State Pap., Dom.*, 1658/9, p. 139.
1657.	Millington, William	*Swarth. MSS.*, iv. 237.
1656.	Mitchell, Lieut. Thomas	Besse (Ireland).
1656.	Moore, John ...	Besse (Ireland).
—	Moorland, Capt. John ...	*F.P.T.*, p. 249.

Date.	Name.	Reference.
1656.	Morris, William... ...	... Smith's *Catalogue.*
1655.	Morris, Capt. William ...	... Besse (Ireland).
—	Musgrave, George ...	... *F.P.T.,* p. 294.
1651.	Naylor, James	... Fox, *Journal.*
1653.	Osborne, Colonel William	... Fox, *Journal.*
1657.	Parish, Thomas	... *Swarth. MSS.,* iv, 237.
1659.	Parker, William... ...	... *F.P.T.,* p. 31.
—	Phayre, Colonel	... *Letters of Early Friends.*
1655.	Pike, Corporal Richard ...	... Besse (Ireland).
—	Pittway, Captain Edward	... *F.P.T.,* p. 277.
—	Pursloe, Captain... ...	... *F.P.T.,* p. 293.
—	Pyott, Captain Edward ...	... Fox, *Journal.*
—	Roe, Major Henry ...	... *Cal. State Pap., Dom.*
1657.	Rowntree, Francis ...	... *Swarth. MSS.,* iv. 237.
—	Sansom, Oliver	... *Life,* p. 203.
1656/7.	Shewell, Thomas (Navy)	... *Cal. State Pap., Dom.,* 1656/7, p. 548.
—	Sicklemore, Capt. James...	... *F.P.T.,* p. 139.
1657.	Simpson, John	... *Swarth. MSS.,* iv. 237.
1655.	Smith, Richard	... *F.P.T.,* p. 106.
—	Stoddart, Captain Amor...	... *F.P.T.,* p. 165.
1654.	Stubbs, John	... Besse.
1653.	Stubbs, Thomas	... *F.P.T.,* p. 68.
—	Taylor, Captain Thomas	... Fox, *Journal.*
—	Turner, Robert	... George Whitehead, *Life.*
1655.	Wall, James	... Besse.
—	Walters, Thomas (Royalist)	... Fox, *Journal,* ii. 48.
1657.	Watkinson, Capt. George	... *Swarth. MSS.,* iv. 237.
1657.	Ward, Cornet	... Braithwaite, *Beg. of Quakerism.*
1652.	Warde, Captain Henry ...	... Fox, *Journal.*
—	Wastfield, Robert ...	... Smith's *Catalogue.*
—	Well, Capt.-Lieut. Thomas	... *F.P.T.,* p. 281.
1652.	Whitehead, John ...	... Besse.
—	Williams, Captain ...	... Fox, *Journal.*
—	Wilson, George... ...	... *Swarth. MSS.,* i. 293.
—	Wilson, William (Royalist)	... Fox, *Journal.*

APPENDIX B

THE TESTIMONY OF THE SOLDIERS, 1657

Preliminary Note.—The captain, William Bradford, mentioned is apparently the same as Dewsbury's visitor at Nottingham (*ante*, p. 47). The manuscript is difficult to decipher, and it is not clear whether the signatory, Watkinson, is " Geo." (the captain of the troop) or " Tho." The former is more probable, as Fox, in his *Journal*, mentions that this year, during his visit to Scotland, " Leutenant Foster and Lt. Dove and Captain Watkinson was turned out of the army for owning truth and several other officers and soldiers, and because they would not put off their hats to them and said ' thee ' and ' thou ' to them " (*Cambridge Journal*, i. 308). Fox and Alexander Parker both carried on active work in Scotland during this autumn, and were eventually banished from the country. The name of the colonel of the regiment is generally read as Kilburne, but no such officer is otherwise known, and it is almost certainly Colonel Robert Lilburne (appointed Deputy Major-General for the northern counties in 1655), who was quartered at York in August 1657, and wrote thence on the fourth of the month, to the Admiralty Commissioners, that his regiment had been ordered to Scotland. Some delay, however, occurred, for on October 13 Captain William Peverell sent a petition to the Protector and Privy Council, stating that, as Major-General Lilburne's regiment of horse much require money to pay for their quarters on their march to Scotland, he has been left behind to receive their pay. Since the soldiers' testimony is dated October 20, the purge of the regiment must have been carried out immediately upon its arrival in Scotland ; or possibly the departure from York had been postponed in order to allow anyone who wished to withdraw from the ranks at a point nearer their homes. (Several of the names are still common in the North of England.) It is noteworthy that Monk's order is dated October 14, the day after Fox appeared before the Council in Edinburgh.[1]

Swarthmore MSS., iv. 237.

A testimony of some of ye souldyers yt were turned out of ye army whoe owned ymselves to bee quakers 1657.

In obedience to an order giuen forth under the hands of Jere. Smith by order from ye L. Genll Monck, bearing date ye 14th of October 1657 wherein is written I desire yu also to certifie under yr hands wat Quakers

[1] *Cal. State Papers, Dom.* (1657), viii. 53.

ether officers or souldiers yu have in yr. troope. In answer theirunto, we whose names are here vnder written beinge officers & souldiers in Capt. Wm. Bradford & Capt. Geo. Watkinson their troopes in Coll. Robt. Lilburne his Regte of horse, doe certifie to all whom these may any way or in any wise concerne, that ye name of Quakers as it is by ye worlde given in much scorne and derision to ye Children of ye Ld who believe in ye Light Xt Jesus and walke in ye same, wee dare not owne. But quakinge and tremblinge according to what the scriptures declares of wee doe owne, and wat they doe declare of by the power and workinge of Jesu Xt in our measures we witnes fulfilled in us. And if we should deny this before men we might rightly feare yt hee yt hath begun this good worke in us, might deny us before his father which is in heaven, accordinge to yt scripture he yt denyes me before men him will I deny before my father which is in heaven. And to the truth here of as by Xt Jesus, it is revailed in us, in ye pure feare, dread & power of ye eternall livinge God who made heauen and earth & knowes ye secrets of all harts are we made willinge to give this testimonie under our hands ye 20 : day of ye 8 month cauled October in ye yeare 1657

Mathew ffoster	Geo. Watkinson
Willm Millington	Tho. Parish chaplin to ye troope
ffrancis Booth	Jonas Langdall
	ffrancis Rountre
	John Simpson

All these were turned out of ye Army by monke with many others wch were tender (in ye army) of Gods truth.

APPENDIX C

g ff to Olefer Croumull, 1654

I, who am of the world called george ffox, doe deny the carrying or drawing of any carnall sword against any, or against thee Oliver Crumwell or any man in the presence of the lord god I declare it god is my wittnesse, by whom I am moved to give this forth for the truthes sake, from him whom the world calls george ffox, who is the son of God, who is sent to stand A wittnesse against all violence and against all the workes of darknesse, and to turne people from the darkenesse to the light, and to bring them from the occassion of the warre, and from the occassion of the Magistrates sword, which is A terrour to the evill doers which actes contrary to the light of the lord Jeus Christ, which is A praise to them that doe well, which is a protection to them, that doe well, and not the will and such souldiers that are putt in that place no false accussers must bee, no violence must doe, but bee content with their wages, and that Magistrate bears not the sword in vaine, from under the occasion of that sword I doe seeke to bring people, my weapons are not carnall but spirituall, And my kingdome is not of this world, therefore with the carnall weapon I doe not fight, but am from those things dead, from him who is not of the world, called of the world by the name george ffox, and this I am ready to seale with my blood, and this I am moved to give forth for the truthes sake, who A wittnesse stands against all unrighteousnesse, and all ungodlynesse, who A sufferer is for the righteous seed sake, waiteing for the redemption of it, who A crowne that is mortall seekes not for, that fadeth away, but in the light dwells, which comprehends that Crowne, which light is the condemnaçon of all such; in which Light I wittnesse the Crowne that is Immortall that fades not away, from him who to all your soulls is A friend, for establishing of righteousnesse and cleansseing the Land of evill doers, and A wittnesse against all wicked inventions of men and murderous plotts, which Answered shall be with the Light in all your Consciences, which makes no Covenant with death, to which light in you all I speake, and am clear.

ff. g.
who is of the world called George ffox
who A new name hath which the world
knows not.

Wee are wittnesses of this Testimony, whose names in the flesh is called

Tho: Aldem.   Robert Creven.[1]

[1] *Cambridge Journal*, i. 1–162, and note p. 425.

Note.—The expressions in this document were early fastened upon by opponents of Quakerism, and in Ellwood's edition of the *Journal* only a very condensed quotation was given. The whole declaration, however, was reprinted in facsimile in 1836 during the " Beaconite Controversy " (in which the value of early Quaker teaching was attacked) by Elisha Bates,[1] who considered it the " outcome of a disordered imagination." On the other hand, it was reported to Fox that its first reader, the Protector, took no exception to it. " My Lord says you are not a foole and said hee never saw such a paper in his life."[2] This may, however, refer to the second letter of personal advice. In regard to the expression " who is the son of God," the Editor of the *Cambridge Journal* writes in his note on the document : " Probably more has been read into these words than they were ever intended to convey. It must be remembered that Fox's mind was not trained to accurate theological expression," and he refers to Romans viii. 14, and John x. 34–6 as the probable inspiration for such a use of the phrase. See also T. E. Harvey's Introduction to the *Cambridge Journal*, pp. xxiv-xxvi, for instances of the unguarded expressions of early Friends before the fall of James Naylor had taught them the need for soberness and restraint.

[1] In his *Appeal to the Society of Friends.*
[2] Captain Drury to Fox, *Camb. Journal*, i. 169.

APPENDIX D

ADDRESS FROM THE RELIGIOUS SOCIETY OF FRIENDS TO THE EMPEROR OF RUSSIA

To Nicholas, Emperor of all the Russias.

May it please the Emperor,

We, the undersigned members of a Meeting representing the religious Society of Friends (commonly called Quakers) in Great Britain, venture to approach the Imperial presence under a deep conviction of religious duty and in the constraining love of Christ our Saviour. We are, moreover, encouraged to do so by the many proofs of condescension and Christian kindness manifested by thy late illustrious brother, the Emperor Alexander, as well as by thy honoured mother, to some of our brethren in religious profession.

It is well known that, apart from all political consideration, we have, as a Christian Church, uniformly upheld a testimony against war, on the simple ground that it is utterly condemned by the precepts of Christianity, as well as altogether incompatible with the spirit of its Divine Founder, who is emphatically styled the " Prince of Peace." This conviction we have repeatedly pressed upon our rulers, and often, in the language of bold, but respectful remonstrance, have we urged upon them the maintenance of peace, as the true policy, as well as the manifest duty of a Christian Government.

And now, O great Prince, permit us to express the sorrow which fills our hearts, as Christians and as men, in contemplating the probability of war in any portion of the Continent of Europe. Deeply to be deplored would it be were that peace which to a very large extent has happily prevailed for so many years exchanged for the unspeakable horrors of war, with all its attendant moral evil, and physical suffering.

It is not our business, nor do we presume to offer any opinion upon the question now at issue between the Imperial Government of Russia and that of any other country ; but estimating the exalted position in which Divine Providence has placed thee, and the solemn responsibilities devolving upon thee, not only as an earthly potentate, but also as a believer in that Gospel which proclaims " peace on earth " and " good will towards men," we implore Him by whom " kings reign and princes decree justice " so to influence thy heart and to direct thy councils at this momentous crisis, that thou mayest practically exhibit to the nations, and even to those who do not profess the "like precious faith" the efficacy of the Gospel of Christ, and the universal application of His command : " Love your enemies ; bless them that curse you ; do good to them that hate you ; and pray for them which despitefully use you and persecute you ; that ye may be the children of your Father which is in heaven."

The more fully the Christian is persuaded of the justice of his own cause, the greater his magnanimity in the exercise of forbearance. May the Lord make thee the honoured instrument of exemplifying this true nobility ; thereby securing to thyself and to thy vast dominions that true glory and those rich blessings which could never result from the most successful appeal to arms.

Thus, O mighty Prince, may the miseries and devastation of war be averted ; and in that solemn day when " everyone of us shall give account of himself to God," may the benediction of the Redeemer apply to thee, " Blessed are the peacemakers for they shall be called the children of God," and so mayest thou be permitted through a Saviour's love to exchange an earthly for a heavenly crown—" a crown of glory which shall not fade away."

APPENDIX E

THE PROTEST OF THE GERMAN FRIENDS AGAINST SLAVERY

This is to the Monthly Meeting held at Richard Worrell's.

These are the reasons why we are against the traffic in the bodies of men, as followeth : Is there any that would be done or handled in this manner viz. to be sold or made a slave for all the time of his life ? How fearful and faint-hearted are many on the sea when they see a strange vessel, being afraid it should be a Turk, and they should be taken, and sold for slaves into Turkey. Now what is this better than Turks do ? Yea, rather is it worse for them, which say they are Christians ; for we hear that the most part of such negroes are brought hither against their will and consent, and that many of them are stolen. Now, though they are black, we cannot conceive there is more liberty to have them slaves, than it is to have other white ones. There is a saying, that we should do to all men like as we would be done ourselves ; making no difference of what generation, descent, or colour they are. And those who steal and rob men, and those who buy or purchase them, are they not all alike ? There is liberty of conscience here, which is right and reasonable ; and there ought to be likewise liberty of the body, except of evil doers which is another case. But to bring men hither, or to rob and sell them against their will, we stand against. In Europe there are many oppressed for conscience' sake ; and here there are those oppressed which are of a black colour. And we who know that men must not commit adultery—some do commit adultery in others, separating wives from their husbands and giving them to others ; and some sell the children of these poor creatures to other men. Ah ! do consider well this thing, you who do it, if you would be done in this manner ? and if it is done according to Christianity ? You surpass Holland and Germany in this thing. This makes an ill report in all those countries of Europe, where they hear of it, that the Quakers do here handle men as they handle there the cattle. And for that reason some have no mind or inclination to come hither. And who shall maintain this your cause, or plead for it ? Truly we cannot do so, except you shall inform us better hereof, viz. that Christians have liberty to practise these things. Pray, what thing in the world can be done worse towards us, than if men should rob or steal us away, and sell us for slaves to strange countries ; separating husbands from their wives and children.

Now this is not done in the manner we would be done by, therefore we contradict and are against this traffic in the bodies of men. And such men ought to be delivered out of the hands of the robbers and set free, as in Europe. Then would Pennsylvania have a good report; instead it hath now a bad one for this sake in other countries. Especially as the Europeans are desirous to know in what manner the Quakers do rule in their province; and most of them do look upon us with an envious eye. But if this is done well, what shall we say is done evil?

If once these slaves (which they say are so wicked and stubborn) should join themselves, fight for their freedom, and handle their masters and mistresses as they did handle them before; will these masters and mistresses take the sword and war against these poor slaves, like, we are able to believe, some will not refuse to do? Or have these negroes not as much right to fight for their freedom, as you have to keep them slaves?

Now consider well this thing, if it is good or bad? And in case you find it to be good to handle these blacks in that manner, we desire and require you hereby lovingly, that you may inform us herein, which at this time never was done, viz. that Christians have such a liberty to do so. To the end we may be satisfied on this point, and satisfy likewise our good friends and acquaintances in our native country, to whom it is a terror, or fearful thing, that men should be handled so in Pennsylvania. This is from our Meeting at Germantown, held the 18th of the second month, 1688, to be delivered to the Monthly Meeting at Richard Worrell's.

> Garrett Henderick.
> Derick Up De graeff.
> Francis Daniel Pastorius.
> Abraham jr. Den graef.

Note.—Both Monthly and Quarterly Meetings passed the memorial on to the Yearly Meeting, as a matter of " too great weight " for their decision. The Yearly Meeting temporized. " It was adjudged not to be so proper for this Meeting to give a positive judgment in the case, it having so general a relation to so many other parts, and therefore at present they forbear it."

Thanks, however, to continued pressure, mainly from one Monthly Meeting (Chester) the subject was kept before the Yearly Meeting until in 1730 it pronounced definitely against the slave-trade.

APPENDIX F

STATISTICS OF ENLISTMENT, 1917

THERE are no complete figures showing the position taken during the war by Friends of military age, either in England or the United States. In November 1922 an English committee, appointed in 1917 to collect such figures, reported to the London Meeting for Sufferings.[1] Application had been made to sixty-seven Monthly Meetings; of these seven did not reply and the information received did not go beyond the year 1917. Returns relating to one thousand six hundred and sixty-six Friends and recognized Attenders at Friends' Meetings were sent in.

40·2% or 670 applied for and were granted exemption as C.O's.

17·3% or 288 applied for and were granted exemption on other grounds.

3·4% or 57 were exempted as not ordinarily resident in Great Britain.

5·0% or 83 applied for and were refused exemption as C.O's.

0·3% or 5 were exempted as ministers of religion.

0·2% or 3 refused to recognize the tribunals.

33·6% or 560 enlisted in His Majesty's Forces.

These figures are admittedly defective. There were no means of checking the Monthly Meeting returns, no knowledge of the total number of Friends of military age, nor of the proportion of " active " Friends included among those who enlisted. The return did not give statistics of the Friends imprisoned either because they were not exempted, or because they received an exemption from combatant service only. In the *Friend*, January 9, 1920, the number is given as two hundred and seventy-nine, of whom one hundred and thirty-four accepted the Home Office scheme and one hundred and forty-five took the absolutist position.

[1] *Vide Friend*, November 10, 1922.

INDEX

Abell, Richard, 527
Abercromby, Lord, 385
Aberdeen, 137, 146
Aberdeen, Lord, 264
"Absolutists," 508, 514, 520, 538
Acadians, 401
Act of Settlement, 101
Adams, John, 400
Ady, John, 208
Admiralty Commissioners, 51, 530
Adrianople, 452
Adult Schools, 254
Affirmation Bill, 108
Afghan War, 297–9
Agriculture, Relief to, 267–8, 498, 500
Aix-la-Chapelle, 191–2
Alabama Case, 289, 292, 295
Albemarle, Duke of, 94
Albigenses, 24
Albright, Arthur, 267 *n.*
Alexander I, Czar, 256, 459–62, 534
Alexandria, Bombardment of, 299
Algiers, Friends captive in, 78–80, 454
Algonquin Indians, 385
Alien enemies, relief to, 494–7 ; in
    Germany, 496–7
Alkmaar, 454
Allen, Douglas, 491
Allen, Ellen, 270
Allen, Henry J., 267 *n.*, 268
Allen, William, 32–3, 210, 215, 243,
    251, 260, 460–3, 472, 523
All Friends' Conference, Reports, 416 *n.*,
    425 *n.*, 427 *n.*, 499 *n.*, 517–19 ;
    meeting of, 521–2, 524–5
Alsace-Lorraine, 294
Alternative service in war, 431–3,
    434–7, 476, 487–8, 490, 492,
    507–11, 513, 517–20
Ambulance Unit, Friends, 494, 501–3,
    509–11

American Colonies, 327–415
Ames, William, 454, 527
Amiens, Peace of, 211, 215
Amsterdam, 139, 454
Anabaptists, 28–31, 40, 60, 120 *n.*, 132,
    143, 311, 472
Anderdon, John, 92
Andersonville, 438
Andrews, Richard, 311
Andros, Sir Edward, 335
Anne, Queen, 166, 177, 329, 337, 340,
    344
Antigua, 307, 318–19, 322–6
Arbiter in Council, 59, 159
Arbitration, 158, 168, 244, 246, 254,
    256, 260, 264, 277, 332, 448,
    493
Arbitration, Hague Court of, 271
Archdale, John, 350–1
Armaments, Limitation of, 168, 271,
    287–8
Armed Associations, 108, 214
Armenians, 272, 477
Arms, Friends in Ireland destroy, 217 ;
    warnings against sale or use of,
    208, 214, 233–40, 394–5
Army, Commonwealth, Friends in,
    45–50, 120–1, 527–31 ; addresses
    by Friends to, 113, 117, 120–3
Army contracts, 208, 214, 233, 259,
    504, 519
Arnold, Benedict, 409
Ash, Dr. Edward, 263 *n.*
Askew, John, 324
Assisi, Francis of, 26, 524
Athanasius, 20
Athlone, 107
Atkins, Sir Jonathan, 311
Atkinson, John, 72
Augustine, 20, 320
Austin, Ann, 307, 327

Austin, Charles, 430
Australasia, Friends and compulsory service in, 487–92 ; Friends during the War, 515–17
Australia, 488, 490–2, 515, 521 ; Australian General Meeting, 488, 490, 491, 492, 515
Australian Freedom League, 489
Austria, 452, 496, 497, 501, 521
Austrian Succession, War of, 170
Ayrey, Thomas, 55

Backhouse and Tyler, *Early Church History*, 20 *n.*
Bacon, Christopher, 56, 527
Baden, Grand Duchess Luise of, 477–8, 493
Baker, Daniel, 52, 527
Baker, Philip, 503
Balance of Power, 291, 293, 297
Balby, Epistle from Meeting at, 48, 52
Balfour, Lord, 483
Balkan Wars, 271, 487
Ballitore, 218, 223, 224
Ballitore, Annals of, 223 *n.*
Ballot, Militia, 197, 205–6, 213, 245, 246, 265
Ballyhagan, 102
Balm in Gilead, 128
Baltimore, 447
Baltimore Meeting for Sufferings, 430, 434, 436, 447
Baltimore Yearly Meeting, 328 *n.*, 446
Bancroft, Major William, 527
Banner of Love, The, 129, 146
Bannian, Lieutenant-General, 456
Baptist, John the, 58, 141
Baptists, 28–30, 39 *n.*, 45, 94, 342, 441, 454
Barbadoes, 103, 179, 307–14, 321, 322, 357 *n.*
Barber, Captain William, 527
Barclay, Alexander, 135 *n.*
Barclay, David (father of Robert), 134–5, 138
Barclay, David (son and grandson of Robert), 192, 201, 205–6, 379
Barclay, Eliza, 267 *n.*
Barclay, Robert, life of, 134–7 ; 329, 454 ; imprisonments, 136, 137, 146
Apology, 30 *n.*, 135, 137–8, 147, 151, 152, 191–3, 456, 458, 463–4, 468, 476, 522, 523, 524

Epistle to Ambassadors, 147–51, 158
R. B.'s Apology . . . Vindicated, 145
Theses Theologicæ, 139, 144
Universal Love, 137, 146–7
Barclay, R., *Inner Life, etc.*, 23 *n.*, 29 *n.*, 30 *n.*, 32 *n.*, 453 *n.*
Bardfield, 215
Barker, Cyrus, 442
Barker, Nathan, 442
Barnard, Hannah, 251 *n.*
Barnardiston, Giles, 527
Barnes, John, 104
Barritt, Cornelius, 512 *n.*
Barton, Colonel, 46
Barrow, Harrison, 515
Barwick, Cornet Robert, 527
Bates, Benjamin, 417
Bates, Elisha, 533
Battin, Dr. Benjamin, 478
Bayley, William, 132, 522
Bayonets, piercing with, 443, 445
Beaconite controversy, 533
Beal, Thomas, 527
Beatus Rhenanus, 15 *n.*
Beck, Ernest, 267 *n.*, 269
Beck, William, 267 *n.*
Bedford, Duke of, 313
Belgium, neutrality of, 293–4
Bellers, John, 165, 523, 524
Some Reasons for a European State, 167–9
Bellows, John, 158 *n.*, 267 *n.*, 271
Benezet, Anthony, 377, 381 *n.*, 384, 401–2, 468, 523, 524
Benezet, Jean, 470
Benson, Colonel, 527
Bennet, Justice, 44
Bennet, Secretary, 71
Berliner Tageblatt, 497
Bermuda, 307, 322
Bernstein, E., *History of Socialism*, 166
Besse, Joseph, 122, 153, 165, 170–1
Sufferings of the Quakers, 50, 55 *n.*, 74, 77, 78 *n.*, 80 *n.*, 308 *n.*, 310–11, 313 *n.*, 315 *n.*, 316 *n.*, 318 *n.*, 319 *n.*, 357 *n.*, 453 *n.*, 527–9
Bethune-Baker, Rev. J., *Influence of Christianity on War*, 19 *n.*
Bewley, John, 219
Bicknell, K.C., 205, 214
Bible Society, British and Foreign, 211, 261

Bible Society, Russian, 460
Biddle, Clement, 412
Biddle, Hester, 453 *n.*
Biddle, Owen, 402
Biglow Papers, 422 *n.*
Billeting of Soldiers, 77, 188, 347, 456
Billing, Edward, 527
Birkbeck, Morris, 236–8
Birmingham, 226, 233, 245, 254, 263, 277, 282, 285–6, 290, 291, 297–8, 303, 482, 502
Birmingham, Bull Street Meeting-house, 233, 240
Birmingham Chamber of Commerce, 263
Birmingham Monthly Meeting, 233–40
Birthright Members, 182, 390, 402, 505
Bishop, Captain George, 527
Bismarck, 255
Black Friday, 191
Black Sea, 295
Blackwell, Governor, 357
Blockade, 291, 497
Bodenstedt, Dr., 256
Bodkin, Mr., 508 *n.*
Bogomili, 23
Bohemian Brethren, 27–8
Bombardment, relief work under, 498
Bonifield, Abram, 77
Booth, Francis, 531
Booth, Sir George, 60
Boston, 327, 333, 335, 341, 343, 392, 395 *n.*
Boswell, *Life of Johnson*, 182, 189 *n.*
Boulogne, 512
Bownas, Samuel, 348
Bowron, John, 307
Boyne, Battle of, 101, 103, 106
Braddock, General, 374
Braford, Edward, 527
Bradford, Captain, 47, 527, 531
Brailsford, Miss, 120 *n.*
Braithwaite, J. B., 158 *n.*
Braithwaite, W. C., *Beginnings of Quakerism*, 40 *n.*, 46 *n.*, 48 *n.*, 527, 529
Second Period of Quakerism, 56 *n.*, 66 *n.*, 69 *n.*, 70 *n.*, 72 *n.*, 75 *n.*, 165 *n.*, 351 *n.*
Brayshaw, A. Neave, 196 *n.*
Brazil, History of (Southey), 249
Breda, Declaration of, 64
Breda, Peace of, 319

Brennan, John, 324–5
Briggs, Thomas, 315
Bright, J. A., 294
Bright, John, 248, 251, 253, 256, 259, 263, 266, 273–303, 423, 428
Exceptions to peace views, 277, 285, 289–91
Letters quoted, 276, 283–4, 286, 287–9, 290–1, 294–5, 299–300, 303
Speeches quoted, 275–8, 280–4, 286–90, 292–4, 296–303
Bringhouse, John, 374
Bristol, Friends and Militia at, 55
Riots at, 203
Bristol Half-yearly Meeting, 234
Bristol and Somerset Quarterly Meeting, 99, 187, 197, 228
Brooke, Sir James, 263
Brown, James, 56, 527
Brown, John, 422
Brown, Mary Willis, 203 *n.*
Brown, Moses, 388, 392
Browne, Sir William, 455
Brownists, 60
Brussels, 268
Bucking down, 442–3, 512 *n.*
Buckley, Colonel, 319
Buckner, Jesse, 441
Bulgaria, 23, 271, 487
Bunhill Fields, 184
Bunker's Hill, 403, 426 *n.*
Bunsen, Amelia de, 267 *n.*
Bunsen, Chevalier, 256
Burgess, Ann, 487
Burke, Edmund, 219
Burlington, 328 *n.*, 344, 347
Burnycat, John, 104
Burritt, Elihu, 254, 256
Burrough, Edward, 118–20, 327
Bush, John, 207
Bushell's Case, 154 *n.*
Butler, John, 324
Buzuluk, 500, 518
Byfield, Colonel, 340–1

Cadbury, M. Christabel, *Robert Barclay*, 134 *n.*
Cadoux, Dr. C. J., *Early Christian Attitude to War*, 16 *n.*
Calendar of State Papers (America and West Indies), 310 *n.*, 311 *n.*, 312 *n.*, 313 *n.*, 315 *n.* ; (Colonial), 89 *n.*,

333 *n.*, 334 *n.*, 335 *n.* ; (Domestic), 51 *n.*, 55 *n.*, 60 *n.*, 83 *n.*, 527–9, 530
Campbell-Bannerman, Sir Henry, 482
Cambridge Modern History, 151
Cambridge Journal (Fox), 8, 42–4, 46–50, 56–64, 66, 68, 70, 530, 532–3
Camels, Army, 299
Camisards, 468
Canada, 271, 339, 342–4, 349, 361, 363, 369, 381, 521
Canonicut, 342
Canterbury, 178
Canterbury, Archbishop of, 494
Cape Colony, 485
Capital Punishment, 354 *n.*
Capper, Samuel J., 266, 267 *n.*
Cardiff, Friends and Militia at, 56
Carib Indians, 309, 315, 318
Carlisle, 190
Carlisle, Abraham, 409
Carlisle, Earl of, 181
Carlow, Massacre of, 223
Carlyle, T., *Sartor Resartus*, 172
Carolina, North and South, 345, 350–2, 353, 393, 396–7, 417, 438–41, 446
Carolina, North, Yearly Meeting, 328 *n.*, 396, 417 *n.*, 489
Carpenter, Samuel, 357
Carrick-on-Suir, 253 *n.*
Carson, Sir Edward, 483
Carver, Richard, 64
Cary, John, 351, 527
Cases, Book of, 185 *n.*, 192 *n.*, 204 *n.*, 205–7, 215 *n.*, 260 *n.*, 264 *n.*, 455 *n.*, 456 *n.*
Catawissa, 410
Cathari, 24
Catherine II, of Russia, 32, 33, 461
Caton, William, 50, 61, 454
Catholicism, Roman, 177, 190, 193
Caudle, Lewis, 444
Cavalry Act, 212
Cavalry fines, 215
Cavour, Count, 260 *n.*
Celsus, 19, 145
Censorship, 514–15
Cevennes, 469
Chalkley, Thomas, 178–9, 321–2, 337–9, 418–19, 523
Châlons Maternity Hospital, 498

Chamberlain, Joseph, 299
Channel Islands, 488
Channing, W. E., 418
Chaplains, Quaker, 514
Chapman, Abel, 230
Charles I, 42
Charles II, 63–5, 68, 88, 136, 139, 309, 327, 353
Charles Edward, Prince, 188
Charles the Great, Capitulary of, 21
Charleton, Robert, 257–8, 260 *n.*, 263 *n.*
Chartists, 245 *n.*, 279
Chatham, Lord, 194, 374 *n.*
Chelmsford, 207, 475
Chester, 205
Chester Monthly Meeting (Pennsylvania), 537
China, 477, 521
Chinese Wars, 254, 263–4, 284
Christ, His teaching on Peace, 29–30, 60, 123, 140, 151, 157, 172, 178, 181, 192, 231, 257, 278, 310, 316, 342, 419, 421, 427, 463, 467, 477, 484, 494, 522, 524–5, 534
Christadelphians, 35
Christianity, War incompatible with, 44, 124, 138, 140 foll., 255, 264, 267, 272, 277, 288, 342, 429, 434, 441, 450, 481, 484, 522
Christy, Thomas, 473–4
Churchill, Lord, 94
Civil War, American, 265, 288–91, 422–448, 489 ; losses of, 448
Civil War, English, 39–40, 42, 138–9
Clarendon, Lord, 260
Clark, C. & J., 259
Clark, Dr. Hilda, 498
Clark, Mrs. W. S., 294
Clarke, Walter, 334
Clarkson, Thomas, 204–5, 244, 360, 401
Clause, John, 455
Clemesha, Samuel, 230–1
Clergy and War, 20–21, 25, 42, 149, 164, 282, 301
Clibborn, John, 527
Clifton, 190
Clifton Union, 243
Clive, Lord, 194
Clonmel, 186 *n.*, 253 *n.*
Cobden, Richard, 208, 244 *n.*, 252, 260, 273, 279–80, 282, 284, 287–9, 291 *n.*, 292, 301–2

Political Writings, 252
Speeches, 208 *n.*, 246, 255 *n.*, 256
Coddington, Governor, 333
Codognan, Paul, 468
Coffin, William H., 422 ·
Colet, Dean, 28 *n.*
Collegiants, 30 *n.*, 453
Coln St. Aldwyn, 165
Colonial Entry Book, 310 *n.*, 311 *n.*, 312 *n.*, 313 *n.*, 315 *n.*, 318 *n.*
Colonial Records, 363 *n.*, 370 *n.*, 380 *n.*
Colvill, John, 76
Commercial treaty, Cobden's, 287
Commutation money (for conscripts), 425 *n.*, 429–31, 434–7, 439–40, 441 *n.*, 442
Compulsory Service *v.* Conscription
Comstock, Elizabeth, 429
Concentration Camps, 485
Conestoga, 385
Confederate States, sufferings of Friends in, 423, 437–47
Conford, 97
Congénies, 468–70
Connecticut, 393
Conscience, liberty of, 66, 92, 144, 260 *n.*, 328, 454, 467, 471, 473, 476, 514–15
Conscience, Nature and Authority of, 521
Conscience, Record of a Quaker, 430 *n.*
Conscientious Objectors, 214, 331, 347, 430 foll., 440–46, 470, 471–5, 476, 488–92, 507–14, 516–20, 522, 538
   cruelties to, 432, 442–6, 473–4, 511–12, 520
   deaths of, 443–6
   sentenced to be shot, 433, 443–4, 512–13
Conscription under Roman Empire, 17–18
   Continental peace sects and, 31–5
   in England, 35, 499, 507–14
   in American Colonies, 339–40, 347, 349
   in United States, 425 *n.*, 429–37, 517–20
   in Confederate States, 437–46
   in Europe, 469–77
   in New Zealand, 516
Conservative Friends, 517 *n.*

Conspiracy, Friends' testimony against, 115 foll.
Constables, Friends as, 76 *n.*, 245 *n.*
Constance, 493
Constantine, 16, 20
Constantinople, 277, 477, 487
Continental Congress, 385 *n.*, 388, 399, 400, 402–3, 405–7
Cook, Captain, 227, 230
Cook, Cornet Edward, 527
Copenhagen, 261 *n.*
Coppoc, Barclay, 422
Coppoc, Edwin, 422
Corbett, William, 64, 527
Corder, Percy, 267 *n.*, 271 *n.*
Cork, 102, 104, 153, 186
Corn, high price of, and Quakers, 210, 260
Corn Laws, Repeal of, 273–4, 278, 303
Cornbury, Lord, 363
Cornwell, Thomas, 340
Coup d'état, 256
Courts-martial, 512–13
Cowper, *The Task*, 194, 197 *n.*
Cranston, John, 334
Crefeld, 454
Crenshaw, J. B., 446
Crimean War, 244, 259–60, 264, 273, 275, 282–4, 289, 302
Crisp, Steven, 90, 454, 527
Croese, Gerald, *History of the Quakers*, 453 *n.*, 464
Cromwell, Henry, 49
Cromwell, Oliver, 47, 49, 57, 532, 533 ; on " Seekers," 40 ; interview with Fox, 58 ; death, 59, 62
Crook, John, 527
Crosfield, Joseph, 244 *n.*, 253, 267 *n.*, 269
Crosland, Sidney, 491
Crucé, Emericde, *Nouveau Cynée*, 159 *n.*
Crusade of 1208, 24–6
Culloden, 171
Culpepper Rebellion, 350
Cumberland, William, Duke of, 170, 190–1
Cumberland, 189
Cumming, Thomas, 182–4
Curraghmore, 253 *n.*
Currency, Depreciation of, in War of Independence, 396, 404–5, 411–12 ; in Confederate States, 439 *n.* ; in Central Europe, 501

Curtis, Ann, 63
Curtis, Thomas, 527
Cyprus, 271 *n.*

Daily News, 245
Daily News Fund, 266, 268
Dakin, Peter, 430
Dale, Dr., 302
Dalencourt, Justine, 270
Daniel, Colonel, 49
Dante, 158, 303
Danzig, 454–5
Darlington, History of, 189
Darlow, John, 324
Darragh, Lydia, 412
Dartmouth, Lord, 201
Dashwood, Peter, 315
Davenport, Captain-Lieutenant, 49, 528
Davies, Quartermaster Daniel 528
Davis, Jefferson, 438, 445
Declaration of 1660–1, 68, 114 foll., 247 *n.*
Defence Acts, Australia and New Zealand, 487–92, 517
Defence of the Realm Act, 514
Defensive war, Barclay on, 142–3 ; Penington on, 126, 128 ; supported, 170–2, 209, 237–8, 361, 398
Delaware, 154, 329, 356, 360, 362–3, 369, 376
Delaware Indians, 369, 375, 379, 384–5
Dell, Jonas, 528
Denmark, 255, 291 ; Friends in, 475–7, 521
Deptford, 458
Derby, 43–6
Derby, Lord, 297, 301
Derbyshire, 200
Deserters, Branding of, 445
Devonshire, Duke of, 186 *n.*
Devonshire House Meeting - house, 188 *n.*, 504, 521
Devonshire House Monthly Meeting, 203
Dewsbury, William, 42, 45–8, 528, 530
Dickinson, John, 388, 399, 403 *n.*
Dillwyn, George, 390, 471 *n.*
Dillwyn, Sarah, 471 *n.*
Dimsdale, Thomas, 461
Diocletian, 18
Discipline, Book of Christian, 247, 490 *n.*, 524

Disownment, 209, 214, 217–18, 224–40, 345, 352, 389–90, 393, 400, 402–3, 410–13, 425, 505
Disraeli, 285, 288, 296
Divine Protection through Extraordinary Dangers (D. Goff), 216 *n.*
Dixon, John, 67
Doe, Mary, 338
Doe, Henry, 339
Douglas, John M., 218
Doukhobors, 33–4, 271, 461–2
Dove, Lieutenant, 530
Draft, *v.* Conscription
Drinker, Elizabeth, 408
Drinker, Henry, 406
Drury, Captain, 533
Dublin, Friends in, 108, 253
Dublin Half-yearly Meeting, 103, 104
Dublin, Yearly Meeting, 217, 224
Dudley, Colonel, 342
Dundalk, 108
Dundas, Admiral, 261 *n.*
Dunkards, 30, 439, 517
Dunkirk, 118, 466–7, 502
Dunn, Colonel Francis, 105, 107
Dunn, Captain William, 106
Dunning, John, 205
Dunning, John, 267 *n.*
Dutch Colonies in America, 327, 330
Dymond, C. W., 250 *n.*
Dymond, Jonathan, 248–51, 523
Essay on War, 248, 277
Dyne, William, 267 *n.*

Easton, 390
Easton, John, 332, 334–5
Easton, Nicholas, 330, 332
Edinburgh, 134, 276, 281, 292, 530
Edington, 98
Edmundson, William (*Journal*), in Irish Wars, 105–7 ; in West Indies, 315 ; in America, 329, 334, 356 *n.* ; 528
Education, Friends and, 211
Egyptian War, 300
Eidinghausen, 473
Elcock, Charles, 267 *n.*
Elizabeth of the Rhine, Princess, 136, 454
Ellis, Edith M., 515
Ellis, J. E., 484
Ellis, James, 79
Ellis, Harold, 485

Ellwood, Thomas, 146, 185, 533
Emden, 454
Emergency Committee, Friends', 494–7, 498 *n.*, 500–1
Emlen, Samuel, 402
Enlistment of Friends, 60, 105, 225 *n.*, 486, 504–5, 507, 515, 519, 538
Enniscorthy, 221
Erasmus on War, 28
Essenes, 22
Europe, Friends in, 452–78, 501
Eusebius, *Church History*, 17
Evans, Governor John, 361–3
Extracts from State Papers, 51 *n.*, 52 *n.*, 58 *n.*, 60 *n.*, 66–8, 71–2

Falkener, Edward, 463
Fallowfield, John, 324
" Family of Love," 30 *n.*
Famine, Irish, 252–3
Farm-burning, Policy of, 484–5
Farmer, Joseph, 233
Fasts Public, and Quakers, 97, 142, 196
Fear God and Honour the King (Fox), 122–3
Fell, Margaret (later Fox), 47, 63–5, 68, 307
Fell, Sarah, 73
Ferns, 217
Fettiplace, Frances, 165
Field Punishment, 512
Fifth Monarchy Men, 45, 57, 65
Fighting Sailor turned Peaceable Christian, The, 52 foll.
Finch, Richard, tract on self-defence, 170 ; returns to peace views, 172–3
Finland, 255, 261–2
Fire of London, Quakers suspected, 72
First Publishers of Truth, 55 *n.*, 527–9
Fisher, Mary, 307, 327, 452
Fisher, Samuel, 406
Fiske, John, *Dutch and Quaker Colonies*, 375
Five Years' Meeting, 451, 517–18
Fletcher, Colonel, 357–8, 360
Fletcher, Widow, 186
Flinn, Christopher, 491
Florence, 284
Flushing, 343, 500
Forgotten Burying Grounds of the Society of Friends (Moberly Phillips), 91
Forrest, 221
Forster, William, 253

Forster, W. E., 253
Foster, Captain, 51
Foster, Lieutenant Matthew, 528, 530–1
Fothergill, Dr. John, 201, 371, 379, 389, 403
Fothergill, Samuel, 372 *n.*, 375, 377, 379, 381
Fox, Charles James, 204, 208
Fox, Edward Long, 469
Fox, George, 26, 35, 60, 61, 63, 64, 66, 68, 115, 116, 120, 122, 464, 486 ; religious experiences, 39–42 ; refuses commission, 43–4 ; on militia, 55–6, 114 ; and Protectorate, 56–9, 122 ; on payment of war taxes, 73 ; addresses to Army, 113 ; on peaceable nature of Christianity, 114, 119, 532–3 ; travels in Europe, 147 ; in West Indies, 308 ; in America, 329 ; letter to Nevis Friends, 316–17
Fox, George, *Epistles*, 48, 60, 73, 113–14, 306, 308, 316
Journal, 40 foll., 56 foll., 66, 70 foll., 115, 146, 455, 531, 532–3
Fox, George, " the Younger," 117, 118, 122, 528
Fox, Dr. Joseph, 469
France, Friends in, 202, 462–70, 519–21
France, Wars with, 78, 138, 148, 208, 243, 279, 313, 318, 322, 335, 339, 349, 357, 371, 374
Franchise Reform, 253–4, 278
Franco-German War, 265–71, 292, 293–5
Francs-tireurs, 270
Frankfort, 256, 258
Franklin, Benjamin, 28, 201, 371–2, 374 *n.*, 376 *n.*, 386, 413
Frazier, Solomon, 441–2
Frederick the Great, 32, 402
Frederick William III of Prussia, 459–60, 471–5
Free Quakers, 238, 387, 411–13, 523
Free Trade, 253–4, 279, 287
Freedmen, Negro, 427, 429, 434–6
French, Thomas, 206
Friedrichstadt, 454, 456–9
Friend, The, 245 *n.*, 263 *n.*, 266, 267 *n.*, 269 *n.*, 274, 470 *n.*, 471 *n.*, 474 *n.*, 482, 488 *n.*, 491 *n.*, 492 *n.*, 493 *n.*, 496 *n.*, 504 *n.*, 509, 510, 512 *n.*, 515 *n.*, 538 *n.*

35

Friend, The (Philadelphia), 375 *n.*, 426 *n.*, 430 *n.*, 436 *n.*
Friend, The Australian, 488 *n.*, 489 *n.*
Friend, The British, 245 *n.*, 246 *n.*, 259, 391 *n.*, 402 *n.*, 482, 488 *n.*
Friendly Association (Indian), 384–7, 401
Friends and the Indians (Kelsey), 333, 343, 375 *n.*, 411 *n.*, 417 *n.*, 449
Friends' Foreign Mission Association, 477
Friends' Historical Society Journal, 200 *n.*, 468 *n.*
Friends in America (Bowden), 358 *n.*, 366 *n.*, 403 *n.*
Friends' Intelligencer, The, 420 *n.*, 424 *n.*, 425 *n.*, 426 *n.*, 436 *n.*, 437 *n.*, 478 *n.*
Friends' Miscellany, The, 417 *n.*
Friends' Quarterly Examiner, 26 *n.*, 101 *n.*, 267 *n.*, 437 *n.*
Friends' Review, The, 426 *n.*, 436 *n.*
Friends' Service Committee (American), 499, 517–20 ; (English), 507, 515
Friends' Service in War-time, 503 *n.*
Friends, Society of, peace principles of, 115, 132–3, 140, 199, 211–12, 216, 276, 370, 397, 429, 486, 493, 504–6, 513, 517, 521–5 ; origin, 40 ; under Protectorate, 57 ; under Charles II, 66 foll. ; obedience to government, 116–7 ; decline in eighteenth century, 177 ; revival of 254 ; other references, *passim*
Frowd, Sir Philip, 72
Fry, Edmund, 244
Fry, Sir Edward, 253 *n.*
Fry, Elizabeth, 211
Fry, J. Augusta, 267 *n.*
Fry, Joseph, 204
Fuce, Joseph, 51 *n.*, 528
Furly, Benjamin, 354

Galton, Francis, 233
Galton, Samuel, junior, 233–40
Galton, Samuel, senior, 233–5
Gardiner, S. R., *Commonwealth and Protectorate*, 55 *n.*
Gawler, Francis, 56
Gawler, John, 56
Gebhart, Emile, *Mystics and Heretics in Italy*, 24 *n.*

Geneva, 501
Gentleman's Magazine, 182, 189, 197 *n.*, 200, 376 *n.*, 385 *n.*
George I, 185
George II, 186, 188, 190, 523
George III, 195, 199, 202, 204
Georgia, 397, 411 *n.*
German Prisoners work for Friends' Relief, 499
Germantown, 356, 386, 536–7
Germany, 492, 493, 501, 521 ; Friends in, 136, 147–8, 154, 453–4, 458, 460, 464, 470–5, 501, 521 ; Yearly Meeting in, 454
Gettysburg, 420, 444
Gibbon, Matthew, 56
Gibbons, James Sloan, 424
Gibbons, Joseph, 233
Gibson, George, 207, 215
Gibson, Milner, 261 *n.*
Gibson, William, 47 *n.*, 528
Gilbert, Benjamin, 410
Gill, Egerton, 516
Gilpin, Thomas, 406, 408, 528
Girdler, George, 76
Girondins, 414, 467
Gladstone, W. E., 260, 273, 282, 288, 291, 294, 296–7, 300, 301
Gnostics, 21–3
Goff, Dinah, 216 *n.*, 220–2
Goff, Elizabeth, 220, 222
Goff, Jacob, 220–2, 224
Gookin, Governor, 363–5
Goree, 182–3
Gortschakoff, Prince, 260 *n.*
Gott, Sarah, 231
Gower, Sir Thomas, 71
Gracechurch Street, 154 *n.*, 458
Graeff, Abraham and Derickden, 537
Grafton, Duke of, 104
Graham, John, 528
Graham, Principal J. W., 35 *n.*, 153 *n.*, 520 *n.*
Graham, Sir James, 261, 282
Grand dessein, 158–9, 162, 169
Grant, President, 448–9
Granville, Lord, 295
Grassingham, Robert, 74 *n.*
Gray, Charles Wing, 267 *n.*
Grcen, J. J., 189, 200 *n.*
Green, Joshua Marks, 215
Green, Nathaniel, 393–4
Greer, Thomas, 104

Gregory, Stoke St., 93
Grellet, Stephen, 32, 459–62, 470, 472, 523
Grey, Lord, 93
Groningen, 454
Grotius, *De Jure Belli et Pacis*, 159 *n.*
Grubb, Edward, 416 *n.*
Grubb, Isabel, 101 *n.*, 105 *n.*
Grubb, J. Ernest, 253 *n.*
Grubb, Robert, 471 *n.*
Grubb, Sarah, 471 *n.*
Guadaloupe, 320
Guildford Court House, Battle of, 393
Guildhall, Trial at, 515
Gummere, A. M., 344 *n.*, 374 *n.*, 392 *n.*
Guns on Ships, Friends and, 89–91, 187, 195, 207–9, 227–32
Gurney, Eliza, 428–9
Gurney, John, 208
Gurney, John Henry, 267 *n.*
Gurney, Joseph John, 251, 428
Gurney, Samuel, 267 *n.*
Guy Fawkes' Day Riots, 186 *n.*

Haarlem, 454
Habeas Corpus, 205, 407
Hack, Daniel, 267 *n.*
Hagen, Jacob, 456, 458
Hague Conference, 162, 271
Hague, William, 324–6
Haldane, Lord, 486
Halifax John, 210
Hall, Joseph, 244
Hall, Rufus, 391 *n.*
Hallatrow, 92
Halleck, H. W., 424–5 *n.*
Hamburg, 454
Hamilton, Colonel, 361
Hancock, Dr., *Principles of Peace*, 216 *n.*, 219 *n.*
Hansard (quoted), 261, 512–13
Hanson, John, 343 *n.*
Hare, Augustus, *Story of Two Noble Lives*, 253 *n.*
Harlingen, 454
Harnack, Professor, 15, 20 *n.*, 22 *n.*, 23 *n.*, 24 *n.*
Harper's Ferry, 422
Harris, Edward, 444
Harrison, Bernard, 205
Harvey, T. Edward, 26 *n.*, 499 *n.*, 533

Harvey, Thomas, 33, 261
Harwich, 179, 512
Haslam, Lawrence, 91
Haughton, Joseph, 216 *n.*, 217–20
Haverford College, 518
Hawley, Major, 395
Hayes, Henry, 74
Hayes, President, 449
Hazebrouck, 502
Heathcote, Dr., 181
Helling, Joseph, 72
Henderick, Garrett, 537
Henry IV (France), 158, 168
Henry, Patrick, 402
Herald of Peace, 208 *n.*, 243 *n.*, 275 *n.*
Herrnhüter, 28
Hessian troops, 221
Hibbert, G. K., 486
" Hicksite " Friends, 416, 424–6, 437, 446, 517–18
Hicks, Elias, 251 *n.*
Higginson, Edward, 463–4
Highwood, Humphrey, 315
Hilary, Christopher, 74
Hildyard, Sir Robert, 67–8
Hill, Richard, 362
Hinde, Luke, 190
Hindenburg, General, 499
Hingston-Fox, Dr., *Dr. John Fothergill and his Friends*, 371, 379
Hinshaw, Amos, 442
Hinshaw, Thomas, 442
Hirst, F. W., 159 *n.*
Hispaniola, 319
Hoag, Joseph, 321, 418–21
Hoare, Samuel, 209
Hobart Friends' School, 490
Hobhouse, Miss, 485
Hobhouse, Stephen, 494
Hobman, Samuel, 528
Hockett, Himelius, 444–6
Hockett, Jesse, 444–6
Hockett, William, 444, 446
Hodge, Henry, 324–6
Hodgkin, A. M., *Friends in Ireland*, 216 *n.*
Hodgkin, H. T., *Friends beyond Seas*, 477 *n.*
Hodgkin, L. V., *A Book of Quaker Saints*, 391 *n.*
Hogbin, John, 75
Holden, Blanch, 102

Holland, Federal Government in, 159 ;
   Friends in, 136, 147–8, 154, 453–4,
   457, 477, 500, 501 ; Mennonites
   in, 30–1 ; religious intercourse
   with England, 29–30 ; wars in,
   136, 148 ; Yearly Meeting, 454
" Hollandische Welvaren," 203
Holmes, Captain, 528
Holstein, Duke of, 456
Holway, Edward, 430
Holy Alliance, 460 n.
Home Office Scheme, 513, 538
Home Rule, 273, 301, 482
Hookes, Ellis, 68, 78 n., 88–9
Hooper, William, 102
Hoover, Herbert, 521
Hopkins, Francis, 490
Hopkins, Stephen, 336, 388
Horetown, 220
Hornould, William, 179–80, 325
Horsemonger Lane, 215
Howard, Eliot, 267 n.
Howard, Elizabeth Fox, 503
Howard, Luke, *The Yorkshireman*, 80 n.,
   203 n., 211 n., 213 n., 464 n.
Howard, Robert, 210
Howe, Lord, 392, 405, 407, 408
Howgill, Francis, 55 n., 72–3
Hoxie, Zebulon, 391
Hubberthorn, Richard, 45, 61, 64,
   68, 115–16, 528
Hughes, Job, 410
Huguenots, 320, 351, 401
Hungary, 280
Hunt, John, 349, 406, 408
Hunter, Jeremiah, 91
Hurd, Sarah, 93
Husband, Hermon, 352
Huss, John, 27
Hutchinsonians, 328, 330
Huterites, 29, 452
Hyde, Lord, 201

Ilchester, Friends imprisoned at, 91–2,
   95–6 ; cruelties to rebels at, 96
Illuminations, Friends and, 186 n., 196,
   199, 203, 409
Illustrated London News, 266
Imitation of Christ, The, 320
Immunity of Friends, in Irish Rebel-
   lion, 104, 218, 221, 223 n. ; in
   Indian risings, 336–9, 343, 367–8,
   375, 384, 390

Income Tax, 213
Independence, Declaration of, 336, 388
Independence, War of, 109, 200 foll.,
   225 n., 383, 388–415
Independents, 45
India, 477 ; wars in, 264
Indian Mutiny, 263, 285–6
Indiana, 417 n., 418, 424, 434
Indiana Meeting for Sufferings, 264 n.
Indians, North American, 28, 330–4,
   336–9, 343, 352, 361, 365–70,
   374–82, 384, 390–1, 410–11,
   417–19, 448–50
Indulgence, Declaration of, 100, 154–5,
   313
Ingle, William, 490
Inner Light, The, 41, 45, 113, 115,
   119, 129, 131–2, 135, 143, 147,
   151, 196, 202, 248, 522, 524
Innocent III, Pope, 26
Inquisition, 121, 452
International Armed Police Force,
   161, 168, 293
Internment Camps, 495, 515
Iowa, 422, 434, 476
Ireland, Friends in, 49, 50, 74, 521 ;
   Irish wars, Friends sufferings in,
   101–8 ; in the Rebellion, 216–24 ;
   famine relief in, 252
Irish Rebellion (1848), 253 n.
Iroquois, 369, 375, 385
Italy, Early sects in, 24

Jackson, Ellen, 267 n.
Jacobites, 108, 170, 185, 188–91, 523
Jamaica, 307, 314–16, 319, 321–2, 521
James II, 69, 77, 88, 96, 100–1, 106,
   136–7, 154, 312, 335, 353
Janney, *Life of Penn*, 100, 153, 156, 367
Jansen, Cornelius, 257
Japan, 521
Jaulmes, *Les Quakers Français*, 470
Jay, Judge, 254, 260
Jeffreys, Judge, 91, 96, 313
Jenkin, Howard, 380
Jerrold, Douglas, 245
Jesuits, 320
Jewish Dispensation ended by Chris-
   tianity, 114, 116, 123, 141
John, George D., 424 n.
Johnson, Doctor, 182
Jones, Augustine, 448
Jones, Quartermaster Daniel, 528

Jones, Eli, 421, 425
Jones, James Parnell, 425
Jones, Paul, 202
Jones, Dr. Rufus, *Later Periods of Quakerism*, 216 n., 416 n., 417 n.; 418 n., 422 n., 424 n., 425 n., 431, 433 n., 446 n.
Quakers in the American Colonies, 307 n., 308 n., 328 n., 331 n., 332 n., 333 n., 335 n., 336 n., 344 n., 351 n., 388 n., 392–9 n.
A Service of Love in War-time, 517 n., 519–20 n.
Spiritual Reformers of the Seventeenth Century, 23 n., 35 n., 453 n.
Studies in Mystical Religion, 23 n., 27 n., 29 n., 30 n.
Swarthmore Lecture, 521
Jones, William, 267 n., 268, 270–1
Julian the Apostate, 20
Julian, Senator, 424 n.
Justin, Martyr, 15 ; *First Apology*, 16 ; *Trypho*, 16

Kansas, 422, 450
Keith, George, 453 n.
Kenderdine, Thaddeus, 424 n., 425 n.
Kent Quarterly Meeting, 75–6, 185, 196
Kenyon, Lloyd, 206–7
Keppel, Admiral, 183
Killo, Ananias, 528
Kilmarnock, Earl of, 171
King Philip's War, 331–4
Kinglake, H., *Invasion of the Crimea*, 257 n., 258–9
Kingston, Duke of, 190
Kirke, Colonel, 91
Knowlman, Richard, 52, 528
Knoxville, 418
Kossuth, 279
Kruger, President, 481

Labadists, 453
Lactantius, 17, 19–20
Lake Mohonk Conference, 448
Lambert, General, 46, 60–1
Lancashire, 189
Lancaster, Fox imprisoned at, 56, 62, 70, 116
Lancaster, Joseph, 211
Lancaster (Pennsylvania), 405, 410
Langdall, Jonas, 528, 531

Langford, Jonas, 323–4
Lansmeer, 454
Lanson, M. Gustave, 462
Latey, Gilbert, 77, 109
Latten, Punishment of the, 474
Laurens, Le Sieur de, 320
Lawrence, Captain John, 528
Le Sage on Friends, 462
Leadbetter, Mary, Experiences in Irish Rebellion, 222–4
Leadbetter, William, 219
League of Nations, Proposals for, 158 Penn on, 161 foll. ; Bellers on, 166 foll.
Lee, General Robert, 442
Leeds, 296
Leeuwarden, 454
Leeward Islands, 315
Leinster, 103, 217
Lesson, The Noble, 25
Letters of Early Friends, 48 n., 61 n.
Levellers, 49, 57
Levenes, John, 528
Lexington, 403, 426
Liberty Song, 399 n.
Lichnowsky, Prince, 497
Lilburne, John, becomes a Friend, 59
Lilburne, Colonel Robert, 528, 530
Limerick, 104, 186 n.
Lincoln, Abraham, 289–90, 427–30, 433, 437
Linskill, Joseph, 227
Liverpool, Quaker shipmaster at, 89
Lloyd George, Mr., 482, 485
Lloyd, Thomas, 356
Loans, War, 208, 238, 519
Lobdy, Daniel, 78
Locke, John, 350, 353
Loe, Thomas, 153
Loflin, Seth, 443
Logan, James, 361–5, 368, 372–4, 380, 383
Logan, William, 380
Loire, 268
Lollards and War, 27
London Friends and Militia, 56
London Friends' Meetings (Beck and Ball), 74, 188 n.
Long Island, 354
Long, James, 266 n., 267 n., 268, 271
Long Sutton, 94–5, 98
Longfellow, *Evangeline*, 401 n.
Londoun, Lord, 374 n., 385 n.

Louis XIV, 138, 148, 158, 318, 320, 453
Louis XVI, 459
Louisburg, 371
Love, John, 178
Lower, Emmanuel, 351
Lower, Thomas, 108, 325
Lowther, William, 66
Luddites, 214
Luke, John, 314
Lurgan, 102
Lurting, Thomas, in Navy, 52–4, 528 ; with Press Gang, 84–5 ; treatment of " Turks," 85–8, 462
Lusitania riots, 496
Lutherans, 365
Luxford, Thomas, 528
Lyons, Poor Men of, 24
Lythall, William, 239
Lyttelton, Alfred, 483

Maccamore, Thomas, 340
Macedonia, 271, 487
Macombe, Linley, 430
Macon, Ahijah, 442–3
Macon, Gideon, 442
Macon, Isaiah, 443
Madagascar, 477, 521
Magistrate, Friends attitude to the, 58–9, 142, 144, 181, 532–3
Mahomet, 121
Maine, 421
Maitland, S. R., on Walderses, 23 *n.*, 25
Majorca, 85
Majuba, 299
Malines, Robert, 528
Mallet, Colonel, 319
Manchester Guardian, 488 *n.*, 508 *n.*, 515 *n.*
Manchester, 276–7, 281, 284
Mansion House Fund, 269
Map, a Quaker, 312
Marcion, 22
Marcus Aurelius, 15–16
Marcy, Daniel, 528
Markel, Dr., 495
Markham, Governor, 356, 358, 366
Marque, Letters of, 187, 195, 203, 208, 229–30
Marriage to non-Friend, disownment for, 226 *n.*
Marryot, Captain, 51
Mars, Scythian worship of, 303
Marsh, Esquire, 66

Marsilac, Jean de, 467–9
Marten, Howard, 512 *n.*
Martin, Josiah, 465
Martin of Tours, St., 17–18
Martinique, 320
Marx, Karl, 166
Maryland, 327, 356
Mason, John, 528
Massachusetts, 327, 333, 335, 340
Massachusetts, Colony Records of, 333
Massey, Daniel, 205
Matlock, Timothy, 412
Maude, Aylmer, on Doukhobors, 34, 271 *n.*
Maximilian, Martyrdom of, 18
Maxwell, Captain, 511
Mead, William, 153, 156 *n.*, 528
Meeting, Quarterly, 69, 226
Meeting for Sufferings, 74–80, 89, 114 *n.*, 165, 178, 185–6, 251, 298, 455, 538 ; in Monmouth Rebellion, 97–100 ; in Irish wars, 102, 108 ; and Barclay's *Apology*, 191–3, 523 ; and illuminations, 196, 204 ; and militia, 197, 200, 206–7, 212–15, 246 ; on French War, 288 ; on corn monopoly, 210 ; on Crimean War, 259–60, 534–5 ; on Franco-German War, 266 ; and West Indies, 312–14 ; Committees of, Continental, 470, 475 ; Australasian, 489 ; Peace, 486 ; on outbreak of war, 493 ; on conscientious objectors, 507, 511 ; on censorship, 514–15
relief given by, to Greek Refugees, 251 ; to Ireland, 103, 253 ; to Finland, 262 ; to France, 266–70, 498 ; to Balkans, 271, 487 ; presents address to William III, 108 ; to George II, 200, 208 ; to Regent, 215 ; to Lord John Russell, 245 ; to Czar Nicholas I, 257 ; on Pennsylvania, 371–9 ; on American Civil War, 427 ; on South African War, 481, 484 ; on Naval Estimates, 486
Meeting-houses, occupied by soldiers, 77 ; sealing of, 471 ; shelter alien enemies, 496
Meidel, Christopher, 475
Mendenhall, Tamar Kirk, 410 *n.*

Mennell, Henry Tuke, 267 *n.*, 269 *n.*

Menno Symons, 30

Mennonites, 15, 23 *n.*, 30–3 ; in Holland, 31, 453, 455 *n.* ; in France, 31–2 ; in Germany, 32, 453, 455 *n.*, 472 ; in Russia, 32–3, 257, 461–2 ; in Pennsylvania, 356 ; in Virginia, 396, 439 ; in Canada, 33 ; in United States, 33, 517 ; work and sufferings during the Great War, 519–21

Meriden, 189

Metternich, 462

Metz, 266, 267 *n.*, 268, 270

Meuse district, Relief in, 499

Mexico, War with, 422

Mifflin, Thomas, 399, 400, 409

Mifflin, Warner, 408

Miles, J. E., 502 *n.*

Military, Warning against assistance of, 214, 323, 490 *n.*

Military service *v.* Conscription, Militia

Militia, Sufferings for, 55, 75–6, 185, 187, 189, 197–9, 202, 205, 207, 211–15, 245 ; in West Indies, 310–16, 318 ; in American colonies, 329–30, 340–4, 348–52 ; enlistment in, 187, 189, 203, 205, 208 ; hire of substitutes, 198–9 ; rate mixed with poor rate, 200, 212, 323

Militia Acts, 54, 197–8, 200, 205–7, 212, 213, 245–6, 264, 280 ; in American colonies, 331, 335, 340, 343, 348–52, 357, 365, 370–1, 417, 421

Exemption of Quakers, 213, 246, 331, 349, 350–2, 398, 417–18, 488

Militia Christi, 15 *n.*, 20 *n.*, 22 *n.*

Militia Commissioners, 43, 54–6, 62

Milledge, Captain Antony, 52, 528

Millington, William, 528, 531

Milton, John, 25

Minden, 460, 471–5

Mirabeau, 467–8

Missions, Friends', among Indians, 417, 449–50 ; in Alaska, 450 ; in Far East, 477

Misson, Henri, on Friends', 462

Mitchell, Lieutenant Thomas, 528

Moddyford, Sir Thomas, 314

Mollison, Gilbert, 457

Molokans, 33–4, 461

Monk, General, 49, 61, 65, 531

Monmouth, James, Duke of, 91–4

Monmouth Rebellion, 70, 91–9, 154, 308

Monopoly, 210, 366

Montanists, 18, 21

Montanus, 21

Montesquieu, 465

Monthly Meetings, 69, 186–7, 214, 224–5, 387, 389, 400, 405, 424–5, 504–5, 536–8

Moor, Thomas, 68

Moore, John, 528

Moorland, Captain John, 528

Moravians, 27–8, 385

Morley, Lord, 480 ; *Life of Cobden*, 208 *n.*, 252 *n.* ; *Life of Gladstone*, 274, 293 *n.* ; *Voltaire*, 463

Morning Advertiser, 210

Morning Meeting, Second Day, 75, 114, 196

Morning Star, 262

Morris, Robert, 407, 409

Morris, William, 529

Morris, Captain William, 529

Mount Holly, 344, 347

Mount Nories, Earl of, 219

Musgrave, George, 529

Nailsea, 91

Nantes, Edict of, 468

Nantucket, 200, 394–5

Napier, Admiral, 261, 281

Napoleon, 31–2, 209, 243, 524

Napoleon III (Louis), 246, 254–6, 287–8, 291

Narragansett Bay, 331–3

Natal, 485

National Biography, Dictionary of, 183

National Service League, 486, 493

Navigation Acts, 388

Navy Bill, 212

Navy, Friends in 51 ; Friends pressed into, 78, 80–4, 178, 185

Navy Rate, 214–15

Naylor, James, 45–6, 58 *n.*, 105, 112, 529, 533

Nazarenes, 34–5, 439

Neander, *Church History*, 15 *n.*, 20, 21 *n.*

Neave, J. J., 439 *n.*, 447

Nebuchadnezzar, 320

Neck and Heels, Tying, 311, 313, 442
Nesbitt, Robert, 391
Nevis, 307, 315–18, 322–4
New England, Persecution of Friends in, 121, 307, 333, 392–3
New England Meeting for Sufferings, 392, 422
New England Yearly Meeting, 394, 434, 436
New Jersey, 138, 154, 211 n., 329, 344, 353, 363, 367, 391–2
New Testament, 18, 23–4, 27, 231, 238, 251, 257, 261, 267 n., 276, 277 n., 278, 288, 317, 421, 458, 522
New York, 328, 343, 389, 392, 425, 430
New York Meeting for Sufferings, 383 n., 392, 427 n., 436
New York Yearly Meeting, 328 n., 434
New Zealand, 488–90, 516, 521
New Zealand Freedom League, 516
New Zealand General Meeting, 490, 492
Newcastle, 266
Newfoundland Fisheries, 200
Newgate, 153, 211
Newman, Sir George, 501, 503
Newport, (Rhode Island), 333–4
Newton, Isaac, 433
Nicholas I, Czar, 257–9, 534
Nicholas II, Czar, 271
Nicholas IV, Pope, 27
Nicholas, Secretary, 60, 66
Nicholson, Thomas D., 267 n.
Nicolay, Baron, 262
Nield, Theodore, 267 n.
Niles' Register, 417
Nimeguen, Treaty of, 137, 151, 162, 192
No Conscription Fellowship, 507–8
Non-Combatant Service, 507–12, 516, 518, 538
Non-Resistance, Doctrine of, 25, 71, 286, 321, 419
Norcott, William B., 267 n., 269
Norris, Isaac, 362, 365, 383
Norris, John, 138
North, Lord, 204
Norway, Friend in, 475–7, 521
Norwich, 208

Oath of Allegiance, 47, 49, 108, 156, 319, 396–7, 407, 410–11, 438, 444, 522
Obedience, Passive, 117

Obernkirchen, 475
Ohio, 418, 428, 434
Ohio Yearly Meeting, 416
Old Testament, Marcion on, 22 ; early heretics and, 23 ; Waldensians and, 25 ; Barclay on, 141 ; Dymond on, 250 ; Gurney on, 251
Oldcastle, Sir John, 27
Oldenburg, Duchess of, 460
Onas, 366, 384
Opium traffic, 254
Oregon boundary dispute, 264
Origen, 19, 22 ; *Contra Celsum*, 19 n. ; *Hom. in Jesu Nave*, 19 n.
Ormond, Duke of, 153
" Orthodox " Friends (in America), 416, 425, 427 n., 430, 434, 447–51, 517
Osborn, Jesse, 444
Osborne, Colonel William, 529
Owen, Robert, 165
Oxford, 153, 185–6

Pace, Edmund, 267 n.
Pacifico, Don, 279
Paine, Thomas, *Common Sense*, 404
Palatinate, 356, 365, 455
Paley, Archdeacon, 248
Palmer, Colonel, 424
Palmerston, Lord, 260, 273, 279–80, 283–4, 287–8, 291
Panics, War, 280, 287
Paris, 260, 267, 269–70
Paris, Peace of, 183, 229, 291
Parish, Thomas, 529, 531
Parker, Alexander, 55 n., 62 n., 530
Parker, William, 529
Parkman, F., *Conspiracy of Pontiac*, 375
Parliament, Convention, 61
Partridge, Richard, 378
Pastorius, Francis Daniel, 356, 537
Paterini, 23
Pattison, George, 85, 87
Paul Thomas, implicated in Monmouth Rebellion, 97
Paulicians, 23
" Paxton Boys," 385, 398
Peace, Friends work for, 215, 503, *v.* also Testimony for Peace
Peace Conference, at Baltimore, 447 ; at Manchester, 208, 275, 281 ; at Philadelphia, 450 ; at Winona Lake, 517

Peace Congress, International, 244, 256, 258, 260, 493
Peace Sects, in Early Church, 21-4 ; in Middle Ages, 24-8 ; since the Reformation, 28-35
Peace Society, American, 244, 418, 448
Peace Society, English, 243-4, 248, 254, 257, 263
Peace, Tracts on, 113 foll.
Pearson, Anthony, 55
Pearson, Professor Karl, 233, 236, 240
Pease, Henry, 257
Pecock, Reginald, 27
Peel, Sir Robert, 264
Peitsmeyer, Ernest, 473
Peitsmeyer, Christian, 473
Pelham Committee, 510
Pemba, 477
Pemberton, Israel, 371, 375, 377, 384, 387-8, 406
Pemberton, James, 377, 379-80, 383, 386, 400, 404, 406-7
Pemberton, John, 377, 471
Pembroke, Earl of, 95
Penington, Isaac, address to Army, 123 ; paper of peace principles, 124-8, 146 ; allows defence to non-Quakers, 126, 128, 171-2, 238, 486, 523 ; on toleration, 128
Penn, Admiral, 153-4, 353
Penn, Hannah, 365, 369
Penn, Richard, 386-7
Penn, Thomas, 369
Penn, William, 40, 100, 114 n., 137-8, 147, 155, 166, 273, 312, 329, 454, 456, 458 ; Life, 153-4 ; and Pennsylvania, 353-75 ; policy to Indians, 365-9, 449 ; preface to Fox's *Journal*, 147, 157 ; to Barclay's *Truth Triumphant*, 157-8 ; *Essay Towards the Peace of Europe*, 158-65, 169 ; *Fruits of Solitude*, 155 ; *Good Advice to the Church of England*, 155 ; *No Cross, No Crown*, 154, 156-7, 456, 468
Penney, Norman, 115, 425, 533
Penn-Logan Correspondence, 361 n., 362 n., 365 n., 374 n.
Pennsylvania, 154, 211 n., 320, 329, 344, 346, 349, 353-84, 398-414, 455 n., 464-5, 467, 537 ; constitution of, 354-5

Pennsylvania, Annals of (Hazard), 366 n.
Pennsylvania Assembly and Council, Friends in, 273, 356-9, 373-82, 383, 400, 523
Pennsylvania, Colonial and Federal History, 380
Pennsylvania, History of (Proud), 368 n.
Pennsylvania Magazine, 363 n., 366 n., 368 n., 377 n.
Pennsylvania, Memoirs of Historical Society, 359 n., 360 n., 361 n., 362 n., 364 n.
Pepys, Samuel, 153
Perrott, John, 452
Petchell, John, 72
Peter the Great, Czar, 456-8
Petersburg Army Prison, 442-3
Petersburg, St., 257
Peverell, Captain William, 530
Phayre, Colonel, 529
Philadelphia, 203, 358, 362, 364, 368, 372, 375, 385, 388-9, 391, 398, 400, 450, 459
Philadelphia Friends' Historical Society Bulletin, 203 n., 374 n., 434 n.
Philadelphia Meeting for Sufferings, 375, 383, 387, 392, 399-400, 403-12, 422, 426
Philadelphia Yearly Meeting, 38, 224, 328 n., 343 n., 345, 373-80, 390-1, 399, 407-8, 413-14, 430, 434, 437, 448, 517 n., 518
Philadelphia Yearly Meeting (Hicksite), 425, 437
Philadelphia Quarterly Meeting, 376, 378-9, 537
Philippines, 450
Phillips, Sir Edward, 95
Philly, John, 452-3
Philo, 22
Pickering Monthly Meeting, 232
Piedmont, 25
Piety Promoted, 307 n.
Pigott, William, 348
Pike, Corporal Richard, 529
Pike, Joseph, 104
Pilgrim Fathers, 29
Pirates, 363
Pitt, Andrew, 186, 464
Pittway, Captain Edward, 529
Place, Francis, 166
Plato, 145

Please, Thomas (or Plaise), implicated in Monmouth Rebellion, 98–9
Plymouth Brethren, 35
Poland, 500–1, 521
Political History of England, 191 *n.*, 193 *n.*
Poll Tax paid for George Fox, 73
Pontiac, Conspiracy of, 385
" Poor Men, Catholic," 26
Poor rate, 200
Poor, Society for Bettering the Condition of the, 210
Pope, Quaker pamphlets against, 118–9, 121
Poperinghe, 502
Popish Plot, The, 68, 155
Porter, Major, 61, 64
Portsmouth (Rhode Island), 328
Prayers for Victory, 142, 149
Predeaux, James, 74
Presbyterians, 64, 339 ; from Ulster, in Pennsylvania, 365, 368, 370, 384, 385–8, 399, 409
Press Bureau, Official, 515
Press Gang, 78, 178–9
Price, Joseph Tregelles, 243–4
Priestley, Joseph, 240
Priestly, Adam, 512
Pringle, Cyrus, 430–3
Prison Reform, Friends and, 211, 514
Privateers, 179, 208, 309, 319, 321, 363, 402 ; Friends concerned in, 187, 195, 202–3, 469
Prize Goods, 195–6, 202–3
Prussia, 255, 269, 460, 471–5
Publicani, 23
" Publishers of Truth," 40
Pumphrey, Stanley, 437 *n.*
Pumphrey, William, 267 *n.*
Punch, 245
Pursloe, Captain, 529
Pusey, Caleb, 368
Pyott, Captain Edward, 529
Pyrmont, 471, 475

Quaker Embassies on Continent, 501
Quaker Family, Records of, 196 *n.*, 274 *n.*, 460 *n.*
Quakeriana (Hicks), 189, 234 *n.*, 236
Quaker, name of, 50, 531
Quakers, Quakerism *v.* Friends, Society of
Quarry, Colonel, 359–60

Quarterly Review, 249 *n.*
Query concerning war, Yearly Meeting, 186, 195, 200, 203, 207–8, 228, 247, 522

Raoul, Daniel, 468
Randall, Francis, 101
Ranters, 40, 57, 150
Rates, Church, 278
Raparees, 102, 105, 107
Ray, James, 189
Raynal, Abbé, 465
Rawlinson, Thomas, 45 *n.*
Rebellion, Irish, narratives of, 216 foll.
Red Cross Society, 268, 503, 518
Refugees, Belgian, 477, 500, 502–3 ; Greek, 251
Register, National, 507, 516
" Regulation, War of the," 352
Relief, given by Friends in Irish War, 103 ; in War of Independence, 202, 211 *n.*, 224, 232, 251 *n.*, 390–2 ; to London poor, 210–11 ; to Greek refugees, 251 ; in Irish famine, 252–3 ; to Finland, 255, 262 ; to France, 266–71 ; to France and Belgium, 497–501, 502, 515, 518, 521 ; from West Indian Friends, 322 ; to Acadians, 401 ; in American Civil War, 427, 447 ; in South African War, 484–5 ; to Balkans, 271, 487 ; to Germany and Austria, 457, 497, 501, 521 ; to Russia, 271, 500, 518, 521 ; to Poland, 500, 521 ; to Serbia, 500, 521 ; to alien enemies, 493–7
Revenue, caution against defrauding, 196
Revolution, American, Friends and the, 388–415
Revolution, French, 208, 395, 465–9
Revolution of 1688, 70
Reynolds, Richenda E., 267 *n.*
Rheims, 498
Rhode Island, 316, 328–9, 330–6, 353, 366, 388, 393–4, 523 ; law to relieve conscientious objectors, 331
Rhode Island Colony Records, 331 *n.*
Rhode Island, History of, 331 *n.*
Rhode Island Yearly Meeting, 328 *n.*, 336–7, 343
Richard, Henry, 212 *n.*, 245 *n.*, 254

Richardson, George, 475 *n.*
Richardson, Isaac, 196 *n.*
Richardson, Major, 50
Richmond, 502
Richmond (Virginia), 439, 442–3, 446–7
Richmond, Duke of, 190
Rickman, William, 392
Rigault, Nicholas, 15 *n.*
Rigley, Walter, 267 *n.*
Riots against militia, 197
Ripa Island, 492
Roberts, John, 409
Roberts, Moses, 410
Roberts, Thomas, 491
Robertson, *Life of John Bright*, 277 *n.*, 280–1 *n.*
Robespierre, 31
Robinson, Joseph, 233
Robinson, George, 452
Robinson, Richard, 55, 72
Robson, Isaac, in Russia, 33
Robson, S. E., *Life of J. Rowntree*, 484 *n.*
Rochdale, 278, 289
Rochester, 476
Rochester, Earl of, 313
Roe, Major Henry, 529
Roman Army, Christians in, 15–18, 20
Ross, Betsy, 412
Rotch, Benjamin, 467
Rotch, William, 395, 466–7
Rotten, Dr. Elisabeth, 497
Rotterdam, 454
Roumania, 487
Rous, John, 307
Routh, John, 231
Royal Army Medical Corps, 503, 515
Rowntree, Allan, 227 *n.*
Rowntree, Francis, 529, 531
Rowntree, Isabella, 485
Rowntree, J. W., *Essays and Addresses*, 79 *n.*
Rowntree, Joshua, 481, 482–5, 523
Royal Prince (man-of-war), 80–3
Royal Society, 169
Royalists, Friends as, 56, 64
Ruinart, *Acta Martyrum*, 18 *n.*
Rupert, Prince, 136
Russell, Admiral, 314
Russell, Lord John, 245, 280, 287, 291

Russell, Lord William, 114
Russia, 162, 168, 456–8, 460–61, 518 ; famine relief in, 271, 477, 500, 518 ; Peace deputation to, 255, 257–8, 477, 534–5
Ryswick, Peace of, 109, 165

Saar Valley, 268
Saccho, Reinerius, *On Heretics*, 25
Saffron Walden, 165, 207, 215
St. Pierre, Abbé, 169
St. Stephen's House (A. B. Thomas), 494 *n.*, 495 *n.*
Salem, 328, 392
Salisbury, prison camp, 438, 445 *n.*
Salonika, 500
Salthouse, Thomas, 61–2
Sands, David, 221
Sansom, Oliver, 529
Sarawak, 263
Savage, Thomas, 190
Save the Children Fund, 501
Scarborough, 70–1, 79–80 ; riot at, 482–3
Scarth, Thomas, 230
Schleswig-Holstein, 255–6, 258 *n.*, 291–2
Schmidt, Frederick, 474 *n.*
Schmidt, Henry, 474
Schomberg, Duke of, 102
Schreiner, Cronwright-, Mr., 482
Schwenkfeldians, 29, 453
Scio, Massacre of, 251
Scot, James, *v.* Monmouth, Duke of
Scotland, Friends in, 49, 50 *n.*, 134–5, 530
Scott, Job, 394
Scott, a Quaker implicated in Monmouth Rebellion, 93, 95, 98
Scullabogue, Massacre of, 220, 223
Sedgemoor, 91, 94, 95
Seebohm, Benjamin, 475 *n.*
" Seekers," 40
Sefferenson, Gerard, 78
Seine, Department of, 269
Seller, Richard, 80–4, 325
Senegal, 182–3
Separations, 69 *n.*, 251 *n.* ; in America, 416, 450
Serbia, 500, 521
Sermaize, 498
Sermon on the Mount, 41, 170, 178, 298

Seven Years War, 183, 194, 196, 343, 346
Seventh Day Adventists, 35
Sewel, Jacob, 454
Sewel, William, *History of the Quakers*, 40 *n.*, 57, 59 *n.*, 100 *n.*, 119, 454, 527–9
Sewell, J. T., 227 *n.*
Shackamaxon, Treaty of, 367
Shackleton, Abraham, 218, 251 *n.*
Sharpless, President Isaac, 359, 400 ; *Political Leaders of Provincial Pennsylvania*, 356 *n.*, 388 *n.*
  Quaker Experiment, A, 357, 359, 364–5, 370, 372, 382
  Quakers in the American Colonies, 403 *n.*, 413 *n.*
  Quakers in the Revolution, The, 369 *n.*, 383 *n.*, 389 *n.*, 400 *n.*, 401 *n.*, 403 *n.*, 404 *n.*, 406 *n.*, 410 *n.*, 414 *n.*
Shawnee Indians, 369, 375, 385 *n.*
Sheridan, General, 438
Sherman, General, 428
Shewell, Thomas, 529
Shields, North, 91
Shillitoe, Thomas, 31 *n.*
Shute, Bishop of Durham, 210
Sibford, 206
Sicklemore, Captain James, 529
Sidney, Algernon, 114, 354
Sigismund, King of Poland, 32
Simcock, John, 357
Simpson, John, 529, 531
Six Weeks Meeting, 316
Skipton, General Meeting, 452
Slavery, Friends and, 194–5, 204, 209, 211, 238, 250–1, 254, 263, 289, 308, 336, 344–5, 388, 401, 416, 422–4, 429, 438, 447 ; protest of Germantown Friends against, 356, 536–7
Sloane, Sir Hans, 166
Slocombe, Roger, implicated in Monmouth Rebellion, 98
Smailes, Thomas, 231
Smiley, Albert, 448
Smith, Goldwin, *United States*, 288 *n.*
Smith, John, 340
Smith, Joseph, 267 *n.*
Smith, Joseph, *Catalogue of Friends' Books*, 122, 527–9
Smith, Peter, 215

Smith, Richard, 529
Smith, William, writings on peace, 128–31, 146
Smollett, *History of England*, 182–3
Smuggling, 196
Smyth, John, 29–30
Snowdon, Thomas, 267 *n.*
Social Reform, 155, 166, 211, 345, 523
Social Science Congress, 266
Socialism, 165
Socrates, 145
Soldiers, sufferings of, 149, 173 ; as policemen, 58 ; disturb meetings, 61, 69 ; occupy meeting-houses, 77 ; converted to Quakerism, 45–51, 74, 170, 527–9
Sole Bay, Battle of, 82–3
Somerton, 92, 94
Somme district, relief in, 499
Soudan, War in, 272
South Africa, 521
South African Wars, 272, 299, 450, 481–5
Southern Heroes (Cartland), 424 *n.*, 428 *n.*, 437–48
Southern Quakers and Slavery (Weekes), 348 *n.*, 350 *n.*, 352 *n.*, 395 *n.*, 397 *n.*, 417 *n.*, 424 *n.*
Southey, Robert, 248–9
Spain, War with, 228, 336, 370 ; (United States), 450
Spanish Succession, War of, 166, 227, 337, 360
" Spanktown Forgery," 406
Spectator, The, 385, 462
Spence Watson, Robert, 267, 269, 270 *n.*, 271, 482, 523
Spies, Quakers suspected as, 270, 390, 393
Spinoza, 30 *n.*, 453
Spitalfields, 210
Spotswood, Governor, 348
Spragge, Sir Edward, 80–3
Stacey, George, 474
Staking-out, 432
Stamp Act, 398
Standon, 205
Stanton, Harry E., 512 *n.*
Stanton, Secretary, 428, 433, 434–6
Stapleton, Colonel, 315, 317
Star, badge of War Victims' Committee, 268

State Trials, 66
Statistics of Friends of military age, 504–5, 538
Stewart, J. Fyffe, 267 *n.*
Stillé, C. J., 377 *n.*, 378
Stoddart, Captain Amor, 529
Story, George, 101
Story, Thomas, 31 *n.*, 101 *n.*, 131, 180–2, 319–20, 337–43, 381 *n.*, 457, 523
Street, 259
Strode, Sir George, 81 *n.*
Stubbs, John, 47, 454, 529
Stubbs, Thomas, 529
Student Army Training Corps, 520
Stundists, 33
Sturge, C. D., 234 *n.*
Sturge, Joseph, 212, 244–6, 253–8, 261–3, 285, 523
Sturge, Wilson, 267 *n.*,
Sully, 158, 159, 169
Sultan, The 452
Sum of the Scriptures, The, 27
Sumner, Charles, 289, 291
Sunderland, 196 *n.*
Surinam, 307
Susquehanna, 385 *n.*
Swarthmore Account Book, 73
Swarthmore College, 478, 520
Swarthmore Hall, 47, 62, 70, 316
Swarthmore MSS., 45 *n.*, 48 *n.*, 50, 55 *n.*, 56 *n.*, 61 *n.*, 62 *n.*, 68 *n.*, 73 *n.*, 78 *n.*, 89 *n.*, 113 *n.*, 114 *n.*, 528–9, 531
Sweden, 148
Swedes in Pennsylvania, 356, 360, 367
Swift, Henry D., 433
Swinton, John, 134
Switzerland, 521
Syria, 477, 521

Talbot, Thomas, 76
Talby, William, 72
Tatham, M., 502 *n.*
Taunton, 93, 96
Taylor, John Burnett, 267 *n.*
Taylor, Captain Thomas, 529
Tedyuscung, 384–5
Temperance, 254
Temple, Sir William, 159
Tennant, Mr. (Under-Secretary for War), 512 *n.*

Tennessee, 418, 438, 440, 441 *n.*, 445
Tennyson, Lord, 302
Territorial Army, 486
Terry, John, 343
Tertiaries, 26
Tertullian, 16, 18–19, 21; *De Corona*, 17–19; *Apologeticus*, 18 *n.*; *De Idolatria*, 18 *n.*
"Testimonies," of Friends, all inter-related, 197, 522
"Testimony" of Friends, for peace and against war, 40–1, 44, 186, 188, 189, 192, 194, 211–12, 214, 216, 243, 247, 264, 309, 343, 389, 399, 407, 430, 434, 487, 504–6, 513, 517, 522–4; failure to uphold, 218, 224–40, 347, 348, 362, 386, 389, 401–2, 409, 422, 424–6, 437, 441 *n.* ; enlistment of Friends, 60, 105, 187, 189, 203, 205, 214, 225 *n.*, 486, 504–5, 507, 515, 519, 538 ; opposition to testimony by individuals, 263, 482, 503–4, 523
"Testimony," against revolution, 89, 99, 108–9, 114–17, 133, 156, 185, 218, 350–2, 355, 403, 408
Thaxted, 207, 214
Thirty Years War, 138
Thomas, Abel, 393
Thomas, Allen C., 425 *n.*, 517
Thomas, Anna B., 494
Thomas, Governor, 370–1
Thomas, Dr. Henrietta, 496
Thomas, R. and A., *History of Friends in America*, 388, 416 *n.*, 425 *n.*, 450 *n.*, 451 *n.*, 517 *n.*, 520 *n.*
Thomson, Charles, 385 *n.*, 399, 406
Thomson, Peter, 412
Throckmorton, Job, 446
Thumbs, Hanging up by, 443, 445
Thurloe, *State Papers*, 49 *n.*, 50 *n.*, 307 *n.*
Thurlow, Lord Chancellor, 206
Tickell, Hugh, 67
Timahoe, 186 *n.*
Times, The, 257 *n.*, 258 *n.*, 261, 266, 282, 289, 292–3, 484
Tithes, 212, 245
Todleben, General, 33
Tolstoyans, 34, 271
Töning, 456
Torbay, 101

Tories, in American Revolution, 389, 399
Tortola, 322
Tottenham, 182, 184
Trade and Plantations, Committee for, 311, 359 ; Board of, 371, 377–8
Trafalgar, 212
Trained Bands, 74, 185
Transportation, 308, 311
Transvaal *v.* South Africa
Trent affair, 265, 289
Trevelyan, G. M., 503 ; *England under the Stuarts*, 77, 117, 155 ; *Life of John Bright*, 274, 282, 287, 291–2, 302
Trevelyan, Sir George, *The American Revolution*, 201 *n.*, 242, 393, 404–5
Tribunals, Military Service, 508–11, 538
Trophy Money, 142, 189, 195
Trueblood, Dr. Benjamin, 448
Tryon, Governor, 392
Tucker, Captain, 94
Tuke, James Hack, 253, 267 *n.*, 269
Tuke, William, 211
Turkey, 162, 164, 168, 277, 281, 487
Turner, Robert, 529
Tverchikoff, General, 33
Tylor, C., *The Camisards*, 470 *n.*
Typhus, 500
Tyrconnell, Duke of, 105

Ulster, 103, 217
Unarmed Ships, Difficulties of 88–9, 226–7, 243, 321
Unitas Fratrum, 27
United States, 254, 263, 264, 265, 416–51, 517–21
Urquhart, Mr., 276
Ury, seat of Barclays, 135

Valley Forge, 396, 408, 411–12
Van der Werf, Jan, 192–3
Varrantrap, Dr., 256
Verdun, 499
Vereeniging, Peace of, 486
Vergennes, Comte de, 469
Vermont Monthly Meeting, 430
Verney, Sir Harry, 42
Verona, 251, 461
Versailles, 453
Vestal, Tilghman, 445

Victoria, Queen, 273
Villiers, C. P., 290–1
Vienna, 251, 461, 501
Vinegar Hill, 221
Vinogradoff, Professor, 471 *n.*
Virginia, 327, 345, 348–9, 393, 396, 407–8, 438, 441, 443, 446
Virginia, Exiles in, 403 *n.*
Virginia, Statutes at Large of, 348–9
Virginia Yearly Meeting, 328 *n.*, 396, 417
Vitry, 498
Vives, Luis, 20, 28, 142
Voltaire, 139, 152, 462–5
Volunteer Movement, 246, 265

Waistcoats, Quaker gift to Army, 189
Wakefield, 215
Waldeck, 471
Waldenses, 23 *n.*, 24–6, 468
Waldo, Peter de, 24
Walker, John, 230
" Walking Purchase," The, 369
Wall, James, 529
Waln, Nicholas, 412, 414
Walpole, Sir Robert, 186, 228
Walters, Thomas, 529
Wanton, Edward, 335
Wanton, John, 335–6
War, economic arguments against, 167, 281, 292, 303 ; moral arguments against, 303
War, the Great, 492–521 ; Friends fined or imprisoned during, 508, 512–13, 515–16, 519–20, 538
War Taxes, payment of, 29 *n.*, 73, 213–14, 341, 346, 358–9, 363–5, 376, 396
War Victims' Relief Fund, Friends' (later, War Relief Committee), 266–71, 487, 497–501, 510–11, 515, 518, 521
Ward, Cornet, 50, 529
Warde, Captain Henry, 529
Warder, John, 203
Warner, Simeon, 192
Warren, William, 178
Warville, Brissot de, 414, 465–6
Waseley, James, 104
Washington, 433–4
Washington, George, 349, 392, 396, 408, 414–15

Wastfield, Robert, 529
Waterford, 186 *n.*, 253 *n.*
Waterford, Marquis of, 253 *n.*
Waterloo, 279, 283, 302
Waters, Thomas, 56
Watkinson, George, 529, 530–1
Watkinson, Thomas, 530
Watts, Arthur, 515
Weardale, Lawrence, 91
Weer, Philip de, 458
*Weighty Question, Somewhat Spoken to
    a* (Penington), 124–8
Well, Captain-Lieutenant Thomas,
    529
West Indies, 307–26
Westminster Meeting-house, 460
Westmorland, 189
Weston Zoyland, 95
Wetherill, Charles, 411
Wetherill, John Price, 413
Wetherill, Samuel, 387, 411, 413
Wexford, 217
Wharton and Drinker, Quaker firm,
    398
Wheeler, Daniel, 461
Wheeler, Frederick, 256
Wheeler, Governor, 315
Whitby, 196 *n.*, 227
Whitby and Scarborough, Quaker
    shipowners at, 188, 227–32
Whitehead, George, 77, 90, 98–100,
    108, 325, 458
Whitehead, John, 108, 132 *n.*, 529
Whiting, John, in Monmouth Rebel-
    lion, 91–7 ; on public fasts, 97 ;
    on Declaration of Indulgence,
    100
Whittier, J. G., 262, 290, 417, 423–4,
    426, 427 *n.*
Whitwell, Thomas, 267 *n.*
Wight, T., *MS.* of, 104–5
Wight and Rutty, *History . . . of the
    Quakers in Ireland,* 103 *n.*, 107,
    186 *n.*
Wilberforce, William, 204, 293
" Wilburite " Friends, 518
Wilkinson, William, 71
William III, 89, 101–2, 108–9,
    148, 154, 277, 295, 297, 357,
    455 *n.*
William and Mary, 313, 335, 357,
    453 *n.*
Williams, Captain, 529

Williams, Roger, 328
Williamson, Under-Secretary, 67
Williamson, William, 102
Willoughby, Captain, 51
Wilmington Yearly Meeting, 450
Wilson, George, 529
Wilson, William, 56, 529
Winchester (U.S.), 443, 446
Winona Lake, 517
Winsor, Justin, *History of America,*
    400 *n.*
Wistar, Thomas, 448
Wooden Horse, Riding the, 74, 315
Woolman, John, 194–5, 238, 255, 336,
    344–8, 375–6, 381 *n.*, 385 *n.*,
    523–4 ; *Journal,* 346–8, 375
A Word of Remembrance to the Rich,
    345–6
Wolfe, General, 194
Worcester, Battle of, 43, 47
Wordsworth, 284
Workman, John, 102
Worrell, Richard, 536
Worship, Quaker, Barclay on, 135, 172 ;
    meetings for, 225, 390, 515
Wrington, 92, 97
Wyatt, Rendel, 512 *n.*
Wycliffe, John, on War, 27
Wycombe, 350

Yarnall, Mordecai, 402
Yarnall, Peter, 402
Yearly Meeting, London, 182 *n.*, 190,
    198, 224, 247, 259, 264, 267 *n.*,
    269, 271, 274, 349, 453, 459,
    470 *n.*, 471 *n.*, 474 *n.*, 481, 486–7,
    489–90, 503 *n.*, 504–9, 513–15,
    523–4
Yearly Meeting, London, addresses to
    William III, 109 ; to Anne, 185 ;
    to George I, 185 ; to George II,
    186, 190–1, 523 ; to George III,
    199, 204 ; petition against slave
    trade, 204 ; Advices of, 198 ;
    Epistles of, 89–90, 185–6, 191,
    195, 202, 207, 211–14, 216,
    229–30, 233, 234, 246, 247 *n.*,
    264–5, 272, 455, 492–3, 506,
    513–14 ; *Epistles Received,* 314,
    322–4, 348 ; *Epistles Sent,* 322,
    324–5 ; Minutes of, 187, 214, 229,
    237, 524 ; *Proceedings,* 267 *n.*,

470 *n*., 471 *n*., 474 *n*., 493, 510 ;
Queries from, 184–9, 196, 200,
207, 247, 523–4
Yellow Fever, 322, 459
York, 502, 530
York, Duke of, *v.* James II
Yorkshire Post, 488 *n*.
Yorkshireman, The, 203, 211 *n*., 213 *n*.,
464

Yorkshire Quarterly Meeting, 188, 200,
202, 227–30, 501
Young Men's Christian Association,
American, 497
Ypres, 502

Zimbricht, Peter, 35
Zinzendorff, Count, 27
Zulu War, 298

Printed in Great Britain by
UNWIN BROTHERS, LIMITED, THE GRESHAM PRESS, LONDON AND WOKING

68984